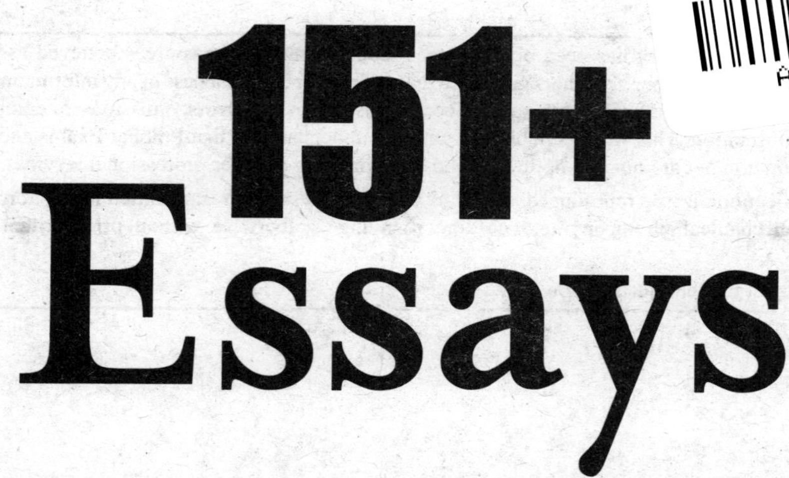

151+ Essays

FOR IAS/PCS & OTHER COMPETITIVE EXAMS

DR. B. RAMASWAMY

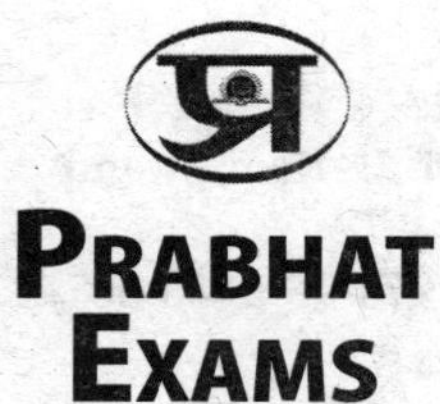

PRABHAT EXAMS

Publisher

PRABHAT EXAMS

Imprint of Prabhat Prakashan Pvt. Ltd.

4/19 Asaf Ali Road, New Delhi–110 002

Ph. 23289555 • 23289666 • 23289777 • Helpline/ 7827007777

e-mail: prabhatbooks@gmail.com • Website: www.prabhatexam.com

Price

Nine Hundred Fifty Rupees

ISBN 978-93-5488-607-2

Printed at

Japan Art, Delhi

151+ ESSAYS

by Dr. B. Ramaswamy

ISBN 978-93-5488-607-2

₹ 950.00

PREFACE

Essay is one of the most important papers in IAS/PCS Mains Examination. Nonetheless, essay is the most taken-for-granted paper in civil services preparation. The students spend months preparing for GS I, II, III, IV, but any of us hardly dedicated time for preparation of essays. It is important to understand that one essay paper is equivalent to almost 1.5 G.S. paper in terms of scoring. It comprises of two essays of about 1,000 to 1,200 words and carries a total of 250 marks. Therefore, it is necessary to have a fair selection of the essay and maintain the flow with regard to one's thoughts. Those who have sociology as optional can make use of various thoughts of various scholars and their theories to enhance their writing. Selection of essay is most important because once you start with it, you cannot look back or start with a new one. The choice of a topic should be clearly based on one's holistic understanding of the subject matter. Therefore, one should choose a topic with which one is most comfortable. At times, we think that the topic is so common that most of the people will choose it, so let me choose some unconventional topic. This is a totally wrong approach; many people end up scoring poor marks as a result of this line of thinking. Therefore, select an essay on which you can write thoroughly. Do not be in a hurry to write an essay. Many people see the broader title and start writing the essay without even understanding the theme of the topic. After selection of the topic, we need to brainstorm to get the material that we can write in the essay. First, break the topic and look for keywords to tinker upon. Another way to think upon is to get points related to the topic. After one selects an essay, think it from a wider dimension and don't confine to a particular sphere. Think from social, political, economic, cultural, legal, international, humanistic perspectives. One can make one's own acronym and add more dimensions to think from. One can look for quotes, examples, events, illustrations, case studies, government initiatives, and facts and figures, etc. So, anything that can make the essay more informative and interesting should be included.

Further, some people will say that they don't have the know-how about how to write such a long essay. It would be better to write good content, say, around 1,500 to 1,700 words will fetch one good marks. It is better to write to the point and explain in a manner that is not repetitive. Try to start the essay with a 'text/quotation' that sets the precedent for one's first paragraph. If one is not able to remember any saying of a popular personality, better to avoid and start with something that is not abrupt but sets a platform for one's topic. The same flow should be maintained in the body of the essay. One should always try to analyse the point one puts forward and never add irrelevant information to the essay. In conclusion, always try to write one's opinion and what is one's stand on the topic. The conclusion should not be more than 200 words. Also, writing constantly on any topic that appears in newspapers, even for 200 words, will help a lot in increasing the chances of getting higher marks. A suitable time division for completing this paper successfully should normally consist of topic selection in 5 minutes; brainstorming/creating outline/structure of essay in 15 minutes; actual essay writing in about 1 hour; and revision of the essay should last 5 minutes.

Remember that possessing the information is one thing but how to put that information in a structured and systematic way is very important. So, we need to focus on few things while structuring an essay. Develop an outline of essay, that is, how will one's essay proceed. Break up the essay properly. Once one has brainstormed the points, create an outline and structured the essay, one is ready to write the content. Write in simple language. No need of flowery expressions. Keep short sentences and small paragraphs. Always use simple English. Explain through the examples or illustrations whatever one is trying to explain. Mention government initiatives, policies and plans wherever possible. Use international examples or case studies wherever possible. Throughout the essay, the theme should be reflected and flow should be maintained from the beginning to the end. Each paragraph should link to the other. So, do not focus only on covering lots of dimensions in the essay. In this attempt, one loses the flow of essay. In addition to knowledge, the essay should reflect one's visions and ideas. The "Introduction" should clearly lay down what the essay will entail, thus giving a brief idea to the reader. One can always use a story, quote, fact/ information or abstract way to create a context and then build your introduction over it. The body part of essay is all about analysis. If the topic is debatable, one needs to discuss both sides. If not, then it will be straightforward presentation. In any case, one should have certain line of arguments to put one's case forward. Try to explain each of them through some examples. In "Conclusion," the focus should be on summarizing the topic; put one's concluding stand; and finally tell about the way forward. One should always try to end one's essay on some positive/visionary note.

One needs to read some good sample essays and learn how beautifully people put up their arguments. These essays don't have diversity but depth. So reading some good essays can tell you how to begin an essay, write arguments, and conclude. Most important, of course, is how to create a well-structured essay. One should take up some common/general topics like women, education, healthcare, internet, and science and prepare some fodder on it, such as quotes, case studies, examples, factual information, government initiatives etc. One should also have a repository of good opening and closing lines. You may find all these through reading newspapers, editorials, good essays of others, etc. One should write at least five to six essays and get them evaluated by experienced teachers or sincere friends. This will help in making improvements.

I hope that this publication proves to be useful enough for all aspiring IAS/PCS candidates.

CONTENTS

PART I

Understanding Essay Writing at its Best

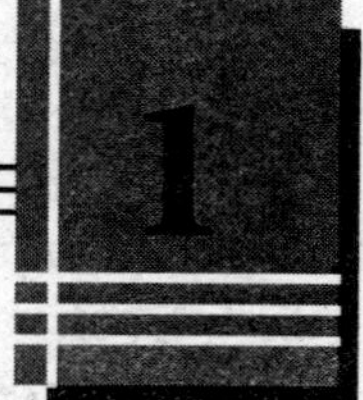

INTRODUCTION

An essay is a piece of writing which is commonly written from an author's frame of reference. Essays consist of a number of sections, which may include literary analysis, political statements, learned arguments, observations of daily life, recollections, and reflections of the author.

Therefore, the essay has a vague definition, which overlaps with the definitions of an article and a short story. Nowadays, almost all modern essays are written in prose, but works in verse have been called essays (e.g., *An Essay on Criticism and An Essay on Man* by Alexander Pope). While a typical essay should be brief, voluminous works like John Locke's *An Essay Concerning Human Understanding* and Thomas Malthus's *An Essay on the Principle of Population* are counterexamples.

Nowadays, essays are becoming major part of formal education in some countries, including the United States and Canada. Structured essays are taught to secondary students to improve their writing skills, and universities usually use admission essays to select applicants, and during final exams in the humanities and social sciences, as a way to assess performance of students.

Today, apart from writing, the idea of 'essays' is extended to other media. A film essay is a movie that includes documentary film-making styles, which focuses on the progress of an idea or some theme.

A photographic essay that covers topics with a related string of photographs may or may not include leading text or captions etc.

DEFINITION

There are a number of ways to define an essay. Among them one is 'prose composition with a focused subject of discussion' or a 'long, systematic discourse'. The genre into which essays fall is very difficult to define. A leading essayist, Aldous Huxley, gave guidance on the subject. Aldous Huxley noted that, 'like the novel, the essay is a literary device for saying almost everything about almost anything, usually on a certain topic. By tradition, almost by definition, the essay is a short piece, and it is, therefore, impossible to give all things full play within the limits of a single essay'. He pointed out that, 'a collection of essays can cover almost as much ground, and cover it almost as thoroughly, as can a long novel'—He gave an example of Montaigne's *Third Book*.

He argued on essays on many occasions that 'essays belong to a literary species whose extreme variability can be studied most effectively within a three-poled frame of reference'.

There are three poles of Huxley, which are as follows:

1. *Personal and the autobiographical essays*: These are 'fragments of reflective autobiography' to 'look at the world through the keyhole of anecdote and description'.
2. *Objective and factual*: In these essays, the authors 'do not speak directly of themselves, but turn their attention outward to some literary or scientific or political theme'.
3. *Abstract-universal*: These essays 'make the best of all the three worlds in which it is possible for the essay to exist'.

The word essay is derived from the French infinitive essayer, which means 'to try' or 'to attempt'. In English, an essay first meant 'an attempt' or 'a trial', and this meaning is still an alternative meaning to an essay. The first author who described his work in essays was Frenchman Michel de Montaigne (1533–1592). He used the term 'attempts' to characterise these to put his thoughts into writing, and the essays he was writing grew out of his common-placing. Montaigne was inspired by the works of Plutarch, Jacques Amyot has recently published his translation of Oeuvres Morales (Moral works) into French, so he began to compose his essays in 1592; the first edition, entitled Essais, was published in two volumes in 1580. For the rest of his life, he continued to revise previously published essays and to compose new ones. The essays of Francis Bacon, published in the form of book in the years 1597, 1612, and 1625, were the first works in English that narrated themselves as essays.

HISTORICAL PERSPECTIVE

In Europe, Robert Burton (1577–1640) and Sir Thomas Browne (1605–1682) were included as English essayists. In Italy, Baldassare Castiglione in his essay 'Il libro del cortegiano' wrote about courtly manners. In the seventeenth century, the Jesuit Baltasar Gracián composed the theme of wisdom.

Polemicists during the Age of Enlightenment aimed at convincing readers of their position through essays as their favourite tool; like the works of Joseph Addison, Richard Steele and Samuel Johnson, they also featured heavily in the rise of periodical literature. In the eighteenth and nineteenth centuries, the essays written by Edmund Burke and Samuel Taylor Coleridge were for the general public. In the early nineteenth century, in particular, great essayists proliferated essays in English—all authors, Charles Lamb, William Hazlitt, Leigh Hunt and Thomas de Quincey, confined numerous essays on diverse subjects. In the twentieth century, by the use of essays many essayists (e.g., T. S. Eliot) tried to elucidate the new movements in art and culture. Whereas essays were also used for strident political themes, lighter essays were written by Robert Louis Stevenson and Willa Cather. Some authors, namely Edmund Wilson, Virginia Woolf and Charles du Bos, also wrote literary criticism essays.

In Japan, essays along with the novel, prevailed many centuries earlier than their development in Europe with the genre of essays. This is known as zuihitsu in Japan, which is loosely connected essays and fragmented ideas, and existed since almost the Japanese literature began. This genre consisted of many of the most noted early works of the Japanese literature. The Pillow Book (c. 1000) by court lady Sei Shônagon, and Tsurezuregusa (1330) by Japanese Buddhist monk Yoshida Kenkô being particularly renowned are some notable examples. Similar to Montaigne, Kenkô described his short writings referring them as 'nonsensical thoughts' which were written in 'ideal hours'. Another major noteworthy difference from Europe is that women have traditionally written in Japan, though it is very formal, whereas in Chinese, at that time, were more influenced by the writing of male and also prized them.

ESSAY WRITING: AN EDUCATIONAL TOOL

Research students of the university are often assigned essays as a way to analyse what they have read in their research. Essays are now a major part of a formal education in many countries, like the United States. Secondary, in these countries, structured essay formats are taught to students to improve their writing skills, and universities often used essays to select applicants. Essays can be used to judge the mastery and comprehension of the material in the secondary and tertiary education. Students are given a topic of the study and asked to comment, explain or assess the same in the form of an essay. During some courses, university students who are preparing topics over several weeks and months are often required to complete one or more essays. Moreover, in some fields such as the humanities and social sciences, students in midterm and end of term examinations are given a time of two or three hours and are often asked to write a short essay. These so-called academic essays are usually more formal than literary ones.

These essays allow the presentation of the writer's own views, but it should be done in a logical and factual manner, with the use of the first person often discouraged. Longer academic essays having a word limit of between 2,000 and 5,000 words are often more discursive. Such essays begin with a short summary of previously been written on a topic, which is often called a literature review.

Longer essays can also have an introductory page in which phrases and words from the title are defined. Most academic institutions require references of all substantial facts, quotations, and other material used in an essay in a works-cited page at the end of the text or in a bibliography. This scholarly principle allows other teachers or fellow scholars to understand the basis of the quotations and facts used to support the argument of the essay, and thereby assists to estimate that to what extent the argument is supported by evidence, and to estimate the quality of that evidence. A student's ability is tested by the academic essay tests to present their thoughts in an efficient way, and also it is designed to test students' intellectual capabilities.

A distinction should be made between research and discussion papers. A US university essay guide states that a 'research paper is intended to uncover a wide variety of sources on a given topic'. As such, research papers 'tend to be longer and more inclusive in their scope and with the amount of information they deal with'. While discussion papers 'also include research they tend to be shorter and more selective in their approach and more analytical and critical'. Whereas a research paper would typically quote 'a wide variety of sources', a discussion paper focuses to integrate the material in a broader fashion.

Students sometimes submit the essays as their own work, which are purchased from paper mill or an essay mill, this is one of the challenges universities are facing the world over. An 'essay mill' serves as a ghost-writer who sells pre-written essays to college students and universities. Hence plagiarism is a type of academic dishonesty or academic fraud, universities and colleges can examine papers, which are suspected to be from an essay mill by the use of Internet plagiarism detection software.

2

TOOLS AND TECHNIQUES

Essays may have many purposes but the basic structure of essays is the same no matter what. An essay can be written to argue for a particular point of view or to explain the necessary steps involved to complete a task. You write it either way, the basic format of the essay will be the same. If a few steps are followed by you, then you will find that the essay almost writes itself. You will only be responsible to supply ideas, which will be the important parts of the essay anyway. Do not let the thought of putting pen to paper daunt you.

There are some simple tools and techniques which will guide you through the essay writing process, they are as follows:

- Decide the topic on which you want to write
- Make some vague idea or diagram
- Write a thesis statement
- Write the body section
- Write the main points
- Write the subpoints
- Elaborate on the subpoints
- Write the introductory part
- Write the conclusion
- Conclude the essay

CHOOSE A TOPIC

Topic Has Been Assigned

You may have no choice as to your topic. If in this case, you still may not be able to jump to the next step. Think about the type of paper you are expected to compose. It can be a general overview or a specific analysis of the topic. If it is an overview, then you are may be ready to move to the next step. If it is a specific analysis, make sure that your topic is fairly specific. If your topic is too general, you must choose a narrower subtopic to discuss. For example, the topic 'Japan' is a general topic. If your motive is to write an overview, this topic is suitable for that purpose. If your aim is to write a specific analysis, then this topic is too general. You must limit it to something like 'Politics in Japan' or 'Culture of Japan'. Once you have decided that your topic will be suitable, you can go forward to write the essay.

Topic Has Not Been Assigned

If you are not assigned a topic, then the whole world lies before you. Sometimes, it seems to make the task of starting a topic even more intimidating. Actually, this means that you are free to choose any topic of your interest, which can often make your essay a stronger one.

Define Your Purpose

First, you must think about the purpose of your essay that you want to write on. Is your purpose to explain, to persuade, to educate people about some person, place, thing or idea, or something else entirely? The topic you choose must fit that purpose.

Brainstorm Subjects of Interest

Once you have decided the purpose of your essay, write down some subjects of your interest. If you are finding it hard to think of subjects, start it to look around you. Is there anything in your surroundings that interests you to write subjects? Think about your life. What occupies the most time of yours? That might be a good topic. Do not evaluate the subjects yet; just write down the things that spring to your mind.

Evaluate Each Potential Topic

If you are able to think of at least a few appropriate topics, you must simply consider each one separately. Think about the topic that how you feel about that. If you choose an educative topic, ensure it is a subject about which you are particularly well-informed. If you wish to persuade, ensure you are at least moderately passionate about the subject. The most essential element in choosing a topic is the number of ideas to include in the topic. Even you do not find any topic particularly appealing, choosing the one you find best to work with. It could be a better topic than you at first thought. Before you are ready to proceed towards the essay-writing process, look at the selected topic once.

ORGANISE YOUR IDEAS

The purpose of an outline or diagram is to put your ideas about the topic on paper, in a moderately organised format. The structures you have created here can still change before the essay is complete, so do not agonise over this. Decide which structure you want to follow, i.e., whether you prefer the cut-and-dried structure of an outline or a more flowing structure. If you start any of the structures and, further it is not working for you, you can always switch later.

Diagram

1. Start your diagram with a circle or a horizontal line or whatever shape you prefer in the middle of the page.
2. Inside the shape or on the line, write your topic.
3. From your centre shape or line, draw three or four lines out into the page. Be sure to spread them out.
4. At the end of each of these lines, draw another circle or horizontal line or whatever you drew in the centre of the page.
5. In each shape or on each line, write the main ideas that you have about your topic, or the main points that you want to make. If you are trying to persuade, you want to write your best arguments.
    - ❖ If you are trying to explain a process, you want to write the steps that should be followed.
    - ❖ You will probably need to group these into categories. If you have trouble grouping the steps into categories, try using Beginning, Middle, and End.
    - ❖ If you are trying to inform, you want to write the major categories into which your information can be divided.
6. From each of your main ideas, draw three or four lines out into the page.
7. At the end of each of these lines, draw another circle or horizontal line or whatever you drew in the centre of the page.
8. In each shape or on each line, write the fact or information that supports the main idea.When you have finished, you have the basic structure for your essay and are ready to continue.

❑❑❑

3 TYPES AND FORMATS

It is important that the essay format should be correct and aesthetic. This ensures the overall success of the project. A proper layout accounts for 10% of the overall grade. Although formatting alone is not a determiner of good grades, it can make a difference between grades. The formatting helps make an essay more readable and trains students to be attentive to details and to follow fixed academic standards. This chapter outlines importance of the correct layout and arrangement of a scholarly paper. This discusses important formatting aspects including the following:

1. Paper selection
2. Correct use of margins
3. Title page formatting
4. Page numbering and paragraphs
5. Spacing between lines; indentation
6. Titles of books, magazines, newspapers, or journals
7. Capitalisation
8. Table of contents
9. End of essay and binding your paper

PAPER

The writer should use clean sheets of good quality paper. Type the text on one side only. Do not decorate the sheets as it is an academic piece of writing. Keep the text of your paper double spaced.

Use standard and approved fonts, either Times New Roman or Arial; font size 12. The font size and the type vary according to the style followed, whether MLA, Harvard, or APA.

MARGINS

It is important to pay attention to what your instructor advises you. Margins vary according to the style of referencing (APA, MLA, and Harvard). MLA format is the most commonly used format.

Normally, margins of the essay should be 1' (2.54 cm) at the top, bottom, left and right sides of each and every page. 1' equals to 14 typed spaces. Exception is made for page numbers which are placed 1/2' (1.27 cm) from the top upper-right hand corner, flushed to the right margin.

TITLE PAGE

Various style guides provide guidelines on a title page. The MLA Handbook provides a general guideline on referencing and documenting sources. In case no style is specified, always follow the guidelines set down by the teacher, for example, numbering of the first or second page, single spacing or double spacing, where to set the title (in the centre or left).

NUMBERING PAGES AND PARAGRAPHS

Keep the pages consecutively numbered, with numbers put in the upper right hand corner, flushed with the right margin and 1/2' from the top. It is suggested that you type your last name just before each page number so that pages do not get misplaced. On page 4 of your essay, for example, your top right-hand corner should show: Mahesh.

Use only Arabic numerals (1, 2, 3, 4, 5 and not I, II, III, IV, V) for the main body of the paper. Avoid decoration on the pages. Do not use a period after the page number.

SPACING BETWEEN LINES

To allow the teacher leave comments, keep the entire paper double spaced; please don't forget to use 1-inch margins on all sides – this is for your teacher's comments too.

SPACING BETWEEN WORDS

The writer should leave one space between words and one space after every comma, semi-colon or colon. Traditionally, it is required to leave two spaces at the end of every sentence whether the sentence ends with a period, a question mark or an exclamation mark. However, nowadays leaving only one space after each punctuation mark is quite acceptable. But, space is not allowed before a punctuation mark.

INDENTATION

The writers typing on computers should indent their essays with 7 spaces or half-an-inch (1/2') at the beginning of each paragraph. Set off quotations should be indented 10 spaces or one inch (1') from the left margin. The exam instructor may give the candidates a choice to indent or not indent their paragraphs. Whichever one is chosen to use, it must be consistently followed throughout the essay. The writers who do not want to indent should start each paragraph flushed to the left margin. It is essential to double-space between lines and quadruple-space between paragraphs. The writers should indent set-off quotations 14 spaces or one inch (1') from the left margin.

TITLES OF BOOKS, MAGAZINES, NEWSPAPERS, OR JOURNALS

The writer should underline the titles of all full-length works such as novels, plays, books, for example, Shakespeare's Theatre. The writer needs to put titles of shorter works in quotation marks—newspaper, journal, magazine articles, chapters of books or essays, for example, 'Giving Back to the Earth: Western Helps Make a Difference in India'. For title citations in the text, every word other than articles ('a', 'an', 'the'), prepositions (such as 'in', 'on', 'under', 'over') and conjunctions (such as 'and', 'because', 'but', 'however'), should be capitalised, unless they occur at the beginning of the title or subtitle, for example, 'And Now for Something Completely Different: A Hedgehog Hospital.' To understand other complex details on how to cite titles and quotations within titles, sacred texts, shortened titles, exceptions to the rule, etc. the MLA Handbook should be consulted.

WRITING AN ESSAY IN ALL CAPITAL LETTERS

The writers should not write the entire text in capital letters and should capitalise only when necessary. Unnecessary capitalisation will eventually lead to unwanted problems of reduced reader comprehension, slow reading speed and consequently would cause irritation.

TABLE OF CONTENTS

Table of Contents is not required for a short essay. However, for a long essay, a Table of Contents relating each section to its corresponding page number could be helpful for the reader. A Table of Contents comprises following sections: Introduction, Body—use main section headings—Conclusion—Summary, Works Cited or References and the corresponding page numbers where each section begins.

END OF ESSAY

An essay does not require any special word, phrase or fancy symbol to mark its end. Rather, a period at the end of the last sentence marks the end of the essay.

THE IMPORTANCE OF BINDING THE ESSAY

Staple the sheets of paper at the upper left hand corner. A paper clip could be used in case of unavailability of stapler. The paper should neither be pinned nor be folded. The candidates taking an important paper might have their paper sheets bound. They should not hand their essay in loose sheets even if these are numbered and neatly placed in an envelope or folder. It is not an easy task to write an essay of an impeccable format and structure. It requires a great deal of practice. It might be very difficult initially for the students to correctly format the essay. However, due diligence and perseverance will help the student master essay formatting.

Various authors, ranging from university students to professional essayists, use different forms and styles discussed as follows:

- **Cause and Effect:** The distinguishing features of a 'cause and effect' essay are causal chains connecting from a cause to an effect, careful use of language and chronological or emphatic order. A writer using this rhetorical method must evaluate the subject, decide the purpose, study the audience, have a critical thinking about different causes or consequences, create a thesis statement, organise the parts, assess the language, and decide on a conclusion.
- **Classification and Division:** Classification is termed as categorising the objects into larger groups whereas the breaking of a larger whole into smaller segment is known as division.
- **Compare and Contrast:** The characteristics of compare and contrast essays are the basis for comparison between two objects, points of comparison and analogies. It is grouped by object (chunking) or by point (sequential). Comparison emphasises upon the similarities between two or more similar objects while contrasting emphasises upon the differences between two or more objects. The writers writing a compare and contrast essay need to determine their purpose, study their audience, analyse the basis and points of comparison, create their thesis statement, organise and develop the comparison, and identify a conclusion. Compare and contrast are organised in an emphatic order.
- **Descriptive:** Descriptive writing is characterised by employing the sensory details that include sight, sound, touch, smell, and taste to capture the attention of the readers. It appeals to the physical senses, and uses details that are appealing to a reader's physical, emotional or intellectual sensibilities. The rhetorical choices to be considered when using a description are determining the purpose, judging the audience, developing a dominant impression, applying descriptive language and organising the description. Generally, the description is organised in spatial order though it can also be in chronological or emphatic order. Keeping the scene in focus, description uses various language tools such as connotative language, denotative language, figurative language, metaphor and simile to arrive at a dominant impression. One university essay guide provides the definition of descriptive writing as 'descriptive writing says what happened or what another author has discussed; it provides an account of the topic'. A significant creative form of descriptive essays is lyric essay.
- **Dialectic:** This form of essay is commonly used in Philosophy. In the dialectic form, the writers create a thesis and argument, then create a counterargument against their own argument and then develop a final and novel argument as a counter to the counterargument. The dialectic form provides the benefits of presenting the theme in a broader perspective while countering a possible flaw that may be present.
- **Exemplification:** In an exemplification essay, the writer makes use of a generalisation and examples that are believable, relevant and representative including anecdotes. Writers need to analyse their subject, determine their

purpose, study their audience, decide on specific examples, and organise all the parts together to present an argumentative essay.

- **Familiar:** In a familiar essay, the essayist describes as if it is addressing a single reader. He speaks about himself as well as a particular subject. According to Anne Fadiman 'the genre's heyday was the early nineteenth century', and Charles Lamb was its greatest exponent. She also states that familiar essays use the characteristics of both critical essay, using more brain than heart, and personal essay, using more heart than brain, in equal measures to provide a balanced view.
- **History:** A history essay occasionally named as a thesis essay, presents an argument or claim based on one or more historical events and provides evidence, arguments and references in support of that claim. The text also provides clarification in support of the argument or claim made to the reader.
- **Narrative:** A narrative keeping its focus on the plot utilises various tools such as flashbacks, flash-forwards and transitions that often lead to a climax. The writers creating a narrative take into account its purpose, study their audience, provide their point of view, use dialogue and organise the narrative chronologically.
- **Critical:** It is a form of an argumentative piece of writing that carry out an objective analysis of the subject matter, focussed on to a single topic. The basic idea of the criticism is to provide the readers with an opinion either of positive or negative implication. Hence, a critical essay requires strong internal logic, research and analysis and sharp structure. Critical essay requires sufficient evidence in relevance to the point made in the support of each argument.
- **Economics:** An economics essay is the form of essay that could be started with either a thesis or a theme. The course of interaction taken by it could be both narrative and descriptive. Writer can even make it an argumentative essay if the need arises. After the essay is introduced, the author needs to make the best use of his ability to bring out the economic rationality associated with it, to analyse it, evaluate it and draw conclusion. If the essay is presented in a narrative form then the writer needs to bring out each aspect of the economic puzzle to the reader in a way that makes it clear and understandable to him.
- **Other logical structures:** The structure of an essay can be organised in various forms and its logical progression can also take many forms. Managing the movement of thoughts through an essay in an effective manner can have significant impact on its overall relevance and its ability to impress. Numerous alternative logical structures for essays visualised as diagrams are available that could be easily implemented or adapted to construct an argument.

MAGAZINE OR NEWSPAPER ESSAYS: IMPORTANCE FOR EMPLOYMENT

Many magazines, especially with an intellectual bent, include essays such as, 'The Atlantic and Harpers'. Many of the essay types in various forms and styles are adopted in magazine and newspaper essays, for example, descriptive essays, narrative essays, etc. Some essays are also printed in the op-ed section in newspapers.

❖ **Employment:** Employment essays provide details of experience in a certain occupational field and are used for applying jobs, especially government jobs, in the United States. Similarly, for applying to certain US federal government positions, essays known as Knowledge Skills and Executive Core Qualifications are required.

Application to the federal government job openings in the United States uses a series of narrative statements known as a KSA, or 'Knowledge, Skills, and Abilities'. To determine the best applicants among several candidates qualifying for a job, KSAs are used along with resumes. Each job vacancy announces the knowledge, skills and abilities required for the successful performance of a position. KSAs are concise and focused essays related to one's career and educational background that presumptively qualify one to perform the duties of the position being applied for.

For applying to the Senior Executive Service positions within the US Federal Government, a narrative statement known as Executive Core Qualification, or ECQ, is necessary to produce. Similar to KSAs, ECQs are used along with resumes to make choice for the best applicants among several candidates qualifying for a job. All the applicants applying to enter the Senior Executive Service, must demonstrate five executive core qualifications established by the Office of Personnel Management.

FORMS OF NON-LITERARY TYPE ESSAYS

❖ **Visual Arts:** An essay in the visual arts is a preliminary drawing or sketch which provides the basis for the final painting or sculpture, made as a test of the work's composition. This meaning of the term, like several of those following, originates from the word essay's meaning of 'attempt' or 'trial'.

❖ **Music:** In the domain of music, a set of 'Essays for Orchestra' based on the form and content of the music, were presented by the composer Samuel Barber instead of any extra-musical plot or story to guide the listener's ear.

❖ **Film:** A film essay also termed as 'cinematic essay' involves the evolution of a theme or an idea instead of a plot as such or the film literally being a cinematic accompaniment to a narrator reading an essay. From another point of view, an essay film could be interpreted as a documentary film visual basis along with a form of commentary that contains elements of self-portrait instead of autobiography, where the signature of the film maker, instead of his life story, is apparent. The cinematic essay uses tones and editing styles to often fuse documentary, fiction and experimental film making. Though the genre is not defined properly, but it might include works of early Soviet parliamentarians like Dziga Vertov and present-day film makers including Chris Marker, Errol Morris (The Thin Blue Line (1988), Michael Moore (Roger & Me 1989), Bowling for Columbine (2002) and Fahrenheit 9/11 (2004), Morgan Spurlock (Supersise Me: A Film of Epic Proportions) and Agnès Varda. Jean-Luc Godard identifies his recent work as 'film-essays'. Georges Méliès and Bertolt Brecht are the two film makers whose work was the antecedent to the cinematic essay. Méliès mixed actual footage with shots of a recreation of the event of the 1902 coronation of King Edward VII to make a short film—The Coronation of Edward VII (1902). Brecht, a playwright, experimented with film and included film projections into some of his plays. Another essay film F for Fake released in 1974 was made by Orson Welles in his own pioneering style. The film dealt specifically with art forger Elmyr de Hory and generally with the themes of authenticity, deception and 'fakery'.

An article from David Winks Gray 'The essay film in action' states that, 'the essay film became an identifiable form of film making in the 1950s and 1960s'. He states that, since that time, the tendency of essay films has been 'on the margins' of the film making world. The essay films are of 'peculiar searching, questioning tone' which is 'between documentary and fiction' but without 'fitting comfortably' into either genre. Gray notes that similar to written essays, essay films 'tend to marry the personal voice of a guiding narrator (often the director) with a wide swath of other voices'. The University of Wisconsin Cinematheque website repeats some of Gray's comments; it calls a film essay an 'intimate and allusive' genre that 'catches film makers in a pensive mood, ruminating on the margins between fictions and documentary' in a way that is 'refreshingly inventive, playful, and idiosyncratic'.

❖ **Photography:** Photographic essay refers to an attempt which covers a topic with a linked series of photographs. Be it purely photographic works to photographs with captions or small notes to full text essays with a few or many accompanying photographs, both comes under photo essays. These can be in the form of non-ordered photographs to be viewed all at once or in an order chosen by the viewer or sequential in nature, where the intention is to view them in a particular order. Though all photo essays can be considered as collections of photographs, but all collections of photographs are not photo essays. Photo essays generally address a certain issue or attempt to capture the character of places and events.

FIVE-PART ESSAYS AND THEIR ADVANTAGE

The five-part essay, often called the 'persuasive' or 'argumentative' essay, is an advanced stage of the five-paragraph essay. The five-part essay is more complex and accomplished having roots in classical rhetoric. Its major differentiating feature is that it is obtained after refinement of the 'body' of the simpler five-paragraph essay. In this type of essay, the names of five parts vary from source to source and are typically represented as:

1. **Introduction:** This segment presents a thematic overview of the topic, and introduction of the thesis;
2. **Narration:** This segment presents a review of the background literature to familiarise the reader to the topic; also, a structural overview of the essay;

3. **Affirmation:** In this segment, the evidence and the arguments in favour of the thesis are produced;
4. **Negation:** In this segment, the evidence and the arguments against the thesis are produced; these also require either 'refutation' or 'concession';
5. **Conclusion:** This segment presents the summary of the argument, and association of the thesis and argument with larger, connected issues.

The five-part essay is less 'thesis-driven' and more balanced and fair as it includes the 'narration' and 'negation' (and its 'refutation' or 'concession') in comparison to the five-paragraph essay in which the 'body' is all 'affirmation'. Rhetorically, contrastive terms such as 'but', 'however', and 'on the other hand' are used to show the transition from affirmation to negation (and refutation or concession). Being purely formal, the five parts can be created and repeated at any length, from a sentence, though it would be a highly complex one; to the standard paragraphs of a regular essay; to the chapters of a book; and even to separate books themselves, though each book, while emphasising a particular part, would, of necessity, include the other parts also.

Another form of the five-part essay consists of:

1. **Introduction**—It is about introducing a topic. An important part of this is the three pronged thesis.
2. **Body Paragraph 1**—It explains the first part of the three pronged thesis.
3. **Body Paragraph 2**—It explains the second part of the three pronged thesis.
4. **Body Paragraph 3**—It explains the third part of the three pronged thesis.
5. **Conclusion**—This part sums up the points and restate the thesis where first part refers to the introduction, the second part refers to the body, and the third part refers to the conclusion. The main emphasis of the five-part essay is in demonstrating the opposition and give-and-take of true argument. Based on the formula of 'thesis + antithesis = synthesis', dialectic is the foundation of the five-part essay.

A writer could also use:

Intro:
Hook (3 sentences),
Connector (3 sentences),
Thesis

Body 1:

Topic Sentence,
Evidence,
Analysis (1),
Analysis (2),
Analysis (3),
Transition,
Evidence 2,
Analysis (1),
Analysis (2),
Analysis (3),
Concluding Sentence

Body 2:

Topic Sentence,
Evidence,
Analysis (1),
Analysis (2),
Analysis (3),
Transition.
Evidence 2,
Analysis (1),
Analysis (2),
Analysis (3),
Concluding Sentence

Body 3:

Topic Sentence,
Evidence,
Analysis (1),
Analysis (2),
Analysis (3),
Transition,
Evidence 2,
Analysis (1),
Analysis (2),
Analysis (3),
Concluding Sentence
Conclusion:
Essayists should sum up all their elements and make their essay sound finished.

❑❑❑

IAS/PCS ESSAYS: APPROACH AND ANALYSIS

It is necessary to have an in-depth understanding of the core concepts on which these essays are based and try to get to the inherent idea, these essay topics carry, in order to have a general understanding of their subject themes.

Examples of few previous essay topics could be taken to figure out the complexities inherent in these essays.

1. Should a moratorium be imposed on all fresh mining in tribal areas of the country?
2. Preparedness of our society for India's global leadership role.
3. From traditional Indian Philanthropy to the Gates-Buffett model—a natural progress or a paradigm shift?

The first essay, 'should a moratorium be imposed on all fresh mining in tribal areas of the country', throws open a difference of opinion and expects the candidates to solve the riddle of development on one hand and preservation of tribal culture, on the other. On one hand, we are bound by developmental responsibilities to find out newer prospects for industrialisation based on cheap and amply available raw materials to boost our production for the elimination of poverty and hunger that in turn improve the living standard. The challenge of improving the living standard of two-thirds of the population can only be overcome by exploring the possibilities of rapid industrialisation. The second five year plan was the envision of Pandit Jawaharlal Nehru—a great visionary, statesman and one of the founding fathers of our nation. Hence, it becomes all the more necessary to mine the mineral-rich places that are often near plateaus and hilly areas. However, it is to be kept in mind that these places are inhabited by our primitive tribes. They represent the rare heritage of our ancient culture, values and practices that have gradually diminished to become endangered today and are on the verge of extinction. Preserving them and their interests is our national, moral and humane responsibility.

Moreover, they have nothing to do with our ambitious developmental projects as the fruits of development hardly reach them. Hence, confronted with this sophisticated situation, a mature, balanced, intelligent and innovative approach is needed to tackle both these critical and important issues in equal measure. At the same time, significant attention has to be paid while expressing opinion in support of or against any of these two needs, as these are very delicate and sensitive issues. Hence, the need of the hour is to take what Buddha preached a middle path or Aristotle's golden mean of the two, that is, granting the permission of mining to only those areas where the mobilisation and displacement of these naturally habituated tribes is low and where they could be provided similar alternate habitat to feel at home even after their displacement.

Though, our previous experiences of displacement failed to meet our expectations and the interests of these tribes, but we can learn and identify the possible areas of their vulnerability out of those experiences. Three categories can be identified: (1) Special case, where tribals have a unique habitat with no alternate option, (2) Where the displacement options are available and (3) Where they agree to adapt to the mainstream development-borne life style, for example, few areas of northeastern states. Regions falling under the first category would not be suitable for mining considerations while the other two cases may allow mining but with utmost care and precaution. Therefore, it can be concluded that a clear cut order banning all fresh mining activities in tribal areas of the country shall be in contravention to our development strategy which forms the basis of our planning and policies. Thus, careful consideration should be given to argue and conclude a middle path that is best suited. A candidate having sound knowledge in the above domain can easily fetch marks ranging from 100–140.

The 2nd Essay: 'Preparedness of our society for India's global leadership role', is something that can be anticipated as a topic preferred by all types of students, including the students of history, sociology, public administration, literature and philosophy. All the students have enough space to accommodate their ideas and reveal a newer dimension to it. Thus, this essay provides immense scope. A survey found that this essay is preferred by over 80% of the students as it helps them in identifying and connecting their studies and understanding of India. Moreover, the selection of this essay requires one to have a deep understanding of Indian society and its progress along with the vision of India as a global leader. Since the very ancient times, the prosperity, spirituality, well-being and welfare-based governance of India made it renowned worldwide as the 'World guru' or the 'World leader'. The societal structure of India, with more than 5000-year old recorded history, can be divided into ancient, medieval, modern and contemporary periods. During all these periods, the Indian society witnessed development in three dimensions, namely, (1) spiritual, (2) psychic or attitudinal and (3) physical. Physically, a developed society is known to be that which fulfils the basic amenities of its people, provides them a decent standard of life and empowers them with prosperity. The fast moving cars, aeroplanes, space shuttle, computers, machines, mobile and internet-based satellite communication, etc. facilitating the humankind nowadays reflects our physical growth in a good light. Nowadays, plenty of Nobel Prizes are won every year. Mentally, the viewpoint of young generation seems far better and coherent than that of older generations. Thus, in terms of mental aspects, a significant leap is taken by the human society. The features of a spiritually advanced society are its openness, liberal thinking and universalistic aptitude that reflect highest degree of human rationality and scientific temper instead of superstition, bigotry and old conventions. In such a society, people have feelings of Brahmanhood within themselves, considering themselves part of a united family, and associate themselves with one universal God. The age-old values of '*Vasudhaiva Kutumbakam*' and '*sarvam khalvidam brahma*' etc. reflects the prevalence of such spiritual practices in ancient India.

A society incorporating all the three dimensions in a balanced state can only claim to be an all-round developed society. As the physical and psychic levels of development, with each and every developmental effort, involve a very critical risk of evolving their negative counterparts also. For example, the development of a fast moving car at physical level also brings with it the simultaneous risk of severe accidents. Similarly at the psychic level, though plenty of Nobel Prizes are won every year, but there has been rise in case of various mental disorders also. In present times, negative tendencies such as frustrations, anxieties and suicide attempts have increased manifolds. Hence, it can be seen that the physical and psychic levels of development carry them their negative counterparts also. Only, the spiritual development does not have any negativity associated with it. Therefore, these three levels are linked together in a complex relationship, which have to be brought to exist in harmony to give the true sense of a developed society.

Since the ancient times, Indian society is said to practise spirituality that was followed with a strong foundation even in the medieval time. Refined with higher standards of values, ethics and morality, the social consciousness was characterised with confidence. People believed in themselves and psychically the society was strong. The people were able to meet their needs and requirements and physically too the society had abundant wealth to take care of its people. The living standard of people was remarkably good and they were satisfied with it.

The medieval period in Indian society during the period of Delhi Sultanate and the Mughals witnessed a little deterioration in the physical well-being of its people, but overall the society was able to manage the intricate balance amongst the three levels.

However, a great deal of harms to the interest of people in India and its societal structure was done in the modern period during the period of European invasion that resulted into British rule and colonisation of India. This was done in two levels—physical level and psychic level. Physically, the Britishers followed the policy of 'Drain of Wealth' and put all their efforts to exploit, extract and export Indian wealth to England. To suit their selfish interests, they exploited the very structure of Indian economy, trade, commerce and occupation of the people without even caring about the grave consequences that followed in the form of long-term destruction because of their lunatic actions. Psychically too they were able to inflict damage to the attitude of the society to such an extent that Indians lost faith and belief in their ability. This caused a remarkable loss to the Indian society and it needed time to heel and revive the society.

Hence, the contemporary Indian society is comprised people who underwent physical and psychic exploitation for over two and half centuries. However, even the alien intrusions could not destabilise them from spirituality. Hence, during all these periods of crisis the base of Indian society in the form of spirituality remained intact.

Post-independence, a strong foundation laid by the visionary leadership of Pandit Nehru, Mahatma Gandhi, Ballabh Patel, Dr. Ambedkar, etc. led to the present form of governance based on modern principles of democracy, socialism and secularism. Our constitution very well incorporates all these principles and enjoys the privilege of being one of the largest written constitutions in the world.

The solid foundations laid by our constitution have resulted in providing a strong base to the Indian society to become self-reliant in food grain production and most of its basic needs. In the present scenario, the country is widely recognised as one of the fastest growing economy in the world and emerging as a leader on many fronts. Even the U. S. President Obama acknowledged that 'When India speaks, the World listens'.

In the 1960s, followed by a series of famines, when our late Prime Minister Smt. Indira Gandhi went to USA to seek help for food grains and other economic needs, she was made to wait half an hour in the presidential corridor to meet the U. S. President. In the present scenario, the situation has changed to such a level that the U. S. President Mr. Obama came to India and sought employments for its people. Today, India is playing a leadership role in international organisations including ASEAN, SAARC, G-20, BASIC, IBSA, etc. Moreover, India has been given an observer status in other organisations like G-8, SCO, EU, etc. which portrays the significant role India plays, its participation and the respect gained by it in the International Forums. India adopted the harmonious and peaceful coexistence principles of Non-Aligned Movement (NAM) based on India's ancient value system of 'Sarva Jan Hitaya Cha' and 'Vashudhaiv Kutumbakam'. It evolved as a result of Indian societal structure and has provided an alternative to the polarised world that followed immature and sentimental principles of polarisation during the second World War. India played a significant role in the formation of the UN even before it achieved independence. Many of the UN institutions are based on Indian's age-old principles of humanism and universalism of which India is also the founding member.

Thus, physically India is able to revive itself within a very short span of time after independence. Presently, India has registered itself as the second fastest growing economy of the world. This has led to a boost in the psychological status of Indian people reflecting growing social awareness and confidence in the society. Nowadays, Indians have regained the sense of belief and pride in being an Indian. This reflects a great sign of improvement the Indian society is going through.

The economic development, prosperity of the people and international position held by its people show the readiness of Indian society for betterment in all spheres of life. The living standard of Indian society has improved in all these fronts. Few social evils such as poverty, unemployment, mass scale hunger, malnourishment, ignorance, illiteracy, and other forms of iniquities that still exist in the present society can be eliminated in future with good development figures, successful functioning democracy, education and good governance. All these developments indicate that India would be able to regain its status of global leader in the time to come. As it is the only country with a social set-up having a harmonious balance in all the three aforementioned fundamental pillars that forms the basis of an ideal society.

A relatively good essay could be turned out by elaborating few of these aspects combined with logical arguments. This essay becomes an obvious choice as a student well versed in these basic aspects of society could get marks in the range of 100 to 145.

The third essay topic: 'From traditional Indian Philanthropy to the Gates-Buffett model—a natural progress or a paradigm shift?' is more of a philosophical tone. To attempt this essay one should have adequate knowledge of the differences that lie in the Indian practice of 'paropkara' and the contemporary western practice of 'philanthropy'. Thereafter, one is assumed to provide comments on whether philanthropy in practice today is a natural progress or a paradigm shift?

Before taking a position, the essayist should elaborate upon these two practices then should logically conclude the topic. The concept of philanthropy in India was called as 'Paropkara', that is, 'Par' + 'Upkara' which means 'service to others'. Therefore, the philanthropy was considered as service or duty to perform whether one had enough wealth or little wealth. The people distributing their money or wealth would consider themselves indebted to person receiving their money and never viewed themselves obliging to the needy or the beneficiary. Raja Harishchandra, Bharathari, Raja Bhoja, Ashoka, etc. are some examples of the kings who testified this system of philanthropy that was prevalent in India since the time immemorial.

In present times, philanthropy in practice is a western adaptation. Influenced by this system, most of the Indian wealthy people, who have become billionaire very recently, are following the western philanthropists, like Bill, Warren Buffett and Milinda Gates, etc. The widespread fame and recognition that comes with this practice motivates these multi billionaires. Thus, most of the Indian philanthropists in their eagerness to transform themselves as a modern western man get drawn into the gaudy power of westernisation and get distracted between the two.

Modernisation does not mean westernisation and is instead a mindset based on the principles of democracy, socialism, equality, secularism and freedom and universalism. Hence, the practice of philanthropy nowadays by Indians who recently turned rich cannot be called as a natural development but a paradigm shift.

Now, enough light has been thrown on core of the issues and one can always make use of his/her vision and understanding to further elaborate on the topic. One can put relevant facts and figures in a meaningful way to make it more substantive. Hence, this essay requires more of a philosophical knowledge than factual knowledge or something learnt from books. A well-written essay on this topic can fetch marks in the range of 100–140.

Thus, we can see that main examination nowadays has become very competitive similar to the situations that we undergo in our daily walk of life in the present scenario. A comprehensive understanding of Indian society, its culture, people, practices and philosophies is a must for an individual who wants to compete in the exam. Writing on some of these topics or on similar issues and getting oneself evaluated is the best way to prepare for essay writing. The importance of essays should not be taken lightly as these could be decisive in changing the rank and portfolio of a candidate and making it to the final list of successful candidates.

SELECTED IDEAL IAS/PCS ESSAY TOPICS

1. Efficient and Smart City: A New World

INTRODUCTION

Worldwide evolution in the twenty-first century is putting a lot of pressure on developing countries for improving their infrastructure and progress rate in various areas. A large number of people are migrating from villages to cities. The rate of this migration is so high that by 2050, about 70 per cent of world population will be living in cities. The same holds true for India, as well. If the migration continues at this rate in India, we would need approximately 500 new cities only to provide basic housing to this influx.

With a high spike in the rate of urban development and the load on rural areas, our government has now understood the growing need for new cities, which can handle the challenges of urban living and become a major source of investment. The announcement of '100 smart cities' by the Indian government falls under this category only. Therefore, 'Smart City' has become a current topic and a popularly known term.

This idea comprises human capital as well as technology for creating sustainable surroundings. Such cities work towards the aim of improving sustainable economic progress, building infrastructure and providing citizens with a better quality of life as they add to the process of progress.

The term 'Smart City' is referred to an urban area, which is technically very advanced with reference to the complete infrastructure, has highly sustainable real estate, communications and quite good market possibility. Information technology plays a major role in providing basic amenities to its people.

The supply and demand of goods in the market is the base of financial progress of smart cities. It is very difficult to attain the economic development as it affects everybody, including common people, businessmen, the government and the surroundings as well.

The revolutionising idea of 'Smart City' came up when the world was facing economic crisis. The year 2008 was the time of creation of this idea when IBM cast its deep sight into developing a smart city by its project 'Smart Planet' initiative. Upon seeing, this project, the whole world got captivated with the idea of Smart City.

NECESSITY OF SMART CITY

Because of the increase in development, India's urban population might (in probability) increase approximately to 600 million by 2031, which would be almost twice to what it was in 2001. Almost half of this population would be living in cities. Based on a recent report on Indian urban infrastructure and services by a high-powered expert committee set by the Government of India, the share of the GDP of the urban areas will probably rise to 75 per cent by 2030 as compared to 62–63 per cent in 2009–2010. This is the major reason why cities are called 'Engines of Economic Growth'. It is imperative that they perform as motivational factors to our economic progress. This pattern of urban progress that is now visible in India will keep continuing for nearby future.

Urban areas will be crucial to the economic growth of the country and will require a massive overhaul to accommodate the influx in future. To cater to this growing urban population, in the future, cities need to provide a suitable environment for future investments, create new jobs and livelihoods, build reliable public infrastructure, provide social services with sufficient access to affordable housing and most necessarily support efficient utilisation of resources for a standard quality of life. This considerable growth also provides impetus for the creation of smart cities, which utilise information and communication technology (ICT) to improve largely the productivity, lifestyle and the prosperity of the dwellers. Moreover, green growth master plans can build environmentally sustainable cities. The vision for 'Smart City' has two major aspects: Technology transportation and energy efficiency. Digital technologies or information and communication technologies (ICT) are used in a smart city to promote quality and performance of urban services, to cut down costs and resource consumption and to remain engaged more effectively and actively with its citizens. ICT discovers the requirements of the area and directs to plan accordingly.

The consequences of climate change, such as sea level rises, melting of glaciers and more frequent changes of extreme weather events with heavy rainfalls and drought periods, pose a great danger to business and livelihoods all over the world. In the attempt to reduce the rising global temperature, the Government of India has set a number of emission targets, which have the potential to improve energy security simultaneously. Energy efficiency is seen conspicuously as a predominant aspect for shielding competitiveness of Indian industry in the longer term. Keeping it in mind, India has committed itself to reducing emissions by escalating the share of renewable energy in final energy consumption to rise in energy efficiency. Besides these, India has prepared a blueprint to shape the low-carbon economy essential for these goals, and thus clarifying a pathway for an India-wide transition to a sustainable energy system. This emphasis on sustainability and climate change mitigation can lead to greater emphasis on cheap energy and competitiveness.

The Energy Performance mentioned in Buildings Directive concentrates mainly on the energy performance of individual buildings with agreeable reasons to address sets of buildings and to determine a common balance of energy for them. It is necessary to analyse the demand and supply of energy for estimating the opportunity of considering sets of buildings one-by-one. Energy demand can be made up for those that are deprived of getting a low energy demand with an agreeable effort provided the disadvantageous conditions affect one or a number of buildings within the same neighbourhood (e.g., shading); while nearby or on-site systems can work as an advantageous substitute to individual systems per building for energy supply. This type of small central supply can produce benefits regarding capital cost savings, higher efficiency and better seasonal storage. Long-term thinking and decision-making plays predominant role for achieving all these.

MANAGEMENT OF ENERGY IN SMART CITY

Energy management by the source nation is essential in a smart city. The main and major objective of integrated energy management is to achieve and maintain sustainable energy realised at the ground level; side-by-side, measures to conserve energy must be executed. Excessive utilisation of any energy source such as coal or oil for generation of electricity causes plights of problems like acid rain and increasing the level of carbon dioxide in the atmosphere.

Hydroelectric power stations and atomic energy stations were championed for curtailing dependence on oil and coal for generating electricity. Huge dams can contribute considerably to economic growth in developing countries' short of electricity like India, but there must be a compromise regarding the case of large-scale electricity generation. Reservoirs deluge wildlife habitats, forests and farmland and even eradicate communities of native people. In order to meet the growing demand, efficient utilisation of energy and its conservation are preponderant factors.

Energy is the key resource to industrial development. It is generated both from commercial sources such as petroleum, coal, hydroelectric plants and non-commercial sources like fuel-wood, cow-dung and agricultural wastes. The index of economic advancement attained by a country is the consumption of commercial energy per head. However, India consumes a very low amount of commercial energy per head—one-eighth of the world average.

Commercial energy supplies a little over half of the total energy used in the country, and the rest comes from non-commercial sources. Since the last two and half a decade, agriculture has been consuming commercial energy at a greater rate. However, now the twin factors, environmental conservation and energy generation, are emerging from exploitative interaction of man with natural resources.

Methodical management of energy is critical to a smart city because it largely depends on power. It is maintained by technologies like smart metering, cloud computing and wireless connected sensors. Smart meters allow two-way monitoring from both the utility providers and the end-user to monitor consumption, loads of peak hours etc.

These systems provide information essential to the citizens in order to help better manage their plan tariffs. Furthermore, smart cities also use 'smart grids', i.e. power grids integrated with controls, automation and latest technologies to boost efficient transmission and quicker restoration of power on outages or other incidences, cut down overall operation and management costs and combine renewable energy systems. Besides these, they offer financial incentives to the consumers for shifting the electrical demand during off-peak hours. Above all, smart grids give opportunities to save energy and at the same time reduce dependence on fossil fuels. Smart city provides seamless and integrated public transport and communication networks in multiple modes—rail, metro, bus and non-motorised transportation (walking and cycling). Preferably, ICT is integrated with the transport networks with a view to allowing real-time tracking and increasing citizen access to information on transportation. Directed parking and volume-based traffic control systems are the measures that help handling traffic challenges and improve flexibility.

Energy policy now has two ways. One leads to the fossil fuels or the hard way, which means to go on as we have been for many years i.e. giving importance to energy quantity by discovering more amounts of fossil fuels and building larger power plants.

The second way is the soft one which leads to the energy substitutes that lay importance on energy quality and are also renewable, flexible and more eco-friendly. The soft way depends mainly on renewable energy that includes sunlight, wind, biomass, tidal energy etc. and waste management to create energy.

This initiative will certainly help cities and regions to undertake ambitious and spearheading measures in order to reduce the emission of greenhouse gas through sustainable utilisation and production of energy. This will need methodical approaches and organisational innovation, incorporating energy efficiency, low carbon technologies and the efficient management of supply and demand. The principal constituents of this initiative would comprise especially steps on buildings, local energy networks and transport.

The final goal of the 'Smart Cities' is the design of energy neutral cities with the least carbon dioxide emissions. In smart cities, people are creators in an urban context where sustainable environment plays a crucial role. Best utilisation of waste to energy helps maintaining a high quality of the use of technology through ICT and many other endeavours.

The pinpointed cities would be designed in partnership with Centre, State and urban local bodies in a public-private partnership (PPP) model. The Centre will pay the viability gap funding (VGF) for undertaking the initiative. The Government of

India realises the importance of promoting industrial energy efficiency for handling competitiveness, reducing total energy demand and the emission of greenhouse gases.

The Govt. of India has built industrial corridors, like Delhi-Mumbai Industrial Corridor, Delhi-Chennai Industrial Corridor etc. in order to make transportation effective with the help of modern roadways that connect the rural areas with the urban ones easily with a view to meet the urban demands and reduce the gap of supply and cut down the consumption of fuel. The venture by the Govt. to build these economic corridors is certainly positive. Apart from the technological challenges, there should be change in the standard of society and lifestyle, and in parallel to this energy saving attitudes must be adopted. Therefore, development of smart cities and sustainable transport systems, where electricity will play as the sustainable carrier, are essential to bring these attitudes into reality, whereas development of smart grid at distribution level helps building smart cities.

CONCLUSION

Energy conservation is considerably a quick and economical way to solve the problem of power shortage and a way of saving the country's finite sources of energy, and the conservation procedures need relatively smaller investments, are cost-effective and also have short evolution as well as payback periods. The smart cities will focus on the development of smart energy efficient buildings, greener environment, and cleaner atmosphere and minimising energy consumption, without any compromise with comfort. Modern technology symbolises the age of energy positive buildings ready at hand for both domestic and office use optimised by thermal storage technology. Therefore, smart cities will meet the energy requirements of India in future and help increasing the sustainable and efficient energy. Further advancements in energy security will help India to become a global icon.

2. Globalisation: A Blessing or a Curse for a Developing Country?

INTRODUCTION

Globalisation has brought a radical change in the business enterprises across the world as well as multiplied the expectations of the entrepreneurs. This term is taken from the word 'globalise' meaning the emergence of international networks of economic policies. Although many scholars have used the term 'globalisation' in the different time spans from 1944 to 1981 and in the 1990s, yet the credit for coining this term goes to Economist Theodore Levitt who, by the article, 'Globalisation of Markets' published in 1983 May-June issue in Harvard Business Review, widely popularised the term by bringing it into the mainstream business audience in the latter half of the 1980s. Since its emergence, the idea of globalisation has motivated challenging denotations and interpretations, with precursors dating back to the activities of colonial and imperial trade and commerce across Asia and the Indian Ocean from the latter half of fifteenth century onwards. Because of the complication of the idea, research projects, articles and discussions often concentrated on the single idea of globalisation.

In 1992, Roland Robertson, professor of sociology at University of Aberdeen, an early writer in the field, defined globalisation as: the compression of the world and the intensification of the consciousness of the world as a whole.

According to economist Takis Fotopoulos, 'economic globalisation' is the opening and deregulation of commodity, capital and labour markets leading towards present neoliberal globalisation; 'political globalisation' refers to the emergence of transnational nobility and a gradual reduction of the nation state; whereas 'Cultural globalisation' means homologising culture across the world. 'Ideological globalisation', 'technological globalisation' and 'social globalisation' are some other terms that he used.

The Global Cities Institute at RMIT University identifies four main practical spheres of globalisation: Economic, political, cultural and ecological, with avoidance of the fifth sphere, ideological from the other four. According to Steger, ideological sphere is filled with a range of rules, claims, viewpoints and narratives about the phenomenon itself.

HOW GLOBALISATION EMERGED?

The rapid use of the term, 'globalisation' has begun from the mid-1980s and especially since the mid-1990s. In 2000, the International Monetary Fund (IMF) recognised four fundamental aspects of globalisation: Trade and transactions, capital and investment movements, migration and movement of people and the promulgation of knowledge. Moreover, some environmental conditions such as climate change, cross-border air and water pollution and over-fishing of the ocean are also considered as parts of globalisation. These proceedings of globalisation affect economics, firms, economic and socio-cultural resources and the natural environment and are affected by business and work environment.

After the Second World War was over, proceedings of the politicians led to the Bretton Woods conference where an agreement by the powerful governments was signed aiming at laying down the framework for international monetary policy, commerce and finance, and setting up several international institutions with the intention of facilitating economic growth and development, various rounds of trade opening simplified and lowered trade restrictions. In the beginning, the General Agreement on Tariffs and Trade (GATT) resulted in a series of agreements to simplify trade barriers. The World Trade Organisation (WTO) succeeded GATT and set up a framework for negotiating and formalising trade agreements and a process for the resolution of disputes. Exports rose to 16.2 per cent in 2001 from 8.5 per cent of total gross world product in 1970. When the perspective of manoeuvring global agreements to advance trade foundered in the Doha round of trade negotiation, many countries shifted to bilateral or smaller multilateral agreements like the 2011 South Korea-United States Free Trade Agreement.

Open skies policies and low-cost carriers have brought competition in the international aviation market. As a result, aviation has now become very affordable to middle classes in developed countries since the 1970s. By the 1990s, the development of low-cost transport and communication networks reduced the cost of communication between countries. Nowadays, manpower is easy to cut down as works like accounting, engineering design and machine development can be done by using a computer from anywhere in the world.

The interrelatedness of the world's economies and cultures which developed rapidly in the late nineteenth and early twentieth century declined from the 1910s owing to the consecutive World Wars and Cold War; but once again it grew quickly in the 1980s and 1990s. A considerable evolution of global interconnection came off across the world following the revolutions of 1989 and the succeeding liberalisation in different parts of the world. Migration and flux of people can also be considered as the predominant characteristic of the process of globalisation. In comparison with the past decades, almost double labour force migrated from 1965 to 1990, and this movement of people happened between the developing and the underdeveloped countries. The inclusion of market-oriented economic policies that stimulate private property rights, free enterprise and competition has helped the economy of Asia to grow rapidly. According to Human Development Report of UNDP 2003, especially in the East Asian developing countries, the rate of GDP grew to 5.9 per cent per capita from 1975 to 2001. In relation to this, Martin Wolf, the British economic journalist said that the earnings of the poor developing countries, which have more than half of the world's population, grew considerably faster than the richest countries remaining comparatively steady in their growth, leading to the minimised international inequality and the prevalence of poverty.

Growth of globalisation too has never been easy and smooth. One of the stiff barriers that came in course of the growth of globalisation was the recession of the late 2000s which was related to lower growth like cross-boundary phone calls and the use of Skype, or short-term negative growth (like trade) of global interconnectedness. The four major cross-boundary flows—trade of goods and services, information, nationals (migrants, tourists and students) and capitals—have been in the study of the DHL Global Connectedness Index which declares that after 2008, the depth of global integration decreased by nearly one-tenth, but it surpassed the pre-fall peak by 2013.

EFFECT OF GLOBALISATION

Societies which are globalised provide a complex series of forces and factors that draw nationals, cultures, markets, faiths and practices into progressively vaster propinquity to one another, and growing international trade and commerce with stiff hurdles to enter corporate consortium.

Active economic liberalisation and international integration brought about certain demographic changes in the developing world that has resulted in increasing social security and, in contrary, decreasing inequality. Martin Wolf asserted that in the developing world, in general, life expectancy increased by four months every year after 1970 and infant mortality rate decreased to 58 per thousand in 2000 from 107 in 1970 because of the developments in the standard of living and healthcare conditions; adult literacy too in developing countries increased to 74 per cent in 1998 from 53 per cent in 1970 and with the passage of time, the illiteracy rate among the young assures to decrease to the lowest rate. Moreover, in the developing world, in general, the fertility rates decreased to 2.8 per woman in 2000 from 4.1 in 1980, which points out the growth of education standard of women on fertility, and control of minimum number of children with more parental care, attention and investment. As a result, a large number of rich and educated parents have come up with fewer children with a view to giving their children opportunities of education by taking them away from labour force—improving the issue of child labour. Consequently, in spite of the apparent unequal distribution of income within these developing countries, their economic growth and prosperity have largely resulted in the progressive standards of living and welfare for the population.

The ASEAN Free Trade Area is a trade union agreement by the Association of South-east Asian Nations that supports local manufacturing in all ASEAN countries. Only the six countries of South Asian Nations—Singapore, Brunei, Indonesia, Malaysia, Philippines and Thailand signed the AFTA agreement on 28 January 1992 in Singapore, then Vietnam (in 1995), Laos and Myanmar (in 1997) and Cambodia (in 1999) signed it, respectively.

An international foundation of legal agreements, institutions, and both formal and informal economic players get together, within the early twenty-first century, with the objective of promoting international fluxes of financial capital for the causes of investment and trade financing. This global financial system appeared during the first modern movement of economic globalisation, marked by the foundation of central banks, multilateral treaties and intergovernmental organisations in order to develop the clarity, regulation and efficacy of international markets. The world economy became progressively integrated financially throughout the twentieth century when nations liberalised capital accounts and deregulated financial zones. A number of financial demands in Europe, Asia and Latin America left infectious effects on other countries, when globalisation was exposed to fraught capital flows. Financial organisations had grown larger with a more advanced and interconnected range of investment proceedings and by the early twenty-first century quickly spread among other nations during the financial crisis suffered by the USA known as the worldwide financial crisis and is considered as the creator of the Great Recession across the world.

COMMENTS ON GLOBALISATION

Regarding such activities in the world and the human costs as well, critiques of globalisation were naturally led to discussion and indicate a 'multitude of interconnected vital consequences—social disintegration, a decline of democracy, more quick and extensive degradation of the environment, the outbreak of new diseases, increasing poverty and separation' which they asserted to be the unexpected outcome of globalisation. Others asserted that, as the forces of globalisation have resulted in the spread of western-style democracy, this has been accompanied by a rise in inter-ethnic tension and violence as free market economic policies amalgamate democratic methods of universal franchise as well as an increase in militarisation to necessitate democratic doctrines as a measure to disagreement resolution.

It is known that with globalisation we have come close to 'the end of geography', but it may not have brought us to 'the end of history'. Since about 1980, the Third Industrial Revolution charged the stiff pressure of time and space which has transformed the mode of our interactions with the international environment. Globalisation, for many, has escalated cross-boundary exchange of capital, goods, services, ideas, information, technology, legal systems and nationals desirably and irrevocably, having guaranteed a rising standard of living throughout the world. Others retreat from globalisation because they find it to be the soft underbelly of corporate colonialism that despoils and benefits behind unrestrained consumerism.

Overseas development assistance from the rich to poor countries has amounted to $50–80 billion per year in the last two decades, and simultaneously about $500–800 billion funds have been brought illegally from the poor to rich countries i.e. for every one dollar of legal fund, the West get in return $10 illegal funds and, for welfare steps, lectures the rest on corruption.

The benefits and costs of linking and delinking have an unequal distribution. Industrially developed countries have mutual interdependence; developing countries, on the whole, have independence in economic relations with one another; and developing countries, to a great extent, have dependence on industrially developed countries. But Brazil, China and India have started to change this equation.

The income levels between countries and peoples have increasingly diverged with expanding inequality among and within nations. Assets and incomes are more focused. Wage shares have declined. Profit shares have swelled. Capital flexibility side-by-side labour rigidity has cut down the bargaining power of labour organisation.

The growing poverty and inequality has left great effect on social and political stability among and within the states—growth for a few countries and people while marginalisation and elision for the bulk. The global markets are growing faster while social and economic organisations are failing to ensure a parallel, balanced, comprehensive and sustainable development. Labour rights have been nonchalantly protected whereas capital and property rights sedulously, and trade and finance rules of the world are discriminatory. This has lopsided effects on rich and poor countries.

The concern of many developing countries, even before the global financial crisis (GFC), was the adverse infringement of globalisation in their economic dominance, cultural integrity and social stability. 'Interdependence' among unequals changed into the dependence of some in international markets functioning under the supremacy of others. The GFC confirmed that the unrestrained transnational forces can inundate absent effective regulatory organisations, markets, states and civil society.

One of the worst sides of globalisation is human trafficking—turning humans into commodities bought and sold in the international marketplace, and women and children are the most exposed ones. In all continents, NGOs endeavour to cope with this dastardly activity and report on those engaged in it.

South Africa has experienced the growth of intricate transnational crime organisations. The illegal trafficking in narcotics, mineral resources, ivory, counterfeit products and stolen property is flourishing. International crime consortiums exploit government weaknesses to profiteer large sums of money. Illegal migration and money laundering snatch the state's valuable human and material resources, in a region that urgently requires them.

Insurgencies flourishing as a consequence of the disproportions created by globalisation have caused a distinct challenge in the world. The 'development dichotomy' explains the substantial national-level progress in India gone concurrently with an ever wider gap between the prosperity of urban, middle-class Indians and the downtrodden who still are in many of its 600,000 villages—the abode of most Indians. The deracinated aboriginal populations (Adivasis) failing to adapt to the demands of modern economy often see rebellious redemption as the only way out of their plight.

On the other hand, Sri Lanka's Tamil Tigers are notably one of the most globalised terrorist movements anywhere in the world. Although it was transitory, yet it was overwhelmingly success mainly because of their effectual reliance on the Sri Lankan Tamil community to gain resources as well as to master strong political support for their inducement.

Jihadists, in South-east Asia, Afghanistan and in Central America, are proficiently using modern IT and telecom technology to boost their cause and encourage their objectives, by building link between the drug trade and terrorism introduced by the CIA. Jihadists, by adopting the ancient methods duplicate the obsolete way Osama bin Laden, remaining head, collected his information through pieces of paper brought by hand by his loyal messengers, transfer funds across the world perfectly and in a definitely untraceable way. Undoubtedly, the negative impact of globalisation will soon be resolved, but it is a matter of fact whether the GFC terminates globalisation, widely known for three decades.

CONCLUSION

Globalisation is considered as the advantageous expansion of liberty and capitalism. Jagdish Bhagwati, a former adviser to the United Nations on globalisation, declares that 'Although there are obvious problems with overly rapid development, globalisation is a very positive force that lifts countries out of poverty by causing a virtuous economic cycle associated with faster economic growth'. Paul Krugman, an economist, a hard-core advocate of globalisation and free trade declares—by disagreeing greatly with many critics of globalisation—that many of them are lacking the fundamental understanding of comparative benefit and its necessity in present world.

The flux of migrants to countries economically advanced has been demanded to introduce a system for gathering global wages. An IMF evaluation pointed out a prospective for skills which are to be transferred back to developing countries as wages with the objective of fostering growth in those countries. Last but not the least, the promulgation of knowledge has proved to be an essential facet of globalisation. With a view to favouring most the developing and least developing countries (LDCs), technological innovation or technological transfer is speculated, for instance, the adoption of mobile phones.

In the late twentieth and early twenty-first centuries, globalisation has resulted in the re-emergence of the concept—growing economic interdependence fosters peace, while in the late nineteenth and early twentieth centuries, globalisation had led this concept to be very persuasive and a predominant principle of classical liberals of that period like the young, John Maynard Keynes.

3. Make in India: A Giant's Step to Promote Manufacturing

INTRODUCTION

The clarion call: Make in India revitalises India's trade and commerce enterprises and entrepreneurs to help the recycling of India's historical monopoly as a trading economy with the inspiration of being self-sufficient and re-emerging as the lord of modern trade imperialism. Historical evidence proves that India was a trade and commerce-based economy supported by an advanced transport system. India was then, as a whole, 'small-scale manufacturing industry', 'handloom industry', and 'art, craft and cottage industry' underwritten by its trade. Then we had a large quantity of manufacturing surplus and the trade greatly supported growth and prosperity by spreading our goods far and wide. India earned name and fame even in European markets, drew the attention of the European trading companies, and for this reason India was then considered a **'Golden Bird'** in trade and commerce.

However, with the arrival of the European trading companies and the establishment of 'British Colonial Empire', foreign trade had been destroyed. 'Indian Cottage Industries' completely declined, pattern of agriculture changed by the forceful replacement of food crops with cash crops—the raw material for most of the 'Colonial Industries' and were in great demand even in European industries. This change made an adverse impact on Indian economic structure and resulted in its complete downfall. Moreover, the drainage of Indian wealth and resources encumbered the economy and ultimately removed the economic cornerstone of the country.

India regained its ground after Independence and partition and endeavoured to rebuild and strengthen its economy. Because of the immature industries and for fear of competition with foreign popular and cheap goods, however, India followed socialistic ideology-based policy of 'Central Plans' by giving initial importance on

'Heavy Industries'. However, the initiative failed owing to the want of latest technology and investment.

When the 'New Economic Policy'—liberal economy came into effect, the current Indian economy was restructured and our required markets were created. With refreshed initiative, India is now endeavouring to improvise and boom its industries relying on the insufficient investment resources and technology. Although Indian economy lags behind other economies in the world for these insufficiencies, yet India is a vast source of skilled human resource largely in service sector, and by its contribution this sector grows rapidly and supports our economy supplying a surplus in the form of 'Balance of Payment'. But the comparative immaturity and deficiency of industries cannot elevate us from the ground, and because of the narrow outlook of intrinsic entrepreneurship our limited exports also suffer recurrent trade shortfall which gives more adverse 'Balance of Payment' and shows current account shortage. So, revenue generation greatly depends on the service sector, the tertiary one, while our primary sector has been overburdened persistently as consequences of marginalised land area, out-of-date agricultural practices, want of irrigation, and unforeseen climate—which, in general, greatly affect our social, economic and political structure. On the other hand, the problems of growing unemployment rate, hike of market price, poverty, health and hygiene, confusion in between the continuity and restructuring education system, access to natural resources like clear water, energy etc. have postulated a risk in Indian economy. At this crucial juncture, the Modi Government has emerged with a clear vision of broad outlook and great expectation with the objective of combating all these serious challenges and bringing a radical change in India. With the firm conviction of building India for its re-emergence as the manufacturing leader, this government has given emphasis on the pro-industry motive, and is striving to enhance growth by learning lessons from the past. This optimistic vision and confidence has created Prime Minister, Mr. Modi's 'Make in India' campaign and it has waved a hope of growth and development across the country. Undoubtedly, it will revive our industries and increase the rate of manufacturing power though it has to go a long way to reach this great goal.

'MAKE IN INDIA' VERSUS 'MADE IN INDIA'

In the connotation, 'Make in India' ignited by Prime Minister, Mr. Modi, 'Make' means that the process of making or developing something should be executed in India in which foreigners can take part, while 'Made' in 'Made in India' implies that only the production is carried out in India and by India. The present government has tendency on the motto, 'Make in India' as to support its manufacturing units, India is greatly in need of infrastructure—the backbone of economy, the key to growth of industrial and manufacturing sector. Including new major initiatives which are designed with a view to facilitating investment, fostering innovation, protecting intellectual property and building highest quality manufacturing infrastructure, the initiative, 'Make in India', has been started with the long-term objective of shaping India as a manufacturing hub and bringing overall change in the economy of India. Now success mainly depends on leveraging human faculty because of faster changes in business dynamics, globalisation, stiff market competitiveness and global involvement boosting the growth of domestic manufacturing by international companies. Furthermore, increasing inflow of investments and technology transfer is expected to make the campaign, 'Make in India' a great success.

CONSTITUENTS AND DIMENSIONS OF 'MAKE IN INDIA'

'Make in India'—a well-devised strategy of administrative reforms and economic prudence—is the national manoeuvre and spearhead of the Government, which concentrates on turning 1.25 billion populous India into a 'global manufacturing hub' with sufficient job opportunities primarily providing a favourable environment to investors—domestic as well as overseas.

The aspiration statement of the official website, *www.makeinindia.gov.in*, promises to accomplish the determined goal giving background to India's manufacturing sector—in January 2010 accounted for fourth-fifth of the total production and grew just 3.3 per cent— by increasing the growth rate of manufacturing sector from 12–14 per cent annually over the medium term, the share of manufacturing in Gross Domestic Product (GDP) from 16 per cent to 25 per cent and emphasising in creating 100 million extra jobs by 2022 only in the manufacturing sector.

Targets to Achieve:

i. Target of an increase in manufacturing sector growth to 12–14% per annum over the medium term.
ii. An increase in the share of manufacturing in the country's Gross Domestic Product from 16 to 25% by 2022.
iii. To create 100 million additional jobs by 2022 in manufacturing sector.
iv. Creation of appropriate skill sets among rural migrants and the urban poor for inclusive growth.
v. An increase in domestic value addition and technological depth in manufacturing.
vi. Enhancing the global competitiveness of the Indian manufacturing sector.
vii. Ensuring sustainability of growth, particularly with regard to environment.

'MAKE IN INDIA': FOUNDATION

Aiming at boosting entrepreneurship in manufacturing as well as other sources in India, the 'Make in India' campaign is based on four columns:

1. **New Methods:** The campaign identifies 'ease of doing business' as the principal determinant to encourage entrepreneurship and has already undertaken some stratagems in order to ease business environment.
2. **New Infrastructure:** The government's objective is to build industrial corridors and smart cities, create highest standard infrastructure with ultra-modern technology and uninterrupted communication. Creative, innovative and research works are supported through a quick registration system and upgraded infrastructure for

IPR registration. The requirement of industry-oriented skills will be marked and initiatives to develop human faculty will be taken up accordingly.

3. **New Zones:** India is open to Foreign Direct Investment (FDI) largely in defence production, insurance, medical apparatus, construction and railway infrastructure.
4. **New Attitude:** The government will work as a facilitator instead of a regulator in co-operation with industry for sake of economic development of the developing country.

OBJECTIVES

i. The dogma of 'Make in India' lies on the backdrop of achieving an iconic identity and global leadership for India by revitalising its manufacturing sector and giving it a first track in global competitiveness.

ii. It aims at identifying substandard infrastructure and traditional labour, improving them in parlance of ultra-modern pattern and training labour as per the industrial job-oriented human faculty in the latest trend in order to foster 'micro, small and medium size enterprises' and 'self-help groups' that can earn name and fame in the world of manufacturing by proving entrepreneurship and producing cost-effective and highest quality products.

iii. The initiative looks for extensive growth seeking everyone's active participation, for instance, Pradhan Mantri Jan Dhan Yojana (PMJDY).

iv. It determines on developing next generation infrastructure to prove food security, healthy, clean, peaceful as well as sustainable environment to live in.

STRATEGIES IN A NUTSHELL

1. **Invest India body:** The investor assistance body founded by the government will play role of the first reference point in order to guide foreign investors on all cases regarding regulatory and policy issues and to facilitate them to gain regulatory clearances. The body will also assist foreign investors from the very beginning to the end of their stay India in the purpose of investing and executing of their project. The information and facts necessary for the potential investors for each sector have been provided in brochures.
2. **Consolidated services and faster security clearances:** The central government is consolidating all central government services in an e-Biz single window online portal and advising the states to introduce self-certification. It has also directed the ministries of home affairs to provide all security clearances for investment proposals within three months.
3. **Committed portal for business queries:** A committed body has been organised to meet the queries from business organisations through a newly developed web portal [*http://www.makeinindia.com*]. The final support team of the body would meet important queries within 72 hours. The portal also boasts of a comprehensive list of FAQs and answers.

4. **Interactions with the users/visitors:** A proactive outlook will be set up to trace visitors for their geographical situation, interest and real time user behaviour. Sequent visits will be modified for the visitor on the basis of the collected information, and registered visitors on the website or standard queries will be followed up with information and newsletter in relation the queries.
5. **Easing policies and laws:** A large number of defence items have been ode licensed, while industrial licences have been validated three years more.

ABATEMENT OF PENURY, EMPLOYMENT AND SKILL DEVELOPMENT

Now India has a population of over 1.25 billion and is not self-sufficient in utilising its resources for most of the concerned population because the majority belong to Below Poverty Line (BPL) and is living an uncertain and wretched life. 'Make in India' initiative promises to bring a radical change in every sphere of manufacturing industry resulting in the increase of job opportunities for the quality human faculty in diverse sectors and opening many scopes, without any limitations, for entrepreneurs and business enterprises. This growth will gradually uplift bulk of common people from BPL to middle class by helping them to grow and develop both socially and financially, making them aware of the necessity of education and vocational training to develop skills, and afford to purchase costlier things essential in their daily life. On the basis of the increase of this transformation, Indian markets will converse into a favourable market for the world.

INDIGENISATION OF GOODS

'Make in India' encourages business organisations and entrepreneurs by the idea of indigenising manufacturing of goods, which will soon make India self-sufficient and help to emerge as a global exporter, and simultaneously creates bulk of scopes to foreign investors and manufacturers of setting up business hubs in major 25 sectors to produce goods in order to supply the growing Indian markets. The ideology of 'Make in India' is to paying equal importance to all buyers which inspires cost effective manufacturing. On the other hand, the foundation of business hubs will grow in parallel with the market demand and India will soon turn into a huge market of diverse products. The production of more affordable goods will raise the market demand as well as profit which will help earning foreign exchange, and at the same time, minimise India's trade deficit and raise the figures of Balance of Payment. Moreover, India has great potential and is in urgent need of highly qualified personalities in respective spheres, for instance, to make successful executions of ambitious missions—Mars Mission.

WELCOMING THE WEST

By 'Make in India' policy, India is out of red carpet with series of measures, acceptable rules, easier norms and conditions, open to foreign investors and manufacturers for the sake of reaching the target of the aspiring India. At the peak season of globalisation, the West as well as the other countries of the world advanced in ultra-modern technology and huge investment looks at the Asian Markets with the aim of making investment and profit. At this crucial juncture, India—a large democracy and diverse demography—with its huge market has appeared as the suitable destination to those investors, and in the meantime many have already set up their business hubs. Therefore, 'Make in India' is on the right track to lead India its goal.

FOREIGN DIRECT INVESTMENT AND FIRST DEVELOP INDIA

The long-term significant initiative, 'Make in India', attracts foreign investors and entrepreneurs through Foreign Direct Investment (FDI) by providing a tremendous opportunity—First to Develop India (FDI), with lots of projects and schemes—beautifying Indian cities, towns, special economic zones and manufacturing areas.

Under this initiative, India has started many schemes such as Swatchh Bharat Abhiyan, Namami Gange (Ganga Action Plan) focusing on the resurgence and rehabilitation of rivers. The ideas of 'smart city' and 'heritage city' improve the standard of township as well as urban areas, and also build affordable houses, fosters India's once neglected civilisation, culture and tradition through sustainable development.

NO DEFECT AND NO EFFECT

No Defect: Goods must be manufactured in a careful considerate manner without defect as the slightest defect has an adverse impact of goods in the market. Therefore, manufacturing world class goods should replace with the highest quality ones with a vaster view to prove the trust and authenticity of products that bear the dream of 1.25 billion Indians.

No Effect: The use of raw materials, energy, water, fuel, land, etc. in industrial units to manufacture the desired amount of goods often interacts with environment and affects it especially in cases of climate change; but by proportionate planning and using advanced technology, alternative energy sources, new and renewable, green and clean energy resources emission of carbon can be reduced to a considerable rate, all as a whole, will help sustainable manufacturing with surplus.

REQUIREMENT OF RESTRUCTURING

The government of India has already taken measures to restructure the social and political standards of India, which are a must to make the mission of 'Make in India' a grand success. The assurance of the honest, foreseeable and growth-oriented governance is encouraging the foreign investors, and which results in the influx of foreign investment in India. By restructuring tax at entry level, the government has opened two ways—automatic and through government—before the foreign investors to invest and carry out business activities easily in India. Through Digital India—a best-in-class physical and online infrastructure—the government has concentrated on skill development inviting private players to actively take in all its schemes and campaigns of 'Make in India' mission executed by Public Private Partnership (PPP) and also has provided a platform of responsibility, transparency and honest and easy access to all its activities. In the true sense, the government assures its efficacy by Digital India, and in near future, it will empower e-corporate governance accountability and responsibility.

Some Slogans of 'Make in India'

- From agriculture to automobiles
- From hardware to software
- From televisions to movies
- From satellites to submarine
- From friendship to partnership
- From paper clips to power plants
- From bridges to biotechnology
- From roads to cities
- From profit to progress
- Whatever you want to make: Make in India

Major Sectors

1. Auto Components
2. Biotechnology
3. Automobiles
4. Aviation
5. Chemicals
6. Construction
7. Defence Manufacturing
8. IT and BPM
9. Electrical Machinery
10. Electronic System Design and Manufacturing
11. Food Processing
12. Leather
13. Pharmaceuticals
14. Media & Entertainment
15. Mining
16. Oil & Gas
17. Renewable Energy
18. Ports
19. Railways
20. Roads and Highways
21. Space
22. Textiles
23. Thermal Power
24. Tourism & Hospitality
25. Wellness

CONCLUSION

The success of 'Make in India' largely depends on the equal and direct participation of states through the federal structure of the nation, as the states have three-tier government with decentralised units like Panchayati Raj. So, 'Make in India' mission invites and encourages all its states to work hand in hand and cooperate actively in the hub-and-spoke schemes with a view to further this to the larger audience through the respective industries.

4. Sustainable Development during Climate Change

INTRODUCTION

Sustainable development, in recent times, is the global issue on which there is a wide agreement. The Brundtland's Report defines sustainable development as: "To meet the needs of present without compromising the ability of future generations to meet their own needs". This definition is mostly accepted as it recommends the concept of 'sustainable development'. The International Union for the Conservation of Nature and Natural Resources (IUCNNR) declares and confirms through the World Conservation Strategy report (1980) that the social, economic and ecological factors must be considered in order to carry out sustainable development.

Some of the definitions by the International Panel on Climate Change (IPCC) explain the relationship between climate change and sustainable development.

CLIMATE CHANGE: SENSITIVITY, ADAPTABILITY AND VULNERABILITY

- **Sensitivity** is the degree to which a system is affected, either adversely or beneficially, by climate-related stimuli. Climate-related stimuli encompass all the elements of climate change, including mean climate characteristics, climate variability and the frequency and magnitude of extremes. The effect may be direct (e.g., a change in crop yield in response to a change in the mean, range or variability of temperature) or indirect (e.g., damages caused by an increase in the frequency of coastal flooding due to sea-level rise).
- **Adaptive capacity** is the ability of a system to adjust to climate change, including climate variability and extremes, to moderate potential damages, to take advantage of opportunities or to cope with the consequences.
- **Vulnerability** is the degree to which a system is susceptible to, or unable to cope with, adverse effects of climate change, including climate variability and extremes. Vulnerability is a function of the character, magnitude and rate of climate change and variation to which a system is exposed, its sensitivity and its adaptive capacity.

CLIMATE CHANGE: A MAJOR CONCERN

Regarding freshwater supply, food processing, health and hygiene, natural ecosystems, etc. humankind is facing many major environmental challenges—one of which is climate change. The latest scientific evaluation confirms that since the pre-industrial age, the earth's climate order has had a verifiable change on regional as well as global levels. The other proofs declare that human activities are responsible for the rise of temperature (at the rate of 0.1°C per decade) observed over the last 50 years. The IPCC predicts that the mean temperature of the world may rise between 1.4 and 5.8°C by 2100 probably affecting the ecosystems, sea level rise, global hydrological system, crop production and other related processes mainly of the developing countries in the subtropical regions including India.

As the climate change is the greatest challenge of sustainable development, effectual climate strategies must be considered in order to make regional and national development processes more sustainable. Otherwise, the different consequences of climate change, the responses of climate strategy, and related socio-economic development will, in turn, affect adversely the ability and opportunities of the countries to accomplish their targets of sustainable development. Especially, the technological and socio-economic features of different ways will adversely affect emissions, the rate, impacts and vastness of climate change, the ability to adjust and the capacity to alleviate.

In the UN Conference on Environment and Development (UNCED) held at Rio de Janeiro in 1992 guided to Framework Convention on Climate Change (FCCC), which founded the framework in order to stabilise the greenhouse gases eventually in the atmosphere, by identifying the common but individualised accountabilities and respective abilities, and social and economic conditions. The Convention was enforced in 1994. Later on, the 1997 Kyoto Protocol came into effect in 2005, and reaffirmed the importance of stabilising greenhouse gas concentrations in the atmosphere in respect to the sustainable development principles. The protocol formulated guidelines and rules concerning the extent to which an industrialised country involved should cut down the rate of its emissions of six greenhouse gases: carbon dioxide, methane, nitrous oxide, chlorofluorocarbon (CFC), hydrofluorocarbons (HFCs) and perfluorocarbons (PFC). The industrialised countries required cutting down the emissions of greenhouse gases by a weighted average of 5.2 per cent adhering to the 1990 greenhouse gas emissions, and to be achieved the target by the end of the scheduled five-year period, from 2008 to 2012. The Kyoto Protocol does not direct mandatorily the developing countries to cut down the emissions of their greenhouse gases.

CONCERNS OF INDIA ON CLIMATE CHANGE

India—the emerging economic superpower in the world in recent time—has about 17 per cent of the total world population, which includes around 35 per cent poor and 40 per cent illiterate people in the world. The economic reform of India has brought about the economic growth, the rate of rise in foreign exchange, IT revolution, export growth and so on, in parallel to the growth of inequality in income distribution. The continuous rejection from the benefits of economic revolution with regard to low agricultural growth—without the reduction of dependent population in the agricultural sector, its share in GDP has been cut down to half, lower employment growth, focuses only on poverty the said certain groups: Scheduled Caste (SC)/Scheduled Tribe (ST); occupation—agricultural and casual labour; low development rate of women and children and sex ratio favourable to men. The sex ratio at birth is 500 females per 1000 males on the basis of the study report of the hospital statistics in South Delhi. The above reasons altogether have caused the growing social and economic discrepancy which is a possible danger to sustainable development, whereas the economic growth in recent years, with a tickle-down effect, creates job opportunities for people from the most educated section to the poorest section of the society.

About 700 million people in rural India depend largely on the climate-sensitive sectors: agriculture, fisheries and forests, and natural resources like water, grasslands, mangroves, coastal areas and biodiversity for their maintenance and livelihoods. Climate change and its negative impacts will gradually decrease the adaptive capacity of the forest dwellers, dry-land farmers, nomadic shepherds and fisher folk. The indispensible natural sources—air, water and soil—for living on earth have been dwindling at an alarming rate. Behind the impending water crisis in India, there lie plenty of factors: increasing demand of drinking water, inequality in regional distribution, lack of appropriate framework for just use, impotent knowledge and resources, major changes in land-use, long-term decline of water level and rising salinity and pollution. India is vulnerable to the vagaries of weather conditions and climate change though it has huge agricultural lands, steps for sustainable development.

India has to bring the comprehensive growth into effect widely including rapid labour-releasing agricultural growth, required employment creation, the reduction of poverty, improvement of social sectors—education and health—and women empowerment in order to combat the challenges posed by those situations. With regard to these improvements, we should learn from our neighbouring country, China, where there are equitable distribution of income through broad-based, high and labour-releasing agricultural growth, ready-at-hand infrastructure, higher rate of literacy and best-in-class skills, incentives for the foundation of business firms in rural areas, and quick and easy access to credit and inputs for the poor section of society altogether which are absolutely necessary for a developing country. Women should be empowered through the substitution of 'Life-Cycle Approach' of the girl child with the main objective of marriage and motherhood for 'Capability Approach'—as propagated by the Nobel laureate Indian economist, Amartya Sen—where the girl child's contributions both in economic and social terms are given due recognition. All measures and initiatives related the girl child, therefore, call for urgent and thorough review by the concerned authority with a view to promoting the status of the girl child as an asset rather than the burden just like conditional cash and non-cash transfer and so on.

Collaborative and continued campaigns are a must to combat the challenges posed by climate change and its negative impacts. In order to handle and carry out a solution to the problems of water scarcity and the decreasing level of groundwater table, the following call for urgent measures to be initiated: Practices of ground water conservation like construction of *khadin* (an Indian term for groundwater conservation popular in Andhra Pradesh, Madhya Pradesh, Maharashtra, Karnataka, Tamil Nadu and Gujarat), renovating dams, recharge shafts, farm ponds, injection wells (in coastal region to fight problems of excessively pumped out aquifers), and contour trenching, detaining surface run-off at elevations and, at the same time, surface water conservation techniques, like construction of *ooranies* (an Indian term for surface water collection ponds with modernised catchments, popular and commonly found in Tamil Nadu). We can also implement rooftop rainwater harvesting and threshing floors by giving proper training and creating awareness among the masses for water conservation. The active participation of the Gram Panchayat/Village Health and Sanitation Committee in operation, maintenance, water quality surveillance can bring about a grand success as they did the National Rural Drinking Water Quality Monitoring and Surveillance Project. Some household measures like using water-efficient household equipment: proper metering of water, low volume flushing cisterns, the concept of a water-efficient home, rational tariff and recycling and reuse of water can decrease the demand of water and encourage its conservation.

By introducing long-term preventive actions such as pasture development, afforestation and livestock management—growing better top feed species surviving annual droughts and providing rich fodder, we can carry out united development in drought-prone regions. We can implement contingency crop schemes by growing diverse combinations of crop, fruits, grasses, and trees in order to decrease the risk of crop failure and keep farm income stable. Methodical land management and latest irrigation technologies: sprinklers and drip systems should be widely used aiming at increasing the production per unit of irrigation water. Other steps like human and livestock population management and creation of substitute methods of non-farm employment can help us gaining far-reaching success. A survey report entitled, 'Comprehensive Assessment of Watershed Programmes in India' conducted by the International Crops Research Institute for the Semi-Arid Tropics (ICRISAT), Hyderabad, has marked that the wastelands decreased by around 8.58 Mha during 2000 and 2005, by using diverse techniques of integrated development of the drought-prone regions. The *National Rural Employment Guarantee Act* (NREGA) is now one of the most dependable programmes dealing with chronic hunger and poverty with the aim of promoting sustainable development in rural India. The government has fixed two-third of the measures under NREGA for water conservation (52 per cent) and land development (14 per cent).

With the objective of boosting the present ecological conditions, India has undertaken a string of strict measures, these are as follows:

i. India aims at registering 31 per cent projects under Clean Development Mechanism (CDM)—the highest number in the world. Under the Kyoto Protocol, CDM or Carbon Credits Mechanism has been devised with a view to rewarding cashable points to eco-friendly projects based on the control of the carbon emissions.

ii. Mumbai has started with the organisation, Sustainable Technologies and Environmental Projects Ltd. (STEPs), which has found out a method of transmuting plastic, electric and organic waste into petroleum without any normal detrimental remnant. Such a plant which costs US $2–3 million can produce about 25,000 litres of petroleum every day, and the operating cost of which is only ₹12 per litre excluding the cost of raw materials. Aiming at reducing the emission of carbon, India is also attempting to substitute ecofriendly biofuels by mixing ethanol, doping, and nonedible oil for 10 per cent of its transport fuels by the next 10 years.

iii. India has now 2 billion square feet (sq. ft.) area of green building projects and is targeting 10 billion sq. ft. by 2022 to be the owner of the highest area of green building expanse. ITC Green Centre in Gurgaon (now Gurugram) was rewarded with the highest level—Platinum rating on November 11, 2004 for the world's largest green building with an area of 170,000 sq. ft.—and the first non-commercial complex in India—by the Green Building Council-Leadership in Energy and Environmental Design of the United States (USGBC-LEED), a non-profit organisation founded in 1993 that has undertaken an initiative to reward certificates at the platinum, gold and other levels by using the 69-point criteria with a view to encouraging green buildings through sustainable development. ITC now reports its performance in financial, environmental as well as social capital.

iv. India invites people to take part in the Corporate Social Responsibility (CSR) so as to decreasing the social and economic discrepancy, and promoting ecological conditions through diverse activities with the inclusion of the corporate sectors: education, health, natural resource management, community support, infrastructure development, non-farm and farm-based subsistence development.

CURRENT DEVELOPMENT AGENDA

The optimism which is based on the proper and practical imperatives of developing an equitable world and a sustainable planet has growingly appeared inevitable is emphasised in an outline prepared by the United Nations Open Working Group on Sustainable development Goals. Because of the moderate but optimistic progress which reduced the extreme poverty to its half five years before the given deadline—achieved on the 2015 Millennium Development Goals—the hope of attaining these ideals has become positive. In 2010, the world clinched success targeted by Millennium Development Goals (MDG) on drinkable water on the basis of access to improved sources of drinking water, but failed to realise on sanitation.

Under the MDGs, the new development criteria set up eight anti-poverty targets the world pledged itself to attain by 2015. Considerable progress has been brought out on the MDGs, showing the value of an integrated agenda supported by goals and targets. In spite of this success, the indignity of poverty cannot be eradicated.

The members of the United Nations are now on their way to defining Sustainable Development Goals (SDGs) considering as part of a new agenda to execute the job of the MDGs, and leaving no job behind.

The Member States at the Sustainable Development Summit in September 2015 adopted an agenda.

They proposed 17 goals of Sustainable Development

1. End poverty in all its forms everywhere.
2. End hunger, achieve food security and improved nutrition, and promote sustainable agriculture.
3. Ensure healthy lives and promote wellbeing for all at all ages.
4. Ensure inclusive and equitable quality education and promote lifelong learning opportunities for all.
5. Achieve gender equality and empower all women and girls.
6. Ensure availability and sustainable management of water and sanitation for all.
7. Ensure access to affordable, reliable, sustainable and modern energy for all.
8. Promote sustained, inclusive and sustainable economic growth, full and productive employment and decent work for all.
9. Build resilient infrastructure, promote inclusive and sustainable industrialisation and foster innovation.
10. Reduce inequality within and among countries.
11. Make cities and human settlements inclusive, safe, resilient and sustainable.
12. Ensure sustainable consumption and production patterns.
13. Take urgent action to combat climate change and its impacts (taking note of agreements made by the UNFCCC forum).
14. Conserve and sustainably use the oceans, seas and marine resources for sustainable development.
15. Protect, restore and promote sustainable use of terrestrial ecosystems, sustainably manage forests, combat desertification and halt and reverse land degradation, and halt biodiversity loss.
16. Promote peaceful and inclusive societies for sustainable development, provide access to justice for all and build effective, accountable and inclusive institutions at all levels.
17. Strengthen the means of implementation and revitalise the global partnership for sustainable development.

CONCLUSION

The most effectual means to discourse climate change is the adaptation of a measure for sustainable development by transferring it to technologies environmentally sustainable and the improvement of energy efficiency, reforestation, forest conservation, renewable energy, water conservation, etc. The most important factor to developing countries is controlling assailability of their natural and socio-economic systems to the assumed climate change. Other developing countries including India will combat the challenge of boosting alleviation and adaptation tactics, bearing the result of such an effort and its significance for economic development.

India is a vast developing country which has about two-third of the population depending only on the climate-sensitive sectors: agriculture, fisheries and forests. The assumed climate change under different situations will probably leave effects on water supply, food production, livelihoods and biodiversity. We have, therefore, a consequential scope in scientific advancement and international understanding to foster alleviation and adaptation which needs advanced scientific understanding, networking, capacity building, and widely acknowledged consultation processes. We can carry out sustainable development successfully by strategically directing all our initiatives to our targeted goal.

5. Judicial Activism: Hope of Justice for the Underprivileged Section

INTRODUCTION

Securing justice is the fundamental duty of our polity. The founders of the constitution have accorded justice, the highest position. The ideology behind drafting the constitution is to give justice, social, economical and political security. People look forward to the Judiciary as the stronghold of protection and justice in times of any injustice.

The Political system of India has introduced Parliamentary form of government that consists of three administrative bodies: The Executive, the Legislative and the Judiciary. These three bodies are independent and have equal significance according to the constitution.

India is, therefore, a federal or representative democracy where administration of justice has special importance regarding protection of the rights of the individuals against the Executive and the Legislative. Judiciary has been kept independent and supreme—with a view to executing this responsibility—from the rest two administrative bodies and which is a must because there is a constitutional division of powers between Centre and States, a functional division of power between the Executive, the Legislative and the Judiciary. Only an independent and impartial judiciary can handle the charge of ensuring rights of the individuals and protecting democracy, and also effectively protect and interpret the meaning of the constitution.

PROVISIONS OF THE CONSTITUTION

According to the direction of Article 50, the Constitution makes Judiciary independent from the Executive and the Legislative, and also directs the Executive and the Legislative not to interfere in the proceedings of the Judiciary.

According to Article 13 of the Constitution of India, the inconsistent laws relating to the derogation of any of the fundamental rights shall be invalid. It means that regarding such cases only the Supreme Court and the High Courts have the power and right to execute a judicial review and also to issue writs.

Article 13(2), the 'heart of the Indian Constitution', prescribes—the provision regarding judicial activism—that the Union or the States shall not make any law that contravenes any of the Fundamental Rights included in Part III of the Constitution, or any law made in contravention of the aforestated mandate shall, to the extent of the contravention, be void.

Article 14 of the Indian Constitution guarantees, to every citizen of India, the right to 'equality before law' and 'equal protection of laws' i.e. all are equal before law and will be equally protected by law. It also prohibits unreasonable discrimination between persons.

DIFFERENCE BETWEEN JUDICIAL REVIEW AND JUDICIAL ACTIVISM

As the guardian of the Indian Constitution, judiciary plays the role of an interpreter and observer over the Legislature. The judiciary can declare any act or action ultra-virus provided it proves to be so in parlance of the interpretation of the Constitution, and can also prevent the Legislature from any steps, if it transgresses the powers provided to it by the Constitution. This process is called Judicial Review (JR).

On the other hand, the process of readily validating the values of the constitution by the judiciary in exercising its power to perform the act of JR actively, quickly and impartially is called Judicial Activism (JA). The quick, accurate and impartial performance of the judiciary proves that JR has gradually acquired the form of Judicial Activism in India.

Judicial Activism is the fundamental duty of the courts to exercise their power of Judicial Review. So, there is a considerable difference between JR and JA.

The Supreme Court and many High Courts of India were given the power to consider the constitutionality of legislative and administrative actions so as to protect and enforce the fundamental rights guaranteed in Part III of the Constitution. Meanwhile, judicial review over administrative action has developed gradually on the lines of common law doctrines such as 'legitimate expectation', 'proportionality', 'reasonableness' and principles of natural justice. Article 246 of the Constitution read with the seventh schedule, contemplates a clear distinction and a zone of junction between the law-making powers of the Union Parliament and the many State Legislatures. So, the High Courts are also approached to consider the questions of legislative competence, mostly in the context of Centre-State relations.

Consequently, the extent of judicial review before Indian courts has, developed gradually in ensuring fairness in administrative action, protecting the fundamental rights of citizens guaranteed by the Constitution of India and considering questions of legislative competence between the Centre and the States. According to Article 32 of the Constitution, the Supreme Court of India has the power to enforce these fundamental rights, and citizens have the right to directly approach it seeking justice against the contravention of any of the fundamental rights.

EVALUATION OF FUNDAMENTAL RIGHTS

The emergency period and the disreputable Habeas corpus formed exemplary moment in history of judicial review in India. The vehement criticism of the judgment resulted in firm base to judicial review succeeded by the extension of fundamental rights. Article 21 of the Constitution of India reads: 'No person shall be deprived of his life or personal liberty except according to procedure established by law'. The exclusive interpretation of this article in the early years of the Supreme Court in A.K. Gopalan's case was altered in Maneka Gandhi's case. In that resolution, it was held that restraints of the government on 'personal liberty' should be en masse assessed against the guarantees of fairness, non-arbitrariness and reasonableness prescribed under Articles 14, 19 and 21 of the constitution. The Court developed a theory of 'inter-relationship of rights' to hold that governmental action which curbed either of these rights should meet the entitled threshold for restraints on all of them. In this manner, the courts consolidated the guarantee of substantive due processes of the United States of America (USA) into the language of Article 21 and were followed by a series of decisions, where the ideas of 'life' and 'personal liberty' were interpreted liberally to put in rights excluded explicitly in Part III. In this regard Justice Bhagwati said, "We think that the right to life includes the right to live with human dignity and all that goes along with it, namely the bare necessities of life such as adequate nutrition, clothing and shelter over the head and facilities for reading, writing and expressing oneself in diverse forms."

PUBLIC INTEREST LITIGATION

The impeccable judicial activism of India is that the poor, penurious and disadvantaged sections of our nation can access to courts through Public Interest Litigation (PIL). The Supreme Court of India led the judiciary, from 1979, in such a way that it became pertinent to the nation and actively took part in the dispenser of social justice far beyond the contemplation of the founding fathers of the Constitution.

Through letters written to sitting judges—in countless occasions—the court took *suo moto* cognisance of matters that include the abuse of bonded labourers, prisoners, and inmates of mental institutions. This practice of legal initiating proceedings based on letters has now been streamlined and has been known as *'epistolary jurisdiction'*, the nature of proceedings itself does not absolutely fix into the recognised common-law framework of adversarial litigation, in (PIL). The courtroom proceedings differ significantly from ordinary civil or criminal appeals. In most public interest related litigations, the judges play a far more active role in the literal sense as well by throwing questions to the parties as well as critical solutions when an adversarial environment may exist in cases where actions are presented to call attention to administrative indifference or the government's condone of abusive practices.

Supreme Court advocate Kapila Hingorani, in 1979, highlighted in the court a series of articles published in a newspaper revealing the plight of prisoners under trial in Bihar, most of whom had served pretrial detention more than the period they could have been imprisoned if convicted. Sunil Batra, one of the prisoners, drew attention of Justice Krishna Iyer of the Supreme Court by a letter to the accounts of torture by prison authorities and the miserable conditions of prisoners in jails. This was considered as a petition. Then the Court put orders into effect for humane conditions in jails. In 1980, two professors of law wrote a letter to the editor of a newspaper by giving an account of the inhuman conditions of detention in the Agra Protective House for Women. The Supreme Court made the instance the basis of a writ petition. By a letter, the Supreme Court's attention was drawn to the exploitation of workmen at construction sites in contravention of labour laws. A social activist organisation took the servile condition of bonded labourers in quarries to the attention of the Court. An active journalist moved to the court against the evictions of pavement dwellers of Bombay. Several cases of this type followed subsequently and was taken preventive measures by the courts in different times.

While dealing with such unthinkable cases, the Court gradually developed a new procedure of rights of citizens and responsibilities of the State and devised new mechanism for its accountability. In 1982, Justice P.N. Bhagwati, definitely affirmed the purpose of PIL based on its origin: 'a strategic arm of the legal aid movement which is intended to bring justice within the reach of the poor masses, who constitute the low visibility area of humanity, is a totally different kind of litigation from the ordinary traditional litigation'.

However, 'public cause litigation', a different litigation, has weakened and outshined the social action sphere of PIL in courts over the years. This type of litigation includes the court's protection for enforcing the rights of the underprivileged or poor sections of the society and simply for correcting the actions or omissions carried out by the executive or public officials or departments of government or public bodies. The court has intervened in many such cases. As a measure for preventing pollution, the Supreme Court ordered to bring automobile emissions, air, noise and traffic pollution under control, control of traffic in New Delhi, made wearing of helmets while driving a bike in cities and wearing of seat belts while in a car mandatory, cleanliness in housing colonies, disposal of garbage, gave orders for parking charges, ordered to carry out action plans to control and prevent the monkey menace in cities and towns, ordered measures to prevent accidents at unmanned railway level crossings, collection and storage in blood banks, stop ragging of college freshes, and for control of loudspeakers and banning of firecrackers.

The Supreme Court's recent direction is to interlink the rivers—the most complex engineering—in India. The Court has also by its order banned pasting of black film on automobile windows. The Court itself has taken notice with reference to the case of the forceful eviction of Baba Ramdev from the Ramlila Ground by the Delhi Administration and the Court's condemnation to it. The court has passed an order to exclude the visit of the tourists to the core areas of the tiger reserves. Orders on such managerial activities passed by the court are dubious jurisdictional step of enforcing fundamental rights under Article 32 of the Constitution of India. Actually, these cases are not at all related to the legal issues of fundamental rights. The court is rather moved for better administration and governance, irrespective of any proper judicial function.

By interpreting most actively and contentiously the Constitution, the Supreme Court withdrew the power of the President conferred on by the Constitution of India to appoint judges with the consultation of the Chief Justice, and appropriated it in the Chief Justice of India. No Constitution in the world confers the power of selecting and appointing judges on the judges themselves.

The Court by the conferred power monitors the conduct of investigation and prosecution agencies whether there are failure or negligence to investigate and prosecute ministers and officials of governments. Some of the cases which are monitored by the Supreme Court are the investigation and prosecution on the involvement of the suspected ministers and officials in the Jain Hawala case; the fodder scam in which Lalu Prasad Yadav, former Chief Minister of Bihar, was involved; the Taj Corridor case in which Mayawati, former Chief Minister of Uttar Pradesh, was involved; and the recent 2G Spectrum Telecom scam in which the telecom ministers and officials are prosecuted.

COURT'S EXISTENCE ON MILITARY AND OTHER ACTIVITIES

There are also instances of the Supreme Court's order even in a military operation. In 1993, the Court passed orders on the conduct of military operations in Hazratbal, Kashmir against the restriction of food supplies to the hostages by the military force. The Court ordered the military authority to supply to the hostages provision of food of 1,200 calorific value on which an Army General wrote: 'For the first time in history, a Court of Law was asked to pronounce judgment on the conduct of an ongoing military operation. Its verdict materially affected the course of operation'.

The Court even controls the proceedings of Legislatures. The Supreme Court, in the Jharkhand Legislative Assembly case, ordered the Assembly to conduct a Motion of Confidence and ordered the Speaker to conduct proceedings according to the prescribed agenda and forbade entertaining any other business, and also ordered to record the proceedings for reporting to the Court. These orders were carried out against Article 212 of the Constitution, which provides that Courts need inquire into any proceedings of the legislature.

The government's policies are also the subject to the scrutiny of the Court. The Prime Minister was compelled to remind the Court that it interfered in the complex food distribution policies of the government, when the Court monitored the distribution of food-grains to the Below Poverty Line (BPL) families. Regarding the 2G Licenses case, the Court declared that all public resources and assets are the matter of public trust therefore; they should only be disposed of transparently to the highest bidder by a public auction. Regarding this the President made a Reference to the Court for the Court's legal advice under Article 143 of the Constitution. In the same case, the Court remained silent to the expert opinion of the Telecom Regulatory Authority of India (TRAI) to sell 2G spectrum without auction in order to create greater tele-density in India.

Disregarding the separation of powers under the Constitution for all practical bases, the Court undertook a general supervisory function over other sections of governments. The tendency to rush to the Supreme Court and 21 High Courts for any injustice against a public authority has also diverted the primary responsibility of citizens themselves in a representative self-government of making legislators and the executive responsible for their actions. In this regard, the Court answered that the other sections of the government proved their failure, so the judiciary was bound to undertake this type of task. Based on this dubious justification, the political sections of the government may overact the functions of the judiciary on its failure, and undoubtedly there are many areas where the judiciary has proved failure to meet the expectations of the public by its inefficiency and areas of cases.

Justice Jackson of the USA is apt in his comment: "The doctrine of judicial activism which justifies easy and constant readiness to set aside decisions of other branches of Government is wholly incompatible with a faith in democracy and in so far it encourages a belief that judges should be left to correct the result of public indifference it is a vicious teaching". If the Supreme Court does not firmly formulate and strictly observe the parameters of PIL, PIL—the significant litigation in current India will be at risk in becoming verbose, unethical, intruding into the functions of other divisions of government and unsuccessful by its random use.

CONCLUSION

Hence, to ensure the fundamental characteristic of the Constitution of India is preserved, the Judiciary has to act within the limits of its jurisdiction and within its domain ordained by the Constitution, and abide by the rule of the land. The independence of the judiciary underlies—on the basis of facts and in accordance with the law—the fair conduct of judicial proceedings and the protection of rights without any partiality, inducements, improper influences, and pressures, threats or interference, direct or indirect. The independent and integrated Judiciary system of India has to abide by the constitutional guidance in every aspect for checks and balances.

6. Empowerment of Women in India

INTRODUCTION

India is one of the oldest and most enriched civilisations, and the largest democracies in the modern world. From the age of cave-dwelling to the modern age of science and technology, and digitisation, Indian women have played crucial roles and have left the proofs of their excellence. Man and woman are the complementary creation of God. In contemporary society, a woman generally plays roles of a mother, daughter, daughter-in-law, sister, wife, friend, etc. Women are, in India, respected and honoured greatly and treated as mother-goddess, and they have immense social significance in Indian society. According to the mythological proofs of the Rig-Vedic period or Indus Valley Civilisation, the word *'Sakti'* connotes 'power' implying women as the image of supreme power. In broader sense, the India term *'paar shakti'* manifests power i.e. 'supreme Goddess' worshipped as a mother and the almighty female principle manifests *'Devi'*, which denotes *'Prakrit'* i.e. nature having association with the subordinate male principle, *'Purush'*. A woman is also conceived as Jagatmata or Jagadamba i.e. Mother of the Universe, and worshiped in the images of Durga, Mahakali, Mahalaxmi, Mahasaraswati, etc. as the source of all powers. So, the empowerment of women is the matter of versatile significance in all ages.

MODERN PROSPECT

Different organisations use the word 'empowerment' in diverse contexts. Empowerment denotes rise of spiritual, political, social or economic strength of individuals and communities, and often includes the situation where the empowered grow confidence according to their own capacities. Empowerment connotes the overall improvement gained by an individual, but not the development for them. Individuals must take part wholly in the decision-making manners shaping their lives. Empowerment is the first opportunity exquisitely necessary for the complete development of the individual and involves individual's access to resources: finance, knowledge, and technology; training in skills and building of leadership, democratic policies, dialogues, participation in policy and decision-making, and techniques for conflict resolution.

EMPOWERMENT OF WOMEN IN MODERN AGE

With the passage of time in the past of India, power of women had gradually faded, and as their power shrank, it became a crying of our society to empower women in order to make an all-round growth of our nation. At present, the poor performance of India in empowering women and controlling gender equality is reflected by many social institutions. According to the Census 2011, the sex ratio of India has increased to 933 females for 1000 males. In 'Gender Inequality Index' conducted by a wing of the United Nations Development Programme, Human Development Report 2016, India ranked 131 out of 189 countries. Women from underprivileged sections: Scheduled Castes (SC), Scheduled Tribes (ST), Other Backward Classes (OBC) and minorities are the victim of deprivation, exploitation, discrimination, and limited employment opportunities.

CONSTITUENTS OF WOMEN EMPOWERMENT

The five major constituents essential for the growth of society: Women's sense of self-respect; their right to have and determine choices; their right to have access to opportunities and resources; right to have the power to control their own lives within and outside their home; and their ability to influence the decision of social change in order to develop a more congenial social and economic order, in terms of national as well as international.

The main and major objective of the Central and States Governments is to realise the development, advancement and empowerment of women. The objective of creating an environment through economic growth and social policies for entire development of women includes:

1. To make them enable to understand their potential;
2. The de-jure and de-facto enjoyment of all human rights and fundamental freedom by women equally with men in social, economic, political, cultural and civil dimensions;
3. Right of women on equal access to participation and decision-making in social, economic and political walks of life;
4. Equal access of women to health care, standard quality of education at all levels, career and vocational guidance, occupational health and safety, employment, equal remuneration, social security and public office etc.
5. Strengthening legal systems targeting the eradication of all forms of discrimination against women;
6. Changing societal attitudes and community practices by active involvement of both men and women;
7. Streamlining a gender perspective in the development process;
8. Eradication of all forms of violence against women and the girl child; and
9. Building and strengthening partnerships with civil society, particularly women's organisations.

So, the three main dimensions concentrated on women empowerment include— Political uprising of women and their participation; economic empowerment of women; and social empowerment of women.

WOMEN EMPOWERMENT IN INDIA

The Constitution has given priority to the issue of gender equality. It grants equality to women as well as empowers the State to adopt appropriate measures of positive discrimination favouring women. The aim of the laws, development policies, plans and programmes of our country, in a democratic framework, is the advancement of women in spheres of life. There has been a considerable uplift in the approach to women's issues from welfare to development, from the Fifth Five Year Plan (1974–1978). The Government of India has recognised the empowerment of women as the major issue in determining the current status of women.

According to the Act of Parliament in 1990—to protect the rights and legal entitlements of women—the National Commission for Women has been established. The 73rd and 74th Amendments (1993) to the Constitution of India have provided provision for reservation of seats in the local bodies of Panchayats and Municipalities for women, by giving priority to their participation in decision-making at the local levels. India has also consented formally various international conventions and human rights organisations pledging to secure equal rights of women.

However, there still prevails a wider gap between the goals enunciated in the Constitution, legislation, policies, plans, programmes, and related mechanisms and the execution and the harsh reality of the status of women in India. This condition has been analysed thoroughly in the Report of the Committee on the Status of Women in India, titled, 'Towards Equality', 1974 and also brought into light in the National Perspective Plan for Women, 1988–2000; the Shrama Shakti Report, 1988; and the Platform for Action, Five Years After—An assessment. The continuous trend of reducing female ratio in the population, social stereotyping and violence at the domestic and societal levels are the demonstrations that manifests the growing gender inequality in India. Girl children, adolescent girls and women still suffer deprivation, ruthless torture and discrimination in many parts of India. The reasons behind gender inequality lie on social and economic structure on the basis of formal and informal norms, and practices. As a consequence, the access of women—especially belonging to the backward and underprivileged sections: ST, SC, OBC and minorities, majority of whom live in the rural areas detached from modern progress and prosperity—to education, health and hygiene, and productive resources, among others, is inadequate and thus women are largely marginalised, poor and deprived.

MODERN INITIATIVES

For appropriate check-out, India has openly endorsed many of the national and international schemes aiming at the upliftment of women and helping them attain a true sense of empowerment. Some of such schemes are: the Mexico Plan of Action (1975); the Nairobi Forward Looking Strategies (1985); the Beijing Declaration as well as the Platform for Action (1995); and the 'Outcome Document' adopted by the United Nations General Assembly (UNGA) Session on Gender Equality and Development and Peace for the twenty-first Century with the title, 'Further Actions and Initiatives to Implement the Beijing Declaration and the Platform for Action'. The initiatives undertaken by India also take note of the commitments of the Ninth Five Year Plan (1997–2002) and the other sectorial policies regarding the empowerment of women. The women movement and a network of Non-Government Organisations spread widely strongly rooted to pay deep insight into women's concerns have contributed in inspiring the initiatives for the empowerment of women. The initiatives undertaken by Government of India for the empowerment of women also include the efforts made to achieve the 'Millennium Development Goals' of UN.

CHALLENGE OF GENDER INEQUALITY IN DEVELOPMENT

In India, gender inequality creates development challenge significantly. According to the 2016 annual Global Gender Gap Index compiled by Geneva-based World Economic Forum, India ranked 108. The ranking is based on a country's ability to reduce gender discrepancies in areas of education, economic participation and opportunity, health and survival, and political empowerment. Violence against women and girls is common phenomenon in private as well as public places. India introduced 'gender-responsive budgeting' (GRB) in 2005 in order to react to such challenges. GRB is a system of planning, programming and budgeting to help advancing gender equality and women's rights as well as to serve as an indicator of governments' commitment to responding those objectives. In India, till now 57 Government Ministries or Departments have established Gender Budgeting Cells which is certainly a bold step to improve the lives of millions of Indian women in near future. An analysis of GRB in India shows that it will be an important indicator of the growth and development of women.

The sum of allocations for schemes relating to women can be by the Gender Budget Statement (GBS) introduced in the 2005–2006 budget. The analysis shows that over the last eight years the allocations for women as a proportion of the total budget have remained constant at approximately 5.5 per cent. Further, only about 30 per cent of the demands for grants, or estimates of expenditure, presented by Ministries/departments to the Union government are reported in the GBS.

Further, allocations to the nodal agency, the Ministry of Women and Child Development (MWCD), for women in the country, show a marginal increase over the last three years—from ₹18,584 crore in 2012–2013 to ₹21,193 crore in 2014–2015. With respect to 'Women Welfare', the allocations actually show a downward trend—from approximately ₹930 crore in 2011–2012 to around ₹920 crore in 2014–2015. And almost 87 per cent of the 2014–2015 budget of the MWCD was allocated for the Integrated Child Development Services Scheme, leaving only five per cent for schemes exclusively meant for women.

The UN Committee on Elimination of Discrimination against Women has emphasised the need for increased investments for the MWCD and for gender budgets across Ministries. Following its review of the fourth and fifth periodic reports submitted by the Government of India (in 2014), the Committee—which monitors States' implementation of the UN Convention on the Elimination of All Forms of Discrimination against Women (CEDAW)—also reiterated the need to strengthen institutions such as the National Commission for Women and the State Commissions.

Schemes focussed exclusively on women either received reduced allocations or were not implemented, as seen from the revised estimates for 2013–2014 vis-à-vis the budget estimates of the same year. Revised estimate figures are presented for the ongoing fiscal year based on the performance in the first six months of that year. The Domestic Violence Act is a case in point. The legislation, enacted a decade ago, received an allocation of ₹20 crore in 2012–2013. Revised estimate figures for 2013–2014 show zero allocation, which indicates that the scheme launched to operationalise the Act did not take off that year. Renamed SAAHAS, the scheme was allocated ₹50 crore last year. The coming budget will reveal how much of this was actually spent.

Some other schemes like restorative justice for rape victims have also proved a failure to gain its objective. The scheme 'Beti Bachao Beti Padhao' by the Bharatiya Janata Party (BJP) government is commendable, but will end in smoke if equal attention is not paid to implement the laws and specific steps for the most marginalised women are not taken, as spotlighted in the election manifesto of the BJP.

By giving their emphasis on women, the increased expense must be ensured in social sections: Education, health, and sanitation. Mostly women handle the heavy burden of unpaid works such as child-care; invalid-care; cooking, washing and cleaning works, etc. The demand for recognising, redistributing and cutting down the number of women's unpaid work has already earned a global impetus. So, it is high time that the sum of allotments to the social sector should be increased.

A PROGRESSIVE TREND

Over the last few years, the Finance Ministry has been organising pre-budgeting consultations with the intention of ensuring women's opinions in the budget-making process. Besides, meeting women's rights organisations, this year the Ministry also arranged a dialogue with UN Women as well as the Ministry of Women and Child Development (MWCD) to discuss key issues relating to Gender Responsive Budget (GRB).

At last, the final budget can have an on-time correction emphasising on the empowering the key institutions, adequate investments for schemes addressing gender concerns and the successful execution of those schemes.

By adopting the post-2015 global development agenda and reviews of countries' performance with regard to the Beijing Declaration and Platform for Action (Beijing+20), in the oncoming months the government will concentrate predominantly on development as well as gender issues. The inclusion of the independent target on gender equality and women's empowerment in the Sustainable Development is undoubtedly a greater achievement for women's rights that advocates across the world. But it will be hard to achieve the target provided not supported by sufficient investments. The first full year budget of the government has a tremendous opportunity for taking restorative measures by recognising the mistakes.

CONCLUSION

Almost everywhere in the world, women have been getting treatment as subordinate citizens since ancient times. The patriarchal society has been relegating women to secondary roles despite their competency in successfully executing the leading roles, in most cases discriminated. This social negligence is the vital reason behind their loss of self-esteem and dignity, though they constitute almost half of the present world's population.

In Indian society, however, women had honourable position in parallel to men and actively took part in social as well as religious affairs. In recent time, Indian women have a considerable growth in diverse walks of life and are successfully handling their responsibilities. But still there are a large number of women prone to superstition and are deprived of modern education. The few must be highlighted with a view to improving the many in our society with appropriate measures and their exact execution on time. Under such situations, we need to think and devise new plans and scheme in order to increase the growth opportunities of women by awaking them from the grassroots of our society where the considerable number of deprived and neglected women live. Men and women together should decisively develop in the fields of health, education, infrastructure, industry and financial services. In India for about two centuries, social reformers and missionaries have also endeavoured to improve the social standards of women and make them aware of their social accountabilities. The female literacy rate has risen to 65.46 per cent (according to 2011 census) from 54 per cent (according to 2001 census) and is about to touch the male literacy rate (over 80 per cent, 2011 census) by the next census. Our past is the testimony of women empowerment of our nation. From the Vedic period to Modern age some of the most significant women figures played leading roles in different walks of life in our society are Lopamudra, Sulabha Maitreyi, Razia Sultana, Kittur Chennamma, Sucheta Kriplani, Vijaya Lakshmi Pandit, Captain Prem Mathur, Indira Gandhi and Kalpana Chawla who are radiating instances of women empowerment.

The Indians should bring a sea-change in their mindset to realise the prospect of women empowerment. It is high time men and women of India should wake and endeavour to grow in parallel to the current growth of the world towards equality and equity. Swami Vivekananda's words in this regard are apt mentioned: 'Arise, awake and stop not until the goal is reached'. In this way, India can be shaped into an advanced nation of integrity, equality, equity, best-in-class science and technology, economic superpower and empowered women.

KSA AND ITS IMPORTANCE IN THE USA

The abbreviation, KSA stands for Knowledge, Skills and Abilities, which are the fundamental qualities required for applying any job openings in the United States of America. Besides the resume, these three qualities determine the selection in the final round in case many a candidate qualifies for a job.

KSAs which are a must for the efficient performance of a position contained on the announcement of each job vacancy. The Office of Personal Management, in 2009, asked Federal agencies that they should no longer ask the job applicants to fill out the questionnaires for which they took a year to eliminate them.

KSAs are the concise and concentrated essays comprising one's education, work history, volunteer and achievements which apparently qualify one to perform the responsibilities of the position being applied for. The KSA statements are essential for applying for most of the federal, state and city government jobs because they are largely considered as the standard to assess the abilities of the fittest applicant in respect of the required ability to perform the accountability of the job. So, most recruitment officials of the government look for the concise and transparent KSA emphasising the results or achievements obtained in the previous work.

KSA statements are known by many terms in different agencies such as 'evaluation factor', 'knowledge, abilities, skills and other characteristics', 'rating factors', 'quality ranking factors', and 'job elements'. Every agency has its own rules and regulations, but in most cases the KSAs must be limited by a half to a half and one page. The name is valueless, but the standard and length of the content influences.

The United States (US) Office of Personnel Management defines KSAs as: 'Knowledge, Skills, and Abilities (KSAs)—the attributes required to perform a job and are generally demonstrated through qualifying service, education, or training.

- **Knowledge:** It is a body of information applied directly to the performance of a function.
- **Skill:** It is an observable competence to perform a learned psychomotor act.

❖ **Ability:** It is competence to perform an observable behaviour or a behaviour that results in an observable product.'

On the basis of the score-scale ranges from 1–100, job applicants essays must score above 70 which determines the qualification for the position applied for. The means of gaining high score is to answer the KSA questions with reference to the previous employment or training that demonstrates your experience and knowledge of handling the responsibilities you undertook. Moreover, a Federal Resume along with KSA statements is a must to apply for the positions in the federal government.

❑❑❑

ESSAY WRITING

Essay writing is an art as well as a science, as it satisfies the urge of creativity of a good writer and requires a discipline of mind, and indeed is a unique blend of intellect and creativity. Essay writing requires skill for a methodical arrangement of the matter. The following are the fundamental characteristics of an excellent essay; hence, they should be kept in mind while writing an essay.

Introduction: Opening paragraph introduces the topic, so it must arrest the attention of the reader with the essential points of the topic.

Body of the Essay: It contains the subject matter in detail. So, the thoughts and ideas must be presented coherently to develop them into a well-arranged excellent paragraph. If arguments arise, they must be presented in separate paragraphs.

Conclusion: In this paragraph, the arguments must be highlighted and drawn to a logical end with clinching effect that can create a lasting impression on the reader's mind. It should support the data provided in the whole essay.

Lucidity of the Language: Simple and lucid language with the exact use of words and phrases is the logo of an excellent essay. Short and to-the-point sentences make reading interesting as well as maximise the grammatical accuracy, which is the most important factor for any piece of writing.

Facts and Figures: Based on the topic, facts and figures out of an extra-edge to the arguments and ensure the weightage of the essay. Not a single irrelevant point or view should be added. The topic must be carefully presented to the point.

Uniformity and Clarity: Above all, the essay should be a logical presentation based on the flow of thoughts and views and related arguments. Continuity is the soul of the essay, and all types of disorderly approaches must be avoided. Always make a proper plan, arrange your thoughts, views and ideas, and write down important points, facts and figures before you start writing an essay, as these are the essential steps for presenting an excellent essay.

KINDS OF ESSAYS

Essays can be broadly classified into five kinds: descriptive, narrative, reflective, biographical and idiomatic essays.

(*a*) Descriptive Essays: These types of essays are generally factual ones, and include the topics based on science, education, politics, economics and current events. These topics need precise knowledge with relevant facts. For instance, describing the climate of a country we need precise knowledge on the weather of the country for more than 20–30 years, for this we need to know neither the trees and plants and types of buildings nor details on the design and points of architectural records of the country.

(*b*) Narrative Essays: This essay is presented in the form of a story. The essay should have a chronological flow and be narrated in an interesting way with episodes suitable for the context of the essay. For instance, the narration of your visit to a hill station should contain the detail on the landscape, flora and fauna, natural scenario and people in around the hill station areas can be presented in the form of a story. Chronological arrangement of events is needed to write such essays. Also the narration should be made as interesting as possible by making use of episodes which fit in the context. For example, the narration of the first day at college should mention some funny incidents. A journey by train or plane should include some exciting experiences.

(*c*) Reflective Essays: It is such a type of essay that requires the writer to be highly imaginative and creative as abstract nature is the essential characteristic of it. The ideas must be expressed in concrete terms.

(*d*) Biographical Essays: This type of essay involves knowledge of the major events in the life of the person whose biography is being described. In addition to that, the essay should mention the qualities or character of the 'hero', his achievements, his struggles and his principles.

(*e*) Idiomatic Essays: Its type says that it needs to expand an idiom or any idiomatic expression with relevance to our everyday life, and even the importance in human civilisation. But before writing this type of essay the writer must comprehend the inner meaning of the idiom or idiomatic expression, otherwise it will prove a wild goose chase. For instance, if you are asked to expand the popular quotation, 'If winter comes, can spring be far behind?' You need not only tell about these two seasons, rather you have to represent the sides contradictory just like these two seasons. In this regard, you have to represent sorrow, adversity or hard time for winter, whereas happiness, prosperity or fortune for spring in relation to the impact of these seasons in nature and the stated conditions in human life.

❑❑❑

STRATEGY FOR WRITING EXCELLENT ESSAYS

SIMPLE PRESENTATION WITH SIMPLE WORDS INSTEAD OF HARD WORDS

Simple style is the best style. So, preference should always be given to simple and familiar words that best express your ideas meant for the topic. Use of complex, hard and bombastic words is redundant. You may choose words like 'help' instead of 'assistance'; 'use' instead of 'utilise'; and 'more' or 'extra' instead of 'additional'.

In this regard keep always in mind the words of the humorous playwright and novelist Enrique Jardiel Poncela: 'When something can be read without effort, great effort has gone into its writing'.

Your essay, therefore, should arrest the reader's attention as well as be easy to understand. The use of simple words makes your essay undoubtedly standard and demands much more attention.

Well-structured presentation: The viewpoints you want to elaborate require a head, body and tail pattern. The traditional pattern is: Introduction, body and conclusion. This structure helps us present the topic in three major parts with a better comprehension scope. In 'Introduction', the context of the topic is told briefly; in the 'Body' the topic is presented in detail in addition to logical arguments; and in the 'conclusion' we sum up the topic highlighting the argument.

On Writing an Introduction: 'First impression is the last impression'. Exactly it is. So, we should always keep in mind that first sentence of the introduction part must be written with careful consideration. We should arrest the attention of the reader at the very beginning, and make him/her interested and enthusiastic to read the essay at a stretch till its end.

On Writing the Body: Now, we need to elaborate the topic with logical arguments, views, ideas, thoughts and with figures (if necessary) and be aware to present it in relation to the introduction—as if we are elaborating every word of introduction part. The body demonstrates the depth in the topic and maturity of the writer as well as his ability to represent a topic in his own skill within the deadline of time. So, before you start writing an essay, scan your brain with the rays of the topic down your memory lane so that your knowledge, ideas, views and instances related to it might dazzle in your brain. Sort them out based on your idea about the demand of the examiner by the topic i.e. exactly what he wants to know from you. Now arrange them according to the manner of presentation just as a military General brings the army of soldiers in order with just a word. This part contains almost 90 per cent information and must satisfy the reader's requirements. Take care so that this part treats a clear understanding of the subject, logical development of your points, and reflection of your grounded reasons.

ON WRITING CONCLUSION

Now comes the finishing point, the conclusion—the last vital part that qualifies your essay and inspires the reader to read it again for his satisfaction. Sum up the subject-matter you presented till now in the body. Trace a logical conclusion to your arguments, views and thoughts or factual statements. Now based on these steps, draw an end to your essay—in tight symmetry—by highlighting the importance, significance, necessity or measures that are in crying need in our society. Remember, the conclusion itself reflects the inner vision of the writer. It should, therefore, serve the voice of the writer to the reader on the said topic. So, it should be up to the mark with a view to convincing the reader and make him well conversant with the whole subject matter presented in the essay. At last, finish the essay with a sentence that leaves a lasting impression in the reader's mind.

On your mark for UPSC/PCS elimination, essay writings are of two types: One for academic purpose, which takes time and comprehensive research, and the other for assessment in competitive examinations. In the former case, greater degree of control can be exercised over the content, while, in the latter, it can be nothing more than a response drawn out of the given stimulus. Under the pressure of scoring qualifying marks out of 200 within time frame of only three hours, there is hardly enough scope to response well but to express one's unique style of perceiving the world. The section of essay writing is devised as a potent tool by UPSC/PCS elimination process in order to sort out candidates of desired profile. Essay writing discovers the diamond in you that the UPSC/PCS requires. Just like personality assessment interview, a candidate needs to keep oneself well-prepared beforehand for orienting his knowledge, ideas and views on the given topic, as essay-writing skills require multifiltering stages.

Try yourself to answer a few significant questions before trying to orient you for an essay. Can you read and realise, in tight timeline, a series of articles assigned to you? Can you discover the essence of those articles and summarise them in only a few sentences?

It is okay, we have conviction that you can, but can you connect the essence of those articles together to form a single symmetric unit by creating a new idea? Can you add thoughts and insights on the basis of the ideas in those articles? Now think and think, and discover the answers we want to know.

So, we have assigned you with an essay to write, as our intention is to challenge you in diverse ways which will assure us that you can face challenges in course of your UPSC/ PCS preparation process and beyond it. But the fact is that where do you begin? How do you know that you're done?

Let's try to resolve all these queries.

REVIEW THE TOPIC AGAIN AND AGAIN

You yourself will develop some questions sometimes on issues of national and international importance. But most of the time you will be provided with topics designed by experienced professors/professionals who are appointed by UPSC/PCS, and you will need to respond them. Scan the topic and think out the issue. Rack your brain for feasible responses or get into that ignites some creative insights. Ask yourself the following questions on reviewing the topic:

i. Do you understand the topic?
ii. Do you know the issues to be addressed?
iii. Do you feel that you can make a blueprint of the topic?
iv. Can you give it a comprehensive outlook?
v. Can you recognise and distinguish, based on the outline, your ideas from the authors'? If yes, try to create a balancing base with a little of critical approach complementing each other.
vi. Do you feel comfortable enough with the language competency necessary for carrying out the planned outlook?

DRAFT THE TOPIC FIRST

Based on the level of flexibility with your writing speed and accuracy, you may choose to invest 10 minutes to 1 hour in order to frame the introduction, successive paragraphs and conclusion.

Just go on writing down your ideas that come out of your brain in flow, and avoid controlling your first responses.

i. What questions do you have for the writers of the various articles assigned to you?
ii. Do you find any inconsistencies in their views/articles?
iii. What problems do you find in the articles?
iv. What mistakes do you identify in them?
v. What is your message on the topic?
vi. Can you present any claims or assertions in support of your message? If you don't have any, you need to check if your message is robust enough.
vii. Do you find any evidence or instances that support your claims? If you don't have any, you should better move to other available essay topic.

CONCENTRATE ON THE INTRODUCTION

After you finish your draft, you should check out your important points. Now think and answer the following:

i. Does your introduction present the context or background for the issue and relate your message? If not, why not?
ii. Is your objective clear and correct?
iii. Do you think it requires explaining your objective?
iv. Can your last sentence give the reader a clear understanding to the rest paragraphs of your essay?
v. Is your introduction relevant to the essay question? If you have any specific essay question, your introduction must be directly relevant to the question. If you have a long essay question, your answer must touch on the issues presented in the question, but generally it does not attend to all the details of the question.

CONCENTRATE ON OTHER PARAGRAPHS IN THE BODY

Once you finish your queries and doubts relating the introduction part, you should motivate on the additional paragraphs of the body by solving the following queries:

i. Do you develop your main theme in the successive paragraphs by asserting and supporting with evidence to make your point stand for the hallmark? If not, you should better start discovering the evidence and examples in support of your points.
ii. Have you included lots of 'shoulds' in your writing? If so, this type of writing can point to assertions without evidence and examples to back up claims. Try to rewrite most of the 'shoulds' out of the response. Try replacing 'shoulds' with 'coulds' to see what happens. Usually you have to offer more evidence and examples to shore up your ideas.

CONCENTRATE ON THE CONCLUSION

Finally, you should motivate on the conclusion that decides the competency of your skills in drawing out considerable and significant resolution. Now try to solve these queries.

i. Have you given a conclusion to your topic essay?
ii. Does your conclusion restate your introduction? If so, rewrite your conclusion, because it is substandard, not at all can hold water.
iii. Have you incorporated the major ideas treated in the essay in your conclusion for offering your reader more insight on the topic? If not, why not?
iv. If not, what do you think your conclusion should contain with a view to further the major theme you have discussed? No doubt it is hard to do, but you should try to master providing such points because they will help rank your essay.
v. Have you drawn all the points of the analysis together in order to provide the reader?
vi. Could you present how the points of analysis work together?

EASY WAY TO WRITE AN ESSAY

It may seem that learning how to write an essay is a confusing or infuriating process, but it is not at all so. It is rather interesting to master it, and once you have learnt the pattern and manner of presentation, it will certainly ignite your interest in essay, it will be funny too.

Just go through the following simple and orderly steps, and try them in your topic of interest.

Research: Your first and foremost duty is to decide a topic, then gather knowledge on the topic from the internet, academic databases and books from the library. Take notes on the things that appear important to you, and think yourself an expert.

Analysis: Now based on your knowledge start analysing the arguments of the topics from different sources. Logically and clearly judge the claims; write down the reasons and evidence. Mark the strong as well as weak logics, and from these you will gather an idea of developing a topic into an essay.

Brainstorming: Now cast your insight on the topic. Ask yourself many probable questions and try to answer them logically. In your study, sit to write down something on the topic, if you fail, walk or be in your own flexible poses and positions; continue thinking until you discover something that you feel to be original insights to write about.

Thesis: Another important step is to record your discoveries. Pick your ideas and put them down in your copy. Those ideas will be the foundation of your essay. In course of all these processes, you will have many ideas—logical and illogical; attractive and less-attractive; interesting and uninteresting. Now it is time to judge them by your own logic.

Outline: Be patient to sketch your essay before attempting to write it down straightway. Write heading sentences and highlight the subject matter that will contain each paragraph. Before you start writing, be sure that from introduction to the conclusion, you have made a draft based on your own logical ideas, and each paragraph is unified. Motivate on the title and introduction again, and ensure that they are well-devised to attract the reader's attention. If not, then try to modify or rewrite these taking some more time. After you are satisfied with it, settle your mind to write the essay.

Introduction: Now you should write down the essay at a stretch. Try to begin the introduction with a sentence that you think is potent to draw the reader's attention. The introduction will demonstrate your views and insight on the topic, and naturally the reader will hear your voice. Maybe it will fail to fulfil its objective at the initial effort. But your readers will give you feedback that will help you carry on your attempts to master this art.

Paragraphs: Next point is that you should pay attention to your successive paragraphs whether they are concentrated on the same topic logically and symmetrically. You should also ensure that they are well connected and express your views clearly and sensibly.

Conclusion: Now in the conclusion, sum up all your views, ideas, and insights within a few compact sentences and finish your essay with a sudden strike, but must have a clinching effect on the whole that can easily leave a deep impression on the reader's mind. At the end of the conclusion, you add a suitable quotation, some call to action or an interesting twist of logic.

MLA Style: Based on the correct guidelines for citation, edit and format your essay. Make sure that ideas and quotations are cited appropriately in your essay, and follow the pagination guidelines. In this regard, the popular MLA Style is best.

Language: The most striking step is the last one which decides the acceptability of your essay. Language is of great importance, because if your language has no grammatical, and punctuation accuracy, it will fail to convey your message. So, assure that your essay is free from language defects, like asymmetry of thoughts; mistakes of collocation i.e. appropriate use of word pairs, idioms, phrases, appropriate prepositions and phrasal verbs, and spelling mistakes. Above all, always try to express your ideas in simple and short sentences, because these will ensure your grammatical accuracy and help you make your essay compact and to the point.

❑❑❑

HOW TO WRITE AN EXCELLENT INTRODUCTION AND CONCLUSION

The title of your essay tells your reader about your topic, but the introduction with its first sentence stir his/her heart whether to continue reading the essay or not. So, introduction must be the spearhead of your essay. The conclusion too is equally important as the introduction is, because it gives the reader a logically satisfying exit that the reader wishes to gather from the essay. Hence, these two paragraphs must be written with strategically and methodically.

INTRODUCTION

Start to draw attention. The attention arrester you use is naturally your own, but here are some ideas:

1. **Remarkable Information:** This is not the new information but common, true and well-known one, but it must be relevant to the topic. It may be a quotation or a proverb with the intention of beginning the essay with an extra value to it. In this regard, you have to write one or two sentences in the introduction paragraph in relation to it.
2. **Anecdote:** An anecdote effectively opens an essay, but its careful use bears the intended result. An anecdote is a brief story-like statement that signifies a relevant topic or explains a relevant point.
3. **Dialogue:** Use of a dialogue as an opener is also highly effective to a relevant topic. The dialogue itself tells the reader its objective that the writer is trying to present in relation to the topic. Use only two to three exchanges of the speakers' conversation. If you introduce your essay with a dialogue, you must elaborate it in the introductory paragraph in one or two sentences that will represent the connection.
4. **Summary Information:** A summary information also plays an opener role. It must consist of only few compact sentences that will gently lead the reader into the topic.

CONCLUSION

This paragraph ensures the acceptability of your essay, as it leads your reader to the end which will sum up his/her expectation from your topic.

The conclusion does not need any specific rule to make it interesting. Just sum up all the ideas treated in the essay with logical resolution only four to five sentences. Take care that the last sentence clearly expresses your clinching voice. But you can add a quotation, or a relevant statement for emphasising your insight.

Finishing Touch

After you have completed your essay, check the paragraphs whether they are okay; if not, format them.

Review the Sequence of your Paragraphs

Now identify the weak and strong paragraphs according to construction. Then try to improve the weak ones into strong ones. If the order too appears asymmetrical and lacking complete sense throughout the essay, format it and bring the symmetry you think is appropriate.

Review the Instructions for the Assignment

Make sure whether the following points are rightly mentioned before you prepare your final draft.

i. Are the margins correct?
ii. Is your title correct as per the direction?
iii. What extra information you have provided?
iv. Have you double spaced your lines?

Review writing

There is no alternative to revision of your work. Check what you have improved by reviewing the essay. Improve the weak points, take care least you missed anyone, because these will be vital for your essay.

i. Do you think your essay has a logical sense? If you are not sure, leave it for a few hours, and then read it again to be sure.
ii. Do your sentences have an orderly flow? If not, check them and try to improve up to your expectation. In this respect, the linking words like, 'however', 'moreover', 'therefore' sometimes make sentences well knitted. Be sure that these words are not missing in your paragraphs that help you making your construction compact.
iii. How do you check your spelling and grammar—by spelling checker or grammar checker? Don't depend on these; these very often fail to check mistakes throughout a piece of writing. So, meticulous and patient editing will help you confident of your work that the work is correct.

GUIDELINES FOR WRITING APPROPRIATE ESSAYS

Essay is an art of composing one's thought in a very coherent, logical and lucid form of writing that create an impact in the mind of the reader or make an individual opinion worthy of due consideration in the ongoing debate. It is the medium to express a point through democratic means. Therefore, it is one of the most popular forms of literature to put one's opinion in the public domain. It is not possible to define an essay due to its varying nature that is based on the subject matter and the writing style of an individual attempting it.

Literally, the word 'essay' means an 'attempt'. It is an attempt to present one's thoughts by writing in a logically coherent structure and sequence. A form of literary composition generally in prose, it deals with a particular subject and brings out its various aspects one by one in a very well-knit composition, with a view to portray a graphic picture of the whole subject-matter. Thus, an essay becomes a test of an individual's knowledge, information, maturity of thoughts and rationality of imagination with the ability to present in writing.

To score high in the essay paper of the UPSC/PCS, one needs to understand the requirement and purposes of conducting this exam. UPSC/PCS looks out for candidates having mature decision-making ability, good administrative skills and an overall leadership quality. So aspiring candidates need to demonstrate all these attributes in not only the essay writing but in all of their write ups including their optional subjects and the G.S. Whatever field the candidate has come from like science, commerce, art, or humanities, he needs to keep in mind that there is always a scope of showing the above-mentioned attributes. He just has to learn to produce them as and when needed. Further, a comprehensive understanding of the nature of the current essay paper and to equip oneself with the changing trends is the necessary requirement.

The ongoing trend in essay is opinion based in nature. Thus, the foremost ability one must have is to differentiate between knowledge and opinion. Knowledge is considered basically a very wide and absolute term that shows things to be in true perspective, objectively and eternally—true forever for all human beings. It cannot be falsified by anyone at any point in time. However, most of our knowledge claims would in fact not fit into these criteria of knowledge, as nothing can be so authoritatively true forever. Therefore, we should not be authoritative in our judgments regarding a particular viewpoint. As such, claims at best can only be considered as one of the sound opinions, not an absolute knowledge. Hence, one must accept this fact and keep oneself at a balanced mindset avoiding the extremes. Moreover, knowledge could also refer to the scientific knowledge that supports the claims with logic and verifiable evidences. Such knowledge that supports your claims with proper evidence and adequate logic is acceptable. Further, most of the time we possess opinions which we often get confused with knowledge. A person makes opinions based on his/her belief system and understandings of the world. Hence, one must show maturity and objectivity considering a democratic outlook of things while expressing his/her opinions. Simultaneously, one must display scientific attitude by providing a logical justification at the time of making one's opinion.

This is the domain where students generally lack or fail to follow and, thus, commit mistakes on a given topic by not justifying their opinions. The first thing to take note of is that the audience (the experienced diplomats checking the essay scripts) is not at all interested in one's 'opinion' for that matter. This surprises the students who believe that they are just trading opinions on various topics. The confusion is created because some students attempt only the first part of a two-part process—they forget or consider the second-part of the process less significant. The experienced readers are interested in a student's argument in explaining his/her opinion instead of his/her opinion. The second-part of the two-part process that students encounter in their writings and discussions is giving an argument that supports and defends their opinion. In general, all opinion-statements should be treated as logical conclusions, and the deep comprehension of the premises, the assumptions and the evidence that led a person to draw that conclusion is the art of good reading and writing.

Similar to that in math classes, wherein it is unacceptable to provide only the conclusion, in essay-writing also a student must 'show his/her work' to support conclusion.

So, an argument comprises, three statements, also called as premises—major premises, minor premises and the conclusion. The examples are as follows:

1. There is smoke on the hill : Major premises
2. Where there is smoke there is fire : Minor premises
3. Therefore, there is fire on the hill. : The Conclusion

The above examples show a logical connectivity between these premises and the conclusion, where the premises logically converse into the conclusion. It is coherent to conclude that when smoke is evident on the hill then there would be fire on the hill, thus establishing the logical relation between the fire and the smoke. This is called the method of drawing logical inferences. In the same way, ideas should be written with logical connectivity to the next idea, thus maintaining the coherence and the clarity of a good write up. It makes the write-up look simple and smooth. It makes the reading delightful for the reader and finally, the candidate is able to successfully impress the examiner and in turn getting good marks.

When a student makes statements based on his belief, as in the following way—'God makes our destiny', or 'abortion is immoral', or 'animals should not be tortured', or 'racism is bad', or 'science is too masculine', etc.—Though he/she has begun with a proper response, it is yet to be justified. The next step is to provide the specific reasons and evidences that led him/her to hold to that belief. This next step is the only genuinely significant part of a good paper, which some students never even begin to provide it in their essays.

Everybody has some or other opinions and nobody really cares about them. A class in which every student expressed his/her opinion in favour of or against the death penalty, for example, would be as fascinating and informative as a class in which every student just stated their favourite ice-cream flavour. The smart reader would be interested in knowing what made a person hold to a particular opinion, but some students are under the false belief of simply stating the opinion, which is not enough. However, writing 'I am against the death-penalty' and then moving on to some additional opinions is not enough in the essay on death penalty. The reasons, experiences and factual evidence leading a person's view against the death penalty must also be explained in detail. One must base his/her arguments against the death penalty on ethical, social, religious, epistemic and economic grounds and so on.

Students must formulate the most compelling grounds for their opinion and express them in the most persuasive and logical terms possible. They need to take notice also that each and every 'controversial' claim made in the sequence of their argument will likely require additional argumentation and justification. For example, it will be disastrous for students to claim that capital punishment is wrong because the Bible says so. They will be required to instantly provide the necessary arguments that their interpretation of the Bible is the only correct one, and then they also will have to give supporting argument for the existence of God, and quickly follow this with a strong argument in support of the reason for God to communicate through this scripture and not, say, the Bhagavad Gita, and so on. All this is a formidable task, especially when the topic at hand is only the death penalty and one should stay focused on that.

The strong attachment of a person towards some issue (say the death penalty, animal rights, the existence of fate, etc.), makes him/her so close to their belief—so familiar and comfortable with it—that they will consider this belief utterly natural and uncontroversial. It will appear to them as evident as to be unworthy of any further explanation and justification. This forms the most common reason because of which students neglect giving arguments for their opinions/beliefs. They believe many of their claims to be so obvious that they do not consider worthy to 'spell it out' which is wrong!

PRECAUTIONS

- ❖ Logical argumentation cannot be substituted with adamant conviction (e.g., the cogency of someone's position cannot be improved by yelling or weeping). Appealing to fear is also a misconception. For example, a lawyer might say, 'If you do not convict this criminal, one of you may be his next victim'. This is false belief because the deeds of a defendant in the future has no bearing on determining his responsibility for a crime committed in the past. At the time of sentencing, it may be relevant, but not during the deliberation of guilt or innocence.
- ❖ A person's passionate believe about x to be true produces nothing, except that he/she passionately believe x to be true. In other words, his/her subjective internal states are of no relevance to the external world to imitate. (e.g., Jim's current status has nothing whatever to do with his/her belief about Jim Morrison still being alive.).
- ❖ Correlation between incidents may not necessarily be the cause. (e.g., it was argued in a recent prime time T.V. programme that since a number of wealthy men had consulted about their investments with psychics, psychic insight induced their investment).

Thus, the subject matter is the most important aspect of your essay. A significant amount of time should be devoted in simply brainstorming ideas for the subject matter before one actually starts writing the essay.

Brainstorming a subject requires deep introspection of one's background, interests, information and aptitudes. Yes friends! The previously learned skills of a person would be a good asset as they reflect his/her individuality and originality. Students need to learn to access them and use them in right perspectives. The following points should be considered for brainstorming one's past and should be incorporated in not only deciding the topic of the essay but also in keeping those skills and experiences intact to write the entire essay.

12

DO'S AND DON'TS

One must consider the title carefully—its meaning and its scope. Whether it asks one to generalise, establish a particular view, or take one's own stand? One should not attempt the essay unless one agrees with what the title states categorically, as generally one is not expected to argue against the title. (It requires flair and self-confidence for a writer to do it.) In this context, one may compare these two titles—'India is not fit to be a democracy' and 'Is India fit to be a democracy?' One need to support the statement in the first title, while in the second title choice of one's own view is provided.

- One must select a perspective and a pattern for developing one's thesis. One should jot down one's points and arrange them in the pattern with focus on one's perspective.
- One should use words effectively. However, difficult words or 'flowery' language should not be used. Each word should contribute to the development or explanation of the idea. Archaic and obsolete usage must be avoided, for examples, albeit, ere, methink and trow. It is better to leave out the foreign words, unless they have achieved currency in English. Usage of slang should also be avoided, oven what is known as journalese, i.e. words coined by journalists and newspapers for effect. One must keep a recent edition of a standard dictionary which will help one identify such slang expressions. Effective usage of words also requires one to know which word to use and where. Though, there are numerous synonymous words, but they are not always interchangeable.
- The usages of clichés or time-worn idioms should be avoided, for example, 'keeping the wolf from the door', 'from the frying spice of life', 'there is no time to stand and stare' have been over used and are thus hackneyed.
- One should firmly resist the temptation to strew one's essay with quotations to emphasise one's point of view even if one has a good memory. Quotations act as dangerous props the presence of which indicates the writer's lack of ideas or inability to express what he or she feels. Quotations should be used rarely and only in context where they give depth to an idea.

- Unnecessary repetition in writing should be avoided. Few examples of avoidable repetitions are Ramesh is never late for work; he is always either early or on time. Mrs. Sharma kept her house spotless, and it was perfectly clean. The butcher was very thin. This thinness was commented on by many of his customers. His customers commented on it because it seemed so inappropriate in a butcher. What would be more appropriate in a butcher, they felt, was a sort of jovial chubbiness.

In all these cases, the effectiveness of statements can be improved by writing it only once.

The following passage exemplifies the kind of mindless word usage one should avoid. Mistaken for argumentation, it merely epitomises the art of saying nothing in so many words.

This paper will attempt to document the way in which the Industrial Revolution changed the lives of so many people. The great technological upheaval known to us as the Industrial Revolution altered the way in which almost all levels of the society of the time functioned. Without this extraordinary Revolution, none of the changes that have made our lives what they are today would have occurred. Probably this period left untouched the life of no one who lived through it. What we are confronted with here is a staggering volcanic eruption in technology, science and manufacturing techniques of every kind that caused the most far-reaching reversals in the life, the existence, the day-to-day habits and the most profound beliefs of almost every soul on this planet. Yes, our society in all its ramifications was destined never to be the same again. No life, however high or however humble, passed through the Industrial Revolution unscathed. In the whole previous history of the world, nothing had wrought such an unforeseen, such a revolutionary effect. Let's take some examples. How many cities and villages, how many families large and small saw the familiar old way of life that they loved and knew so well slipping away from them as the new ways took over? No subject has attracted more research or more detailed scholarly comment than this: we know more about this period than perhaps about any period before or since. In conclusion, what this mass of evidence points to is the extent to which the Industrial Revolution did indeed inexpressibly affect the hard but rewarding lives of so many of our American forebears.

- One should check one's writing for correctness. Ungrammatical sentences have no place in an essay. The words, phrases, expressions about whose meaning or correctness one is not sure should not be used. Long and rambling sentences which are difficult to comprehend should not be used.
- An essay reflects the views and personality of the writer. Thus, from the point of view of an examination, keeping extreme opinions to oneself and not express idiosyncrasies would be considered pragmatic too.
- One should be clear, lucid and simple so that one cannot go far wrong.

- Starting essay with brief introduction preferably with a small relevant anecdote/story/incident is a better way to create some genuine interest in the examiner's mind.
- It is not very pragmatic to start an essay with definitions of the terms in the essay topic, because most of the times it is difficult for us to define the terms precisely. Moreover, the essay topics in recent times are highly subjective in nature that requires our personal opinions and views. Therefore, it will put constraint on our creative ability of writing to start the essay with objective definitions of terms and problem may arise in flow of essay and lucidity of expression from one idea to other etc.
- It is a nice option to start with a popular quotation. However, it is very important to write quotation relevant to the topic and thus one should know numerous quotations. A quotation however good it is if not 100 per cent relevant to the topic, it becomes a liability rather than asset, because it needs to be substantiated in line with given topic in our essay. Quotes of various scholars should be added wherever required and should be linked with recent happenings, events, etc. Enriching the essay with several quotes and examples has a lot of potential to fetch good marks.
- In an essay, the best option to start with is writing about the most relevant recent news item or a small anecdote with 100 per cent relevance to the given topic. We need not prepare specially for this.
- Do not provide lengthy introduction prior to actual topic to test the patience of the examiner who have little patience to go through supposedly irrelevant matter.
- Indicate the salient points of the essay in bulleted form to give the examiner an idea of what has been written in the entire essay without going through it.
- It will also help in ensuring that any major topic covered by the writer is not missed by the examiner due to a casual glance at the papers. But, make certain to introduce it in second or third page of the essay. Moreover, incorporate it in the regular flow of the essay rather than making it appearing like an index.
- The writer should write as many examples and case studies as possible to logically substantiate his/her arguments.
- The grammatical errors and interpretation problems in an essay could be reduced by writing simple sentences.
- Conclusion is another important part of an essay. One should has a fair idea about how to conclude the essay during the brainstorming session itself. For the writers having clear introduction and conclusion in their minds, streamlining the thought between these two objectives becomes easier.

- It is better to write about introduction and conclusion in their full length while forming the essay structure itself. The writers will have enough time to refine it during this stage. Especially with conclusion, it works very well as conclusion may not be a best piece of writing just before the closure of the prescribed time.
- One can overcome the language barrier by concentrating on content and smooth transition between various ideas with interesting introduction and conclusion. One should not worry about flowery language and adhere to use of simple meaningful sentences logically linked to maintain the flow of the essay.

Taking care of all these things results in good writing, and if time permits, you can highlight key assumptions, analysis and conclusion by simply underlining them.

There is no doubt that essay writing is challenging, but if one thinks of it as a way to teach oneself about the important issues and ideas, it could be a possibility that one of these ideas turn out to be the rank-deciding factor for the writer.

PART II

SAMPLE ESSAYS IN ALL SUBJECT AREAS FOR IAS/PCS EXAMINATION

ESSAYS ON SOCIAL ISSUES

1. Tackling Hunger Globally is Need of the Hour

Hunger is an indicator of the enormity of social injustices prevailing globally. The existence of hunger can be traced back to many years back. It has been one of the driving factors behind the French Revolution in the eighteenth Century where the lack of bread in Paris was also the reason other than demands for political freedom. It has been the cause and effect of many riots occurring due to unjustified government policies causing severe economic hardship and clashing with the basic human right to food. Tea, a non-edible food item, was used as a protest tool to protest the British tax on tea imported to the colonies by a group of Boston citizens. The food crises around the world led to the immediate establishment of the World Food Programme. Moreover, many other United Nations agencies have incorporated hunger or food security in their work programmes, which include the United Nations Children Education Fund, the World Health Organisation, the United Nations Development Programme and the different United Nations missions to war-torn countries.

The loose definition of term 'hunger' has led to adaptation in its meaning often to serve the purposes of those experiencing it. In affluent countries, especially, hunger is the gnawing pain in the stomach for many on missing a meal. On the contrary, another form of hunger is the physical debilitation of those affected from chronic undernutrition. However, hunger that encloses the emotional and political aspects of the society is multidimensional. It involves the anguish of a farmer who in a dilemma to pay the rent for the land or feeding his family has the only option left to sell the produce from his farm. It includes the pain of suffering one goes through to see in helplessness ones loved ones die for violating the practices and policies set by the few dominant elites. Imposition of laws and regulations is just to ensure that the poor and hungry are compelled to provide their labour in lieu of low wages or small quantity of food. Regulations are imposed to reduce the chances of self-sustenance in poor so that their existing condition remains unaltered. The schemes run by the Indian government on providing rice and wheat at extremely subsidised rates are also of little help to the poor as either the grain is black marketed or its quality is too poor for consumption by any human being. The main cause of hunger in some parts of the world is considered to be the population growth, which put pressure on the limited resources of the world. Thomas Malthus, an English economist, argued that food and water supply at some point would be unavoidably outstripped due to fertile land and safe drinking water being finite resources. Therefore, a disastrous consequence of high population growth rate would be anarchy and mass starvation. Some drastic measures have been taken to reduce the population growth rate based on this belief and the problem of addressing their needs.

Hunger, which is the cause and effect of poverty, is responsible for the depletion of people physically, physiologically and psychologically. For the poor to earn a living, the most abundant asset available is labour. However, this labour is of no avail due to hunger that further entraps the poor in hunger and poverty. The everyday struggle of finding food for the family relinquishes any thought of long-term development in the miserably poor. Even after the discovery of many innovative ways by the modern technology and medical research to fight various pests and diseases, famines have been a serious trouble for a long time. The increasing pressure to resolve the food crisis among world's population has led to the utilisation of marginal, erosion-prone lands and deforestation. This causes the environment to be more inclined to famine situations and undermines the fertility of the land. Natural disasters do not discriminate the poor from the rich and affect them alike. Reconstructing agriculture to be more self-reliant and discouraging specialisation could be an alternative solution to the hunger in modern day. Increasing self-reliance can result in reducing the help from aid agencies, thus attaining this long-term measure. Farm cooperatives should be developed to support and facilitate the farming activities of farm workers and those urban migrants who wish to return to their rural homes. Food security can also be enhanced by increasing the amount of arable land under cultivation. It would be an incentive to reduce or cancel debts owed by farmers to increase their contribution towards ensuring food security. The inability of farm workers and small farmers to claim a fair price for their labour and the goods produced by them in a monopoly-controlled market leads to their exploitation. It has been the major cause of frequent suicides in the rural districts.

The skeletal look of people in places, such as Ethiopia, Somalia, and closer home in Andhra Pradesh, Maharashtra, etc. will cause frequent embarrassment to us unless urgent warlike steps are taken up to tackle this menace across the world.

2. Closely Knit Families are Being Replaced by Nuclear Families

Once India was renowned worldwide for its culture of joint families. Bringing up in a joint family was believed to inculcate in an individual the necessary values of adaptability, adjustment, understanding, etc. to live in society. However, the trend seems to have changed now. This is because the people now prefer nuclear families more than the joint families. Living in a nuclear family leads to a stronger bond between a child and his parents, is the general feeling among the modern-day parents.

In a nuclear family, the parents get more time to focus on the development of their child. This is helpful for the proper grooming of their children. There are minimum chances of conflicts between the two generations—parents and grandparents—which interfere with the child's development.

Positive and negatives traits are associated with both these types of families. However, keeping in pace with the present day lifestyle, nuclear families are more appropriate to handle. The present generations wanting to settle in nuclear families could be due to this advantage.

Another argument made by some parents is that the level of scrutiny in a joint family is higher on a child, even though it gets lot of love and care in joint families. For example, in case of the child making a mistake, both the parents and other family members may shout on him or counsel him, thus, making the child uncomfortable.

In joint families, the probability of difference in opinion may also be much higher. It becomes increasingly difficult to maintain harmony among all the family members as the family gets bigger. Hence, in such families, risk of stress also increases.

However, the level of celebration and fun and enjoyment associated with it, such as festivals, birthdays, etc. is unforgettable and much higher in joint families.

However, most of the middle-class families have working parents who believe the nuclear family system to suit their living style, giving them more time for themselves and their children. A section of sociologists also agrees with this viewpoint that the scope for parents to pay attention to their children increases a lot in a nuclear family.

However, another section of sociologists have counterarguments on the failure of nuclear families to instil in their children the importance of strong family bonds, close knit relatives and social norms.

As, this debate will continue forever, the family type should be decided after due consideration involving the consensus of all the family members and making everyone comfortable and happy. The nuclear families can help reduce the inconvenience of staying together as a joint family, but the bond among the family members should remain intact.

3. Justice Must Reach the Poor

INTRODUCTION

The term justice refers to acting in a 'just and fair' way. During trial in courts, Judges all over are addressed as 'My Lord'. This implies the power they have to exercise for bringing justice to the needy people, which they must do. Unfortunately, people nowadays have a counterview that most things including love and respect could be purchased and thus have complete disregard for ethics or laws.

The judiciary by exercising its power could be of great help to the underprivileged section of the society, as it is an important pillar of democracy. In order to ensure better survivability of poor people, they must be provided with basic amenities. They rarely get any respect in the society and suffer a lot.

Unfortunately, the long process of justice in India makes it very difficult for them, and it is rare to get. However, those getting it consider themselves very fortunate.

IMPORTANCE OF JUSTICE

The ideals such as hard work and honesty in a world of receding morality may be unable to ensure prosperity of a person. The judiciary should ensure doing justice to the poor where a large section is even not aware about the injustice it goes through. They are even willing to work on lower wages and, hence, get exploited by their employers.

Many poor people go through the harassment at the hand of *sarkari babus* for getting their work done. Thus, unethical practices like bribe should be abolished so that such people can also live with dignity. All the segments of justice that includes social, civil, economic and political justice must be taken into consideration. Under the British rule, India suffered enough and the poor class had the belief of getting fair share in a free country. Unfortunately, the poor still remains in a baffling state as the clumsy and complex Indian social structure failed to bring any respite to them from this melancholy. A segment of the country's population is still getting exploited at the hand of upper caste. Even though the Constitution of India has so many provisions in place to uphold their rights against any atrocities, in real terms, the objective is far from being achieved.

One of the foremost causes behind elusion of justice is the lack of information. It is ironical that the poor are not aware of numerous schemes which the government brings in for their welfare. The rural population is still detached from the rest of India undergoing tremendous digital revolution and this is one of the foremost reasons for the unawareness.

Many poor people because of not possessing any knowledge or financial power find it difficult to bail themselves out from the arrest over false accusations. Same is the situation in case of small farmers in villages who suffer at the hands of bigger landlords.

An NGO or public group can file 'Public Interest Litigation (PIL)' which is a vital part to preserve the rights of children, disabled person in courts and giving priority to women.

A leading example of this is 'the Manual Scavenging Bill 2012' that was introduced in order to ban it by law so that the poor do not have to go through such atrocities, yet many of them are still working in such detestable situation. Hence, in rural areas as well imparting education can lead to better life conditions. It is really depressing that even after being termed as one of the world's fastest growing economies; India is still marred by issues of caste and class leading to exploitation of poor section of the society.

Many people have undergone the depression caused by the rampant corruption, piling of cases, and the endless time to get justice that has led to distrust in the Indian judiciary system. The maxim 'Justice delayed is Justice denied' cannot be truer than in a country like India. Though reservation has been of great help to a chunk of the lower class of the society, the merits of this policy is being questioned because of undue advantage taken by a large number of people in getting what they are unworthy of. Moreover, a large section of political class is using this as a tool to score political points over its opponents in terms of vote bank politics.

However, a lot of steps have been taken for the welfare of the poor over the last few years. Various schemes such as Janni Suraksha Yojna, Kanya Vidya Dhan, etc. introduced by the government and the active engagement of NGOs are helping people at the grassroots level. NGOs are also contributing to the cause by taking the responsibility of arousing awareness among the poor about their rights. All these steps taken together will be beneficial to the lower strata of the society including the rural people and would be of great help to fill the gap between them and the upper class and urban people. This equality in social and economical terms will transform India into a developed country in the days to come. Providing amenities to the poor and eradication of poverty will also act as a catalyst towards deliverance of justice to them.

CONCLUSION

Even though our constitution has made so many provisions to protect the interests of all the sections of the society and the Indian judiciary system possess uttermost authority and strength, development of the lower strata of the society and the poor to bring them at par with the upper segment are the only means to impart justice to the poor.

4. Crime Would Reduce with Harsher Punishments or Moral Teachings: Do You Agree?

The effectiveness of stringent punishments or moral teachings in reducing crime rate is quite debatable. The followers of the Bible would abide by the principle of retribution that believes in punishment in proportion to the seriousness of the crime.

However, the inherent objective behind punishment must also be understood. If the purpose is merely causing physical suffering on the offender, strident punishment should be the approach. However, if the purpose is to strengthen the moral values in the wrongdoer, then the right approach would be imparting moral teachings to him. In my view, following the balanced approach would definitely be helpful in effectively handling the crime—the right mix of punishment and moral values that show him the right path to follow in life. The convicted ones should also get a chance to reform themselves. For example, breaking the habit of stealing in a person would be more significant than putting him behind bars. However, imprisonment is equally necessary to stop the incidents of wrongdoings further.

Social boycott of the convicted and negative public perception against them leads to further aggravation in their behaviour inclining them permanently towards crime. A far better approach to reduce the crime rate significantly would be to make stringent laws in a country and an efficient police force with a watchful eye for the implementation of the laws. Moreover, passing fast verdicts by the court can also help in reducing the crime rate as the unnecessary delay in court proceedings leads to increase in crime rate. At times, it becomes absolute necessity to enforce stringent punishments. The probable reason for this is that the decision-making in some people towards whether to commit a crime or not is based on the punishment it carries. Such people are more prone to commit crimes which carry little punishment/penalty or provide enough loopholes to escape. Thus, stringent punishment is an effective way to prevent such people in committing crime and, thereby, decreasing the crime rate.

Several psychologists are of the opinions that media also has a big role in increasing the crime rate. Television shows with highly violent programmes are often telecasted that are reflecting in the behaviour of the society.

Some crimes are committed due to forcible circumstances while some are committed out of passion and logic. The decision to punish and on its harshness should be taken based on the nature of crime and the inherent intention associated in carrying it.

5. Role of NGOs in India's Development

The state has a primal and significant role to play in a democratic set up in devising and enforcing the development programmes based on social and economic perspective. Unfortunately, in the present-day society, the poor are facing much more complex problems. In a country like India, this particularly holds true as a large chunk of the society is still vulnerable facing discrimination at every level.

Non-Government Organisations (NGOs), the groups or institutions or organisations that act independent without any administrative hold, work on the foundation of principles of equality, selflessness and human development. Currently, approximately 25,000 NGOs are operating with a pan-India presence.

Social service holds significance since ancient times in India. Even Mahatma Gandhi, after India getting independence, is alleged to have expressed his desire to transform the Indian National Congress into a public service organisation. His proposal was declined, but later many of his ardent followers emulating on his principles setup several voluntary organisations across the country to carry out constructive works. However, in the early 1970s, the process of identification, verification and registration of these organisations came into operation and led to emergence of NGOs in India. Following their formal inception, the government took great interest in promoting them in different ways.

The Sixth Five Year Plan of India was launched with the famous slogan 'GARIBI HATAO' where the government acknowledged the significance the NGOs hold in the development of India. Later, the government came out with the seventh FYP, where it put the onus on NGOs to develop 'self-reliance communities' for promoting development of rural sector. The government brought out the eighth FYP with the objective of promoting the network of NGOs across the nation. The ninth FYP visualised the main role of NGOs in the promotion of PPPs in the country. The tenth FYP came out with a vision over the significance of NGOs to raise awareness among the peasants about various modern farm techniques and government initiatives being adopted for their benefits and the development of the agricultural sector. In addition, government has come up with various assistance programmes and financial aids to promote the development of NGOs.

NGOs with the backing of government have speeded up its development activities by working on specific issues like poverty alleviation, social inequalities, children rights, child labour, caste stigma, women rights, rural development, water and sanitation, environmental issues, etc. The last two decades have witnessed the proactive role played by NGOs in the development of social sector including education, health, etc. An important role the NGOs have played particularly in rural sectors is in causing the school dropouts return to their school, thus, upholding the Right to education. Moreover, the initiatives taken by NGOs for the development of health sector such as programmes on the eradication of leprosy, TB and malaria and improving water and sanitation facilities have been of great success.

The most significant contribution of NGOs is witnessed in successfully persuading the government to come up with several development-oriented policies and laws that include the following: Right to Information, Integrated Child Development Scheme (ICDS), Integrated Child Protection Scheme (ICPS), MNREGA, Juvenile justice, Nirmal gram initiative, Rashtriya Swasthya Bima Yojna (RSBY) and various policies on women development, forest and environment development, anti-trafficking and people with disability, etc.

NGOs in reality have been very active in safeguarding the interests of the poor and impoverished and hold significance for protecting the democratic values of the country. However, several NGOs operating in India have come under the scanner for suspicious functioning because of lack of accountability and credibility loss. Recently, the Intelligence Bureau (IB) came up with a report on few NGOs, which in the pretext of protests against the developmental activities taken by the government, are causing great harm to the interest of the nation. The report mentioned that the nations bore a loss of 2–3 per cent of GDP due to consistent protests made against the government's initiatives by 'foreign-funded NGOs'. The report has raised discussions and debates putting a question mark over the accountability of NGOs. The NGOs has the right to protest over the rights of the people but they should come up with alternate options without hampering the developmental initiatives taken by the government. Merely hampering and disrupting developmental activities in the name of protests would be detrimental to the growth of the nation. Hence, it becomes all the more essential for NGOs to ascertain effective policy research and suggest alternative solutions to the government, working as a think tank, since the basis for their set up was to help the government with the most effective options in pursuit of national interest.

It is well-known fact that several NGOs funded by the foreign agencies for their activities played a major role in raising protests against government initiative to set up coal and thermal power plants and Kudankulam Nuclear Project in the respective states leading to power shortages in the region. After the release of IB report, few voices were raised from various quarters to stop the flow of foreign funds to those NGOs. However, in a country as vast as India with little income source and high difficulties in raising funds for the sustenance of NGOs. It would not be prudent to stop flow of foreign funds. The better alternative to blocking the funds would be to ensure more transparency in their classification based on their fund sources. An effective approach would be to beef up the scrutiny procedures through the Foreign Contribution (Regulation) Act, 2010. Moreover, NGOs must be instructed to ascertain transparency in their governance framework and the functioning of their board.

In brief, the NGOs functioning with added accountability, coming up with alternative developmental approaches, in tone with the government and market can work wonders in boosting further the development process in India.

6. Secularism Opposes All Forms of Inter-Religious Supremacy

The favouritism of one's own community or its members while discriminating against another community or its members on the basis of religious identity are the cases of religious abuse and reflect inter-religious supremacy.

One can assume that detachment, disaster and agony are endemic to any individual, but a large part of one's agony is man-made itself and hence eliminative; at least some of our suffering is not man-made. One finds respite in religion, art and philosophy as a counter to such miseries of life. Secularism too believes in this faith and, therefore, approves such religious practices.

Religion also associates with itself some ingrained problems. In some religions, there has been a relentless inequalities in some sects. A visible example of this is barring the Dalits from entering temples. In some cases, women are banned entry to temples. In any organised religion, it is the most conservative faction which dominates its religious beliefs and does not tolerate any dissension.

Religious fundamentalism has become a big trouble across the country and the entire world and pose a great threat to peace within and outside the country. The frequent sectarian violence among various religious sects inside most religions leads to abusing of dissenting minorities. This religious dominance of one particular sect over the other is known as inter-religious domination.

As Secularism is against all such discrimination based on religious doctrines by any form of institutionalised religious community on any other community, it rejects not only inter-religious domination but also intra-religious dominations. It advocates for promoting freedom within all religions and, thus, denounces inequality between, as well as within all religions.

Further, we will go through the ways in which a state adhering to the ideal of secularism need to treat its various religions and religious communities. Most of the inhibitions, biases and mistrust could be reduced by mutual help and sharing among communities. Working together for mutual enlightenment is a way to encourage religious equality. Such psyche of people can only be changed by imparting education.

However, merely education and benignity of some persons will not help the cause of establishing religious equality. The society and states of present-day times possess enormous public power.

Theocratic state is a peril: Theocracy implies the governance of a state by the head of any religious organisation in a priestly order. It leads to complete disregard for other religions and should not exist in any state. A few examples of theocratic states are Papal States of Europe in Medieval period and Taliban-controlled states in current times.

Thus, the states lacking any form of coordination between their religious and political institutions are quite notorious for their grouping, tyranny and persecution of other religious groups and not allowing freedom of religion. To some extent, this could be controlled by the states detachment from any particular religion at the primary level, however, that is not enough.

States should be non-allegiant towards any religion in any formal or legal way. Neither should they have close alliance with any particular religious group which many non-theocratic states have formed.

For example, in the seventeenth century, though the governance of England was not in the hand of any priestly class but it favoured the Anglican Church and its community. The official religion established in the states of England was Anglican religion. At present times, Pakistan is such country having Islam as the official state religion. Such states have high intolerance towards any internal protest on religious equality.

A secular state must adhere to the principles and objectives derived from non-religious sources to a certain extent (i.e. means). The purpose behind such objectives should be to maintain peace, religious freedom, freedom from religion-based persecution, promote equality and discourage religious boycott in terms of inter-religious and intra-religious equality.

The states must not show any attachment towards any organised religion and its institutions to achieve these objectives. Not any specified pattern or form is there to propose such detachment.

To further understand the concept of secularism, we will discuss two models—the Western model, best represented by America and the Indian model of Secularism.

WESTERN CONCEPTS OF SECULARISM

In western concept of secularism, state and religion both hold their own exclusive domain with independent jurisdiction without any interference of state or religion i.e. state and religion are mutually excluded against any unlawful invasion on the respective domains of each other.

The state is not allowed to grant any type of assistance to any religious institutions. State is not allowed to hamper the functioning of any religious community which is running its operations within the constraints of the law of the land.

For example, in case of a religious community opposing its woman to become a priest, the states cannot enforce its will on the matter. Similarly, in the case of a religious group prohibiting the entry of a section of its community in the sanctum of its place of worship, then the states has no authority to interfere on the matter.

Thus, the practice of religion is an individual choice and does not come under the purview of state policy or law. This model represents freedom and equality to an individual. It also grants liberty to an individual. It promotes equality among individuals and leaves very little scope for bias against any based on community-based rights or minority rights.

However, this has few drawbacks. The focus of these states is on intra-religious domination and advocate for strict detachment of state from church to attain individual freedom. The issues related to inter-religious equality and thus minority rights are often ignored. This model does not take into account the idea of state-supported religious reforms.

Nehru's perception in this regard was different and advocated for the state to provide equal protection to all the religions. The ideal secular state which he wanted to establish was that which is protective towards all the religion but is not biased towards any specific one ignoring others and against the discriminatory policy of adopting a particular region as its state religion.

Indian secularism in this context follows basically a different approach than western secularism. In addition to its focus on Church–State separation, it also emphasises on the idea of inter-religious equality.

Inter-religious 'tolerance' was already inherent in the Indian culture. Though, the compatibility between tolerance and religious domination exists and it may leave space for everyone to go together but put a limit on such freedom.

The arrival of western modernity highlighted upon the ignored and marginalised beliefs of equality in Indian context. It focussed these beliefs and helped us to put spotlight on equality within the community. It also introduced ideas to replace the beliefs of hierarchy with the concept of inter-community equality. To achieve its objective, it takes into account the following factors—scientific and rational education, legislation, social reforms, urbanisation and industrialisation.

So, Indian secularism reshaped into a distinct form resulting from the fusion of the already existing patterns of religious diversity and the ideas coming from the west. It resulted in equal emphasis in the context of intra-religious and inter-religious domination.

The strength of Indian secularism has been tested time and again in various wars. For a long period, Kashmir has become a symbol and test of Indian secularism.

Punjab terrorism due to communal politics was dealt in a manner to keep the secular fabric of India intact in 1966. Nehru dealt with militant agitations and their demands following a few basic rules. First, he rejected any negotiation or political transactions with the leaders of such movements having secessionist policies, using violence or raising demands on the basis of religion or communalism. Second, Nehru dealt firmly with both Hindu and Sikh communalism taking up the cause of minority issues.

India in its endeavour to keep secular fabric of the country intact is facing challenges in the form of communalism, politicisation of caste and religion, the rise of religious fundamentalism and obscurantism, etc.

At times, Indian secularism draw criticism for being anti-religious, which is false, as it works against institutionalised religious domination. It is also criticised for promoting and favouring minorities, but it only encourages minority rights to protect their fundamental interests. It is also blamed for being Interventionist, which means that secularism intends to be forcible and interferes extremely with the religious freedom of communities.

However, this is misinterpreted as it allows state-supported religious reforms. Personal laws can be reconstituted to suit and represent both minority's rights and gender-based equality. However, such reforms are neither expected to be enforced by state or religious groups nor a policy of detachment from reforms is recommended. The state must encourage and facilitate the liberal and democratic opinions within every religion.

Other nations disapproved the Indian model as an impossible project, but India rejected their criticism to be false. In reality, globalisation has led to increase in migration and a situation is arising where Indian model could be of great help. The increasing diversity of cultures and religions in other parts of the world such as Europe, America, and some parts of Middle East has made the structure of their society resemble India. In the hope of arriving at a solution for their society, these countries are keeping a watch on the future of the Indian experiment with keen interest.

Some countries like Bangladesh have a unique form of secularism. It's state religion is Islam and follows secularism as a basic tenet of the Constitution.

As far as China is concerned, the Communist Party of China follows Atheism, but five religions are in practice and recognised by the state: Buddhism, Taoism, Islam, Catholic Christianity and Protestant Christianity. Normal religious activities are encouraged and enforced by the state (e.g., prohibition on using place of worship as a medium to preach violence or anti-state rhetoric) for the stability of China. In addition, the religious practices are controlled by the state in China.

7. Labour Issues in India

Developing countries face frequent challenges in the process of development to pass the benefits to the impoverished section through generating employment for them and provide for respectable way of living. Universal adult Franchise is a landmark of democracy and raise voice for the interests of labour force which is large in numbers.

These countries have to take into perspective labour interests in favour of industry and capital. On the contrary, developed countries approved the eligibility of workmen to exercise their franchise only after long period of industrial development. The capitalists of the country amassed great wealth during this period and, due to repeated labour movements, workers getting right to vote, activism of International Labour Organisation and New Deal of Roosevelt in latter period, the western governments assumed the duty of wealth redistribution. In India, the government at the time of independence assumed the dual responsibility of creation and redistribution of wealth simultaneously.

To achieve this, investment inflow in competition with developed countries is required. Investment will come only on offering low cost advantage, be it domestic or foreign. In the initial phase, cheap labour in surplus amount allows the industries to extract the low cost advantage. In consequence, industries start to expand, which gives rise to shortage of adequate skilled labour and the simultaneous rise of trade unionism. By now, low cost advantage begins to decline and governments find it very difficult to maintain equity between labours' privileges and industrial growth through legislation. The government undertakes various initiatives like easing of infrastructure bottlenecks, tax concessions, etc. to keep the low cost advantages intact. This can be seen in the development of Chinese economy since the last two decades.

Trade unions like Bharatiya Mazdoor Sangha or Centre for Indian Trade Union are pressure groups with the objective of protecting the labour interests through 'collective bargaining'. The labour force need to organise to influence the capitalists as the individual labour's demands are not paid heed to by the management. They frequently deal for higher wages, safety at work place, social security, job security, etc. To achieve this, they hold demonstration, strikes and file petitions to higher authorities. The first organised strike was held in the Great Indian Peninsular Railways in India in 1899. At times labours use violence while protesting, the recent example being a jute mill in West Bengal and Maruti Udyog Ltd. They form a different class as vote bank, and political parties try to woo them before elections. However, in the past decade there has been significant reduction in the frequency of strikes, lockouts and man-days lost. The behaviour of labour force as separate vote bank has also changed which signals towards growing cordial relations between them and the higher authorities.

The employers also got organised in the need to deal with labour unions and to present their consolidated viewpoint, which resulted in the formation of the All India Organisation of Employers, the first such organisation, in 1932.

Three parties are involved in such cooperation called Tripartite Cooperation System that includes (1) government, (2) employer and (3) trade union. The government in such cases acts as the mediator between the two parties generally having conflicting interests. However, in reality all the parties work on a common ground of industrial growth and are mutually dependent upon each other.

There are many articles in our constitution which are focused towards their interests. A few examples include Article 23 that prohibits forced labour, 24 that prohibits child labour below the age of 14 years in factories, mines and other hazardous occupations. Moreover, the forty-second amendment introduced Article 43A—which directs the state to take steps making sure the participation of workers in the management of industries. (Gandhiji described the employers to be trustees of workers' interests and directed them to ensure the welfare of their labour force.)

One of the fundamental features of welfare state is labour protection legislation with the objective of rendering social justice. The chief objective of such laws should be creation of more, safer and rewarding job for the upliftment of labour. It includes criteria on minimum wages, working conditions, overtime controls, rights against unjustified retrenchment, strengthening of labour unions, right to compensation of workers in case of accident at workplace, post-retirement benefits, personal progress, skill development, social security and dignity of labour, etc.

Around 85–90 per cent of workforce in India is employed in informal sector which are micro firms employing about 5–10 persons where these laws are inapplicable. A great number of regressive laws are in operation to discourage such employers from expanding their businesses. Moreover, they do not have that much knowledge of laws and do not avail the services of lawyers ensuring that conformity to law is much expensive. In addition, a large number of workforce do not get any formal training, which results in low productivity and low value addition.

Modernisation of workplace is mostly good for workers in long term. For example, when telecom revolution took place, few thousand workers lost their jobs because of transformation from manual landline networks to digitised cellular network. However, the telecom sector in present times is one of the biggest employers in India and pays decent perks to its employees. Similar adverse reactions were reported from the employees during the introduction of computers in various departments and PSUs.

Enforcing the retention of a disproportionately large number of workforce on an organisation, would cause the business to suffer and over a period of time closing of its operation. When it affects large number of firms, this in turn will hamper the whole economy as the investors will take into account costs of these crises as well. Their preference would be on capital-intensive production or lower production causing lower employment and higher prices of products. On the contrary, is the relaxed criteria of easy entry and exit, will result in growing manufacturing firms, with option for more investment, more number of factories, causing more employment and lower costs of products. This over a period of time will lead to a robust manufacturing sector having the capacity to employ any retrenched workers in productive employment.

❑❑❑

ESSAYS ON ECONOMIC ISSUES

1. Impacts of Demonetisation

Demonetisation, considered as a mother of all reforms in India, taken by the government has begun to show its positive indications in a very short span of time. The demonetisation moves terminated the legal validity of ₹500 and 1000. As expected, though this reformative action made it a bit difficult for common people to deal with the situation, it will be overcome soon. The people of this country were willing to take this pain cooperating with the government move and reacted in a matured manner. This is a perfect example of democracy where the government and its people go parallel in building the nation and deciding the policy.

The manyfold impacts of the demonetisation move on country and society are detailed as follows:

- **Attack on Black Money:** Black money is cancerous to the economic growth of a country. Acting as a parallel economy, it cripples the foundation of any nation. The total worth of black money being in circulation in India is estimated to be ₹3 lakh crore. It is quite big amount in comparison to the total money in circulation, which is only ₹17 lakh crore. The demonetisation move is a single masterstroke played by the government that will put shackles on black money which will either come to account book or be destroyed.
- **Blow to Fake Currency:** The Indian Statistical Institute (ISI) claims that the total fake currency being circulated in the Indian economy is around ₹400 crore at any given point of time. Around ₹70 crore fake currencies are also estimated to be injected in India every year.
- **Impact on Bank Deposits:** It is widely known fact that the 500 and 1000 currency notes constitute about 86 per cent currency circulation in India. As a result of this move, people deposited the money in the form of ₹500 and 1000 notes into the banks. The RBI also made a declaration of receiving deposits worth ₹5.12 trillion until 18th November, which can boost Indian GDP by 0.5 to

1.5 per cent. The State Bank of India (SBI), India's largest public sector bank, also received cash deposits worth ₹1.27 trillion.

- **Effect on Lending Rates:** The banks may be able to reduce the cost of funds due to this move because the huge cash deposit base will substitute the high cost of borrowing and cut down the overall costs of funds. The banks are expected to trim the deposit rates by approximately 125 bps over the next six months. The new Marginal Cost of Funds-based Lending Rate (MCLR) directives will instantly take into account the reduced cost. This will lead to a decline in lending rates that will be effective in boosting the economic activity in the medium term.
- **Real Estate Cleansing:** The real estate industry is alleged to be established on black money. The amount of black money circulated in the sector is quite big. A report says that about 40 per cent of the real estate transactions in Delhi-NCR are being made through black money. The demonetisation move will keep a check on such transactions in the real estate sector.
- **Attack on Hawala Transactions:** The Hawala transactions have also been severely struck because of demonetisation. Hawala is a way to channelise money without any actual movement of it. Intelligence reports suggest that Hawala route acts as a medium to ease money laundering and terror financing. The sudden elimination of black money from the market have brought a stop to the Hawala activities.
- **Financial Inclusion:** Banks will be inclined to offer subsidised loans and other facilities to Jan Dhan account holder because of cash inflow. The Jan Dhan accounts has a share of below 1 per cent in total deposit base of the Indian banking system. The demonetisation move based on higher denomination notes might thrust cash flow in Jan Dhan accounts. Moreover, the Jan Dhan Account holders will get accustomed to banking system.
- **Government Finances:** The flow of unaccounted money into the formal channel because of demonetisation will increase the income tax collections. This amount produced from income tax will enable the government to cut down the fiscal deficit in fiscal year 2017. This will result in shifting of economy from the unorganised to organised sector. The formalisation of unaccounted money will also aid in the smooth implementation of GST scheme.
- **Bond Market:** The call for government bond will increase in the market due to ban on currency notes. As the cash flow in the banks will improve, it will eventually generate the demand for higher statutory liquidity ratio (SLR).
- **Unrest in Kashmir:** The demonetisation move has strongly hit the terror operations on Kashmir Valley in a very short time. The four-month long turmoil in the valley has come to halt due to lack of monetary supply. In a recent report from the intelligence agency, it is claimed that ₹1,000 crore are funded annually from Pakistan to separatists through Hawala route for causing disturbance in

the valley. At present, the separatists are clueless as demonetisation entirely blocked Hawala transactions. The counterfeit Indian currency syndicate running its operations both inside and outside the country has been severely hit.

The stone-pelting incidents also decreased in the valley because of demonetisation. The separatists are unable to engage young people in the agitation against the army or the state due to demonetisation causing a deadly impact on their funding.

- **Naxalites and North-East Insurgency:** Naxalites and insurgents in North-East also sustain their treacherous motives through black money, which is a lifeline to their operations. They are the worst affected by demonetisation scheme. This made them term this move as 'Financial Emergency'. Their annual turnover is estimated to be over ₹500 crore through terror funding, NGOs, forgery, extortions and local taxes. This enormous amount of money is used for recruitment, arms, foods, medicines and shelters to spread anti-national activities.

  The demonetisation move turned all these stash of money to no more than a worthless paper. However, it is discovered that Naxals are using villagers for depositing the money in their accounts. The authority must take this matter seriously and put a stop on any further deposition of such money in their accounts. The recent data on crime showed that many places like Delhi, Pune, and Mumbai, recorded a dip in the crime rate like theft, snatching, dacoity, etc. after demonetisation.

2. NPAs: The Bane of Indian Banking Sector

INTRODUCTION

Non-performing assets (NPAs) are categorised as the loans that are in risk of default. A loan is considered as a non-performing asset once the borrower fails to make interest or principal payments for 90 days.

In general terms, NPAs are assets/projects that are unable to generate cash flow in the period and to the extent originally expected. By translation alone, banks may not be able to timely recover the entire amount lent and hence, set aside certain amount for a known liability in future. However, in reality, the factors causing rise in NPAs are wrong assumptions/inefficiencies, genuine reasons and violation of law.

THE MAGNITUDE OF NPAs

A recent survey found out that in the banking system net NPAs constitute only 2.36 per cent of the total loans. However, on taking into account the restructured assets also, 10.9 per cent of the total loans in the system will be stressed assets account. According to a report released by the International Monetary Fund (IMF), the debt at risk in India constitutes around 37 per cent of the total debt.

State Bank of India (SBI), the largest lender in India, reported that in the third quarter of the 2015–2016 financial year, a massive 67 per cent decrease took place in consolidated net profit at ₹1,25,949 crore and loans worth ₹20,692 crore were termed as bad loans.

The cumulative gross NPAs of 24 listed public sector banks that includes the market leader SBI and its associates as on 31 December 2015 was found to be ₹3,93,035 crore as per an estimate.

The Economic Survey 2015–2016 also raised apprehensions over the possibility of growing bad debts hampering the future growth prospects of the banks.

CAUSES OF RISING NPAs

In reality, factors that cause rise in NPAs are wrong assumptions/inefficiencies, genuine reasons and violation of law. These could be classified as external and internal environment.

The causes in the external environment category are global slowdown, drop in domestic demand, setback in policy and disputed contracts.

The factors causing NPA rise under the internal environment category are as follows:

- *Banking sector*: Poor credit appraisal; weak risk management; governance deficit, all debt-no equity; chasing quick growth; power-faulty FSAs, infra financing particularly highways—'gold plated' contracts; pass through arrangement, termination payments; pretend and extend.
- *Beyond corporate universe*: Small/medium enterprises—lack of timely support and delayed payments; Kisan Credit Card and agriculture distress vis-a-vis crop insurance.
- *Corporate India*: High leverage; complex web-holding company; overseas acquisitions; step down entities; unhedged exposures; siphoning, diversion and so on.
- *Value sale versus distress sale*: Minsky's Financial Instability Hypothesis—three types of borrowers (Hedge, Speculative and Ponzi).

EFFECTS OF RISING NPAs

- A major chunk of NPA is formed by the public sector banks, which provide around 80 per cent of the credit to various industries. Last year, banks provided a huge amount of loan to Kingfisher, which was marred in financial crisis, but it is unable to recover from it.
- The falling of any Indian industry into crisis is bound to impact the banking sector causing their NPA to rise.
- Not only PSBs but the economic policy of the government and the politician-corporate nexus are behind the rise in NPAs of banking industry.
- The consistent rise of NPAs in the present scenario as in case of some public sector bank & private bank will lead to closing of bank, thus, creating a serious economic crisis in the nation.

- One of the critical factors behind the rising NPA is relaxed lending norms, especially for corporate chiefs. Often, a proper analysis of their financial status and credit rating is not carried out. Moreover, in the face of competition, banks are resorting to hugely selling unsecured loans that causes a rise in the level of NPAs.
- Global economy can cause a very minor impact on banking sector. The policies of RBI and government can, however, improve the situation.
- There is a need to keep the NPAs in check otherwise a bank may go bankrupt. This would result in the dismantling of entire credit distribution structure of the economy causing a major financial turmoil in the country.
- When the financial crisis hit the United States, it was because of the lenient lending norms and due to huge number of loan defaulters in banks. The US economy went into panic when big banks filed for bankruptcy. Thus, NPA problem should be seriously taken.

STEPS TAKEN BY THE RBI

- RBI has recommended the lenders to carry out their independent and impartial credit appraisal in all cases without relying on credit appraisal reports put up by outside consultants, in particular, the in-house consultants of the borrower company.
- Banks/lenders should perform sensitivity tests/scenario analysis, specifically for infrastructure projects, including project delays and cost overruns. This will aid in decision-making on vitality of the project at the time of deciding the Corrective Action Plan (CAP).
- RBI further recommended that Asset Reconstruction Companies (ARCs) should be interpreted as a supportive system for stressed asset, instead of considering it as a last resort to dispose of NPAs by banks. It is recommended to sell the assets to ARCs at only that stage when there are good chances of revival of the assets and obtaining fair amount of realisable value, for rehabilitation and reconstruction is encouraged.
- Banks will be encouraged to use floating provisions, without obtaining prior permission of the promoters of the company, as per their approved internal policy towards accelerated provisioning/additional provisions aroused at the time of sale of NPAs. Defaulting borrowers shall be barred from repurchasing the asset directly/indirectly from the ARCs. RBI suggested to examine and address the potential legal issues involved.

RBI'S ACTION PLAN FOR EARLY IDENTIFICATION AND RESOLUTION OF BAD LOAN CASES

- Borrowers with suspicious credit worthiness should be offered expensive loans.
- Debt restructuring plan should be set up within 17–100 days instead of the 180-days time limit followed earlier.

- Action should be taken over payment delay of 30–60 days instead of earlier prescribed limit of 90 days.
- Setting up a joint lenders forum for borrowings of ₹100 crore and more.
- Special branches to be set up for speedy disposal of SARFESI (Securitisation and Reconstruction of Financial Assets and Enforcement of Security Interest Act) cases.

3. Impact of Oil Prices in World Politics and Indian Economy

Most of the global economies rely on oil, which is one of the major commodities in recent times. Hence, prices of oil affect almost every economy including India.

India being one of the largest importers of oil in the world imports around 70 per cent of its total oil requirements accounting for one-third of its total imports. Consequently, the price of oil has a huge impact on India.

There had been a consistent decrease in crude oil prices globally which drop 17 per cent to 46.59 US dollars per barrel in 2015 after slipping 47 per cent in 2014. The current crude oil price is floating around 46 US dollars.

FALL IN OIL PRICES: REASONS

- The primary reason for the falling crude oil prices is said to be caused due to tensions escalating between the Iran and the Saudi Arabia—the two top oil-producing nations in the world.
- This is reflecting in decreasing demand, specifically in Asia where China, the biggest economy and energy consumer, is seeing the most sluggish economic growth in a generation.
- It has become very troublesome to cope up with storing excess oil in storage tanks around the world due to large overhang. In USA itself, the domestic crude production reached 9.6 million barrels in July 2015. Canada also went through a sharp rise in production, as heavy investment in tar sands began to yield good result.
- In recent times, shale gas revolution in the United States has reduced its dependence on import of crude oil. For the global oil market this revolution is of significance as around 20 per cent of the oil production in the world is consumed by the United States.

IMPACT ON GLOBAL POLITICS

- *Political realignment*: Oil being one of the most essential commodities in the global world, this is bound to reflect into a major jolt to the political order, where petroleum-producing states from Saudi Arabia to Russia are going to lose their prominence and geopolitical clout.

- *Relevance of OPEC*: Oil is not in scarcity today. The geopolitical battle is more over global market share than mere access to resources. Saudi Arabia seems to export to the global markets in abundance to push out higher-cost producers, especially in the United States. Further, Iran is reluctant in cooperating with the Saudis on oil. That implies the unlikely revival of OPEC.
- *Role of Saudi Arabia*: It does not hold the same clout it had in the global oil market. Even after the crash in oil price, it is producing at full sway. In the past, Saudi Arabia played a balancing role for the producers in maintaining an elevated price for supply of oil in the market for both low-cost and high-cost producers guarantying an income stream for all producers.
- *Role of the USA*: The USA will be moving in the direction of self-sufficiency in oil and gas if its domestic shale industry is able to maintain production at lower prices. Its interest in ensuring stability in the Middle East might also decrease which may increase geopolitical tensions.

ADVANTAGES TO INDIA

India, as a major importer of oil in the world, will have the following advantages due to decreasing oil prices in the global market:

- *Current account balance*: Due to decreasing price of crude oil, India as a major importer of crude oil is able to save billions of dollars. The drop in prices would bring down the value of its imports, which will help in narrowing down India's current account deficit.
- *Inflation*: The entire economy is impacted by variation in oil price especially because the transportation of goods and services is almost impossible without it. A decrease in oil price also results in decrease in cost of all petroleum by-products like tyres, paints, etc. The reduced input costs would also be beneficial to many other industries associated with it.
- *Oil subsidy and fiscal deficit*: In relation to the market price, the government fixes the fuel price at a subsidised rate. Hence, decrease in oil prices results in reduction in government fund transferred to oil marketing companies owing to subsidies and thereby, leading to low fiscal deficit.
- According to the 2015–2016 Economic Survey report, reduction in global crude oil prices primarily helped in restraining the petroleum subsidy bill to ₹30,000 crore in 2015–2016 against ₹57,769 crore spent in 2014–2015.
- *Rupee exchange rate*: Low oil price implies favourable exchange rate for Indian rupee in terms of Indian rupee as it will reduce its dependence for oil payments on reserved currencies like the dollar.
- However, the negative effect is the strengthening of dollar every time the value of oil falls. This neutralises any benefits in favour of India due to reduction in oil prices, as it is a major service exporter in the world.

- According to the Economic Survey 2015–2016 report, India exported services worth 155.6 billion US dollars' in 2014 which made the country the eighth largest services exporter in the world.

DISADVANTAGES FOR INDIA

India may benefit as a result of the fall in global oil prices, but it still has its repercussions which are given as follows:

- *Petroleum producers*: The fall in global oil prices affects the exporters of petroleum producers in the country. It negatively affects exports from India, which is the sixth largest exporter of petroleum products in the world.
- In addition, for India, buyers of its exports and many of its trade partners are net oil exporters. A drop in oil price may affect their economy and hinder demand for Indian products.
- *Remittances*: According to a report released from the World Bank's Migration and Development Brief 2015, India is the world's largest recipient of remittance of 72 billion US dollars. The Indians staying in Gulf countries are the major contributors of this money.

Hence, any drop in oil prices negatively affects the economic prospects of the Gulf Cooperation Council and, thus, remittances to India, which plays a significant part in funding the Current Account Deficit (CAD).

4. Electrification of Rural India to Reduce Energy Poverty is Need of the Hour

It has not passed more than a year after the agreement on Sustainable Development Goals (SDGs) was carried out at the UN General Assembly. SDGs comprise a set of 17 goals with the intention to dramatically improve lives across the world by 2030. SDG7 is one of the major goal that aims to ensure global access to affordable, sustainable, reliable and modern energy. In fact, it could be considered a necessity for meeting all of the SDGs.

Developing national priorities in alignment with the SDGs is crucial as mainstreaming SDG7 would vary across countries. Here, two critical indicators are of significance—access to electricity and cleaner cooking options for all.

The advancement made towards accomplishment of SDG7 in India appears noteworthy with electricity having been delivered to 97 per cent of the villages. The launching of the Ujjwala scheme by the government is another initiative taken to provide LPG to 50 million underprivileged households. However, a deeper analysis raises concerns.

The yearly growth rate of rural households, taking into account the decadal population growth, is estimated at approximately 2 per cent, while the number of households being electrified are increasing at an average annual rate of around 3 per cent. Around 58 million un-electrified households are still there, as estimated by the government, which will be covered under the scheme 'Power for All' by 2019.

However, the Grameen Vidyutikaran (GARV) data gives a different perception and seems to suggest that the yearly household growth since the last 2011 census has not been looked at. Taking into account the annual growth, it is found that increase in the number of un-electric households is almost 23 per cent. This shows that the household electrification are not being carried out at a desired pace.

In Madhya Pradesh, the access rate dropped from 62 per cent in 2001 to around 57 per cent in 2016 according to the Census and GARV data for States. A mere 1 per cent rise in household electrification was observed in Assam from 2001 to 2016, and is now at 35 per cent. West Bengal, on the contrary registered a big growth from 20 per cent in 2001 to 95 per cent in 2016.

The main concern is to find the way to connecting and sustaining un-electrified households in the states which are lagging behind. A grid infrastructure for these households may already be present in the villages they are situated. Most of the times, government records do not provide a true picture of the social structure. Several un-electrified hamlets in the electrified main village are shown as electrified. There is a need to identify such habitations and cover them under government schemes or through renewable energy-based mini-grids engaging the private sector also and adequately incentivising them for this.

Although the pace of village electrification has slightly increased, the intensification has been comparatively slow. There is a marginal difference in the financial status of above poverty line households and below poverty line households, who are provided free connections, in most villages. The households that are interested for electrification but lack the financial means should be helped by financing their wiring, metering and connection costs to bridge this gap. Selecting such households for subsidised connection by using the deprivation framework of the socio-economic and caste census could be another alternative.

Ensuring access to clean cooking options is another important aspect of SDG7. TERI studies suggest that fuel stacking is a major issue in most villages, though considerable progress has been made under Ujjwala scheme.

Most families prefer LPG for emergency cooking only instead of using for cooking their major meals. Higher expenses incurred for using commercial fuels could be one such reason. A family of 5–6 members availing the subsidy of an LPG cylinder is expected to spend a monthly amount of around ₹500 to cook their meals. According to the last SECC, nearly three-quarters of the rural households earn ₹5,000 or less, and an expenditure of more than 10 per cent of their total income on fuel will bring them under energy-poverty. Thus, in addition to providing rural households with cleaner fuels to reduce household air pollution, it is equally important to ensure a substantial increase in rural income so that part of the added income of such households is used to meet clean energy requirements.

The use of electric induction cook stoves as complementary to LPG should also be promoted. It has almost the same cost and fuel expenditure as in case of LPG. The usage of induction cook stoves will ensure optimum possible use of the electricity infrastructure being created.

At present, most of the power plants are not running to their full capacity. Thus, higher plant load factor and better revenue sustainability for DISCOMs could be achieved through the electrification of the cooking energy demand which will also lead to preventing the cost towards creating a supply chain for cooking fuel. The promotion of star-rated energy-efficient cook stoves with lower electricity consumption, higher efficiency and no emission of harmful pollutants will be another feasible rural solution towards achieving SDG7.

5. Miseries of Contract Labour

INTRODUCTION

The workers employed by or through an intermediary or a third party comes under the category of contract labour. Such kind of labour differs from the permanent labour in following aspects:

- Absence of names on the muster roll of principal employer/establishment
- Absence of employee-employer relationship
- No direct relationship with the principal employer
- Method of wage payment

As per Section 2(b) of the Contract Labour (Regulation and Abolition) Act, 1970 ('Contract Labour Act'), a workman shall be deemed to be employed as 'contract labour' in or in connection with the work of an establishment when he is hired in or in connection with such work by or through a contractor, with or without the knowledge of the principal employer.

PRONOUNCEMENT OF APEX COURT

In an important judgement, the Supreme Court gave a ruling that payment of contract workers should be same as permanent workers because denial of the principle of equal pays for equal work

- is a violation of human dignity,
- led to exploitative enslavement,
- is against the provision of Article 39(d) of the Indian Constitution.

Due to a lack of job security and social security, the contract workers suffer. They lack bargaining power and are not adequately remunerated for the work performed.

TRADE UNIONS

Industrial Revolution resulted in trade unionism. An association of wage earners to ensure safeguarding the workers' interests and improving the working conditions is termed as trade union.

Trade unions render various benefits that include the following:

- ❖ Worker empowerment
- ❖ Socialism and welfare of workers
- ❖ Proper regulation of personnel matters
- ❖ Dispute settlement and grievance redressal
- ❖ Partici ative decision-making and enhanced bargaining power

However, the trade union movement in India does not give contractual labour any membership or voting rights, to which other members are eligible, and hence suffers from a major problem. The reasons behind this are as follows:

- *Greater Management Hostility*: There is a general belief among the workers that including the contract workers in the union may turn the management hostile to their demands.
- *Management Attitude*: Managements do not like to discuss any issues in concern with contract workers.
- *Vulnerability of Contract Labour*: The highly insecure and vulnerable nature of job of contractual workers make them more probable to be dismissed from the company for their indulgence in union activities.
- *Attitude of Permanent Workers*: Permanent workers themselves are unwilling to include contract workers for union membership for the fear of getting marginalised with numbers of contract workers more at a workplace.

PROVISIONS AND CHALLENGES OF CONTRACT LABOUR IN INDIA

The contract labour in India barring those from some PSUs in select sectors such as steel and coal is heavily exploited and largely un-unionised. There are various legislations and provisions existing with respect to such labour, but to ensure their welfare, effective enforcement of these acts along with additional labour reforms is required.

TRADE UNION ACT, 1926

Under the Trade Unions Act, 1926 ('Trade Union Act'), Section 2(g) defines workman as any person employed in trade or industry whether or not in the employment of the employer with whom the trade dispute arises and any workman who works in a factory can join a union of that factory. However, only permanent workers constitute trade unions as its members due to absence of direct relationship with the principle employer.

CONTRACT LABOUR (REGULATION AND ABOLITION) ACT, 1970

The Contract Labour Act was enacted to abolish contract labour. This Act on the other contrary offered a legal operating framework to labour contractors and secured workers' exploitation at their hand. Both permanent and temporary workers were eligible for claims as members of the same union before this legislation was enacted.

The Contract Labour Act, however, increased the scope of hiring contract labour by introducing a distinction between an 'employer' and a 'principal employer'. Hence, it is proposed to drop the term 'abolition' from the name of the Act.

The Contract Labour Act was enacted with the intention to prevent the contract labour recruitment for core production work. Hence, workers are employed for non-core jobs such as cleaning or gardening. However, after the worker is hired, he is engaged in production activities, and no documentation is available to show engagement of a contract worker in production.

CONCLUSION

The growing exploitation of contractual labour requires immediate attention to stop. It will be good for both the companies and the society to realise the implications associated with it. Moreover, reforming the labour to deal with such issues is also important for the success of Make in India and for India to raise its rankings on World Bank's Doing Business Report.

6. Are MNCs Harmful to the Economic Development of a Country?

MNCs, a virtue of modernised enslavement, has become a new culture prevalent not only in India but across the world. A cautious analysis of the pros and cons of the MNC culture shows how appalling and painful it is to see the sole wealth of the nation, our youth, totally captivated with the greed of wealth, losing themselves to their entirety.

Several arguments have been made in favour of MNCs and their culture, especially suggesting them to be contributory factor in our economic development. However, in practical, MNCs have acted as impediment to our economic development. A careful analysis shows that development of an economy is based on the wealth and standard of living of its people, which comes from its manpower, their health and capability. When we think of ourselves, our standpoint is surging down on daily basis in terms of our manpower. We can briefly discuss them as follows:

Wealth that denotes the economy of the country is divided into three classes in the society, namely, rich, middle and poor. Although the rich and poor class manage to be within their blocks, the lucrative offers of these companies draw in the middle class with their desire to achieve beyond their reach. The middle class are ready to compromise everything in a bid to live a life of luxury. In turn, they fall victims to circumstances where they get trapped in the quicksand of multiple loans.

Although the status of an average Indian has gone up, yet the lack of strength and confidence stops him to represent his luxurious life as his own. A bi-product of these MNCs is the pervasiveness of EMI. Everything these days is purchased on EMI, and the day we finish paying the instalments for a thing and make it our own, we would need to replace the product having undergone too much wear and tear. Moreover, the human being in its preference for a higher ranged product out of greed get trapped in the same vicious cycle time and again. The lucrative salary offered by these MNCs give us the confidence to bear the EMI. On introspecting, we find that what we possess today with that high salary is simply 'Nothing'. However, in present times, this living standard with a high burden of loan is being called Economic Development.

Young India, the backbone of India, in their greed for money is blindly following the currency like a sheep herd, which is quiet disheartening. A few of them prefer working abroad serving other nations, while the remaining are serving these MNCs within our country. This is what we call as 'Brain drain'. Our geniuses are working harder round-the-clock economic development of other countries. Hence, these countries are termed as the developed ones while ours still remain as the 'Developing Nation' and will remain so, with our manpower putting all their efforts to further develop the Developed Countries. It would be very difficult for our economic development to compete and find a status in this world, with our own men playing a role of rivals.

Again, the success of our mission in the race of life is being established at the cost of health. 'Rotational Shifts' have been the new term coined by the MNCs in its pursuit of development. Our youth is willing to follow it without foreseeing its negative impacts on his health and personal life. In his blind rush for money, he works round-the-clock, forgetting family and friends, which alter his biological clock and affects his immune system. There has been an increasing number of health-related issues faced among the 20–30 age group, which is alarming. This raises the question whether these MNCs causing such negative health effects on our manpower are really promoting the Indian economy. A famous quote from Billy Graham says, "When wealth is lost, nothing is lost; when health is lost, something is lost; when character is lost, everything is lost". India was always renowned for its great influencing culture. MNCs spoiled the Indian culture and most of the teenagers are frequently visiting pubs, bars and disco. This is badly affecting their morality, and the drunken youth are resorting to violence and losing their ethics, which in turn is leading to criminal and sexual offenses even putting relationship to shame.

In brief, the MNC culture is ruining the Indian youth, causing the society devoid of its cultural values with 'No' brain working for us, 'No' health, 'No' concern for family, 'No' moral, 'No' character. All this blind rush for money has contributed to the economy nothing but loans, the priceless gift of MNCs to our country.

7. Globalisation and Its Impact on Indian Culture

INTRODUCTION

Globalisation has spread its wings in all spheres of life all across the world and is going to play a major role worldwide. The interchange of views and ideas have transformed the living standard and life style not only in India but the entire world. Indian culture is no exception to this change and its deep-rooted culture and traditions have loosened up their grip with the emergence of globalisation. Indian culture with its ingrained cultural values and pride is quite renowned world over. Globalisation has resulted in exchange of culture between India and the world, thus, inculcating the western values in India and vice versa. Culture and traditions of any geographic region are unique to that particular region and differentiate the population living in that geographic entity from the other. This uniqueness has been neutralised to some extent in varying levels because of globalisation. In a developing country like India, such impacts are very much noticeable.

GLOBALISATION: A BIRD'S EYE VIEW

Globalisation provides an international platform to maintain uniformity in the life style of people across the globe, as the term 'Globalisation' is itself self-explanatory. The interchange of views, opinions and the various cultural aspects all around the world results in globalisation. It acts as a medium for people of various sectors, culture and dialect all over the international community to intermingle with each other and move forward in coordination with mutual respect for each other's dignity.

Globalisation began with the movement of masses in other geographical entities for exploration and further spread initially for travel and personal enjoyment and later in search of employment opportunities anywhere on the globe justifying the 'survival of the fittest' concept. Every human advancement helped globalisation in spreading its reach all over the world. In present times, the role of Internet along with different modes of telecommunication and social media is significant in the spread of globalisation.

Globalisation has both advantages and disadvantages associated with it across the world. Globalisation is also responsible in playing a negative role across the world in the exploitation of scientific advancements, raising their ill-effects with environmental challenges such as the air, water, soil pollution etc. and technological challenges such as cybercrime. Globalisation has its outreach on the economic and financial position of a country including its business, trade and work exposure or any other field.

INDIAN CULTURE

In any country, culture is representative of not only its region and language but also the mindset and mentality of its inhabitants. Due to cordial approach of its citizens and abundant with various heritages and resources, Indian culture is quite affluent. It may be compared with a bouquet of flowers containing various flowers such as varying religion, dialect, tradition, edibles, custom, art, music and architecture, etc., all bundled into a single unit of patriotism and unity. The common thread connecting all these diversities is the Indian mindset of cordiality, greeting and celebrating in a united way with immense affection and togetherness. The rich character of Indian culture is appealing to many foreigners who prefer to stay in India and mingle into its eternal fragrance.

Analysing this affluent culture in the globalisation scenario, we find that this beautifully woven blanket is incorporating many punch holes of westernisation and other traits and cultures mixed into it. A close analysis of the impacts of globalisation on Indian culture provides the following outcomes:

Family Structure

A significant effect of globalisation has been on the falling apart of the attractive Indian tradition of joint family culture. The joint family culture has become a shock to the Indians especially to those metropolitan city residents living in small flats as nuclear families and are spreading in the city just like mushrooms in the rain. Living in the nuclear family, the virtue of patience and adjustment to surroundings have been lost which existed in joint families where imbibing the values of the elders and getting the young ones brought up under the shadow of their grandparents was inherent in culture. The spread of nuclear family culture has caused a distortion in the ethical values where children treat grandparents like guests or visitors, and such kind of upbringing is mainly responsible in increasing old age homes, as those children on reaching adulthood begin to consider their own parents burden on them.

Marriage Values

There has been a rise in incidents of divorces and extra-marital affairs that indicate that marriages have also lost their values. Gone are the days when marriage was considered as bonding of two souls meant to be linked even after death, but today marriage is considered as a professional bond or a so-called commitment to live the life together without intruding upon their self-interests. The ego factor trapping the Indian youth is also an outcome of globalisation.

Adultery

For a long time in our culture, too many restrictions and limitations were imposed on both the genders to come in contact with each other. The globalisation and western culture along with it have made it possible for the youth to mix up well with each other. Although the friendly approach and the socialising feature are well appreciated, the overindulgence without any restriction has adulterated the Indian mindset leading to physical relationship. This has led to rise of new relationships in India like live-in relationships. Moreover, the incidents of rapes and sexual abuses have increased due to perverted minds, which are a result of values imbibed from a culture very much alien to the ancient Indian culture.

Social Values

The Indian culture has the inherent values of treating the guests as God, maintaining cordiality, respecting elders and festival celebrations with great enthusiasm, enjoyment and togetherness. Such a vast gathering with great exuberance is hardly witnessed nowadays. People today have self-imposed restrictions for social interaction. The interaction nowadays is highly diplomatic in present generation based on financial status and wealth. Our social values and affection for each other no longer exist. In comparison to Holi and Diwali, the present generation are more happy in celebrating Valentine's Day.

Food, Clothing and Dialect

Food, clothing and languages in India vary with respect to different states. Every food has nutrient value unique to it and it varies in taste across the region. Moreover, every region has its own specified method of preparation rich in its medicinal values with home remedies. The clothing also varies in different states with focus on maintaining the dignity of woman. The cuisines across the world vary with different flavours to add, yet the food ingredients that are most popular among the present generations are the junk food items which in turn have resulted in increased health disorders in the country. The dressing like the suitings for the males are an unsuitable match for the Indian climate. Moreover, the perverted minds find the female dresses quite distracting.

Even the Indians today are shy in promoting their mother tongue or our national language. They consider it quite shameful to speak in Hindi, their national language. The growing prevalence of foreign languages in India such as the French, German and Spanish, from the school level itself, is an example of the level of importance we provide to the Indian languages in comparison to the foreign ones.

Employment and the Agricultural Sector

India was especially an agriculture-based economy. However, with the spread of globalisation and appearance of MNCs, the farming has lost its significance in India. The youngsters nowadays not the least interested towards agricultural science and find it as an unworthy profession. MNCs are luring most of the manpower with lucrative perks and employing them for other countries working as their customer care. Gradually, we are entering into the age of economic slavery, losing our health and status because of MNC culture emerged as a result of globalisation.

CONCLUSION

In summary, globalisation is a gradually spreading risk agent that has enveloped almost the entire country with its graveness. Although it imparts some positivity of having a generalised knowledge of the culture, the happening and incidences across the world, yet the major negative impacts it causes are quite alarming for the country. Hence, we need to be more cautious in our approach to the globalisation process preserving the pride of the nation and keeping our cultural prestige intact.

8. Sustained Economic Development: Role of Ecology and Environment

INTRODUCTION

Today, economy of a country holds great significance, especially when every country is endeavouring hard in its efforts to take the lead for its survival and emergence as a supreme power. The development of any country is associated with its overall economic development. The country needs to assign priority to the things associated with the upliftment of economy in order to match the pace of the world. The market value, shares and dividends are preferable to the priceless emotions, affection and love. Many ecological and environmental factors are responsible for such an economic development.

The ecological and environmental resources available in a country yield the per capita income that provides the impetus to thrust its economy forward. All the biotic and non-biotic things of any community or country taken combined comes under the wide sectors of ecology and environment. Both the terms 'ecology' and 'environment' has a very thin line separating them and coincide their inference at many inferences. We briefly examine what constitutes ecology and the environment, which has a deep-rooted impact on the economic growth.

Ecology: The interaction between the biotic and abiotic community amongst themselves and to their surroundings is called ecology, thereby giving an entirety called ecosystem. Ecology comprises various forms of life and species, their utilisation in the environmental affairs, effects on the atmosphere and every possible aspect that can be collated to express a sound interaction. For the existence and survival of species, the ecological aspect of life holds utmost significance.

Environment: Environment similar to ecology deals with the existence of various resources, its utilisation by the living species and their impact. Environment, which is more of an abstract term, is better explainable by the words like atmosphere or surroundings in physical world; or situation or circumstances, in terms of vitality. It is the space, the void which enables the life providing them a comfortable atmosphere to reside.

Being acquainted with a brief account of environment, we now elaborate on the core issue, the role of ecology and environment in economic development.

ECONOMIC DEVELOPMENT AND ECOLOGY

Ecology and economic development are interrelated in an inversely proportional manner. As the one increases, the other suffers a decline. Few of the various factors influencing the economic development are as follows:

- **Population:** It is one of the most crucial issue faced by any developing country like India. The population index of a country is the standard to determine the per capita income and expenditure for it. The citizens of a country are the contributors in its revenue. The revenue is directly proportional to the number of people in a country, considering the honesty of public as a default note. But contrarily, the population also increases the expenses of the country taking into account the basic utilities of food, clothing, shelter, employment, etc. Thus, for the economic development of any country, the increased population is a set back unless the manpower is appropriately utilised.
- **Manpower:** The biggest resource for any nation is its manpower. However, a majority of the countries do not realise this and prefer instead the fast spreading

epidemic of computerisation and online take over the rich manpower. Most of us do not utilise this resource to its optimum. For the best outcomes in terms of net productivity in any country, it needs to channelise its manpower well. For the economic development of a country such a productive manpower is definitely a boon, but the utilisation of this manpower is disrupted by the factors like illiteracy, ignorance, super ego, high status consciousness, poor infrastructure and the absence of a good competent governance to overcome the obstacles and get the task accomplished.

- **Wealth Distribution:** Another major obstacle in the economic development of a country is the improper distribution of wealth. The improper wealth distribution has resulted in making the rich more rich, while there is decline even in the middle class, which is approaching towards the poverty zone in reality. The high profile lifestyle reflecting a high status of the people in reality does not give a real picture of the situation the majority class is going through suppressed with the burden of loans. Most of the products projecting high status are bought on EMI and are not completely owned till the entire payment made. By that time, the product loses its strength. This fake reflection of lifestyle is in no way contributory to the economic development. The increasing loan on citizens leads to growth in actual economy. The distribution of wealth in proper manner that helps the masses reach above the poverty line contributes greatly to the economic development.

ECONOMIC DEVELOPMENT AND ENVIRONMENT

Environment and economic development are also interrelated in an inverse manner. An enlivening development of the economy is carried out at the cost of gross destruction to the environmental resources, as the economy is measured on the tradable resources alone. The environmental factors influencing the economic growth could be explained further as follows:

- **Minerals, Ores and Other Resources:** The role of resources in boosting the economy of a country is significant. These tradable forms of resources bolster rich transactions with various countries and thus add to the revenue of the nation. Moreover, these resources produce a big improvement in the financial market having a direct impact on the country's economic growth.
- **Soil and Land:** Another productive resource which requires a good acumen to be converted into fruitful wealth is land. The prudent utilisation of land can result in more income for the country. The most judicious move would be to utilise the productive soil for farming and the barren land for construction purposes. This in turn would help in more export of the raw materials and contribute to the national treasure.
- **Water Utilisation:** Another feasible great source of economic growth is project like hydroelectric power. The utilisation of such conventional forms of energy

instead of nuclear energy as the only reliable option for power generation could reduce the amount of national expenditure incurred towards monitoring and safe handling of the nuclear reactors and disposal of the radioactive wastes.

FEEDBACK MECHANISM OF ECONOMIC DEVELOPMENT TO THE ECOLOGY AND ENVIRONMENT

Although economic development is an appreciable trend, widespread hazards to the ecosystem, environment and nature are evident because of sustained economic development activities. There is no doubt that natural resources get replenished but causing an irreparable loss to the natural resources just for the sake of economic growth is not a wise move. The feedback mechanisms in relation to the sustained economic development are given as follows:

- **Population** leading to overconsumption and overutilisation of the available resources, which results in the surge in economic development.
- **Employment:** Lesser opportunities for employment impelling the increase in child labour, causing severe medical emergencies.
- **Corruption** resulting in accumulation of wealth to a selective group of people, which is resulting in poverty.
- **Environmental** hazards including the nuclear explosions and the disposal of radioactive wastes is causing health hazards for many generations ahead.

These are a few examples of the repercussion of economic surge just in a greed for having a faster economic growth.

CONCLUSION

In conclusion, we may compare the economic development with an open sword, which calls for a tentative management in order to protect the available resources. Economic development provide opportunities that appear lucrative always, but a reasonable mind should be able to evaluate and examine the positives and negatives associated with the measure taken. A prudent approach would be to make a steady economic growth, preserving our ecological and environmental resources, which will always render us with their goodness.

9. Should Rich Countries Provide Loans to Poor Countries without any Interest?

INTRODUCTION

Borrowing financial aid has become the perquisite of poor countries to relieve themselves from poverty. However, few issues regarding interest associated with loans need consideration. A favourable approach would be to provide loans to poor countries without charging any interest. For the world to become a better place, impartial growth and development is necessary. The inequitable growth opportunities are leading to increase in crime rate in poor countries. Providing loans at low interest rates would enable poor countries to stay out of debt. For the improvement in infrastructure and promotion of social welfare programmes, poor countries are dependent on richer nations for crucial financial aid. To alleviate the evil of world poverty, rich countries need to lend money without interest.

THE PERSPECTIVE

High interest rates have made it a big problem for the poor country to borrow financial aid from rich countries. Charging high interest rates seem unreasonable if the loan is taken with the purpose of improving the socioeconomic status of the poor country. Financial aid has become a subject of dispute between rich and poor nations because of this reason. It cannot be held correct to burden a poor country with heavy interest rates if the sole purpose of the loan is to initiate social welfare. As it will cause the poor nations to get trapped in the debt cycle, this will cause the problem to get more intense.

The motive of rich countries in making profit rather than help poor nations becomes obvious because of their charging interest on loan. A major problem faced by many developing countries is poverty, while developed nations in contrast enjoy the best infrastructure economic growth that is stable. Many poverty-stricken nations lack adequate food security, sanitation, health-care facilities, infrastructure and educational institutions. There is critical requirement of adequate capital to bridge the gap between the developing countries and the developed world. Borrowing international loans will be beneficial to its recipients only if they are able to repay the loan without the added burden of high interest rates.

Loans borrowed with hefty interest rates are harmful for poor countries. Availability of adequate resources along with favourable social, economic and political conditions combined together has been fruitful for the rich countries for their unprecedented economic growth. Such a scenario further aggravates the adverse circumstances for poor countries already going through untoward incidents like war or famine to catch up with the developed world. The rich countries must follow the principles of social justice to contain the unjust rate at which the world is growing and the problems associated with this. Social justice in this context implies that rich nations need to adopt a more reasonable approach by supporting and assisting the developing countries to help them reach a fair enough state of economic growth.

Poor nations need huge amount of capital to develop infrastructure, open more educational institutions and impart adequate health care. A poor nation stuck with the liabilities of heavy interest on the loan will not be able to release adequate capital to tackle the challenges of inducing desirable growth and development in the country. Financial aid in the form of too much loans coupled with interest could be really damaging to the poor countries. The needy countries can have better growth opportunities and protection from insolvency if rich countries give them loans without interest.

THE WAY FORWARD

Loans should be provided to the poor nations without causing added burden that hampers their economic development. Charging interest rates put the rich countries in the same league as any bank or lending institutions, which serves no purpose. To comply with social justice, rich countries should be able to provide easily repayable loans. One way of ensuring this is to charge no interest at all. To initiate positive social transformation and desirable economic growth in poor nations, loans without interest is an ideal way.

10. Our Traditional Handicrafts Are Doomed to a Slow Death: A Comment

INTRODUCTION

The ability of a business to differentiate itself from the rest is crucial for its success. Businesses which are able to utilise their best features in the best possible manner to woo customers looking for unique products ultimately rise far ahead in the race from the competitors.

The Indian handicrafts sector is renowned in the world and has buyers from all over the world drawn towards it. India was a centre of attraction for traders across the world since time immemorial because of its quality fabric.

SLOW DEATH OF HANDICRAFTS: REASONS

Handicrafts industry is comprised of various categories, the 'premium' segment being the first that include luxury products for export to overseas markets. Kanjivaram Sarees of the south or Pashmina shawls of Kashmir are a few examples of 'premium' products.

The other product category includes those for sale to local markets and are relatively cheaper. Both the categories are easily noticeable in terms of huge difference in both reach and quality. However, the important point to be taken into consideration is position of the business in modern context. Its ability to utilise modern management techniques or technology is one of the essential factors that would give it a unique identity and keep it ahead from its competitors. It is essential to have a know-how of the particular business for it to stay afloat and grow.

Moreover, businesses must be able to form good external and internal linkages in the supply chains. This implies that a business would not be able to get the desired result even after producing something worthy if it does not develop a network of distributors or other people to have a good reach among the consumers. Finally, other factors include government policies or regulations that actually affect any business in modern context.

We need to look at the position which the Indian handicrafts industry holds, taking all these factors into account. The Indian handicrafts are struggling as the exports of this business did not increase post WTO contrary to the expectations. Handicrafts worth a mere amount of ₹8,000 crore was exported in 2010 and have been stagnating ever since.

However, China holds a major share in the global handicrafts market and its business has been growing rapidly after the meltdown that shook the world community for 3 years.

The biggest impediment in the growth of the handicrafts sector is that a part of it comes under the unorganised sector. The irony is that on one hand, the government wants to promote entrepreneurship, while on the other hand, poverty and other social injustices make it difficult for a part of the entrepreneurs in this sector to survive. Such situations make it very difficult for an entrepreneur to take risks. This is why they have their own apprehensions to adopt the vital element of today's business, such as, the latest technology or skill-based training to labour in the industry.

Businesses have witnessed rapid expansion through economies of scale. Unfortunately, in the handicraft sector, the units are small and the people are poor who are unable to set up the required infrastructure to expand the business. Their inability to manage costs put them at a huge disadvantage than their overseas counterparts. Finally, our governments did not come out with enabling policies previously to favour the sector.

No organised structure was established to provide 'cheap credit' to the handicrafts manufacturers contrary to the case with so many other industries. Over 90 per cent of the units were estimated to have no access to any form of credit. Many disadvantages are hampering this powerful sector today. However, the handicrafts sector provides many opportunities that should be borne in mind.

India is renowned worldwide for its rich cultural heritage and the handicrafts sector should be able to make the optimum use of this feature in its endeavours to grow. Indian villages do not have easy finance schemes available to them, yet they have the necessary social capital, which they can make use of by forming self-help groups to overcome the problems of economies of scale in this sector.

A crucial step to be immediately taken is to provide them incentives for getting credit ratings done from standardised agencies. It would help in addressing the issues of scale and information and bring in the required capital in the sector.

Banks could be crucial in financing these self-help groups, as has been the case with other sectors in the past. It will enable the self-help groups to bargain better and improve the efficiency by improving supply chain, conduct skill-based training and investing in technology. Entrepreneurs should adopt a cluster-based approach to prevent infrastructure bottlenecks faced by the sector. It would enable them to take maximum advantage of the developments.

A crucial feature of any business to be successful is its risk appetite. Thus, ensuring quality education for people in rural areas would enable them in taking better decisions. Finally, the National Skill Development Council, a government agency to bridge the skill gap in the country, could be engaged to address the lack of skill development.

CONCLUSION

A systematic approach needs to be adopted to make handicrafts feasible as adopted in some other big sectors today. Instead of huge sums or grants, a pragmatic approach making use of education, policy and core competencies effectively can redeem the past glory of India's culturally rich heritage sector.

11. Cashless System

Cashless society describes an economic state where financial transactions are not conducted with money in the form of physical bank note. Cashless payments will bring transparency and help to minimize the effects of corruption. It is very usable and will help India move towards paperless society. The Digital India Program is a flagship program of the Government of India with a vision to transform India into a digitally empowered society and knowledge economy. "Faceless, Cashless, Paperless" is one of the professed roles of Digital India. The Cashless Mission was started by the Government of India under the leadership of Prime Minister Narendra Damodar Modi. The denomination currency note of ₹ 500 and ₹ 1000 were banned by the Honorable Prime Minister on 8th November 2016. This denomination was the first step toward achieving the goal of cashless system. The Digital India campaign 2015 plays a major role in moving a step forward to achieve the dream of Cashless India. The Cashless system means there is the exchange of monitory value through either plastic currency or digital mode of payment. Plastic currency includes 2 types of card payment such as Debit card and Credit card. Digital and Online transactions include several electronic fund transfer systems such as NEFT (National Electronic Fund Transfer), RTGS (Real Time Gross Settlement) and IMPS (Immediate Money Payment System). Digital and Online payment also includes several mobile applications such as Paytm, Mobikwik, Google pay, Airtel Payment Bank etc. Moreover the concept of Bitcoin have given a new phase to cashless economy. The Covid-19 Pandemic had given a push to the concept of cashless economy. People are more concerned for their health and safety so there has been witnessed a large shift of traditional exchange of currency to cashless and digital mode of payment. Advantages of Cashless India are reduction of black money and corruption. Black money is the amount earned through illegal means or money which is earned but not recorded for tax payment. It can be kept hidden. Thus Cashless economy can keep a check on black money. The transaction in online mode is being recorded so as to avoid corruption and encourage transparency. Moreover, it has been made sure that no personal information of the user is being misused. It can be reduced to grate extent if the technology behind cashless system is well updated. On the other side cashless system facilitates us to ease of transaction through Phonepe, Google pay, Paytm, Debit card, Credit card and many other cashless options. Further the Government of India has announced a platform such as UPI (Unified Payment Interface) for cashless transaction. The burden of carrying cash is eliminated. Shopping, paying bills, mobile recharge, booking movie ticket, booking travel ticket many where made easier. Complex payment has been made easier by this system. In this one can get proper detailed information of transaction and payment schedule easily. The currency exchange while travelling Internationally is also made easier due to cashless system.

- **Saves time:** Cashless transfer saves time as well. One can do small to big transaction by sitting comfortably at there room or shop. The ease of managing financial transaction is one of the biggest motivations to go digital.
- **Health Benefits:** Cashless system of transaction also help to keep us away from germ that can be spread easily through hand to hand. The boost in the need of cashless system is being witnessed during Covid-19 pandemic where people are more conscious about there health, so prefer going with digital.
- **Reduction in production cost of Coins and Paper currency:** The production of paper currency and coins is expensive and paper currency also have a chance to be torned out. Moreover it has a life span of approximately 6 years. Going cashless can result in reduction in production cost of currency notes.

Though there are plenty of benefits of going cashless, there are some major downsides associated with a cashless system of transaction respectively which is need to be witnessed. Some of them are:

- **Privacy and hacking risk:** Cashless and digital payment may not be proven as safe as such payment. We need to trust the organization and we might have nothing to hide. Hackers and robbers are the gangsters of electronic world. If our account is targeted, they may drain our accounts. However it will still be inconvenient to restore our financial standing. Reports of online thefts and hacking have made people think twice before making large amount of transaction online.
- **Lack of knowledge and Infrastructure:** Though our country is moving a step forward for going digital, there are still many problems faced by people mostly in the rural parts of India. Smartphone, electricity for charging the phone and data connectivity is a must for going digital. Yet there are many people in our country who are unable to afford a smartphone and data connection. Further there are many parts of our country where there is a lack of uninterrupted power supply.

In addition to it, there are many people in our country who has there infrastructure but literacy creates lack of knowledge of having bank account, digital payment and online transaction in many parts of our country specially in rural India. These are the problems which need to be addressed.

Cashless system came up with many pros and cons. The benefits have been encouraged and positive outcome has been witnessed by the growth of digitalization in India. In the other hand disadvantages need to be observed. Some of them are addressed by Government of India. The Central Government has taken many steps to spread awareness regarding online theft and hacking. In addition to it, Cyber forensic facility has been improved to keep an eye on such crime, spread up investigation and prevent it. Woefully it is very difficult to stop cyber theft completely, but it can be prevented. Each individual should take responsibility to protect themselves from online robbery. They need to follow some steps such as do not share OTP with stranger, secure mail id by changing password time to time, always have a security lock on the phone or laptop. Do not click on the link provided by untrusted site.

Though it is a quite difficult task for a developing country like India with a population of approximately 130 Crore to adopt cashless system completely, we need to understand the fact that cashless system is the need of progress in present scenario. Whether it is pandemic or advancement of technology, we need to adopt the cashless payment system not only to stay safe but also to cope up and move forward with growing digital world. Hence the cashless system paved the way for greater transparency, ease and convenience in monetary transaction. Digital transaction is detected smoothly due to which it will be mandatory to pay taxes to all so that the means of black money will be closed. Now people have come to know that digital media is safe, convenient and transparent and there is no scope for black money.

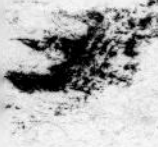

❑❑❑

ESSAYS ON POLITICAL ISSUES

1. Judicial Activism and Indian Democracy

INTRODUCTION

Democracy can be understood as a system where people elect their government, a small elite body, for being ruled by them. As per the Constitution of India, the main aim of this body is to frame laws and work for the betterment of society as a whole. The issues of validity of laws framed by the government and methods of control on government have been debatable since decades as the representatives of people (elected body), once elected, remain in power till the end of the term even if people are not contented with the policies of government. Not only does the government enjoys immunity because of the constitutional provision, but also its members tend to engage in wrongdoing as the Constitution does not provide 'call back' power to the people. The lack of transparency and popular participation in the system created a vacuum in governance, that is, who shall monitor the validity of law.

The judiciary, as per the principle, cannot take suo moto action till victim files a petition, resulting in substantiating vacuum. To bridge the gap between the principle of democracy and the essence of democracy, 'Power vacuum filling' theory states that it is important for judiciary to extend its influence in its sphere. Many argue that it is against the principle of democracy. May be it is true. Concerned with the view that vast hegemonic growth of the form and procedure of democracy may pose a grave threat to the ideals of democracy, it is of utmost importance to decide what is more important: the procedure and principles of democracy like the legislative supremacy or the spirit of democracy, i.e. welfare of people. They may be a means to an end, but the end is always the spirit of democracy. So if means are abridged to attain the ends, then democracy will be more successful than anything else. So judicial activism is important for this basic spirit of democracy.

JUDICIAL ACTIVISM

Although judicial activism can be defined in a number of ways, it cannot be discarded as an intellectual void as the main aim of the same is survival of law. It is also important to understand the difference between judicial activism and judicial review and other process of jurisdiction. On the one hand, judicial review can influence the executive and the legislative, the two pillars of democracy. On the other hand, judicial activism is a form of judiciary which not only limits itself to the interpretation of law, but also monitors the situations where law has an adverse effects on people. Considered as a safety valve, judicial activism has contributed a lot in making the judiciary more competent.

OUR CONSTITUTION AND JUDICIARY

India's founding fathers created three arms during writing the constitution: Parliament, Executive and the Judiciary. These three were the keepers of the ideals inculcated in the constitution. In the present scenario, the Parliament is not functioning properly, the Executive has refused to perform its duties and even the Judiciary is using their authority to make everyone work very hard. Many realised that it is cracking the whip a lot. But according to me it is not the same. The role of active judiciary is to defend the fundamental rights of the people and their liberties against the evil acts of the state. According to a judge, the policy formulation is the job of the Executive and Judiciary does not need to interfere but another could believe that even in policy formulation, there is also a requirement of Judiciary to guard fundamental rights. When the Executive fails to discharge its statutory, constitutional obligations, this type of situation often arises, and as a result, the fundamental rights of people are violated.

To make sure that system is functioning properly within constitutional boundaries, the Constitution has given the power to Indian Judiciary to motivate and direct the Executive and Legislature to work for the betterment of people. If any law turns out to be beyond Parliament's competence or violates the norms of the Constitution, the Judiciary has the power to strike down the same. The same applies to any illegal Executive action. As Article 142 vests an extraordinary power to our Supreme Court (SC) to do 'complete justice' in any matter presented before it, the apex Court's judgement becomes the law of the land. However, this power has often been wielded unpredictably. For example, the Court granted a divorce to a Hindu couple on the ground of irretrievable breakdown of marriage, even though no such ground exists under the Hindu Marriage Act.

There are two theories that best explain the nitty-gritty of judicial activism. The first theory, 'Power vacuum filling', states that if lack of any organ or its inaction creates a vacuum, then the others are ready to fill that vacuum by raising their concern about the issue. Nature does not allow the vacuum to remain as such. In some spheres in the government, lack of interest in executive or legislative or owing to the inaction and indifference in their part creates a vacuum that is filled by a dynamic judiciary called as the judicial activism. As the theory of 'social want' states that something that is provided by neither the executive nor the legislative is wanted by people, judiciary took the responsibility to satisfy the wants of the people. Hence, this proactiveness is called as judicial activism.

Montesquieu, while explaining the necessity for separation of powers, given in our constitutional scheme, wrote: "There is no liberty where judicial power is not separated from both legislative and executive power. If judicial and legislative powers are not separated, power over the life and liberty of citizens would be arbitrary, because the judge would also be a legislator. If it were not separated from executive power, the judge would have the strength of an oppressor..."

HISTORY

On 13 November 1608, Stuart King James I, Ruler of England, after entering the royal courts, claimed that he has the power to take and remove any case from the courts and decide it in his royal person. However, Chief Justice Coke, referring to the law of England, confronted him that this cannot be done as the cases have to be determined and adjudged in a court of justice. Offended by the answer, the King replied: "This means that I shall be under law which is treason to affirm". Following which Coke stated: "The King should not be under man but should be under God and law". This can be seen as a perfect example of judicial activism as Justice Coke's reply was an affirmation of the judicial power while upholding the rule of law against arbitrary decisions of the sovereign.

In the another example of 1801, in the case of Marbury v. Madison, the judicial review power of the American Supreme Court was highlighted and reaffirmed by Chief Justice John Marshall in invalidating Congressional statutes. The decisions by US Chief Justice Earl Warren, regarded as one of the great activist judges who have profoundly influenced the Indian Supreme Court, played a pivotal role in the following: legitimising affirmative action by the courts, removing racial discrimination in schools by desegregation, reapportioning obsolete electoral districts and enhancing the rights of poor accused and defendants.

INDIAN CONTEXT

The following cases stake their claims when considering the judicial activism in India.

1. **Golaknath vs. The State of Punjab:** Retracing from its own judgement in the Shankari Prasad case and Sajjan Singh vs. the state of Rajasthan case that the fundamental rights can be amended, the Supreme Court in Golaknath vs. the State of Punjab clarified that no constitutional amendments can be made on the part III of the Constitution, thereby fundamental rights cannot be abridged by the legislature.

For empowering the legislature with the power to amend the constitution, Article 368 was amended by the government in the 24th amendment.

2. **Keshavananda Bharti vs. the State of Kerala:** Stating that the legislature by virtue of the amending power cannot change the basic structure of the constitution, the Supreme Court overruled the case and parliament regained the power of amending. However, the court did not explain what constitutes the basic structure. Hence, to make the process of amendment hassle free, Clauses 4 and 5 were inserted in Article 368 by the government which mentions that limited power of amendment is a basic structure of constitution.
3. **Minnerva Mills vs. The Union of India:** The Apex court in this case stated amending power to be a basic structure of constitution. By this time, the legislative and the judiciary in India were at loggerheads.
4. **Sunil Batra vs. Delhi Government:** In this case, the writ of Habeas corpus was reinterpreted by the Supreme Court as not only producing a person in the court but also preventing a prisoner from the inhuman treatment with the bars.
5. **M. C. Mehta vs. The State of Tamil Nadu:** In this case, the Supreme Court ruled child labour in hazardous factories is unlawful and provided various guidelines for the welfare and betterment of children.

Recently, a recent review petition was filed by the Centre after the recent order of creating a Special Investigation Team (SIT) to probe the black money in the Supreme Court. In a first, appointment of a former judge of the Supreme Court as a chairman of the SIT and another former judge of the same court as the vice-chairman was done to start the investigation. A high-level committee including revenue secretary; Deputy Governor, RBI; Directors, IB, CBI, (financial intelligence unit) and ED; Chairman, CBDT and DGs, Narcotics Control Bureau and Revenue Intelligence was appointed by the Union government. Later, three more members, including two former judges and Director, RAW, were inducted in SIT. Even as police will investigate the case, what is unprecedented is that the SIT will report to a former judge. According to the Cr.Pc., the court cannot take over investigation, although someone can be appointed to impartially investigate the case.

In the another case, Nandini Sundar vs Chhattisgarh, under the policy of arming of a civilian vigilante group, the Salwa Judum, the appointment of special police officers (SPO) was declared by the apex. The court while lambasting the neoliberal economic policy of the government, held the government responsible for black money growth and invidious inequality which has led to the menace of Naxalism. Both judgements are replete with condemnation of the state's 'amoral' economic policies in florid language. The question is whether judges are competent to do it? While speaking at the Motilal Setalvad Memorial Lecture, Chief Justice of India S. H. Kapadia cautioned his colleagues against breaching the doctrine of separation of powers: "We do not have the competence to make policy choices and run the administration...Under the doctrine of separation of powers, each of the above organs must stay within the powers allocated by the constitution". The issue of accountability was rightly raised by Justice Kapadia.

It is clear from the above cases that judicial activism seem to be against the legislative hegemony. However, the question remains whether it is against democracy? Legislative gains its authority from people as it is a democratic body. Because the judiciary is not backed by popular mandate, it is an independent authority. As per the principle, judiciary ratifying the legislature is against the principle of democracy, although arriving at any such conclusion is easy. There are many loopholes in such straightforward criticism. For example, if the law formulated by the legislature affects the liberty of people which is a gross violation of human rights, should the judiciary remain silent and follow the rule of law principle even if the law is inhumane? One needs to reinterpret the word democracy to understand its far-reaching significance.

In America, the process of appointing judges is different. The presidents choose the judges on ideological grounds after being grilled by the Senate live on television. Thus, people are already aware of the ideological commitments of future judge of the Supreme Court. Still, they tenaciously stick to the constitution. While in India, because of being apolitical, judges have to interpret laws strictly within the mandate of the constitution. In the black money order, the court has clearly overstepped on the ground of protecting the fundamental right to equality (Article 14) and the right to life and personal liberty (Article 21). It is important for justifying judicial intervention that some kind of amorphous connection can always be established with these rights.

In India, liberalising access to justice and giving relief to disadvantaged groups and the have-nots under the leadership of Justices V.R. Krishna Iyer and P.N. Bhagwati helped judicial activism to become a significant force. The courts on several occasions in the past have issued directions in public interest litigation (PIL) covering a wide spectrum such as road safety, pollution, illegal structures in VIP zones, monkey menace, dog menace, unpaid dues by former and serving legislators, nursery admissions, and admissions in institutions of higher learning. There is no doubt that sometimes righteous indignation and emotional responses trigger these orders. Due to the widespread corruption and non-performing administration, the common citizens have now a useful tool in the form PIL to seek justice. Is it the duty of the court to intervene if a child is bitten by street canine or cattle, etc.?

IS DEMOCRACY UNDER THREAT?

No, given the above scenario, if the judicial activism is practiced within the boundaries, it may not be a derailing force. In fact, it will be important to keep democratic functioning on track. Independence is not over interference. It should be understood that judicial activism can only be effective, if the same is sparsely used. Media need to be more responsible and mature as overhyping judicial activism will only have negative effect on the society. Even political parties need to show maturity and rather than branding the verdict as conspiracy against democracy, should avoid the collision course. If all the sections show restraint and maturity, judicial development's rise can potentially lead to stable democracy.

Acting as a safety valve in a democracy, judicial activism in India has given hope that justice is not beyond reach. As long as the Judiciary maintains its respectable image in the hearts of people, judicial activism will prosper and help people in getting justice without negative perceptions, which have overtaken the executive and the legislature. Last few years have seen people being concerned about the lack of transparency in judicial appointments and a sense of increasing unease due to lack of a credible mechanism to deal with serious complaints against the higher judiciary. For example, even if laws to prevent children from working in hazardous occupations exist, due to economic necessities, parents themselves are willingly sending their children to work. The condition worsens further with the inspectors being bribed by factory owners to escape any wrongdoing that is punishable in the eyes of law. While hearing such cases filed by NGO, a court has the authority to direct the state to enforce the laws because failing to implement it is akin to violate the children's fundamental right to a healthy life. That is activism in the right sense.

CRITICISM

Many critics opine that proactiveness of judges is for gaining the limelight as they are devoid of the same in comparison to the legislature and executive. As anyone can file PIL for any reason, the chances of PILs being misused are very high, resulting in huge volumes of litigations lying pending on the floor of court.

Because judges have always enjoyed a respectable position in the society, the idea concerning judges' craving for limelight does not seems to be apt. This issue need not be hyped as being a human being, judges might sometimes crave for popularity, and it cannot be seen as a sin. Concerned with the increasing cases coming to fore regarding the abuse of PILs, some guidelines for the PILs and their usages have been mentioned by the apex court.

CONCLUSION

Judges should be aware of thin line between judicial activism and judicial adventurism, and hence should avoid interfering in issues out of their ambit, for example, the court has the power to direct the government to frame a scheme, but not the power of framing it itself. Judiciary being the only ray of hope for common people against the arbitrary actions of the Executive, India cannot let this pillar to fall prey to corrupt practices and media headlines for popularity. Our constitutional scheme has the doctrine of separation of powers, and the soul of our constitution should be kept intact.

2. Judiciary vs. Executive: A Conflict in Appointment of Judges

The issue of appointment of judges for some time has been a bone of contention between the judiciary and executive. The recent accusation of the Chief Justice of India (CJI) against government for delaying appointment has strained the relation between two even more. Later, a contempt of court notice against secretaries in PMO and department of justice was also contemplated by the CJI before being assured by Attorney General for action before next hearing. As a result, even though the appointment of 10 Delhi and Guwahati High Court judges was then cleared by the government, the debate regarding the process of appointment of judges with the revised Memorandum of Procedure (MOP) continues as the government and SC collegium failed to reach any consensus.

CAUSES OF CONFLICT

With both parties wanting to keep the power of judicial appointment to higher judiciary to themself, they have been engaged in a struggle of power of sorts and game of one-upmanship.

Despite both parties claiming to make appointment on the basis of merit to make judiciary more efficient and accountable, it is surprising that no consensus has been made until now.

Even when there is no better way to reach an amicable solution via dialogues, the two sides are maintaining status quo by not meeting in this regard.

The tussle between the two started with the 1993 judgement that formed the collegium system to appoint the judges of higher judiciary, a power that was earlier enjoyed by the Executive before the above-mentioned judgement. Even after the SC asking the government to frame the memorandum of procedure, it is stuck for last 10 months as the executive and judiciary have been at loggerheads.

The issue of merit has been the centre of debate. It is sought that the candidate should be eligible as per the requirement and the data of the same have to be made public. This is where problem arises. The disagreement is about induction on both sides of people who may not ultimately prove to be not worthy of selection for a constitutional post.

The present tussle aggravated after the National Judicial Appointments Commission (NJAC) judgement, which was not taken well by the government. Hence, any amicable solution is far from reaching in the near future.

Acknowledging that there were many loopholes in the procedure of the collegium after the NJAC judgement. The SC after having detailed hearings on procedures left it on the government to come out with new MOP. Now, government continues to sit on appointments as the SC did not clarify that until the new MOP was put in place, the old memorandum would continue. Confronting the government's action, the CJI rightly asked, if this was the reason, how government has been clearing appointments piecemeal. Either it did not clear any appointments or come back to court and say it cannot clear appointments until new MOP in place. The present appointments give the impression that government is selectively appointing judges.

It is to be noted that deadlock of 10 months will delay the process further. Hence, it is the duty of the court to find a solution quickly to frame a proper MOP. If deadlock continues further, it is the court's responsibility to help both parties settle the difference and come out with a framework that fits all.

CONFRONTATION AND ITS DEVELOPMENT

In democracy, cosy relations between judiciary and executive pose a challenge as the bond can influence the decisions. The issue of distrust in appointment of judges came to fore in the early 1970s when Indira Gandhi hoped for committed judiciary, committed press and committed bureaucracy. That distrust further deteriorated during the time of emergency. Later, in a quest to ponder over the issue, super session of judges came to the understanding that obliging and convenient judges are wanted by the executive so that they can amend constitution as per their convenience. Informed about the loopholes, the SC has made it clear that essential core of constitutional cannot be amended even by majority, and appointment of judges is one of it.

The issue of attaining the supremacy on the appointment of judges has made this an even bigger debate as both the parties fear of loosing their authority to each other: on the one hand, the judiciary feels that executive may interfere in judicial process; on the other hand, the executive fears that judiciary is overstepping its limit.

JUDICIARY AND EXECUTIVE

The clash between these is not that of personalities, and the constitutional scheme itself defines this kind of difference in their relationship. The executive is vested with all the powers to make policy, execute it and hold the perks. On the other hand, judiciary plays the role of watchdog to keep a check on what executive does. Being checked or scrutinised is not liked by anyone unless one is staunch follower of the constitutional schemes. Just as bureaucrats do not take judicial orders in good taste because the same upset their plans, also no political class takes it well when its policy is upset by a judicial review.

The instances of political class retracting from any issue where it was important to take a stand lead to judiciary's 'sense of self-importance' which is sometimes perceived as being possessed by the judiciary. Instead, the political class decided to take a back seat and let the court take a decision, subsequently resulting in the growing stature and importance of Judiciary.

As the problem is inbuilt in the institution, it is important for proper functioning of democracy that both executive and judiciary should have professional faith in each other to effectively avoid confrontations on petty matters.

In addition, they both have a common goal to work for the system which is law of land by not getting engaged in the blame game and daily battle through media.

The power of appointment has a certain element of patronage in system. There can be merit but the power of appointment has certain political connotation. It can be used in wider sense like use of power in university, judge's decision or political process.

As the real issue, how judges are appointed and whether there is transparency or not, got lost amid other controversies and debates, consensus seems to be difficult to attain in the near future. It is yet to be decided whether the judge be appointed under

NJAC system is declared unconstitutional by SC and constitutional under collegium system. In both cases, there is no surety of transparency. It is needed that SC should ensure there is transparency. There are opinions coming from within the judiciary about lack of transparency in the functioning of collegium system. Sans transparency, desired results will not be achieved.

Transparency in appointment and established procedures should be the primary aim of the judiciary. Lack of proper systems is causing problems for the judiciary in managing functions like time management, docket management, etc. And the time has come to rope in management expert to handle such functions. Just as high-level appointing bodies lay down their procedures, also there should be some defined procedures for the collegium. It is the fact that judiciary has failed to establish above procedures even after they being debatable for many years.

3. Balochistan: Carrot-and-Stick Policy or Simply a New Paradigm Shift in Indo-Pak Relations

Balochistan, the largest province in Pakistan, was a princely state that annexed by force. Home to approximately 13 million people, mostly from Baloch community, Balochistan is the least developed region.

The issue after partition, annexation of NWFP, Balochistan and certain areas into West Pakistan as a single polity was opposed by Khan Abdul Gaffar Khan of NWFP. Baloch nationals who inhabit south-west Pakistan, south-eastern Iran and southern Afghanistan have been demanding greater autonomy and higher share in revenue from natural resources from the governments of Pakistan and Iran.

Recently, the issue of Balochistan conflict attracted much limelight from media after the prime minister of India endorsed the freedom struggle waged by Baloch nationals against Pakistan's seizure. Later, Prime Minister Modi also reiterated that the concerns of people from Balochistan, Gilgit and PoK against Pakistan's mayhem will be discussed in the international arena.

INDIA'S STAND

Although India under Nehru, keenly followed Non-alignment policy and Panchasheel since independence, the nation has followed different path in certain circumstances by expressing its concern for other nations and aiding Bangladesh, Sri Lanka and Nepal with respect to freedom struggle movement or human rights movement.

India in last few years have tried to shed its image of soft nation as the regular efforts to bring Pakistan on the peace table and solve issues bilaterally have seen only failures. Although Indian government did not react in Balochistan issue back in 2009 when during Shaem El Sheikh joint statement Pakistan was stressing on India to acknowledge its involvement in Balochistan, today's PM appeal to save Balochistan and support their freedom struggle has seen a great turn in India's foreign policy for countries, such as Pakistan, sponsoring terrorism.

REASONS FOR INDIA'S STATEMENT

1. **To curtail Pakistan's interest in Kashmir:** It has been seen that Pakistan is running a propaganda to defame India on the international platform by claiming that India is exploiting people of Kashmir. To give Pakistan a taste of his own medicine, PM statement to help Baloch people has been a really apt reply to silent Pakistan.
2. **To Distract Pakistan from Kashmir:** With a view to expose the hypocrisy of Pakistan, India has recently started raising the following issues concerning Balochistan:
   - Why the Baloch nationals do not participate in the formation of government?
   - Why is there no appointment of them at government posts?
3. **Strategic Interest of India in Balochistan:** Although it is evident that India is trying to curtail Pakistan's evil strategies, there also exist some strategic interests of India in Balochistan:
   - Geostrategic location of Balochistan
   - Untapped mineral resources
   - Very close to oil lanes of Persian Gulf
   - Common border with Iran and Afghanistan
   - Iran-Pakistan-India pipeline

   It will prove to be beneficial for India in future if condition in Balochistan normalises as it being a mineral-rich area will pave the way for trade relationships.

   In addition, the IPI project that has been delayed too much owing to the instability in Balochistan region will also get a boost and help India in reducing its dependence on other countries for oil.
4. **To Keep a Check on China:** China with its string of pearls strategy is trying to encircle India by developing strong relations with Pakistan and an economic corridor that will span from Pakistan to Balochistan. With a view to increase its influence in the region and make route to import oil and raw materials from Middle East and Africa, China has plans to develop Gwadar port of Balochistan which will facilitate export through land corridor from Gwadar to Sinkiang province of China.

CONSEQUENCES

If India comes out winner in exposing Pakistan's atrocities on people of Balochistan on international arena, it will be a major setback for Pakistan as the forces aiding Pakistan to influence Kashmir issue will stop their agenda and Pak-China plans for infrastructure development will be surely affected.

CONCLUSION

If we scrutinise recent developments regarding India's stand on Balochistan and PM's statement, it is still early to say whether a carrot and stick policy is being adopted by India against Pakistan or a major paradigm shift in India's policy towards Pakistan exists. However, it is evident that India is ready to shed its image of being a soft state by retaliating via diplomatic channels keeping in view the long-term goals.

4. Article 356: Use and Misuse

The news to invoke Article 356 of the Indian Constitution for imposition of president rule in a state was in circulation once again over the last few months. The states in news were first Arunachal Pradesh and then Uttarakhand. In both the cases, the news for the imposition of president rule emerged due to withdrawal of ruling party lawmakers and the resulting political crisis. Even now, the legal battle in the case of Arunachal Pradesh is going on in the Supreme Court, while in the case of Uttarakhand it is going on in the High Court.

In this context, it is necessary to understand Article 356, its uses and the ways in which the ruling parties have often misused it.

ARTICLE 356 FOR EMERGENCY PROVISION

Article 356 is an Article in part XVIII (Articles 352–360) for imposition of the emergency provisions of the Indian Constitution. The Article originated from Section 93 of the Government of India Act 1935, which was constituted for the accession of the provincial government by the governor.

The National Commission to Review the Working of the Constitution in a consultation paper on Article 356 of the Constitution states in Clause 1, Section 1.4 of the Emergency Provisions of the Constitution that if the President, on receipt of a report from the Governor of a State or otherwise, is satisfied that a situation has arisen in which the Government of the State cannot be carried on in accordance with the provisions of this Constitution, the President may by Proclamation—

(*a*) Assume to himself all or any of the functions of the Government of the State and all or any of the powers vested in or exercisable by the Governor or anybody or authority in the State other than the Legislature of the State.

(*b*) Declare that the powers of the Legislature of the State shall be exercisable by or under the authority of Parliament.

(*c*) Make such incidental and consequential provisions as appear to the President to be necessary or desirable for giving effect to the objects of the Proclamation, including provisions for suspending in whole or in part the operation of any provisions of this Constitution relating to anybody or authority in the State.

The constitution-makers' intention was to invoke Article 356 only for an emergency provision, similar to ordinances. Dr. Ambedkar asserted during the constituent assembly debates that "Whether there is good government or not in the province (state) is not for the Centre to determine"; he further expressed a hope that Article 356 would remain a 'dead letter'.

THE MISUSE OF ARTICLE 356

However, in reality, even a casual glance at the data show huge contradiction from the assumption made by Dr. Ambedkar. A report by Sarkaria Commission found that since independence, it has been used over 100 times.

Even the absolutely justifiable state governments have bore the brunt of being fired to either make them conform to the union government or to provide the ruling party a chance to obtain power in the state. To prove the authenticity of its decision, Union governments have taken up exactly the same role Dr. Ambedkar feared of—that of centre interfering and deciding on the quality of governance in the states.

The most vindictive use of Article 356 was made in Indian politics in 1970s and 1980s. It was invoked 59 times from 1971 to 1984, with maximum use in the period 1977–1979 during the rule of Morarji Desai government. It was invoked by the post-emergency union government as political grudge against Congress-ruled state governments. Later, Indira Gandhi played the revenge politics after coming back to power in 1980 and invoked it 17 times during the period 1980–1984 till her party was in power.

Even Pandit Jawaharlal Nehru misused Article 356 by invoking it to displace the majority Communist government of Kerala. However, Indira Gandhi is identified of having exploited it as a weapon to settle political scores over opposition-ruled state governments. Moreover, there was sharp increase in Article 356 being invoked post-1967 after the defeat of Congress party in several states of India.

In reality, Indira Gandhi imposed Article 356 through the 38th Constitutional Amendment during emergency barring judicial review of even the Presidential order. Fortunately, the Morarji Desai-led government brought forth the 44th Constitutional Amendment Act in 1978, restoring the original Article 356, as visualised by Dr. Ambedkar.

Article 356 has been invoked the most number of times in Manipur. The state is going through profoundly disintegrated internal politics and violence for long periods that have often been the cause behind the Union government's imposing its decree on the state.

The politically significant states of Uttar Pradesh and Bihar, other than Manipur, with their disintegrated polity, have been under the watchful eyes of the government in centre.

FALL IN THE MISUSE OF ARTICLE 356

There has been a great reduction in the frequency of invoking Article 356 since mid-1990s despite the opposition ruling in an increasingly large number of states.

Two factors are responsible for this reversal: strengthening of regional parties and Supreme Court's intervention.

RISE OF REGIONAL PARTIES

A significant change was observed in the nature of union governments in the mid-1990s. Prior to the 1990s, even when coalition governments were bestowed the power in Delhi, the government was mainly dominated by a few national parties.

The mid-1990s in Indian politics witnessed the rise of regional parties that changed the nature of government giving an increasingly diplomatic and elusive character to Indian polity. Now the national parties were constantly looking to seek new regional allies for coalition, and hence were cautious towards invoking Article 356 against their governments.

In addition to registering their presence in the governance system and thus causing direct political impact, the strengthening of regional parties also led to reinvigoration of institutional safeguards like courts and the President to challenge any discriminatory imposition of Article 356.

SUPREME COURT INTERVENTION

The Supreme Court passed the notable SR Bommai judgement in 1994, when the Court deliberated upon the provisions of Article 356 and related issues. This case proved to have remarkable effect on Centre-State relations. This judgement turned crucial in preventing the misuse of Article 356.

In the Bommai case, the apex court pointed out the rise of regional parties to conclude that determining the governance quality in states was no longer the privilege of union government, and dissolution of an opposition-led state government cannot be held valid.

GUIDELINES LAID DOWN BY THE SUPREME COURT

In the aforementioned case, the Supreme Court set certain guidelines to prohibit the misuse of Article 356 of the constitution.

1. The majority enjoyed by the Council of Ministers shall be tested on the floor of the House.
2. Centre should give a warning to the state and a time period of one week to reply.
3. The court cannot question the advice tendered by the Council of Ministers to the President but it can question the material behind the satisfaction of the President. Hence, Judicial Review will involve three questions only:
   (*a*) Is there any material behind the proclamation?
   (*b*) Is the material relevant?
   (*c*) Was there any malafide use of power?
4. If there is improper use of A 356, then the court will provide remedy.
5. Under Article 356(3), it is the limitation on the powers of the President. Hence, the president shall not take any irreversible action until the proclamation is approved by the Parliament, i.e. he shall not dissolve the assembly.
6. Article 356 is justified only when there is a breakdown of constitutional machinery and not administrative machinery.
7. Article 356 shall be used sparingly by the centre; otherwise, it is likely to destroy the constitutional structure between the centre and the states.

5. Section 377 of IPC and its Constitutionality

INTRODUCTION

Introduced during the British rule in India in 1860, Chapter XVI, Section 377 of the Indian Penal Code (IPC) terms sexual activities against the order of nature as illegal. It states that a person indulging voluntarily in carnal intercourse against the order of nature with any man, woman or animal would be punishable for life imprisonment or with imprisonment of either description for term extendable up to 10 years, and shall also be liable to fine.

Any sexual conjugation that involves penile insertion, would come under the ambit of Section 377. Thus, it would count even the consensual heterosexual acts such as anal penetration and fellatio as punishable under this section.

THE HISTORY

In 1991, a movement to abolish Section 377 was triggered by AIDS Bhedbhav Virodhi Andolan. They raised the problems associated with Section 377 in their historic publication, Less than Gay: A Citizen's Report, and demanded its withdrawal.

The case proceeded at a slow speed and extended over the years. The Naz Foundation (India) Trust, an activist group, again raised the issue in the next decade. In 2001, a public interest litigation (PIL) was filed by the trust in the Delhi High Court, which demanded that consensual homosexual intercourse between adults should be legalised.

DELHI HIGH COURT HISTORICAL JUDGEMENT

The Delhi High Court passed a historic verdict on 2nd July 2009 that repealed the 150-year-old section and thus legalised homosexual activities between consenting adults. The Court justified its decision to repeal Section 377 by declaring the essence of it going against the fundamental rights granted to the citizens in the Indian Constitution.

A bench of Chief Justice Ajit Prakash Shah and Justice S. Muralidhar passed a 105-page judgement stating that Section 377 of the IPC unless amended, would lead to violation of Article 14, 15 and 21 of the Indian Constitution. However, the court ruled out that penile non-vaginal sex and non-consensual penile non-vaginal sex involving minors will continue to fall under the ambit of Section 377.

Another argument was made that Article 21 includes the right to live with dignity and the right to privacy and Section 377 IPC intrude upon a person's dignity by criminalising him or her solely on the basis of his or her sexual orientation and thus violates Article 21 of the Constitution.

SUPREME COURT'S JUDGEMENT OF DECEMBER 2013

Nevertheless, the historic judgement of the Delhi High Court was overturned by the Supreme Court on 11 December 2013 in Suresh Kumar Koushal vs. Naz Foundation case. The apex court reinstated Section 377 with full force.

The Supreme Court further issued instructions to the parliament to deliberate and decide on the issue of Section 377 over its repealing.

The Union Government responded by submitting a review petition on 21 December 2013 putting forward that the rights under Articles 14, 15 and 21 of the Constitution are violated by the judgement.

Moreover, a review petition was submitted by the Naz Foundation against the judgement issued by the Supreme Court on Section 377.

The apex court in response on 28 January 2014, dismissed the review petitions claiming that Section 377 is constitutional and holds for sexual acts regardless of age or consent of the parties involved.

NEW THRUST

The Supreme Court on 15 April 2015, acknowledged the right to identity of transgender persons in National Legal Services Authority (NALSA) vs. Union of India case. The apex court also particularly took into notice of exploitation of Section 377 for the harassment and physical abuse of transgender persons.

In response to the NALSA judgement, DMK leader Tiruchi Siva, a member of the parliament, initiated a private member's bill called the Rights of Transgender Persons Bill, 2014 in the parliament. Though the bill was approved in the Rajya Sabha, it is still pending in the Lok Sabha.

Both the Supreme Court and the parliament are determined to protect the rights of all citizens including transgender persons that reflected in the NALSA decision and the Rights of Transgender Persons Bill, 2014. In 2000, the Law Commission of India, another state institution, in its 172nd Report recommended towards repealing of Section 377.

REVIEW OF SECTION 377

The Naz Foundation filed the final hearing of the curative petition on 2 February 2016, and others came to the Supreme Court for hearing.

A three-member bench led by the Chief Justice of India, T. S. Thakur, ordered a fresh review of all the submitted eight curative petitions by a 5-member constitutional bench for an in-depth comprehensive hearing.

The open court hearing, resulted after two years of filing the batch of eight curative petitions, which included the parents, civil society, scientific and lesbian, gay, bisexual, and transgender (LGBT) rights organisations as the petitioners, in March 2014 against the 28 January 2014 apex court verdict. The final hearing on repealing of Section 377 is expected by September 2017.

REPEALING SECTION 377

Various institutions and organisations expressed concerns against the repealing of Section 377 citing counter arguments as follows:

- Apostolic Churches Alliance opposed the petitioners arguing giving an account of the Bible that homosexuality was an abomination in the Bible.
- It is further argued that decriminalisation of homosexuality would cause the Prevention of Immoral Trafficking Act, 1956 baseless.
- Repealing Section 377 would result in further spread of sexually transmitted diseases like AIDS that would do more harm to the people.
- Its consequences would be detrimental to the society causing severe health hazards and degradations of morality in the society.

CONCLUSION

Section 377 poses a serious threat to the dignity and self-esteem of LGBT persons who are consistently affected by the Act, suffering for a peaceful indulgence in terms of sexual orientation and family life across the country. Hence, all the stakeholders need to work in coordination to arrive at a solution that protects the dignity and rights of LGBT.

Moreover, amendment is also required in Section 375 of the IPC in agreement with the Justice Verma Committee recommendations to extend protection from rape to all persons irrespective of their gender or sexuality.

6. Status of Democracy in India

INTRODUCTION

There has been an in-depth relationship between democracy and India and it is inherent in Indian context. India, despite having diverse cultures, is the largest democracy of the world. There is no country other than India having so many customs, religions, casts, traditions and linguistics. Even then, we have been successfully running an efficient democratic set-up for the last 60 years since our Independence. Indian democracy is undoubtedly going to have its influence and eternal charisma throughout the world.

DEMOCRACY

It is the system of governance of the people, by the people and for the people. In a precise manner, in a democratic set up, all the importance is given to the citizens of the country who act as the creator, protector and destroyer of the government in their nation. In democracy, all the citizens irrespective of their status, castes or religion are considered equal and are free to exercise their veto power.

Prerequisites for a good democratic set-up are as follows:

- Electoral group which are educated enough to cast their vote wisely, keeping in mind the efficiency of the candidate and the pride of the nation.
- Unbiased and independent judicial system, which is free from any governmental or political interference; so that the judicial system could not be influenced by anyone in the country.

- Freedom of Press, which is free from the hold of any politician, VIP or any other strong person in terms of power or wealth. The freedom of press is like an entry ticket for a call to fight against corruption.
- Unblemished moral integrity is another main requisite for a smooth democracy.

ROLE OF OPPOSITION IN DEMOCRACY

In democracy, the opposition has a good hold and a strong role to play in the efficient working of the government. An efficient, undeniably honest, brilliant, strong and courageous opposition is a must to bring out the best output from the government. They can unlock and reveal all the loopholes within the government and their ministers to the outside world. Without an opposition, a government would be more like an autocracy, especially if the supreme power is in the hands of an autocrat.

INDIAN DEMOCRACY

Indian democracy, being the largest democracy in the world, bestows us with enough power to participate and enjoy the free and fair elections with an unlimited freedom of exercising our franchise in a secret manner. Indian democratic set-up, which is just like a puzzle, needs much efficient handling to maintain peace, taking into account people of diverse cultures from various sectors having different interests and requirements. Even a single outrageous step could result into violent agitations and disorder in the whole country.

IMPACTS OF INDIAN DEMOCRACY

Indian democratic set-up has given many positive outcomes till now. Our country is gradually developing to be a supreme power. We need to utilise the different traits inherent in our society, viz. manpower, brilliance, skill, determination, efficiency, etc., in the best possible manner to enjoy the freedom in its full entirety. A few areas where democracy has a clear advantage are as follows:

- **Fundamental rights and secularism:** Our fundamental rights are safeguarded all the time. Our constitution ensures proper shielding of our rights, which is the major motivating factor in democracy. We also maintained the best provisions to keep our esteem up as an ideal secular state, since our declaration to be a secular state.
- **Agricultural sector:** Agriculture and farming are the inherent foundations on which our country stands. Although a major chunk of the present generation is not associated with this field, yet a lot has been explored in this sector and few of the youngsters are still making a mark in this sector to improve and increase the yield more.
- **Industrialisation:** Industrialisation has left its footprints all over the globe including India also within its reach. An outcome of Industrialisation has been the improvement in the standard of living of an average Indian citizen and a civilised lifestyle.

- **Employment opportunities:** Instead of lack of employment opportunities, the ever-increasing population has been the major cause of unemployment. In fact, a marked increase has been noticed in the number of employment opportunities, quality of work and salary on careful monitoring of employment index.
- **Education and literacy:** Indian education system has a reputation of being the best in the world. The demand and market of our geniuses is great worldwide. Our insatiability for much higher payrolls leads to the brain drain. Otherwise, India would have been in the forefront as a leading economy in the world because of its supreme education and literacy level.
- **Independence of Press and Judiciary:** The press and judiciary in India functions with an unlimited sovereignty. For an effective democratic set-up, we have tried to maintain this major requirement in the best possible manner.

DEMOCRATIC SET-UP IN INDIA AT PRESENT

With the spread of globalisation, we are falling apart from our customs and tradition in a blind rush to emulate western lifestyle. Even after leaving aside the external factors, a few internal challenges within our country are also obstructive to our progress. A few of these factors are given as follows:

- The inability to stagnate the ever-increasing population by application of stringent laws
- Corruption
- A major chunk of our population still lingering on and below poverty line
- Communalism, casteism, fundamentalism, religion and inter-state tensions
- Inappropriate law and order situation in the country
- Coalition government and its impact on the economy of the country.

CONCLUSION

In conclusion, our democratic establishment are efficient enough, but we need to keep an eye on the negative factors seriously affecting our economy. It is necessary to curtail the flow of negative influencing factors to preserve our pride of being the largest democracy of the world.

7. Social Activism is a Key to Survival of Indian Democracy

INTRODUCTION

The importance of social activism is crucial in ensuring that the democracy survives in India though, it is not the lone instrument for promoting democracy. Social activists' attempts for engaging civil society in a dialogue about key issues affecting the society, really counts for promoting democracy.

However, in order to ensure continued progress of democracy in India, not only the social activists but its citizens and civil society also need to take active action towards the cause. All the factors including the alert media, objective judiciary, sincere political leaders, ethical businessmen, courageous social activists, visionary intellectuals, keen civic sense and patriotism combined together, are crucial for the survival of democracy in any nation across the world.

THE PERSPECTIVE

Social activism is not the lone factor responsible for the advancement of democracy within a nation. Democracy in a nation can be secured and flourished only through the active involvement of all other members of the society.

Social activism lacking principles will be of no help to any democratic nation. Moreover, it will be damaging for our nation. Activists with the intention of malicious agendas or campaigns for gaining power or money will be exposed in the long run. They will not be of any help to the Indian democracy.

Though, social activism is essential to the maintenance of democracy, it loses its worth for the survival of democracy in a country with incompetent political leaders and unethical businessmen involved in corrupt means of bribery and money laundering.

Such circumstances make it almost impossible for even the most determined social activist to be able to campaign successfully for any cause. Social activism will be of little help to preserve the sound functioning of democracy unless the society is observant about the various developments taking place in its surroundings. It is in the interest of the nation that media keep a distance towards any temptation to paid news or remain uninfluenced from any political interference resorting to slur campaigns, otherwise the Indian democracy will be left in anarchic state. Merely social activists' sacrifices for the cause of democracy would not be sufficient unless the government and corporate leaders come out of their nexus to achieve their self-serving interests.

The objective of democracy is to assign the power in the hands of the people. However, social activism is worthless and of no use if citizens themselves are indifferent and unwilling to participate in key issues of importance to societal growth. Social activists can raise their voice for the people's cause only when the media or the lobbyists do not suppress them. Parties with selfish motives are a hindrance to the democratic set-up and reduce democracy to a laughingstock in the country.

An example of how much destructive political camouflage could be for the democracy in our nation, is the recent censorship of the parliamentary proceedings on national television during the discussion on the Telangana bill. In addition, a direct violation of the democratic principles is being committed by the businessmen who, in pursuit of their petty self-interest, offer bribes to exploit the economic resources in the country.

Continuous support of celebrities, common man and principled media to social activism can, help achieve transparency and accountability in India that in turn will re-establish the previous glory of Indian democracy.

CONCLUSION

It could be difficult for even the leaders to raise social issues if they face stiff opposition from rivals or warring factions. Leaders from various parties in India are involved in such political scuffle. It is necessary for the survival of democracy that the administration works in tandem with the leaders for effective implementation of reforms. Social activism is only part of the solution.

8. Indian Judicial System

A famous quote from William Edwart Gladstone (1809–1898), a great English political leader who was also a former Prime Minister, says "Justice delayed is justice denied". The meaning of this phrase is that if justice is not done at the right time, then even its commitment at a later holds no significance because a period of time was spent committing injustice.

The credibility of Indian judicial systems is reducing in the eyes of common people because of long delays at all levels of judiciary and the reluctance of all the judges to pass the verdict and the inevitable adjournments. This is the reason behind mafia finding favour among the people who believe in instant justice.

However, it is very difficult in reality to describe the delay in justice without clarification. Since the time of seeking justice, there are so many prerequisites and formalities in the form of rules and regulations and prescribed procedures regulating court proceedings which are again time consuming but impossible to evade that it gets very difficult to deliver justice in time.

Indian judicial system is the last ray of hope for Indian citizens. However, the Indian judiciary pass judgement on the basis of facts and evidences, not conscience or morals. Once the facts are in hands, all it require for the fast deliverance of justice are arguments and hearing. A judiciary which takes into account only evidences and facts should deliver fast justice rather than weaken the spirit of the complainants and the defendants with unnecessary expenditure and time delays. This compels them to engage in 'out of Court settlements' which are relatively cheaper and quicker, thus, leading to trust deficit in our Judicial System.

The Preamble to the Indian Constitution, among other things, announces that: "We the people of India having solemnly resolved to constitute India into a sovereign, socialist, secular, Democratic Republic and to secure to all its citizens—Justice, social, economic and political". However, even after six decades of Independence, numerous laws are available but of little help to impart justice. The founders of our constitution had set 'Justice' as the top priority and our preamble to the constitution also establishe justice at a higher order than other features like liberty, equality and fraternity. People look up to judiciary to seek justice.

Indian judicial system is regarded as one of the vital pillars of democracy, and is held in high regard along with media while the other major pillars such as administrative system and police are considered to be highly corrupted. Political class, bureaucracy and police are often blamed to be corrupt in India, while judiciary in comparison is seen as an institution that answer for the grievances of Indian people.

As Chief Justice Burger noticed: "A sense of confidence in the courts is essential to maintain the fabric of ordered liberty for a free people and three things could destroy that confidence and do incalculable damage to society: that people come to believe that inefficiency and delay will drain even a just judgement of its value; that people who have long been exploited in the smaller transactions of daily life come to believe that courts cannot vindicate their legal rights from fraud and over-reaching; that people come to believe the law in the larger sense cannot fulfil its primary function to protect them and their families in their homes, at their work, and on the public streets".

It is well known that as on 1 January 2015, 62,794 cases were pending for judgement before the Honourable Supreme Court. According to the available data, the total pending cases up to the year ending 2013 for the 24 high courts and lower courts were found to be 44.5 lakh and a huge 2.6 crore, respectively. Out of the 44 lakh cases in pendency in the high courts, 10,23,739 were criminal and 34,32,493 were civil in nature.

Major factors responsible for Delay in Law: The most important factor is the unnecessary delay in the disposition of cases are as follows:

(*a*) One of the main cause behind this gloomy situation is the hopelessly insufficient number of courts along with judges in the country.

(*b*) Another reason in addition to inadequacy of the number of judges is the incompetency and inefficiency of judiciary.

(*c*) Lawyers with hidden motives in the habit of seeking adjournment are another reason behind the delay.

(*d*) Another reason is numerous amendment of laws.

(*e*) Another significant reason for delay is absence of work culture in the courts.

(*f*) Incompetent nature of justice impedes building of peace culture in the society and also undermine the internal security of the country.

The Arrears Committee led by Justice V. S. Mallimath in 1990, found the following primary factors responsible for delays in law:

(*i*) Litigation explosion;

(*ii*) Accumulation of first appeal;

(*iii*) Inadequacy of staff attached to the High Court, i.e. vacancy crisis in Indian Judiciary;

(*iv*) Inordinate concentration of work in the hands of some members of the Bar;

(*v*) Lack of punctuality among judges;

(*vi*) Granting of unnecessary adjournments;

(*vii*) Indiscriminate closure of Courts;

(*viii*) Indiscriminate resort to writ jurisdiction;

(*ix*) Inadequacy of classification and granting of cases;

(*x*) Inordinate delay in the supply of certified copies of judgements and orders etc.

REMEDIES TO OVERCOME DELAY: SOME SUGGESTIONS

More courts should be established in the country and more judges should be recruited in proportion to the population to address the pendency of cases, as the ever-increasing population and the cases associated with it far exceeds in comparison to the number of courts or judicial staff available. According to an estimate, India has the lowest ratio of number of judges per million population in the world, standing at 11 judges per million population. Hence, the number of judges need to be increased especially at the local level to attend to the grievances of common people.

The Supreme Court judges Doraiswamy Raju and Arijit Pasayat quoted the aforementioned poem of Julia A. F. Cabney in 'Little Things' while passing judgement on the infamous Best Bakery riot case in Gujarat on 12 April 2004.

In conclusion, the disappointing figures on the chronic backlog of court cases over the last six decades indicate the growing trust deficit in the Indian legal system. However, taking measures for multi-pronged reforms is a long-term project and it will need the engagement of judges first to bring out any significant changes to their profession. A crucial step towards fast settlement of sexual crimes was taken to address the trust deficit through the opening of Fast-track courts all across the country. However, speedy justice also has its own challenges.

It is true that 'justice delayed is justice denied' but, the opposite also holds true that 'swift justice is injustice'. There is some resentment among the judges and observers that the quality of justice administered through fast track courts is questionable despite their reducing the backlog in terms of cases.

9. Achievements of UN over Past 70 Years, its Relevance and Needed Reforms

The United Nations (UN) held a huge celebration on 24 October 2015 to mark 70th anniversary of its establishment. A special annual general assembly was held to mark the historic occasion at its New York headquarters and the Sustainable Development Agenda 2030 for the transformation of the world was given the node at the assembly. The agenda further extended the objectives of Millennium Development Goals (MDGs) that guided the global policy dialogue for the past 15 years towards ending inequalities and promoting prosperity.

The devastation caused by the Second World War and the consequent anxieties over recurring use of nuclear bombs or arsenals in the context of Hiroshima and Nagasaki incidents led to the formation of the United Nations on 24 October 1945.

The United Nations is the successor to the ineffective League of Nations that came into operation in 1920 in reaction to the First World War to resolve international disputes.

The United Nations is established with the dual objectives of maintaining peace and security across the world and promoting worldwide cooperation to solve international disputes of an economic, social, cultural or humanitarian character.

ACHIEVEMENTS: PRE-COLD WAR ERA

The primary phase of its formation was up to the expectations when it did not allow regional tensions to escalate up to the level of initiating the Third World War. The role of UN was also appreciated and well regarded for its effective handling of the Suez Canal crisis (1956) and the process of decolonisation in Asia and Africa.

COLD WAR ERA

During the Cold War era, the UN was in the maturing phase following its inception. Its main task was to efficiently handle the cold-war era diplomacy and politics between the USA and the USSR and not letting them escalate into full-fledged real war. The laudable feat during this period was the peaceful dissipation of the Cuban missile crisis of 1962 using diplomacy at its best.

POST-COLD WAR ERA

During the 1990s when the UN was relishing the accomplishment of 50 years of its establishment, the disintegration of the USSR and the emergence of the USA as the sole global super power brought a distinct responsibility for it.

It executed its responsibility by not allowing it to drift towards the sole ambitions of the USA and proving its relevancy for the betterment of the poor and marginalised nations.

THE MODERN ERA

In recent years, its role in promoting international cooperation and resolving international disputes is described as follows:

- Its role is to promote special grouping among the major countries of the world in line with their objectives for mutual cooperation and resolution of international disputes or crisis. Few of such examples are WTO (trade), G20 (to deal with financial crisis) and UNFCC (climate change).
- It played a major role in rehabilitation of millions of Syrian refugees in neighbouring countries like Lebanon, Turkey and Jordan.
- The deployment of peacekeeping and peace-building missions to resolve the disputes in Africa.
- It is effectively playing its role in promoting the concept of development, human rights and influencing the civil society to maximise its potential for the progress of the society and empowerment of the poor and marginalised sections.

However, the UN has also drawn criticism from several corners for its inability to contain US-Iraq war and growing imparity in income levels.

Particularly, in the case of Israel-Palestine conflict, its failure to arrive at any viable solution has drawn wide criticism.

IMPORTANCE OF THE UNITED NATIONS IN THE PRESENT SCENARIO

The United Nations still holds importance because of the following reasons:

- The world is still facing consistent nuclear threat.
- The religious, ethnic and regional conflicts are continuously increasing in Africa.
- The poor in the world constitute around one-third of the global population and they are in constant need of support through joint development action by global multilateral agencies.
- The need to eliminate consistent disparities in wealth distribution and achieve balanced and sustainable development worldwide.
- Promoting concerted efforts among nations to tackle growing threats of terrorism from violent non-state actors, such as ISIS, Al Qaeda, etc.
- The importance of the UN get even more significant in achieving global security when it is not possible for a single nation to solve all the problems in the interdependent global world.

VARIOUS REFORMS THAT ARE NEEDED

The United Nations need to take various organisational reforms to effectively equip itself to tackle modern day challenges such as follows:

- There is a need to expand on a priority basis the present structure of permanent and non-permanent membership of the UN Security Council that still reflects the realities of 1940s.
- It need to give more chance to both the developed and developing countries to express their opinions and have their say in the decision-making of the specialised (WHO, UNESCO, FAO, etc.) and subsidiary agencies (peacekeeping missions).

CONCLUSION

During the period of 70 years since its inception, the United Nations has successfully transformed itself from a mere organisation into a global institution. It has been able to meet the expectations for playing its part as a global policy agency and a mediator in resolving international disputes.

Finally, it has been able to successfully interconnect international community building mutual trust and using diplomacy instead of coercion and aggression to resolve conflicts.

10. Interrelationship of Good Fences with Good Neighbours

INTRODUCTION

A fence is a barrier or boundary to keep privacy. A famous poem by Robert Frost uses the proverb 'good fences make good neighbours' and beautifully describes the idea of barriers between friendship, communication, people and a sense of security it gives. This implies that maintaining fencing between neighbours, can preserve harmony between them and the absence of boundary can lead to conflict of interests resulting in bitterness between the two parties.

THE IMPORTANCE OF FENCE

The poem presents the similarities between home and the country in terms of both reality of life and scenario. The chances of intruding upon each other's zone are eliminated by making a fence. The above fact also holds true in terms of relationships, colleagues, neighbouring countries or everything else in life.

However, to maintain communication instead of building a stonewall, a low fence should be built just to maintain a distance that allows privacy.

The Berlin Wall, the Great Wall of China, walls separating Israelis from Palestinians or Americans from Mexicans are few of the famous walls in the world. Nations worldwide are trying to ensure robust boundaries to stop cross-border infiltration. One living example is that of India which in its bid to prevent any possible dispute with its land-locked neighbours has tried to make good boundaries. Some of the major border areas made by India keeping an eye on immediate neighbours, China and Pakistan, are the Wagah Border, Siachen glacier and Arunachal Pradesh. There are many instances in the past when the creation of weak fences led to infiltration from either side, which disrupted the harmony between the countries and resulted in discords and violent encounters. Taking lessons from the past, countries have been able to create fences resulting in reduction of border disputes.

One school of thought is also of the view that keeping some kind of boundary evokes feelings of great longing and thus maintaining harmony amongst people. An obvious example is the affectionate way the people meet after long period of separation.

Neighbours may be in friendly terms with each other but keeping a fence is essential as it ensures some kind of separation to maintain privacy. There may arise a probability of too much friendliness leading to intrusion on privacy of an individual.

In present times, people want to avoid getting affected by any sentiment or words and thus have begun to keep a certain distance from others. Hence, in addition to preserving the privacy, keeping fences or boundaries also helps one in maintaining harmony and peace both at home and surroundings.

DRAWBACKS OF CREATING A FENCE

However, creation of a boundary also has its side effect of leading one to isolation. In past, porous fences enabled neighbours to discuss their daily affairs and share each other's concerns. However, in the present times, people are not even aware of their immediate neighbours because of boundaries. Due to creation of boundary, people may not be able to share common concerns over their needs and come out at a solution that can lead to dispute in the long term as people have difference of opinions. It could be difficult to cross borders for the citizens of one country sharing relationship with their neighbours as the long procedures and delays in getting approval for the same could be cumbersome.

The same holds true even in building personal relationships, when people, who build walls around them, before even talking to others, lose out the opportunity to know someone as good as a friend, bearing some preconceived notions in their mind. In future, such people would be devoid of close friendship or true intimacy because of the barrier they created towards their relationships much before.

Man is a social animal and creation of a wall leads to less movement of people, which in turn, results in elimination of any social interaction. For the world witnessing fast unwarranted changes, this can have severe outcomes on society where people even after having all means of communications are drifting apart fast from their near and dear ones. The progress of civilisation is caused due to different social, cultural and technological aspects. Without social interaction, it would not be possible for people from various cultures to come together resulting in elimination of free exchange of ideas and growth of society and its citizens. This in turn can have a serious impact on the growth of human beings over a long time.

CONCLUSION

The proverb 'Good fences make good neighbours', in line with the age-old belief, is applicable even in the present context. However, it is to be noticed that these boundaries do not become communication barriers for people to interact with each other. Robert Frost, the poet, may have had his own view in favour of removal of barriers to ensure hassle-free communication but he failed to visualise the multifaceted aspects having both advantages and disadvantages associated with it. The purpose of putting barriers should be to ensure that privacy is kept intact, no intrusion takes place on the borders and there exists goodness of relationships at various levels all times.

11. Importance of India in Promoting ASEAN Cooperation

INTRODUCTION

The all-time strategic significance of the Association of South-East Asian Nations (ASEAN) region in the Asian continent is widely recognised. The region comprising Indonesia, Malaysia, Philippines, Singapore and Thailand as its members has gained prominence in the eyes of the world community due to expansion of trades amongst other reasons. Over the period, few more countries such as Brunei, Cambodia, Laos and Myanmar also joined the ASEAN.

OBJECTIVE BEHIND ASEAN FORMATION

The purpose behind creation of ASEAN was to promote growth, cultural development and to ensure political and economic stability in the region through mutual cooperation. There were some apprehensions initially when India wished to join ASEAN because of its huge size and population.

After India's engagement with ASEAN through sectoral dialogue partnership in 1992, the India-ASEAN partnership moved a step further in various sectors that included tourism, trade as well as science and technology. India received invitation to join as a full dialogue partner from ASEAN in 1995. Over the long time, India has signed pacts with various countries, which adjusted the tariff so that even the East Asian countries find it suitable for them.

India is involved in dialogues with Singapore to form a Comprehensive Economic Cooperation Agreement (CECA). It committed economic cooperation to push the trade turnover further up to $12 billion. Malaysia and Singapore have been the most prominent trading partners for India.

The tourism sector is also a beneficiary of the boost in intra trade. Other things anticipated to play a significant part in ASEAN are counter-terrorism, disaster management and maritime security. The future of ASEAN seems bright and the prospects of bilateral trade links is expected to be significant in future.

India in its firm commitment to the 'Look-East' Policy is looking to foster partnership and build links with countries in the region. The foreign policy of India should be good enough to meet its ambitions as it is gradually emerging as a power to reckon with in the Asian region.

To register its benign presence in the entire Southeast Asia regardless of neighbouring China, India needs to spread its zone of influence using diplomacy and cordial approach. The government is more focussed in its approach towards 'Look-East Policy' with the liberalisation of Indian economy and working on further expansion of its relationship with South-East Asian countries.

The signing of free trade area pact between India and Thailand allows import of 84 items at half the normal duty charge existing in India. The objective of this move was to keep the same tariff across the Southeast Asian countries.

India and the ASEAN countries, in their endeavours to take the cooperation between the two countries to the next level, have taken concrete steps in the form of the Mekong Ganga Cooperation (MGC) and the Comprehensive Economic Cooperation Agreement (CECA).

The relations between India and ASEAN have improved further with regular India-ASEAN summits taking place and the ongoing transformation in international politics over the last two decades. The trading between India and ASEAN has been facilitated further due to improved relations in political and security aspects and signing of many other trade pacts.

In the twenty-first century, which is being termed as the Asian century, India and China are slated to be the major players. India's cooperation with ASEAN is expected to resemble the Eurozone with less trade restriction, freedom of movement without visa requirement and good interconnectivity in the form of highways and other infrastructure.

CONCLUSION

ASEAN countries should perceive India's rise as a major international power as an asset that can raise the reputation of the country multi-fold. India's emergence as a powerhouse of Asia should encourage the countries to hold a positive perception of the opportunities that would come across their way to development, by engaging with India along with a healthy and peaceful Asian order.

Ensuring stability in the region by maintaining cooperation between the countries and facilitating trade in achieving its objective of expanding trade to boost the economy and provide employment opportunities to people in the region, would be some kind of litmus test for Indian policy-makers which they have to pass.

The reputation of India being a peacekeeper amongst many disturbing elements in the region find favour among the other countries in the region who would look to associate with India to make growth and to maintain peace and harmony.

12. India-Africa Relations: The New Dynamics

The third India-Africa Forum Summit with the theme—Partners in Progress: Towards a Dynamic and Transformative Development Agenda—was hosted in New Delhi on 29 October 2015. The forum was formed in 2008.

The summit called for transformative relationship in the future adopting the Delhi Declaration. The 2015 India-Africa Framework for Strategic Cooperation and Plan of Action also got approval at the summit with the focus on transforming shared aspirations into reality.

INDIA'S ROLE IN AFRICA

Development Assistance: India is an important ally in the development of Africa along next only to the United Nations, Japan and China. It has been contributed around 17.4 billion US dollars in promoting developmental activities in Africa since 2008.

Moreover, India offered 600 million US dollars of grant assistance in the 2015 summit. It included 10 million US dollars of India-Africa Health Fund and 100 million dollars of India-Africa Development Fund.

Education: The Indian government awarded 50,000 scholarships to African students in the summit for availing higher education in India. India initiated the Pan-African e-network project for 54 African nations in 2007 to promote tele-education, e-commerce, telemedicine, e-governance, resource mapping, infotainment and meteorological services.

Civil Wars and Conflicts: India also took part in four UN peacekeeping missions—Ivory Coast (since 2004), Congo (2005), Sudan and South Sudan (2005) and Liberia (2007) and is a major contributor to UN Peacekeeping operations in Africa.

AFRICA'S RELEVANCY FOR INDIA

Source of minerals: Africa, with its rich mineral resources, offers ample opportunities to build trade relationships. India's trade relationship with Africa covers crude oil imports in addition to gold and silver. May 2015, Nigeria replaced Saudi Arabia as the largest oil exporter to India. Presently, India imports around 26 per cent of its crude oil from Africa with Nigeria and Angola being the major contributors.

The strengthening relationship of India with Africa, in oil exploration and production, could be witnessed from the presence of ONGC Videsh Limited (OVL), international arm of ONGC in five African countries— Libya, Mozambique, Nigeria, Sudan and South Sudan.

Moreover, India's association with Africa, the next global provider of rare earth minerals, in exploring rare earth minerals will be fruitful to curb China's dominance in this strategic sector, which forms the basis of modern electronics industry.

Market for Indian made goods: Africa in present times has become one of the major destinations for Indian-made goods due to improvement in lifestyle and standards of living in the continent.

In a report issued by the World Bank, Africa's GNI is higher than India, and the GNI per capita of a dozen African countries are higher than China.

India's production is expected to increase over and above the consumption level under the Make in India initiative and, thus, Africa could be the best partner for India in future.

Many African countries come in the least developing countries (LDCs) category and India's decision to extend preferential treatment to LDCs in trade in services in the WTO can enhance the mineral resource-led trade momentum to even the services sector in the coming years.

In the last 15 years, there has been an increase of 20 times in the trade with Africa, but it was much less than the specified target of 100 billion US dollars set for 2015.

Even this 100 billion US dollars trade target of India is much less in comparison to 250 billion US dollars trade partnership of China with Africa.

India's chances of achieving the UN Security Council permanent membership will be further strengthened with more than a quarter of UN members being representatives from African Union of 54 countries.

It would not have been possible for India, without the support of African nations, to get elected to the UN Security Council for seven terms since 1945 and in important organisations like UNICEF, UN Habitat, World Food Program, etc.

AREAS OF COMMON INTEREST

Demography: Even after having demographic variation in terms of size, India and Africa share many commonalities as follows:

- Both the regions share equal population of around 130 crore forming one-third of the global population.
- Both the regions share similar proportion of young population with Africa having 200 million people in the age group 15 and 24 and India with 18 per cent of the population as young.

❖ India and Africa share similarity in terms of ethnic and linguistic diversity also.

In the context of large youth population and increasing rate of unemployment, India and Africa can learn from each other's experiences and can work together for development of desired skills and reap demographic dividends.

Security: Considering the expanded ambit of security, India and Africa share similar concerns with threats emanating from both internal and external sources in various forms such as unemployment, hunger, poverty, insurgency, drug trafficking, money laundering, human trafficking, terrorism, diseases, piracy, etc.

New International Order: To promote democratic global order, it is necessary to carry out structural and procedural reforms in the global political and financial institutions such as the United Nations, International Monetary Fund and the World Bank. Deeper engagement are required between the two partners to achieve this objective.

CONCLUSION

While the factors considered to be binding the world politics till the 1990s were the Non-Alignment Movement (NAM), the resistance to cold-war politics along with racism, the modern age Indo-Africa relationship is differentiated by bilateral and multilateral cooperation with focus on trade, people-to-people exchanges, investments and broad-based development aspirations.

The leadership in India and Africa should immediately take notice that their people are their true resources, as realised in the Delhi Declaration and go all out in their endeavour for improving their living standards as laid down in the UN Sustainable Development Goals.

❑❑❑

16

ESSAYS ON SCIENCE AND TECHNOLOGY

1. The Work and the Work Culture have Changed with the Emergence of Information Technology

Information technology (IT) has brought the office to home by destroying the limitations of the office. It has created a tremendous opportunity to work irrespective of the physical conditions and disabilities of people. Before ITs arrival, work meant to going office and working only there. Information technology has changed this trend. With the help of information technology, one can work from home even at one's own flexible time. This revolution is no doubt the excellent means for a nation to grow and develop.

Information technology has boosted up the speed and accuracy and saved time. For instance, in the field of communication, it has brought revolution. In earlier times, a letter would reach from India to the United Kingdom in about twenty days. But by dint of information technology now, an e-mail (electric mail) is sent anywhere in the world within fraction of seconds. Online videoconference, chatting and web cams have destroyed distance and brought the families, living in two ends of the world, close together and effectively enabled their communication. The business partners also in different countries enjoy the communication boon of IT very easily and effectively. IT has multiplied the efficiency of business many times.

Online education and distance education have opened a vaster vista for the students and young professionals who have become able to pursue various courses at their own flexible time in order to boost their career. Online tests and exams are rapidly replacing the notebook exams as well as reducing the use of pen and paper which, is certainly a positive aspect.

The revolution in the field of robotics has also increased speed of our work as well as helped us do a strenuous and heavy task at ease. With the invention of remote, the olden days are gone when we had to frequently get up from a cosy seat for changing the channels or increase, decrease or modulate the volume of the television. The strenuous job that humans cannot accomplish because of the requirement of many labourers, is now being done easily by robotic machines. In the construction sites, we can see wide use of robotic machines. It has saved labour and reduced time as well.

Information technology, in words, is a boon that has been upgrading our life greatly with its latest incessant developments, by making our life more and more comfortable, and largely saving our time day-by-day. The growth and development of digital knowledge has made our life adventurous.

2. Machine Translation is Slower and Less Accurate than Human Translation

Human is the producer of machine, but not the machine. So, machine does a thing by command of the knowledge that a human provides. So, the above cliché goes exactly and highlights the fact. Success largely depends on the effectiveness of communication. The current trends of globalisation have resulted in the rapid growth of trade and commerce. It has also collected people and brains close together from across the world. The humans communicate through a common language that is essential for better understanding as people belong to different countries with different languages. Humans are prone to bring rapid speed and accuracy in this communication too as they do in other sectors at a great speed within fractions of a second. The art of translation should also be done with so high speed.

Business meetings between people of different countries, having no common language, reams of documents or even exchange of words between officials of different countries are all solved by either interpreter or translation software. Since the last few decades, the demand for interpreters and translators has been steadily increasing.

In order to handle this bulk pressure of translation, there emerged many outsourcing companies. They get their work translated by humans and also by machines in their offices in the country. Still it fails to meet the day's demand of the companies abroad.

So, various websites have also started providing translation services. Google, the most popular search engine, provides its free of cost translation services popular among millions of people.

But, the fact is that, the translation done through any such machine-based sites is not at all perfect. There are many common grammatical and logical errors. Moreover, a machine translator does the work slower than a human.

But, a human has the outstanding ability to learn and speak many languages. The understanding of a human being of any language and its culture gives far better translation than any software translator. Besides this, a machine translator merely interprets everything verbatim, whereas a man does it by applying much logic and with detailed explanation if necessary.

So, politics, sports, BPOs, beauty pageants among many others largely depend on human translators though simple software is easily available with onetime minimal purchase cost because it is well known that human translator does the work precisely, accurately and intelligibly. Though machine translator can solve most of the problems as well as ease many tasks for us, the primary understanding or ability to communicate intelligibly and successfully with others is best managed by human beings.

3. Genetic Engineering has more Negative Impacts than Positive

INTRODUCTION

The production by means of advanced biotechnology is known as genetically modified (GM) crops for human consumption. The objective of this type of production is to meet the bulk requirement with the healthiest crops flawless in the seeds and its produce in parlance of health and hygiene. Genetic engineering increases qualities in the crops as well as reduces the need for pesticides, by boosting the crop's resistant power to pests. Maize, wheat, rice, BT cotton, potatoes, etc. are some of the most common crops that are genetically produced.

GM CROPS—A BLESS OR A CURSE?

With rapid and widespread popularity of genetically manufactured (GM) crops, there rises voices across the world for and against their hygienic qualities. Scientists and economists argue that GM crops are unique in the interest of economy as well as society, whereas environmentalists and other groups of scientists reply that GM crops are harmful to the environment and hazardous for health in the long run. Let's try to discover the good and bad of GM crops.

ADVANTAGES

i. **Low production cost:** Although the GM crops are costlier comparatively, but the overall costs it sums up is less as, these crops do not need pesticides or insecticides. Moreover, it yields in greater quantity which brings higher profits. Besides this, GM crops are tolerant to drought and salt in the soil, highly disease resistant, and immune to herbicides destroying weeds.

ii. **Increase in employment opportunity:** The advanced technology used in this field of research works creates employment opportunities for several people. Besides the employment in research sector, there is a greater demand of manpower in the harvest season because of the rapid growth in yielding crops.

iii. **Profitable for farmers:** Some specific studies have revealed that the profits of the farmers go up especially because of the rise in yield for the genetically modified seeds.

iv. **Beneficial to cost and health:** GM crops directly provide better health for the consumers because of the genetically produced healthy qualities. These crops also stop consumption and the probable harmful effects of the chemicals widely used in the insecticides and pesticides.

DISADVANTAGES

i. **Damaging cell tissues in the modification process:** The process includes invasive modification. As a result, it maximises the chance of damage to the cell tissues of the plant.

ii. **Cancer threat:** GM products have the risk of carrying carcinogens.

iii. **Probability of allergic diseases:** The GM crops can also cause allergic diseases because of the procedure involved in it.

CONCLUSION

It is clear that the advantages of the GM crops are much more than their disadvantages. These crops can, moreover, meet the huge demand of the growing population across the world with much better hygienic qualities. While the negative impacts are much lesser than the positive ones, the consumption of GM crops is far better than the traditional health hazardous crops and go on meeting need of the hour.

4. Concept of Cloning Human Beings for Replacement of Body Parts: Scary but Not Fiction

INTRODUCTION

Technology has been advancing and improving with its diverse fields of novelty. Medical science has got an extra-edge by dint of technology in many cases—saving lives from fatal diseases, and increasing the average lifespan. Disregarding the moral and sentimental bases, we must encourage and enhance the studies and research in the field of science.

SCIENTIFIC VIEW ON CLONING

Cloning denotes the procedure of developing a genetic copy of a living organism with the exact DNA. In the case of twins, this takes place naturally or it can even be manmade. For some time, horticultural cloning has been practised. Science has been slowly progressing to cloning more animals from 1996 when a sheep, Dolly, was cloned successfully. After processing it in a lab, it was carried to term by a surrogate sheep. Winnie the two became the first British dog to be cloned which was born in a lab at Seoul, South Korea in April 2014.

Because of a set of legal and moral limitations, the scientists have not yet tried cloning on human beings. Different religious groups are arguing against cloning that it is against the natural order of things that God has created. But the fact is that there are various other scientific practices going against the discerning natural order. For example, scientific progress has helped countless couples to have a child of their own when they have failed by natural process—the God gifted natural process. Again, hearing aids as well as the transplants of corneal, help the deaf hear, and the blind see. There is, therefore, no reason for looking at cloning against humankind.

ADVANTAGES OF CLONING HUMANS

Needless to say, the benefits of cloning human beings, is immense, especially in medical emergencies. If a patient requires an urgent replacement of any organ, she or he need not have to wait for the uncertain period of time. Moreover, there also could not be found a better match. But cloning produces a duplicate of a person's DNA, there is no chance of rejecting it.

Besides this, there are countless health advantages for the human race-age reversal, correcting defective genes, preventing heart attacks, preventing Down syndrome, etc.

DISADVANTAGES OF CLONING

It may cause population explosion. As a result, it will certainly make things worse, as there are not enough resources to support the present population of the world. The people will also suffer financial repercussions the worst. Despite, several health benefits, it will be certainly beyond the reach of common people—the mass. This will, instead, be favourable for the few rich.

CONCLUSION

We must, therefore, think of the advancement of science and research with a liberal point of view, and consider the advantages of humanity. Before we accept or reject any idea, we should better judge and analyse it thoroughly from different points of views.

5. Human or Technical Intelligence: Which has more Importance in Combating Terrorism?

The only grievous word is 'terrorism' that creates the feelings of chill running through the spine, shivering of the body, and panic and horror in the minds of people irrespective of status, colour and religion all over the world. We hardly pass a single day without hearing some terrorist activities that take place somewhere, killing or harming innocent people in any part of the world. The entire world is infested with terrorists and the problem is now faced largely by developed as well as developing countries. Terrorists kill in some cases massacre a large number of innocent humans causing the governments incur the massive financial costs in confronting the menace posed by the terrorists. Different terrorist groups have divergent objectives and ideologies.

However, their critical operation strategies and the resultant impact of their activities have similarity as they engage in violent activities and carnage to spread their message. With the objective of curbing the extensive security threat many countries employ diverse defensive and preventive techniques against the terrorist activities. Human intelligence (HUMINT) as well as technical intelligence (TECHINT) is engaged in combating the challenges being posed day-by-day by different terrorists groups across the world.

WAR AGAINST TERRORISM

Terrorism is the established ethos and ideology which is based on occurrences. In recent times, it is quite difficult to challenge and combat terrorism unlike any social crime.

Different terror groups carry out their operations in highly effective, clandestine, and constantly changing landscape to be successful in their objectives. A highly expertise intelligence network is a requisite part of a country's arsenal in its struggle against terrorism. Therefore, intelligence capacities and capabilities are the backbone of a country's ability to avert terrorism.

HUMAN INTELLIGENCE (HUMINT)

Human intelligence (HUMINT), the oldest and the cheapest method of gaining intelligence, is served by a human source or contact. The examples of the means of gathering intelligence via HUMINT are developed informant networks and infiltration of terrorist movements through espionage. The training and experience of the human operative lies behind the information derived out of this form of gathering intelligence. An untrained human operative will have diverse insight into the target he or she is incumbent to monitor. So, this form of intelligence gathering needs the human operative to be trained rigorously on a distinct kind of target monitoring.

TECHNICAL INTELLIGENCE (TECHINT)

Technical intelligence (TECHINT) denotes the employment of advanced technological apparatus in order to determine terrorist activities in a secret manner. TECHINT does not include the use of human source of information, rather it uses the highly advanced set of techniques—electronic intelligence (ELINT), photographic or imaging intelligence (PHOTOINT), communication intelligence (COMINT), signal intelligence (SIGINT), measurement and signature intelligence (MASINT), telemetry intelligence (TELINT), and the most recent computers and internet intelligence (HACKINT). TECHINT can help in snooping huge amount of information from all over the world by means of decoding techniques, remotely piloted aircrafts, computer exploitation techniques, traffic analysis, cable and phone tapping, satellite pictures, etc.

HUMINT Vs TECHINT

Human or technical intelligence (HUMINT) as well as technical intelligence (TECHINT) is the backbone of the intelligence system of any nation. But the extraordinary advancement of technology has made TECHINT replace HUMINT on the basis of the effective and efficient usage and the distinct methods of collecting intelligence. The downsides and failure of HUMINT is the major factor to minimise the reliance on this discipline. HUMINT includes time-taking processes like identification, screening and recruitment of agents. Moreover, a human is more persuadable and vulnerable which may result in compromising, a backlash fabrication of information, and great risk to life due to high awareness of the informant or agent to the counterspy units.

The aspects of TECHINT make clear its advantage over HUMINT. TECHINT is largely dependable on advanced technological equipment with minimum human involvement and helps in deriving information easily and safely. A TECHINT operation can be effectively and efficiently executed without any risk of getting misleading or fabricated information in complete secrecy. TECHINT also helps in collecting serious information within so short a time by maintaining higher degree of security. However, technology too has its own limitations. Besides, the counterparts are also operating their activities by command of the advanced technology, so a slightest mistake can cause great risk. TECHINT is very expensive to develop and can be encountered using certain measures by the terrorists. For instance, terrorists hiding in the underground cannot be easily traced and gauged even by the advanced satellite pictures or remotely piloted aircrafts.

CONCLUSION

Above all, even if the technological intelligence reaches the highest level of advancement, it cannot be used independently and safely. There must be a strong synergy between human intelligence and technological intelligence. The intelligence derived from any of these disciplines must be validated and supplemented by the other reliable techniques. The intelligence community should always keep reliance on HUMINT because of its capability of providing first-hand information, which will probably have no substitute or be out-of-date. So, a nation should not rely on any one of these disciplines, as there is a greater chance of failure which may result in the loss, suffering and death of innocent people at large. The Pearl Harbour (under the United States of America) bombing (7 December 1941) by Japan was successful because of the absence of HUMINT cooperation. The USA military force was very confident on their TECHINT, but the bombing taught them a lesson for their reliance on only one intelligence discipline. So, it can be sum up that these two disciplines of intelligence must work together as integral parts of each other in order to provide better security to the nation, and negligence of one must invite perils for the nation as well as the world.

6. Advancement of Science versus Erosion of Human Values

INTRODUCTION

The advancement of science and technology has brought about a radical change in the lifestyle and living standard of human beings. By each and every invention day by day, science has been gradually adding one after another machine and tool for the ease and comfort of mankind, and helping in releasing pressure of works and headache to execute them as well. So, our life on this earth is constantly undergoing evolution and, in some cases, we still feel the lack of latest technologies that will help us boost the pace of our life. With the evolution of latest technology, we are happy and comfortable with it until its random use, abuse or misuse results in bad effects by hampering our normal life. Hence, the scenario is not at all positive in terms of our living and values. Human values have been extremely hampered and affected by the current progress of science and technology.

SCIENTIFIC ADVANCEMENT: THE DEMAND OF THE TIME

Today, life seems to be competing with natural forces like sound, light, etc. as every human being is constantly moving here and there in search of something they want or in some cases unknowingly. They are hurrying to and fro, competing with themselves or one another to be the winner in the world. But if one of them is asked about his destination, he gets stuck what to answer, or what would be his correct response; it is common among millions of people because of their ignorance about their ultimate situation.

Now, the most essential requirement of time is to live happily and help our neighbours and the people around us to live happily as well. Happiness is the motto of our life, but different people define happiness differently. A poor leads a simple life with the bare necessities of life and his life yields much more happiness and satisfaction than that of a rich man because riches begets more and more riches become the firm conviction of the rich man, and hence he becomes restless to hoard more and more. This results in stress, fear of uncertain failure or success, and frustration in the end if he fails, and if he succeeds—he rushes more and more for the more. Thus, he leads his life through scarcity missing the feeling of satisfaction and happiness. In reality, a man thus struggles day-night in order to give the best standard of life as per his expectation to his family failing to enjoy the blissful life, losing the pleasant moments of togetherness, family and even children. But when he gets manages plenty of times, by then his next generation begins rushing with a load of responsibilities. Our life is sophisticated enough with the want of satisfaction.

HUMAN VALUES: THE BLISS OF MANKIND

The specific characteristics of humans are human values: respect, emotion, mercy, gratitude, etc. We have six senses to realise, feel, understand and even develop them and make our neighbourhood a comfortable place to live in. We have a great source of intellect to analyse and judge our deeds in terms of human values. But the fast advancement of technology and its gadgets have swallowed our brain and, as a result, we remain absorbing in them almost round the day, and we have with us hardly a little bit of time to think of our values. The faster growth has made us selfish, heartless, brutal and even loose commonsense. Today, our only and foremost aim is to achieve success at any cost—may be love, breech of family bond, life or happiness of other persons. But we have neither any sense of feeling our dignity nor carefulness to respect other's emotions or feelings that we encounter in course of our success.

IMPACT OF SCIENCE ON HUMAN VALUES

Science Devoid of Abstracts of the Nature

Man has won his dominant position on this earth by his command of science and technology, but he has failed to sense the abstracts of the nature and, as a natural result, he suffers and lacks them greatly. Man can develop his science and technology;

impart his intellect to his latest gadgets which can never mimic the natural living forms. Thus, science advancing faster on the contrary abstracts of nature is decreasing from humans in parallel. Today, we are surrounded by machines and machines, but lacking the values. Our brain has surrendered its freedom to the science and technology as they give us hassle-free life devoid of the abstracts of nature. We can explore the land, the water or even the space that is limitless and immensely vast, but we have neither power nor patience to explore ourselves, the self in us, where our values are dying out of our knowledge making us poorer and poorer. The crying need of the world today is the human values, not the so-called happiness and satisfaction, as the values, the abstracts of nature, are the treasure house of those feelings for which we are blindly hankering after.

Internet, the Boon of Science, the Consumer of Our Time and Energy

One of the mightiest inventions and gadgets of the current science and technology is undoubtedly the internet that attracts us, captivates us and consumes our quality time out of our knowledge. The charms of the inventions are really untameable. The days have gone when children passed their time with the old and their playmates. Now children often leave their assignments to enter the world of internet and enjoy the thing they want and hang out for hours together. The most popular social media, like Facebook, WhatsApp and Twitter, powered by the internet, are the only medium of spending time by chatting, exchanging SMS and videoconferencing with friends, relatives and even with strange people. This is the latest trend developed from young to old, and even to get their shopping, interactions, communications and the work tasks done through internet.

Our wishes of getting things done are bonded to machines, the gifts of science. We hardly do anything that does not need a machine. We wake up by the alarm of the clock, now mostly by alarm of the clock of our mobile phone, make our room comfortable by a fan or cooler or an AC, take exercise with scientific devices, get a bath hot or cool, cook food, press dresses, travel, work in office off-or on-line, and till we return home and switch on the television or turn on the computer, connect to the internet and go to bed. In a word, our days start and end with machines. We are lacking time for our family, friends and loved ones. In our mechanical life, we only suffer the unhealthy body and mind.

Deterioration of patience and elevation of exasperation in fast age

The scientific advancement has fastened and multiplied the pace of the world. We are in need of different gadgets and benefits that make our life comfortable and happy. Our endeavours to obtain all these make us move faster. But the science and technology move so fast that we are hardly able to move in parallel to them, and often could see the ominous. Definitely, this hankering is not a positive sign for the well-being of mankind. In this course of life, we are not only impatient, but we are losing also the level of our gifted emotions. All these as a whole, deteriorate our patience at the slightest concern, exasperate our power of elevation, and make our life miserable.

Science, the bearer of comfort, inculcates greed for money technology and highly sophisticated gadgets are behind our increasing demand of more comfortable and luxurious living, which also in return demands money. The luxury and comfort have charged us with the aim of hoarding more and more money, and encourage us always to run faster day by day. This run has no end as science and technology are providing us with their latest boons that allure us more and more. Under such circumstances, what we should keep in mind are as follows:

i. Nothing is lost, if wealth is lost.
ii. Something is lost when health is lost.
iii. Everything is lost the moment the character is lost.

But in today's mechanical world, we are really ready to lose everything for the sake of wealth, but why?

LIFE WITH OR WITHOUT SCIENCE AND TECHNOLOGY

Effect on Health and Hygiene

The byword goes, 'health is wealth'. But where is health and hygiene that keep us physically as well as mentally hale and hearty? Science has also snatched the natural process of keeping us fit as a fiddle in both those terms. The constant rush for money and wealth by dint of science and technology has been gradually deteriorating our health for the lack of exercise. As a result, we look out for the scientific devices in artificial or closed gymnasiums as a status symbol, instead of walking and jogging in the open grounds in the lap of nature where fresh air prevails. Particularly, these activities have burdened us with loads of stress and strain, and made our body the factory of new or artificial diseases which even science fails to help us fight or cure.

Education

Despite our extensive research in the field of education, the books till now deteriorate the power of our concentration. We have also forgotten the olden days of learning just by hearing. At the advent of the twenty-first century, we are about to lose the art as well as skill of writing as the widespread use of computers in this age of advanced technology has considerably replaced pen and paper with computers. As a result, the next generation is certain to lose another important art, writing. Moreover, the rate of literacy has, by this time, increased but few of us are able to make the best use of our knowledge. It is hard to feel that our trend of giving value to our art, culture and human values are at great risk.

CONCLUSION

At last but not the least, we should remind our past, learn day by day and undertake just measures at the right time to prevent the odds and ills of science and technology. We should grow and advance with science and technology, rectify our mistakes and blunders as well with an intense focus on human values so that the next generation might not lack the things we are lacking right now. We should not fall in the alluring trap of science and technology that mar our moral values. We must save and cultivate our moral values in parallel to the technological advancement with a view to the betterment of mankind. Both human values and science are need of the time, if we give up science, we cannot walk; and on the other hand, if we lose moral values, we suffer lots of stress and strain, and die every day.

7. Lure of Space: Unveiling the Obscure

INTRODUCTION

Man has explored land and water and discovered countless things, and still now has been carrying on this action. But space is always a never-ending attraction to the mankind. Since the discovery of science, man has been making the use of his science to explore the space in order to satisfy his curiosity. At the beginning of the twenty-first century, this is the most innovative field of study and research that lures and makes the human mind curiously jump into the vicious circle of the vast universe. Countless participants and students are enthusiastically joining the branch of Space Science and Technology and contributing their intelligence towards the goal of discovering more and more of the universe. This demands the expertise in physics, aeronautics, engineering, etc. Space exploration highly demands the corroborative efforts from all the fields to put in their best efforts for an effective result. Moreover, the space science is very lucrative, and has the chance of winning name and fame with the successful experiments. Petty knowledge we have gained about the space, while the vast unknown is lying in front of generations to come. These unknown and unexplored things also allure the inventors. The lure of space has the greatest opportunity to answer many unknown questions regarding the universe as well as the resolutions of major concerns of human beings, and to feel pride not only for the nation, also for the mankind.

SPACE EXPLORATION

Space is no doubt the storehouse of knowledge on facts and fictions. So space exploration has infinite opportunity to study, prepare hypothesis, carry out experiments and draw rational inferences that may be prospectively help mankind in ways. We do not know whether the space exploration may discover some other life forms primitive to earth.

At the beginning of the twenty-first century, we only come to know that the universe consists of many a galaxy, and the galaxy that we belong to is the Milky Way. We are in a system of the universe; we call it the solar system and we have not yet completely know about this system. Our exploration and research works are going on as usual with the aim of gathering more and more information about our neighbouring planets. Let us know only the brief highlights of the most significant research and exploration records:

1. 21 August 1957: **First Intercontinental Ballistic Missile** (ICBM)—R7 Semyorka; USSR

2. 4 October 1957: **First artificial satellite**—First signals from space Sputnik 1; USSR
3. 3 November 1957: **First animal in orbit (dog Laika)**—Sputnik 2; USSR
4. 17 February 1959: **First weather satellite**—Vanguard 2-NASA (NRL) 1; US
5. 7 August 1959: **First photograph of Earth from orbit**—Explorer 6-NASA; US
6. 14 September 1959: **First impact into another celestial body (Moon)**—Luna 2; USSR
7. 12 April 1961: **First human spaceflight (Yuri Gagarin)**—First orbital flight of a manned vehicle—Vostok 1; USSR
8. 16 June 1963: **First woman in space (Valentina Tereshkova)**—First civilian in space; Vostok 6– USSR
9. 20 July 1969: **First man to step on the lunar surface (**Neil Armstrong)—Apollo 11; USA
10. 1971: **First space station**—SALYUT1
11. November 1998: **First International Space Station;** Russian Zarya; USSR
12. 20 September 2004: **Three-stage Geosynchronous Satellite Launch Vehicle (GSLV**); India
13. 21 October 2008: **Chandrayaan-1: The Lunar Mission; Included a lunar orbiter and an Impactor**; India (ISRO)
14. 5 November 2013: **Mangalayan: Explore and observe Mars surface features, morphology**

EXPECTATION ON THE EXISTENCE OF LIFE BEYOND EARTH

Human curiosity and imagination is the founding father of science and technology. This curiosity can one day discover a lot of unknown things in the universe. As its intuition has been expecting life beyond earth is possible for ages, there must be something beyond our earth. We expect to be some form of life on Mars, but the matters remain unsure with regard to its practical existence. Based on our knowledge on solar system, we have only found some vague phenomenal evidences of life expectancy on Mars. Only earth has a surface, water and the gravitational force probably due to its iron content in its core which has a magnetic effect, while the rest of the planets have only a surface. The possibility of the existence and survival of life on earth is only for the biosphere—a combination of atmosphere, lithosphere and hydrosphere.

By the command of our science and technology, we are always curious to know life beyond earth and understand them. Maybe our science is a mere child to discover the unknown by exploring different galaxies far beyond the reach of our science. The living forms may vary, in terms of kinds and species. But they may be older or younger than ours, more or less civilised than ours.

UNIDENTIFIED FLYING OBJECTS

In the night sky or in some cases by day, some unidentified flying objects (UFO) have been seen in various places on earth. These facts are still under discussion whether they have any real existence, and if they really have, what they are. As these ignite the mythical ideas and stories told by the older ones, so inspire the space research works with the ray of hope for the existence of some kinds of lifeforms in the solar system or beyond it. Thus, we are fond of imagining that maybe those are the different form of living beings and have invented some different types of space vehicles and are exploring we are doing. Whatever these are, either myth or reality, will soon come to light by the command of our science and technology.

IMPORTANCE OF SPACE EXPLORATION

Space exploration has added an extra-edge in improving our lives on earth. Our forecast and foreseeing will be realistic based on our factual knowledge on the space and the happenings in the universe. We can combat many natural calamities effectively by knowing real reasons, and also can be safe gathering knowledge prior to the phenomenon. Our space research also focus on the following fields of studies:

i. Transmission and broadcasting of television channels
ii. Telephone calls, especially the mobile phone network, signalling—subscriber trunk dialling (STD) and international subscriber dialling (ISD)
iii. Weather forecast
iv. The frequency of Radioactivity used for frequency modulation (FM) radio signals
v. Marine industry—used for steering the boat using global positioning system.

Space exploration widens our expectation for gaining much more benefits on being successful in the endeavours by different researches. Space science and technology is very lucrative as well as accolade-achiever. So, most of the countries are greatly interested to carry out research works in this field of technology with the objective of gaining benefits and name and fame as well. We are not far away when our research and exploration will help improving the condition of our life on earth by various means and discovering the unknown to a great extent.

CONCLUSION

The current trends of research works and explorations on space and wide culture of space science are really a praise worthy adventurous endeavour. Our inquisitiveness fosters, our endeavours, are leading us far and far in the space. In course of these endeavours, we must not be indifferent to the adverse impacts on the life forms and environment on earth. We must follow sustainable methods while using the fuels for combustion and conducting other experimental works. We have to go on checking simultaneously the pollution index and other measures for controlling pollution. Needless to say, these innovative works have the potential to provide us knowledge to fill our curiosity, pleasure and a happy life in near future.

8. Cyber World: An Illusion

INTRODUCTION

Cyber world is the illusion of science and technology. The advancement of the science and technology encourages mankind to try to exert their proficiency in order to challenge the natural creations by means of the cyber world. The immensely great use of the internet, in current times, makes the mankind think it to be an integral part of their life. In this modern age, we are dependent on the internet so much that, without the internet our life will almost come to a standstill. By this time, we are unknowingly in the illusion of the cyber world which has only the entrance, but not the exit.

THE AGE OF COMPUTERS AND INTERNET

Reliance on the electronic gadgets like computers, laptops, androids, internet, etc. has made us dependent to them. It is very hard to imagine that a non-living component, popularly can be called the second idiot box after television, absorbs our quality time. The whole world is directly or indirectly has become the slave of the internet. The educated and the literate who use internet themselves are the active users, while the rest are the passive users as almost all the organisations, business enterprises, and governments and companies are constantly executing their work proceedings through internet across the world.

CYBER WORLD

Cyber world too has its advantages and disadvantages. It is like a star that is as attractive, hot and dangerous as a star that burns when anything comes within its range. As much it is beneficial as it is hazardous to people. People are well aware of the hazards of this advantageous technology that is hardly traceable by an average skilled people. It has the power to vanish the balance of your bank account within the little fractions of a second, and has been causing adverse effects on the human emotions and health. But, cyber world's service to the comfort of our life and living standard is incredible.

ADVANTAGES OF CYBER WORLD

Behind our latest sophisticated life, there is cyber world. Let us know the advantages of cyber world.

Social and Business Networking

Cyber world is a space where, everyone is living a networked life, and the business of the world stands on it. We have left behind the days when business needed huge infrastructure and a large sum of money in order to spread it throughout the country. Moreover, then it was restricted to the local circles. But in this age of internet and networking, business is completely dependent on cyber world which has enhanced the business spread worldwide by means of just a few clicks.

The social networking sites are the incredible blessings for the human beings. Networking has brought the world at your desk and helps you interact with anyone in any part of the world and also helps you to expand and promote your business.

Brand Building

Networking, moreover, has reduced physical labour and time as well for increasing sales and promoting business brands. Internet has proved to be the genuine medium for brand building. Today, businessmen are comfortable and happy with the internet as they are easily and simply executing their business from brand building to selling their products. Above all, internet is giving them cost-effective service.

Mobile and Online Banking

Mobile and online banking is another important service provided by the internet. Now, people solve their concerns of money transaction sitting at their desk comfortably and easily. People now go to banks and financial organisations only for some specific criteria for which their visit to the bank is a must. It has also decreased the pressure of the crowd of customers at any branch of a bank. As a result, the employees can now work freely and without stress and strain in the calm atmosphere of the bank.

Billing and Payments, Shopping, and Ticket booking

People could not even imagine a few decades ago, that they could shop different products, send and pay bills and book tickets of buses, trains and flights from their own home. It is the excellent service of the internet that has helped people save their invaluable time and energy, and ended the days of standing in long queues or going through crowds while shopping.

e-library with e-books

e-libraries with e-books have arrived at the readers table with the books after their choice. Book lovers now can collect and read more and more books they want sitting only at their desk. Many sites even provide reading samples free of cost. Now, we don't even need sufficient space in our study room for so many hard copies of books. We only need a computer with internet connection on the table and that is all.

The World at the Door

The next blessing that the foreign and overseas workers and employees enjoy to their hearts' fill is destruction of distance of communication and interaction. Chatting and video conferencing have brought the hearts so to each other that they even could hear their heartbeats.

Game Zone

The internet is the storehouse of the wide varieties of fascinating games for children and adults. They can be downloaded from any part of the world at any time through internet.

News and Publicity

The news through the internet reaches every part of the world within the fractions of seconds. The days of physical newspaper has gone. People get the update news from time to time. The publicity of anything can now be done very quickly, safely and genuinely to the large mass through the internet.

Entertainment

The internet serves a wide variety of entertainment. From the oldest to the latest, all kinds of music, movies and many more things can be watched and downloaded through the internet.

Education

The service of the internet in the field of education is immense. Education has diverse fields which has plenty to do through the internet. The cyber world has a wide range of information necessary for the students. They can gather knowledge from the internet.

Mobile Applications and Androids

The mobile apps and mobile internet has brought a revolution in the world. This advantage has enabled people carry the medium, in their pockets, by which they can do maximum works: speaking with people, listening music, watching videos, playing games, downloading whatever they want, remaining update with latest news of home and abroad, paying bills, booking tickets of modes of transports, transferring money and a lot more. In a word, the world is in the pocket by means of an android cell phone enabled with internet.

THE CHALLENGES WITH THE CYBER WORLD

Reduction of time and emotions

The internet hardly lets people to interact, move and pass some affectionate hours with family or kith and kins. Moreover, it has also made people forget the value of family, friends and relations.

Health

Cyber world is the cause of health hazards. From the early twenties, people suffer lifestyle disorders. The sedentary life is result of internet proneness and the cause of abhorrence to physical exercise. As a result, some new diseases take forms that cause many health hazards.

Hacking

Hacking is another dangerous and worst side of the cyber world. It involves great risks in internet dealings and transactions. Despite the security check at various levels carried out by the websites before processing the transactions, the hackers can break through the cyber security measures and carry out their operations tactfully and successfully.

Voyeurism: Voyeurism is another bane of the cyber world. The practice of voyeurism has spread widely with the introduction of the internet. In the social networking sites, porn videos and photos are easily uploaded, accessed and misused.

Dangerous to women

Cyber world is not at all safe for women. The gullible girls who are easily fooled through interactions in social networking sites like Facebook, Twitter, WhatsApp, Instagram, etc. often suffer the fatal consequences, and some cases they face even death. The cyber world is at the root of the rapid decrease of human values.

Freedom of Access

Cyber world has eased the access to the unwanted stuff into the young minds. Allured by the adventurous and interesting games, children are often facing death. Parents may allow their children to access internet for the educational purposes, but the adverse impacts pop-up every now and then, and divert the concentration of the children.

CONCLUSION

The cyber world is the world of illusion. It plays with give and revert policies. As it saves time, so it destroys the opportunities of pleasant moments. It provides us with comfort and sophisticated luxury, but destroys our moral values, and makes our life miserable. We could feel all the serious and adverse effects and consequences of the cyber world. But because of our too much dependence on it, we can get out of its charms and attractions. But we should not forget that human brain is the creator of this wonderful and incredible world. It has the power to control and destroy it in fractions of seconds. We should learn and practise the just use of the cyber world. We should enjoy the blessings of it and find out the genuine resolutions for the hazards that often create in our life as well as lifestyle. At all costs, we have to cultivate human values as usual, and restrict our stay in the cyber world.

9. Mars Orbiter Mission

INTRODUCTION

The launching of the Mars Orbiter Mission (MOM) is the second largest initiative by India after the success of the Chandrayaan, the lunar mission. MOM was launched on 24 September 2015. It collected a large data set acquired by all five payloads successfully completing one year of the mission life around Mars. On this occasion, a Mars Atlas containing a compilation of images collected and sent by Mars Colour Camera (MCC) was brought out by the Space Applications Centre of (ISRO) at Ahmedabad. Mars Global Data (MGD) had showed the clouds, dust in atmosphere and surface albedo variations, collected from its apoapsis at around 72,000 km.

INDIA'S MAIDEN INTERPLANETARY PROBE

Mars, one of the nearest planets to the Earth, has attracted people towards itself since the beginning of space research. Till the beginning of the twenty-first century, many unmanned orbiters, rovers and landers have been launched in order to reach Mars since early 1960s. The successful ones of these missions have sent a large numbers of data on diverse scientific aspects of the Mars.

The space research was revolutionised by the Missile Man, Dr. A. P. J. Abdul Kalam. Following his paved ways, India joined the club of space faring nations to explore Mars in 2014 by launching its first, interplanetary mission, Mars Orbiter Mission (MOM). It is also known as Mangalyaan. It reached the Red Planet at night on 23 September 2014, only two days after the touch of Mars orbit by NASA's Mars Atmosphere and Volatile Evolution probe (MAVEN).

Mangalyaan is a Sanskrit term meaning, the Mars craft. It costs India 73 million US dollars just a tenth of NASA's Mars mission Maven and took a record period of less than two years to design, build, and launch to its mission. Naturally, it was a matter of pride for the Indians.

INSTRUMENTS OF MOM

Mangalyaan carried five science instruments with a view to collect data on atmospheric processes, surface geology, surface temperature, morphology, and atmospheric escape process. These are as follows:

Mars Exospheric Neutral Composition Analyser (MENCA): It was capable of analysing the neutral composition of particles. This payload was adapted from Chandra's Altitudinal Composition Explorer (CHANCE) payload aboard the Moon Impact Probe (MIP) in Chandrayaan-1 mission.

Lyman-Alpha Photometer (LAP): It could measure the relative abundance of hydrogen and deuterium from Lyman-alpha emissions in the upper atmosphere.

Thermal Infrared Imaging Spectrometer (TIS): Its operation could be conducted both by day and at night, and could measure the thermal emission. It could also map mineralogy, surface composition and atmospheric CO_2 and turbidity of Mars.

Methane Sensor for Mars (MSM): It could measure methane, if any, in the atmosphere of Mars and map its sources.

Mars Colour Camera (MCC): This tricolour camera could collect and send images and information about the composition of the surface of the Mars.

INDIA'S PRIDE IN THE SUCCESS OF MANGALYAAN

The injection of Mangalyaan into the Martian orbit and its completion of some 120 orbits brought cent per cent success to India.

Undoubtedly, the Mars mission achieved the acknowledgment in the field of space science and technology also by the speech of US President, Barack Obama: 'India and

America are two countries that have reached Mars'. China too praised the success of Mangalyaan and terms it as the pride of Asia.

Previously, the United States of America (USA) tried to scuttle Indian Space Research Organisation (ISRO), but now it seeks joint venture in the space research and exploration. However, Mangalyaan helped get rid of the shackles and its success brought ISRO and NASA together to build and launch NASA-ISRO Synthetic Aperture Radar (NISAR) mission, an Earth Observing Satellite with the aim of studying climate change in the next five years.

The success of the maiden interplanetary mission of India, the indigenous Mangalyan mission, proved the capability and power to execute successful space research and exploration in near future. Consequentially, it has given extra-edge to the encouragement and curiosity of India's endeavour in the field of space science and technology and inspired to undertake next greater initiatives.

10. Cryptocurrency and Bitcoin

Cryptocurrency is a type of digital asset, which is medium of exchange in different types of transaction using cryptocurrency. This medium of exchange helps in controlling the creation of additional currency units. Bitcoin is an electronic coin was the first cryptocurrency which was introduced in the year 2009. Bitcoin is a part of decentralized and distributed digital cash system which is measure using the digital ledger known as block chain transaction database.

A Cryptocurrency is a digital currency that is secured by cryptography. The word 'Cryptocurrency' derived from the encryption techniques which are used to secure the network. A defining feature of cryptocurrency is that they are generally not issued by any central authority. Cryptocurrency uses decentralized control which means that they are not controlled by one person or Government. It is a form of payment that can be exchanged online. Cryptocurrency work using a technology called Block chain. Hence, Block chain is decentralized technology spread across many computers that records transaction. Bitcoin else is collectively known as an 'Altcoin' i.e., a combo word derived from "Alternative coin". Cryptocurrencies are a type of digital currency, virtual currency, alternative currency. The validity of each cryptocurrencies coin is provided by Block chain. A Block chain is a continuously growing list of record called Blocks, which are linked and secured using cryptography. It is directly transferred between peers and the transaction are confirmed in the public ledger. After bitcoin numerous other cryptocurrencies have been created. Day-by-day cryptocurrency are gaining popularity they provide lower entry barriers, privacy protection, caused effectiveness. Every transaction is transparent, autonomous and secured. Cryptocurrency have gained significant transaction over the last half decade. At present there are around 969 cryptocurrencies in across the globe. Despite these advantages cryptocurrencies face criticism for a number of reasons including their use of illegal activity, exchange rate volatality and vulnerability of the infrastructure underlying them. It is denounced in many countries due to their uses in gray and black markets.

Some advantages of Cryptocurrency:

- It is a cheaper alternative compared to other online transaction.
- You can only access the own part of cryptocurrency via digital key.
- Payments are safe and secured.
- Funds transfer between two parties will be easy without need of third party like Debit, Credit, Government, and Banks.
- It is helpful for a country that has weak economy.
- Funds transferred are completed with minimal process fee.
- Protection from payment fraud.

Some disadvantages of Cryptocurrency:

- Payment is not irreversible.
- Rate of crypto currency are very volatile.
- Prove to be threat to official currency and monitory system.
- Crypto currencies are not accepted everywhere.
- The almost hidden nature of cryptocurrency transaction makes them easy to focus on illegal activities.
- Black market activity takes place.
- High volatality and potential of large losses.

The most common way of earning money from cryptocurrencies is buying coins such as Bitcoin, Ripple, Litecoin, Etherum and many more, wait until the value rises. Cryptocurrencies are now come under the regulatory net in order to check misuse. Japan has become the first country to regulate cryptocurrencies.

In India recently, the Government of India announced to introduced a bill, cryptocurrency and regulation of official digital currency bill 2021, to create a sovereign digital currency. In India the funds that have gone into the Indian block chain startups accounts for less than 0.2% of the amount. The top cryptocurrencies in India are:

- Bitcoins (BTC)
- Cosmos (ATOM)
- Tron (TRX)
- Binance coin
- Dogecoin (DOGE)

The top 5 cryptocurrency exchange apps in India for online trading are: -

- WazirX
- Coin DCX
- Zeb pay

- Unocoin
- Coin kuber

Types of bitcoin wallet in India 2021

- Bitcoin mobile wallet
- Web bitcoin wallet
- Desktop bitcoin wallet
- Hardware bitcoin wallet

However, in 2018-19 budget speech by the Finance Minister announced that the Government does not consider cryptocurrency as a legal tender. In 2018, RBI banned all the functions and entities which is related to the sale and purchase of cryptocurrencies. In 2019 July, Government completely bans on all cryptocurrencies and also said to implement new rules to fines and punishments for violations of rules. As per the cryptocurrency and regulation of official digital currency bill 2021, The Indian government want to create an official digital currency to be issued by the RBI and also prohibits all the other private cryptocurrencies in India. Although cryptocurrency transaction is taxable in India in cases where the person earning such gains is an Indian tax resident or where the crypto is said to be domiciled in India. However, the need for a new policy arises as the recommendations by a committee headed by former finance secretary Subhash Garg, to impose a blanket ban on digital coins is now outdated, the report said. The new panel is likely to examine the working methods to operationalize the RBI proposed digital rupee. Moreover, RBI raised multiple concern about cryptocurrency and waiting for government decision.

The future and the further success of cryptocurrency depends upon the way regulatory frame work. Different countries have approached in different ways so the regulatory environment remains uncertain. The Government will have to take considered steps, given the risk from possible use of cryptocurrency in terror financing, tax evasion. Despite all risks, the encrypted technology in cryptocurrency can prove to be an asset for the financial market place. Most countries are opting for a regulation on cryptocurrency rather than banning it.

ESSAYS ON HEALTH AND MEDICAL ISSUES

1. Sedentary Lifestyle: The Cause of Health Problems

Sedentary lifestyle, unquestionably, is the reason behind most of the health problems. It is a very slow lifestyle almost without any physical activity. Cyber world is also accountable for creating countless sedentary jobs that increase the sedentary lifestyle.

People sometimes follow sedentary lifestyles as per their choice and, in some cases, situations lead them to do so. The nature of jobs, however, needs to one to sit for eight to ten hours at a stretch. As a result, people drive back home, or return by other vehicles and instead of unwinding the day's stress and strain in open grounds by walking, jogging or taking some exercise, mostly they pass time sitting in front of the television. Cyber world add to this injury. It has brought the world home and provides all sorts of comfort and amenities of sophisticated life ranging from paying bills to shopping and many other laborious activities. We may not realise it, but these casual habits of stay sitting on a chair or lying on a couch for hours are the causes of many health hazards.

A research on lifestyle in Australia, in January 2010, reports that 'each hour spent watching TV is linked to an 18 per cent increase in the risk of dying from cardiovascular disease, perhaps because that time is spent sitting down'. Now, this has reached almost an alarming situation and demands urgent attention. It is unbelievable that human beings evolved as walking beings, and their brain children have made them glued to seats for hours together. In the past people roamed about and explored the world on foot. But today, their lifestyle has changed greatly.

There is no medical remedy for the diseases and health hazards caused by sedentary lifestyle. The only way out is to adding physical or laborious activities as many as possible every day before or after the sedentary office work or homework to prevent and gradually cure such disease. Morning walk as well as morning exercise keeps one active throughout the day. Some form of cardiovascular exercise, at least for five days, also plays a remedial. Yoga is a unique exercise which can keep us hale and hearty both mentally and physically not for days but for years. Self-motivation and self-discipline are the indispensible parts of our life which enable us lead an active lifestyle.

2. Stress: A Major Concern of the World

INTRODUCTION

Stress, in the recent years, is the household name of kind of physical condition which is considered the creation of modern hurry and lots of pressure of works and unmatchable ambitions, and cyber world is also considered as the passive factor of this widely known word of concern. Stress is anything that poses a threat or challenge to our well-being.

STRESS: POSITIVE AND NEGATIVE SIDES

Stress does not always pose negative effects in our mind sometimes, it helps boosting our morale or performance. It also makes us dynamic and performing best in our respective fields. For instance, the pressures of exams do not pose stress on students; rather it helps in exerting their best and results in outstanding performance. Strangely enough, without any stress we even suffer boredom, and our existence would seem futile.

STRESS: ITS ADVERSE EFFECT

However, we suffer stress only when the intensity of it goes beyond the capacity of our endurance power. It starts interfering with our mental as well as our physical health, and creates psychological imbalance.

SITUATIONS: STRESS AND EXCITEMENT

The probable causes of stress are varied and many. Same situations or incidences cause stress in some people while, in others simultaneously become the source of excitement or pleasure. There are different reasons behind such cases. For instance, a speeding bike may be a source of great excitement for a person while another person on the same bike, at the same time, may be afraid of the high speed or the possible danger.

CAUSES OF STRESS

The work pressure, busy schedules, peer pressure, health issues, personal relationships, financial problems and various irritants like noise; sometimes unpleasant people are also the causes of stress.

TYPES OF STRESS

Steps to control or relieve must be taken at the prime time as it can pose severe effects on one's health and even, in some cases, causes death to the person suffers. Some of the most common effects of stress on our heath are: hypertension, diabetes, herpes, insomnia, multiple sclerosis, etc.

Stress is sometimes considered accountable for suicides, family fights, marriage breakups, road rage, and violence.

CONCLUSION

We should, therefore, identify the factors and probable causes of the mental conditions that are behind our stress. Then, we must take appropriate steps to control or get rid of the stress. In this case, the sooner is attempted; the better it is for our physical as well as mental well-being. William James is praiseworthy in this regard for invaluable word, 'The greatest weapon against stress is our ability to choose one thought over another'.

3. Passive Smoking Harms More

INTRODUCTION

'Smoking is injurious to health' declares the statuary warning on the cover of a cigarette packet. Then, both active and passive smoking is harmful for health. Again, survey reports declare that passive smoking is more harmful than active smoking. So, it is better and high time that smoking should be banned, simultaneously should be strictly enforced. The cover of a cigarette packet also declares the statuary warning: 'Taking tobacco causes cancer' with cancer affected picture of lungs. All these attempts have failed. Still, the number of smokers is increasing. What are the healthy and probable reasons for the proneness of smoking from young to old irrespective of ladies and gentlemen? However, active smoking affects the health of the passive smokers i.e. people around the smokers. It is the major concern for the world. As it is more injurious since it cannot be controlled. Because of smoking, the entire atmosphere of a certain area becomes contaminated and therefrom the health hazards of non-smokers start getting affected.

SIDESTREAM SMOKE: THE DANGEROUS ONE

The smoke comes from the burning end of the cigarette is known as the sidestream smoke which is inhaled by the passive smokers. The combustion at the burning end of the cigarette at lower temperature releases the half burnt chemicals, much more carcinogenic in nature, into the atmosphere. Moreover, the smoke containing tiny sized invisible particles easily percolate deeper into the lungs. Hence, passive smoking is much more injurious, and seriously affects the lungs than active smoking.

IMPACT OF PASSIVE SMOKING

'Passive smoking causes lasting damage to children's arteries, prematurely ageing their blood vessels by more than three years', declared the research report prepared by a constellation of medical experts and was broadcasted by the BBC news on 4 March 2014. This is the startling fact and cannot be overlooked and ignored. By endangering our children's health, we are leading the whole mankind to great risk.

NATIONAL MEASURES

The failure of the State and Central Governments are leading the nation to danger. So, the governments should formulate more strict rules on banning smoking along with punishments in relation to criminal acts and successfully implementing them. Simultaneously, the programmes and campaigns on mass awareness should be frequented with short intervals.

GLOBAL MEASURES

Exposure to passive smoking is very injurious to health is the widespread scientific consensus. Moreover, World Health Organisation and other organisations across the world are becoming increasing vigilant concerning the matter. The Governments of 168 nations have recently signed and 174 nations have ratified 'The World Health Organisation Framework Convention on Tobacco Control'.

CONCLUSION

The initiatives are positive and widely praiseworthy. Growing awareness along with such initiatives at national and international levels are sure indications for the eradication of this dormant violence. The mass should be made aware of precautions from their end, for instance, standing far away from smokers in public places, or forbidding the smokers to smoke in public places, etc. These simple and small steps can certainly provide safety. Right to a healthy environment is the fundamental right and smokers should not be allowed to avail it.

4. Covid-19 Pandemic

Covid-19 pandemic which is said to have emerged from Wuhan (a city of China) has caused a serious impact worldwide. World Health Organization declared it as a global pandemic on 11 March 2020. India reported its first case on 27th January 2020 in Thrissur (Kerala). People were forced to stop travelling. An unexpected challenge was faced by people globally. Whole world faced a drastic downfall in GDP Rate.

A developing country like India had to face many downfall and challenges during the ongoing Covid-19 Pandemic. Decision of Lockdown was taken by Prime Minister Shri Narendra Modi. The first lockdown was implemented on 22nd March 2020. Industries, factories, were shutdown. School, college, premises were closed. The whole market (except essential services) were shutdown. The nation faced never happened challenges to employment, health, food system, education, economy and lots more. There has been a heavy loss of human life worldwide. Millions of people lost their loved one.

There had been a dramatic fall in cash flow of aviation and tourism sector. The tourism sector served approx 43 million people in FY 18-19 had to face downfall during pandemic year. India is the 3rd largest energy consumer behind USA and China and contributes to 52% of global oil demand. The lockdown across the country led to slowing down in demand of transport fuels. Due to shut down of factories and industries millions of people were at the risk of falling in extreme poverty. The service sector employees were allowed to work from home. There had been significant change in the demand of telecom and broadband connection due to work from home. Online classes demand had been increased by about 10%. Pharmaceutical companies witnessed 144% growth in sales of hand sanitizer in 2020 as compared to 2019. The rise in demand of mask and sanitizer resulted in rise of pharmaceutical companies. Unfortunately, like other countries, India faced an economic downfall and contraction in GDP rate. Moving from economy, the impact of pandemic had been witnessed in education sector, school, college, universities are conducting exams online. Moreover some sections of students are being promoted on the basis of previous performance. These have lessen the fear of exam among students. This many led to lack of knowledge.

World bank in a report has titled 'Beaten or Broken Informality and Covid'. World bank had said that there will be a long-term impact on the productivity of students of this generation. Moreover shutting down of school and college and shifting traditional class to digital platform is affecting the mental health of students. Online classes was something for which no one was prepared for. However in a developing country like India not every house has an access to internet. As a result learning has become tough for many kids. There are several problems which students are facing specially in their young age and adolescence. Due to closed premises of school and colleges children are less exposed to other environment and extracurricular activities which is must for their development. Online classes created a gap between the students and teachers. The major factor affecting the mental health and peace of children such as lack of proper schedule, less interaction with friends, social isolation may lead to long-term personalities issues and lack of self-motivation like students, children also have some emotional need that sometime parents fail to acknowledge them. The need of how parents should interact more and more time with their children. They should engage them in extracurricular activities. They should manage to boost the confidence in their children.

There are some other sections of people who faced hardship during pandemic. Some of them are daily wage workers, migrant worker, delivery boy, cab driver. During shutdown the industries and work place, lockdown imposed in whole country there workers had to deal with loss of income and daily need to survive. Due to low income they were forced to work in unsafe condition exposing them and their families to risk. These workers depend an earning on daily basis. They barely have saving for emergency. Millions of workers who worked on daily wages faced high level of who were not able to survive in that situation moved to their respective villages. The struggle was not over yet. As a result of lockdown whole country and lack of transport facilities, they were forced to walk bare foot towards their village. Many of them walks miles with their child and pregnant wife.

There is a proverb "Tough time are great teacher" the Covid-19 pandemic taught us many lessons of life. It taught us the importance of saving, importance of our loved ones and many more. People are more concerned towards hygiene and cleanliness as compared to earlier time. Though social distancing created a gap in social life. We got closer towards our family members. It has been witnessed a large drop in crime rate in National Capital. In addition to it, there are many other positive effects of this unfortunate pandemic outbreak. There had been gradual decrease in pollution especially in air and noise pollution. Air is clear and environment is greener. People got some time to relief from their busy schedule. We got time to spend with family members which is priceless. We got enough time to learn new things and boost our hobbies. Although we were digitalized earlier, we have become more familiar with digital world now. The greatest lesson we learn is humanity. This many be an action of reform for India as well as whole world.

Covid-19 symptoms are very common like fever, dry cough, and breathing problem. Apart from this symptom like fatigue, muscle pain, and loss of taste and smell. Prevention of covid-19 are washing hand regularly with soap or sanitizing hand regularly. Avoid unnecessarily outing on public places. Maintaining a social distance of at least 6 feet. Also maintain proper hygiene and cleanliness. Avoid touching your eyes, nose and mouth and main thing wear mask conclusion. Coronavirus is one of the severe issue that are facing by people around the world. It is necessary that we come out of this situation as early as possible. So people should stay informed and maintain good hygiene. Togethere we all can bring an end to this unfortunate pandemic.

5. Nutrition During Covid-19 Pandemic and its Impact on Health

Proper nutrition is one of the most essential elements to being healthy and living a long life. What we eat becomes our diet and our diet plays a major role in deciding how wealthy and healthy we are. Without proper nutrition our body cannot carry out the function what it needs to perform. A healthy diet promotes healthy growth and development and also helps to maintain a healthy body, reduces risk of chronic disease.

Nutrition is the process of consuming, absorbing to receive adequate, appropriate nutrition people need to consume a healthy diet. Which consists of variety of nutrients. There are 7 main elements that body needs they are protein, carbohydrates, minerals, vitamins, fiber, and water. Nutrition is the physiological and biochemical process by which an organism uses food to support its life. It includes ingestion, absorption, assimilation, biosynthesis, catabolism, and excretion. Nutritional deficiencies result to chronic diseases. This is the condition where, there is an inadequate supply of essential nutrition. So diet should be taken in balanced way to avoid diseases. People from different age group require different diets because their dietary requirements vary with the activity they perform.

Health refers to the absence of deficiency, illness, diseases. One can be healthy if they get all the nutrients that body need every day. A healthy person has a strong immune system. Proper nutrition is one of the most important ways to become a healthy person. Certain nutrients prevent the condition that makes healthy and make immune system strong specially they are Vitamin C and Zinc that supports our immune system.

The Covid-19 pandemic is pausing severe threats to health and economy. Covid-19 is caused by specific coronavirus (SARS- COV) i.e. severe acute respiratory syndrome.

The outbreaks of SARS demonstrates how coronavirus affect can be when they cross the specific barrier and infect humans. Symptoms of Covid-19 is fever, cough, respiratory syndrome, shortness of breath, fatigue, sour throat. To cure and to relax to some extent with this disease, one needs healthy pattern of eating optimize the function of immune system, improve immunometabolism.

Nowadays, with so many people falling ill from the coronavirus, unhealthy diets are contributing to pre-existing condition that put them more at risk. Covid has many visible impacts both proximal and distal. But one of the silent and invisible crises got effect on malnutrition. To fight with this problem, the government has prioritized addressing malnutrition through the Prime Minister, scheme for holistic nourishment (Poshan) abhiyaan which updated guidelines announced in January 2021. The focus is on the 1000 days between a mother pregnancy and her child's 2nd birthday, addressing their nutritional deficiencies through fortification and provision of take home rations. Poshan abhiyaan also emphasized the importance of data driven approach to plan and manage delivery of nutrition services. The Government of India has now clearly said in each district to setup a district nutrition committee, review progress, and take appropriate action if needed.

Good nutrition can reduce the likelihood hood of developing other health problems, the food should avoid during Covid-19 is snacks which is high in salt and sugar, limit the intake of soft drink and sodas instead of this choose fruit juice specially fully loaded with Vitamin C. Drink enough water, eat green vegetables, eat moderate amount of fat and oil. During Covid-19 pandemic, the nutritional status of individuals has been used a measure of resilience towards destabilization. An adequate intake of Vitamin A, B12, B6, Vitamin C, Vitamin E is essential for the maintenance of immune function. So a balanced diet is needed which guarantee a strong immune system which can help withstand any assault by the virus. Also a vitamin C is one of the major vitamins which tends to make a strong immune system. Daily recommended dietary allowance for Vitamin C is 90 mg per day for men and 75 mg per day for women. Eating nuts like almond, walnut, pistachio is also a beneficial in this time. The high rate of consumption of diet high in saturated fats, sugar, refined carbohydrates can contribute to the prevalence of obesity, diabetics and could place these at the risk for severe Covid-19. However peripheral inflammation caused by Covid-19 may have long-term consciences in those that recover, leading to chronic medical conditions such as dementia. Thus people should focus on healthy foods thinking as top priority. Data suggest that minorities have increased barriers to access healthy food choice and nutrition education due to increased rate of poverty. So governments have duty to take care of there health and should provide healthy food to them so that they cannot face the problem of malnutrition and also government should keep addressing that generation should not suffer in future for this present pandemic.

Hence a proper diet can help to ensure that the body is in strong position to fight the battle of virus.

18

ESSAYS ON ETHICAL AND MORAL PRINCIPLES

1. Discipline is Success, Anarchy is Ruin

INTRODUCTION

'Discipline' bridges goals with accomplishment, while absence of disciple i.e. 'anarchy' brings chaos and uproots the widely acceptable and healthy goals. Discipline helps us realise our dreams and goals in the healthy and amiable ambience, while indiscipline or anarchy destroys our calm, peaceful and progressive environment, and prevents us from the course of happiness and success. Anarchy is at the root of oppression, exploitation, violence, sorrow, misery and unhappiness. Self-discipline tames our lusts and desires, while anarchy makes us slave to our lusts and desires, and ultimately jeopardises our life. The word 'discipline' comes from 'disciple' (a learner or follower of a teacher or guru) which is originated from the Latin word, 'disciplina' meaning 'instruction' and 'knowledge'. On the contrary, 'anarchy' means lawlessness or indiscipline. Originally, it is originated from the Greek word 'anarkhos' meaning 'without a ruler'. Anarchy keeps one or a nation in extreme chaos or lawlessness which often leads to destruction. Anarchy snatches away our normal balance between work and our goals, as well as destroys our human values.

IMPORTANCE OF DISCIPLINE

Discipline has immense importance in our life. Discipline is teaching and training obedience, self-respect, and other sets of required skills, rules and knowledge through a systematic way. It is the foundation of the whole universe, without it nothing is practicable even the creation of the world and subsequently diverse lives on earth would not have been possible. When the universe will lose discipline, it will be in anarchy and definitely come to an end.

So, the inculcation of discipline is a must from very childhood. Talents and greater ideas blossom in a disciplined person, not in an undisciplined one. Discipline is behind the all-round progress and prosperity of a person as well as a nation. Discipline is, therefore, essential in all walks of our lives. The earth revolves around the sun following the universal discipline. Certain discipline is in the lives of animals, birds and insects. So, to keep peace, progress and prosperity in social, political and economic dimensions, we must maintain discipline. In family, society, educational institutions, public and private offices, games and sports, army, transport and communication, discipline predominantly plays the vital role. There lies discipline behind the accomplishment of success in our life in any field. Without discipline a person cannot live or even do his work well.

SELF-DISCIPLINE AND ITS IMPORTANCE

The inculcation of self-discipline is a bit hard. Self-discipline means to govern oneself by controlling lusts and desires—both good and bad. In broader sense, it means to always keep one's awareness and conscience active, which helps one to take right decision at the right time. The waning of self-discipline among the young people often leads them to lots of social crimes as well as evils. As a result, they are deviated from the main course of social lives. The lack of self-discipline also ruins human values in the young people and leads their lives to darkness and at large out of their knowledge. This problem is one of the major concerns of the world. The lives of eminent persons of diverse fields like, Albert Einstein, Rabindranath Tagore, Mahatma Gandhi, APJ Abdul Kalam, Bill Gates, Steve Jobs, Mahatma Gandhi, Milkha Singh, Sachin Tendulkar, Shahrukh Khan, are founded by stern self-discipline and hard-work. Life in their sense is, 'ninety-nine per cent perspiration, one per cent inspiration'. Even in our everyday life, we see many glamorous celebrities of various professions in newspapers, news headlines or sometimes in stage shows. If we glance at their lives till that time, we discover that their lustre and accolade is founded by perseverance, hard-work and steady endeavour charged by their self-discipline day-night. Success is not a magical action; it is rather the outcome of self-disciplined diligence for years. A person can accomplish such luck lustre success, only if he inculcates self-discipline from the very beginning of his life. Our self-discipline largely determines our success. That is why children are advised and encouraged to start their life with a combination of varieties of work along with their studies. Cultivating hobbies they like, playing outdoor games and sports, taking exercises, yoga and practising meditation, practising awareness, judging things and actions by their human values, passing time with superior ones, following news, pursuing their studies, and above all obeying their superiors. The combination of all these activities in the routine life of a child helps him blossom his potentials and leads him towards the goal he has posted. To maintain a routine life, one must inculcate self-discipline.

ANARCHY AND ITS ADVERSE IMPACTS

On the contrary, lack of discipline is anarchy which is considered the greatest evil of mankind. The slightest loss of our awareness and indifference to discipline give birth to anarchy and from that very moment it begins gradually prevailing in our life by hoarding unruly elements of our life, even tempts us to those for transitory happiness and comfort. This result in complete loss of discipline, then anarchy rules our life by making us slave to our lusts and desires. Anarchy also destroys our moral and ethical principles, and being blind to our lusts we turn ourselves brutes. We ruin our lives unknowingly as well as mar other lives in the society. Our activities will then appear just in our own viewpoints, but in reality we only go on doing one after another misdeed. Such cases of anarchy in a human's life often come out in the news headlines. The respective countries then highlight these cases with legal proceedings for mass awareness.

Similarly, anarchy in a country means the situation of lawlessness or political disorder when subordinates and leaders do according to their own intensions without the rules and regulations of the country. A democracy like India too was threatened by its dangers in the period of emergency in late 1970s. There was a possible situation of anarch during the tenure of then Prime Minister Mrs. Indira Gandhi. However, before it could assume its massive form, a new government was formed timely within a few years. Anarchy makes people unhappy and becomes the cause of their uncertain life full of worries and threats day in and day out. For instance, during the capture of a country by its militant groups there prevails a situation of extreme disorder and chaos as we have seen in cases of Iraq, Afghanistan or Sudan in recent years. The consequences of anarchy are violence, suffering of the mass from oppression, exploitation, injustice, eviction, threats and a lot more. The anarchists in such situations think themselves the lords of their lands, but ultimately they are punished, or lead a perilous life.

IMPACTS OF DISCIPLINE AND ANARCHY

Nations like Union of Soviet Socialist Republication (USSR) or Russia, Japan, China, etc. have witnessed the fruition of rigorous discipline over years which led them to success in accomplishing social and economic development. On the contrary, nations like Iraq, Iran and Libya have experienced a great social, economic and ethical loss for the anarchists. The redundancy of anarchy on individuals as well as on nations has proved repeatedly that people must ensure that they learn the art of discipline for better social order, peace, progress and prosperity.

CONCLUSION

There is no alternative to discipline that can help people transform their life from adversity to prosperity, from ignorance to renaissance, and above all, to achieve far better social, political and economic developments. It also promotes people as well as nations towards perfection. Contrarily, anarchy halts all mighty positive forces and deviates people and nations to worse situations. In every realm, discipline appears to be a shackled habit, and in some cases seem difficult to inculcate, but its fruits are very sweet that set up the foundation of greater accomplishment, growth and development and above all, the throne of wide acclaim. It also leads a man to live in deeds not in years.

2. The Paths of Glory Lead but to the Grave

INTRODUCTION

This is the 36th line that occurs in the ninth stanza of the poem, 'Elegy Written in a Country Churchyard' by Thomas Grey, the eminent British professor and poet, renowned for this poem. Thomas Grey has artistically threaded the words into a garland which provokes a deep sense and leaves a grand message to the mankind. The quotation implies that people, from all walks of life, who accomplish pre-eminence and glory by heroic, generous, reforming and redressing activities either by their talents or by exercising power over the mass will end in the grave. So, they should not boast of themselves by exaggerating their transitory impression and influence over the mass. With their death all these will efface from the memory of the poor.

GLORY

The word 'glory' appears to different people with different meaning, but in the broader sense, it implies the success or accomplishment. People feel and realise the glory of any achievement which is hard-earned and hard-obtained and worth-rewarding and appreciable. In any sphere, achievement requires talent and efficiency charged by diligence, perseverance and a lot more sacrifice and strenuous activities.

PATHS OF GLORY

The very phrase, 'Paths of Glory', reminds us the bravery of the soldiers in the battle fields. They confront and combat the challenges posed by our enemies, and defend our nation as well as save from the dangers by sacrificing their lives for the sake of our security and safety. Their chivalric deeds indicate that those are certainly the paths of glory.

The phrase has, however, no narrow limited sense; rather it has broader sense that means the heroic and stout deeds in all walks of life. Every person struggles throughout his life to achieve something he/she has posted as his/her goal in life. There are also many people who eat to live but do not do anything for the well-being of their fellow citizens. In both these cases, we face great difficulties in our everyday life, just to meet the bare necessities of life like, food, shelter and rest. Some people live to eat and only think of the means of gathering their food, while the others concentrate on their performance and their duties. People have growing tendency to work for wealth, pride, prestige, dignity, name and fame, property and much more. Aims and objectives in life vary from person to person. The Path of Glory implies the paths people follow and stick to till they accomplish their targeted goals.

Glorious paths lead to grave, and our paths of glory have mainly two contradictory outlooks, which are defined as follows:

POSITIVE OUTLOOK

Some people who consider the paths of glory with their positive outlook always feel confidence and bravery, and hardly care for the obstacles that appear in course of their life. They proceed ahead with great enthusiasm and courage and lead an uncertain life full of dangers and perils. The pace of our life decides our destiny, i.e., as fast people march towards their goal and achieve it ultimately, so the glory of their success follows them even after the end of their life. The honourable soldiers and leaders do the same thing.

NEGATIVE OUTLOOK

The same extract means differently to some other people. People hanker after the materialistic things like money, wealth, etc., or they stick to gaining the abstracts like power, popularity, etc. to find their glory. Their glorious life makes them satisfied and proud, but even with that glory, one day they go the grave; so there is no cause of being proud of this transitory glory. If we observe the lives of people around us, it will be very clear that people with ambition go through various hazards of their lives and often are found in stress and strain. There are also some people who do not care for money and wealth; rather they are much careful of the abstracts like love, affection and care and enjoy their lives to their hearts' content. But the ambitious people stick to their by sacrificing even many moments of joys and happiness. As a consequence, they suffer sometimes from serious diseases which often hasten their lives to the graves.

Though, the glorious people are successful to meet their goal, to fulfil their desires and wants, they fail, no doubt, to enjoy the pleasant moments in their life. So, they can hardly value the priceless things like love and affection.

CONCLUSION

The ambiguous words or extracts are difficult to decide in this mundane world. People with negative attitudes are growing faster and create a negative atmosphere in their circle. It is high time that we should try to create and value the positive aspects that this extract hints at by adding the varieties of life: time to get together with kith and kins, friends and other near ones, enjoying our pleasant moments in eternal sources of happiness—the wonders of nature.

3. There is Nothing Either Good or Bad, but Thinking Makes it so

INTRODUCTION

William Shakespeare, the magnificent observer of human behaviour and nature, discovered the key to destiny of mankind as well as this world, and artistically presented it for the coming generation in his specific creation 'Hamlet' (Act. 2 Sc. 2 at page 11). In course of conversation with Rosencrantz and Guildenstern, most intelligent and perspicacious Hamlet uttered the above extract.

If we think and observe even our own activities and their results—good and bad, successful and unsuccessful, well and woe till now, we will discover that everything happened and are happening on the basis of our decision and perception. Our thinking process has two opposites: one that ushers in healthy and favourable outputs is known as positive or good which always keeps us active and encourages us stoutly and confidently undertake one after another action or adventure, while the other results in unhealthy and vulnerable outputs that jeopardise our lives is known as bad or negative. Our positive thoughts and decisions, the output of our thinking, always lead us to growth and improvement while the negative lead us to perils and dangers. This power makes us decide the good and bad based on the human values we own. Our conscience, awareness, knowledge, experience, love, hatred, and other qualities influence us greatly in course of deciding the status of anything. It is natural or God gifted. Only human beings avail this opportunity out of the six senses that God has given all living beings in this planet. We have won the dominant position on this planet by the command of our thinking that has helped us develop our science and technology over time.

SHAKESPEARE'S ELABORATION

Shakespeare was once asked to elaborate the above extract. He replied intelligently, "A man cheerfully observed a religious fast seven days a week. His neighbour starved to death on the same diet".

This very statement makes it clear that our perspective and thinking work differently in a same situation. A thing appears differently to different people. We differ in our thinking, behaviour, acceptance, grasping, mannerism, and reactionary power to a stated situation.

In our head there are two functionaries: Brain and Mind. Brain is analytical while mind is persuasive. There occurs a conflict between our brain and mind, when we take decisions upon a situation. Our ability determines our strength to win over this persuasive mind by making decisions especially based on the output of our analytical mind. Interference of our mind in our activities proves our inability to decision making power. Shakespeare is also considered a wise psychologist who founded the background for psychological therapy formed in future. The modern 'Cognitive Behaviour Therapy (CBT)' has been developed on the very idea of the thought process that determines things good or bad. The above extracts prove that Shakespeare had the power of keen observation and intellect.

INFLUENCE OF FACTORS IN THINKING PROCESS

Human morals, preconceived nature and external factors greatly influence our thought and perception. All these factors intermingle in our head together. We can hardly trace the process that goes on constantly in our practical life. Our life is what our thinking produces.

HUMAN VALUES

Human morals play crucial role in our thinking process. These are our inborn qualities while we acquire some other qualities since childhood. Our fundamental learning remains subconscious in our mind but comes out naturally through our reactions to different situations. Our reactionary power is hardly discernable which comes out in fractions of a second. Our mind reins our intellect as the mind processes the perceived information with regard to its understanding and then stores into our subconscious mind. This has no relation to our practical perception.

The proverb, 'Where there is a will, there is a way', elaborates the significance of the will power that has the capacity to help a man come out any difficult and invincible situation. This willpower is generated by our positive thinking. It energises and encourages us to constantly look for the genuine solution for the prevailing stiff situation. It generates hope for life and makes us feel its importance. This power also charges our sinews and revitalises our lost and defeated power and even leads us to success. It is, therefore, our positive thinking process. Our ability is moulded by our perception and understanding. For instance, we can call a half filled cup as 'half empty' or 'half full'. This is our response that the analysis process of our brain gives on the situation. Our positive and negative notions reflect themselves automatically through our regular expression of words and behaviour both consciously and unconsciously. Again attraction to a thing varies from person to person. For instance, the rose has thorns; still people like to pluck the rose while a few dare not pluck it. Why?—The formers are charmed and captivated by the beauty of the rose though conscious or unconscious of the thorns, while the latters though captivated by its beauty, dare not pluck it because they find the thorns risky.

INFLUENCES OF NOTIONS

The act of processing information is carried out by our mind before storing it in the subconscious mind. The understanding once gets settled into our mind becomes a notion. This notion highlights the exact situation instead of providing any scope to our healthy intellect to analyse the situation, in case we perceive anything in a similar altitude.

We are excelled in creating the best out of odd circumstances; still in some cases, we surrender to circumstances. But we can definitely control our thoughts if we try. Again, we give uncertain time to any matter for our brain to analyse and carry out the details without any fit of immediate reaction. Thus, we can create the 'good' out of any stiff or negative situation. However, it is not an unhealthy situation; it is rather our reaction which determines our outlook and mindset for life.

SITUATIONS OF THE SOCIETY

Society has immense influence in the process of our thinking. Man is a social animal. He is always fond of living through sun and shower in a society. This society plays significant role in his life; every moment it creates diverse situations before us. These situations make different people act, react and perform differently. In some cases, the society makes us accept a situation that seems adverse or negative to our life because either it is accepted by the majority or it is a custom based one. Such situations create depression in our mind as we are by heart and soul against the situations. Depression is nothing but our silent reaction to the situation that we cannot accept as true, good or positive. Mostly it is actually our negative judgement on the situation and in that case it is better we change our mindset. A depressed mind begins to expect the negatives or impracticable to happen and this expectation leads the good moments of our life to the worst. This unhealthy state of mind is dangerous to our normal life as it fails to acknowledge the bright sides of life and in reverse it tries to discover the bad in the positive. Thus our thinking entirely changes the course of our life and jeopardises it by snatching away all its good moments and happiness.

EVERYTHING IS SUBJECT TO CHANGE

Change is the law of nature. As day alternates with night, the opposites: good and bad; sun and shower; success and failure; rise and fall; up and down; joy and sorrow; adversity and prosperity constantly changes with each other. It is eternal. Nothing can come out of the mighty clutch of change. So, there is no reason to be worried or depressed with the point appeared negative in life. Cheerfulness begets happiness and energises us to proceed afresh. A smile on our face can energise us and others too and even give them power to face the adverse situations as we know every cloud has a silver lining. One can enjoy the enriched flavour of gentleness provided he has ever experienced the feelings of 'bad' anytime in his life. The process of our thinking too is transitory positive alters with negative. We sometimes call things bad in comparison to some good old ones. The same situation can be considered good provided we can logically compare the situation with some worst ones, though not from the experience of our life.

CONCLUSION

'Good begets good, not bad', should be our mindset. We should have tolerance enough to accept that our thinking is behind everything we act, react, enjoy and suffer. Body is the engine while thinking is the driver. So the driver should be always aware and attentive to the road the engine is moving along, but neither on its truck that it left behind immediately nor on the passengers it carries. A veteran driver is always aware of his duty, so he can drive the engine along the good and bad condition of the road steadily and safely. On the contrary, a careless, unaware and inattentive driver very often faces accident the road is either good or bad. Consequently, he blames the condition of the road instead of blaming himself. We, therefore, simply develop the habit of judgement, for instance, the road is neither good nor bad, the driver is good or bad. A good driver drives well and safely goes miles after miles while the bad driver faces accidents after accidents before covering even a mile. We should always concentrate on the process of our thinking, not on the situations time presents in course of our life.

4. Tolerance of Dissent is the Base of Democracy

INTRODUCTION

'Democracy' in Abraham Lincoln's opinion is 'of the people, for the people and by the people'. It is the sole objective of the democracies across the world. As a result, in the democratic ministry there are representatives from diverse background and of course with different objectives and mind-sets. So, there must be tolerance of dissent as it is crucial to the democracy. 'Dissent' and 'tolerance' are two integral part of democracy, except these the democracy cannot exist.

The word 'Democracy' is originated from the Greek word 'demos' which implies 'the people' i.e. the whole population of a country, especially the adult population. Practically, the entire population or the collectivity consists of a large number of individuals as a unit. No two individuals in a collectivity—either mechanical or organic—can be alike, since their requirements and aspirations vary even with regard to their physical and mental compositions. Obviously, their views, beliefs, notions and habits are dissimilar and yet the concept, rule and practice of or by those people, however disparate, are significantly acceptable and much in existence.

REASONS FOR THE EXISTENCE OF DEMOCRACY

The philosophies and ideologies of politics as well as religions have successfully hold human beings together in different parts of the world for ages, both by their advantages and disadvantages, and also by their strict laws of punishment according to the interpretation in their constitutions and holy books respectively. Some of the rules are unchangeable as they are the decrees. A democratic constitution is in fact much more significant than a writing on a piece of paper since it conceives of the cultural and moral loyalty to certain values that the law of the states incorporates. Citizens interact in their daily lives to the work procedures that are led by the power of this meta-juridical ethos. This principle is the sovereignty of each individual as well as the sovereignty of individual political judgement. The majority of the people are meant by the phrase, 'by the people' and the entire population execute what the majority decides. But it does not mean that the majority is entitled to dominate over the minority; rather the enthusiastic cooperation of the minority and the protection guaranteed to the rights and freedoms, and tolerance of—though not in agreement with—the views and beliefs of the minorities help the democracy thriving. As a result, there may be people with different thinking from the ideas of the majority and official ideas. Dissent offers an alternative to the existing ideas, institutions and system, and prevails even in non-democratic systems. So, dissent is not a negative concept.

IMPORTANCE OF THE EXPRESSION OF DISSENT

During the dominant and established principles of the Soviet Socialist Republics, Boris Yeltsin's views that expressed dissent are worth-mentionable. People often voiced their dissents against the monarchical government of Nepal. Though the decision of the government is taken by the majority, in a healthy and working democracy, the minority voice against it and their dissents are considered by the majority. Debate and discussion make the air transparent as well as create a situation of compromise and despite the opposition there exists a certain amount of accommodation.

People will be dissatisfied and raise growing anger provided the positive phenomenon of dissent is attempted to subdue. Subsequently, this resentment would result in the revolt against the established system and a revolution would break out causing violence, bloodshed and destruction. Therefore, in the larger interests of democratic setup, it is much better to tolerate voices of dissent with a view to ventilating pent-up feelings and different views. However, extremes of dissent can jeopardise democracy, so the permissive limit of dissent is fixed. People enjoy freedoms of expression, association, economic pursuit, belief in political, religious and other matters, etc. in a democracy. These freedoms of an individual or a group of people, however, are restricted so that they may not be the cause of injury to another individual or the collectivity, or may not even affect the social or national fabric adversely. All possible measures are taken against fascism and is not allowed a little room to grow although people passionate to apply it as an alternative to the existing democratic government system. So, anything that goes against democracy is against people too. Hence, the dissent of people must be checked as the most vulnerable aspect of democracy is freedom which makes people avail its advantage and ultimately overturn the existing system by controlling the voice of dissent that goes against them.

REASONS FOR THE EXISTENCE OF DISSENT IN DEMOCRACY

There are two vivid sides of dissents: Inter-party (that is, one party against another) and intra-party (that is, within the same party) in the domain of politics. Despite the principles and the particular modus operandi, sometimes, the members of the same party express their guaranteed dissent against the malfunction of the leadership or taken decisions that appear to be inappropriate based on the situations. Then these cases should be immediately controlled by strong hand by the top leaders, and must be restricted within the party-platform not allowing it to be public, otherwise the party will get an authoritarian image among the mass or split into bits which is not at all yielding to the party. Democracy, similarly, permits the foundation and continuation of political parties with diverse views. The several modus operandi of the democracy allow parties to express their voice of dissent; moreover, the system itself leads the parties not to allow any strong party attack and subdue the weak because the strong party always aims at suppressing the weak and subverting the system, and also has tendency to establish its own dominance which has the maximum chance of destroying democracy and giving birth to dictatorship. In case of Indian politics, it was seen the political parties showing an intolerance of dissent and either breaking up by themselves or the people being forced to experience a bitter period of authoritarianism. In 1969 and 1977, the Indian National Congress Party broke several times and it resulted in the authoritarian emergency rule in the country from 1975–1977. But today, the tolerance of dissent in the Congress Party leads it to remaining united and controlling the unrest among the members in different times. The existence of various parties like Rastriya Swayamsevak Sangha (RSS), the Samajwadi Party (SP), Bharatiya Janata Party (BJP), the Communist party and other national and regional parties plays a major role in Indian democracy to allow the successful existence of the tolerance of dissent in different situations. In a democracy, people enjoy the freedom of choosing occupation and economic pursuit in order to earn their livelihood. As a result, there are various occupations and this variety may cause dissent rise, especially in respective of the macroeconomic policy. For instance, some may speak deliberately for mixed economy, others liberalisation or capitalism while a few others voice in support of the socialistic approach or nationalisation. These diverse dissenting views must be given a patient hearing, though not supported from the official viewpoints. This response shows the respect for these diverse viewpoints which encourages official spokesmen as well as ministers to clarify or in some cases even to modify policies and programmes with the intention of facilitating a broader plan of action. In a democratic society, it is common that a group or class may vary in respect to its form and pattern from the majority. But the majority should not intervene in that form or pattern, or even resort to value judgements. Each and every form and composition of any social group is comfortable with its members, and in case of any outside forcible attempts to bring changes would certainly destroy the aim of democracy. It is against democracy to ask some ethnic groups like a group of Kerala or the North-East to change its matrilineal form of family with the issue that it does not follow the practice of mainstream. The value of democracy will be marred if any group tries to impose their social norms upon other. In this regard, 'Live and let live' must be the fundamental motto of democracy.

The world has diversity in the dimension of culture. India too is not an exception; rather it is a multilingual and multiethnic country. Some of the cultural groups are smaller minorities and as a result, they may seem to others as backward or ridiculous. In such cases, instead of making fun and keeping them in the same status, we should respect them and undertake measures to improve their standard. Temples, mosques, churches and gurudwaras are the sacred shrines where God is believed to exist are of equal value to their respective religions. So, a person from any group cannot vilify or utter demagoguery words against any of these shrines because it will hurt the religious sentiments of the stated religion and break the favourable norms of democracy. The freedom of speech can then be valued in the democratic sense and enjoyed by people. Based on the nature and philosophy of a democracy, it can be deduced whether its people are enjoying democracy where the dissent is discernable in its absence.

Freedom to dissent, pluralism and tolerance are limited by the constitutional morality of democratic society. The constitutional democracy guarantees the legal freedom to each individual challenging its fundamental principles. Since the constitution defends the right to dissent, the citizens as well as the society must maintain civil sentiments that help developing the social fabric. Tolerance and moral limitations of individual freedom are essential to the ethos permeating democracy itself and centres round the individual as a predominant wealth which denotes necessarily Socratic habit of the mind. The person in its main focus is simply a rational agent moved by preferences as well as an individual to ask for explanations for the obedience owed to the laws of the state. Contemporarily, democratic deliberative institutions are founded on the premise of free debate and their training to the public's free will and judgement are widely appreciable for the free flow of ideas and pluralism of information, and above all through freedom of alliance and the right to express personal views. The democratic citizen is called upon to argue using his own knowledge to vote as an individual as well as in solitude, to cooperate and interact with others, to change his or her mind and then change it again. Ultimately, the democratic citizen is asked to come face-to-face to those in power. Democratic deliberating institutions are predominantly formed in order to educate citizens gradually so that they can make out that they are able to change their mindset and give value to their right to question authorities and enquire why they should obey or share or believe. They can also render accountable to those who in their name govern or perform their duties in the parliament.

The sovereignty of individual judgement justifies that democratic government is the government by debate and the fixed point which holds democratic society together, and it does not need any discussion regarding its acknowledgement. The sovereignty of individual judgement is also the principle of private morality as well as a value giving democracy its own ethical specificity. In a word, it is neither a metaphysical rule nor an abstract principle; rather is the gradual acquisition of civilisation and inherent to human history in its fundamentals. It is, thus, deeply rooted in the depths of the psyche as it were a commonsense or moral garment.

As in the democratic society, there exists the relationship between individuals as the symbol of codification relationships of equality between different people, the value of individuality gains moral legitimacy and judicial. It is demonstrated in two forms: Ethical i.e. as feelings of cooperation and partiality and legal form i.e. as the right to political and social equality as well as individual freedom. These two dimensions comprise democratic moral constitution which pervades and orients the deliberative competence of the citizens in a representative democracy. In the same time, it preserves political and legal order from the fundamentalist propensities of the powerful and conceited majorities and anti-egalitarian tendencies which are grounded on the economic and corporative interests.

The sovereignty and dissent of an individual are inextricable within a democratic society because of the anti-authoritarian or the reactive role of the majority to power of dissent; self-culture being a public and private virtue for individuals and the Socratic kind of democratic ethics. Dissent is a constitutive virtue of democracy as the base of democratic legitimacy is reciprocal respect of ideas, consensus and autonomy of judgement. Dissent strengthens favouritism and cooperation between citizens instead of eroding the social ideas like authoritarians and conservatives. We are aware that beliefs of individuals and commitment are strengthened by dissent and a free public discussion as we discuss about our favourite things linked by bonds deeper than rational principles and assent. Moreover, dissent reveals a primary loyalty to a community, society or country. Even a religious community based on the compliance to principles and no option to appeal the hierarchy, an interpretative authority, like the Catholic Church, preferably allows active and spiritually effervescent believers instead of apathetic and passive believers.

Dissent strengthens the acceptability of majority rule as a means for taking decisions on the basis of acknowledgment of the equal unreliability of citizens and on the contrary, diminishes the inclination to cultural uniformity fundamental to democratic society. Equality to review opinions and decisions is similar to acknowledge none as infallible and demanding irrefutable opinions. There is no serendipity in Albert Hirschman's definition. The attitude of those attempting to 'win an argument rather than listening and discovering that one can at times learn something from others' as that of someone with a susceptibility for authoritarian rather than democratic policies.

CONCLUSION

Dissent does not indicate undermining or disharmony; rather it humbly acknowledges every decision that can become the object of revision, even accepted and voted by a vast majority since the foundation of democratic measures is opinions of the people not the truth. The unique form of government is democracy which is devised with a view to yielding a constant process of the amendment of laws or decisions taken without endangering the stability of civil and legal order. Hence, dissent is at the base of decision-making process and is one of its fundamental elements. In this regard, John Stuart Mill can be supported that 'formidable evil' is not in 'conflict between parts of the truth', but instead in the 'quiet suppression of half-truths'. However, the critics of democracy have often stressed on the conservative temptation of the political model, where the principle of the sovereignty of individual hardly endorses the ideal of a harmonious society rather a society that learns how to synchronise dissent using methods for solving conflict through a free debate instead of using force. Tolerance of dissent, last but not least, is the foundation of democracy in all dimensions.

5. A Man is the Product of his Thoughts; What he Thinks, he Becomes

INTRODUCTION

This statement by Mohandas Karamchand Gandhi (popularly known as Mahatma Gandhi) precisely connotes the statement by William Shakespeare (in Hamlet), 'Nothing is good or bad, our thinking makes it so', and the proverb, 'Man is the architect of his own fate'. If we try to discover the themes of these extracts, we find that they mean the same thing in a little roundabout way. However, these quotations stoutly encourage us to give up the blind reliance on the theologies of God and completely depend on ourselves, to be realistic and logical while confronting the barriers of life, day in and day out. The fact is that our destiny is nothing but the complete output of our thinking process and the subsequent actions based on it. Our thinking and decision together is the predominant driving force of our life, health and hygiene, career, future, well and woe, prosperity and adversity, everything of our life. We make our life heaven as well as hell based on our thinking process. Positive thinking always yields positive outlook, awakes our indomitable dormant will power, and generates iron determination to move forward with unflinching ambition to accomplish something that we long to obtain, whereas the negative thinking makes our life miserable, destroys our potential, replaces our strengths with weaknesses, gauges out the power of our self-reliance and injects blind beliefs, makes us the slave of the belief of God—the word that greatly influences the human life-process on land.

IMPACT OF POSITIVE AND NEGATIVE THINKING

'Alas, I live in a hut while my neighbours are residing in a palace! I suffer in sun and shower, no food, no bare necessities, not even a bellyful meal. The mud walls break down in monsoon, then nowhere to stay. Oh, God, how can I survive!'.

This statement only focuses on the penury of the person and how he wastes his time and energy on thinking about his survival in his badly off situation. Whereas his neighbour, of the exact status, cried out in utmost satisfaction, 'Wow, I have a hut to live now. This is more than enough to live more days with a shed over my head. But my neighbour lives in a palace—no doubt, it is the fruit of the sacrifice of his forefathers or his own. Oh God, I'm very happy with it, but from this very moment I begin discovering the genuine means to build a royal palace to the rest of my life'.

This statement certainly demonstrates the poor person's prosperity, happiness and indomitable willpower that make him dream to live in a royal palace one day.

'I could not pursue higher studies; I cannot even understand these work processes. I'm weak and feeble, my hard days will never end, and my life is in great danger'. This should be rather far better to state, 'My studies are nothing but the means of gathering knowledge and building character, there are diverse walks of life, there many various careers, it does not even if I do not make out this work process, I cannot do manual labour; it does not mean that I'm not fit to do other works. Who said, I suffer from poverty. Nicholas James Vujicic, the born tetra-amelia syndrome, became a world class motivational speaker. He has no legs and hands, how can he won the world. I've hands and legs and even some education. I've great potential. I've to discover the way-out; I'm sure one day I will definitely find out the solution. I've gone on trying in other fields of work'.

'Where there is a will, there is a way'. No thinking based on any stiff situation, no exit. Our positive thinking gives us motion, grows hope and leads us according to our thinking and belief. It even gives the true taste of life. On the contrary, negative thinking makes us static, breaks the backbone of great potential and compels us live the life like a creeper till we die. Helen Adams Keller was deaf and blind, yet she mastered the skills: Reading, writing and speaking, and also reign over the world. Sudha Chandran with her artificial leg cheered the stage after stage. What was in them? They were led by their positive thinking not the God's grace. He who waits for God's grace dies in hunger, lives in primitive age. There are countless instances across the world, who believe and prove that 'we're handicapped by our negative thinking not by birth, or devoid of any limbs. These are our situation to awake our dormant mighty and magical power to fulfil our heart's desire'.

FRUITION OF OUR THOUGHTS

We, therefore, think always to discover the keys to overcome the stiff situations in our life, not wasting time suffering the worries, pains and pangs as well as the bear the stress and strain posed the prevailing miserable situation. Deep analysis of our misdeeds or misery deteriorates our health as well as the valuable time that is ready to help discover the silver lining in the prevailing cloud of hard-time. We should cheer up and resolve to compensate the loss little by little. That very resolution will awake our magnificent magical power.

So, we say 'I can finish this project within due date, coming across any difficulty in handling this project I need my senior to guide me', instead of saying 'sorry, I cannot do this project'.

TWO EXTREMES COMMON TO ALL

Be sure that good and bad, strong and weak, virtue and vice, adversity and prosperity are the natural fundamental components of each and all on earth. As there are day and night, there are strengths and weaknesses in every one of us in this world. Moreover, 'to err is human being', 'no man is perfect in this world', still there is nothing that invincible to man. Man has discovered his knowledge, applied it to his best and now is the lord of this planet. There is neither magical nor God-gifted power that has helped human being from time immemorial, but positive thinking and stern and stout decision to execute the work leading towards the goal by patience and perseverance. Just simply think 'if I don't sow a seed, how can I reap the produce'. Again sowing is not the be-all and end-all, we have to take specific care so that the plant may grow and help it in its course by all necessary means till it bears rich fruits. Negligence of a little moment may destroy or harm, or even stunt its growth, then the fruition too will be late.

CONCLUSION

Come what may, what you believe will become one day. The germination of a seed tells us that the seed has life potential; had it no potential, it could not germinate. You, therefore, have certainty and potential to be so, so there rise a thought or belief or even the imagination comes in your mind. Nothing but our knowledge matters, it does not mean the bookish knowledge; rather it is the knowledge that shows you, in vision, the probable way-out from your misery or the trouble you are suffering from. The factors that help shaping us in the form or pattern we deserve are our love, discipline, punctuality, and iron determination, steady methodical and strategic course with necessary infrastructure, dedication, patience and tolerance that keep our ambition and will power fresh and up-to-date. So, think and think; hope and believe the best; and discover the shape you like to be in the next days, and at once put yourself into action, since we know well that 'life is action, not contemplation'.

6. I Object to the Violence Because When it Appears to Do Good, the Good is Only Temporary; the Evil it Does is Permanent

INTRODUCTION

Non-violence generates no-violence and ultimately in the long-term sense, promotes peace, progress, prosperity and heavenly harmony, whereas violence stirs and instigates more and more violence that poses threat, horror, tension, colossal waste of life and property, animosity, in some cases even complete destruction. In this regard the statement and stout step in his life course in worth mentionable. Gandhiji made the above statement in the crucial time during the freedom struggle movement of India, which reflects his supreme surrender and worship to peace and peace process because he felt and knew the consequences of it in the core of his heart. Violence gives temporary gains and sense of victory, but in the long-term sense it has adverse consequences, the destruction and great damage at large in social, economic and ethical spheres.

NON-VIOLENCE AND ITS SIGNIFICANCE IN THE HISTORY

The history of India has witnessed many immortal worshipers and propounders of non-violence; some upheld the means by understanding its power by heart while a few by means of their self-led violence. The magnificent ones who conquered the world are Lord Gautam Buddha, Mauryan king Ashoka the Great and Mohandas Karamchand Gandhi. The Mauryan king Ashoka taught himself practically by his self-led annihilation of hatred bloodshed in the Kalinga war. By dint of his mighty clutches of power, he turned the vast kingdom of Kalinga into graveyard packed of corpses and carcass. The vast Kalinga was gasping in emptiness at the edge of Ashoka's strong sharp sword. That war taught and overnight reincarnated king Ashoka into Ashoka the Great. He destroyed his sword, gave the policy of hatred warfare, and took up the policy of peace and love that had been established by Lord Buddha. He promulgated the concept of Dhamma i.e. the policy of non-violence. The latter policy established his kingdom in the heart of mankind while the mighty wind of time wiped out the former.

Current Indian history also reflects some instances of violence that led to huge loss of lives and property and stunted growth and development and life process are the Repression of the Rebellion of 1857, during the Partition of India in 1947. There are countless instances of violence that led almost destruction. The vital ones of them are the First World War, the Second World War, and the latest violent operations in Yemen and Libya.

The consequences of violence are also witnessed in social backdrop. Physical abuse of children hinders their physical and mental development, perils their potential, and endangers their lives making them exposed to alcohol and drug abuse. In India, often comes out the incidents of ruthless violence on women in the news headlines as consequences of the patriarchal mindset. The worst of all violence in current India is the perpetuation of caste system that exploits and represses the innocent ignorant Indians as well as deprives them of their birthrights. Since independence innumerable communal riots, major or minor, that have been breaking out every now and then in India mar the peace and communal harmony and damages on life and property. The ruthless suppression of the riots of tribal people for demanding their fundamental rights also result in great damage.

CONSEQUENCES OF RECENT VIOLENT ACTIVITIES IN AND AROUND INDIA

Recently, Naxalism and terrorism are mighty challenges perplexing our policy. Violent modus operandi at times fails. Violent operations against Maoists have unintentionally caused the loss of lives of local people. Laws like Armed Forces Special Powers Act (AFSPA) have withstood their utility by causing more damages than advantages. In this respect, anger of people is seen in the areas where AFSPA is imposed. The success acquired through anti-terrorist laws by the act like Prevention of Terrorism Act (POTA) and Terrorist and Disruptive Activities Act (TADA) are also hotly debated as well as controversial. The neighbouring countries like Sri Lanka obliterated the Liberation Tigers of Tamil Eelam (LTTE) through a destructive war in 2009, which resulted in a large scale violence and the suffering of the displaced people and in the creation of permanent wedge between people of two communities Sinhalese and Tamils. The colossal violence in Bangladesh post-war crime trials have come up at cost of the loss of thousands of lives simultaneously grew targeting the minority.

SUCCESS OF NON-VIOLENCE

The dhamma i.e. the non-violence policy brought peace and progress in the Empire of Ashoka. The all-round measures of Ashoka led to the considerable success, he could do by this policy what he had failed to execute by the sharp edge of his mighty sword. The glorious history of his kingdom is the bright instance of the non-violence.

Other instances are Champaran and Kheda Satyagraha, Indigo revolt in Bengal (1859–60) and Pabna Unrest (1870–85), where the non-violent movement accomplished remarkable success.

India got independence largely by means of non-violent movements though, many diverse methods of movements were executed.

In the post-independence period some non-violent movements like Chipko Movement, a forest conservation movement, Dongria-Kondh Resistance by tribals against bauxite mining were successful by means of non-violent protest.

Nationalist Socialist Council of Nagaland-Isak Chishi Swu and Thuingaleng Muivah (NSCN-IM), after the struggle of 37 years, is on the march to obtain a state. The recent die-hard activities by NSCN-IM have created confusion and chaos in the region.

CONCLUSION

Gandhiji observed, realised and encountered the consequences of an eye for an eye. So, he remained firm in the policy of Ahimsa i.e. non-violence. He thought of the vast success long-lasting result instead of the petty transitory victory attained by violence. Needless to say, the results of non-violence leave no scope of doubt or dissatisfaction; rather they become the driving force of peaceful process of life on earth. It is, therefore, high time the entire world should mitigate their violent feelings and think and judge deeply on the impending consequences of the world, for which they are planning to execute operations they are preparing. Non-violence has no alternative to solve each and every problem or stiff situation the humans encounter in their day-to-day life across the world. Violence is brutality, while non-violence is humanism.

7. The Weak can Never Forgive, Forgiveness is the Attribute of the Strong

INTRODUCTION

Forgiveness and vengeance are the words that lead our heart and soul to two opposite dimensions: Destruction and prosperity. Forgiveness has the magical power to mitigate the hearts and souls of two rivals as well as instil immense peace in their minds, whereas vengeance mars both of them and only results in violence, restlessness, and makes the lives hell. Vengeance, in some cases, leads to bloodshed. Forgiveness is the strongest power that helps a man forgive anyone for his mistakes or even crime, while weakness is the worst means of the weakest who himself is neither safe nor confident of his security. So, Mohandas Karamchand Gandhi, the father of India, said, 'Forgiving is the attribute of the Strong'. Precisely, forgiveness leads us to peace and progress, while vengeance takes us back to terrible and restless past events and keeps us lingering on those things that bleed our heart incessantly, and even blocks our humanistic progress of mind. Vengeance is the worst power of the weakest, out of humanity, strength and security.

STRENGTH AND WEAKNESS

In reality, it is difficult to forgive the person who harmed us anyway. Our strength of mind and courage always help us to stand up those who hurt and try to denigrate us. None, but the weak people are offended and hurt with any derogatory remarks or activities of the offenders. Weakness makes us lead uncertain, worried and vulnerable life as we always suffer and miss our strength and security. As a result, it is impracticable to bear and forgive those who harm us any way. On the contrary, strength makes us confident to solve or destroy at any moment, so there is no question of any such feeling; rather it generates feelings of forgiveness towards the culprit.

Strengths broaden our heart while weaknesses wrinkle our heart and make it narrow where there nourishes narrow-mindedness, narrow ideas, thoughts and feelings. While strength broadens our heart, helps open our hearts to all irrespective of status, caste, creed and religion, makes our heart immense like the vast endless universe where there everything grows peacefully. Only then does it become able to hold greater human values like mercy, forgiveness, generosity, kindness and charity and above all, love.

The weakness of our heart bears the means of violence, malice and hatred and forms a vicious circle that makes us more and more violent. Since the day of our independence struggle till now, the communal riots that have been happening in different parts of our country at different times manifest our weakness, not our strength. The sole reason behind this unrest and disharmony is the narrowness of the communities. They are the victim of their petty and narrow ideas that are not at all fit for humanism and philanthropy.

CONTEXTS OF CRIME AND SIN

It does not, however, mean to forgive a criminal, and let him go on doing one after another crime; it is rather our weakness, fear for life. The matter of retribution and rehabilitation of criminals largely depends on their crime. Punishment should be the first treatment, then comes the matter of rehabilitation, chance of reformation as it is crucial to bringing harmony, security and solidarity in the society.

'An eye for an eye makes the whole world blind', said Gandhiji. This attitude keeps us without benefits and fruition, simultaneously results only in damage and loss as taking revenge, neither benefits nor brings peace on either side. It is, however, not always just to forgive some offender, especially who commits a sin. In this regard faith in humanity is important to judge and decide to forgive someone. This faith comes from assumption, which assures and makes you believe that the sinner's act will be an instance to others to commit something offending the same race. The assumption also may be that the sinner will now begin to change himself or even be a changed individual, he will repent of his sin and resolve to reform himself radically for the sake of his own life, his community as well as the human race. It also seems that raging for revenge is far more impractical and inhuman than forgiving someone, but it practically depends on the level of crime or sin in relation to the exiting conditions and situations.

The Dadri case is an epitome of the rising intolerance among the communities instigated by various other social factors which help increasing spread of intolerance between each community because of coexistence in the web of dissatisfaction due to a broken ground past. Bringing peace and progress in such social situations, it calls for the initiatives undertaken by the government and non-government organisations along with the persons from either community enlightened and practising broader humanistic senses, rather narrow communal feelings and interests. Then comes the matter of forgiveness for creating better and greater feelings among them.

CONCLUSION

However, recent proceedings of activities show a different scenario. The committers find it easy to avoid with crimes by just plead. Money and influence have replaced regret and guilt. It is high time to draw a line of demarcation between the acts of forgiveness and improvisation.

8. Being You

INTRODUCTION

It is immensely easy to get lost in the rise and fall of life forgetting ourselves and our purpose. There are thousands of attractions and repulsions that can easily divert you to different paths and ways of life. In all confusion and mystery, we are haunted by the questions: 'What is my purpose? Who am I? Why am I in the way I am now? Am I doing what I love and enjoy? Have I found my life's objective and meaning? Am I happy and contented with, who I am right now?'

BE YOURSELF

The absolute necessity is to be you; rather it is not a mere choice. You have to find out that inner position in your life where you can live and grow peacefully and certainly. The discovery of your true identity relieves you of all the unnecessary strife and struggle you are undertaking day night.

The purposeless and meaningless life always bears pains and pangs and sufferings, there is no sign of peace and comfort. Life is an uncertain long and painful journey to who still has not framed out what they want to be and do. Each and every moment reminds them of their uncertain identity. They are haunted by the strangeness of their daily experiences.

The first and foremost question you have to ask yourself is: Who am I and what is my objective here? Some of us often avoid such questions that do not give any immediate answer to our problems. Only those who have gone through their life without asking any such questions realise the importance of getting to the core of their beings and living from there.

Life is what it is supposed to be; it is neither beautiful nor ugly, neither good nor bad, neither this nor that. The only problem is that very few people are interested in life; rather they are interested in money, comfort, recognition, success but very rarely do they explore the fundamentals of living.

Being you is a crucial assertion of your personality. You are the sole symbol imprinted on all your experiences. Once you discovered your identity, you will understand everything happening around you. A constant and steady pursuit of your objective is to discover the key that makes life a grand adventure. The ways of living is grander than succeeding or failing which are simply matters of statistics and opinions.

CONCLUSION

Whatever you do: Ask a question, understand, argue, fight, love, care, explore, etc. the ultimate aim of life is a quest for your grander self. Remain indifferent to the responses of the people to your ideals and your ways. They have no idea about your reality. What they know about you is just their point of view. Try hard to discover the diamond in you and stick to your course of adventure from the core of your being, let your personality grow and shine out in the midst of the darkness of commonness and crudeness. Do not let that light of your uniqueness die. The grandest gift to you from God is you and there is no experience grander than being you.

9. Faith versus Reason

Faith and reason looms large in our life. We often get confused on: What is the most essential thing for a successful, happy and peaceful life?—faith or reason? The age-old argument between faith and reason is—which one is the right way of living?

Faith and reason play a very important role in our daily living and in course of our decision-making. The debate between faith and reason is not a philosophical one; rather it is a very practical aspect how we organise our life and the way we want to live it.

Faith is a way of believing in the passage of something through the ages as right. It is the way of considering a set of rules as true and final. It could be about either wearing certain clothes, eating certain foods, visiting a temple, or even our other habits.

Reason is the process of questioning mind to logically enquire and understand the meaning and essence of the something told or said. In reasoning, we apply commonsense in matters of faith and belief. Reason is a scientific and argumentative method of knowing more about ourselves as well as surrounding.

A young mind attempting to make sense of our world should understand the difference between reason and faith logically, if not taken in conflict. Our faiths on traditional things and beings come down as a system from parents to parents. Children always want to lead a lifestyle of their own choice on the basis of their reasoning which assumes a conflict.

The only means to bring resolution is to accept both faith and reason as two very different dimensions of life. There are innumerable situations where reasons fail, and faith succeeds; on the contrary, where faith fails and reason succeeds. The difficulties we encounter in our everyday life because of our ignorance of justly and rightly applying faith and reason. We often use reason by questioning on certain primary beliefs such as religion, God, tradition, etc. without being aware that they are merely a matter of faith. Simultaneously, we apply lots of traditional blind beliefs and faiths in the matters requiring reasoning and logic. Reasoning is a short term analysis of a situation for understanding its impact, but faith is a durable viewpoint on the whole meaning and objective of life. Logic is moving step-by-step carefully and awarely least you fall down. But faith is to believe that there is a usual path throughout the course which has no cause of accident or falling down.

The precisely logical mind can achieve many things; it can obtain wealth, gain accolade, even can live a luxurious life, etc., but hardly with meaning, happiness and fulfilment. On the other hand, a mind completely relying on faith finds peace of mind, certainty and happiness but hardly with wealth or success. The most ideal combination of life is a precisely logical mind blended in a faithful heart. Your realisation must find that reasoning is the quality of the mind while faith is the quality of the heart and that is the foundation of resolution to all your day-to-day difficulties.

10. Your Identity is Your Attitude

Attitude, in reality, is your true identity. But your misconception is that your talent and capabilities make the world recognise you. Your success or failure depends on your efforts, actions as well as your attitude i.e. how you look at the world around you, and how you look at yourself.

Attitude is not the mask you wear to show people that you are kind, nice and responsible; it is in fact your internal behaviour. Attitude displays the core of you, your feelings, thoughts and emotions that linger within you and hidden from the external world.

Your attitude and understanding are hidden from everybody, and in their hide they are hard to manage and control. The world can only see the output of your attitude which largely relies on the ability of your managing skill. The output is commonly known as behaviour. Most of you try to change your behaviour, but it is very hard to try for it without changing the attitude.

Again, change in behaviour is also a change in response to the environment around you. Change in attitude requires the fundamental change in you. For instance, if you find it difficult to interact with yourself because of your seriousness much beyond normal extent, addition of smile more often during your conversations is a behavioural change. When you search within you the reason of your serious behaviour, change your prospect of people to perfectly connect with them better. It is called shift in attitude.

Change in behaviour is easier than change in attitude. The change in attitude calls for conscious and constant effort over a period of time to look within, review and evaluate your activities as well as yourself critically.

Despite your expected behaviour, be it in a casual conversation or a formal interview people will recognise the flaw in your attitude. In fact, most behavioural evaluations deal with your attitude not your behaviour and this is why lots of you fail and fail even to recognise the real reason of your failure. You might have conversed well, or answered perfectly in the interview, or even prepared yourself precisely for the oncoming challenge, but could have done nothing about your attitude, the most important thing that matters.

You test your attitude in your solitary existence, but in presence of people your behaviour is tested. Again, your attitude displays your behaviour. So, observe yourself and your thoughts, feelings and emotions closely from the bottom of your heart when you are alone. Try to discover the ways you think and act in your vision. If something seems unjust about you and the way you are looking at things fundamentally, change and continue to work at it until it becomes your natural habit. Remember, you are not your behaviour, you are your attitude. Above all, your attitude is your identity as well as your humanity.

11. Corporate Governance in India

The procedure of governing the corporate world with sets of rules, processes and practices by which a company is maintained and controlled involving the balance and interests of the stakeholders like management, shareholders, suppliers, financiers, customers, government and the community is corporate governance. It also prepares the framework for achieving the objectives of a company and hence involves every sphere of management, from action-plans and internal controls to corporate disclosure and performance measurement.

The Ministry of Corporate Affairs (MCA) and Securities and Exchange Board of India (SEBI) have undertaken many initiatives in the past in order to achieve success in corporate governance. Consequently, SEBI emerged with recommended changes to ensure effective governance in corporate sector.

The corporate governance agreements by various companies have been brought under trial of corporate governance by the recent disagreement between the TATA Sons and the expulsed chairman Cyrus Mistry. This incident has raised concerns about the level of compliances in the reputed companies including smaller organisations with a lesser reputation.

The objective of effective corporate governance is to allow the companies manage autonomously and prevent dominance by the owners so the differentiation between the management and shareholders is a must.

The Board of Directors influence corporate governance as they are the direct stakeholders. Again Shareholders or other board members elect or appoint the directors so shareholders of the company are represented by them. Hence, the task of the board is taking important decisions, such as compensation, appointments and dividend policy.

The boards often comprise the inside, as well as independent members. Inside the body comprises major shareholders, founders and executives, while independent directors have no ties with the insiders, but they are opted as they are experienced in managing or directing other large companies. Independents are thought to be helpful for governance, because of their possibility to reduce the concentration of power, they also help aligning shareholders' interest with those of the insiders.

As a result of the TATA Sons debacle, in addition to this, the clear message came out in open that the controller of dominant shareholders has the strong responsibility for making major decisions.

Such shareholders play the role of alternative power centres devoid of any responsibility or accountability. India is full of family-centred companies which have dominant shareholders. Hence, it is difficult to organise a Board that can be able to bring the dominant shareholders under the control of discipline because the shareholders give the Board all its powers. The idea of shareholder democracy appears to be imaginative as power in a company depends upon the block of shares. Hence, The TATA Sons debacle also exposed the harsh reality that the guidelines on corporate governance are showy; rather they hide the reality of exercising power within the companies. The compliances of these guidelines are only official formality. They only execute manipulations. Practical obedience is the way behind the theoretical compliance just as the audit reports show to mislead the stakeholders.

Corporate governance is highlighted through reports and awards by organising decorative exhibition and fantasy-view of programmes. So, the true scenario is completely different from it seems on its outward views witnessed in the cases of the Satyam, Sahara and the Shardha scams.

Such major and vital problems are dangerous to India alone; these can even plague the most advanced economies like the USA. The banks in the USA have compelled to pay a large amount as fines to the authorities in order to avoid prosecution.

The regulators have already taken over steps the years to address abuses of power. The standards of corporate governance require standardisation and the interests of minority investors calls for the safeguard in the best possible way with a view to attracting investments from across the world, simultaneously preventing any untimely flight of capital. In the 2016, ease of Doing Business report by the World Bank, India ranked 13 in the world on the basis of 'protecting minority investors' while in overall index ranked 130.

The concentration of the controllers on governance standards needs companies to make a cooperative effort to assure compliances and provide an opportunity to match with the global standards and deliver additional gains for their stakeholders.

❑❑❑

ESSAYS ON EDUCATIONAL ISSUES

1. India's Contribution to World Wisdom

INTRODUCTION

The ancient ideas of traditional India are the foundation of world today. Though the ideas are old, they bear the messages with innovative appeal. India has great significance in the wisdom of the world. The words of Max Muller, German Scholar, expresses the fact: "If I were asked under what sky the human mind has most fully developed some of its choicest gifts, has most deeply pondered on the greatest problems of life, and has found solutions, I should point to India".

In the various domains of life, India has significant contribution which has taken a long way to promote the lifestyle of mankind. The influences are found in the field of medicine, mathematics, the vibrant art, literature, etc.

THE DOCTRINE OF UPANISHADS

Max Muller, the German Scholar, exactly appreciated the Upanishads: *'There is no book in the world that is so thrilling, stirring and inspiring as the Upanishads'*.

The Indian philosophies have the answers to all mysterious questions of people what is after life, what comes after death, what is the real form of heaven, etc. Indian literature also guides the confused generation. The Upanishads is a complete philosophy of life. The doctrine of the Upanishads is followed by the world. It is one of the excellent works by human mind; it transforms the abstract thoughts into actions in the practical sense, which is presented in the form of poetry with spiritual thoughts.

ART AND CULTURE

The unique history of art and culture of India has made it famous in the world, and it has excelled in expressing in the wonderful literary works. The ancient paintings, the varied dance forms, the sculptures, and the different forms of literature have impressed the people across the world. The words of Keith Bellows, National Geographic Society expressed the respect and affection for the art and culture of India: "There are some parts of the world that, once visited, get into your heart and won't go. For me, India is such a place. When I first visited, I was stunned by the richness of the land, by its lush beauty and exotic architecture, by its ability to overload the senses with the pure, concentrated intensity of its colours, smells, tastes and sounds. I had been seeing the world in black and white and, when brought face-to-face with India, experienced everything re-rendered in brilliant Technicolour".

VEDAS

The significance of the power of Vedas is accepted by the world. The learned people have appreciated the Vedas as a luminary source full of universalism. The Vedas shows the way how to attain the true knowledge, is enriched with the pure form of Sanskrit language and conveys the purest divine message through the ancient scriptures.

MATHEMATICS

The world is indebted to India for the most significant concepts of Mathematics which was provided by the intelligent personalities of ancient India. They introduced the principles of decimal number system, the place value, algorithm, algebra and geometry which made their way into the world of mathematics from India. The rock edicts of Ashoka show the Arabic numerals. Even the importance of zero was discovered by Aryabhata, the famous Astronomer of India. In respect of mathematics and science, India is in leading position and its knowledge is spread all over the world. The base of many concepts like the concept of the earth's circumference, the solar system, eclipse occurrences and many others are the sources of the wisdom of India.

MEDICINE

In the sphere of medicine too, India has immense contribution.

Ayurveda, a branch of medicine created in India, uses herbs to treat various diseases. The other branch is the Homeopathy. Both Ayurveda and Homeopathy treat the complex diseases without any side effects. Moreover, the cost of medicines is very low so they are affordable by all.

CONCLUSION

India is the house of diverse culture with excellent human minds that are rare in the world. The world has taken the wisdom in diverse fields from India. Besides these, the world is indebted for the message of love and oneness and the ways of living together peacefully which is the result of the co-existence of the people from diverse castes, creeds, religions, and culture. India is the unique land where unity in diversity is existing, and naturally it preaches the countries across the world to do it.

2. The Building Blocks of Our Society are Paid Peanuts

The building blocks of our society are teachers, doctors and nurses, but unfortunately paid peanuts, but in the corporate world people earn almost double than them. The transmutation of our society also means the new jobs opportunities which people choose for today. But the traditional careers such as becoming doctors, teachers and nurses are still very popular with young people only because of the opportunities for helping people directly. But the lucrative salaries and world-class working environment attract the younger generations and naturally it has opened a new avenue in the professional world. Moreover, the increasing influence of businesses, sports and media in the corporate world raise the importance of the corporate world.

The building blocks of our society are paid a lower salary. Our nation is suffering the shortage of teachers and professors in its educational institutions only because of its lower salary. Though the medical professions are popular career options for people since ages, a large number of the excellent doctors join private hospitals or try for higher remuneration in the western countries like the USA, UK, Canada, etc. while the minimum numbers are seen in small nursing homes or inefficient government hospitals.

Whereas nursing is a crucial element of health industry, the government has not given importance without an aid to the doctor. Nurses are crucial for both war patients and general patients. So, the well-trained and excellent nurses too try their luck in the western countries for better salary with higher remuneration and world-class working environments. As a consequence, India is also lacking well-trained nurses.

The corporate world and entertainment industry of the country has earned great importance and naturally a large amount of money is being invested in the fields of movies, advertisements and even in sports tournaments. The government has not taken any such attempt that ensures the lucrative pay packages for the building blocks of the society with a view to encouraging people to take up these careers.

We have no fundamental system for deciding the remuneration in various spheres of professions, but there is a need to standardise the wages or remuneration for the professions such as medicine, nursing or teaching. Due to our own negligence of acknowledging the importance of people engaged in these professions, the significance related with these professions is being lost. A quick buck is spent on a movie or a show or even for providing a television but we hardly think when we consult a doctor or even look a good teacher for the child.

3. Technological Education and Human Values

INTRODUCTION

Human values are the most essential parts for our survival. However, in this age of modern technology, the human values have lost their grounds and are about to vanish into the glamour of modernisation. It marked a considerable inverse relationship between human values and the modern technological education. As the technology advances, the emotions of human beings are about to be vanished. Humanitarian behaviours and human values have been remarkably deteriorated by the radical change brought in the field of education with the technological advancement.

HUMAN VALUES: THEIR SIGNIFICANCE

Human values generate abstract feelings necessary for a lively living. Love, mercy, care, affection, simplicity, honesty, understanding, sharing the pain, helping tendency and happiness, etc. are the common human feelings bear great value and are the fundamental factors to judge humanity as well as differentiate them from brutal nature and attitude. The memory of our childhood tells us the importance of the moral stories from the Panchatantra, the Ramayana, the Mahabharata and many other epics and ethics. However, in the advanced civilisation influenced by globalisation we have failed to implement our childhood knowledge into our practical life.

IMPACT OF TECHNOLOGY ON EDUCATIONAL SYSTEM

Materialistic Gain

As the technologies developed, the course of the education system has been further increased and it was beyond the knowledge of our ancestors. Our great scholars and philosophers have no materialistic certified degrees which are considered the standard of education and intelligence. We are abounding in certificates, gadgets, applications and appliances which have immense materialistic importance in recent times. The technological advancement is responsible for the diseases assumed today for the lack of physical work.

Gurukul

Education system in the Gurukul period was different. Then pupils used to learn from their gurus and the teachers or Gurus were respected next to God. The pupils had to leave their homes and used to stay at the Gurukul. They grasped the teachings and preaching on human values which were important and relevant to their customs and traditions. In this period, human values were adopted in the educational system.

Schooling

With the passage of time, there came the period of schooling. The children used to attend their emotional values. This distracted their focus on their studies. In this period, the skill schools from home. The parents supervised their children and gave some sort of EOF writing was initiated. The learning aptitude just by dint of listening began to diminish.

University and Graduation

This was the further advancement in the field of education. The advanced skills of practical learning through laboratories were introduced in the age of computers. The University education gave more freedom to the children and the hold of parents started getting loosened up. This advancement paved way to over socialisation, westernisation and intermixing of the genders under the friendly ambience. As consequences, the world has seen a remarkable increase in the crime index especially in respect to the safety for women.

Multiple Degrees

The higher studies have created a strong sense of ego among the youngsters and this ego has made them feel superior to all others in respect of their knowledge and intelligence which in turn has made them lose their sense of respect to their elders as well as their knowledge and skills.

Internet Age

The age of latest technology is marked as the cyber age. Now, we have fully air-conditioned institutions. The soul focus is on the outward beauty, extra-curricular activities and the physical comfort. Education has the least value in these educational institutions. Internet has brought lots of teachings to the latest generation. They can understand and grasp all the wanted as well as unwanted, and even malevolent contents at their age. The mental setup gets adulterated. This generation wants quick and easy access available for prompt success at every cost. They cannot trace any loss in terms of the loss of their human values. They feel the importance of wealth and materialistic things throughout their life.

NEGATIVE IMPACTS OF TECHNOLOGICAL ADVANCEMENT

The impacts are as follows:

i. Man-made things have everything except emotional values.
ii. Values, patience as well as tolerance have deteriorated.
iii. This generation fails to apply their knowledge and value success happily and respectfully in spite of their sufficient knowledge.
iv. Rat race for the top position has greatly created pressure on children.
v. Increases greed of more wealth.
vi. The gadgets, the gift of science, divert our attention and snatch our invaluable time from our loved ones. So, they are in reality a curse for the human beings.
vii. Dissatisfaction, mercilessness, is common among younger generation.
viii. Man has ambition to explore the moon but don't have the heart to help or serve his neighbours as well as fellow humans.
ix. Above all, this education system has encouraged the growth of violence and terrorism.

CONCLUSION

The modern technological education appears to be Devilish in nature. However, modern technological education is undoubtedly a precious gift; still it is the civilised production of the brutality. This education has also resulted in modern violence, terrorism, and a total malfunctioning status of law and order in the country. The human emotions have been deteriorated by the introduction of various subjects of study at each level of educational system. It has also affected the humanitarian grounds to further a level down. Frankly speaking, the modern technological education calls for the rectification as well as modification of their background in order to cultivate the human values as a compulsory subject of teachings.

4. Formal Examinations versus Regular Assessment with Projects

It is the question of discussion in recent times in India. Education experts are in discussion on this issue with learned men from various walks of life. There are already various methods of evaluation under consideration with a view to introducing an effective evaluation system to judge the students' qualities on maximum parameters.

However, hardly any method seems exhaustive to judge a student's qualities entirely. Hence, evaluation system should be designed in order to broaden the options and make it suitable to the curriculum, the type of students, teaching and learning strategies. Our education systems are dependent solely on formal examinations to finally assess the students. However, as the new courses of study and new curriculums per year owing to globalisation have emerged, the formal examination seems just one mode of evaluation but is not at all suitable enough to evaluate multiple skills of the students except their mere performance on one single day.

However, the arrangement of regular evaluation can be more effective since it decreases the stress on students and makes the students more attentive in the class throughout the course. It maximises the research inclination of the students. Many non-conventional techniques and skills like project reports, case studies, presentations, etc. help to judge diverse skills of the students: analytical skills, communication skills, ability to work in a group, time management skills, and many more which cannot be evaluated in a formal traditional examination system.

Many educational institutes are now adopting a stressful blend of the two systems because of these advantages of the regular evaluation over the formal examination. For instance, management institutions like MBA colleges have introduced an evaluation system with equal weightage to multiple factors such as presentations, case studies, projects, group presentations, course work, etc. are popular for effective assessment system.

Various skills of the students: expression, presence of mind, confidence, spontaneity etc. are assessed by online quiz and role plays which are getting popularity today.

Hence, a good assessment system is the one which has the highest level of credibility and reliance and sufficient chance for giving feedback to the students for their improvement.

5. Credit-Based Higher Education System—Status, Opportunities and Challenges

INTRODUCTION

The most essential part of Indian culture is education. In ancient India, gurus or teachers had a great influence on their students. The act of imparting education was not considered a business.

Then students had no financial pressure in terms of education. India was an ideal destination of higher studies since students and teachers were inclined to financial issues. During British regime, the transformation of education was undertaken because they thought that free education had no values to the natives.

Jawaharlal Nehru, the first Prime Minister of India, however, ensured that in spite of insufficiency of funds the institutions were open to the best-in-class minds. Liberal state grants made this possible by ensuring a small amount of fees for students. This system worked well till the structure was begun to change in 1990s. The free Indian economy made it compulsory to look into the matter of education with up-to-date mindset. Hence, the time to update higher education had begun. At first, the change of economy made students to complete their college education to gain skills and relevant testimonials. This department invested a huge amount of money to train the younger generation with a view to enabling them work with new technologies and management practices. Moreover, India had an average record in the prospect of higher education. It had even no sign to continue with the purpose of lifting the economy to growing trajectory. Under such circumstances, the government did not appear to be dependable even the public funds were insufficient.

STATUS

At this crucial juncture, the credit-based education system emerged. Simultaneously, the higher paying jobs too enhanced the process of change and as a result, students were interested to pay more for higher studies. In addition to this, the amalgamation of the domestic economy with that of the world boosted the rate of migration of the qualified people including even teachers for brighter prospects.

With the passage of time the tendency of huge investment in private institutions was increased. The government institutions and banks took the advantage of the opportunity by raining the fee. During this time, a large number of foreign universities were established in India.

OPPORTUNITIES

The higher education system on the basis of credit has the prospect to groom best-in-class human resources. Once the ultra-modern infrastructure is built, it would base the retention of the required world-class teachers and ensure positive feedback mechanism from students. The model has the potential to improve the soft skills of India immensely and that could go overseas and even develop a different identity altogether.

CHALLENGES

There are some grave concerns that call for urgent attention. The system definitely creates lots of pressure on the students disregarding their sensitivity because of the higher stakes in the new system. Some students are compelled to commit suicide or take other drastic steps being unable to bear the depression caused by the pay back credit drives. The other disadvantage is that both students and their guardians are at the mercy of colleges because of the effective regulatory mechanism. Even an average institution charges higher fee pretending a good institution. Here paid rankings are common which are the darker side of information circulation. As a result, some institutions cannot be discredited because of their coexistence. At last, students would have to be in search of research-oriented jobs as well as lucrative side of the market. The higher fees are the bar to the poor students to enter the best management colleges. With the objective of making the system effective, the introduction of regulatory mechanism is a must. Without establishing the effective checks and balances system, it cannot be ensured that India is a true powerhouse of education. Despite the remarkable growth of engineering and Information Technology, the provision of large incentives for the growth of India, especially in the fields of research and development, worldwide is a far cry.

CONCLUSION

The credit-based higher education system is the trend of the day. Although it provides great potential to India's future, yet only the sufficient steps relevant to the concerns can ensure the growth of education sector in near future.

6. India Must Delink Classroom Teaching from Student Learning

The burning matter of discussion in India is that 'education and innovation' or 'education or innovation'. Almost every discussion withheld in dispute. The education system mars innovative skills and makes students to take risk. It also forces students to comply with the standardised template, and it dissuades failure as well as departure from the standardised average. But it remains indifferent to the outliers.

The refrain is true because there many components that lead to lots of problems from beginning with admission in the education course at the pre-school level. For instance, in higher education the rate of attending lectures by students is poor and one more fact that the duration of their concentration on the lectures is also mediocre.

But generally, in the USA and Western Europe, the average duration is 15 hours, and there is difference between learning hours and classroom hours. The aim of their classroom contact is to make the students learn instead of teaching, and this process can happen even outside classroom contact. In those countries it appears that through instructive teaching and classroom contact, a student spends two hours on direct learning, so 15 hours of classroom teaching turns into 45 hours of weekly learning.

The University Grants Commission (UGC) announced a choice-based credit system in 2015. This made higher education more pliable but still is controversial as there were other reasons too. This new system defines education as follows: 'Credit: A unit by which the course work is measured. It determines the number of hours of instruction required per week. One credit is equivalent to one hour of teaching (lecture or tutorial) or two hours of practical work/field work per week'. A student earned credits in every semester are a summation of lecture with tutorial and practical work.

On the other hand, practical work and field work are meant for science subjects and, in cases of social sciences, student learning includes classroom contact and tutorials. According to a survey, some students of Delhi University said, "We attend around 28 hours of lectures every week and around 40 hours including tutorials and practical work". But the duration of lectures was typically 55 minutes, not one hour, so a minor difference was traced. It is supposed that 40–45 hours is the norm for almost all of the universities in India. It is clear by this that the students either have no time to learn on their own or spend 120 hours on learning including the multiple of two times.

The learning process generally goes on for around 80 hours per week instead of 120 hours, as there are only 168 hours in a week. But according to the Factories Act one should work between 18 and 48 hours per week, but not more than that. So, this principle should be applied in case of students; we should not make them slog for 80 hours. The norm should also confirm that students who do not learn on their own should be marked that never think on the subjects they are learning. The classroom teaching from student learning should be delinked as maximum number of students reproduces their lessons by rote learning. The advanced countries have now accepted that fifteen hours of classroom teaching is good enough for the students while their outside classroom learning duration is longer.

What is the output of classroom learning? In other cases, the difference between input and outcomes are appreciable. Why cannot it be possible for higher education? That norm of 40 hours of lectures every week is the result of workloads incumbent to teachers. There is a minimal difference between assistant professors, associate professors and professors as they have to teach for about 15 hours per week inclusive of 30 hours of tutorials in total 45 hours per week. Tutorials involve physical contact with the teacher as don't form any independent student learning.

In short, students have to attend 40 or 45 hours of lectures every week since teachers teach for 45 hours. However, in the USA, credits emanates the duration in Carnegie Units, pioneered by Carnegie Foundation to decide retirement pensions for professors. Contemporarily, Morris Llewellyn Cooke prepared a report, entitled 'Academic and Industrial Efficiency', for Carnegie Foundation for the Advancement of Teaching in 1872. The objective was to systematise faculty workloads, simultaneously to use this as a measure to deliver education. Obviously, it goes on well parallel to factories and industrial production, a little like Ford Motor Company which uses mass production to manufacture Model T cars: 'Any customer can have a car painted any colour that he wants so long as it is black'.

But higher education is unlike factory production in reality. It is quite logical to repeat Henry Ford, "I will build a car for the great multitude. It will be large enough for the family, but small enough for the individual. But it will be so low in price that no man making a good salary will be unable to own one". But other countries, especially the European ones, have achieved a considerable improvement in the field of education by overcoming such dysfunctional ideas on the basis of their standards and guidelines for quality assurance, the European Higher Education Area 2015. It is high time, India should undertake such initiatives.

7. New National Education Policy (NEP) 2020

'Education is the most powerful weapon which you can use to change the whole world',

Nelson Mandela.

The National Educational Policy 2020 is approved by the government of India on 29 July 2020. The policy has sanctioned by our cabinet in India after a gap of 34 years after 1986. The education policy in India was first announced in the year 1968 on the report and recommendation of Kothari Commission. Then a New Education Policy was formulated in the year 1986. After making some amendments it was reintroduced in 1992 by P.V Narasimha Rao Government. The National Education Policy 2020 is the first education policy of 21st Century in India which aims at promoting better education. Under this policy the Ministry of Human Resource Development is renamed as Ministry of Education. The policy was developed and formulated under the leadership of former Chairman of Indian Space Research Organisation (ISRO) K. Kasturi Rangan. The change in the existing education system has been done to make education reach up to all, whether rural or urban. The policy is aimed to focus on overall development of a child/student. In addition to it, the policy is aimed to increase the investment of GDP in education to 6% and increase gross enrollment ratio up to 50% by the year 2035. The new education policy is an initiative taken by our government to make education more accessible. The policy has been recommended to bring out transformation in school education and higher education system. The policy aims at reformation of school education by adapting measures such as focusing on early childhood case, reforming examination and assessment program. The transformation includes a shift from 10+2 pattern to 5+3+3+4 structure. The 12 years of school and 3 years of preschool or anganvadi. The first five years is named as foundation stage. In this initial stage initial 3 years will be pre-school. It includes children between the age of 3-8 years. Thus, children will have an experience of schooling at an early age. After 3 years of pre-school students will study in class 1st and 2nd for which no exam will be conducted. This will reduce stress of examination among children. The focus of student will be on activity-based learning. This stage is the framework to build early childhood care and education. The next 3 years is named as preparatory stage. This includes children between age of 8-11 years. In this stage from class 3 to class 5 will be taught. School will focus on enhancing education building by focusing on activity based learning, plays, discoveries, and will also begin in cooperate same light textbooks studies. This includes the subject such as physical education, science, arts, mathematics. Moreover child is not bound to study in English language up to 5th grade. The children can study in their regional language. This had been done to make a child familiar with the books and studies and to lessen the burden. The next 3 years named as middle stage includes students the age group from 11-14 years of age. The grade system will include in this stage from class 6th to class 8th. The student will be taught according to subject based learning. Children will be taught about coding and programming from class 6th. Skill development course will also be started from middle stage. This will include vocational and technical learning on the subject as per their interest. Moreover, there is a compulsion opt for anyone of the Indian language. The subject also includes mathematics, science, arts etc. Last 4 years of education in school is for student from class 9th to class 12th. This includes the students of age group of 14-16 years. The major change in this stage is students can choose a variety of subjects combination as per their choice, skills and interest rather than being restricted the arts, science and commerce stream. This will create a flexibility in thought process and will result in greater critical thinking. There is a shift of exam pattern from early based to semester based. This will increase consistency for studies among students. These will be semester based assessment of exam from class 9th students. Students are also allowed to learn any of one foreign language as per their choice.

National education policy 2020, is also set bring a drastic change in higher education system. The bachelor degree course will be of 4 years. However students can opt for 3 years also which they will be provided a bachelor degree certificate. Moreover a new concept of multiple entry and exit in the course has been introduced. If a student leave in between will get a credit transfer certificate. This will give them a change to complete their degree after a break. The students will also be given other 3 options during their bachelor degree course, i.e., one who completes 4 year bachelor course will be provided a certificate of graduation research, in completion of 2 years course the student will be provided an advance diploma certificate and graduation certificate on completion of 1 of course. This new education policy emphasises on degree taking only but it lays emphasis on creative thinking, reducing the burden of higher education and mental stress. Innovation and employment education among students. Introduction of vocational skill in new educational system will help them to do part time job during graduation course. According to the policy, there will be no M.Phil. course after master degree. The Post-graduation will include 1 or 2 year course as per the graduation course.

There are many other changes in the New Education Policy. There is drastic change in traditional exam assessment system of school. The result of the student in school will not be based only on marks obtained in examination, rather it will be collectively based on marks obtained by student, marks given by their teacher, marks given by their friends, and marks given to themselves. This will help them in personality development. There is also a change in teacher recruitment and education. A 4 year integrated B.Ed. program is made essential for teaching. The policy aimed at limiting high demand of school fees. Thus, the school will not be allowed to charge excessive fee.

The National Education Policy 2020 aim to increase standard of education at International Level by allowing Top 50 Universities to open a branch in India. The policy is designed to achieve its objective by 2030. The National Education Policy 2020 is laid down with several initiatives and changes that are utmost need of the present scenario. If worked accordingly, the policy will propel our nation towards progress. It makes education system flexible, holistic to the needs of 21st century.

❑❑❑

20

PHILOSOPHICAL, RELIGIOUS AND SPIRITUAL ESSAYS

1. If Youth Knew, if Age Could

INTRODUCTION

The quotation "If youth knew, if age could", implies a deeper message that highlights the relation between the young and the old from one generation to the other. It depicts that young and the older people should cooperate to apply their knowledge and power for the better accomplishment. The young and the older people are in an inverse relationship in most cases. Concepts in maximum cases result in their disagreement. This disagreement is generally termed as 'generation gap'. We have encountered generation gap but have hardly tried to analyse this gap make a common resolution.

GENERATION GAP

Currently, this concept calls for urgent analysis and understanding in parlance of 'Young Generation' and 'Older Generation'. In course of our discussion, we fumble upon the very quotation that makes us young or old. But the fact is that the young should try to consider the knowledge and message delivered by their elders, whereas the old people too should try to be patient enough to compete the worldly affairs in contestant manner. At this juncture, we should approach towards the practical situations in the following ways:

Rational Thinking for the Young while Retaining Strength for the Old

The young are warm-blooded, so they often sparkle in moments. They should start thinking logically and rationally being patient enough to listen and understand the opinions and views of their elders and argue them in relation to those in order to make a complete compilation of our requirement to overcome the barriers that come in course of our life. To the contrary, the elders too should retain their patience, strength and power in their actions on the basis of their knowledge and experience in order to argue logically.

Young and Elder People Cooperate as a Single Unit

The result of cooperation of a dynamic enlightened young and a veteran old in any field of work is always better. In this combination, the older official reciprocates his experience and knowledge while the young enthusiast implicates them seriously and meticulously with a view to delivering the best-in-class output.

Out of these two approaches, the latter appears to be the best and more practical and acceptable in any work pattern.

AGE-OLD HINDU MYTHOLOGICAL CONCEPT

According to the age-old Hindu mythology, the human life consists of childhood, adulthood, married life and the old age i.e. Vanaprastha. This concept explains that a person is successful in his mundane responsibilities by making his children established and subsequently handing the complete charge of the family over to them. Ultimately, the older persons leave for forests to live the rest of their lives by concentrating on the spirituality leaving the sparkling and booming materialistic city behind.

During that period, the elders had no opportunity to lead and guide their successors with their knowledge and experiences. The elders left the family life and the women being refined into the narrowness of the society, while the children were the head of the family as well as handled outdoor responsibilities. Naturally, the young had to live of their own experience. However, the elders had neither right to involve in the worldly affairs nor to discuss their strength and physical potential and experience.

IMPACT OF GENERATION GAP A DECADE AGO

The ancient concept of life is obsolete and has been abolished with the passage of time and has now developed entirely. The Vanaprastha is no longer in vogue. It has now opened a period of interaction between the experienced elders and the young. However, the above quotation was not orientated with the situation and a defined shape in this age. People led their life simply with grandchildren in their old forties by handing over the responsibilities of the family to their children before their age of retirement.

In this age, the elders guided their children regarding their family and other related matters with their knowledge and experiences despite the curtness of their children. However, they would obey the words of their elders. It means that their experiences were implemented. But as the task accomplished by the young was done without any enthusiasm and interest, it didn't attain the expected input of the young potential in the performed result. This is because of the stubborn nature and disregard to the words of their elders. The elders used to work hard during their lifetime. Then there was not a single point of discussion with regard to their physical stamina to confront the young and have the best performable.

GENERATION GAP TODAY

In our present age, we live in the age of technology. People are civilised and understand the value of literacy and education very well. Men and women take part in worldly affairs and the age of marriage too has been increased. The average retirement age is sixty plus. At that age, people maintain their physical and mental strength and more inclined to remain hale and hearty and try to utilise their knowledge and experiences for better purposes.

Today, the young generation is more educated and have much patience to retain their temper and understand the requirements and importance. They are now more open minded. They have enough patience to listen to the elders and consider and even comply with the fresh thoughts and views. The young are neither diffident nor reluctant to learn from the experiences of old people and gather knowledge from their success as well as failure. With such an attitude, they have enough potential to brighten the world with their excellence. The young clearly and vividly make out the difference between the requirements of the time as well as execute the accurate measures in order to satisfy their needs.

The latter approach holds water for the present trend of lifestyle.

CONCLUSION

Needless to say, the extract is appropriate for our present age. We have pretty plenty of scopes open to reform and redress the human society, the world today into a more welcoming age and an age of recreation for the generation to come. The young knew the age could, above all, successfully implement their knowledge and experiences in the most practicable ways.

2. True Religion Cannot be Misused

INTRODUCTION

The word, religion implies manipulation. The mass, various communities as well as political parties use religions in their respective fields. Actually, it means the unity of a particular group of people usually by creating a line of difference from the others with a view to living in peace and progress. But does it work practically to meet its objective? The fact is in inverse. Religion has now been reshaped a means of political parties that force people to search the belief, values and peace outside their self.

THE ESSENCE OF RELIGION

Religion awakes the sense of contentment and satisfaction within our inner self. All religions of the world preach the same beliefs differently in their own languages. The religion in true sense promotes peace and progress instead of harming others. The first and foremost step of true religion is to establish peace in one's own self. By making peace with oneself, the person gains the power and ability to make peace with the external world, and at this moment he is ready to submit himself for the betterment of mankind. Religion implies this submission.

The Message of Religion

People should try to understand how the religion brings inner peace and nurtures relationships. It influences the relationships of: family, community and even the society. The light of internal peace of a person contributes to the peace of the world even by breaking the barriers of castes and creeds and races leaving any room for war. The holy books of all religions convey the message of being in peace by welcoming people from all religions.

War in the Name of Religion

The history is impregnated with innumerable instances of war that took place regarding religion in different parts of world in different time periods. In those wars people, communities, states and even countries fought against each other. War was, however, considered a means of bringing peace; in reality, it is nothing but a blind belief. It is rather a form of violence, a means of annihilation, not creation or redress of mankind. People should war for self-defence for justice, but not in the pretext of religion and peace. The Mahabharata, the epic war, depicts a war that was fought between good and wicked for putting an end to the malpractices followed in the name of religion accompanied by torture and oppression unleashed upon the mass and, above all, for establishing a religion, a mode of lifestyle where all would enjoy their rights equally and lead a life of peace and progress.

RELIGIOUS INTOLERANCE: ITS INSTANCES

The problems of socio-economic, racial and religious factors were behind the aggressive war in the name of religion which resulted in violence, unrest, suffering and destroyed peace.

i. Kashmir is the age-old point of religious controversy between India and Pakistan and this station is known to the world. India as well as Pakistan claims Kashmir to be the integral part of their land. Since the day of independence, the two countries have been at war. Hundred thousands of people have already been killed by either country to include the land in their own geographical boundary.

ii. India is well known as a land of enjoying unity in diverse cultures. It is also true that it cannot free itself from the religious, political dramas happening since the Independence Day. These are happening at loss of the common people at large. In Orissa, the Christians often become the innocent victim of the militant Hindu extremists.

iii. The world knows the problems posed in Afghanistan. It is considered by the world the hub of radical, fundamentalist and extreme, terrorist groups. Al Qaeda is supposed to be headquartered in the country by the late supremo of the Al Qaeda, Osama Bin Laden. Now this group is safe and secured by the Taliban dictatorship in the country and is freely executing frameworks for operating destructive operations in different parts of the world. These extremist groups are led by the orthodox and narrow beliefs of their religion.

RELIGION: ITS IMPLICATION IN HUMAN LIFE

The above are three of the most vital instances of war going on in the name of religion and clarifies that still at the age of ultra-modern technology and generosity religion is the centre of war and disharmony. What prevails is nothing but the narrowness of religion. True religion includes the entire world irrespective of religions as a single entity. It stops killing and massacre in the name of religion, even generates generosity in human race and abolish any sense or reason for their destruction. Truth rests in falsity and narrow belief of religious supremacy. These inhuman activities clarifies that neither the Gita, nor the Bible, nor even the Koran is responsible for these hatred blindness, it is rather the name of true knowledge by which people cannot differentiate themselves for beasts because they always think that they are not animals, they are human beings.

CONCLUSION

Religion in the true sense makes people think differently and always makes them follow the path of peace and harmony, not of any malice and war. The actions are led by the blind mania of man not by religion. Religion always considers human a part of the diverse creation of the Almighty, all livings beings are created for all, not for the survival of humans. But another blind belief of humans is that for the sake of humans God has created all other living beings. Until people understand the essence of religion as well as its truth, they cannot execute any activities based on religion. Man-made religions lead them to the course of destruction, while God-made religion i.e. the true religion leads them to the redress and reformation of mankind as well as for the sake of existence of this wonderful planet with its diversity.

3. Science and Religion

Science is based on the yardstick of proofs and testimonies, while religion only on ideas. Science treats the material world comprehended by senses, but religion is concerned with a metaphysical world. Reasons are the legs of science while intuition is the base of religion. The scientist is busy at his laboratory of the material world, whereas the religious teacher is in the recess of his experiences. The end of science is the beginning of religion, while the answer of science to the 'First Cause' is still unknown. Again religion declares that the discipline of religion helps us know and understand everything as God is self-revealed as well as self-existent. Hence, there goes on a strong rivalry between the man of religion and the man of science.

There is a wide gap between science and religion. Science treats concrete things, whereas religion on abstract things. Science is the representative of fact, while religion of faith. Science deals with all material things: Living and non-living, but religion deals with human and nature. It is human mind that is the father of both science and religion. Science has certain principles: reason, fact, believe on seeing or proving by experiments and research works while religion has principles like faith, reverence, experience and supreme reliance. Religions are again based on personal experiences and venture, be that but of Christ or Ramakrishna, is not visible to all but be believed, while science is founded by impersonal venture, the results of which are eternal and believed by all. Religious enlightenment is felt by personal experience, religion is subjective.

An individual himself needs to experience religion otherwise he cannot enjoy the taste and pl asure of religion. In ethical situations, the moral as well as religious rules are combined and must be followed by individuals. Religious gains are individual property but are applied on the mass. On the contrary, science treats the objective side of life and all scientific inventions and discoveries are common to all. Achievements of science are not mysterious and their truth is universal. A methodical scholarship and focus is essential to reach the scientific truths subsequently tested and adjudged by theorem and experiment. Until the perfection of scientific knowledge is proved, the faith on religion as well as God will continue to be highly pertinent. In this sense, science and religion generally meets at a point. Scientists and spiritual teachers have to embark on solitary travels into the regions beyond the knowledge of human mind depending on themselves. When a line of separation comes between them, their ways bifurcate and take separate paths.

Human knowledge was undifferentiated in the beginning of human civilisation. The sort of complexity of human mind that masters over the modern times was lacking then. Religion too had scientific implication. During the period of Rig Vedas, the worshipping of gods and goddesses and the subsequent religious practices and customs were inseparably formulated with scientific pursuits. For instance, the common practice of offering *jal* i.e. water to the rising sun-god in the morning has a scientific truth that the first rays of the sun are good for the eyes. The practice of fasting too has scientific truth; it improves patience and willpower in the faster. The customs such as the *holme* or *hawan* during a *puja* or a *Vagya* also has the truth that it purifies the atmosphere. But in the later Vedic period, the scientific sides of the religious customs and practices were abolished by superstitions and nameless fears which were cultivated by influential the priests allured by their inclination to misuse religion for their own mercenary interests. Religion is age old.

Since the beginning, man believed that a mighty invisible force existing and controlling the universe. This belief guided and governed the human thoughts and ideas. Then man worshipped serpents. Science is supposed to develop latter than religion; it may grew about four or five thousand years ago and from fifteenth century, the modern science began. However, the supremacy of religion was behind the rise of many evils, and overtime it also encouraged superstition and evil practices and unjust activities. The heads of different religions exercised their powers over their followers just like a dictator. The Brahmin priests in India and the Roman Catholic Church in Europe and others exercised their despotism and tyranny over the mass and the true spirit of religion was destroyed by them. But the rapid growth and development of science and logic many of these evil and unjust practices began to diminish from mankind. Once there was a time when the conflict between science and religion was very bitter. Then it seemed that science would lose its growth tracks before the mighty and authoritative force of religions.

The establishment of truth by the argument of science was not at all easy. Men of science had to confront innumerable difficulties and inhuman torture over time. For instance, Galileo Galilei was imprisoned forcefully by the Pope for his new theories on heavenly bodies. Nicolaus Copernicus too faced difficulties and, in the nineteenth century, Charles Darwin too became the victim of the Churchmen who raised the voice 'Religion in Danger' and demanded the persecution of such a scientist. In the late nineteenth century, Robert Mayor the German scientist was kept in a lunatic asylum for his discovery of the theory of Conservation of Energy. In those days who discovered something and that was against the accepted Biblical theories about God, and universe were punished regarding as the enemies of mankind and religion. The voice of reason and truth was thus attempted to suppress the Church authority as the preacher of the Bible. But over time, science and reasoning got its ground. The critics of science turned to be its supporters and followers. By nineteenth century, science got its firm ground and grew and developed faster since then on.

The advancement of science and technology has brought a considerable change in the world. It conferred the mankind with incredible comforts and conveniences. The wonders of science have confused mankind but man enjoys innumerable blessings of science in his life. Man has conquered time and distance, fatal diseases and pain by dint of his science and technology. These developments make people believe that man is all-powerful while God a supernumerary being. By the magical of his science, human has forgotten to believe in Heaven or Hell, God or the Almighty. Religion now seems to be redundant and the shrines of worshipping the God have begun to lose the respect as well as power. Once there was a time when the shrines enjoyed religion immense power and authority, then it seemed science to be dethroned from the hearts of man.

But the path of science was not at all smooth. The moral and spiritual development of man brought bodily comforts and turned a man sceptic. Man became selfish, dishonest and proud, destroyed his simple faith, affection, fellow feeling, and kindness. The blessings of science have also created new social problems. The gulf between the rich and the poor grew wider. The machines are used widely and naturally, it leads millions of humans to the evils of unemployment, economic exploitation, congested cities, crowded and the growth of slums. Many workers have lost their independence and happiness and cut down the position of a clog in the modern industries. Science and technology have also enhanced the rate of manufacturing of weapons which poses the possibility of increasingly horrible and destructive form of wars. The very existence of humanity and civilisation is now in danger. But science is unable to answer the primary questions relating to the mystery of life and death. Science even in this age of technology has failed to give us peace and happiness. So, it is high time that science should be jointly led with religion. Science makes man materialistic, while religion makes him keep faith in God and helps him lead a peaceful life of higher and spiritual values. Besides, there are many things in Heaven as well as on Earth, which are still beyond the range of our science. Without moral and spiritual values, man's life turns futile. Man then turns into a beast out of his own knowledge.

In ancient times, the magician played the role a doctor as well as a high priest. The act of taking Hippocratic Oath by doctors even today is considered a religious belief of the Greeks-Hygeia, the goddess of health. It is noticed that there is nothing antithetical ideas in it that it demands of speaking between the two for ages. Besides, intuition is crucial medium to apprehend the existence of God or belief in any religions. In the same way, a great scientist continues his research without any pre-plan for the invention or discovery of any certain thing. For instance, millions of apples must have fallen to the ground in presence of many thinkers and scientists, and maybe before Newton. But the day his supersensitive insight worked extraordinarily and revolutionarily that the fall of an apple led him to the laboratory and ultimately made him discover the famous law of gravitation. The following couplet exactly demonstrates the concept of the agreement between science and religion:

'Nature and Nature's law lay hid in the Night,
God said, let Newton be and all was Light'.

Science and religion seems to be the two opposite dimensions of human's consciousness. Though these repellent to each other, they converse in the mind of human. Religion without science is debased and superstition clogs its course. On the contrary, science without religion leads humans to materialism and snatches their faith, belief and other moral values. Science purifies religion, while religion gives a touch of beauty and mystery to science. The wonders of the Supreme Being brought to light by the discoveries of science and its conquest of Nature and it supports the work of religion. A scientist does in fact believe in God and is not even an irreligious person; rather he is a real worshiper of God and his magnificent creations. Thus, the blind worship of superstitious man is the fruit of true knowledge of the scientist. The modern scientists have realised that the limitations of science as well as religious insights have given better understanding of the wonders and miracles of Nature and the Creator. The cry of conservatism and superstition has no scope in the rational approach to the problems of the universe which is the religion of science. In this current age, the rivalry between science and religion has ended, and a sense of cooperation has come to exist with a view to providing humans' better life as well as discovering the truth behind the mystery of life and death and many other mysterious things.

4. Eastern Religions and Western Philosophy

It is supposed that India is the only land without any historical moral codes or regulations to rule and govern its people and flourished precisely based on its religious and spiritual roots. People here simply led their life just by understanding the process of life around them. There was none to lead and guide them. They were imparted knowledge and wisdom through natural process of experience and understanding.

There is a fundamental difference between the western philosophy as well as its approach to life and Indian religion as well as their lifestyle. The Greek philosophy pioneered the western philosophy as the Greeks discovered the concept of 'state' and its administrative system.

The religious and spiritual wisdom of the east originated in India and came down through ages as the lofty human ideals, while the western philosophy of state and patriotism to it is the highest of human ideals. Thus, the East and the West were in total contradiction in ancient times.

The book, 'Eastern Religions and Western Thought' by Dr. Sarvepalli Radhakrishnan, explores this contradiction as well as conflict quite logically and argumentatively. It deals with the origins of the modern society and the fundamental reasons of conflict and contradiction between modern men.

The greatest ideal in the world is the one that helps an individual to discover himself and stand at the climax of his aspiration. On the other hand, the philosophy of a state helps a man with the root framework of survival, but it fails to satisfy the longing of the soul to know him.

Life is meaningless if it has no means to understand oneself and reach to one's perfection when one is struggling for survival. Eastern religions are impregnated with the necessary means to understand and explore oneself through systems such as meditation, yoga, etc.

In western philosophy, however, logic and reasoning is the highest system of thought. This commands human life to understand the happenings around us through logic and reasoning. Evidently, this system works on the very individual human experience almost in the heartless mechanical process continuing devoid of individual and spiritual needs.

As the modern man becomes wealthier, safe and secure, he also becomes more worried, frightened, empty and uncertain. Now the mankind is gradually realising the critical mistake it did by adopting a baseless logical system devoid of sympathy and awareness to an individual spirit which is behind all happenings around us.

There can be no reasoning on the system of thought to lead man to his higher self. The wars, struggles and politics of the last two hundred years, undoubtedly proved the logic and reasoning to be a giant to chew and spit out the human spirit, only to prove it true.

5. History Changes but Not Geography

It is history that draws and redraws borders and demarcation lines and changes geography over time. But geography gives the identity of a place with all its physical characteristics which remain the same for years to come, while history decides the politics of the place which changes over time as the generations as well as civilisations change.

There are two apparent ways in which the history changes: One is with the passage of time and the other by the writer. History is supposed to be written by the conquerors.

So, what is a fact today, tomorrow it will be an assumption.

For instance, the existence of India with its natural borders has been clearly visible more than since 10,000 years before. On the north, it is bordered by the lofty Himalayas, while south is by seas and oceans on two sides. In this natural existence, India witnessed the development of the Indus valley civilisation from about 2500BC in its west, subsequently the movement of the Rig Vedas from about 1500–500BC towards east and Indo-Gangetic plains. With the passage of time, history travelled further and brought changes in the shape of India with the emergence of the Mauryas around 300BC; the Guptas in about 400 AD; the Mughals and ultimately the mighty British in around seventeenth century onwards who drew and redrew the borders of India. The last power left India in its present shape. However, the geography of India has been the same from time immemorial. Whoever comes, enjoys the same climate of India and it will remain intact till its doom's day.

But history can never stop. It changes not only rulers of the country, its borders, but the style and manners of the lives of its people even influence the religion of the land. For instance, the phallus worship of the Indus valley civilisation turned into nature worship of during the Rig Vedic period. India witnessed the absorption of bhakti cult as well as Sufism and also the idolatrous worship of Lord Vishnu, Lord Shiva, Shakti and so on. With the development of religion, the customs and practices changed the social life of people. For the lack of logical and reasoning-based education, castes system dominated the society; women were subjugated through the practice of sati, but modern India witnesses the higher importance on gender equality and wide participation as well. Economic life also underwent some changes. Modern industries and services have replaced the pastoralists and agriculturists with a new process of economy, the gross domestic product (GDP). In the dimensions of architecture and culture history also witnessed significant changes. India witnessed a considerable change in this dimension. Several techniques were evolved as they developed over time. The monolithic rock cut architecture continued till sixth century AD in India. Its instances are in Ellora, Ajanta and Mahabalipuram. There is a remarkable change in the temple building styles in Puri, Bhubaneswar and Khajuraho. Paintings have also changed from the base of religion to the base of secularism during the Mughal period again towards religion in the form of Pahari miniatures.

However, the writer too changes the history with the script of their time. History is subject to controversy while geography is static in its fact. For instance, the colonial rulers with orientalist views gave the history of India today. The view represents that the Aryans migrated from somewhere in Europe. But the contention on the context of the original inhabitants of India is still a burning topic.

History is also re-written. For instance, the Islam between fifth and sixth century AD was at the beginning a peaceful and progressive religion and was considered one of the most approachable philosophies during that period behind the prosperity of Arab world. The magnification of their trade relations with Rome, India and Africa was quite remarkable. With the passage of time, Islam has been witnessing the rise of extremism with fatal components such as Al Quaeda, ISIS, Taliban, etc. Surprisingly, the word, 'jihad' has got diverse interpretations to different sects of Muslim religion and has brought a striking change in the philosophy of the Islam.

While geography provides a land with neighbours, history considers them as allies, partners or enemies. In this regard, the Israel-Palestine conflict is worth mentionable. The subjugation of Jews is a historical incident. The Jews experienced multiple attempts of ethnic cleansing, but the worst one was certainly during the Second World War under the inhuman hands of the Nazi Germany led by Adolf Hitler. The Jews at last got their homeland, Israel that emerged on the erstwhile Palestinian territory. The city of Jerusalem is holy to both the Jews and the Muslims. Now, this Jerusalem has been the context of chronic bitter conflict between Palestine and Israel, just as Kashmir has been to India and Pakistan.

However, in some radical widespread colossal natural powers like the movements of plates, tsunami, earthquake, water-submerge, etc. may help change geography too. In this case, it reshapes a land as well as its climate and natural vegetation. The recent, onslaught of the mighty tsunami, especially in the Andaman islands, a part of India with its primitive tribal groups, has witnessed a change in the lives of its people under the measures of rehabilitation. In such cases, geography too influences and brings changes to the history of a land. Over time the tribals may lose their traditional culture and be involved into the mainstream of modern life.

In the time table of History, the land remains intact but the politics, culture, economics, people may have radical change. Europe too has witnessed many changes under the hands from the Greeks, Iranians and the romans. With the passage of time, it has been feudal, and then the pioneer of the industrial revolution. The geographical characteristics bordered with the Urals and the Alps have been intact but the dynasties have evolved it into different shapes and ultimately into the present European Union. By the hand of history, the land witnesses the change of its frontiers, such as disintegration, assimilation, and integration again. Till now the countries of European Union fought two World Wars and they are now in collaboration with one another for their common good to live in peace and progress. History is to them, as it were, a great teacher.

Change is the law of nature as well as history. So, history is written each and every day as it passes. It is repeated and sometimes rewritten if there is a significant change in conditions and situations. History is, in fact, a story changing constantly for the same land with its people, nature and vegetation just like a sentinel.

6. Happiness is when what you think, what you say, and what you do are in Harmony

To define happiness is quite difficult for subjectivity. The face of a little baby declares it on getting a new toy and also on the face of an old parent on being loved and cared by their own children. Happiness, in general term, is all about the freedom of our choice. It is freedom to do things we like in our life. Again it is the, quest for knowing one's self. In a word, 'happiness is when what you think, what you say, and what you do are in harmony'.

'Men', in the opinion of Rousseau 'are born free but everywhere he is in chains'. Obviously, the limits to freedom are behind unhappiness of people. When a parent does not allow its child to go out and play in rain, the child is unhappy. But the parent is happy to restrict its child as it is sure of its positive result. People may become unhappy for the lack of actual knowledge in life. In this regard, happiness is relative as well as subjective.

A robber is happy as well as unhappy by the very act of stealing when he gains wealth and on the contrary he is caught and beaten black and blue, respectively. The consequences hardly usher happiness in people, some cases it depends on the act, while in the other in the consequences. In this context, the case of human bombs is worth mentionable. By the sacrifice of their life based on their belief, they find happiness as well as blind blessing that they sought.

Happiness is a matter of circumstances too. A gift on any occasion is certainly the sign and cause of happiness but not at all on the demise of a dear one. A woman in dire need always wishes to get a job in order to win over the hard time. Naturally, she will be happy only when she gets her wish fulfilled. She should be able to speak out her wishes for her family provided she is afraid of speaking out will be unhappy forever; or in situations when her family members are against the idea of her interest for a job. So the freedom is very important to be happy in life.

The government and other organisations have, at present, undertaken initiatives for promoting happiness as a sign of development. Bhutan has initiated the measure of Gross National Happiness as a step for the Development of happiness in its people. People have many unlimited and never ending wishes and it is impracticable to fulfil the wishes of human beings. Life is all about limiting the choices of our wishes and expectations. Some people fulfil many of their materialistic wishes: A nice palace, a costly and luxurious car of the latest fashion, latest costly and fashionable dresses, etc. while some fulfil find it difficult to meet their wishes mainly because of their financial or in some cases situations. Yet it is baseless to consider the rich people happier than the poor on the basis of their freedom to choose the materialistic things in life. Regarding the perfect definition of happiness, philosophers as well as thinkers differed in their interpretations. 'Happiness lies' in the opinion of Lord Buddha, 'in achieving nirvana, in conquering the real self or getting rid of the flame of desire'. Gandhiji, Vivekananda, Sister Nivedita, Florence Nightingale, Mother Teresa and many other noble people discovered happiness in their service to the people as well as the nation.

Happiness exists in the heart of people and largely in their mood of accepting things irrespective of small, minute things in life or even in the admirable achievements. In this regard, the words of Helen Keller are worth mentionable: 'The best and most beautiful things in the world cannot be seen or even touched—they must be felt with the heart'.

Happiness appears differently to different people, but it largely depends on their choice in life of doing things that they want as the freedom of choice also paves the path to happiness.

7. Love in a Glass Jar

The most illogical as well as profound of the senses is the sense of love. Love appears in various forms: love towards people, an object, family, kith and kins, friends, work, etc. Love is in general different from logic. A lover cannot be asked questions regarding it. It is even hard to give justifications and reasons. One can simply love or not.

There are a few basic differences between liking and love they appear to be similar terms like, desire, interest, curiosity, love, etc. in order to express feelings positively towards someone or something. But we very rarely use the word love. Love differs from all other words of feelings quite distinctly.

Love falls into its own category due to its grasp beyond the mind. Love always baffles us by its mystery and magic far beyond our endeavour and ability to understand. We almost always experience that we love someone, but in reality we hardly like them. It does not just happen with people; this happens with emotions, objects, as well as places. Despite our disinterest to visit a place, we have deep feelings of visiting it in some other context.

Liking is rather acceptable than love in case of giving perfectly logical reasons for our likeness to someone or something. Like is always suitable to the confined rules and regulations of the mind. So, it is always easier to understand and express.

On the contrary, love always appears that it is beyond the reach of our understanding. Love is, moreover, too transcendental to accommodate things such as fear, hate, frustration, worry and so many other negative emotions. We can fall in love easily despite having some negative points probably because of our miseries. We might have fallen in love with our troubles because of our unawareness. Naturally, it raises the most important question: Can we make out our reality as well as the world around us by using our minds only?

Regarding the mystery of the mind as well as its inability to understand the harsh reality, Albert Einstein's words are citable: 'The human mind, no matter how highly trained, cannot grasp the universe. We are in the position of a little child, entering a huge library whose walls are covered to the ceiling with books in many different tongues. The child knows that someone must have written those books. It does not know who or how. It does not understand the languages in which they are written. The child notes a definite plan in the arrangement of the books, a mysterious order, which it does not comprehend, but only dimly suspects. That, it seems to me, is the attitude of the human mind, even the greatest and most cultured, towards God. We see a universe marvellously arranged, obeying certain laws, but we understand the laws only dimly. Our limited minds cannot grasp the mysterious force that sways the constellations'.

Finally, it is supposed that love is the mysterious force, referred by Einstein, which is governing the universe. The secret of our existence can be discovered only when our science can grasp the grip of love. Above all, love is the basic constituent of our life.

❑❑❑

ESSAYS ON CULTURAL TOPICS

1. Customs and Traditions of Indian Culture

INTRODUCTION

The human civilisation in India is about 4,500 years older. So, Indian culture is considered to be the oldest in the world. According to the All World Gayatri Pariwar (AWGP) foundation, 'Sa Prathama Sanskrati Vishvavara' i.e. it is the first and the supreme culture in the world. Indian culture is the most enriched as well as the oldest. Christina De Rossi, an anthropologist at Barnet and Southgate College, London, once said, 'Western societies did not always see the culture of India very favourably'. There was a time when culture and the aspects of human development were considered as the evolutionary processes by early anthropologists. On the basis of this view, the societies, especially of India, African countries and the Far East, which were not following European or Western manners of life or outside of Europe or North America were supposed to be culturally primitive and inferior.

INDIA'S EXCELLENCE IN DIVERSE DIMENSIONS

Indians, however, have achieved considerable advancement in the fields of art and architecture with the instances in the Taj Mahal, the Sun Temple, Meenakshi temple; mathematics with the incredible example of the invention of zero; and medicine and hygiene, especially in the branch of Ayurveda. With the passage of time, India has accomplished remarkable development in diverse dimensions and emerged as the rare land of unity in diversity with the second largest population (more than 1.2 billion as per the record of the CIA World Factbook) in the world.

INDIA: ITS STATES AND VARIOUS RELIGIONS

According to the current record of the World Health Organisation (WHO), India consists of twenty-eight states and seven union territories. On the basis of the verdict on the language issue by the Gujarat High Court, 2010, India has no national language but two link languages: Hindi and English. According to the report of The Times of India, 'Many people speak Hindi in India, but 59 per cent of Indian residents speak something other than Hindi'. Other major languages of India are Bengali, Telugu, Tamil, Marathi and Urdu.

Hinduism and Buddhism which are the third and fourth largest religions, respectively, in the world originated in India. Again, the Handbook of Research on Development and Religion edited by Matthew Clarke and published by Edward Elgar Publishing, 2013 mentions that about 84 per cent of the population world population is identified as Hindu with variations in four principal sects: Shaiva, Vaishnava, Shakteya and Smarta. India, with approximately 13 per cent of Muslim inhabitants, is one of the largest Islamic nations in the world while Sikhs and Christians cover smaller per centage of the total population, and Buddhists and Jains make up the smallest per centage.

Indian cuisine is influenced by most other countries of the world. According to the Agricultural and Mechanical College of Texas (Texas A&M University), 'when the Moghal Empire invaded during the sixteenth century, they left a significant mark on the Indian cuisine'. The large assortment of dishes and its liberal use of herbs and spices are also well-known to the world. India is a land of diverse communities and creeds so cooking styles vary from region to region.

INDIA: ITS DIET TRADITION

The staples of Indian diets are enriched with Basmati rice, wheat, and pulses with Bengal gram or *chana*. The spices: Ginger, cardamom, coriander, dried hot peppers, turmeric and cinnamon, etc. also enrich Indian food with curries. Various fruits and vegetables: Tomatoes, tamarinds, cilantro, mint and other herbs are used to prepare *chutney* i.e. thick condiment and spread. Indian food is, thus, proud of its wide variety.

The non-vegetarian Indians commonly enjoy the dishes of chicken, goat and lamb while vegetarians live on varieties of vegetables and milk products such as ghee, butter, paneer, etc. According to the report of The Guardian, 'between 20 per cent and 40 per cent of India's population is vegetarian'. Most of the Indians eat their food with fingers and sometimes with bread used as utensils. Oven-baked flatbread, naan, a leavened, bhatoora, a fried, fluffy flatbread popular in North India and eaten with chickpea curry, etc. are some of the varieties of bread are common in Indian diet.

INDIA: ITS ARCHITECTURE

The Taj Mahal is one of the seven wonders in the world. It was built in an artistic combination with the elements from Indian, Persian, Islamic, and Ottoman Turkish architectural styles by the Mughal emperor, Shah Jahan in memory of his third wife, Mumtaz Mahal. Some of temples with rare architectural flavour are the Brihadeshwara Temple (Tamil Nadu), the Kailashnath Temple (Ellora), the Chennakeshava Temple (Karnataka), the Adi Kumbeswara Temple (Tamil Nadu), and the Golden Temple (Amritsar).

BOLLYWOOD: INDIA'S FILM INDUSTRY

Bollywood, the film industry of India, is famous in the world. According to the Hollywood Foreign Press Association, India began its journey since 1896 when the Lumière brothers displayed the art of cinema in Mumbai. The films of present India are well-known for their intricate thematic background, dancing and singing.

ART AND CULTURE OF INDIA: ITS CLASSICAL DANCE AND MUSIC

Even in the domain of dance and music, India has displayed the surprising hallmark as the advanced civilisation challenging the blind belief of the west. According to *Contract Law in India* by Nilima Bhadbhade, the unique and most enriched dance, music and theatre of India began from more than 2,000 years before and have been continuing till today through innumerable political ups and downs. Bharatanatyam, Odissi, Kathak, Manipuri, Mohiniattam, Kuchipudi, and Kathakali are some of the major classical dance traditions themes drawn from mythology and literature with rigid rules of presentation.

CLOTHING OF INDIA

Variety is the spice for enriched life. Indian clothing too has wide variety especially with the silk saris various colour-flavour worn by the women of India while the dhoti, and an unstitched piece of cloth tied around the waist and legs are for men. Men are often seen wearing a kurta, and a loose shirt long up to the knee. Sherwani i.e. a long coat buttoned up to the collar and down to the knees and the Nehru jacket i.e. a shorter version of a sherwani are commonly worn by men in special occasions.

INDIA: ITS SIGNIFICANT DAYS

India as the culturally and socially advanced country with its hoary traditions and customs, also celebrates many important days round the calendar. The Independence Day, the Republic Day, the Mahatma Gandhi's Birthday, Birthday of Rabindranath Tagore and birthdays of many other important national figures who sacrificed their lives for the sake of the land are celebrated with solemnity and pride. Diwali, a five-day festival of lights symbolising the inner light that protects people from their spiritual darkness, is the largest and mostly observed holiday in India. Moreover, different religions and communities observe their religious festivals and important days throughout the year. The Holi i.e. the festival of colours, the Durga Puja, the Ratha yatra are some of the famous Hindu festivals and the Eid, the Ramjan are some of the Muslim festivals which are celebrated with pomp and fanfare in India.

CONCLUSION

In a word, India is the land of unity in diversity. The astounding cultural intermingling is seen only in India. The east, west, north, south and central India populated with diverse communities and different language speaking people live and flourish in peace and progress caring a fig to some sudden outbreak of communal riots and violence in different parts of India in different times. India is the land of varied and unique culture and customs since its beginning and has been flourishing with immense varieties and grandeur. India is not only culturally varied, but it is varied also in its climate and landforms. Different parts of India enjoy different climatic and atmospheric conditions. In any respect, the customs and traditions of Indian culture is unique and surprising, and impressive in the world.

2. A Problem of India: Lacking Toilets

'Is India's lack of toilets a cultural problem?' is the burning question of the day. The mindset of Indians is at the root of the derogatory situation which makes raise this question. The existence of low caste and backward classes, and the existing negligence by the rest of the Indians are responsible for the unawareness of those people. As a result, in many parts of our nation people lack toilets and prefer the open defecation. The context of lacking toilets may be a cultural issue. In the villages, the situation appears to be worse as two-thirds of the villagers have no toilets. Evidently, open defecation is common to them, and it is the major barrier in the course of achieving millennium development goals with the inclusion of reducing by half of the total number of people with no access to basic sanitation by 2015. In the opinion of a biographer, Mahatma Gandhi, the father of India, had a 'Tolstoian preoccupation with sanitation and cleaning of toilets'. With reference to an incident experienced by Gandhi during visit to inspect the toilets in Rajkot city, Gujarat, he said: "He (Gandhiji) reported that they were 'dark and stinking and reeking with filth and worms' in the homes of the wealthy and in a Hindu temple. The homes of the untouchables simply had no toilets. 'Latrines are for you big people', an untouchable told Gandhi".

Years later, Gandhi took a step of encouragement for his disciples to work as scavengers and sanitation officers in villages. In this regard, Madhav Desai, his diarist and hardworking secretary, recorded the villagers' attitudes: 'They don't have any feeling at all. It will not be surprising if within a few days they start believing that we are their scavengers'.

Obviously, the cultural attitudes of India are at the root of this enduring shame. More than half a century passed after the Independence of India, yet many Indians go on littering implicitly and relieving themselves in the open. However, they keep their domestic areas clean and tidy. The state has become unsuccessful in extending the facilities of sanitation, for the unawareness of the people at large.

The city dwellers as well as residents of Indian cities are also remarkably blatant and blameable. For instance, once in the suburb of Gurgaon a rich and sophisticated and educated resident sent his servants with pet dogs outside for open defecation of the dogs, and the rich man refused to clean up the mess on demand by the other neighbours and said that his apartment was clean and tidy and no place for his dogs. This is not a rare case; it is common in all cities in India. Such situations tell us that not only the ignorant villagers but the educated city dwellers also are equally responsible for such problems.

However, the situation in villages is gradually getting better. The rate of access to sanitation facilities rose from 40 per cent (in 2002) to 51 per cent (in 2008–2009). According to the survey reports, more than 60 per cent homes in the states of Jharkhand, Bihar, Orissa, Madhya Pradesh, Rajasthan, Uttarakhand and Tamil Nadu are still lacking toilets. The behavioural and cultural indicators show: More than 70 per cent Sikh and Christian households have access to improved sanitation while Hindus only 45 per cent.

India campaigns on sanitation and hygiene by providing subsidies to build toilets and increased the integrated expense on sanitation by nearly three-fold in 2005. The government of India started a scheme to award the councils of villages with a view abolishing the act of open defecation in rural areas. The village councils of Kerala performed with 87 per cent and picked up the awards while 2 per cent of councils in badly off Bihar won in a dull commentary with respect to its sanitation.

Haryana and Himachal Pradesh can be the role model for other states as both have been successful by using and empowering local people for tackling open defecation. They are also succeeded in building toilets and adopting good waste management. Providing subsidies to poor households to build toilets, Haryana leads campaigns with women volunteers encouraging people to build toilets in its patriarchal and less progressive condition. According to the government survey reports it is said: 'Himachal Pradesh has toilets today in its every home'.

Above all, the condition will go on till people stick to their age-old cultural attitude of community sanitation. The mass awareness and active initiatives of the people irrespective of their status, is a must to make the target successful in near future.

3. India and China: The Management of Cross-culture

The two eastern developing countries: India and China are the lands with more than five thousand year-old civilisations as well as enriched cultural and traditional heritage. The geographical existence prevents the countries to interact since time immemorial. Still since ancient times, some scholars such as Fa Xian and Xuan Zang travelled to India from China, Buddhist monks, especially Bodhisattvas, travelled to China from India. Despite this restricted exchanges, cultural differences did not avert two peoples to interact their motives regarding their search for knowledge or spiritual search. From the beginning of modern age, the active phase of social contacts has started between India and China.

However, due to the rapid globalisation process, these two nations have come closer, and economics have unveiled a new horizon crossing the border. Both China and India are rising for their reform policies. By means of their conditions, both nations are compelled to promote their trade and commerce in mutual interests.

A precondition is at the root of these countries for their social, economic and political understanding with regard to their cross-cultural communications. China is aware of the crucial fact of India, a multilingual and multiethnic land, and its democracy with multiparty political system, independent judiciary representing pluralistic interests.

China should predominantly mistake neither the unity in diversity of India nor its economic reforms initiated in early nineties and its course of transformation into the encouraging market of liberalisation and foreign direct investment. India has got a real growth which showed the positive side of India in its Gross Domestic Product (GDP) at an average of 8.6 per cent in the last few years. In the global domain of Information Technology (IT), Indian companies have proved their success. China should recognise India in regional and global sense as a rising power of Asia. India too needs to realise the unique political, economic, social and cultural conditions of China. Since its reformation in 1978, Chinese economic liberalisation adheres to a centrally planned economy, 'socialist market economy', by predominantly awarding the basic superiority to public ownership. The State-Owner undertakings (SOEs), has now been reformed and its plays a crucial role in the national economy. The output of SOE to the GDP of country is now 50 per cent against 70 per cent in 1985 while the corresponding share of the state sector in India was 14.1 per cent in 1990. The encouragement of Chinese entrepreneurship is undoubtedly at the highest point and the private sector too is booming. In the 15th Chinese Communist Party (CCP) Congress in 1997, China boosted privatisation and subsequently undertook a crucial practical measure in 2005 by introducing a share conversion pilot reform programme. The south-eastern coastal China having been open to the foreigners for a long time is ahead of other parts of the country in respect of growth in private sector market and cultural development.

In the field of politics, CCP is the all-in-all force in China as well as the state and the entire nation is submissive to the party. The CCP decides even the macroeconomic policies and as a result the State easily implements in the absence of any credible opposition, in contrast to the scenario in India. The party vets all senior appointments in business enterprises and its trade unions are operating within all the companies.

The Chinese economic model is based on the discipline and central control, while Indian economy is marked by chaos and decentralisation. Simultaneously, China has some weak areas to focus on. For instance, legal and banking infrastructures are considered by the foreigners as obstacles to their business operations.

Foreigners involving themselves with China should have in the back of their minds the idea about the unprecedented economic growth of China in recent times. Over the last 20 years, the country has registered an impressive 9.5 per cent growth every year. It has become the third largest economy (second in terms of PPP) in the world with its per capita GDP US$ 3260 in contrast to just US$ 50 in 1949, whereas on the basis of market exchange rates, India is the 12th largest economy in the world fourth largest in terms of PPP with its per capita GDP US$ 830. China could pull out 500 million people out of poverty in past few decades. The profile of China in international trade has gone up, with the volume now at US$ 2.6 trillion, a hundredfold rise from US$ 20.6 billion, 30 years ago. Three decades ago there was no Foreign Direct Investment (FDI) into China, but now it has reached the level of US$ 92.4 billion, first accomplishment among developing nations. The Chinese mass exodus has been very active in investing largely in China.

Undoubtedly, China is still a developing nation, and in terms of per capita GDP ranked 104th in the world. A balanced development is the main and major target of Beijing's policy and a rise from its former GDP-centric growth model. China positioned its goal towards the tetrad of the 2000 GDP by 2020 to become a medium level advanced nation by 2050. However, China encounters big challenges: environmental questions, income disparities and ensuring of the efficacy of the government investment towards development.

China is also leading an active military modernisation programme raising concerns in the region. It badly needs foreign resources for its development but it hunts energy in global sphere. Apparently, China is utilising its economic strength to accomplishing a political influence in the global domain and its outlooks have become crucial for decision-making by world powers. A rising China has naturally drawn attention of the world business community along with India to trade with and invest in its territory. The major countries of the world are more and more establishing joint ventures or wholly self-owned enterprises in China to produce goods for the Chinese market or export to other countries. The neighbouring country, India is not exception in this regard, its trade and investment relations with China are gradually on the pick. By 2010, India-China trade almost touched US$ 60 billion. China has proved to be India's largest trade partner.

The cross-cultural management calls for a holistic approach from India and China. Indians and Chinese are in search of a way-out to resolute the problem of transcending the cultural barriers. The task will be easy the moment they know each other in respect to the traditions and culture of their nations. The base of Chinese culture is its rich language and literature, spirituality, its culture of clothing, health and hygiene, and food habits. The knowledge of Chinese language will be important to foreigners for communicating effectively with the Chinese as English has not yet spread widely in China as a link language. Chinese too has an opportunity to be acquainted with the unique characteristics of the Indian civilisation, philosophy as well as democracy.

The following are some of the ideas helpful to the Indian businessmen interested to deal with China:

i. The Chinese have a traditional mindset of a 'Middle Kingdom' with the belief of their country being the 'Centre of Universe'. During the Ming (1368–1644) and Qing (1644–1911) dynasties, there was the system of tribute. The dynasties of Korea, Burma, Siam (present day Thailand) and North Vietnam used to convey their tributes to the Chinese emperors, when the latter favoured them. In this way, Chinese assumed their cultural superiority and even in this present context the mindset is common among the Chinese.

ii. Business community of China, especially the younger generation, does not think the Sino-Indian territorial conflict of 1962 to be a hindrance in their business relation with India. Simultaneously, the Sino-Indian conflict may still have influenced the Chinese traditions of territory as in the Chinese concept of 'Under the Heaven' (Tianxia), i.e. all territories belong to the emperor, the Son of God, the term 'territory' has no importance. However, the Chinese now demand that this age-old concept is out of vogue. In relation to this, there is another point that the two nations are rivals in the political as well as territorial positions, and it will certainly ward off promoting their business relations.

iii. The Chinese are not interested to give equal status to stability as well as reforms because of their firm belief in stability. Their past was guaranteed with stability by the leaders, Mao Zedong as well as Deng Xiaoping and in future they look for the same by the Chinese Communist Party as the civil society supports the government in this regard. Therefore, the Chinese business concept hardly has any intention of being involved in bureaucratic terms because of the importance of the government's charter in the country's economy. Hence, Indian businessmen should establish dealings with the Chinese governments as well as their sponsored enterprises simultaneously; China should think of the contributions of Indian ventures for the development of China.

iv. Indian executives familiar with the business climate of China are keen to select local Chinese partners and employ more Chinese at senior and middle management levels in the staff of their companies with a view to entering the local markets.

v. The CCP has great influence over business of China and it distinguishes China from India in parlance of the prevailing conditions in both countries. That is the question for the Indian businessmen.

vi. The staff of the Indian companies should be trained in Chinese language, social and culture conditions in this way the West establish their markets.

The Chinese too in India face cultural barriers such as the cases of governance, language and infrastructure problems. The following are some of the crucial ones:

- As per the reports from the observers, the Chinese construction companies confront indignation of the unemployed engineers of India.
- India is not willing to allow Chinese entrepreneurs in the sensitive sectors like telecommunication and port projects because of security reasons. The Chinese companies better be familiar with Indian compulsions for better business opportunities.

The Chinese companies interested to deal with India should understand the legal system of India functioning in the foundation of a democracy. For instance, the case of the Chimney collapse, in Central Chhattisgarh causing death of 41 persons, subsequently 80 Chinese workers were not allowed to return China until the enquiry was completed by the authorities. It is, at last, clear that the fundamental systems of India and China differ and it may influence their business relations. Indian system is chaotic and prone to communal as well as ethnic conflicts and decentralised in decision-making, flexibility oriented and resilient preventive social pressures for the country's overall stability, whereas the Chinese system is disciplined and people oriented and centrally controlled. The growth and success of the India-China cross-cultural management largely depends on the cooperation of the two to harmonise their strengths as well as weaknesses for the betterment of their business understandings.

4. Challenging Cultural Values Affecting Food Security in India

The government of India considers food security as a fundamental right. Hence, it has introduced schemes with a view to improving the conditions of access to food and nutrition. However, a project initiated in the rural areas of northeast India, Uttar Pradesh displays that gendered patterns in case of food distribution within the households often rest out of their chance to intervene because they are very deeply fixed within the local culture and tradition.

In rural areas, women solely manage the nutritional and other needs of their families while tending crops and other duties. Men often scruple to share domestic activities because they are in the age-old tendency to it as 'women's work'. Women play crucial role in ensuring the food security in their families even by neglecting their own nutritional needs. There is a tradition in rural culture that the male breadwinner eats first. Then, children, particularly sons, eat while women and girls last, by then there will be very little or no food left. Women get neither enough food nor are taken care of even during their pregnancy. As the family is based on the traditional culture women are even deprived of nutritious food and sufficient rest during sickness or pregnancy.

5. Does Indian Cinema Shape our Popular Culture or Merely Reflect it?

Our popular culture is shaped by Indian Cinema by reflecting our culture from fashion to lifestyle as the temporal and physical distances reduce.

The common values and themes determine the popularity of the culture any society which has tendency to grow and develop. We can see our culture in Indian Cinema as cinema features the social values, norms, beliefs and customs of a society. Culture itself is dynamic and constant changing in a gradual manner as a society goes on with time. But the implication of culture assumes different meaning too. Since the first movie *Raja Harishchandra* released in 1913, our culture has undergone lots of changes.

The Indian cinema has always displayed largely the belief of the people and the future course of the society. The movies such as *Pyaasa* and *Do Bigha Zamin* reflect the incidents of our society like exploitation of labourers by zamindars, after the British regime, the vibrant culture that throve on kinship and family, and the dire poverty. Gandhian and Nehruvian ethics predominantly influence these movies of the pre-independence era. The major and heart piercing happenings of our society were viewed on the silver screen clearly. Superstition grew in parallel as it was in the past and movies were produced based on mythologies like *Jai Santoshi Maa* which emphasises honesty and idol worship.

As the political conditions of India changed, society underwent some changes, especially during the emergence of Mrs. Indira Gandhi in power, contemporary problem of unemployment and emergency imposed on the people. Movies like *Zanzeer* and *Deewaar* reflected the way of integrity in such disorder; showed the anger of honest working class; the suppressed ambitions of the young people and frustration and rage against the corrupt system. With an angry young man, the anger of crowd was reflected in the cinema. At this critical juncture of the social as well as cinema of India, there emerged superstar like Amitabh Bachchan, who voiced for the mass and the mass resounded his voice.

The death of Rajiv Gandhi influenced the political as well as Indian cinema. After his death, the uncertainty of the country was viewed on the screen. The cinema declined with the deterioration of the social situations of India. The movies of the new millennium produced newer narratives into public domain. *Rang De Basanti,* released in 2005, reflected the power of youth and newer patterns of protest. Many national protests across the nation were inspired by the protest with candles in hand at India Gate. Recently released movies like *Namastey London*, reflected rare change in backdrop since 1970s when *Purab and Pashchim,* starred by Manoj Kumar, showed the differences between western and native Indian culture sarcastically. The movie like, *Bhaag Milkha Bhaag* shows the life of the hero who made India proud in their field of struggle on the screen. The popularity of the films gave us the demographic record of our country because maximum people in the 19–45 years of working age could reproduce with these stories especially on the path of dedication and hard work.

The movies like, *Taare Zameen Par, Stanley ka dabba,* etc. reflected new types of understanding on child psychology as well as problems of children. This highlights the evolution of our culture through cinema. The economic growth of India was more than 8 per cent for few years and nation could afford more, there is more scope for executing research on the unexplored areas and producing grand budget movies like *Jodha Akbar* indicates us the economic development and bearing power of people because of growth. Once there was a time when the north and south were considered different domains. But as the actors from Bollywood started working with Tollywood as well as Kollywood this distance reduced. This indicated the growth of the people's wisdom transcending the frontiers of the regions. It has proved to be an instance to represent the relevant values and lifestyle of society.

Cinema as the popular mode of media has also played a critical role to shape our culture as we learn many things from this popular resource. The facts of reflection and influence were not important as the popularity of our culture by means of cinema. Indian cinema is mirrors happenings of society while it lefts minimal modification or influence on the popular culture.

6. Advancement of Civilisation versus Cultural Declination

INTRODUCTION

The growing trend demonstrates that civilisation and culture are inseparable and are keenly involved with the human behaviour as well as characteristics. Civilisation and culture attribute to life in the same way, but differ at different contexts regarding the human lifestyle as well as standard of living. Culture is the yardstick to determine a special group of people separated with regard to small areas, while the civilisation requires a vast geographic area with people with same characteristics art and skills. Further, it can be clarified on the basis of culture differentiating different groups of people within the same civilisation. But it is usual instance that humans have a proneness to lose their culture when the civilisation advances. There is no exception in the present age to follow the same practice from the Old Stone Age civilisation.

CULTURE

The term 'culture' has significant impression on deciding the approach of human life. Food, clothing and shelter are inclusive to our culture. Languages, art and architecture, dance and music, the various customs, religions and rituals vary from region to region. The cultural significance for, however, a country uniquely presents its culture. The hoary tradition and heritage of a country demonstrates its historical significance and enriches its culture. The culture represents the prestige of a nation by displaying the mentality of the people as well as the proneness of the human beings living in the region.

CIVILISATION

Civilisation too is equally significant to the humans of a particular place, region or country. Civilisation denotes the manner of living including the social behaviour and performance of people, the abstract inclinations of the human components, and the utilisation and development of the artificial and natural technologies. Civilisation is constantly changing with time. The evolution process cannot be experienced while living in the age. If we read the history right from the Old Stone Age to the modern age of Nuclear and Cyber civilisation, we can vividly realise the alterations in the civilisation. Our growth began in the metal age which we have left far behind even beyond the reach of our ancestors' memory, and are in the course of inclusion from the electronic age to the cyber era.

The simple division of the world into different civilisations on the basis of the various differentiating factors assemble the population of the entire world in the single gridiron when we start discussing history with regard to developing civilisation and culture. The civilisation that has been constantly developing certainly created calderas in the surface of culture which leads to confusion in diverse looks and aspects.

VARIOUS FIELDS AFFECTED BY THE RAPID GROWTH OF THE CIVILISATION

Agriculture

Food is our fundamental requirement of life and it is largely based on agriculture the driving force of any civilisation. Agriculture has been the only means of food, since the dawn of civilisation, for the humans who began growing different food crops. However, with the advancement of age, he developed the habit of eating flesh and now the existing generation has developed tendency to ignore this vital field. Agriculture has developed in parallel to science significantly but unexpectedly the modern generation young men are indifferent to this sector of farming and providing food to the society. Despite appraisal and respect to the farmers like God, for their contribution to feeding the people throughout the nation, they have appeared valueless and regardless in the minds of Modern sophisticated younger generation.

Industrialisation

The process of industrialisation and its rapid growth is one of the most responsible factors for the deterioration of our culture. The adaptation of the industrial sector in the civilisation has created greater employment opportunities and in parallel to it the arrival of the MNCs in the different developing nations has resulted in the use of the manpower throughout the world. The utilisation of the human resource i.e. the manpower has enhanced the value of brain power for growth of the economy of the developed countries and it is considered 'brain drain' by the developing as well as the under developed countries which have proved failure to value the manpower for the lack of adequate financial support. Moreover, industrialisation has also caused the considerable decline of the small scale as well as cottage industries, the traditional part of the culture. The home-made products and the handicrafts could not compete with the machine made products regardless of clothing, edibles, and other utilities of everyday life.

Society

The act of togetherness is the predominant part of society as well as human behaviour. Naturally, the bond and interaction of humans with the biotic and the abiotic species in the environment is greatly important. In a word, these factors are the significant part of the culture. The culture hints at the firm connection with regard to the togetherness, affection in festivities and celebrations which are the primary family values of agreement and unity. The radical change and evolution of it into the small units of nuclear family patterns are gradually losing the flavour of warmth and affection.

In this advanced civilisation of modern, people have discovered a fake prestige by mimicking the trendy speech of the English language disregarding and neglecting the natural pride of using their own dialect and languages. It is now a common instance that people often seem to be unable to communicate with each other in their own language though they have good knowledge of their mother tongue. They are ashamed of speaking their own language.

Lifestyle Regarding Clothing and Standard of Living

Our lifestyle has developed from the ancient age of earthen pots to the modern age of stainless steel for the microwave, and plastic utensils. Our clothing has also evolved considerably from the covered clothing to the undue exposure that leads to the over socialisation, attraction and cases of increasing sexual abuse. Medical science has advanced from the obsolete home remedies to the advanced medical dimension, but we have unfortunately failed to perceive the value of home remedies as well as the nutritious food items, and even the usage of earthen pots.

The advanced sophisticated technologies like television, air-conditioner, social media, internet and various telecommunicating devices have developed the artificial pride in us by arresting our attention to their fascinating usages simultaneously we don't care to acknowledge its adversely negative effects for both human beings and the atmosphere.

The sports, like cricket and other lots of games and sports, have increased craziness among people. As a consequence, people prefer to enjoy watching sports as an audience and are not interested to engage themselves in the physical activities. Despite the automated devices for physical exercise and even for walking, for instance, tread mill, developed by the advanced civilisation, people do not have enough time to apply their abilities to these valuable requirements governing their health.

CONCLUSION

Finally, it is evident that the context demands the value of culture in contrast to the advancing civilisation. There are innumerable instances and activities with regard to enlisting the importance of the growing civilisation by constant provision of comfort to the humans and calming the lifestyle. Undoubtedly, the adverse and irreparable impacts of the rapidly evolving civilisation are discovered in the 'hole we have created in the ozone layer'. The vandalisation to our culture is really distressing. Still it is high time to consider the greater and long-lasting values of our ancient culture as well as strictly follow the immortal values in them and integrate them in our day-to-day life.

7. Mass Media versus Cultural Invasion

INTRODUCTION

Mass media is the driving force of this cyber age. The media has proved to be a style-of-the-time rather than the essential necessity. People nowadays depend mainly on the media for every fundamental requirement of their everyday life. The invention of the form of mobile internet has enabled people to keep the world in their pockets. From childhood to old-age, we are in the trap of the media and thus we are gradually sacrificing our invaluable freedom to the mighty media. We cannot find a place in our country devoid of the media as well as its wastage.

Media has established its firm base in the artificial culture of modern era. Despite the fame of our enriched culture and its tradition the present status with regard to its culture as well as disorder makes it hard to feel proud of. As the western business concerns arrived in our nation with the hand of globalisation, our culture has got an uncontrollable shock resulting in great flexibility in our prestige as well as pride.

MASS MEDIA

Once, a simple landline telephone appeared to be a big deal. The age of television followed by the emergence of computers and the world was turned upside down. The Internet has given a great scope to bring the world just a click. The social media such as Twitter, Facebook, have made communication faster. The video calling mediums such as viber and skype bring us very close to each other and people are pleased to being able to interact face-to-face. The news channels too have reduced the wide gap between the mass and the government and made democracy well established. Media has established its crucial position in our everyday life.

SIGNIFICANCE OF INDIAN CULTURE

India is well known for its hoary cultural tradition with immensely great evidence of our customs and traditions. India is unique in the world for its united existence with diverse cultures. India has diverse traditions, customs, linguists, creed, caste, etc. with equal importance to every Indian. Indians endeavour their best to convey equal respect to every tradition and for this reason India has succeeded in paving the way to the westernisation. India has incorporated the western culture by adapting it and hence, it is in course for following the values and trends. When the westernisation appears to be negative and bad traits become apparent, the wide gap peeps in.

IMPACT OF MEDIA ON INDIAN CULTURE

The media has played the critical role in highlighting various dimensions of Indian culture:

Values of Family and Marriage

The family as well as marriage has lost their values as the younger generation is inclined to television and internet. As a result, the influence of the western culture is growing among them. It has introduced some new relationships such as live-in together relationship in the country, where the marriage and joint family structure has the great importance as well as the major preference for the nuclear family structure.

Adultery

The internet has given the unwanted twaddle easy access to the young minds, and naturally it lightens the sparks for the background of the country to get their identity and pride destroyed.

The growing women insecurity in India is the consequence of the damage caused to our cultural tradition. The cultural degradation has resulted in the growing fear factor in India. Certainly, this is the major reason for cultural degradation.

Governance and Democracy

Media has accomplished great success in connecting the mass to the government. Media has definitely made the citizens aware of the proceedings of the government, which is very important for our democracy. Media has helped greatly to grow up the Indian culture regarding the socialising and community interaction.

Human Values

Social values in India have already lost their ground with considerable progress of media. Media is providing the common man with more along with the information. The culture of conveying respect to the elders is no longer in vogue. With the fast evolution of the new culture and trends, the situation has turned upside down. Everyone has developed the desire for money, property and power instead of caring a fig to anyone or anything coming in course of their path to attain the goal. Naturally, people have the policy of honesty for gaining the short-cut ways to attain their desired target.

Lifestyle

Indians have developed inclination to fast food, as well as the international cuisines as their updated status rather than the delicacy.

The clothing too are about to lose their existence. Males prefer the suiting in the hot summers imitating the foreigners. Females have proneness to the western culture and Indian dresses now appear obsolete to them. Indian female prefer dignified outlook set in western dressings. Now the traditional Indian trend has been redesigned with the fashionable westernised touch. The mother tongue seems shameful to them, rather they feel pride in Indianised English. The adults as well as the kids keep up their conversation in English. The growing trend, in the recent times, is preferring to send kids to convent schools for better English fluency. Many Indians do not even know their mother tongue.

CONCLUSION

In a word, loss of culture means the loss of a nation's value, pride and dignity in the International level. Media is behind all these successes as well as consequences. Despite bringing the world at the corner of our home, media has opened many means to which our society is vulnerable. It is high time that we made the technology dependent on us; rather making it our lord. Now we should realise the situation, take initiatives to upgrade our society by controlling its vulnerable sides for saving our culture and our country from impending ominous.

8. Being Proud to be Indians

INTRODUCTION

Humans are proud of their motherland. India is our motherland. Naturally, we pride ourselves on being Indians and nurturing respect for it in our hearts and soul. The feeling of being its citizens is great as its cultural tradition is unique in the world. The depth of our emotion betrays our great patriotism.

Indians are honoured and given dignity by the world because of its hoary cultural traditions which are matchless. The amplitude of our emotion betrays the immenseness of our patriotism in times of safety India. The whole Indians always forget all their existing misunderstandings, problems and shortcomings, and tie themselves by the bond of a family and it becomes visible to the Indians and their supreme strength.

THE PRIDE OF UNITY AND POWER

Our distinct way of living differentiates us from the rest of the world. The largest democracy of the world gives us lots of comforts. It has tremendously great secrets behind all these—its power as well as its unity.

UNITY

The special characteristic of our land is its unity in diversity. The diversities are geographical as well as cultural, religious, on castes, traditional etc. even of the fundamental utilities of life such as food, clothing and dialects. Irrespective of all these diversities, people enjoy the equal status in respect of their own social and economic background. These diversities astoundingly get united and make the world wonder and always make them think discover the secret behind our unity. During national crisis our patriotism too impress the world.

DEMOCRATIC BACKGROUND

India is a large democracy. To a democratic government, it is a challenge in itself to execute successfully by keeping a healthy balance in the demands of so many varieties of people. The Indian democratic government overcome these difficulties and come forward to satisfy the population united under all the sects and sub-sects as well as provide them equal status and importance.

SECULARISM

This feature too is visible in the lives and culture of Indians. Hardly do few nations pay equal importance to all the religious and ethnic groups in their lands. Every religion is freely performing their religious rituals simultaneously conveying respect to all other religions. They are surprising secularity is incredible, they seem as they are children of the same mother, though in reality they belong to diverse religious and ethnic groups and follow their own rules and principles.

JOINT FAMILY

The joint family culture is the unique social and cultural emblem of India. We keep strong family relationships so we are happy and feel the bond of it greatly. It also helps us forget our religious narrowness. Love, affection and care are prime importance. The whole family lives together at a place where the kids are brought up and taken care of by the elders. Here the flavour of love, respect, unity and integrity is predominantly practised. So, our family becomes the first school for our children where they learn developing their moral values. The unity incorporates the feeling of oneness.

ENVIRONMENT

The beauty of environment in India is the by-product of the freedom and liberty in every sphere of life. We breathe the fresh aroma of the air without any restrictions. Every citizen enjoys freedom in all considerable aspects to the extent that it does not hurt others in any way. Indians live after their choice and build their own lifestyle after their free choice.

EMOTIONS

India, the land of emotions, is tied together by means of this very invisible power. It pulls us to one place though we live in different parts of the world. Our family, relatives and friends play significant roles in our lives. Our younger generation is struggling in many parts of the world for providing themselves good living for their family.

LIFESTYLE

Indians also have freedom to live the life according to their own choice. But the Indian lifestyle is 'simple living and high thinking'. This too is quite awesome and appreciating. Our respect for the women as well as for the physical relationship makes our land unique and precious. The special framework and dignified outlook of the Indian women is rare in the world. Our clothing betrays our traditions diverse cultural background. Every style of cloths that we wear has its specific significance. Be it a saree or suit for the females, the kurta-pyjama or dhoti for the males, the way of wearing the dress imparts the dignity and respect among the people around us.

MEDIA: NEWSPAPERS AND NEWS CHANNELS

India has maximum number of newspapers in different dialects. In recent times, the news channels too have succeeded in reaching this goal, these serve in many regional languages in addition to the major languages. The maximum number of agencies are rushing and pushing us ahead with their provisions to the necessary details to the other parts of the world.

THE DECLINE OF OUR CULTURE

We have some other sources to feel proud of, but the advancement of science and technology is gradually transforming the reality into a different sphere. As a consequence, our culture is on decline. Globalisation has paved ways to the intermixing of the cultures and westernisation especially, the younger generation is greatly influenced. Westernisation is marring our culture. Fooding and clothing are on the way to rapid change. All these are the consequences of globalisation.

CONCLUSION

Precisely, India can be called a heaven in respect to its diverse natural as well as cultural beauties with its rare fragrance of nature. The different colours of the Indian culture give unique pleasure making one forgetting anything and everything. But the recent situation tells the tale of degradation of all these. It is high time Indians needed to discover the evils and set straight to reform and redress the culture as well as its economy in order to get united and pledge to save our motherland from the impending danger.

9. The Culture of the Younger Generation

INTRODUCTION

The younger generation today emerged as overcivilised on earth. As change is the law of nature and the evolution process too constantly undergoes changes. Our youth have also developed impressively by incorporating the best as well as the worsts greatly. The youth have moulded and modified themselves as well as their lifestyle in much faster pace that is beyond imagination. Their trend has not only surprised a country, but the whole world.

YOUTH TODAY: THEIR POSITIVE SIDES

The youth today, the backbone of next generation, have many positive and praiseworthy aspects. They have certainly power to move ahead and succeed in their attempts which draw attention as well as inspiration. Some Special Aspects of the Youth Are as Follows:

Iron Determination and Dedication

The youth have an iron determination which gives them strength and immense stamina for endeavouring to accomplish their goal in time perfectly. If we cast a peer glance, their sincerity and dedication in the work will be visible to us.

Resisting the Stress

They have excellent capacity to cope with the stressful circumstances. They are able to manage almost all stiff situations successfully. Gender is not the bar to this generation. Male and female in equal gallop are proving their excellence in the spheres of work and achievements. They have qualified the performance and excellence parameters in the competitive world.

Patriotism

The zeal of patriotism is no issue to the generation. They are promised to serve their nations till their life. In the worst situations, they are desperate to defend the congenial station of their motherland. Everyone performs and devotes their part in the best possible means.

Approach to Life

They have a practical approach to their life. They have developed some specific qualities to win over the practical situations coming in course of their life. They are always ready to face the endangered situations and are well equipped beforehand to confront them efficiently.

Refined Approach

They have gained maturity and have ability to analyse the situations keeping a healthy balance of mind to clinch the best resolution without any bias. They do not rush for solution; rather they buy time to discover the exact ways for the resolution.

Awareness: Social and General

They are aware how to balance the situations with their life. The Intelligent Quotient (IQ) and the social awareness make them able to uplift the segments of the countryside to the fore. They preplan and boost the development in the underdeveloped areas.

YOUTH TODAY: THEIR DARK SIDES

As none is perfect in this world, the younger generation too have some pitfalls. The obvious side is that some of them are deviated from their mainstream and are prone to the extremities of the abstracts of their own emotions. This tendency has resulted in growing concern of violence and rage the society.

Oversocialisation

The gender partiality cannot be overcome existing in our society because of the socialising nature of the youth. The oversocialising nature has changed the relations and the physical relationship is considered a game. This attitude of the younger generation leads them to lots of medical complications in the later part of their lives.

Craze

Their warm blood occasionally makes them impatient and heated up much and leads them to violent activities. Their craze to complete their task has the utmost priority. Different forms of terrorism in the world are indicating their rage and effective tendency.

Pub and Disco Era

Their proneness to the western culture lead them to some new sorts of entertainments like, disco going and pub visiting. They are becoming the slaves of some bad habits such as drinking and smoking. The pub culture is their latest fashion of pride which is the sure negative sign for the next generation. Life appears as a game to them and enjoyment is their prior choice. It is good to lead the life at present but for precocious plan for the future. But it is a matter of sorrow that most of the younger generation fail to adopt with the peak years and plan for their life. The junk food is a trendy habit.

Complete Dependence on Technology

The generation has shined as the tech-savvy talents. They can complete every task by the click of a mouse. The ease and comfortable they enjoy is the boon of the cyber world. They have forgotten the importance of physical exercise and naturally are suffering poor health with lots of artificial health hazards in tender age. We are in the era when our youth are unable to recognise anything without the help of technology as they completely rely on the technology. The technology itself is managing and controlling them.

Loss of Moral Values

They are remarkably losing their moral and human values which are essential to lead a life in humanistic approach. Money, wealth and property are their sole concern. So, they have no time for their family, friends and kith and kins. They have failed to develop moral values like respect, care and affection.

REFLECTION IN SOCIETY

Society too has predominant role in shaping and reshaping the youth. The congenial environment certainly produces significantly positive results. But our society has been losing its moral situations because of the egoism and self-centeredness of the majority of the well aware people. There are hardly people to appreciate and value the quality in their environs. Everyone has developed the habit of portraying their false face up. This demotivating atmosphere too is responsible for the moral decline of the present generation.

CONCLUSION

We are aware that there are many factors behind our progress and regress. Similarly, the younger generation too faces the same case. It is society where we grow and flourish. So it is the responsibility and accountability of the older generation to determine the course of the younger ones, as they are vulnerable. The social negligence is the crucial factor that leads us to our results and consequences. They are now in need of our special attention as well as appreciation. They are much like the mould of soft clay in hands of the sculptor and the society is the very molder. The more careful the molder is, the better the statue takes form. Our youths are in urgent need of molding in careful and tactful manners. We should encourage and uplift the young generation with a view to creating a better future for oncoming generation.

10. The Composite Culture of India is Captivating

INTRODUCTION

Indian culture has earned wide dignity and respect in the world. The Indian culture is unique and diversified since the beginning and has developed and assumed the current form through lots of ups and downs. This is the incredible facet of India that earns the credit from across the world. India boasts of its maximum religions, cultures and dialects, geographical varieties, by keeping in healthy and equal balance, respect and prestige by means of its magical unity.

Indian culture has a special flavour and grandeur, which maximises and encourages the pride of the nation. India has also succeeded in spreading its culture almost across the world. Foreigners are often captivated by its grand diverse culture. Some of them prefer even to settle in India. This is another speciality of our culture and tradition. Indians are always liberal and exercise broader sense and outlook, so they have kept their gates open for all who want come and settle and share their ways of living and lifestyle, of course with equal respect and freedom. The composite characteristic of our culture is its own identity which gives an open choice to the outsiders to begin their journey from here. Naturally, it is a matter of fact that it captivates foreigners. The inquisitive of a person makes him more inclined to get into the knowledge of India culture and traditions and its diversity in lifestyle, customs, traditions, region, outlook, caste and much more.

RELIGION

In India, Hindu, Muslim, Sikh, Christian, etc. all coexist together in peace and progress. They freely practise their religious rituals, clothing and even eat the food as per their choice. All religions preach their followers to live a peaceful and successful life; to convey their prayer to their respective or all existing forms of God; to be secular at heart; to not attack anyone in anyway; and above all to contribute to betterment of the society. They are thus an integral part of Indian values.

MARRIAGE AND FAMILY PATTERNS

Arranging marriages too are the integral part of Indian culture. It is also rare in the world. Customs like cohabiting, live-in relationships, and love marriages are popular in western countries. The growing trend of love marriage in India is adding flavour to this custom and increases it variety. But the arranged marriage is major and even many love marriages are fruited in arrange marriage. People have growing tendency to nuclear family. But there are still innumerable joint families. But the present generation also feels the importance of joint family and are some of them inclined to retain the custom because there are wide scope to take care of the old generation; passing time with the elders as well as grandchildren sharing and helping them to be aware of the world as well as grow with knowledge on moral values and ethics. In reality, it is a boon to be in a joint family. In the hard time one can have lots of well-wishers and guide and support from within the family and encouragement for moving ahead with confidence.

THE DIGNITY IN CLOTHING

Indian traditional way of dressing is still prevalent though vulnerable to western culture. It is the fact that many westerners appreciate Indian dressing style and some even can wear a saree or suit as an original Indian does. In a word, Indian clothing style is intended to cover the body sufficiently in order to hide the unnecessary parts of our body that are against the custom of decency in public. It has a significant side while westerners think it savage and are prone to show their shame as the parts of attraction in public.

INDIAN CUISINE WITH VARIOUS TASTES AND FLAVOURS

Since the beginning, India has been the breeding ground of many diverse groups of people. Evidently, it has diversity in cuisine too. There are varieties of dishes with different taste and flavour in different states. The cuisine has taste and nutrition as well as tradition. Some of the most popular ones are bhel puri and batata pao of Mumbai; Delhi's chat; biryani of Hyderabad; daal baati choorma of Rajasthan, peda of Mathura; Agra's petha, Goa's seafood and so on. Moreover, India is land of spices, so the dishes do not lack a little scope of lacking taste. Various spices are blended in unique manners in each dish to enrich the best-in-class taste.

DIALECTS

India is again a land of many ethnic groups, castes, creed and sub-castes, besides the upper classes. Normally, there are languages as well as dialects. They are even enriched with their own dialectic flavour. People of different parts of India attract outsiders by the specialities of their dialects as they are the only source to know more about their origin and development through ages.

MUSIC AND ART

Ancient India betrays the flavour and superiority of music and dance forms. Each state practises their own folk tales, folk dances and folk songs. They are unique in their charm. Some most well-known of them are bhangra, kuchipudi, bharatnatyam, uttamthullal, etc. Music too has its various forms ranging from classical, Hindustani, soft light music, high beats to the western music forms. The world is attracted by different dance and music forms of India. India has also given birth to many great artists who have enthroned our art in the world and have left a significant impression in the world of art. The art ranges from various sorts of paintings, sculpture, the craftsmen and many more.

HERITAGE

Since the ancient times, our heritage has shown its evidence as the superior and enriched culture and civilisation. So, our heritage too attracts people from across the world. The governments are taking possible measures to preserve this National Treasure for the future generation.

FESTIVALS

A land with various religions has many festivals and celebrations. Indians celebrate some days of national significance like, the Independence Day, Republic Day and birthdays of national leaders and freedom fighters. The festivals are mainly based on different religions. Hence, they are celebrated by the respective religions in their own ways. The most popular ones are Diwali (festival of lights), Holi (a festival of colour), Christmas, Easter, Eid, Ramzan, Guru Purab, Budh Poornima, and so on. Each festival has its own speciality and grandeur. The happiness is not limited to people of one religion, with the passage of time and people's awareness on the festivals, it spreads among the other too.

RHYTHMIC COMPOSITE CULTURE

The composite culture as well as its unity in diversity is always challenging to maintain integrity, peace and communal harmony as every sect and religion has people with different outlook which very often stirs communal riots and violence. In this regard, the role of the government as well as the citizens in general, undoubtedly makes endless efforts to satisfy the ego and the demands of the people from all communities of the society.

CONCLUSION

Above all, the cultural compositeness of India is captivating. There is nothing in the world that only gives happiness, but sorrow. But our sole accountability is to maintain and keep a healthy balance so that we may get the brighter sides always. Hence, the Indians irrespective of religion, creed and community feel to be Indians, incorporate possible measures for the betterment, peace and progress of this enriched nation, not to be blind by narrowness of religion or community. Our composite culture needs strong bond among its people as well as for the whole world.

ESSAYS ON ENVIRONMENTAL, GEOGRAPHICAL, AND DISASTER MANAGEMENT TOPICS

1. Animals Deserve the Same Treatments as Human Beings

Some people are in the opinion that animals deserve the same treatments as humans and they shouldn't be used by human beings for food or research purposes while the majority contradicts it.

Animal exploitation is considered a treatment causing harm to them. But the cruelty depends on the amplitude of treatment. The organisations of India as well as the world, aiming at preventing exploitation of animals often face questions against their intentions.

The animal protection laws and regulations demand the rise of conscience in order to enhance sensitivity towards animals. Cruelty to animals is considered a moral issue. By giving them the same treatment as human beings seem impractical, but they demand that they should be prevented from exploitation.

It is a matter of judgement and decision to find out the ways which are considered animal exploitation. Besides, billions of animals are killed for testing animals every year. Passive and active are the two evident ways of cruelty towards animals. Passive cruelty indicates the abuse that is because of negligence and dehydration. Starvation, lack of shelter and medical care etc. are involved in this category. On the other hand, evil intentions of people towards the animals are considered active cruelty. It indicates the intentional afflictions on animals. Hide and leather business is one of the very profitable businesses, but simultaneously includes both animal exploitation and innocent killing of large number of animals every year.

In research activities, a large number of animals are killed every year. For instance, human beings share 95 per cent of their genes with that of mice. So, mice are appropriate model for research regarding human body simultaneously the vaccines like tetanus, penicillin and insulin would never have been invented without animal research. The ban on animal research can be foolish but certainly care should be taken for reducing misuse.

The animal protection laws should be meant to determine animal exploitations. The research aiming at inventing a medicine or for advancement of treatment should be considered valid. On the other hand, business thriving on animal husbandry for personal needs must be invalid and marked as punishable crime. Animal exploitation without a valid objective should be considered crime and penalised heavily and punished. These measures will be an attempt to bring a balanced animal exploitation and research for inventions for the welfare of mankind.

2. Rain Forests have Vital Role in the Ecosystem of the Earth

Rain forests play a crucial role in keeping proper ecological balance by providing habitat to a wide variety of animals and other living beings. But the deforestation of rain forests poses impending dangers for the living beings in those forests as well as for the mankind.

Rain forests nurture the oldest ecosystems in the world. They are featured by hot and humid climate and the highest amount of rainfall throughout the year. The unbelievable fact is that they cover only 6 per cent of the earth but they have more than half of total plant and animal species in the world.

About 30 million plant and animal species live in these forests and are the sources of various foods as well as medicines. They help balancing the climate of the world, prevent floods as well as draughts and support tribal people to earn their livelihood.

Though, we have so many advantages from the rain forests reckless felling of trees goes in different parts every year. The exploitation of the rain forests is only getting wood for timber, buildings construction, road construction, extraction of minerals as well as energy to name a few.

Felling of the rain forests is going on because it is a source of huge profit.

However, mankind will soon realise the severe consequences of felling rain forests. Severe climatic changes are because of felling rain forests. For instance, in the recent decades, Indonesia has seen several severe draughts because of felling trees recklessly. Felling rain forests also interrupts the water cycle and subsequently, causes the unequal distribution of rainfall and soil erosion as well. Besides, various animals and plants become homeless and some other species endangered and become extinct.

For thousands of years, man has only been satisfying his requirements by taking things from the environment. Now, even the existence of earth is jeopardised. It is high time humans should take stout measures to stop exploiting the ecosystem of the earth.

Humans should create mass awareness and initiate preventive campaigns with a view to salvaging trees for the ecological balance of the earth.

3. Nature and Climate Change

Wetlands, forests and oceans absorb and store carbon and these qualities make them important resources for countries following the Paris climate agreement's targets for the reduction of CO_2 emissions. So, what are the ways to use these resources most effectively?

The Paris accord was ratified by 196 governments at the 21st Conference of the Parties of the United Nations Framework Convention on Climate Change (UNFCCC) in Paris and accepted by consensus/agreement on 12 December 2015. In 2016, the meeting was held on 7–18 November in Marrakech, Morocco, for the annual UN climate change conference. For the year 2017, this annual meeting is scheduled on 6–17 November in Bonn, Germany. The aim of these conference events is to focus on how countries can use natural resources to meet their CO_2-reduction targets.

As the climate-change challenge is extremely high, so, it is the time to speed-up the sustainable development and ensure a better future for the planet. Under the Paris agreement, governments have promised to reduce their countries carbon emissions in order to keep global warming below 2 degrees Celsius. To achieve this goal, various signatories' countries have presented and described their national action plans and these plans will become more ambitious with time.

These national action plans consist of renewable-energy targets and proposals for sustainable transportation, energy efficiency and education and countries should consider adopting policies to manage natural capital better. The Paris agreement itself identifies the important role that natural ecosystems play in controlling the emission of carbon in the atmosphere, and governments should not avoid such powerful tools.

There is the need to conserve existing ecosystems in a people-friendly way and government should take action in this direction and it is particularly true of wetlands that include all land areas like lakes, floodplains, peatlands, mangroves and coral reefs that are covered with water, either seasonally or permanently.

Peatlands cover only 3 per cent of the world's total surface area but they have the capacity to store twice as much carbon as all forests combined, so, peatlands are particularly important. Peatland soils are composed of carbon in the form of decomposed plant material that has accumulated for thousands of years and when peatlands are drained or burnt, that carbon is released into the atmosphere. In fact, the amount of carbon released in the atmosphere from draining peatlands is two times more than the aviation industry does.

In 2015, fires erupted across Indonesia's forested peatlands. This raised concern all over the world about the quantity of carbon was being released into the atmosphere, to say nothing of the far-reaching health effects. Indonesia's government estimated that peatland fires and deforestation alone account for more than 60 per cent of the country's total greenhouse-gas emissions.

Conserving and restoring peatlands is the most effective method to reduce global CO_2 emissions. In 2015, the Nordic council of ministers committed to preserve the region's peatlands. About half of Nordic countries' peatlands have been vanished, and this ecosystem degradation contributes 25 per cent of their total carbon emissions.

The Paris agreement indicates that there is global momentum for concrete action to address the causes of climate change, and its effects also, for example, the disastrous floods, water shortages and droughts are already affecting many countries.

According to UN-Water, as climate change worsens, then, 90 per cent of all natural hazards which are water-related will increase in frequency and intensity. But natural systems can alleviate them: wetlands act as sponges that reduce flood, delay the arrival of droughts and provide fresh water and are the food source for nearly three billion people; and mangroves, salt marshes and coral reefs all act as barriers that prevent storm surges.

Countries have a convenient platform to use for their future wetland-conservation efforts. The Ramsar Convention on Wetlands and an intergovernmental treaty under which 169 countries have committed to conserve and sustainably manage their wetlands, is an ideal medium to achieve their CO_2-reduction targets, as well as to meet the UN Sustainable Development Goals for 2030.

Achieving climate-neutrality is the long-term objective of the Paris agreement—no net greenhouse-gas emissions—in the second half of this century. To keep global warming below 2 degrees celsius, climate-neutrality is compulsory and to achieve this target, we must reduce emissions to that level that they can be fully and easily absorbed by nature. This was the natural cycle for millions of years before anthropogenic climate change began.

There are different ways to achieve climate-neutrality which includes political willpower, imaginative policies, new green technologies and clean-energy sources and a multi-trillion-dollar shift in investment towards sustainable economic areas and infrastructure and needs cost-effective investment in protection and expansion of natural wealth. To achieve success of a clean and rich future is only possible through nature-based resources like wetlands and forests.

4. Do you agree that 'To Keep Ganga Clean, Puja Should be Performed on the Bank of the River'?

The quote 'melting pot', a land that promises 'unity in diversity' is given by Pandit Jawaharlal Nehru, the first prime minister of India and we find it to be true. India is declared as a secular country and a land crowded with people of different religion, belief, culture and heritage. Indian culture is one of the oldest culture and known worldwide for its uniqueness. In the modern view, different culture is the root of different ideology. A behaviour which is very idealistic that it sometimes takes toll on an unseen scale, and in this case it's our holy river Ganga. Present Prime Minister also said that 'The diversity of India, of our civilisation, is actually a thing of beauty, which is something we are extremely proud of'.

River 'Ganga' is considered as the holy river and stretches miles of kilometres over the entire northern hemisphere of the geographical India. It is the only river mentioned time and again in every major Hindu script and has of *Vedic* importance too. The Ganga which is shelter of various life forms is now a victim of the sole cruelty of the human race. The reality is we have developed ourselves in technology, but we have failed to understand nature in its true form and it is the result of our activity that the entire ecological system is out of balance. So, the question is: to keep Ganga clean the puja's should not be performed on the bank of the river, do I agree? Yes, I do, in fact, not just I, any responsible citizen of the nation would agree on the same statement. River Ganga is the largest river in India with numerous streams. The origin of Ganga is the Himalayas which covers a large land and makes it fertile, and rests in the Bay of Bengal. Since, Ganga is a water body, it is the major source of irrigation, fishery, supports large per centage of Indian agriculture and adds to the economic spectrum of our country. To avoid the wrath of floods, Dams are built on river in order to serve as partial-reservoir. Also, it is the only river mentioned time and again in every major Hindu script. So it's of Vedic importance too.

According to early Vedic legends, holy river Ganga always was time immemorial. People believe from the ancient time that after bathing in the sacred river, they are bound to get salvation in afterlife, or maybe they will end up in heaven directly after ones death, washed away of all their sins. After bathing in the river, their souls become clean and the 'atma' becomes pure is the solid notion embedded and every Hindu, once, in their entire lifetime wishes to take a bath in the holy river to clean his soul. Many cities host the 'kumbha-mela' and various other pujas stretching over days like Varanasi and Patna. To become witness of the spectacular view of these pujas, thousands of local people and tourists gather and take part by offering prayers and wishing goodwill to the Ganga. The most important aspect is the outcome, i.e., the ecological effects of these pujas, what are the effects of pujas on the river?

The survey done by ecologists mentioned devastating effects to the river. The amounts of organic wastes offered during the puja like flowers, bangles, leaves, mud plates with oils, carbon wicks, were in huge amounts that their decomposition takes a long time. Also the whole process of funeral pyres on the banks affect the river a lot which includes death of a person, soon after ones death the body is prepared for final rights by decorating it with flowers, colours etc., then prayers are chanted through pujas and rituals and the body is set ablaze and burnt. Even before the body is completely burnt, it is dumped into the river along with the pyre. Another issue which affects a lot is the industries that treats the river like a disposal ground and tons of chemical wastes, non-biodegradable materials, and reactant elements are directly let into the river without treating it. In some other parts, the city's sewage is also let into the river, in fact the local people also use the river for recreational purposes such as washing clothes, bathing, cleaning cattle etc., is a common site along the river bank. All the activities are performed everyday and no one stops these activities. Everyday, we treated the river as divine, and on another side we do such cruelty.

To stop these inhuman activities, various programmes have been initiated by the government and NGOs from many decades. Yet, Ganga fails to get its name out of the list of most polluted river which is such a disappointment for us. For clean Ganga project, billions of rupees sanctioned by the World Bank fail to make Ganga pollution free. Public interests litigations (PIL) filed against industries and actions taken against them are all long forgotten. Some actions must be taken at least to save what is left of the river because it serves multiple services and it is even regarded as a national river.

River Ganga or 'the great Ganges' known to be as important source to various aspects is indeed on an edge of failing. Failing for its existence and originality, soon the river may disappear. We can see clearly that aquatic life is vanishing. People and animals consuming its water are suffering from different diseases such as large scale cholera, skin infections and fatal being death etc., due to inhuman activities. Before the river lost its originality and we become late to undo the wrongs, local masses need to be educated. To protect the river, propaganda should spread widely otherwise most of north India will suffer a lot without its major river.

According to philosophers and thinkers, civilisation changes on the edge of precipice. It makes us realise our originality and it is the time to save the Ganga river by changing ourselves that means a mindset that needs to be uprooted.

5. Deforestation: A Road to Self-destruction

It is the harsh truth that humans are engaged in activities and practices that can be said to be self-destructive. Over the centuries, humans have been exploiting and cutting forests to satisfy their need, and this regular process has decreased the density of forest to a large extent, making difficult for millions of species of plants and animals to sustain. This practice will also leave the earth's ecosystem and ecological balance shattered, and the consequences of this will be felt not only by plants and animals but by human beings as well because we are reliant on plants and animals for all our needs.

The fact, that forests have high significance to humans, is established by the information that forests are the sources of foods and medicines, aid to stabilise the world's climate, shelter against floods and draughts and are also a great support for tribal people.

Despite all the advantages of forests, humans are leaving no stone unturned to earn profits by exploiting forest in a way that will affect our future generations. The process of deforestation is carried out mainly to get wood to be used for various purposes, to build roads and buildings, and to extract minerals and natural resources.

Also, paper-making companies exploit large proportion of forests to earn big bucks by selling paper.

Therefore, it is important for mankind to soon understand the negative effects of destroying the forests. The effects of cutting down of forests include severe climatic changes, loosening of soil, decreasing fertility of soil and increasing intensity of floods and draughts. For example, Indonesia has experienced several severe draughts in the recent decades due to the same.

This also results in an interruption in the water cycle, thereby causing a disparity in the distribution of rainfall followed by soil erosion. Loss of habitat and extinction are the problems that arise due to deforestation.

For many centuries, man has been continuously misusing the environment to fulfil his selfish needs. But a time has come where everyone has to take responsibility to not damage the environment further. Like they say, excess of everything is bad. So, if we humans do not stop exploiting environment, we will be the biggest sufferers as we are dependent on forests for the simplest to the most complex needs.

6. Climate Change: A Concern

INTRODUCTION

There has been much hue and cry over the issue of climate change over last few decades. This change in climate can be defined as a long-term shift in weather conditions identified by changes in temperature, precipitation, winds and other indicators.

Balance between incoming and outgoing solar energy, which plays a role in determining the Earth's energy balance, regulates the earth's climate.

ASPECTS RESPONSIBLE FOR CLIMATE CHANGE

Factors that are mainly responsible for the problem of climate change can be divided into three categories, viz., external natural factors, man-made factors and natural internal factors.

External natural factors are deviations in volcanic activity, solar output and the Earth's orbit around the Sun. These factors mainly influence the volume of incoming energy and generally have a short-term effect. On the other hand, natural internal factors comprise changes in ocean currents or atmospheric circulations.

Man-made factors, normally caused by human activities, are of much concern. Since they affect both incoming and outgoing energy, far-reaching environmental, social and economic consequences could not be avoided.

CONSEQUENCES

If the problem of climate change continues unabated at the present rate, it will have a catastrophic effect on people and the planet will no more be liveable. Climate change has already started showing its negative effects as in the form of changes in precipitations (Chennai floods in 2015); rise in sea levels; visible changes in seasonal periods with no fix period for winters, summers or rainy seasons; warmer sea surface temperatures mean stronger and frequent typhoons (in 2015, almost every other typhoon or hurricane was a category V storm); and finally, the rise of environmental refugees which will cause a huge political, economic, social and strategic cost for countries living on the fringe of coasts.

ATTEMPTS TO SAVE EARTH

The first attempt to highlight the issue at the international level was made in 1962 by the Club of Rome's publication 'Limits to Growth' and later on Brundtland Commission in 1987 emphasised in sustainable development.

But the first serious efforts in controlling climate change were made in Montreal Protocol (1987) that emphasised on limiting ozone gas to decrease the size of ozone hole. This treaty has earned the title of being the most successful treaty in environmental space.

To control the Dracula of climate change more efficiently, United Nations Framework Convention on Climate Change (UNFCCC) was established in the 1990s. The UNFCCC led to constitution of Conference of Parties (COP) that saw the coming together of all the UN member nations. To date, 21 COP have been conducted, with the COP 21 being held in Paris, France.

PARIS CLIMATE SUMMIT 2015

United Nations Climate Change Conference, COP 21 or CMP 11 was held in Paris, France, from 30 November to 12 December 2015. Being the 21st yearly session of the COP to the 1992 UNFCCC and the 11th session of the Meeting of the Parties to the 1997 Kyoto Protocol, the conference discussed the Paris Agreement, a global idea to reduce the speed of climate change. The agreement enables application of global greenhouse emission reduction measures in the post-2020 (post Kyoto Protocol) scenario.

This agreement if joined by at least 55 countries which together epitomise at least 55 per cent of global greenhouse emissions will become legally binding. The parties who agreed to the clauses need to sign the agreement in New York between 22 April 2016 and 21 April 2017, and also adopt it within their own legal systems.

TAKEAWAYS OF THE SUMMIT

- One major goal achieved in this agreement is that average global warming was limited to 2 degrees Celsius (3.6 degrees Fahrenheit) above pre-industrial temperatures, and a target for a limit of 1.5 degrees Celsius (2.7 degrees Fahrenheit) was set if possible.
- Each country has to submit their plans every five years. Moreover, there needed to be a more transparent and comprehensive reporting and monitoring system. Especially, emerging and developing countries that now dominate emissions like China will be part of that system.

- It will be the duty of developed countries to raise at least 100 billion dollars annually to help developing countries.

HURDLES IN THE ACCORD

- COP 21 falls short of deciding exactly how much each country must reduce its greenhouse gas emissions. In addition, it devises a bottom-up system in which each country will set a 'nationally determined contribution' and then explain how it plans to achieve it.
- Although the accord sought formation of an expert committee to 'facilitate implementation' and 'promote compliance', it will not have the power to punish violators.
- Although one of the main issue is that will the nations, which have suffered irreparable damage from climate change but have done almost nothing to cause it, be compensated, not much is achieved on this.

Although less has been achieved, the Paris summit is a move in the right direction. As is evident, it will be of interest for humanity to limit the pace of climate change to avert the possible disaster looming large at the Earth. It has been observed that despite being committed to the accord, the growth of the world economy has been more than the fall in emissions per unit of output. To save the mother earth while not sacrificing growth, it is necessary to increase this rate of decline.

The thing that takes centre stage is not the Paris agreement, but how the committed terms were executed by the member nations for meeting the desired targets. To be able to reach a united goal of reducing emissions, national plans must be ambitious and swift, and new and innovative technologies are needed that are more environment friendly. It is far too early to feel confident that the curve of emissions will now bend downwards.

7. Green Bond: A New Financial Tool

INTRODUCTION

With the large investment requirements in infrastructure space, it is acknowledged extensively that current project financing sources may be insufficient for capacity enlargement.

Thus, the need of the hour is to introduce new ways of financing and innovative financial tools that can influence a wider investor base such as pension, funds, sovereign wealth funds, insurance companies, etc. that can make investment in the area of infrastructure.

To achieve India's global obligations: According to an estimate, to complete India's Intended Nationally Determined Contribution (INDC) goals about 2.5 trillion US dollars (at 2014–15 prices) will be needed between the years 2015 and 2030.

In this context, the INDC document makes a mention of the initiation of Tax Free Infrastructure Bonds of 794 million US dollars in order to fund renewable energy projects during the year 2015–16.

To achieve India's renewable energy objectives: India has adopted an aggressive target of building 175 GW of renewable energy capacity by 2022 and, for this, a massive estimated funding of 200 billion US dollars is required.

Thus, the financing requirements of renewable energy space need new methods to be discovered which could provide not only the desired financing, but may also help in lowering the price of the capital. Green bonds as a part of corporate bonds space may be one of the answers to this dilema.

WHAT ARE THE ADVANTAGES OF INTRODUCING GREEN BONDS?

Positive Public Relations: Green bonds can go a long way in strengthening an issuer's reputation, as this is an efficient method for an issuer to show its green credentials. It exhibits the issuers' obligation for the development and sustainability of the environment. Further, this may also lead to some positive publicity for the issuer.

Diversification of Investor: There are specific global pools of capital, which are allocated for investment in Green Ventures. This source of capital puts an emphasis mainly on aspects associated to environmental, social and governance (ESG) of the projects in which they desire to make investment.

Thus, green bonds give an issuer access to such investors which they otherwise may not be in a position to tap with a regular bond.

Potential for Pricing Advantage: The green bond issuance have the ability to attract broader investor base and this in turn may help the issuers in the form of better pricing of their bonds with regards to a regular bond. Further, with growing focus of the global investor community for green investments, it is believed that new set of investors will make an entry into this space resulting in reduced cost of funding for green projects.

Global Experience: Issuance of green bonds began in 2007 and in the initial years, green bonds were a niche product, pioneered by a few development banks. The duration between 2007 and 2012 was characterised by the issuance of green bonds by the multilateral organisations namely the European Investment Bank and the World Bank, and governments etc.

The size of green bond market has nearly tripled between the years 2013 and 2014, with approximately 37 billion US dollars issued in 2014.

In India, the green bond market is still in the budding stage. Till now, only four entities, i.e., Yes Bank, CLP India, IDBI Bank and Exim Bank of India have issued green bonds in the country.

On the one hand, Yes Bank and CLP India have issued bonds worth 1315 and 600 crore rupees, respectively, while Exim Bank of India raised 500 million US dollars in March 2015 to supply fund to eligible green projects in countries which also include Bangladesh and Sri Lanka.

For designating the status of the bonds as Green, the investment of such money must be done in renewable and sustainable energy, clean transportation, climate change adaptation and so on.

8. Effects of Uneven Distribution of Monsoon on Indian Economy

INTRODUCTION

'Monsoon' is the word that has originated from the Arabic word 'Mausam' which refers to the seasonal reversal of wind direction. In India, south-west monsoons make their arrival in early June till September. This is the period during which India receives maximum rainfall.

The monsoon arrival and its evenness is very important in determining the growth and inflation prospects of the Indian economy in a specific year.

However, in the June and July months of 2015, the rains received were 9 per cent lesser than normal, with sharper shortages in a few regions. Further, according to the Indian Meteorological Department (IMD), rainfall received during August-September months of 2015, the remaining two months of the rainy season would show a poor outcome of 84 per cent.

Rainfall is described to be normal when it ranges between 96 and 104 per cent of the long-term average. Kerala, where the monsoon hits first and has usually witnessed rains much more than the national average, has also seen a deficit rain of 30 per cent this season.

The rains so far have shown uneven distribution, which means while some areas have experienced excessive rainfall and even terrible flooding, other areas have witnessed drier spells. When plotted on a rainfall map, a minimum of 35 per cent of the country's area shows deficiency of rainfall, while 35 per cent of area has witnessed normal rains. In another 30 per cent area of the country, rainfall has been in excess.

EFFECTS OF PATCHY MONSOON ON DIFFERENT ASPECTS

Effect on Growth: It is being projected that by the end of the ongoing year, agricultural growth would get reduced by 5 per cent as compared to the previous year. This will also take away 0.7 per cent per centage points out of the whole GDP growth of India. This will also have an adverse effect on the non-agricultural sector demand in the country.

Effect on Agriculture: India being an agricultural country, about 60 per cent of population is dependent on agriculture for their subsistence and also it contributes to around 16 per cent to the GVA. Thus, the importance of monsoon cannot be ignored. A total of 40 per cent of the cropped area in India is completely dependent on rainwater. For sowing, July is the most crucial month and thus shows the strongest correlation with the production of foodgrain. Although cumulative rainfall is shown to be only 4.1 per cent below normal (till 24 July 2015), it is believed that the shortfall in rains during the first three weeks of July will dampen the production of food grain to some extent. Sowing of rice—the main Kharif staple—has shown a great progress because of good amount of rain received in the northwest which accounts for 29 per cent of total rice production. In states such as Andhra Pradesh and Telangana, sowing of rice has been badly affected. Both rain deficit and uneven distribution of rains have proved to be problems, for example, in West Bengal, sowing of rice got affected due to floods. However, due to poor rains and low reservoir levels in the states of Maharashtra and Gujarat, coarse cereals, pulses and oilseeds suffered drastically. Also deficient monsoon also causes the soil become drier as against normal and leaves lesser water to be used for irrigation. All these factors will lead to lesser production during the Rabi or winter season.

Effect on Rural Demand: In March and April months of 2015, unseasonal and pre-summer rains caused a severe damage to crops in regions already suffering from deficit monsoons. A second year of weak monsoon will cause a decrease in the efficiency of India's irrigation system and could hit farm production and farmers badly. Already the growth of rural wage has collapsed to around 8 per cent. This will impact the rural demand negatively.

Effect on Food Inflation: Poor monsoon could affect food prices, which have been rising steadily, with retail price inflation reaching quickly to 5.4 per cent in June 2015, compared to a 4.8 per cent hike in April 2015.

Effect on FMCG Sector: A number of detrimental effects can be experienced on the FMCG sector due to poor monsoon. The demand can go down—this can happen mainly in the rural areas—and input costs increase significantly. Currently in rural areas, volume growth in sales of FMCG products is about 11–13 per cent but the weak monsoon may bring it down to 8–10 per cent.

Effect on Power Sector: Because the water levels will be lesser than normal in many hydroelectric dams, lesser electricity will be produced. Across 91 water reservoirs touched 87.09 billion cubic metres (bcm), which got reduced by 13.2 per cent from 100.36 bcm a year earlier and is even lower than the normal 10-year average of 90.68 bcm. During the period of May and June when intense heat is round the corner, rains bring a cooling effect to the regions and when there is less rainfall, the use of electricity will be more than the normal.

CONCLUSION

Under the present circumstances, a multi-pronged strategy is required to permanently deal with the deficiency of monsoon, this would require finding newer drought tolerant and climate-conducive crop varieties, reducing our dependence on rainfall by strengthening irrigation ecosystem, increasing the opportunities of employment to non-farm poor, bettering skill sets at the farm gate, introducing sea change in farm-to-fork transaction chain etc.

9. Environmental Pollution

Environmental pollution is one of the major threats nowadays. The environment is surrounding in which we live. All living things that live on earth comes under environment. But the contamination of our environment by pollutants is environmental pollution. Pollution has negative effect on natural elements that are necessary for life. Environmental pollution refers to undesirable changes occurring in physical, chemical, biological composition of natural environment. Consisting of air, water, soil etc. It plays a vital role in keeping living things healthy in environment but pollution makes environment unhealthy. Also environment is the source of natural beauty and is necessary for maintain physical and mental health. Environment gives us countless benefits as they are connected with the forest, animals, soil, water, plants, air. It also regulates the vital system which are essential for ecosystem. Thus the life in an ecosystem depends upon the environment which provides energy in the form of sunlight a nutrient. Waste matter and irregular manmade activities can create disturbance in the natural environment or in ecosystem. Disturbance in any component of the environment is likely to have a harmful effect on the ecosystem which causes the pollution known as pollutant. There are 2 types of pollutants:

1. Qualitative pollutants
2. Quantitative pollutants

Qualitative pollutants: These are not occurred in nature but are added by human. i.e. Insecticides

Quantitative pollutants: These substances normally occurring in the environment. When pollutants concentration gets increased due to unmindful activities of human. For example- Using of automobiles and regulating industries. As a result carbon dioxide in atmosphere becomes high then normal.

Environmental pollution means pollution which degraded the environment. Due to increase in pollution, global warming also increases. There are five main types of pollution:

A. Water pollution
B. Noise pollution
C. Soil pollution
D. Radioactive pollution
E. Air pollution

As a result there is an imbalance in nature birds, plants, animals are on verge of extinction day by day. The smoke that is emitted from factories, from vehicles is the mixture of poisonous gases. These poisonous gases are very harmful for human beings. Carbon and dust particle string up with the air in the form of smog, damaging respiratory system. Besides, it also effects the body system and body organs. The activities of humans that cause environmental degradation in pollution, defective environmental policies, global warming, ozone depletion. Ozone is another pollutant which is toxic for environment. It reduces photosynthesis and slower the growth in plants. In humans, it can affect the respiratory system. Above all increasing human activity is giving more pressure on the surface of earth as a result causing of many disasters in an unnatural form.

The main cause of soil pollution are chemical fertilizers, industrial waste, domestic waste. All these gives serious impact on environment. There are other pollutions as well which plays a vital role in degrading environment like Air pollution. The main sources of air pollution are burning garbage, industrial air pollution, radioactive elements, automobile pollution etc. All these happen due to global industrialization and modernization. The serious effect of air pollution on environment are Global warming, smog effect, acid rain, climate change, extinction of animal species, health problems etc. Though high levels of air pollution can cause an increased risk of heart attack, coughing, breathing problem, irritation of eyes. Due to environmental pollution, the worst sufferers are the plants and animals as they are extinct day by day. The destruction of Ozone layer on the earth surface threaten catastrophic consequences such as rising of sea levels, tropical diseases submersion of many islands, melting of glaciers etc. Agricultural activities also produce emissions to pollute the environment. Nitrous oxide and ammonia are the key pollutants released from this.

The continuous degradation of air quality demands effective measure to curb air pollution. In India to fight with this various policy measure are being introduced by Government of India to reduce the vehicular and industrial emissions. There have been various efforts to study the air quality in Indian cities. Several policy measures have been taken by the Ministry of Environment, Forest and climate change. The Government decision to adapt compressed natural gas as an alternative fuel to petrol and diesel. Moreover, there should be need to study the impacts of pollutant emissions on various forms such as ecosystem, biodiversity and health risk.

Environmental education is playing an important role to save the environment. It is the study of relationships and interaction between natural and human system. It is a process which allows individuals to explore environmental issues, take action to improve the environment. In this one should develop understanding of environmental issues. It gives the effort to make the general public aware of knowledge of environment and environmental challenges through print material, media, videos, etc.

The only way to eradicate environmental pollution is to plant many trees by which we can rid of many harmful poisonous gases. Also it provides a lot of benefits to the environment and helps with the release of oxygen. The concept of recycle and reuse is also beneficial to eradicate the pollution. It is not just conserve resources but also is helpful for air pollution as it helps in reducing pollutions emissions. Some other ways are also there to make environment pollution free. The use of plastic products could be very harmful to the environment as they take a very long time to decompose instead of plastic bags uses of paper bag is better alternative as they decompose easily. The fire takes place in forest during dry seasons is a huge factor of causing air pollution so reduction for forest fires and smoking should be necessary to reduce the pollution. The gases that is emitted from factories are dangerous for living beings. The use of filters should be used to reduce the harmful gases absorbing in the air. The practice of planting trees.

Environmental problems have attracted attention and public concern. Scientific research has played an essential part in solving environmental problems. Pollution control laws should be imposed. There should be restriction on use of fossil fuels and encourage the use of CNG Gases should be encouraged. Hence, it is responsibility of every individual to protect from environmental contamination agents and should be involved in helping to control the pollution. So that we can maintain the environment in better situation for future generations.

❑❑❑

ESSAYS ON ADMINISTRATION AND GOVERNANCE ISSUES

1. Government should not Invest in Arts and Heritage, this Investment should be Made in Public Services —Do you Agree?

Usually, art is considered as the presentation of human creative skill and imagination to create a pictorial form such as painting, sculptures etc., which are valued for their aesthetics and emotional connections to a culture or life forms.

'The aim of art is to represent not the outward appearance of things, but their inward significance' said by the Aristotle. I can say confidently that art is one of the valuable inheritances of a country and culture. In the developing countries, like India, the governments should invest more in art as it is the heritage of nation. From the above mentioned, it can be said that preserving any nation's heritage is not wastage as it is significance of the culture, rather than an investment which is done to develop the cultural heritage of a country and to portray its strong grounds.

People can use their personal strengths in expressive ways and offer opportunities for self-expression with the help of art. Various means of expressing is the significance of healthy nation, and art is one of them by which people express themselves. Art is responsible for improving the social, critical and creative skills of people and provides a sense of independence and teamwork, both of which are needed to create a happy and vigorous nation.

India is on the top of the list of tourism, for tourists from all over the world and it is all due to art. Tourism helps in any nation's economy by generating huge amount of income. Every year, millions of tourists come to India due to its art heritage, for example, Indian paintings which have their roots in the Indus Valley Civilisation, Indian pottery, sculptures dating back to the Harappa period, various dance forms such as Bharatanatyam, Kathakali, Manipuri etc. In fact, Indian theatre is one of the oldest in the world, and world still has number of dedicated fans of the same.

It is the real fact that public services are basic necessities that every citizen has a right on and in developing countries and there is also a lot of scope for their improvement and development. But I think, diverting the investments from the field of arts into public services is not a better idea. Both these fields have their own importance in their own ways and need attention but not at the cost of each other. The government should focus on both and funds for both should be raised through more effective approaches and financial arrangement, rather than reducing funds for each other.

Practically, no one can survive without public services like fire brigade, army, paramedics etc. and no one can live in a concrete jungle without colours, patterns and sculptures, or to put it together—without art.

2. Transparency in Public Administration

INTRODUCTION

Transparency is a small word but it has a very deep meaning. People keep on boasting about the transparency in every ground of life, but the efforts are limited to words only and never get converted into actions. People have always stayed divided in opinions in the section of transparency in public administration. According to some people, it is really desirable, while the other group thinks it is just a threat to privacy. The question arises why there is need of transparency in public administration? If it is really important, what are the actions that should be taken to succeed it?

RIGHT TO INFORMATION

Transparency in public administration is the right of people and they have freedom to know the details of the steps and actions taken by the different fundamentals of the system. It can be better called as the right of public access to the key information and it convinces the deep belief on the actions of system. If public finds the decisions are forced or manipulated, they have the right to know the details of the taken decision. As system is there for people and so it has to work accordingly with the needs of people. Therefore, it is not only the need, but can be better named as the right of public to demand for transparency in public administration. It should be open for the public to observe the pros and cons of the system, and local crowds can arise the questions behind making the important decisions.

ELIMINATION OF CORRUPTION

The existing system of Public Administration is the major part of life, which can be termed as more administrative run and administered by the officials. It has given rise to the decision-making democracy. The corrupt officials have no right and are not allowed to make administrative branch a playing tool, and administrative branch is meant for the welfare of societies. But corruption is rooted deep in the system, and the benefits are not passed on to the individuals. The right to access of information can be proved a best tool to deal with the corruption existing in the system. Transparency in the system is a clear sign of reduction of corruption, and it also encourages comprehensive public involvement.

DEGREE OF CREDIBILITY

A lot of risks are related with the lack of transparency in the public administration system in which usage of funds is one of the risks. The public funds are composed of the taxes paid by the taxpayers of the country. This money is used by the government for welfare schemes. The clarity in the public administration permits the public to know where the taxpayers' money is used in the procedure. It is a matter of trustworthiness of the system. Public can get the selected information, after all, an understanding into the proceedings will bring no issue to the system.

MAKE THE PROCESS SYSTEMATIC

The execution of transparency in the public administration should be in terms of both public and the system. It is the right of public to verify the information that is not sought and used by the illegal components for fulfilment of their selfish purposes. The public administration system should deliver the overall information in the form of electronic and visible data. In terms of the content and processes, this information should be general but informative. It should be accurately directed and scrutinised so that it cannot be misused by any illegal element.

THE EFFECTIVENESS OF DATA

The information available to the public should contain the basic elements and available only on limited application boundaries. It should provide uniform access to the public. The contents should be appropriate in terms of quality and relevance. It should origin from the central system so that it does not lose its importance. The basic point is to maintain the data security in all cases. Remember, if the data are damaged it is again the loss of the societies. If the illegal elements misused the data then the transparency can be proved costly.

THE PATH IS TOUGH

The implementation of transparency in the public administration system is tough but is not impossible. However, there are technical issues, which should be sorted out by experts. For transparency, the rules and regulations should not be held at stake. The cooperation from all the participants including the officials, politicians and people is important to make the process efficient and effective and to get a transparent public administration system.

CONCLUSION

Transparency is always for the welfare and it makes officials more responsible in the case of public administration. The modification provides the authority in the hands of public and eliminates the corrupt rule of the powerful administrators. It allows the government to have a stable foundation for its people. The free flow of information will eliminate the complex issues existing in the system.

3. Direct Benefit Transfer Scheme and Government Subsidies: A Welfare Scheme for Underprivileged

INTRODUCTION

For the underprivileged section of the society, the government of India has launched welfare schemes from time to time demanding huge cost to the exchequer in the form of sponsorships.

Indian government has been providing subsidy on both merit and non-merit goods, which include subsidy on education, health, fertiliser, power, oil, food grains, kerosene and LPG. The major challenge in front of the government is managing subsidies on petroleum, food grains, kerosene and LPG under the Public Distribution System (PDS).

According to the Economic Survey 2017–2018, the subsidy bill is placed at 3.0 per cent of GDP. There has been an increment in the subsidy bill from time to time.

The revised non-plan expenditure for year 2015–2016 was ₹26,000 crore and expected budget for 2017–2018 is ₹24,700 crore.

The expected direct financial cost of petroleum and food subsidies is about ₹3,78,000 crore or about 4.24 per cent of GDP.

Prima facie, price subsidies did not affect so much the living standards of the poor, though they have helped underprivileged families, withstand price rises and price volatility.

To overcome with the challenges of managing subsidy, the Direct Benefit Transfer Scheme (DBTS) was introduced in 2013.

WHAT IS DIRECT BENEFIT TRANSFER SCHEME?

The DBTS offers direct transfer of currency into the bank accounts of eligible persons known and covered under several government welfare programmes.

The scheme has been compared with the Brazilian Bolsa Familia which is the social welfare programme of the Brazilian government. The scheme has brought together the delivery of a various range of existing social programmes in India, for example social pensions, student scholarships and employment guarantee scheme payments.

INITIAL PHASE OF DBTS

Dilli Annashree Yojana is the centre of DBTS and launched by the Delhi Government in December 2012, which used DBT tool for delivering privileges. Under the scheme, an amount of ₹600 per month was transferred to the account of the seniormost female member of the eligible family, and this was the first cash transfer scheme for food security in the country.

Afterwards, DBTS was launched on 1 January 2013 in 20 districts of India by the then Prime Minister of India, Manmohan Singh. The inauguration ceremony of the scheme was organised at Gollaprolu in East Godavari district on 6 January 2013. By the end of March 2013, it was planned to cover 26 social welfare programmes in 43 districts of 16 states.

To avoid duplication, the scheme was launched by linking it with biometric-based Unique ID programme, Aadhaar. Duplication means one person getting benefits multiple times, and 'ghosts' i.e. non-existent people getting benefits.

In addition, use of micro ATMs and banking correspondents (BCs) was planned to influence the core banking infrastructure of commercial banks for transfer of benefits.

DBT FOR LPG CONSUMERS (DBTL) SCHEME

On 1 June 2013, the Union Minister of Petroleum and Natural Gas, M Veerappa Moily, launched DBTS for LPG consumers (DBTL) at Tumkur near Bangalore in 20 high Aadhaar coverage districts. After that, in these districts, the subsidy on LPG cylinders was provided directly to consumers in their Aadhaar-linked bank accounts.

On 15 November 2014, Prime Minister Narendra Modi-led NDA government introduced the modified Version of DBTL Scheme in 54 districts in 11 states including all in Kerala. Under this scheme, LPG consumers not availing the benefit will get cash subsidy transferred into their accounts to buy Liquefied Petroleum Gas (LPG) cylinders at market price. It was extended in the remaining parts of the country on 1 January 2015 under the scheme PAHAL.

On 1 January 2016, after observing the financial success of DBT in LPG, the Union Government planned to launch the similar DBT for kerosene subsidy. The aim of the scheme was to cut down the diversion and black marketing of the fuel.

DBTS FOR KEROSENE

According to government approximations, the subsidy outgo for kerosene for the financial year 2014–2015 was approximately ₹24,799 crore, and the distribution of subsidised PDS kerosene at 86.85 lakh kilolitres was more than the consumption at 71.3 lakh kilolitres.

The Union Government announced in January 2016 to launch the DBTS in kerosene which will cover 26 districts across eight states from 1 April 2016 including Chhattisgarh, Haryana, Himachal Pradesh, Jharkhand, Madhya Pradesh, Maharashtra, Punjab and Rajasthan.

The government has given cash incentive of 75 per cent of subsidy savings during the first two years, 50 per cent in the third year and 25 per cent in the fourth year to incentivise states to implement DBT kerosene.

CONCLUSION

From the viewpoint of welfare function of any government, these subsidies is necessary, however, demands well-organised management so that the subsidy reaches the right person and in time without becoming a load on the financial situation. After numerous surveys and studies, it has been revealed that subsidised goods and welfare benefits have not been reaching to intended beneficiaries.

4. PPP Model of Infrastructure Development and its Viability

INTRDUUCTION

Infrastructure development can be defined a pre-condition to achieve broad based and inclusive growth on continuous basis. The 12th Five Year Plan (2012–2017) has an ambitious goal of infrastructure investment at 1 trillion US dollars. The huge requirement of funds and limited availability of public resources made it necessary to explore new possibilities of funding infrastructure development.

One such possibility is PPP (Public Private Partnership), which has been accepted globally. PPP is the contract between a public sector authority and a private party, in which the private party offers a public service or project and take responsibility of important financial, technical and operational risk in the project. There are various models in PPP such as Design-Build (DB), Operation & Maintenance Contract (O&M), Build-Own-Operate-Transfer (BOOT), Build-Own-Operate (BOO) etc.

Benefits Associated with PPP

- It bridges the gap between demand and supply of funds for creation of infrastructure projects.
- It provides much needed expertise, operational competency and managerial efficiency of the private sector.
- It brings in new and cost effective technology.
- It puts contractual accountability on the private party to ensure timely and quality infrastructure service to the end users.
- PPP is an 'off-balance sheet' method of financing the delivery of new or refurbished public sector assets. It is because project borrowing is done by the private sector.

PRESENT SCENARIO

According to PPP India database, currently, 758 PPP projects has been awarded underway status whose costing is ₹3,833 billion. The leading states in terms of number and value of PPP projects are: Karnataka, Andhra Pradesh and Madhya Pradesh. The National Highway Authority of India (NHAI) is the leading user of the PPP model at the central level.

GOVERNMENT INITIATIVE TO ENCOURAGE PPP

- Setting up of the Public Private Partnership Appraisal Committee (PPPAC) responsible for the appraisal of PPP projects in the Central Sector.
- The Government has created a Viability Gap Funding Scheme for PPP projects. It provides financial support in the form of grants to make infrastructure projects commercially viable.

- The Government has set up India Infrastructure Finance Company Limited (IIFCL) with the mandate to provide long-term debt for financing infrastructure projects.
- The scheme for 'India Infrastructure Project Development Fund' (IIPDF) has been launched to finance the cost incurred towards development of PPP projects. The IIPDF supports up to 75 per cent of the project development expenses.
- Web-based tool kits are available to improve decision-making for infrastructure PPPs in India.
- An infrastructure projects database (*www.infrastructureindia.gov.in*) was developed to provide key information on the status of infrastructure projects.
- The Public Private Partnership (PPP) Cell is responsible for matters concerning policy, schemes, programmes and capacity building.
- Government has also set up a Committee on Revisiting and Revitalising the PPP Model of Infrastructure under Dr. Vijay Kelkar. The committee has submitted its recommendations.

CHALLENGES AND ISSUES IN PPP IN INDIA AND KELKAR COMMITTEE

Regulatory Environment: Presently, no independent PPP regulator exists in India which led to private sectors losing bargaining control due to fluctuations in environment over time leading to Obsolescing Bargain. Further, a major number of PPP projects have been delayed by legal challenges relating to financial issues.

According to the Economic Survey 2014–2015, the delayed projects added up to ₹8.8 trillion or 7 per cent of India's GDP. This burdened banks with enormous amount of bad loans.

Lack of Information: The PPP programme lacks a complete database. The database includes feasible reports, agreements etc. regarding the projects/studies to be presented under PPP. In this situation, the committee has spoken against unwanted proposals (Swiss Challenge) as they bring information irregularities and result in lack of transparency and fair and equal treatment of potential dealers.

Lack of institutional Capacity: One more issue associated with PPP is limited institutional capacity to accept large and complex projects at various stages hampers the PPP projects. There is the requirement of structured capacity building programmes for different stakeholders need to be advanced.

The Kelkar Committee recommends '3PI' which has the ability to enable research, review and support cultured models of contracting and dispute redressal in addition to functioning as a centre of excellence in PPPs.

The committee also suggested structuring a host of other institutions like Infrastructure PPP Project Review Committee (IPRC), Infrastructure PPP Adjudication Tribunal (IPAT) and a national PPP policy.

Financing Availability: Raising debt for the PPP project is an issue, and private sector is dependent upon commercial banks. However, with commercial banks reaching the sectoral exposure limits, and large Indian Infrastructure companies being highly leveraged, funding the PPP projects is getting difficult.

For sourcing long-term capital at a low cost for PPP projects, the committee suggested that the government should encourage banks and financial bodies to issue zero coupon bonds or deep discount bonds.

Allocation of Risk: The possibilities of PPP failures can be disorganised and biased sharing of risk in PPPs. A balanced sharing of risks can be assumed in sector and project-specific backgrounds.

CONCLUSION

To speed up infrastructure development in India, PPPs in infrastructure represent a valuable tool. With huge young population that will need good jobs and a vast pool of global savings that can be selected for constructing infrastructure, India is currently in a win-win situation.

For the economic growth and development of the nation, PPP is the key policy. The government must move the PPP model to the next level of maturity and sophistication due to the urgency of India's demographic transition and the experience India has already collected in managing PPPs.

5. Creation of Smaller States and the Following Administrative, Economic and Developmental Implications

INTRODUCTION

'India is a Union of states' is the statement of Article 1 of the Indian Constitution. This means that states were created for governmental convenience and states have no right to separate from the union and hence states do not have a say in their foundation. The underdevelopment of certain regions of the country is the reason of the demand of separate states, but it is not compulsory that these demands are always acceptable. The formation of smaller states is actually for national benefit.

Before understanding the significances of the formation of smaller states, we need to know why smaller states should be formed in the first place. For the creation of a new state, there are certain parameters which can be considered as following. After the formation of a new state, a proper machinery should be set up to execute administrative tasks. An issue can arise if the regions which are taken for formation of the new state should have similarity, keeping dissimilar culture under one label. The state should have the wealth which can make it economically sustainable to survive on its own expenses. Finally, the Country belongs to its citizens, so people's goal should be given a due share in the formation of a new state.

Demand of a separate state based on etymological terms too can be proved disaster for democracy. A question arises: When India claim about unity in diversity, how can smaller states be formed just on linguistic lines? Such creation will initiate demands for other smaller states. Formation of smaller states on the basis of linguistic is unacceptable as India has more than 700 local languages, dialects, etc. How can we divide and accept such demands?

ADMINISTRATIVE IMPLICATIONS

The administrative function is easier and better in small regions and it will have a direct contact from the head of state i.e. Chief Minister. Smaller state will get better control and command on minute disputes of development, more specificity in administration is possible then.

However, India being a union of states, for smooth functioning of centre-state relations, there is a partiality of powers in the favour of centre. Such division is declared in the Constitution.

The formation of smaller states will weaken the central's mechanism, as there will be several smaller entities to monitor the progress, and later more effort for already burdened centre. This may seriously impact centralised structure of the country and at last lead to poor administration.

Always, formation of new states is not the solution to cure poor administration. For example, Jharkhand, formed in 2000, has gone worse due to political variability.

However, I am unable to understand how it will make much variances at the ground level. In fact, to administer the smaller regions within state, there is already an appropriate system including Gram Panchayat, District Collector etc. This functioning machinery at the ground level will still be the identical and at last will be at the functional end of governance. As the system of orders and stabilities is already in place, so the formation of smaller states would not improvise much.

ECONOMIC IMPLICATIONS

Economic development need to be given its due share. Actually, liberal thinking clarifies economic development in more detailed way. People expect more growth as creation of states gives more funds to a smaller region. However, there is no direct relation between development of smaller state and perfection in the economic conditions because more funds give more leakage in the system and hence exploitation.

Now, the better evaluation of natural resources is possible, which was not present prior. For example, Chhattisgarh was the energy generating source of MP as seen during the formation of the State, and it benefited a lot by selling the same electricity to M.P. which was free earlier. But mostly it depends on political will and the government that how much they want to consume them for development otherwise a state can go down in smuggling of resources and environment issues due to inappropriate regulation authority. Other resources such as handicrafts, native culture of the place also helps smaller state to get a different individuality and more attentiveness for its uniqueness.

More infrastructures will bring more opportunities for employment in the state, as it has been formed recently.

DEVELOPMENTAL IMPLICATIONS

Development will be a fusion of social, economic, political and other aspects, and it will be the end outcome. According to simple theory, it is easily concluded—smaller state—more funds—better spending—more vigilance—more development. But, reality is very far from this workflow.

Although, for me it is unbelievable that matter of development will get a cure in small states.

Development is a wide term, and it requires contribution of many performers. It could go either way, it may initiate demands across the country for creation of smaller states, hence creating unrest and disturbing society.

The smaller state may lose the advantage it was receiving from the being a part of big state, for example non-payment of certain duties, getting benefits of state schemes and getting resources unavailable within the smaller state from the bigger state. Now, it will have to buy them from other state and this may create load on already strained new economy of the small state.

But at the same time, it can be boon for the smaller region as it does not need to take burden of the entire region. Now, a small state can progress based on its own resources.

Further, it can be an irony for the nation that even after taking steps for balanced regional development, the most resource rich areas are the least developed.

It clearly shows for the development, a lot of will and other elements are required for development and not just a spree of creating smaller states.

CONCLUSION

The central government has given 'special status' to the states provided them monetary help irrespective of their dimension, but still they figure low on development. Reduction of the size of states is not the remedy for all problems in relation to underdevelopment, language differences, regional identity etc. of a people. This solution will only create differences among people, but it is also not easy to overcome these differences. It will require a robust commitment on both sides of people and the government to formulate other ways to resolve these problems and to work for welfare.

6. Role of Media in Good Governance

INTRODUCTION

Media are the most important dynamic way for broadcasting of information. Media have spread its roots in an extremely terrific manner from cranky radio signals in villages, your daily cup of tea that is incomplete without newspaper, catching up on the prime time news shows to know the updates throughout the day or even catching up a quick piece of news on the internet through your smartphones.

Hence, for smooth functioning of democracy as it helps in forming public opinion on various vibrant topics, the role of media is extremely critical. As the fourth estate, as it is not a non-state element aimed at protecting citizens. All forms of media have a specific set of followers and, therefore, they together guarantee better governance.

DIFFERENT REACHES BUT COMMON IMPACT

The journey of advancement of media is interesting. Broadcasting the information regarding freedom struggle of great leaders was the responsibility of Print media. Despite strong competition, Print media is still popular and is the preferred medium for reaching out to common people as well as classes.

On the other side, the Radio is a simple medium as well as portable. Radio wields its impact greatly in rural areas where majority are not well educated. Since a large number of the population is still illiterate, this medium is critical for government as well who would like to communicate any urgent information like weather related warnings.

It is a well-known fact that visual medium does have the greatest impact and television is a medium that continues to grab the maximum eyeballs. The presentation and the attractive visuals do ensure that maximum mass of the country is tuned in for both entertainment and information. Internet is the latest medium that combines the audio and visual effects to reach out to millions of users globally. People can access internet according to their convenient time which is not possible by television or radio. The power of social media and internet is now widespread. To reach out the maximum youths, the government is now increasingly focusing on the internet.

WHY MEDIA ARE PARTICULARLY IMPORTANT FOR INDIA?

Media have an important role in ensuring the criteria of good governance are met from time to time and the criteria of good governance involve accountability, transparent, responsive, equitable and inclusive as well as effective and efficient. Good governance basically means how public institutions conduct public affairs and manage public resources.

The involvement of media is more important in developing country like India which still reels with superstition, communalism and casteism. For eliminating poverty and other social evils, it is the responsibility of media to bring backward and underprivileged people forward and introduce them with modern ideas.

Another reason why media is of paramount importance for the country is because of the vast inequality that is widespread. Despite being one of the fastest growing economies of the world, it is ranked sadly lower than even its neighbours in the Human Development Index. While a large number of journalists cover the more glamorous and glitzy events and news, less report on the number of deaths or the unemployment scenario is introduced. The prudence of media lays in helping the government in fighting diseases for example AIDS, Polio and Cancer along with promoting latest technologies for the advancement of its citizens.

Media should be attentive about the laws of the country and that they are not dishonoured by institutions of the government or any other rogue components. In this aspect, it has demonstrated its excellence in bringing to book some of the law breakers, recently, in fact, it has gone an extra mile by putting pressure to make sure that justice is given to victims. However, often we find that it exceeds its role of a supervisory body and instead efforts to give the judgment, which is the Judiciary's responsibility.

A lot of administrations across the world have faced charges of corruption emphasised by media and that has often led to either dethroning of corrupt administration or bringing in more transparency into the system. Hence, the fourth estate can help in effectiveness to the existing scheme of things as well.

One of the toughest roles of media is that it tries to involve millions of viewers, listeners or readers. In this manner, the major role of ensuring contribution of its citizens in the decision-making process of the nation is done by media very well.

CONCLUSION

The role of media has risen over the time and it would achieve more importance in the future as many across the world still desire for better governance or at best governance itself and not repressive rule. While media does highlight some of the issues from time to time, it does not investigate deeper into the real issues. The orders and stabilities which media guarantees by reporting issues in an objective manner can go a long way in confirming that governance by government would be fair and productive.

❑❑❑

24

ESSAYS ON PSYCHOLOGICAL ISSUES

1. Religion and its Humanist Face

Today, religion is wrongly being associated with the violence and hatred prevalent in society. Staunch followers of faith use religion as a catalyst for satisfying their political or personal goals by influencing general followers, resulting in evolving a catastrophic vision of what religion 'should' be in contemporary society. If not addressed urgently, this disturbing phenomenon with the mixture of a particular kind will leave no stone unturned to damage the social fabric of democracy.

In addition, it is also important to understand how a humanist approach and world view, which addresses the human condition in its tenet and practice, are influenced by religion. If this understanding of religion is given a cold shoulder, it is likely that we will not be able to determine the role played by religion in the Indian society. Interfaith harmony, of keeping differences aside through the practice of compassion and service to others, comes out as the main aim of all the religious discourses.

We also need to ponder over the persistent characteristics of religion, for completely understanding the role played by religion in contemporary India, that are far from the angles of political gains and personal exaggeration. The contributions of the Kashmiri Shaivite mystic Lal Ded, Guru Nanak, the saints and poets of the Bhakti tradition and many, many others are the examples of ancient noblemen. A present-day exemplar is the teachings of the 14th Dalai Lama, Tenzin Gyatso.

A sense of awe, stillness and anticipation in the air prevails among the people in the packed hall of a temple complex in McLeod Ganj, Himachal Pradesh to acquire the knowledge of the Nalanda Shiksha teachings on an eighth-century Buddhist text, Shantideva's Bodhicharyavatara, or A Guide to the Bodhisattva's Way of Life. Over 1,200 people who have come from far-off places, some crossing international borders, await for the next three days the arrival of their Buddhist teacher. Respected around the globe for not only being as spiritual avatar, but also for being a preacher of peace and well-being, and one who does not worship at the altar of pelf and power, the 14th Dalai Lama respects and speaks of many religions. With a view to promote interfaith harmony, this 'Guru' seeks religious unity by not only through his private meetings with religious leaders, but also through discussions among them to develop mutual understanding, trust and goodwill.

Spiritual practice can be regarded as an important factor in uniting people in the hall from different cultures and faith. It is only their love for a man who is as distant as he could be from a 'religious' teacher: humble, gentle, and jocular—about himself ('I talk too much... blah, blah, blah...'), about politicians, and the strange upside-down world we live in that people from far off places come here to seek blessing from him.

This unusual teacher in unique ways encourages the audience to not accept anything he says blindly out of faith. He believes 'Skepticism is essential' and states that it is good to reason and question the values of teaching. To understand oneself and one's relationship to society, it is important to doubt, question, analyse, discover and practice, so that blind faith, ardent devotion and ritual can be side lined. One should emphasise on 'oneness with humanity', and the principle of fixed self has no place in this doctrine. He adds: 'I am a global citizen'. He even tries to underline the interconnectedness between people, religions and nationalities.

This event is considered very important not only for the Buddhists, but also for the many others who want to understand Buddhism as a science. The Dalai Lama said: 'Buddhism is not a religion; it is a science of the mind'. It is about human psychology. The possibilities for training the mind through mindfulness and introspection lie within each one of us. It is our wish to choose our future path to live with either conflict, despair and suffering, or by using human intelligence to make an effort to rein in negative thoughts, and live a life of harmony with other individuals.

Concerned with the conflicts surrounding religion, created by 'mischievous elements', and the distinctions of caste that create differences and exclusion, he stressed the need to at the same time, the Dalai Lama is well aware of the conflicts surrounding religion, created by 'mischievous elements', and the distinctions of caste that create differences and exclusion. There is a need to know our connectedness with all people.

Over few decades, the Dalai Lama has initiated to indulge with scientists to establish a scientific temper among young monks. Science education has emerged as an essential component of monastic education in the Dalai Lama's monasteries. He has also been working to include secular ethics into the curriculum. With the help of Dalai Lama, a draft curriculum on secular ethics has been prepared by Emory University in Atlanta, Georgia, for implementation in schools. In India, attempts to reinstate religious-based or classical tradition-based 'values' in education are expected to have disastrous consequences in its implementation and outcome as children would unwittingly become firm supporter of particular religious traditions and see others as 'different'. The focus on values coming from religious discourse and not religious harmony will only serve to reproduce conflict. The initiative by Emory University is the first of its kind to keep completely secular approach to the preparation of a curriculum that seeks to restore 'ethics' (without any religious connotations) as a core value in school curriculum.

It is in this sense that we may speak of religion with a humanist face. The view that religion must only be used to divide and destroy, to manufacture and indoctrinate, to motivate and engender violence is very limited. Being citizens who want a future sans violence and fear for ourselves and our children, it is important to ensure that larger goals of humanity and its enduring potential should not be overshadowed by petty political ambitions with a narrow world view.

2. Religious Neutrality: An Accepted Behavioural Script

INTRODUCTION

Our Constitution framers were conscious of the fact that there was a need to transform society for bright future. Even though the main aim of the nationalist struggle was to overthrow the British Raj, the need of the hour was to transform a society that had a dismal record and understanding of human dignity and worked on the tyrannical hierarchy of caste that disproved self-evident individual rights. This idea helped our leaders to make a conscious choice of institutions and symbols that formed the basis of such a transformative articulation of politics. For example, Ashoka's Wheel of Law, a symbol from a Buddhist era, on our national flag was a reminder for every citizen and the state to commit to dharma. The nature of dharma practised by Ashoka was secular, and the dharma aims to undone the worst practices prevalent at that time in India. After the India attained independence in 1947, the commitment to secularism in India did not only mean a commitment to freedom of religion, but also a commitment to eradicate with religious practices considered being at odds with liberalism. In other words, secularism not only relates to state neutrality towards all religions, but also to the desire to undertake social reform.

DESTINY OF THE SECULAR SCRIPT

Two issues have complicated the project of secularism in India. First, the state may be impartial towards religion, but it is not that state actors and individuals in society are impartial towards religion. Second, there exists no agreement in India of religion being relegated to the private sphere. In fact, the opposite is true. In India, there is freedom for people of all religions to pray in large numbers in varying frequencies every week, and they do so collectively and in public. This fact points out to the idea that political appeals are usually made through religious spaces and spokespersons.

In India, because of societal and individual decisions are still based on and influenced by religious conditioning and imperatives, the state cannot manage to be indifferent to religion. After pondering over the issues of secularism and religion for over 65 years, it has emerged that the state has accepted religious neutrality as its accepted behavioural script, but society and certainly individuals (even when they are state actors) have failed to accept the same.

This fate of the secular script has garnered much limelight in the recent times. As observed over the period, bureaucracy has majority of tacitly Hindutva supporters, and some court judgments over the last two decades have highlighted religious morality or interpreted Hinduism in particular ways. It is also noted that Hindutva has increasing spread its base among the urban middle class in tier-one and tier-two cities and business persons.

Democracy provides the right to every person to support any ideology, for example, if the left can exist and be supported by many people, so can the right. However, Hindutva is not only the statement of a political ideology, but also a process which is claimed to make Hinduism and Indian nationhood almost coterminous. No heed was paid to this issue by the Constitution framers, even as elected representatives from the right actively argued in favour of a Hindu nation in the Constituent Assembly, but the same was denied by Nehru and the Congress.

BREAKDOWN OF TOLERANCE

Although the idea of secularism as per the Indian state can be understood as the impartiality of the state towards religion in addition to the necessary interventions in the religious domain to safeguard some rights, Indian society cannot be said to have attained secularism completely. This concept can be better suited to the idea of 'scale of tolerance'. For example, in some places, society is more tolerant of other religious and caste groups and, in some places, it is less, but nowhere in India is society perfectly secular.

Being a deeply patronising value, tolerance is an independent, individual choice, and no one can be forced to be tolerant. As tolerance is influenced by the perceptions an individual possesses about another community, its implementation is a matter of individual dispensation and benevolence.

Communal riots that took place in recent years have testified to an extent the breakdown of religious tolerance in society. As we live in a society where tolerance has a weak societal foundation, it is easy for the anti-social people to incite the mob for political gains to vandalise public property and kill innocent people. We as a society have failed to make ourselves tolerant to many issues, even as many have been treating it as a sought-after value. Hate speeches by various politicians only make the case worse.

Let us take few examples to understand the level of tolerance. First, many Muslims, single women and men and people from the northeast face difficulty in getting accommodation in the cities they work. The logic offered for this includes reasons such as that such people may be involved in 'bad' or 'immoral' acts or may cook and eat food that according to the landlords is not good or acceptable. Icing on the cake is that some local society associations also prohibit certain types of people to live in their places. Even if they manage to bag an accommodation, higher rent and charges are levied on them. The lack of any law that prohibits a landowner from discriminating against people on the basis of religion, race, gender or marital status also helps this intolerant rental discrimination to go unabated. In essence, a person's perception of what a group represents (single women, Muslims, people from the northeast) allows that person to informally institutionalise his intolerance of such groups.

Second, majority of parents warn their children not to marry a person who is dark and of different caste and religion. Even as study by Ahuja and Ostermann reveals that the idea of same-caste marriage has seen a decrease, many matrimonial ads still want same-caste marriages. However, majority of those having intercaste marriages mainly belong to lower castes, Scheduled Castes and Other Backward Classes (OBC). In addition, khaps have their ways in northern India to kill those who they considered as having bad marriages or marriages within same gotra.

Third, it has been observed that the recruiters in private organisations scrap resumes on the basis of last names, prefer people of the same caste and sometimes profile people based on region. For example, a call centre recruiter revealed that they don't recruit people from Bihar as it is assumed that they don't have such a good English. She even said that they also reject the resumes of Muslims. A research in 2005 in Chandni Chowk, New Delhi, revealed that banks often are unwilling to lend money to Muslims as they are seen as defaulters. To make a matter more serious, some even reported to be detained by police without any reason.

DOMINATION OF THE MAJORITY

Finally, it has also come to fore that many private schools don't induct underprivileged OBC students under the government's initiative of Right of Children to Free and Compulsory Education (RTE) as they are of the view that their behaviour and language will have a bad influence on other students and schools.

Essentially, the problem is that even if the state formulates a law to protect religious and caste groups, the whole process gets interrupted by a society that fails to understand and value the rights of other groups or individuals. There is a section of people that can't stand the empowerment of certain religious minorities, majorities or outsiders supports the Bharatiya Janata Party, the Shiv Sena and other politicians like Mr. Owaisi.

It is also observed over the period that majority in India doesn't want to share their rights and facilities with other minority groups, and it is the reason that benefits and rights, economic opportunity and social equality are not properly extended beyond the majoritarian fold. Even as it is evident from the studies that Hindus most often capture the benefits of reservation, recently Muslims have been granted reservations in some states, via an incorporation into the State's OBC list.

CONCLUSION

Growing the culture of tolerance in society is need of the hour, broadly through legislation if necessary. Like social evils such as untouchability and the practice of Sati have taken long time to be eradicated, it will be a good step to also starting to create institutional mechanisms to deal with hate speech.

3. India's Struggle against Leprosy

The mere mention of 'leprosy' has been hunting people across the world for centuries. Leprosy patients face multi-faceted problems, spanning from medical, social and psychological to economic and legal. Leprosy is known to primarily affect patients' skin and peripheral nerves and is mainly caused by a slow-growing bacteria called *Mycobacterium leprae* (*M. leprae*), resulting in disfigurement and nerve damage.

Research in India has played a significant role in developing the medicine to shorten the treatment and increase the cure rates, that is, Multi-Drug Therapy or MDT, which is now recommended by the WHO. The complete eradication of the disease faces many challenges such as the lack of a simple and accurate diagnostic test, long duration of treatment and most importantly, the social stigma which prevents patients from seeking care.

Although the cases of leprosy have decreased to a greater extent, the fight to eradicate it completely will take much more efforts and time. In India, even as we claimed to have achieved leprosy eradication (<1 new leprosy case per 10,000 population) in 2005, 60 per cent of the world's leprosy cases are reported in our country. Further, it is estimated by the Indian Council of Medical Research (ICMR) in 2008–2011 that there may be 2,50,000 new cases every year.

With an aim to focus on both prevention and cure, National Leprosy Eradication Programme (NLEP) has been strengthened and modified to work especially in endemic regions. In addition, a Leprosy Case Detection Campaign was initiated in March 2016, involving house-to-house screening and referral of patients for diagnosis. Till date, 65,000 suspected and over 4,000 confirmed cases have been detected after screening 68 million people in 50 districts and seven states. Accredited Social Health Activists (ASHAs) under the National Health Mission for the last seven years have been working to detect and treat patients.

In addition to the pain, disfigurement and loss of function, the leprosy patients also goes through social stigma that results in isolation, depression and loss of livelihoods. In the past, many patients were forced to leave their homes live in selected colonies, or they would be admitted to asylums and sanatoriums. In view of such discrimination, Mahatma Gandhi famously said the ultimate measure of success would be the day the disease would be eliminated.

Sensitivity presented by our society plays an important role in fighting this disease as stigma often force people to not reveal their condition to anyone. Half the battle will be won once the attitude of people for patients changes, discrimination ends and steps are taken to preserve their dignity and privileges.

We need to devise and implement a clear and effective plan to make our country free of this curse. The government has planned to run a door-to-door and person-to-person complete detection and screening programme to ensure no one is left out. In addition, many initiatives have been devised by government such as covering 163 endemic districts and revisiting ones surveyed in preceding stages, increasing the number of active case detection days and initiating a drive to encourage patients to approach nodal centres for detection, with or without financial incentives and to motivate survivors of the disease to spread awareness and prevent stigma.

New inputs and ideas will be integrated and assessed while carving out a move to move ahead with the fight against leprosy. Apart from developing newer molecular-based methods in addition to slit skin smear diagnostic technique, on-ground infrastructure will also be improved, care-givers will be trained and a follow-up system will be established to monitor abnormalities after treatment completion.

As the government stands committed to these actions, a novel vaccine, developed in India, will be launched on a pilot basis in five districts in Bihar and Gujarat. If the results come out to be positive, the leprosy vaccine programme will be used comprehensively in other high-prevalence districts.

4. Complications of Adolescents in Indian Context

One goes through many phases of life accompanied with difficulties since taking birth. Among many phases is the stage of adolescence in which one goes through transition from childhood to adulthood facing developments and problems. Following can be seen as some of the outstanding problems of Indian adolescence:

Perplexity with Regard to Somatic Variation: Every adolescent to go through many hormonal changes related to puberty and adjusting to them is a difficult task initially. Fear and anxiety grip girls, in connection with the flow of blood during menstruation, and boys, in relation to nocturnal emission. Ours being a conservative society, these physical changes during puberty are not talked about openly in family, resulting in youngsters having less information about the issue. They try to satisfy this anxiety and lack of scientific information about sex hygiene and philosophy by gaining crude and perverted knowledge about sex-related matters. Considered a sin, this makes them an introvert and secretive personality, thereby affecting their growth process.

Problems Related Intensification of Sex-consciousness: The sudden urge to know about sex-related topics results in intensification of sex consciousness. As the Indian parents generally do not talk sex problems openly with their children as compared with the parents of Western countries, Indian children opt for unacceptable and unwanted ways to satisfy their curiosity and satisfy their sexual needs. In addition, misguiding information in print and electronic media finally results in sexual maladjustment in adolescents.

Adjustment Difficulties with Parents: The stage of adolescence comes with the rebellious attitude where one longs for freedom and independence. However, often this freedom is curtailed the intervention of parents. In Indian context, parental opposition extends areas such as choices of friends, choice of education, recreational interests, dress, lifestyle, going from and coming to the home, mode of behaviour, etc. This normally leads to a conflict between children and parents as adults find it difficult and unnecessary to meet the demands of parents. Failure to adjust with the parents may result in revolting against parents and authority.

Childhood-Adulthood Conflict: In our society, the adolescent is considered as a phase between childhood and adulthood. On the one hand, one has to be depended on parents for all the needs to be fulfilled; on the other hand, one wants to work as per his/her discretion and be independent. Being treated in an ambiguous manner by parents and teachers leads them to a state of confusion whether they need to behave as children or adults.

Adjustment Difficulties with School Discipline: Adhering to discipline in schools turns out to be a very difficult task for adolescents as they want a life free of shackles and interventions. Schools should not implant habits of unquestioning obedience that inhibits the growth of young people towards true independence.

Adjustment Difficulties with Community: Societal pressure and expectations play a negative role in the life of adolescents. They are always pressed to do as per required by their seniors keeping in view the competitiveness in the society. As the expectations build very rapidly, they find it difficult to live up to the demands of the community. At this critical stage, most adolescents react by withdrawing into a non-demanding and non-working world of pleasure and satisfaction.

The Ideal and Reality Conflicts: It is during adolescence that an adolescent goes through the maximum changes, and others may not know how they feel about themselves, but we should.

Confusion and maladaptation can raise due to disparity between ideal and actual, or this disparity can be a source of motivation and aspiration for adolescents who are searching for identity. Characterised by the emergence of new-found cognitive capacities and changing societal expectations, adolescence represents an interesting transitional period.

Parental help and initiatives, such as deliberate expression of affection, concern about the adolescent's problems, harmony in the home, participation in family activities, availability to give organised help when needed or asked for, setting clear and fair rules, understanding peer influences on self-esteem, etc., can be very important to tackle adverse effects of the adolescents to a great extent.

Adolescent-Parent Attachment: Encounter between adolescents and parents is not the result of poor quality of relationship, but it is mainly due to the rapid neurological, cognitive and social changes that make them anxious and rebellious. Adolescents then have the responsibility to maintain connection with parents while exploring new social roles away from the family and developing attachment relationships with peers and romantic partners.

This issue arises a new question, what adolescents expect from their parents to sustain healthy attachment? It is a fact that the successful transition of adolescence cannot be achieved by making distance from parents, and to make sure of healthy transition to autonomy and adulthood, it is necessary that they secure attachment and emotional connectedness with parents. Parents clearly know that adolescents who understand their opinions and stay committed to the relationship, even in the face of conflict, can easily move forward toward early adulthood in a hassle-free way.

The capacity of parents, teachers, the elders, etc. to maintain a 'goal-directed partnership' with adolescents in their daily life by all means will help in making them confident and keeping away from all modes of newly emerged social evils that are nowadays proving out to be really dangerous.

5. State of Mental Illness in India

Stable mind is an important factor to live a healthy and purposeful life. In India, at least 13.7 per cent population is suffering from various mental disorders, and it is reported that around 10.6 per cent of them require immediate interventions.

Although nearly 10 per cent of the people suffer from common mental disorders, 1.9 per cent are reported to have severe mental disorders.

The National Institute of Mental Health and Neurosciences (NIMHANS) has recently conducted a National Mental Health Survey to assess the condition of mental health in India.

That is not all. The higher dominance of schisophrenia, mood disorders and neurotic or stress-related disorders are found to be the main reasons for high mental morbidity in urban centres. Some of the important causes to this are fast-paced lifestyles, experiencing stress, complexities of living, a breakdown of support systems and challenges of economic instability.

In 2014, worried over the rising problem of mental health in India, the NIMHANS was appointed by the Union Ministry of Health and Family Welfare to assess the condition of mental health in the country.

Post conducting a feasibility study in Kolar District, Karnataka, with a sample size of 3,190 individuals, the survey was initiated in the states of Punjab, Uttar Pradesh, Tamil Nadu, Kerala, Jharkhand, West Bengal, Rajasthan, Gujarat, Madhya Pradesh, Chhattisgarh, Assam and Manipur by a team of senior professors from NIMHANS: G. Gururaj, Mathew Varghese, Vivek Benegal and Girish N.

With a sample size of 34,802 individuals, all important traits of mental illness including substance abuse, alcohol use disorder, tobacco use disorder, severe mental illness, depression, anxiety, phobia and post-traumatic stress disorder among others were assessed. A team of researchers, local teams of co-investigators and field workers used computer-generated random selection for primary data collection in the 12 states.

Although 10.6 per cent of people in the total surveyed population were currently evaluated to be having mental disorders, substantial variations in overall morbidity ranged from 5.8 per cent in Assam to 14.1 per cent in Manipur. Rates of prevalence less than 10 per cent were reported in Assam, Uttar Pradesh and Gujarat. The rates of prevalence were between 10.7 per cent and 14.1 per cent in 8 of 12 states.

Even after it is revealed to the Union Health Ministry that, approximately three of four persons are experiencing severe mental disorders, huge gaps still exist in treatment.

The gap in treatment for all mental health disorders is reported to be more than 60 per cent except for epilepsy. In reality, accessing treatment and care for these mental disorders proves to be a costly affair as the affected families have to spend nearly ₹1,000 to ₹1,500 a month.

The pathetic state of the progress in treatment is evident from the study that around 80 per cent population with mental disorders failed to receive any treatment despite being ill for over 12 months because of the stigma related with mental disorders. Improper execution of schemes under the National Mental Health Programme is stated to be mainly responsible for this.

Highlighting that mental disorders are not given high priority in the agenda of public health and, health information system itself does not prioritise mental health, Dr. Gururaj also points to the fact of lack of mental health specialists in India.

He further adds that keeping in view the poor state of mental health treatment, it is of utmost importance to form a national commission on mental health by taking on board the specialists from the spheres of mental health, public health, social sciences and the judiciary to frame and monitor the mental health policies.

Below is the data concerning the prevalence of mental disorders in different states of India:

- Manipur: 14.1 per cent
- Madhya Pradesh: 13.9 per cent
- Punjab: 13.4 per cent
- West Bengal: 13 per cent
- Tamil Nadu: 11.8 per cent
- Chhattisgarh: 11.7 per cent
- Kerala: 11.4 per cent
- Jharkhand: 11.1 per cent
- Rajasthan: 10.7 per cent
- Gujarat: 7.4 per cent
- Uttar Pradesh: 6.1 per cent
- Assam: 5.8 per cent

IMPORTANT FINDINGS

- Common mental disorders such as depression, anxiety and substance use as amount to as high as 10 per cent in the total population.
- Depression affects almost 1 in 20, with females in the age group of 40 to 49 years at higher risk.
- Substance use disorder is prevalent in 22.4 per cent of the population above 18 years.
- Tobacco and alcohol use disorder affects the highest people.
- Nearly 1.9 per cent of the population have severe mental disorders.
- These are detected more among males in urban areas.

- Although mental illness affects males more (13.9 per cent) as compared to females (7.5 per cent), some specific mental illnesses like mood disorders (depression, neurotic disorders, phobic anxiety disorders, etc.) are more prevalent in females.
- Women seem to be more vulnerable to neurosis and stress-related illness.
- Prevalence in teenagers aged between 13 and 17 years is 7.3 per cent.

As the trends have it that mental illness is emerging as one of the most important problems that India faces now, there is an urgency to take corrective and preventative steps, especially for the section that is more at risk due to such mental problems.

❑❑❑

ESSAYS ON RURAL AND AGRARIAN ISSUES

1. Rural Uplift Programme in India

The rural uplift programmes in free India were launched in 1952 under community development programme with the objective of transforming the look of the countryside and developing a new perspective among the village folk.

Keeping in mind the challenging objectives of community development programmes, the development of scientific methods in agriculture has enabled enhanced production of rice, barley, wheat, cotton and other crops and further efforts are being made in this direction. Cottage industry is the mainstay of rural workers and the production of cottage goods based on agro, marine and natural products or bio-products is significantly enhanced that has led to increased employment opportunities in this sector.

Co-operative credit societies have emerged in an effort to meet the increasing demand of capital by small farmers and workers engaged in cottage industries. Moreover, efforts are in continuation to perform tasks for the benefits of the village community, such as village roads, gas plants, tanks, adult education units and technical know-how centres in the rural sector. The distinguishing features of the village uplift programmes are rural industrialisation, enhanced agricultural production and transforming the vision of the rural community.

The outcomes of the community development programme during the five-year plans have been quite appreciable. Significant improvement has been made in areas like village link roads, electrification, rural water supply and sanitation and mass education. Medium of entertainments such as radio and television are also common in rural areas now. Schools, colleges, and other educational and technical institutes are spreading in rural and semi-rural areas.

A large amount of harvesters, tractors and tubewells have cropped up in villages. Seeds and fertilisers of high quality are provided to the farmers near their locality. Minor irrigation schemes are coming up leading to improved production and the village industries are expanding. Setting up of primary health centres and veterinary health care units has resulted in improved living and livestock. Various developments and the resulting benefits have emboldened the spirit of village boys and girls who are heading for loans to set up new venture.

Panchayati Raj as an important community development aspect has been brought in all the provinces. The major purpose of introducing Panchayati Raj is to decentralise and democratise the administration of community development. The system envisions a significant transformation in the dimensions of local administration and rural development. With the objective of involving all the people of rural areas for their own development and betterment, the Panchayati Raj government will manage rural water supply, irrigation facilities, housing programme, consolidation of assets, roads, schools and health centres. The new set-up places large numbers of women at high positions in these panchayats.

Village entrepreneurs are being helped by banks through easy schemes in the setting-up of new projects and generation of employment opportunities in the rural regions. Banks are coming up with easy instalment schemes for large amount of money, seeds and machinery at cheaper rate for increased production and launching of various development projects.

The Indian villages are rapidly transforming due to initiation of these large-scale programmes under different names by various financial institutions. The government these days is also aware of its duty towards the huge rural population.

India's villages depict the real life of India and not its town. Hence, village uplift programmes should be given the highest priority. This is the reason that plans are always underway to ensure that the farmer is felicitated to get all his input requirements at a subsidised price and sell his produce at a fair price.

Though the village uplift programme is going well, but much needs to be done. Though the living standard of villages has begun to flourish, yet the concerns of landless agricultural labourers still require considerable attention. Hindrances to the prosperity of villages in the form of red tapism, unprincipled and corrupt administration need to be eliminated. The village lifestyle has also begun to suffer due to rise of dirty politics and vices like gambling, drinking and litigation have entered into the lifestyle of people and even causing loss of life. The rural people need to acknowledge their new responsibility in the new set-up and come up with solutions to their problems. Considerable attention is still required in areas like rural employment, education, health, sanitation, storage of wheat and rice, co-operative farming and increase in agriculture and industrial production so that villages in India regain their old glory, health and prosperity.

2. Drought Management in India

The condition of decreased availability of water below the statistical requirements is termed as drought. The high temporal and spatial variations in rainfall and climatic conditions cause droughts almost every year in varying magnitudes.

A region is said to be in the grip of drought when the rainfall deficiency vary from −20 to −59 per cent (early warning), −60 to 99 per cent (drought) and −1005 of normal (severe drought) conditions. India's 68 per cent area is drought-prone in varying degrees. Out of which 35 per cent of India's region receiving rainfall between 750 and 1125 mm is considered drought prone whereas, 33 per cent region receiving less than 750 mm rainfall is severely drought prone.

CAUSES OF DROUGHT

The prime factor responsible for droughts in India is climate change like variability in the volume and rainfall pattern from the southwest monsoon. Another factor behind droughts in India is the El Niño phase of the Southern Oscillation (ENSO).

Factors like improper agricultural practice, land-use changes and drainage issues reduce the water retention capacity in the soil.

Degradation of natural resources, deforestation and poor water management have caused more severe drought occurrences and vulnerability.

IMPACT OF DROUGHT

The impacts of drought are of varying degrees at economic, environmental and social scale.

Droughts have caused agricultural losses to the farmers badly affecting their income and purchasing power resulting in unemployment of farmers. The drought in India in 2002, is considered one of the severest affecting the livelihoods of 300 million people and 150 million cattle in 18 states impacting 56 per cent of its geographical area.

Few other consequences of drought are shortage of drinking water supplies, food insecurity, malnutrition, starvation, fodder deficit, distress sale of animals, lowering of soil moisture and groundwater table, etc.

Typical examples of areas with drought-related deprivation are regions of Rajasthan, Bundelkhand, Karnataka and Odisha whereas improper agricultural practices and poor water management leads to drought in states like Punjab, Haryana, Chhattisgarh, etc.

DROUGHT MANAGEMENT IN INDIA

India's drought management strategies over the years have been fruitful towards overall development. Few examples are the drought of 1965–1967 encouraging 'green revolution' and the 1972 drought causing development of employment generation programmes for the rural poor.

Over the years, there has been a shift in India's focus towards adopting a relief centric approach to the drought management strategy that includes institutional mechanisms, employment generation, community participation, operation of EWS and social welfare practices.

INSTITUTIONAL MECHANISM

India has an institutional mechanism in place to ensure implementation of its scheme through coordinated action across ministries. The National Disaster Response Fund (NDRF) and State Disaster Response Fund (SDRF) have been constituted under the 2005 Disaster Management Act to provide immediate relief to the drought-affected people. The National Agricultural Insurance Scheme (NAIS) in 1999 and Weather-based Crop Insurance Scheme in 2007 were also introduced to combat the adverse financial impacts of drought.

For coordinating the efforts in dealing with drought in various states, the Drought Management Group was constituted. For monitoring the drought situation in different states, the National Disaster Management Cell was constituted and National Calamity Contingency Fund was constituted to deal with calamities of severe nature.

The government started the Drought Prone Area Development Programme and Desert Development Programme to mitigate drought effects through implementation of plans based on integrated estimation of resources from remote sensing data.

Some other institutes dedicated to drought management tasks include, the Central Arid Zone Research Institute, Indian Grassland and Fodder Research Institute, the International Crops Research Institute for Semi-arid Tropics (ICRISAT), Indian Council of Forestry Research and Training etc.

EMPLOYMENT GENERATION AND SOCIAL WELFARE PRACTICES

The Government of India has come up with several programmes to help build communities' adaptability of communities against drought. The National Mission for Green India is launched with the objective of improving the quality of forest cover. Presently 2.14 billion dollar is allocated for a period of 2012–2017, to address 2.8 million hectares (mha) of degraded lands and enhance livelihoods of the people dependent on them.

The Mahatma Gandhi National Rural Employment Guarantee Scheme (MGNREGS) is launched with focus largely on land, water and afforestation activities.

Similarly, the Integrated Watershed Management Programme (IWMP) has been initiated with the objective of developing 75 million hectares of rainfed/degraded area during 2007–2027 in a phased manner.

India's draft National Water Policy is launched with focus on issues such as the water scarcity, inequities in its distribution and the lack of planning, management and use of water resources.

The National Watershed Development Project for Rainfed Areas, National Horticulture Mission, Rashtriya Krishi Vikas Yojana, National Food Security Mission, and National Mission on Micro Irrigation are the other programmes.

COMMUNITY PARTICIPATION

The effectiveness of government efforts could be enhanced through community participation approach. In this approach, the Gram Sabha or Panchayat recommend relief works and Districts and Block-level committees play the role of sanctioning and monitoring relief works and NGOs provide training and motivation.

3. The Developmental Challenges in Rural India

India is being acknowledged as a major power with its economy growing at a high rate and it is beginning to reflect in the transformation of its cities and urban centres.

However, this development is non-uniform and the rural area has not been able to reap their benefits. The benefits of economic growth are not spreading to more than two-thirds of the population consisting of more than 70 per cent of the population and 80 per cent of the poor population living in rural areas. The obvious symbols of development do not reflect the problems of rural areas which need attention.

The growth pattern of the Indian economy despite being the fourth largest in the world is not uniform. Though there has been substantial improvement in the growth rate for manufacturing, services, and communications sectors, yet the performance in important sectors such as agriculture, infrastructure development, community and social services and rural development as a whole is not up to the mark.

A country can be considered developed only when the development has reached to its rural people. There has been alarming decrease in agricultural growth in recent year and so have investment and profitability of agriculture, the area under irrigation and net sown are under crops. The Economic Survey 2006–2007 also raise grave concerns about the low yield per unit area across almost all crops becoming a regular feature.

The crisis gripping the rural India is reflected in the words of Dr. M. S. Swaminathan, the distinguished agricultural economist, who stated, "The agrarian crisis has its roots in the collapse of the rural economy. Unemployment leading to outmigration of the assetless is growing. The minimum support price mechanism is not operating for most commodities. At every level of the livelihood security system, there is a tendency to make profit out of poverty. Something is terribly wrong in the countryside".

In current situation, the peasantry in various parts of the country is helpless to take extreme measures in their inability to face the various kinds of adversities. Unpredictable climatic variations, increasing debt burden, inability to meet the rising cost of cultivation are leading to recurrent crop failures causing frustration among the farmers. In this backdrop, it becomes all the more necessary to tackle the challenges of rural reconstruction.

Agriculture is the backbone of Indian economy and it needs strong attention and action to devise a comprehensive and time-bound programme to release the sector from stagnation. The need of the hour is to provide larger irrigation facilities, better seeds and agri-inputs and fertiliser at reasonable costs to farmers, along with marketing, finance and infrastructural facilities. Farmers should not be left at the mercy of variations in weather, financial resources and market conditions.

Support prices and provisions of cheap credit are not sufficient to increase productivity and employment generation in the sector and strong land-related structural reforms is the need of the hour. A better rural growth strategy would be to realise the importance of small family farms to bring out reforms, thus, providing the poor with access to land.

Some facts about the agricultural turnaround made by West Bengal through extensive land reforms measures undertaken by the state government over the last three decades are presented as follows:

In West Bengal, land reforms comprised of two important elements: redistribution of land and tenancy reforms, known as Operation Barga (share croppers). Under Operation Barga, 1.5 million bargadars or registered tenants consisting of over 30 per cent Dalits and 12 per cent Adivasis were granted permanent and heritable right to cultivate leased land.

In total, 2.9 million landless and marginal farmer families consisting of 55 per cent Scheduled Castes and Scheduled Tribes were redistributed around 1.1 million acres of agricultural land. In addition, 6.8 lakh households below the poverty line were distributed homestead land.

As a result of these institutional reforms in agricultural land ownership, too many peasants helped in production activities that led to enhanced production of food grain at the rate of 6 per cent per annum. As a consequence, West Bengal emerged as the country's largest producer of rice and the second largest producer of potato.

Cropping intensity also increased as a result of these reforms from 136 per cent in 1980 to 180 per cent in present times, the second highest in the country. This contributed a consistent share of 3.6 per cent for agriculture in the State's GDP much better than the country's figure of 1.53 per cent. The population per centage below the poverty line declined from 60 per cent in 1977 to 21 per cent in present times due to the highest growth of per capita net state domestic product registered during the 1990s. The per capita calorie intake in rural Bengal rose by 9.6 per cent during 1983–1984 while nationally it decreased by 3 per cent during the period.

In India, 87 per cent of the villages are in population group of 2000 or below. Hence, the farmers living in these villages get small markets without efficient linkages and financing options thus falling prey to middlemen and moneylenders. Many a times, productivity is also affected by agricultural inputs of low quality, sometimes even spurious products, that may trap the farmer deeper in poverty.

The agriculture sector cannot be left at the mercy of imperfect market fluctuations. In addition to adopting short-term measures such as cheap agricultural credit and remunerative support prices, substantial long term investments should be made by the state in water conservation, minor irrigation, electrifying villages, building rural roads and markets, providing robust primary education and health facilities in the rural areas.

The cooperative movement proved to be quite efficient and accomplished in addressing the problems of rural India. Rural development involves adopting a multi-disciplinary approach, and an in-built mechanism should be devised that involves people's representation in the conceptualisation, planning, and management of any rural development programme, especially relating to crop production, water conservation and minor irrigation. A large network of grassroots entrepreneurs as self-help groups (SHGs) are emerging in India and generating incomes in rural areas, justifying self-help as the best help. These groups are examples of the new 'social economy' emerging in India. In present times, more than 25 lakh SHGs are operating with nearly 75 lakh 'swarojgaris'. They should be encouraged, for they play a big role in transforming rural India by unleashing the entrepreneurial energies of common Indians.

It is not about deciding on implementing industrial development directives or pressing for agricultural growth that development challenges in rural India would be met. It does not make good economic or political sense to reduce the whole issue to one of a choice between one sector or the other. The way that must be followed is by helping the rural sector realise its own potential for development by making best possible use of gains of modern science and technology and industrial development.

Our vision towards future advancement should use the modern concept of Gross National Entitlement where people even from the vulnerable sections, instead of being forced to accept what is being distributed by the system, get the right to have quality education, earn their living, access good healthcare, obtain basic needs and have the freedom to live in dignity.

This objective is possible to achieve by determined efforts as accomplished by several countries in short time in recent decades by effectively overcoming underdevelopment problems and inequalities. A living example is that of Vietnam, which has undergone incredible developments in a short period both in its urban and rural areas even after enduring exploitation by long periods of colonialism and devastated by imperialist wars. Our political leadership should take into consideration issues of rural India, where agriculture is the basic occupation; as major national issues. It should overcome the political and geographical barriers as well as factional considerations with focus of our national endeavour on fast and comprehensive development of rural India. To accomplish this objective, the prime responsibility of the nation will be to ensure adequate health care, quality education, sufficient infrastructure for development and improved living standard of rural people. The future progress depends in the development of rural India and partisan political confrontation should not hinder this objective.

India stands at a critical juncture that has potential to bring rural India into the mainstream of economic development. Every challenge brings with it some opportunities also. This provides us with an unparalleled opportunity to effectively utilise the maturity in our economic system, the potential of a global market and the technological advancements brought about by the InfoTech revolution to bring in a new dimension of development to rural India.

The realisation and emphatic acknowledgement is apparent in India and the world that India is going to play a pivotal role in making twenty-first century the Asian century. To realise this assumption India needs to bring in its large rural population also in the main stream to accomplish the dream of turning India into a developed nation. The emergence of a prosperous rural hinterland with strong agricultural base only could facilitate the wheels of industry and commerce to rotate smoothly.

4. Agricultural Challenges to Overcome in India

Agriculture policy, impelled by sudden apprehensions and enthusiasm, reflects upon the psyche of politicians worldwide in a very poor light. The political leadership resort to providing short-term solutions for public worries over food security and appease shamelessly to farm (and fishing community) voters.

However, this does not provide any good policy to achieve permanent growth in output. It is not the prerogative of any country to monopolise the agricultural trade with expensive, counterproductive and trade-distorting agricultural policy. The present World Trade Organisation (WTO) Doha Round has collapsed several times due to reluctance of the United States and the European Union to cut down on subsidies that has been damaging to the agricultural interests of others. The U.S. action on biofuels earlier significantly crippled international stocks.

India was placed at the top of international achievement in agricultural innovation. In India, pioneers of high yielding hybrid seeds, in particular M.S. Swaminathan, using to their advantage, a wide variety of international grain types, were able to achieve a real 'green revolution' in India in the 1960s and 1970s that impressively boosted the agricultural productivity and made the country fully self-sufficient in its main food requirements for the first time in modern history. Energetic policy at the Union and State levels well supported the scientific innovation to achieve one of the world's most striking agricultural successes of the twentieth century. However, a purposeful policy could not be executed well and dissolved into politicking and piecemeal implementation.

Without the support of any rigorous policy, unsustainable use of water resources encouraged by free or subsidised electricity for farm pumps and excessive use of fertilisers, led to depletion of sub-surface aquifers and soil degradation. At the same time, an expanding population, climate change and a sudden boost in agricultural commodity prices in 2007–2008 due to lower international grain stocks and a sharp rise in commodity prices, notably oil, raise a warning to India that its agricultural policy needs to be revisited. This was followed by impulse buying on international markets simultaneously when export of some items was prohibited (affecting mainly other developing countries, as the industrialised world cornered all the food it required). A healing step taken by Delhi was the lowering of tariffs on some essential international food imports. However, by November 2008, the government again raised tariffs on some products (soya) protect the interests of the domestic producers.

These set of measures taken together are certainly not a coherent set of policies to raise productivity over long-lasting periods. Instead, as in any place in the world when governments face similar pressures, such measures reek of political opportunism and whim.

India is going to face a persistent crisis in agriculture and a serious threat to its food security. It is not the situation for short-term panic. India will keep doing well in terms of managing its main needs and simultaneously of earning fairly large sums from agricultural exports. However, the factors causing anxiety would be the combination of Indian demographics with the rising success of its overall economy and environmental stress that create a challenge where increasingly prosperous Indians will be consuming more and probably wasting more also, as do middle classes everywhere.

There has been stagnation in global rice production in the past decade, whereas the price has increased four-fold. Earlier, a comment from President George Bush drew huge criticism from Indian commentators when he blamed expanding demands from India and China to be the reason behind international food crisis. Probably his mistake was in not differentiating in terms of consumption between the two countries because while the population in China consumed more than double the food after 1990, that in India also consumed more but at a much more modest rate, by roughly 30 per cent. However, anybody would hardly believe that the food consumption of a significantly more prosperous India will not be greater, including of meat that is so expensive in grain to produce.

To better understand this difference, diverging path of early economic reforms in India and China need consideration. In case of India, its major economic reforms in the early 1990s focused on liberalisation in favour of manufacturing and services sectors. In case of China, however, the key reforms were started earlier, and its prime focus was on agriculture anticipating that a decline in rural poverty might help in gaining favours politically of those raising suspicion of change due to other reforms in the pipeline.

Shenggen Fan and Ashok Gulati produced a fine article in Economic and Political Weekly in June 2008 that presented the outlines of China's revolutionary attempt in the late 1970s for raising agricultural production on the basis of promoting multiple experiments at the local level, termed as 'learning by doing'. Following this approach by analysing the outcome of various experiments helped Beijing in forming a full-bore nationwide reform process, a process Deng Xiaoping described as 'crossing the river while feeling the rocks'. This process was greatly successful in raising productivity and significantly reducing rural poverty. India needs to follow similar steps to reduce rural poverty.

In the scenario of a global slowdown, rural India should be better equipped to cushion the impact in comparison to its Chinese counterpart because of the availability of a large number of Indian anti-poverty programmes constituting a fragile but hopeful safety net.

However, it is not the matter of agricultural policy only to improve productivity and nutrition.

It is widely known and equally surprising that India has higher levels of child malnutrition cases than Sub-Saharan Africa. However, it does not imply that the basic Indian foodstuffs are less nutritious than Africa's. Though an important contribution was made by Canada's global micronutrient initiative, co-funded by U. N. agencies and the World Bank, in fight against malnourishment, but stunting and wasting in India (all at disappointing levels, all with life-long effects) is not as successful as expected. The major factors behind this complication are poor rural health, education and physical infrastructure that prevent the free flow of foodstuffs thus naturally alleviating nutrition problems.

Hence, food security is not only about agricultural incentives and disincentives but wider national policies and programmes are equally important. However, despite Indian democracy being vibrant enough, active civil society and admirably free and crusading press, little progress has been made in recent years.

It is high time India take the required steps in the interests of its own food security.

In India, an unwanted phenomenon of ice melting in huge quantity is happening in the Himalayas. This does not augur well for India's northern belt as it may cause changes in water supply that could have devastating effects on the foundation of the country's food self-sufficiency. The country needs to take prudential steps urgently to lessen and adapt to the effects of these upcoming shifts in water supply.

The U.S. and Canadian rural development model succeeded in creating non-farm rural jobs within decades of the first European farming settlement to avoid the sub-division of farms and unemployment. These jobs were created mostly to facilitate a growing agricultural sector and processing food in order to get as much of it as possible to distant markets intact and this is a major challenge which India needs to overcome with respect to fresh produce. India needs to adopt coherent government policies to encourage good non-farm jobs in rural areas to draw in the rural migrants instead of misdirected attempts towards forcing the rural migrants from urban settings they have reached in search of livelihoods.

India has a vast agricultural land and per capita, same as Italy and Germany, when both are highly efficient agricultural producers. What India needs is full range of policies necessary to boost agricultural production and nutritional progress. The country may devise sensible water management policies and programmes as is not short of water with perennial monsoons, with some fluctuations, which can be relied on. More importantly, India has plentiful human capital, which is optimistic, hardworking and endlessly entrepreneurial and having such admirable workforce, India can definitely succeed in boosting world agricultural production. However, this need a range of sound policies with a balanced approach taking into account rural interests and perspectives in a more systematic and meaningful way along with determined implementation of those policies.

5. Decentralisation for Rural Development is the Way to Overcome Challenge

The rural development trajectory in India has been appreciated for successful interventions, yet the country has a long way to go in terms of eradicating poverty and bridging the development gap between rural and urban centres. A look from a historical perspective on the developmental strategies in the country give us a fair idea of approach to rural development having undergone an ideal shift over the last few decades, from that of a 'top-down' to a 'bottom-top' approach.

India adopted a development strategy of centralisation until the 1990s, but the centrally administered support programs and planned interventions like community development and integrated rural development were not as effective in substantial rural poverty alleviation as expected. These shortcomings led the think tank in India to realise the ineffectiveness of the top-down approach or the 'trickle down' effects of economic growth in taking too long to reach the poor, and hence the need for decentralisation was envisaged.

The transferring of power and authority from the central/state government to the local level and to non-government and private organisations is termed as decentralisation. It enables the participation of rural poor in decision-making that affects their daily lives, minimise chances of misunderstanding, assess the outcome of their own decisions, understand the problems and complexities of administration, planning and management, accept responsibility for failure and develop a sense of belonging and commitment to civil society.

For the formulation and execution of various programmes of economic development and social justice, Article 40 of the Indian Constitution provided for decentralisation in the form of a general directive to the state to establish Panchayati Raj institutions at the village level. Presently, plenty of central and state-sponsored schemes are being enforced in a direct or indirect way through panchayats on many aspects including education, health, income security, water and sanitation, housing and roads.

Unfortunately, either political pressure or changes in growth strategies and policies of the government in most states caused the promising start towards decentralisation to fade. The progress of the decentralisation process was hampered by not following up the devolution of powers and resources to panchayats.

The launching of Sansad Adarsh Gram Yojana (SAGY), by Prime Minister Narendra Modi, has revived the concept of gram swaraj or village democracy into reality by empowering all the sections of the society to participate in various aspects related to village development, in particular, decision-making and resource allocation. This programme is initiated with the objective to strengthen local democracy through robust and transparent gram panchayats and active gram sabhas, facilitating overall good governance. Each Member of Parliament under this flagship scheme is assigned the task to motivate and drive development of best quality amenities and opportunities in these villages. MPs are required to lead and foster these villages and mobilise the participation of local community as they are transformed into 'model villages' which could be a shining example for replication elsewhere.

With a comprehensive approach towards development, the scheme is unparalleled. It conceives of overall development of the village across various fields such as agriculture, education, health, sanitation, environment, livelihoods, etc. Apart from supporting activities related to development of institutional and social infrastructure, it stresses on raising the living standards of village people along with accumulation of social capital. Under this scheme, each MP can adopt any village for the Adarsh Gram initiative except their own village or that of their spouse. Lok Sabha members are free to opt for any village under their constituencies, where urban MPs can select one from the nearest rural area. For Rajya Sabha members, the selection of the village should be from the state where they represent with members. Every member was instructed to adopt one village initially and two others later on, out of which the first village was to be transformed as model village by 2016 and all the three villages were to be ready as model villages by 2019. Thereafter, members need to adopt one village every year with the objective of ensuring five model villages by 2024. Following this approach, the entire team of MPs combined together can give their contribution in turning up 6,433 model villages by 2024. Total number of Gram Panchayats covered under the scheme will be 2,65,000.

The success of this flagship scheme depends on the role played by technology and innovations. Application of advanced and cost-efficient technologies in the field of livelihoods, agriculture, building and road construction would vastly improve quality of life and expand the horizon of opportunities, apart from facilitating improved monitoring. The first state to formalise this approach as a development strategy as part of its Smart Village/Smart Ward Programme is Andhra Pradesh. This programme is launched with the vision to implement an integrated local development process around the principles of inclusion, empowerment, bottom-up participation, equity, social justice, inter-sectoral convergence and self-management.

Individuals, institutions or private organisations were encouraged to partner villages and strengthen the development process by facilitating the communities, in particular, women, youth and deprived and marginalised communities in society while integrating different sectoral verticals of the government under the Smart Village programme bringing a new dimension to governance.

Their role is to act as a bridge between the village body and the government to determine the development requirements, plug them into the relevant government schemes, and monitor their implementation. Their responsibility will also include mobilisation of any additional funds and relevant technical support for development projects.

The desired outcomes of the approach to development can only be achieved by effective coordination and systemic monitoring towards its implementation.

The state government will also play an effective part in the implementation of the programme by setting up various committees at state, district, mandal and village level for an independent monitoring of the development process. Moreover, taking the participatory approach that involves self-monitoring as well as learning will ensure that all the key stakeholders in the Smart Village Programme, including sponsors and service providers, partake and understand the process, degree of participation, performance, progress, and maintain persistency towards sustainability of the development initiatives.

Moreover, advisory boards have to be set up at the village level with the authority for decision-making and implementation of the approach for effective governance. The crucial part of this approach is the provision for basic social and economic infrastructure, creating human and institutional capacity, creating more jobs and aim at growth areas in sectors recognised for increased resource use efficiency.

The aforementioned participatory approach is based on the belief that marginalised people of community are the best judge of the challenges they face and how to overcome them. However, to make any participatory approach to rural development successful, people having the requisite information and incentives and bearing the responsibility for both political and economic consequences of their decisions should be given the control rights in governance structures.

However, this devolution of power to local authorities and communities most of the times lead to disappointment as the local power elite authorised for the development process may thwart the process of achieving public delivery of social services. Hence, decentralisation through participatory approach should also include serious efforts to transform the existing structures of power within communities where disadvantaged sections of the community also get the opportunities for participation and raising their concerns.

6. Agriculture: Second Green Revolution

It is very well known that the present state of agriculture in India is the result of green revolution taking place since the late 1960s, well supported by government. It effectively tackled the criticality of food crisis and delivered India food security and sufficiency at that time. However, this progress and security came at a cost of environment and economic viability. Green revolution brought with it rampant use of fertilisers and other chemicals that resulted in making food and water toxic to some extent. It promoted extensive use of water aiming at rice production to be the main target of revolution, which led to consumption of 80 per cent of fresh water of India by agriculture, especially, by rice farming.

Moreover, Green Revolution in past led to consistent increase in yields per hectare of various food crops. Earlier, yield per hectare for rice was merely 1 ton which has increased to over 3 tons. The same in case of wheat has increased to around 2.4 tons. Over all these years, this increase was consistent with increasingly cultivated area constantly coming under high yield varieties, irrigation and fertilisers. However, in recent past, these measures have started to show fatigue and yield growths are dropping. Also, the increasing costs of fertilisers have led to increased agro costs, thus, turning food unaffordable for masses. Also, careless use of fertilisers is causing the nutrients in the soil to deplete rapidly.

In brief, the original means taken up in the green revolution are to some extent exhausted. Indian lands lag far behind world average in terms of agro yields and our policy makers need to look at other alternatives to bring it at par with world average. The present state of agriculture is unsustainable. Hence, India has devised a new agriculture policy that aims at sustainable agriculture, popularly known as 'second green revolution' or 'evergreen revolution'.

The second green revolution covers almost all the present policies making use of revolutions in bio technology, information technology and research and development as well as targeting of specific crops, etc. Information Technology will be utilised as a support service like customer care to create awareness among the farmers and make them acquainted with various cost efficient technologies. Hence, using this service information deficit on part of farmer will be addressed and it will enable them to make choice among different alternatives. The main feature of biotechnology revolution is improvement in genetic traits of crops, by making them pest, weed, draught and climate resistant. This is to be achieved by continuous modification of the crops using genetically engineered methods. However, there is some controversy about use of genetically modified crops and its benefits. Another feature of biotech revolution is use of biopesticides and biofertilisers keeping in view a bigger strategy aimed towards organic farming.

Organic farming, which makes use of organic wastes, is being followed by India from ancient times. It cultivates the land and raises the crops in such a manner that the soil remains alive and in good health. In this method, soil is nourished using organic wastes, such as animal and farm wastes, crop and aquatic wastes, and other biological materials along with beneficial microbes, such as biofertilisers, to release nutrients to crops, thus, leading to increased sustainable production in an eco-friendly pollution-free environment.

A central scheme called 'National Project on Organic Farming' is initiated to promote organic farming. The scheme creates awareness among farmers and promotes use of organic fertilisers, conducts training and programmes for capacity building, etc. This scheme also provides financial assistance through Capital Investment Subsidy Scheme for biofertilisers/biopesticides production units, agro-waste compost production units, human resource development, development and implementation of quality control regime, etc.

Northeastern India with its distinct agro-climatic zone and soil immensely rich in organic matter offers the highest potential for organic farming. Moreover, it was devoid of any green revolution and as a result farmers there still use traditional methods. This clearly provides a perfect opportunity to encourage organic farming in a rigorous manner in the northeast. The 'Horticulture Mission for North East and Himalayan

States' is a scheme that provides financial assistance to adopt organic farming and establishing vermin compost unit and is also available in other Himalayan states. The 'Indo-Israel Agricultural Cooperation Action Plan' is another area of coordination in which Israel shares its expertise in organic farming and related technologies with India. This cooperation covers in its ambit methodical interactions between governments, experts and mainly the farmers. This includes bilateral cooperation through sharing of knowledge and technologies, exchange visits of experts and farmers, setting up of Centres of Excellence in various agriculture sectors all over India and post-doctoral scholarships for Indian agriculture researchers in Israel.

Five projects have been launched under the plan, out of which two Centres of Excellence have been made functional including one for vegetables in Gharaunda in Karnal and the other for fruits in Mangiana, Sirsa in Haryana, while work for installation of three more centres is in operation in Maharashtra for a Citrus Centre in Nagpur, a Pomegranate Centre in Rahuri and a Kaisar Mango Centre in Aurangabad.

Widely perceived as a solution to the problems of chemical-based agriculture, second green revolution that opts for organic farming is quite important. Though, heavy dependence on chemical-and water-intensive techniques, leaves little scope for any significant change in near future. However, with the passage time, traditional means of farming will get even more expensive and this, combined with increasing water security concern, will compel farmers to use sustainable methods. Recently, organic farming is finding favour among the farmers. It brings many advantages of being environment-friendly, nontoxic and offering far better value in monetary terms than normal crops. Interestingly, non-farmers are also making investments in this sector. Moreover, research and development is being done with the objective of developing water-efficient technologies. 'System of rice intensification' is one such technology developed to save not only significant amount of water, but also to increase yield of rice.

7. The Dynamics of Changing Rural Economy in 21st Century

World Development Report 2008 from the World Bank found that poverty reduction through agricultural growth is at least twice as effective in comparison to growth emanating through non-agricultural sectors. This holds true for India, also, where 80 per cent of the population formally counted as poor came from rural sector in 2011–2012. The report indicates that poverty reduction is possible only by causing the rural incomes to grow at a faster rate. Over the years, the gap between consumption levels of urban and rural sectors has widened. Studies undertaken recently have shown that even though there has been growth in rural incomes between 2005 and 2012 due to increase in commodity prices and terms of trade favourable for agriculture, the increase registered in the level of non-farm incomes is at least three times that of farm incomes even in present times.

The rural economy in the present context depends a lot less on agriculture than it used to be in past. As the average size of landholding has decreased, the number of farmers who fall in the small and marginal category have now grown over 90 per cent and over 50 per cent of the cropped area is being cultivated by them. Smallholder farmers facing unfavourable circumstances are increasingly compelled to combine non-farm work with work on their own land. A report based on the data collected from the 68th round of the National Sample Survey (2011–2012) found that there has been a shift of around 36 million workers from agriculture to non-agricultural sectors between 2004–2005 and 2011–2012, which implies that a major share of their income is generated from work other than agriculture. Owing to this inter-sectoral shift, the agriculture share in the total manpower has dropped below the 50 per cent mark for the first time post-Independence. While there is some dispute about the veracity of this number, it is the fact that substantial numbers of workers are now being employed in sectors like rural construction. The working conditions in these sectors being poor and the quality of employment in the economy undergoing comprehensive decline, many observers consider this to be the result of an exchange of low-income farm work for low-quality non-farm work.

Therefore, there is a growing need to tackle the huge challenge of employment generation. According to the Economic Survey 2014–2015, regardless of the data source used, employment growth, which is 1.40 per cent, has fallen behind labour force growth, which is 2.23 per cent, between 2001 and 2011. It is obvious that employment elasticity of growth, which shows the effectiveness of the economic system in generating employment, appears to have undergone a decline over time. Over the last decade, around 5 crore rural households have been provided relief employment every year by the Mahatma Gandhi National Rural Employment Guarantee Act (MGNREGA). Unfortunately, the number of person days of employment generated and the number of households covered under MGNREGA as a whole since 2012 in the country has undergone a sharp decline.

THE IMPORTANCE OF PUBLIC INVESTMENT

For the vivaciousness of rural India, the future initiatives require addressing the twin challenges of reviving the dynamism of the farm sector by strengthening its climate resilience and generating quality employment in non-farm sectors of the rural economy at the same time.

Public investment could provide the solution to address the long-term structural constraints of the rural economy. Official land use statistics show that irrigation facilities are not yet made available to 55 per cent of cultivated area. This rainfed segment of Indian agriculture is extremely vulnerable to variations in the pattern of seasonal rainfall. As experienced in the case of watershed projects over the past three decades, local harvesting of monsoon run-off which provides supplemental irrigation to crops at crucial periods of plant growth could be a good measure for drought mitigation in the near future. There is a need to converge the investments under MGNREGA and watershed programmes in this entire framework of drought-proofing rainfed agriculture. Taking into account the food security, there is an urgent requirement to make investments in rainfed agriculture because it contributes about 40 per cent of our foodgrain and a major share of pulses, millets and oilseeds.

Another critical area that requires immediate attention is soil where investments are needed to improve the soil composition. The quantity of organic carbon in soil is not up to the required level in most parts of India due to poor organic matter incorporation. Soil health is further deteriorated with the careless use of chemical fertilisers. Various methods of soil enrichment have been evaluated by scientists as well as farmers that include conversion of 'waste to wealth' and recycling of organic matter. There is a great need to speed up these measures for greater farmer uptake. The present fertiliser subsidy regime, which is highly partial in favour of synthetic chemical fertilisers, needs to be reframed. Even though the public awareness about the harmful effects of chemical pesticides on environment and human beings is growing, yet the use of chemical pesticide has been escalating over the years. The pesticides are causing more harmful effects in India than in many other regions across the world. Immediate steps need to be taken to eliminate the use of synthetic pesticides in agriculture and make it chemical-free by developing alternative ways of pest management, such as non-pesticidal management (NPM) practices.

PROMOTION OF CROP DIVERSIFICATION

Another big challenge that need immediate attention is crop diversification. Though there is consistent change in consumption patterns in the country, pulses are still the major source of protein for the poor. They play a crucial role in the food security framework of the country. Millets are known to contribute higher resilience to the cropping systems against climate risk in conventional millet-growing areas. Most of the farmers growing pulses or millets are unable to meet even the Minimum Support Prices (MSPs) and there is no proper mechanism in place to procure these crops to the public. Taking a cue from the recent experience of States like Madhya Pradesh, decentralised procurement of pulses and millets could be made possible in those rainfed states where they constitute a major part of the cropped area. The growing malnutrition among children, adolescent girls and pregnant women in India could be effectively cut down by the procurement of local foodgrain, supplementary nutrition such as Integrated Child Development Services Scheme and the Mid-Day Meal Scheme.

The role of agricultural research is very crucial in the promotion of diversified cropping systems. There is an urgent need to raise the public expenditure on agricultural research by at least three to four times the present expenditure of a meagre 0.7 per cent of the agricultural GDP. At the same time adequate attention must be given to include crops like pulses and millets and measure should also be taken to develop climate-resilient cropping systems. The agricultural transformation in the country has been made possible by the huge contribution of scientists and extension workers of the public-funded agricultural extension system. Unfortunately, in many regions of the country, in particular, in the rainfed tracts, this system is virtually not in operation. Hence, a focused action-oriented approach should be taken to revive the agricultural extension system in these parts and effective utilisation of human resource and technical know-how to build its capacities. There is an urgent need to invigorate and empower organisations like the Krishi Vigyan Kendras and the Agricultural Technology Management Agency to become active agents of change in rural India.

Creation of employment opportunities is another major challenge that need to be tackled. Projections based on current trends of employment growth indicate that it will require creation of at least thrice the number of non-farm jobs than those at the present growth rate of 5–6 million jobs per year to meet the requirement of unemployment in future. A great number of these jobs need to be generated in the rural non-farm sector. Therefore, the sectors within the rural economy which provide potential for high growth and employment generation need to be identified and well supported through the implementation of a carefully worked out policy package. The chances for local employment control of the local producers over the value chain could be significantly increased by involving sectors like agro-processing and through value addition to agricultural produce. Public investment in rural infrastructure could help in leveraging substantial private investment in this sector and significant local employment multipliers could be generated. Available evidence shows that though there has been a decline in the overall rate of women's labour force participating in agricultural-related work, but participation of women from poorer households has been high in the labour force, particularly, in times of increasing agrarian distress. The importance of MGNREGA in providing relief employment to a large number of rural women cannot be underestimated and there is an urgent need to revive it.

8. Arhar: A Solution to Pollution

Environmental pollution has taken a heavy toll on the nation's capital and its surroundings over the years due to extreme weather conditions involving the process of thermal inversion that aid the settling of particulate matter and other pollution, dust arising out of construction activity, and vehicle-related emissions. Especially, the burning of paddy every year after the kharif harvest is a cause of concern.

A multi-faceted approach would be required to tackle multiple causes of environmental pollution, but one of the permanent ways to tackle the pollution problem is to address paddy burning. This is where the importance of pulses in containing environmental pollution is realised. A new variety of arhar, pigeon pea, developed by K.V. Prabhu and his colleagues at the Indian Agricultural Research Institute was discussed as the possible solution to the environmental concerns based on Subramanian Committee report on pulses submitted earlier to the ministers of finance, agriculture and consumer affairs.

The paddy-growing regions of Punjab, Haryana and Uttar Pradesh and, eventually, all of India could be used to grow this variety known as Pusa Arhar16 as an alternative to paddy crops. This variety has a yield of about 2000 kg/hectare that is significantly greater than those of the existing varieties and is of uniform size that will also be amenable to mechanical harvesting thus drawing in the farmers in northern India to adopt it who currently use this technology for paddy.

The most important feature of arhar straw is that unlike paddy straw it is green and can be ploughed back into the soil for decomposition. The high silica content of paddy straw makes it difficult to decompose. However, growing arhar provides the added advantage where after combine harvesting the farmer will just need to run a rotavator to cut the left over straw into pieces that can be ploughed back to decompose very fast. In comparison, left over paddy stalks are difficult to salvage or plough back because they are very firm forcing the farmers to simply burning them.

Replacing paddy with pulses, in over half million hectares or more eventually, will provide other social benefits such as use of less fertiliser, less water and fewer emissions. Moreover, growing pulses will help in restoring the soil with nitrogen unlike paddy, which depletes the soil of nitrogen or other important ingredients. In addition, it is expected that pulses production could result in social benefits of ₹13,240 per hectare. Based on this ground, an MSP of close to ₹9,000 per quintal for pulses over the medium term is suggested to make it competitive with paddy and to preserve the incomes of farmers. It would help in preserving the environment and reduce pollution as less paddy would be burnt.

The broader policy lessons outlined in the pulses report have acquired new salience in the light of the pollution problem. However, few constraints are there which need to be paid attention for the full implementation of the aforementioned measures to counter environmental pollution.

First, for the future of sustainable agricultural science and research must be promoted and its research institutions must be accorded autonomy to work freely without any political intervention. Especially, the hard and creative work of India's scientist must be appreciated and proven talent must be rewarded.

Second, implementation of this scientific finding as a commercially feasible option will require re-evaluation of price incentives. A complicating factor that determines the relative incentives between pulses and paddy is the amount of risk involved. There is a guaranteed MSP in paddy which makes it less risky to grow than pulses. According to an estimate by the Subramanian Committee, the risk associated with pulses production was about six times more than paddy production. The required MSP for pulses to compensate this risk should be about ₹ 1100 per ton greater than otherwise.

Third, setting the pricing in India must be based on externalities, positives and negatives associated with the commodity. In the context of agriculture, that refers to readjusting the present methodology of setting MSPs that the Commission for Agricultural Costs and Prices use with its focus exclusively on private costs and benefits. This causes promotion of socially wasteful production and specialisation, which includes excessive paddy production in north India, with all the attendant consequences harmful to the environment and the society. As stated by Professor Ramesh Chand of Niti Aayog and recommended by the Subramanian Committee report, social costs and benefits should be taken into account for MSP setting.

The burning of rice stalks provides an opportunity for the policy makers to devise a policy with major shift in approach towards reducing pollution, promoting indigenous research and science, incentivising pulses production and rationalising pricing on a broader context. After all, the hallmark of a good public policy is to convert crises into opportunities.

❑❑❑

ESSAYS ON URBANISATION-RELATED ISSUES

1. Urbanisation and its Menaces

INTRODUCTION

For the last few decades, cities and urban spaces have seen large influx of people all over the world. With the growing concern of population explosion, while some cities have been able to cope with the increase in the city population by putting in place-required infrastructure, many failed to achieve the same.

Urbanisation is the process in which large number of people migrate to urban centres to find better employment opportunities. The reasons such as erratic monsoon and failure of crops, which forced many farmers to commit suicide, are a setback for rural people. In addition, lack of quality education also becomes one of the reasons for migration.

BEGINNING OF URBANISATION

Although origin of urbanisation dates back to Renaissance times, it started becoming a common phenomenon during the Industrial revolution of eighteenth and nineteenth century. However, Asia has faced massive urbanisation only in twentieth century. As per the estimates by experts, cities around the globe will be accommodating over 60 per cent of the world's population in the near future.

SIDE EFFECTS OF URBANISATION

So, what are the broad issues that arise as a result of urbanisation?

Owing to the population explosion in cities, there arises a problem to find suitable accommodation. Also, failure to find an affordable place results in the creation of slums which are considered to be the breeding ground for various crimes. It is also noticed that lack of any regular source of income also drives them to indulge in illegal acts to earn some quick buck.

Rising population also leads to increase in demand as well as consumption of water. Although demand keeps on increasing with time, limited availability of potable water results in serious consequences as people suffer and die of many health hazards. Besides posing a water problem, heavy influx also affects traffic system, built keeping in view a limited capacity, with heavy traffic jams being a normal phenomenon.

URBANISATION AND ITS EFFECTS ON HEALTH

The large-scale urbanisation leads mainly to health hazards. The pollution of water, air and land is the main source of disease. Air pollution caused by large-scale traffic also has significant impact on the health of people. Even as the amount of waste generated has been on the rise, the efforts of government to curtail it to the minimum have not been enough. This toxic waste ultimately causes diseases such as malaria and dengue.

Sanitation can be considered as another grey area because diseases related to hygiene because of inappropriate drainage system also take the life of millions of people.

The sudden change of younger generation's mood to leave farming and move to cities for better opportunities also presents a challenge to food production. Now, the question arises that, even as food production being the very important aspect of any economy, if every person starts migrating to urban area, who would grow crops?

Because of the large number of people present to consume limited resources, price of essential commodities rises to leave a common man in discomfort. Urbanisation affects not only environment but also psychological issues due to the lifestyle that people lead.

Urbanisation has also caused deforestation on a large scale to accommodate increasing population in high-rise buildings, resulting in disturbing the balance of environment. Besides this, the increasing number population has resulted in increase in temperature.

Hence, it is evident that rise in revenues and lifestyles has negatively affected the overall quality of human life as well as the emotional aspects connected with it.

PROS OF URBANISATION

In contrast to its cons, urbanisation has a lot of advantages, such as good education and living facilities, that cannot be ignored. These conditions ultimately help in improving economy.

Urbanisation has also provided an opportunity to people from various cultures to blend together with harmony. For example, Mumbai is a classic example where people from different regions live together, making social integration more acceptable.

Besides many advantages, it cannot be disregarded that lifestyle, health facilities and quality of infrastructure in urban areas are far better.

CONCLUSION

Therefore, it is of utmost importance to chalk out a plan for the betterment and welfare of population not only in the upcoming cities but also in existing cities, which have to bear the brunt of poor planning and population explosion.

As urbanisation has largely transformed the landscape of cities in the twentieth century and it will continue to do so in the times to come as well, it is sought to formulate a plan that would help in improving lives of millions and not lowering it.

A combined and concentrated effort is required by the governments of major cities to cater to the growing needs of people and provide them with the better quality of life.

2. Homes and Safety Norms in Indian Context

All the political parties while attracting the voters promise to provide them the basic amenities of life, that is, food, clothing and a decent home. Given the vast expanse and dense population in India, it is an impossible task for the government to build homes for all single-handedly. This paves the way for a new player, real estate companies, and government entities like MHADA to make homes to accommodate the rising population in urban centres. It is required by the private builders to get the proposal sanctioned by various important authorities and complete the construction as per the government norms.

As people pump in their hard-earned money to buy homes, it is the responsibility of the government and builders to serve hand in hand while keeping interest of people in mind. To avoid any mishappening and accidents, the government needs to devise some safety norms and builders have to work as per those safety norms.

A number of incidents have happened in recent times where buildings have collapsed, as the norms were not followed by the builders, resulting in the monetary loss and deaths of many people who were merely the victims of corruption.

Even the media reports fail to show the plight of victims as the government and builders keep on blaming each other for incidents.

Fearing protests and opposition from all fronts, governments suspend some officers as a formality to depict their seriousness. Later, as the case dies a natural death, those officers are reinstated.

Many experts even blame buyers of not conducting proper inquiries of a housing project, builder's profile, etc. before finalising the home. Even those who try to investigate the credibility of builders are satisfied with the false claims made by builders to attract buyers.

Even though the government has different legal, technical and inspection teams to monitor proposals and pass building plans submitted by builders and the government gets stamp duty, VAT, service tax, registration tax and development tax from home buyers, which has to be utilised for protecting the interest of buyer, corrupt and greedy officials pass defaulted projects to make money.

Regarding the wrong practices, the government should punish those who violate building norms, ignore safety norms and cheat buyers. In addition, both builders and government have be held accountable while building homes for the general public.

3. Better Access is Important to Inclusive Cities

Easy accessibility is regarded as the most important feature of most planned and inclusive cities. Chandigarh can be seen as the best example of inclusive city with each well-organised sector, in an iron grid pattern, having a shopping complex, a school, a hospital and other basic amenities. All major transport routes (State Highway or National Highway) can be accessed within minutes. The city also boasts of dedicated parks in almost every sector for recreational activities and dedicated sectors for wholesale market and shops.

Even in ancient civilisations, accessibility used to be the main factor in city planning. This is evident from the Indus Valley Civilisation where cities were said to have planned in iron grid pattern, and important public structures such as the Great Bath were accessible to all. Even the British Empire effectively used coastal cities' (Mumbai, Kolkata, Chennai) port for easy transportation of goods and people for economic interests.

Transport being an essential part of accessibility, is really important for inclusive cities to build a planned public transport system comprising bus service, metro rail, etc. to make travelling across the cities easy, time-saving and cheap for all sections of the society. This efficient system will also lead to marked reduction in air pollution. Nowadays, the concept of TOD (Transport-Oriented Development) has been doing the rounds for urban planning. This concept centres on urban planning which revolves around major public transport routes such as metro stations, bus depots, etc. It will help the residents to have easy access to the transport routes which will be environmentally beneficial.

Easy access to healthcare is also important for inclusiveness. The lack of sufficient number of government primary health care centres makes a situation difficult for residents. Even as our country has seen a significant increase in the numbers of private hospitals, costly treatment makes it tough for the deprived sections of society to get correct care. For tackling the lack of government hospitals, the Delhi Government's initiative to open Mohalla Clinics in localities has been a commendable step.

For Government's initiative of Digital India to be successful, it is important to have access to internet and develop digital infrastructure to bridge the digital divide between cities. Even as nowadays almost every service is available on the Internet, socio-economically deprived sections still have no access to digital world. Internet access should be ensured to all to help people in many ways such as taking inclusive decision making, people can file e-grievances, share their expectations on public portal, avail e-services easily, give suggestions on various issues and thus can be a part of urban decision making.

Among the most inclusive cities in the world are the Scandinavian cities because of information accessibility. Transparency in the functioning of the government is the main characteristics of these cities. For example, all the details of meeting and commitments made by the representatives of urban local bodies are put on public portal. All the information concerning the progress of work, the expected time of completion and the availability of e-services is just a click away.

Access to public services facilitated to the vulnerable sections of the society decides the efficiency of urban governance. Despite the fact that there are about 2 per cent disabled people in our country, but no heed was paid to their issues. As the lack of ramps, escalators and continuous footpaths force them to be depended on others, the recent initiative of Government to ensure universal accessibility under 'Sugamya Bharat Abhiyan' is a welcome step. To avoid cases of acid attacks, rapes and molestations, which have seen a rise in recent years, women should have accessibility to ensure safety. For being called an inclusive city, law and order needs to be strengthened in addition to gender sensitisation of the masses.

The inclusiveness of a city can also be determined by the easy accessibility to clean environment and recreational facilities. The process of unplanned urbanisation over the years has concretised cities, and metro cities have almost no parks, waterbodies, etc. left. As all the parks and empty spaces have been encroached and used to build high-rise buildings, children are forced to play on roads and people jog on footpaths in even the posh areas of Delhi and Mumbai.

With basic features such as inclusive decision making, considering the needs of vulnerable sections, adequate facilities for migrant population, public transport, transparent and accountable governance and availability of basic amenities at convenient distance, the idea of smart city, represents the easiness of accessibility to all.

It is only through combined efforts of local bodies and residents that the better accessibility will be ensured to all the sections. Difficulties faced by the authorities should also be kept in mind. Our moral obligation includes aiding the disabled, providing security to women, reporting about suspicious activities to the public authorities etc. After all, had the bystanders taken her immediately to hospital instead of ignoring, Nirbhaya's life could have been saved.

The World Bank has estimated that approximately 50 per cent of India's population will be living in cities by 2035. Therefore, it is necessary to make concentrated efforts to ensure that basic public services are accessible to all sections of society. After all, smart governance and responsible citizens make up a smart city.

4. Future of Smart Cities in India

A 'smart city' is an urban space that boasts of highly advanced infrastructure, sustainable real estate, communications and market viability. It is a city where information technology is the principal infrastructure and the basis for providing essential services to residents. Among various technological platforms involved in this region are automated sensor networks and data centres.

When the world was reeling under economic crisis in 2008, the idea of smart cities was coined by IBM when it started working on a 'smarter cities' concept under its Smarter Planet initiative. The idea caught the eyeballs of many nations worldwide by the start of 2009.

Soon, nations like South Korea, UAE and China started investing largely into their research and formation. Today, India can keep on motivating itself by a large numbers of examples from such as those in Vienna, Aarhus, Amsterdam, Cairo, Lyon, Málaga, Malta, the Songdo International Business District near Seoul, Verona, etc.

Almost every state has stake its claim for being named among the 100 smart cities ever since the Prime Minister's ambitious 100 smart cities initiative was announced by the Ministry for Urban Development. Recently, the government has announced a list of 98 cities that will be developed as smart cities in the next 5 years. The strategic components of development include city improvement (retrofitting), city renewal (redevelopment) and city extension (Greenfield development) with a pan-city initiative in which smart solutions are applied covering larger parts of the city.

The way to the future of the smart cities initiative is a difficult task, and time will play a key role in deciding the success of the mission. The process will start with the formation the legislative and governing authorities for developing smart cities that are Special Purpose Vehicles (SPVs), which will monitor planning, appraisal, approval, releasing funds, implementation, monitoring and evaluation of the development projects. The foundation of public–private partnerships, joint ventures and subsidiaries will be an important task in guaranteeing an adequate revenue stream as well as providing technology support that is required.

Being a centrally sponsored scheme, the central government will inject a funding to the amount of ₹48,000 crore over a span of 5 years. Approximately, same amount will be pumped in by the state/ULB, which means funds worth nearly ₹1,00,000 crore will be available for smart cities development. Models and capacity will decide the project cost for smart city proposals. It is also necessary to create attractive investment opportunities and scope for economic expansion so that government can receive returns on the expense.

Multiple stakeholders also pose a great challenge to the project. More than eight ministries are involved to monitor the process of making smart city. Because in many cities different civil systems and operations are managed by different private companies, it is necessary for the government to work harmoniously with private companies to constitute a consortium to manage the smart city.

Security and privacy will play a critical role in building smart cities. Because providing internet access to all may pose a threat to safety of the city, intelligent safety and security solutions will be needed to aid in protecting cities against crime, terrorism and civil unrest. These solutions are thought to allow law enforcement monitor public areas, analyse patterns, and track incidents and suspects, permitting quicker response. By integrating statistics from video surveillance cameras, social media, citizen reports and other sensors, the solutions make it a point to tackle the issue of safety on priority.

As India has taken the first step by announcing the names of smart cities, the government is required to make a developmental plan and prioritise the needs of individual cities. To carve out a niche for itself, India needs to shape its own unique smart cities while keeping strengths and weaknesses in mind. The template is there, but the model will be unique. In future, as more people in India gear to move to urban areas, our cities will be the defining units of human habitation. The future of generations to come will depend on how smartly we build, manage and operate our cities.

5. Messy Urbanisation Poses Challenge to India

INTRODUCTION

Estimates say that among the total population of 1.21 billion in India, approximately 377 million people reside in urban areas. As more than 10 million people are moving to cities and towns from rural areas every year, it is expected that the urban population will surge to about 600 million by 2031. In addition, it is estimated that urbanisation is likely to grow at a compounded annual growth rate (CAGR) of 2.1 per cent, which will be almost double the growth rate of China.

The problem of messy or disordered urbanisation arose due to the lack of urban centres that promise better prospects than most cities and towns. This is evident from the fact that people living in urban slums and sprawls amounted to almost 65.5 million according to the country's 2011 Census.

'HIDDEN' URBANISATION

The World Bank's Agglomeration Index, a globally applicable alternative measure of urban concentration, states that the proportion of population living in areas with features of urban cities in 2010 was 55.3 per cent compared to an official urban proportion of the population of over 31 per cent, suggesting the existence of considerable hidden urbanisation.

This population, which is mostly not included by official data, generally resides on the borders of major cities. It is seen that this hidden urbanisation is indicative of the failure to effectively address congestion problems that are caused from the pressure of urban populations on infrastructure, basic services, land, housing and the environment.

Keeping this situation in mind, it is necessary to bridge this gap in the urban housing. According to the Economic Survey of India, it is necessary to address the problems of significant segment of population including EWS (economically weaker sections) and LIG (lower income groups) which amount to 95.6 per cent of lack of the urban housing.

In India, the housing shortage has reached 18.78 million due to the rapid increase in urbanisation. As around 56 per cent of households in urban India now have four or less members and smaller families have become a trend, the demand for housing in urban areas has increased tremendously.

In India, even as the number of households kicked up by 60 million between 2001 and 2011, there has been an increase in the number of houses by almost 81 million at the same time.

However, the recent official Economic Survey reveals the shortage of around 20 million homes in India. The reason behind this is that only middle-income and affluent population has been the focus of builders, resulting in soaring the prices of homes over few decades.

CHALLENGES

Even as the lack of availability of land and soaring prices of the same have been the major supply-side constraints in providing low-cost and affordable housing, the demand has been increasing due to the increasing urbanisation.

Private players in real estate developers have mainly focused on luxury, high-end and upper-mid housing segment because of the higher returns from such projects.

Furthermore, high gestation period of housing projects, limited and expensive capital, spiralling land and construction costs, high fees and taxes as well as unfavourable development norms are some of the issues that are the mainly restricting the expected increase in housing stock in India.

CONCLUSION

The current five-year plan focuses to increase the living conditions in urban spaces by virtue of smart city programmes.

The success in providing affordable housing will only be achieved by efforts on land and housing policy reforms, allocation of power to urban local bodies, nurturing innovative housing finance and the decline in project costs and schedule overruns.

With the aim of providing better facilities to citizens, the government needs to opt for planned urbanisation and other initiatives so that slums could be eradicated and suitable opportunities for employment is provided, especially for the marginalised section of the society.

6. India's Problem of Slow, Messy and Hidden Urbanisation

The process of slow, messy and partly hidden urbanisation has been a concern for India and neighbours for several years. This is evident from serious problems of livability and congestion that makes the cities unattractive for rural migrants. The World Bank report on urbanisation in South Asia reports that whatever benefits urban agglomerations could have offered in terms of economic advance are getting diluted.

The report tries to provide some solutions to problems faced by the country over messy urbanisation. Money for infrastructure comes out as a main factor for developing a better future. The report taking in account the recent growth trends provides that during the period 2010–2050, urban population in India is expected to increase by approximately 497 million. Therefore, nearly $600 billion (at 2004 prices) will be required just to get an access to adequate water, sanitation and roads.

At current exchange rates, it is estimated that about ₹40 lakh crore for 40 years or about ₹ 1 lakh crore per year will be required. This does not include housing, electricity, transportation, education or health, to name a few essential requirements for a decent life. The costs are expected to double, if above requirements are included. As per recent trends, local bodies will be responsible for raising at least a third of this amount.

The World Bank debates in this report that 'urbanisation leads to concentration of economic activity, improves productivity and spurs job creation, specifically in manufacturing and services'. This has the 'potential to transform economies to join the ranks of richer nations in both prosperity and livability', it says.

As per the World Bank data not incorporated in this report, more than 54 per cent of the world's population now lives in urban areas, creating 80 per cent of global GDP, consuming two-thirds of global energy and accounting for 70 per cent of greenhouse gas emissions. Almost billion urban people are poor and deprived of decent housing and basic services.

This report delves with some exciting perceptions on the growth of Indian cities. The main being that the pace at which the physical space of cities is increasing is outpacing the rate at which the population has been increasing. Satellite analysis of night lights reveals this 'messy' nature of sub-continental urbanisation, with an observed growth rate in urban areas of more than 5 per cent per year in contrast to population growth of under 2.5 per cent per year, which means low-density sprawls at the peripheries. As per the night lights data, multi-city agglomerations of two or more 100,000+ cities went to 45 in 2010 from 37 in 1999 in India.

The 'hidden' nature of Indian urbanisation has come to fore while scrutinising Census 2011 data. Between 2001 and 2011, the country has seen an increase in the number of census towns from 1,362 to 3,894 because of reclassification, resulting in approximately 30 per cent urban population increase. In contrast, majority of these towns are still considered as rural for all other purposes.

After many years of uncertainty to the issue of urbanisation, it is observed that it has been increasingly at a significant rate in India. It is evident by the importance that these cities have seen in the distinct 'worlds' of government, business, think tanks, academia and civil society. Each of these 'worlds' comprises specialists in specific 'fields' within the urban sphere such as planning, environment, transport, housing, finance and health. The multiple 'fields' within these parallel 'worlds' act as storehouse and do not relate with the other 'fields' and 'worlds'.

7. The Significance of the 'New Urban Agenda' for India

The 'New Urban Agenda' aims at sustainable urbanisation for the next two decades. It is the final document that has developed from the UN Conference on Housing and Sustainable Urban Development (referred as 'Habitat III') held in Quito, Ecuador, recently. With earlier meeting conducted in Vancouver (1976) and Istanbul (1996), the UN's Habitat conferences are held in a bi-decennial cycle. Even as the draft was approved by representatives of national governments, it took two years for being prepared after preparation lasted two years and involved consultations with various stakeholders, including local governments, civil society groups and urban scholars and practitioners.

The idea of 'New Urban Agenda' received a major boost after the approval of a new international development framework to succeed the Millennium Development Goals. Last year, the 2030 Agenda, for Sustainable Development with 17 Sustainable Development Goals (SDGs), was approved by the UN general assembly. The aim of Goal 11 on Sustainable Cities and Communities is 'make to cities and human settlements inclusive, safe, resilient and sustainable'. Expectedly, sustainability is the main characteristics of the 'New Urban Agenda'. With themes like social inclusion, urban prosperity and resilience in view, a significant part of this draft is devoted to various 'transformative commitments for sustainable urban development'.

This agenda seeks an 'urban paradigm shift' to readdress the way 'we plan, finance, develop, govern, and manage cities and human settlements'. It basically is devoted to a 'vision of cities for all' where 'all inhabitants' are expected to 'inhabit and produce just, safe, healthy, accessible, affordable, resilient, and sustainable cities and human settlements'. One of the major obstacles in the dialogues for Habitat III was related to the insertion of the provision on 'Right to the City', a term used to describe the collective right of 'all inhabitants', regardless of their legal status, over the city's resources and spaces. Despite this phrase being referred in the draft, it has been extensively neutralised because of compromise between its supporters—Latin American countries—and its more powerful opponents: the US, European Union, Russia and India.

The contribution of India in the drafting of the 'New Urban Agenda' has been quite less. Even as more comprehensive recommendations for revisions were proposed by other member states, India mostly gave short, cryptic comments voicing dissatisfaction over certain sections. India was in support of provisions to help refugees and migrants circumscribed by a proviso stating 'where applicable as permitted by laws of the land'. A more generic commitment on the right to housing instead of one that denounced discrimination and forced evictions was proposed by India. Also, restrictions on rules that increased local government autonomy over taxes were also sought by India. The way in which India has been engaged in this draft is bound to attract concern about the government's seriousness in empowering cities and their inhabitants.

Despite following an urban-centric development agenda seriously, the priorities of India do not seem to comply with those of the 'New Urban Agenda'. The current urban policy framework adopted by India is not based on a method that offers 'all inhabitants' a 'right to the city'. What is more interesting is that even as 'smart cities' form the major attraction of India's urban agenda, only fleeting appearance has been made in the 'New Urban Agenda'. Equity, inclusivity and sustainability are instead the regular themes (even though, much to the chagrin of some urban activists, it also uses the language of 'leveraging' agglomeration, competition and productivity).

This shift in priorities hence poses questions about the appositeness of current urban development approach of India.

The main question that arises is: Will the 'New Urban Agenda' be able to create a paradigm shift in the way cities are built and governed? Because of its non-binding nature without solid mechanisms for application, its ability to effect change is limited. However, instead of dismissing it as hollow proclamations, India should consider whether it can harness some of its key ideas. For example, various policy papers on topics such as urban governance, municipal finance and urban spatial strategies are included in Habitat III proceedings. As proceduralism or adhocism mainly decides the course of decision-making processes in Indian cities, it is worthy to discover alternative strategies and processes. Even as India is expecting to have magnificent cities with good facilities, in contrast to present scenario, the 'New Urban Agenda' offers a normative framework for guiding India's urban future.

ESSAYS ON WOMEN EMPOWERMENT-RELATED ISSUES

1. If Women Governed the World!

INTRODUCTION

Since ancient times, men and women have been playing a fixed role. One the one hand, males have been blessed with more importance due to various factors such as building of civilisations, hunting, getting food as well as other explorations over ages. In contrast, women have not been appreciated for their subtle contribution in fostering culture amongst many other things. As change is the truth and essence of life, even old traditions and policies have to give a way to new ones. Over the course of time, women have been proving their worth in diversified fields, even as a large chunk of male population continues to be the breadwinner of the household.

TRANSFORMATION IN WORLD ORDER

Last few decades have seen the time where women have proved their mettle. Among the examples signifying the empowerment of women in today's world are the election of Julia Gillard in Australia or even Dilma Vana Linhares Rousseff in Brazil.

This change in order poses interesting question like what if women played a more decisive and powerful role and come to dominate the world in the times to come! It is evident from the role women have been playing in today's society. Even as males are not comfortable with the idea of women being equal, they have to accept that women power is here to stay and is only likely to increase. First Woman Prime Ministers such as Indira Gandhi of India and Margaret Thatcher of England have proven their leadership quality. Not only in politics, now women have their involvement in intellectual, creative and scientific fields with superb elegance. They have also managed to set high standards for world to see and get motivated through outstanding examples of social service. Mother Teresa, Oprah Winfrey, Coco Chanel, Marie Curie, Madonna, Angela Merkel, Indra Nooyi, Aung Sang Suu Kyi amongst others have proved their mettle in their respective fields and are role models for many to follow the same path. Although they may be small in number, there are still many who are making best efforts to make their mark in this male-dominated world. This new scenario has given a hope to young women as traditional societies only witnessed women lending a shoulder to men in their various pursuits, whereas their own power or abilities remained untapped.

Women are regarded as multi tasker by being perfect in roles of mother, sister, etc. Women bring a certain level of compassion, love, beauty and virtue to the everyday life making it more meaningful. A World Bank study had discovered that in countries where parliament has higher number of women, there is lower level of corruption.

India has taken many steps in empowering women over time by introducing steps such as reserving one third of seats in parliament and various welfare schemes. Increasing number of women in business world such as Biocon founder Kiran Shaw also states the fact that women have good business acumen. There are different views on the topic that if women do rule the world, the chances of wars that caused so much loss to the world may have been lesser. Despite males being physically stronger, women are more emotionally stronger than them. Diversity of people plays an important role in infusing better and fresh ideas.

While men are easy to please in some reliable ways, women are more devious and complicated making them capable of being nasty in a silent manner. In addition, the kinder nature of women would also make them more determinant to fight for ensuring better condition for children of the world.

FLIPSIDE

As there are always two sides of coin, there is also a flipside to things. Even though they do possess the right attitude and ethics to get the work done, being gentle in nature makes it difficult for them to handle a situation where they have to crack the whip on people. Although women are considered to be headstrong, the way men impose their decisions and authority is uncommon with a lot of women.

CONCLUSION

We can only ponder over the issue, but it is really impossible to predict the result if women started ruling the world. However, there exists one strange truth that men want to remain in power, whereas women do not wish to have it so much that they can make them let go of it.

Yes, it is difficult for sceptics to swallow this, but this phenomenon may arise sometime in future. If it does come true, the world would never be the same place again.

2. Women Need More than Empowerment

INTRODUCTION

Although the times have changed since ancient time, it is sad to see the current state of crimes committed against women. Not only empowering women is necessary to make the life better, but also a change in mindset is important to bring change for good in society.

UPBRINGING AND ITS IMPACT

Although everyone boasts of our culture and values, crimes against women show the different picture altogether. As we already consider ourselves to be among civilised people, it will be a difficult task to bring a change in mindset. It is necessary to inculcate these values in children since the initial stage of upbringing. This should also be included in the education system. Later, the same should be inculcated in the Human Resource Development in corporate and government employment.

NECESSITY OF LEGAL ENFORCEMENT

Strict law and order must be maintained in order to ensure no individual can commit crime against women. Flexibility in law should exist to choose punishment, which will set examples for others. At present, the judicial system has certain limitations in punishing the minors calling them to be under-aged, in the same way as adults (recollect the December 16th incident, the Nirbhaya case); what if the judicial system was empowered to sentence the offenders with life imprisonment and family planning. Keeping in view the gravity of crime committed, how can a minor walk free in lieu of law?

AMENDMENTS SOUGHT AT SECURITY FORCES LEVEL

As it has become a common practice for police personnel to repeat the crime with complainant, protect the criminals and create a barrier for women to seek justice, there should be a system in place such that these complaints are dealt by female police. It must be mandatory for each police station to have at least one senior female police officer. Alternate channels should be devised to raise complaints, and possibly one complaint should be shared or raised with different authorities (for example, a copy to district magistrate, district collector, home ministry, police commissioner etc.) with the faith that they will act with honesty fearing one or more of the others may not co-operate in hiding the crime.

SOCIETY'S ROLE

As empowerment of women alone is just a part of whole process, it is needed that all individuals should respect others irrespective of gender, caste, colour, etc. As it is not possible for police to assign a protector to every woman, it is also the duty of society and individual to respect and work for betterment of each other. It is the duty of every citizen to raise a voice against any crime as the same can happen to anyone if not resisted at a perfect time.

THE ULTIMATE POWER: SELF-DEFENCE

Gone are the days when women were weak and vulnerable to threats and crimes. Society has side lined many taboos against women since the ancient time. Female foeticide during the 1980s was so prevalent that male : female ratio was greatly affected in the country. With a view to eradicate evils against women, our society has come a long way in overcoming the social and moral torturous and superstitious customs and tradition like sati, child marriage, etc. In addition, divorce was introduced in the society to relieve women of her struggling incompatible life.

It is need of the hour for women to understand their strength and raise a voice against any crime. Women's confidence in society has seen a significant dip with respect to the violence with respect to the sexual assault and rape cases

Introducing the self-defence mechanisms right from the schooling age can be of great help to the girls and women in protecting themselves and others from awaiting danger. It is important to imbibe a culture in society where girls and women are given basic self-defence training to protect and spread the same culture forward.

EMPOWERMENT AND RESERVATION

Although reservation is seen as an epitome of empowerment of women, in reality, it categorises women as the weaker section of society. A smart move by politicians, reservation rules are silly strategies to gather their vote bank. Even as women speak out a lot today regarding the equality, but we can rarely hear any voice to remove the rule for reservation. In essence, reservation is again a type of discrimination of gender in the society.

CONCLUSION

With a view to make this society safe and sound for women, it is time that women understand their positives and negatives to have a confident outlook in the society. It is high time for our women to shed any attempt for backdoor entry for escaping the scenario, to nourish themselves with the good traits and to fight back the evils in the society, instead of being settled with the issues of reservation and empowerment of women.

3. Women: Delicate or Strong?

With the rising frequency of terrorism and crime in our nation, the role of armed forces, army, air force or naval forces, has only increased with the passing time. Although these forces were earlier considered as a career option only by males, government's increasing focus on woman's liberation has seen rising number of girls joining sectors such as aviation, engineering, military forces and law amongst others. The rate at which the number of women has joined armed forces has significantly rose from the 1st batch of lady officer joining the Indian armed forces in 1992 to a share of over 3, 4 and 10 per cent in army, navy and air force. The brave acts by women in the field have led to shedding their delicate image entailing greater protection.

To change their image just in a span of two decades, a large number of women had been allocated the task of UN peacekeeping mission half a decade back. Irrespective of the fact that men are physically strong as compared to women, but women can efficiently handle difficult times with courage and good managerial skills. Being mentally more strong, women have been able to go through the rigorous trainings as well as face harsh challenges that are a part of being in the armed forces.

As India boasts of the third largest army in the world, one may find more uniform-clad women officers in the army if gender disparities are addressed properly. The likes of Kiran Bedi, India's first lady IPS officer, and Lieutenant General Punita Arora, a lady officer from the Army Medical Corps, heading the prestigious defence institution, have motivated millions of girls across the nation to follow their dreams irrespective of the disparities against women.

Despite being this path regarded as tough for women, with their courage and spirit, they will also be taking parts in combative roles shoulder to shoulder with their male counterparts in the future.

4. Women's Depiction in Advertisements: Gender Bias or Mean Attitude of the Society?

INTRODUCTION

How many of you have seen an attractive male model standing alongside cars being advertised in promotional events? Normally, curvaceous women of different nationalities are used for advertising campaigns to sell everything from luxury cars to sports goods. What is disturbing is that women in scant clothing are portrayed by advertisers to sell their products.

It is a fact that if gender bias can only reflect in advertisements it exists within the society of a nation. Gender equity has still been a dream of many nations. Women are still being abused and exploited in different parts of the world. One way of doing the same is through negative and stereotypical portrayal of women in print ads and commercials.

PERSPECTIVE

- There are many examples in Indian advertising agency where women have been used in derogatory and subservient ways to promote a variety of products. Going against the tide, some brave advertisers have endeavoured to give women more respectful roles in commercials and ads by depicting them with respect and sincerity.

It is through the evolution of society that sexist advertising will eventually cease to exist, but advertisers can certainly hasten the process by ensuring that their ads do not reflect any gender bias.

Consumerism is a process of alluring investment and promoting economic growth in the country. If irrelevant advertisements depicting women in poor light are used, they will not be able to catch the sight of consumers. Advertisers should remember this if they want their products to sell

Regarded as the gift of god, fair skin is of utmost importance in India as many celebrities participate in demeaning ads which promote unrealistic standards of beauty. Fairness cream ads always portray dark women as being at a huge disadvantage, which is ludicrous and racist. This fact presents the state of mind narrow minded Indian society lives with.

- The most worrisome trend is habit of showing women as being incapable of thinking or acting for themselves. Some ads like TVS Scooty commercials that go against the wave to show women in good light are refreshing change and are being followed by many.
- With society going through so many changes, it is important that ads also reflect reality and changing trend instead of traditional stereotypes. As women today are modern, progressive, independent and intelligent, their true identity should be reflected in ads to bring a change in society.

CONCLUSION

What is more problematic is that Indian women continue to be looked down upon and as a result be portrayed in negative terms. Today's outmoded belief systems define the advertising campaigns and commercials. Instead of following the stereotypes, ads should show women in a good light.

It is expected that the change in mindset will set a path for future to be free of all disparities and discrimination against women which will change the face of advertising in India for the better.

28

ESSAYS ON CHILDREN AND VULNERABLE SECTIONS OF SOCIETY

1. Do You Agree That Violence on TV Directly Influences Children's Behaviour?

Everybody would agree with the title of this essay. Research conducted on this issue has revealed that exposure to violence is not limited to television only but also video games, cell phones and internet increases the susceptibility of the child towards fierce behaviour.

Random research carried out on children by exposing to violence on TV and video games had revealled shocking facts, which indicates the possibility of the child getting influenced by violence and becoming aggressive in the short run. A lot of psychological experts and neuroscientists have observed that children's exposure to violent electronic media including violent games is an indication of long-term increases in their possibility for behaving aggressively and fiercely. These long-standing effects are the result of influential observational learning and desensitisation processes that take place automatically in the human child.

Due to thrilling activity, these acts of violence shown on television have long-lasting effects on children. After watching these activities, they start thinking over these scripts and start connecting these acts in their real lives. However, if the same is not observed, it can also change the permanent behaviour of the child, in fact, sometimes this risk is great enough to be treated as public health threat.

For every parent, it is very important to monitor their kids' television activity and how they are spending their spare time. We know children learn from both experience and social learning or role modelling as a result, when children watch violent activities, it is difficult for them to decode which ones are actual and to what extent. In this situation, the parental or adult guidance can come to their help and stop them from getting misguided. Even cartoon channels show lot of violence these days that influence the children's mind.

According to medical science, there are chemical changes that take place in the brain which are very similar to those that happen in post-traumatic stress disorder after watching violent activities for a long time. Since, the brains of young children are in developing situation, this can impact them badly.

Hence, the children need proper parental guidance in selecting which television programmes to watch and which video games to play. Parents should encourage their kids to watch the inspirational or the entertaining programmes on television. Developing interest in knowledge conveying channels such as Discovery channel, History channel etc. can be wonderful for the development of their mind.

2. Children Should be Encouraged to Think Individually

INTRODUCTION

The practice of developing a viewpoint through one's own thought and capabilities rather than have faith on the word of others is called independent thinking. The capability to believe one's own decisions, acting according to one's beliefs regardless of mistakes or imperfections forms part of independent thinking.

The formative years of a child are the real time-period for shaping up their independent thinking. Childhood is considered one of the most critical and essential parts in life, which leads to development of independent thinking that can go a long way in shaping their individuality. At this age, children are at their creative best, energetic and raw. This encourages them to develop habits which ingrain a sense of self sufficiency, which can lead to fewer problems while growing up.

IMPORTANCE OF THINKING INDIVIDUALLY

There are a lot of reasons that make it essential that children should be inspired to think independently.

Innovations in science or medicine have been made possible because of the courage shown by some children, who decided not to follow others. The real fact is, for developing and strengthening the mind, it is important to introduce independent thinking in early childhood. The end result of independent thinking is innovation and without the same, we would be a part of dark ages.

But, some parents end up shaping up their children's minds the way they want like if parents are of the view that learning a set of questions are important to do well in examinations, then the same thought is forced upon a child without understanding that those answers will not help their children to face questions that do not come with ready solutions.

For development of creative thinking, the parents must encourage their children to do something new which would take their minds into creative thinking process without fear of being wrong or different.

To judge a student on the basis of failure or success, the pedagogy followed in school is 'teach to test'. However, creativity needs to be considered as benchmark of independent thinking.

There are many methods that can be followed at home in order to develop independent thinking in children. First, they should be encouraged to talk imaginatively. Second, children must be taught to acquire listening skills so that they would respect various perspectives in life. In addition, parents should ask children to resolve their own issues instead of spoon feeding every time.

At last, children must be encouraged to write, i.e. putting words to paper for story or drawing something out of imagination can go a long way in improving their talent.

Encouraging independent thinking in the childhood is ideal otherwise children may fall prey to some unwarranted elements that may lead them into negative thoughts.

Parents must show flexibility towards children as they must not unnecessarily pressurise children and understand their limits. Another way to encourage their independent thinking is by asking for ideas in order to make plans. The creativity and eagerness of children is unparalleled and hence it can quickly translate into good planning along with providing motivation to their creative thinking.

The simple tasks for example cleaning study table, doing laundry, tying shoelaces or doing homework on own without parents' help are common and important responsibilities for a child.

Individually thinking is also the source of information and knowledge. Another major advantage of independent thinking is that it supports children to learn and master many skills that are needed before they leave home for higher studies.

As we know, everything has pros and cons and encouraging children to think independently too early can have its own negative consequences. Sometimes, few independent people may find it difficult to work in a group or a team. Since there are chances that individuals turn out to be far more efficient and somewhat superior, a sense of pride with respect to their own self and a feeling of deprecation towards others are possible. However, apart from these demerits, encouraging independent thinking in a child is far more likely to produce quality individuals who can make a huge difference in the mundane scheme of things.

CONCLUSION

The saying 'beginning well is half the work done' can be best demonstrated with respect to encouraging independent thinking from childhood days. Children's minds are filled with wonderful energy and if the energy is channelised in a fruitful manner through nurturing, it would result in developing individuals with better capability in addition to higher mental toughness. As the future of this world rests in the hands of generations who are growing up then it is the responsibility of everyone from parents, teachers as well as other individuals to ensure that the children will develop proper independent thinking to make a difference as these elements play a very important role in the growth of the children.

3. HIV and Drug Abuse in India

HIV is human immune deficiency virus which causes HIV infection, and AIDS is acquired immune deficiency syndrome which is the advanced stage of HIV. HIV virus breaks down the in-built defence system of the body. AIDS was first clinically recognised in the USA in 1981. In India, the first case was identified in May 1986. The Government of India established the National AIDS Committee within the Ministry of Health and Family Welfare after registering the first HIV case in India. HIV virus spread through attacking and destroying the CD4 cells (T cells) of the immune system. Scientists found that the source of HIV infection in humans was a type of chimpanzee in the Central Africa. India is the third largest country in the world with higher per centage of identified HIV-infected patients. To analyse that how much HIV has infected Indians, the health authorities of the government of India has organised the screening of high risk groups in October 1985. The HIV/AIDS is not confined to any one class, community, religion, age-group, sex or profession, in fact, the HIV infection is spread over all religions and all groups. According to the Indian Health Organisation, women and children are believed to be more infected with AIDS. In India, National AIDS Control Organisation (NACO) is responsible for preparing and implementing programmes for the prevention and control of the HIV disease.

HIV is not easily transmitted through the environment like air, water food etc. although HIV is an infectious disease and the main reasons through which the virus enters the body are:

1. Sexual intercourse with an infected person.
2. Through the transfusion of HIV infected blood, the blood products or through infected blood in needles, syringes and other such instruments.
3. Transmission from an infected mother to her newborn.

According to a study conducted by the Directorate of Health Services, Manipur in 1991, in the analysis of 6,680 specimens of HIV, the highest risk factor (93.9%) in spreading HIV was found among the drug addicts followed by blood donors (2.93%) and homosexuals (2.61%). Prostitutes infect their customers and in turn also get infected by them. Drug addicts who take drugs by injection carry the possibility of spreading the HIV infection through shared infected needles. According to one approximation, the level of HIV infection increased from 1% to 30% among the sex workers in Mumbai during 1989–1991. In Manipur, 40 to 50% of intravenous drug-users are HIV positive and many of them are sent to jail in some crimes even by their own parents.

The transmission of HIV infection is also possible by the blood donors. There are estimated 2000 blood banks in India which supply about 20 lakhs bottles of blood every year and half of these blood banks are government banks and the remaining half is unlicensed.

The devastating effect of the disease in our lifetime and beyond is very difficult to imagine. Initially, the disease appeared confined to few homosexuals who later has affected millions of men, women and children worldwide. AIDS is not only a health issue rather it is a societal problem who affects important social, cultural and economic dimensions and it threatens the basic social institutions at the individual, family and community levels. If the needs of AIDS patients are not meet fully then its economic consequences will equally serious as it could claim up to half of the national expenditure for health. Not only HIV patients but families of HIV patients too suffer economically, psychologically and socially.

Programmes that provide information, condoms and HIV testing to persons in high-risk groups are extremely important to prevent the further spread of the disease. In its official policies and statements, the Indian government has realised the importance of reaching out to women in prostitution and homosexual men as an essential element of its HIV/AIDS response. The national AIDS program led by AIDS control society of India, financed largely through a $200 million World Bank loan, invests in programmes that target persons in high-risk groups. Bill and Melinda Gates Foundation assured international funding amounting to $ 200 million for battling the disease but still the potential costs of battling the disease are staggering. However, the services available for the care of AIDS patients are sadly insufficient.

To help the patients in overcoming fear and hysteria, effective strategies have to be designed and developed. Counselling families, neighbourhoods and members of social-support networks are also an important need because ultimately they have to bear a major responsibility for the sick and the survivors. The trained medical staff can provide information about AIDS to the patients and to their relatives. Since persons suffering from STDs are also a significant risk factor, so it is important to give high priority to the programmes for the prevention and control of STDs.

The blood or blood products should be tested for HIV before transfusion and HIV tests should be made free and confidential for persons who indulge in high-risk activities. The medical staff should make sure the use of disposable syringes and other operation equipment. The condoms should be freely distributed and its use should be encouraged among the sex workers who are the most susceptible group. The drug users should be convinced to not using intravenous drug abuse and voluntary organisations should aware the people using innovative and community-based approaches.

AFFECT OF HIV/AIDS ON WOMEN

HIV/AIDS have an adverse impact on women worldwide. Indian women are already economically, culturally and socially needy lacking access to treatment, financial support and education. They have no power and right of decision making and even they lack the opportunity of participating equally within the community and are subjected to punitive laws, norms and practices exercising control over their bodies and sexual relations. Women are supposed as the main sources of Sexually Transmitted Infections (STIs) referred generally as women diseases. The traditional beliefs about sex, blood and other type of disease transmission have become fertile ground for the stigmatisation of women within the context of HIV/AIDS.

The route of transmission of HIV infection in women is similar as men. Few women become infected through artificial insemination from an infected person, and lesbians do get HIV/AIDS by using drugs, sharing needles and sharing sex toys with an infected partner without washing. Unborn baby also get infected by their mother during pregnancy, birth and breastfeeding.

MISCONCEPTIONS

There are few misconceptions related to HIV disease:

- Withdrawal during intercourse
- Douching
- Birth control pills and diaphragm does not protect from being infected with HIV/AIDS
- HIV can be spread through casual contact with an HIV infected individual
- Mosquitoes can transmit HIV
- Homosexual men and drug users can be only infected through HIV

HIV/AIDS AND PREGNANCY

Women with HIV can transmit the virus to their babies before, during and after birth—this is the important biological difference between men and women that leads to additional social and cultural consequences with regard to HIV/AIDS and this type of transmission is referred as vertical transmission. Only a minority of children gets infected during early pregnancy and most infected infants acquire their infection during delivery when the infant exposed to large amount of infected maternal blood and secretions. The additional risk of transmission of HIV/AIDS is through breastfeeding.

WHY WOMEN DO NOT SEEK TREATMENT

The reasons why women do not seek treatment are as follows:

- Low self-esteem and abusive relationship.
- Fear of being recognised and ostracised from the community.
- Distrust in health care system.
- Partner's failure to disclose status.
- Women are restricted by household responsibilities and lack of mobility.
- There is restricted access to prescribed treatment due to poverty.
- Women oriented health services do not include STD related services.
- Services that only focus on STD treatment carry a greater stigma than integrated services.

Awareness and Empowerment of Women To prevent HIV, there is a need to aware women on this topic and at the right age also. Here are few points mentioned below:

- Women have the right to say 'NO' to unsafe sex and they can even refuse to share needle and syringes.

- Women can insist their male partner to use condom always for sex.
- To have sex with one partner but the partner should not be infected with HIV/AIDS and who is not engaging in high risk behaviour.
- To prevent STDs, women should go for regular sexual health care check-ups.
- They must use disinfected needle and syringe each time to inject.
- Women should freely talk with their partner on the topic of HIV/AIDS prevention.

There is the need of counselling for women to make them aware on reproductive health issues, family planning and safe infant feeding and also need for active networking for complete healthcare and social support for positive women and their family. Pregnant women and infants who are in high-risk category should be tested. There should be quick assessment for anti-retro viral therapy and other additional supportive treatments should be given side-by-side for their recovery.

DRUG ABUSE IN INDIA

International Day against Drug Abuse and Illicit Trafficking is celebrated on June 26 every year. This day is celebrated by the world community to alert the people in general and youth against the negative effects of drug. If data are collected worldwide on the drugs scenario, then result would be very grim. Next to petroleum and arms trade, it is the third largest business in the world with a turnover of around $500 billion which is huge. Approximately 190 million people worldwide consume one drug or the other. The result of drug addiction would be immense human distress and the illegal production and distribution of drugs have produced crime and violence all over the world. Presently, there is no part of the world that is free from the curse of drug trafficking and drug addiction, and Millions of drug addicts worldwide are leading miserable lives, between life and death.

India too is affected by the drug abuse, and the numbers of drug addicts are increasing day by day. According to a UN report the registered number of heroin addicts is one million in India, and unofficially there are more than five millions. Inhalation of heroin alone has given way to drug use, that too in combination with other narcotics and painkillers and has increased the intensity of the effect, speeded the process of addiction and made difficult the process of recovery. The most frequently abused drugs in India are Cannabis, heroin and Indian-produced pharmaceutical drugs. Due to the association with some Hindu deities, Cannabis products often called charas, bhang or ganja, are abused throughout the country because it has achieved some amount of religious holiness. The International Narcotics Control Board in its 2002 report released in Vienna stated that Indian persons addicted to opiates are changing their drug of choice from opium to heroin. The medicinal products containing narcotic drugs and intravenous injections of analgesics such as dextropropoxphene etc. are also reported from many states, as it is easily available at 1/10th the cost of heroin which is very less. Drug abuse is the habit of taking illegal drugs which has many social, cultural, biological, geographical, historical and economic characteristics. Some of the reasons behind the drug abuse are: the disintegration of the old joint family system, absence of parental love and care in modern families where both parents are working, decline of old religious and moral values etc. These reasons are the cause to an increase in the number of drug addicts who take drugs to escape from the hard realities of life. The nature of the drug abused, the personality of the individual and the addict's immediate environment are the major reasons of drug use, misuse or abuse. The processes of industrialisation, urbanisation and migration have led to loosening of the traditional methods of social control, rendering an individual vulnerable to the stresses and strains of modern life. The fast changing social environment, among other factors, is largely contributing to the increase of drug abuse, both of traditional and of new psychoactive substances. The use of synthetic drugs and intravenous drug has led to HIV/AIDS has added a new dimension to the problem, especially in the northeast states of the nation.

Society has affected a lot due to drug abuse and it has led to increase in the crime rate. Addicts choose the way of crime to pay for their drugs. Drugs remove shyness and impair judgment encourages one to commit offences. The incidences of drug abuse are of eve-teasing, group clashes, assault and impulsive murders. In addition, addiction increases conflicts and causes indefinable emotional pain for every member of the family. With most drug users being in the age group of 18–35 years, the loss in terms of human potential is infinite and damage to the physical, psychological, moral and intellectual growth of the youth is very high. Adolescent drug abuse is another area of concern in adolescent and young people's behaviour. It is estimated that, in India, by the time most boys reach the ninth grade, about 50 per cent of them have attempted at least one of the gateway drugs, however, there is a wide regional variation across states in term of the incidence of the drug abuse. For example, a larger proportion of teens in West Bengal and Andhra Pradesh use gateway drugs (about 60 per cent in both the states) than Uttar Pradesh or Haryana (around 35 per cent). The health care system is burdened due to increase in incidences of HIV, hepatitis B and C and tuberculosis due to addiction adds the reservoir of infection in the community. Indian women face greater problems from drug abuse and the consequences include domestic violence and infection with HIV and the financial burden also. Maximum domestic violence is directed against women in the context of demands for money to buy drugs. Eighty seven per cent of addicts being treated in a de-addiction centre run by the Delhi police recognised being violent with family members. At the national level, drug abuse is basically linked with racketeering, conspiracy, corruption, illegal money transfers, terrorism and violence threatening.

The country has faced the threat of drug trafficking effectively at the national and international levels. Several measures involving innovative changes in enforcement, legal and judicial systems have been brought into effect against the threat. The introduction of death penalty for drug-related offences has been a major step taken by the government. The Narcotic Drugs and Psychotropic Substances Act, 1985, were passed with strict provisions to control this threat with minimum term of

10 years imprisonment extendable to 20 years and fine of ₹1 lakh extendable up to ₹2 lakhs for the drug offenders. The Act has been further modified by making provisions for the loss of properties derived from illegal drugs trafficking. For the reduction in use of drugs has been developed by the various government agencies and NGOs and is further improved by measures like education, counselling, treatment and rehabilitation programmes and India has bilateral agreements on drug trafficking with 13 countries, including Pakistan and Burma. Before 1999, extradition between India and the United States occurred under a 1931 treaty signed by the United States and the United Kingdom, which was made applicable to India in 1942. However, a new extradition treaty between India and the United States entered into force in July 1999 and in October 2001, a Mutual Legal Assistance Treaty was signed by India and the United States. India also is signatory to the following treaties and conventions:

1961 U.N. Convention on Narcotic Drugs

1971 U.N. Convention on Psychotropic Substances

1988 U.N. Convention Against Illicit Traffic in Narcotic Drugs and Psychotropic Substances

2000 Transnational Crime Convention

There is a need to prevent the spread and entrenchment of drug abuse, as the cost to the people, environment and economy will be colossal. Moreover, the spread of such unacceptable habits among the relatively youth segment of society ought to be arrested at any cost. To find the solution of drug addiction issue, there is a need for the government enforcement agencies, the non-governmental philanthropic agencies, and others to collaborate and supplement each other's efforts through education and legal measures.

4. A New Assertion of Dalit Politics in India

Today, Dalit politics is taking charge of various affairs in their own hand and extending their terrain of struggle rather than limiting it to political power or religious conversion.

At present, a new swing in Dalit politics can be easily noticed in the way Dalits have raised their voice against violence towards them. They have devised modes of struggles, the kind of alliances forged, and the nodal concepts and norms appeal for action. While old methods of doing Dalit politics—paternalism, quotas, sub-caste appeal, conversion, bahujan (including sarvajan)—are still active, more in a client-patron mode, Dalits are taking more and more charge of affairs in their own hands.

Some features of this turn are remarkable: caste is back into reckoning; for networking and communication, the use of social media has increased; left politics and its limitations are under examination; Babasaheb Ambedkar has reinforced his presence as the flagpole; there is a highly literate Dalit leadership deeply aware of historical injustice and electorally decisive numbers in support; an idea of Brahmanism is highlighted as the enemy; a search for a new civil society-state axis is on; and a new form of concepts and slogans are being deployed as the battle cry. Dalits have started developing layers of folklore and alternative nationalist imagery to forge skilful use of signs, symbols and representations.

All these features are part of the Dalit movement at one time or the other, it is their combinatory which is proving itself fatal. Above all, this commotion is situating itself on the ground of India's distinct democratic politics, utilising its resources as much as possible. For this movement, there is no single political party at the head although many political parties will have much at stake in it.

REACTION TO VIOLENCE

The atrocities on Dalits were largely limited to police records and the bulky records of the National Commission for Scheduled Castes for long. But cases like a suicide note by a research scholar, Rohith Vemula, that stated 'My birth is my fatal accident' seems to connect the whole issue with a bad taste of caste of a dalit son. The incident is being identified as the squeezing the life of youths by the institute management on account of caste and special identity. Dalits felt that the opportunity to right to use the legal and institutional resources of a democratic polity has gone and relocate them into a caste grid, consigning all their efforts, again in Vemula's words, to 'immediate identity and nearest possibility'. Their life prospects are much lower to those of its other beneficiaries. This sense of 'unfair inclusion' connects them to the vast numbers in the Indian subcontinent who are kept in Ambedkar's cryptic phrase, 'outside the fold'.

According to Valerian Rodrigues, 'The denial of access to equal opportunities and rewards is not merely economic but ways of life, and abilities to define one's own and collective futures'. Such a state of affairs may not be played out in the open but built into the common sense of everyday life. Therefore, Dalits tend to fill those levels that are not important, prone to routine and fake rather than inventive and decision-making. In institutions of higher education, Dalits fill social sciences and humanities that are able with very little institutional expense or vision, and can generate very few sought after jobs or opportunities.

The effect of land improvements and agricultural transformation has pushed Dalits and social segments similar to them further to the restrictions. There is a new dependence ranking at the workplace rather than enablement and companionship.

The *Hindutva* agenda of inviting all Hindus to the feast table but assigning lower castes to their predetermined places has further aggravated the sense of being unsolicited. 'The fatal accident of birth' connects all the sites that have witnessed Dalit upsurge recently, from Tughlakabad to Una, from Hyderabad to Udupi. But it also occurs between skilled and unskilled, organised and informal, rural and urban, and male and female labour.

MODES OF STRUGGLE

The social relations, in which Dalits are struggling, are not merely against external domination like capital, caste or power, but also against rejection of their very humanity.

With the movement, Dalit are widening their terrain of struggle rather than merely limiting it to political power or religious conversion. Given this task, there are new elements in place in Dalit struggles: the social media does not become simply a site to network, but also to inform, to criticise, to assess as well as redefine concerns. In fact, the social media is supporting today as the backbone of the new Dalit growing as could be seen in the solidarity movement with Rohith Vemula across the country, in 'Azadi Koon' (March for Freedom) from Ahmedabad to Una in Gujarat, or the 'Udupi Chalo' walk that brought thousands of Dalits from various parts of Karnataka to the temple town, Udupi.

Various marches and rallies across distant villages and small towns have united people physically and emotionally and there are slogans emphasising pride in being a Dalit, with a sub-caste enumeration as an add-on, not infrequently. There is a rebirth of folklore, sites of violence have changed into pilgrimage, traditional musical instruments of Dalits have thrown up fusion with rhythmic dances of great power and self-confidence, and broadsheets, songs and street plays, evocative posters and imaginative slogans challenge dominant opinion and sensitivity. Women and men are helping each other in this struggle, something that the late Sharmila Rege portrayed in her writings. Ambedkar makes a rich and ideal presence across such performances, and there is almost none beside him in importance. In present scenario, sites of Dalit rallies are crowded with a rich display of books and publications, a widespread practice in Left rallies of yore.

Cleavages between Dalits and backward castes, Dalits and Muslims, and the gender divide have come in the way of improving the democratic dividend from their devastating numbers. The positive support of Dalits to the backward castes in the Mandal protest did not create long-term political alliances. The Dalit and Muslim alliance never materialised on the ground at any point of time in right sense. And, less said the better so far as the alliance between backward castes and women is concerned.

The slogans in the Dalit movement these days indicate a softening of position: the banners read, and slogans echo: 'choice of food', 'right to land', 'Swabhiman' and 'Atmabhiman' (self-respect), 'Azadi' (freedom) and 'dignity'. They decided to take oppression head on to assert their own self-hood. Dalits also seem to assert the equality of women and choose the kind of life they wish to live and never accept moral policing on them by the Hindutva brigades. The murder of Mohammad Akhlaq by a local Hindu mob on the charge of storing beef at his house in Dadri, Uttar Pradesh, has become an important matter in Dalit struggles, woven around the right to food. As a result, the bonding among these large number of associations of these groups and communities are found.

The current Dalit movement has appealed for the registry of norms while explaining and justifying its objectives and actions has much to separate it from its previous expressions. It is more of human dignity and worth, and one's ability to achieve one's best as per the potential should achieve the high ground. Identifying freedom to one's birthmarks, or social structures, institutions, partialities and interactions is a state of affairs today which is seen as new form of dependency.

From the time of Jyotirao Phule and Iyothee Thass, the term Brahmanism that Dalits have employed to rally against a specific mode of dominance has acquired new meanings of sustaining a social order based on graded inequality, servility and deference, and self-aggrandisement at the expense of misery and inhumanity meted out to others. Even, India's so-called modern and democratic institutions are recognised as sustaining a Brahmanical allowance. The central concerns of Muslims, women and backward castes are supposed as being consistent with these concepts and norms.

The new Dalit politics senses that it holds the key to some of these concerns and strivings while there is much that unites the social groups and communities computed above, there is much that divides them too. There is a need to fill the gap and to build a bridge, and Dalits are yet to reach out to *Adivasis* in a meaningful way.

5. Old Age Problem and Our Responsibility towards Old Age

The old age people are the important part of human being. They have lots of experience, and using these experiences youths can success in their life, in fact, their experiences and views are the base of a well-cultured and traditional society. In this essay, we will discuss about the old age: problems associated with it and our responsibilities towards old age. Life expectancy has increased dramatically over the past century and in coming days, the world will have more old people than children and this social transformation represents both challenges and opportunities.

To cope with the demographic shift, countries and health care systems will need to find innovative and sustainable ways. John Beard, director of the WHO Department of Ageing and Life Course, says that 'with the rapid ageing of populations, finding the right model for long-term care becomes more and more urgent'. The plan is a resource for policy-makers, suggesting ways for governments, non-governmental organisations and other stakeholders to reorient the ways in which their societies observe, interact with and care for their older citizens, as by 2050, two billion people will be aged 60 and above.

Old age is defined as the ages nearing or surpassing the average life span of human beings. The United Nations World Assembly on Ageing, held in Vienna in 1982, conveyed a package of recommendations which gives high priority to research related to developmental and humanitarian aspects of ageing (United Nations, 1987). The plan of action specifically recommends that 'international exchange and research cooperation as well as data collection should be promoted in all the fields having a bearing on ageing, in order to provide a rational basis for future social policies and action. Special emphasis should be placed on comparative and cross cultural studies in ageing'.

In later life related to ageing (e.g., arthritis) or the beginning of a chronic disease, (e.g., lung cancer, diabetes and peripheral vascular disease) or a degenerative illness (e.g., dementia), many people develop disabilities. But disabilities associated with ageing and the beginning of chronic disease can be prevented or delayed.

In protection of the social and economic security of the elderly people, the traditional Indian society and the age-old joint family system have been instrumental. With the rapid changing society and the trend of nuclear families in India in recent years, the elderly are likely to be exposed to emotional, physical and financial insecurity in coming years.

The Ministry of Social Justice and Empowerment, Government of India, adopted a 'National Policy on Older Persons' in January 1999 after realising the increasing need for intervention in area of old age welfare, and the policy provides broad guidelines to the State governments for taking action for the welfare of old age in a proactive manner. It defines 'senior citizen' as a person who is 60 years or above and struggles to ensure their well-being and improve the quality of their lives by providing specific facilities, concessions, relief and services and helping them cope with problems related with old age. For ensuring that the existing public services for senior citizens are user-friendly and sensitive to their needs, the policy proposes affirmative action on the part of government departments.

To make aging a positive experience, longer life must go hand in hand with continuing opportunities for health, participation and security. The World Health Organisation has introduced the term 'active ageing' to underline the need to achieve this vision.

WHO launched a new campaign during the International Year of Older Persons in 1999, Active Ageing, which highlights the meaning of social integration and health throughout the life course. The aim of Active ageing is to extend healthy life expectancy and the quality of life for all people as they age, including those who are weak, disabled and in need of care.

Active ageing depends on many factors or 'determinants' that surround individuals, families and nations and these apply to the health of all age groups, while the emphasis is on the health and quality of life of old age persons. To achieve this goal of active ageing will require action in a variety of areas, including education, employment and labour, finance, social security, housing, transportation, justice and rural and urban development.

For the prevention of the abuse of older people, WHO has recognised the need to plan and develop a global strategy within the framework of a working partnership between the WHO Ageing and Life Course unit of the Department of Chronic Diseases and Health Promotion, the WHO Department of Injuries and Violence Prevention, the International Network for the Prevention of Elder Abuse (INPEA), HelpAge International and partners from academic institutions in a range of countries.

Some recommendations of WHO are: promote and live a healthy lifestyle across the life-course, create age-friendly environments and policies to engage older men and women, make primary health care age-friendly ensure easy approach to health care and rehabilitation services for older people and adapt physical environments to existing disabilities.

For Active Ageing, lifestyle choices should start at the early stage of life which should include participating in family and community life, eating a balanced and healthy diet, maintaining proper physical activity, avoiding smoking and excessive alcohol consumption.

It is the period to set a new example, one that views old age as active participants in an age-integrated society and as active participants as well as beneficiaries of development.

6. Human Rights Issues in India

There is serious requirement for the intervention of National Human Rights Commission (NHRC) to deal with human rights problems that come in front of everyone related to violence by the police and security forces, including extrajudicial killings, torture, rape, and corruption at all levels of government.

The world's largest democracy is also single-minded by separatist violence, life-threatening prison and police custody conditions, sex trafficking, environmental destruction and a general environment of impunity. A large per centage of population live in poverty, and women, children (especially the girl child), religious minorities, Dalits, *Adivasis*, and members of the LGBT community face discrimination and violence and physically and mentally challenged person often have no choice to decent employment and/or sufficient treatment.

This is the real fact and very hard to deny that a large number of exploitations of human rights occur as a consequence of a mindset of 'superiority' and 'privilege'. This is often a result of upbringing, as individuals have learnt from the society itself to compare themselves with people of different status or identity as they believe they are 'different' and 'superior' to others.

There are other issues exist related to sustainable livelihood as well as social and political involvement of vulnerable groups. Even administrative authorities have failed to guarantee rights to the common people and people belonging to vulnerable groups are mostly unable to have equal access to their rights.

To constantly review and uphold the available safeguards for human rights protection, National Human Rights Institutions (NHRIs) have been set up across the world. They do so through the authorities permitted to them that include monitoring human rights violations, advising their governments on pertinent human rights concerns, establishing and maintaining relations with other regional and international organisations, promoting human rights education, while exercising their quasi-judicial powers. In order to implement these authorities, NHRIs have been provided a clearly defined and broad-based order, including all human rights—civil, political, social, cultural and economic.

The NHRC deal with the activities related to human rights in India, and has the authorities of a Civil Court while looking into cases of human rights violations. After completion of its investigation in a case, the Commission advises to the concerned authority to initiate actions against those responsible for human rights violations. Usually, in almost all cases recommended by the Commission, concerned government authorities take the initiatives to investigate and compile report in cases of human rights violations but because of the non-binding nature of commission's recommendations, it raises a kind of sentiment that such bodies are usually ineffective in bringing right results on the ground. This requires urgent attention and change.

Constant efforts have to be made towards consolidating the rights which have been achieved through a lot of pain and struggle over centuries. Combined effort of individuals, communities and even governments are important to fight against the abuses of human rights.

In future for human rights, the nature and quality of national-level legislations, policies and execution mechanisms will be the crucial factors. The responsibility of the State would be to make sure of the universal access to human rights, guarantee a life of self-respect, and equal access to various public goods and services are further emphasised by international human rights conventions, to many of which India is a signatory.

The base of the development of the nation should be on the objective of securing human dignity and assuring fundamental human rights to all. It is not possible for any police station, commission or court to monitor every nook and corner of the country to prevent human rights abuses so it is at last up to the citizens of this country to treat each other as equals. It is our responsibility to inculcate a human rights culture in our neighbourhood. In addition, we also need to remember our duties as declared in Article 51A of the Constitution. There are many human rights institutions but still there exist violations of human rights across the whole world. There is, therefore, some sting, which is very true in the cynic's lament that 'the only thing universal about human rights is their universal violation'.

On the 66th anniversary of the Universal Declaration of Human Rights (UDHR) this year, revelations of mass human rights violations have raised the question regarding the commitment of governments in guaranteeing the protection of fundamental rights and highlighted the need for greater responsibility.

Globally, this year is the witness of various human rights violations for example executions, amputations, and lashings by terrorist groups, assassination of captured belligerents by governments, violations and crimes committed during clashes, among other egregious rights abuses.

Still, a large number of countries just talk about democracy but in reality mock the rights important to democratic rule. This requires deep contemplation as it directly impacts the life of individuals.

Pointless to state, governments which secure human rights are stable, more committed, and able to contribute to and strengthen international peace and harmony while countries which are ineffective in safeguarding and promoting human rights will in the long run face economic deficiency and international seclusion.

The true test of 'good governance' is the extent to which it fulfils the promise of civil, cultural, economic, political and social rights. Thus, the key yardstick to evaluate effective governance is by knowing if public institutions are effectively providing rights in the form of right to health, housing, food, education and justice along with effective safety in the country.

7. Suicide in Youths and Reason Behind it

Every year thousands of youths follow the route of suicide. The problem of suicides of young people in India is little mystery. The numerous reports from the National Crime Records Bureau and independent investigations of mortality show that suicide is a leading cause of death in youths. According to the latest government data, there is an approximation of 60,000 deaths of youths each year; with independent studies showing that these data underestimate up to a third of youth suicides by misclassifying them as accidents—the true figure may even go up to 1,00,000 a year.

The recent case of suicides of three young women students in a medical college in Tamil Nadu has mentioned the awful conditions in their institution add to the increasing number of suicides among young Indians in the past year. Consider few examples that have hit our headlines: the suicide attempts by four female athletes in a sports facility in Kerala; the 29 suicides of youth preparing for national entrance exams in coaching institutions in Kota; the suicide of Rohith Vemula in Hyderabad; and the most recent loss of Saira Sirohi, a national-level swimmer, in Ghaziabad.

Each of these events has been studied separately and in detail with commentators emphasising the relationship of the deaths of these youths to the particular social issues they found themselves facing with such as from caste-based oppression and gender discrimination to the pressures of academic performance etc. In the noise that has surrounded each of these tragedies, with the predictable hysteria in TV news debates and the slugfest between rival ideological camps, one common thread running through all of these suicides is the loss of hope in the young educated victims trapped in a system that had failed them.

The reason behind suicide of youths globally in this period is because this is the phase of life which is characterised by rash behaviours, is associated with dramatic changes in one's self-image and objectives, and is when some of the most important life decisions related to education and relationships are made. This is the reason why suicide attempts in youth, unlike suicide in older adults, are often impulsive—triggered by severe disappointments like poor examination result or the loss of a romantic relationship. In some cases, there is a history of a longer-term period of social issues causing a clinical depression. A research has shown that the major zones of youth suicide are in the most developed states of India, like in the south of the country. One of the key reasons for this is the increasing gap between the ambitions of educated youth, such as to freely choose their life partner or live a life free of social biases, and the reality of a tough, inflexible, and uncertain society in which they find themselves struggling.

The suicide was impulsive or well-planned is the secondary matter, one thing is for certain—no one tries to end their lives unless they become hopeless for their future. Many other countries have started to work in this direction and implemented a range of interventions which target not only the social conditions that trigger the hopelessness that leads to suicidal activities, but also the more immediate individual interventions to encourage youths to recover their hope to live.

Despite the evidence testifying to the huge toll of suicide in our youths and the knowledge of effective interventions to prevent suicide, there remains no coordinated effort to address suicide as a public health issue in India. Thus there is no need to surprise that the suicide rates of youths in India are among the highest in the world and in this regard, our response to these tragedies is similar to that of suicides in other groups in our society. This is no better demonstration than by the discourse on farmer suicides being viewed almost completely through a socio-political lens. Similarly, the response to the heart-breaking suicides of the parents of a young child who had died because of dengue in New Delhi in September 2015 highlights the actions of the hospitals which denied treatment of the dying child. There was no attention to the fact that the suicide of the parents might have been prevented with suitable counselling. It appears that our gut response to each suicide tragedy, not least in our news media, is to hold someone responsible for the social aspects that trigger the loss of hope. Sadly, we never question whether the suicide might have been prevented had there been supporting environments for the recovery of hope and what lessons we may learn to prevent further suicides.

A question arises here that if social elements play such a major role in understanding suicidal behaviour, why should we emphasis on interventions targeting individuals? Some says that this may even divert attention from the social factors that must at last be held responsible for all suicides. The reason is that most youths who are exposed to the same social factors do not lose hope and, if they do, they do not try to end their lives. The huge majority of youths in the same institutions of Kota or in the decrepit medical college in Tamil Nadu survive their ordeal and move on. Self-harm behaviour is a relatively rare outcome of a unique confluence of factors in a person, both social and related to psychological well-being, and we must aim both of these to prevent suicides.

There should be an open dialogue to challenge the stigma surrounding mental health; the development of life skills in schools to strengthen emotional regulation, which can help build resilience to overcome with the phases of loss of hope that are expected in the transition from childhood to adulthood; parenting interventions to minimise the pressures on youths to perform academically and to choose their intimate partner; ensuring freedom from violence, gender discrimination, and social rejection of young people, not least in campuses; a campaign to make sure the safe storage of pesticides, the most commonly used method for suicide; and easy contact to trained personnel to deliver psychological treatments in educational institutions and health-care facilities.

The Indian Constitution has provided the opportunity for an expansive expression of basic rights after its adoption. It has moved to an interpretative practice that supports the spirit of the fundamental rights to life, liberty and equality with dignity, among others. There is little confusion that it has provided the framework for the declaration of fundamental rights mainly against not only the state, but also private sectors, providing the standard of constitutional principles that must in all cases defeat public, including religious, morality. This is especially critical where the latter is found to carry out stigmatised identities that reduce the dignity of persons and dominate them in countless ways.

8. Disability is Not Divinity

In 'Mann Ki Baat', Prime Minister Narendra Modi spoke about disability: 'Those in whom Paramatma has created a deficiency in the body, those for whom some part of the body does not work properly, we call them 'viklaang'. But sometimes, when we get to know them, we realise that although there is the deficiency that we see with our eyes, God has given them some extra power, there is a different kind of shakti that God has created within them which we cannot perceive with our eyes. But when we see their capability, we are taken aback, 'Arre wah? How does he manage to do this?' Then, we had a thought: 'From our eyes we feel that he is 'viklaang', but from experience we find that he has some extra power, atirikt shakti'. Then we had another thought: 'Why don't we, in our country, replace the word 'viklaang' with the word 'divyaang'? These are those people who possess divinity—divyata—in one or more parts of their body; whose bodies are possessed by divine power (divya shakti), which those of us with normal bodies (saamaanya shareer) do not have. Compatriots! Can we adopt 'divyaang' instead of 'viklaang' in common usage?' In other words, that which is divinely fated shall not be questioned. The 'deficiency' and the 'divya shakti' are the factors that constitute the disability stereotype.

The bail application of Delhi University professor G.N. Saibaba was rejected on medical grounds by a single judge of the Nagpur Bench of the Bombay High Court, emphasising his involvement in a 'serious crime', and passed an order that the activities of a 'banned organisation' overrode any concerns for his physical health and comfort while in state custody and all struggles to secure bail for him on medical grounds are nothing but 'subterfuge'. It is useful to accept in mind that we are speaking of a person who has been placed under arrest, but has not yet undergone trial and has surely not been convicted for any offence under the Unlawful Activities (Prevention) Act.

The court accepts that 'the applicant suffered 90 per cent disability from his childhood. He had also undergone cardiac surgery about 8 to 10 years before'. The medical certificate trusted by the court states that Dr. Saibaba suffered from a known case of post-polio residual paralysis with 'chief complaints of reduction in left shoulder movements and pain in [the] back ....' He was advised to go through regular treatment for three months and a coronary angiography by the doctor in the super-specialty hospital at Nagpur. On the basis of these medical accounts, the court concludes that the 'present health condition of the applicant ... is perfectly normal and is in the same position as it was when he was in jail'.

The reality that his disability and related medical conditions has put Dr. Saibaba at an unfair disadvantage in conditions of custody —that the standard of care need for a person with severe disabilities is of a different from the standard of care for a non-disabled person; that the standard is not met by only ensuring the maintenance of *status quo*; that conditions of imprisonment worsen the risk to life disproportionately in the case of a person with disabilities—does not enter the balance sheet. The tenor seems to be that the diabolical acts that the complainant is alleged to have sympathised with offset any need for state and judicial benevolence. The Constitution hangs in suspended disbelief.

Trapped between the divine and the diabolical, it is time, yet again, for us to understand afresh that the discrimination results in disproportionate disadvantage, rejection, and stigmatisation suffered by persons with disabilities, and are caused by cultural, social, and physical obstructions that obstruct their effective contribution in social and political life. Disability is not a divine gift—this declaration is a serious misconception of the place of rights in realising human dignity, and the role of the state in ensuring protection against discrimination. Similarly, it is important to recognise that ease of access and support services for persons with severe disabilities are necessary to the protection of their right to life, bodily integrity, and dignity under the Constitution. Imprisonment of persons with severe disabilities worsens their suffering disproportionately in comparison to other prisoners, crushing the fundamental right to equality. We need to accept, at least by constitutional courts, that our prisons are not well-equipped to provide custodial treatment that does not erode the fundamental right to life, equality, and dignity of prisoners with disabilities. There is an urgency with which we must wrest constitutional ground for disability rights in these worried times. Importantly, we need a re-education on the Constitution at the highest levels of our juridical-political order.

❑❑❑

29

ESSAYS ON CONTEMPORARY ISSUES

1. Terrorism and World Peace

INTRODUCTION

There have been many unforeseen events in the 21st century that have changed the course of history forever. Apart from the advancements in the field of technology, the most noticeable change no doubt has been the emergence of terrorism which has been considered one of the biggest threats for the whole world. All over the world, terrorism has been continuously affecting the lives of people all across the globe. This has adversely affected the world peace at an alarming rate. Terrorism has affected all countries, be it a superpower United States of America or a developing country like India. The scourge of terrorism continues to spread its roots with the world having no concrete solution to tackle this. This has literally not only compromised the national security but has also led to a state of anarchy in different countries.

FAR REACHING CONSEQUENCES OF TERRORISM

Terrorism and its Long-term Effects

The word terrorism has its root in the French revolutionary reign of Maximilien Robespierre, when millions of people were put to death in 1793–94, mostly at the guillotine.

In fact, it was after the 9/11 attack on the twin towers in United States, the world recognised terrorism as the biggest global threat and could no longer turn a blind eye to it as it was highly significant for the domestic or international security. The far-reaching adverse effects of terrorism have to be comprehended candidly to understand why so many countries are investing billions of dollars to wipe out the scourge of terrorism from their regions. First of all, any terror attack can be a triggering factor to change foreign policies that may impact the relationship of a country either with its neighbouring countries or with some of those countries involved in trade partnerships.

The display of fear and distrust by countries for each other has been indeed very disappointing, though none of them may be at fault. A typical example for this can be of India and its neighbouring country Pakistan which have broken trade ties off and on in the wake of a terrorist attack. They have not even come to an understanding to keep some essential items away from the restricted list which has ultimately halted the realisation of potential opportunities that are highly crucial for the mutual growth and understanding.

Terrorism is known to kill innocent citizens and disturb peace in the region. There have been ulterior motives in the minds of terrorists who cause such heinous acts. But, the ultimate loser in the process is the common innocent civilians. The issue has become an everlasting one because of the world's slow response on the issue and because of many other pressing issues like environmental damage, sanitation, food security that are at hand to be tackled. Traditionally, terrorist acts are mainly performed for religious reason; however this is not the sole reason for this. Terrorists can even be politically motivated to carry out attacks. Religious strife is one of the many ways that has been used to upset peace and harmony between people of different religious communities, leading to change in hostility between communities and a change in the policy for people of particular religion.

The situation of strife and distrust between countries like India and Pakistan or Palestine and Israel and Muslims who are waiting for opportunities to terrorise US and UK in the name of Jihad or Holy War has resulted in a number of terrorist attacks, causing the killing of a number of people in these countries. In recent past, even Latin American countries like Mexico, Peru, Columbia and Argentina have witnessed a number of terrorist activities. The recent terrorist attacks of London, Madrid, Chechanya (Russia) among others underline the cruelty of this threat. There have been a number of terrorist organisations like Al-Qaeda, Taliban, Indian Mujahideen, Lashkar-e-toiba that have become synonyms of terror in countries both in the East and the West. Names like Osama Bin-Laden, Dawood Ibrahim, Maulana Mashood Azhar among many others have become infamous because of their involvement in a number of terrorist activities across the world.

While India would like to spend a large portion of its GDP expenses on basic needs like education and health, unfortunately, it has to provide a large share of budget allocation to non-productive activities like defence so that the safety and security of the country could be kept intact. Problems like cross-border terrorism from Pakistan and turmoil due to naxalism within the country have compelled the country not to ignore terrorism and in fact, they have become a countrywide topic of discussion during multilateral meetings. However, a part of the reason for people getting attracted to become a terrorist is that they are not being provided enough opportunities of employment in the country for making a living. Wrong or anti-national elements of the country take advantage of such situations and try corrupt young minds as part of their bigger strategy to kill or threaten people in lieu of getting money.

Therefore, terrorism is seen in countries where people are not able to realise their basic needs for living because of a number of constraints existing in their countries.

CONCLUSION

Though countries have recognised terrorism as a global threat, much more is still required to tackle the menace. All the countries are yet to work harder so that world peace is not at stake. To ensure global peace, all the countries have to join hands together in countering the growing menace of terrorism and end violence, fear and bloodshed. A huge task but certainly not an easy one is at hand before the world to counter terrorism for which the countries would require to collaborate and reach a consensus to ascertain a terror-free country and in turn a world free of terror. It can be concluded that in recent times, if countries have to find a lasting solution to many of the problems blocking their progress, they should come together and make all efforts to restore world peace.

2. India: A Land of Young Talents and Few Innovations

INTRODUCTION

India is bestowed with the most sophisticated, talented minds, especially in the field of sports, economics, literature, commerce, law, social activism, science and academics. The country is known to have one of the largest young populations in the world. Besides being the third largest Asian economy, the country is also leading the world when it comes to democracy. With a rich cultural heritage, the scholars in ancient India were revered because of their wisdom, knowledge and intelligence. The field of cinema and entertainment in the country also offers a huge talent that is well recognised by the world. However, on innovation front, we lag a little behind at the global stage. Many brilliant minds in India decide to go abroad because of a high living standards and access to wide-ranging opportunities.

VIEWPOINT

- In India, it is said that the scientists and academicians do not get enough respect and recognition as compared to what they deserve. In a land where once upon a time, sages got enough respect in the society for their knowledge, today's professors and lecturers in India have to go through a number of problems like inadequacies in infrastructure and salaries. They do not get approval for teaching posts at right time and students are often left on their own fate. The Indian educational system is not at the best today as it lacks the ability to innovate and advance in order to face the challenges of the present century adequately. The researchers and scientists in India choose to work in foreign countries as they do not get enough incentives for their progress in India. Because of this, Indian innovations are not in plenty and rather much below the desired potential.
- The Indian government has been spending a huge amount to provide subsidised education in the fields like medicine, law, engineering and technology. Students

are taking advantage of this and ultimately using their qualifications, knowledge and skills to get cushy jobs abroad instead of looking for an opportunity to work in India for the betterment of the country. A mass migration of IIT students to countries like US and the UK can be observed very easily. This has happened because they aspire for a better job and spend a comfortable living in more advanced countries. Though innovation is known to be born in India, it is patented in the US along with other developed countries.

- ❖ The Indian people are facing an outdated education system that has no scope of encouragement to students so to enhance their critical thinking skills. The trend is simply to mug textbooks, attend the coaching classes and attend the exams. Students are no longer free to learn and understand at their own speed after critical analysis so that they could think out of the box and unique. Parents are more eager to push their children into safe occupations instead of encouraging them to indulge in critical thinking and innovation to become entrepreneurs or leaders.
- ❖ The mindset of Indian people is more inclined to follow rules rather than discovering new things. Be it administration or management, everywhere there are strict processes, methods or steps to be followed for every project and thus, usually no one gets a favourable condition to come up with new ideas. If one tends to propose innovative solution to something, it is seen as if a person is trying to oppose the existing establishment. In such a situation, it becomes extremely difficult to generate courage to innovate.
- ❖ Though India is full of talent, it is also a fact that it offers fewer opportunities as against advanced Scandinavian countries or the US. It takes a long time for business clearances and permissions to fructify and the system is so badly plagued with bribery and graft that it usually takes days for a single file to move and reach the authorities. So far as start-ups are concerned, funding has always been a problem. Indian companies attracting foreign funding are usually those that can develop and sustain innovation in field of production and manufacturing.

CONCLUSION

India has to cover a long way before it would be able to catch up with the talented people who are Indian citizens. Radical thinkers do not get appreciation for their ideas as the aim is simply to stick to something that is considered safe and viable. Therefore, people need to change and step out and challenge themselves to innovate and discover new ways. The system particularly needs to change if it expects people to deliver better results. Though all parties in India constantly promise positive change, the question always remains as who will be actually delivering the result.

3. Can India Become a Superpower by 2030?

Is India capable to be a superpower by 2030?

Corruption is an issue which is a cause of concern for a country like India. It is such a burning issue that the upcoming Indian elections are being fought on this issue. While newly formed anti-graft parties are trying to capitalise on the issue of corruption, older parties are making all efforts to launch an offensive.

The situation seems to be turned into the battle of Mahabharata with a politician recently describing the election to be a 'battle for India's soul'.

The elections and their outcome will be meaningless unless parties coming to power take all necessary steps to reverse the serious problem of corruption in India. By doing so only, India can become a superpower by 2030. Actually, the common Indian citizens are not at all bothered about which leader emerges victorious. What they are interested in is the tangible outcomes on the ground like well-constructed roads, power supply without any interruption, safety and security along with ensuring the constant economic growth of the country.

These issues also mean a lot to global investors. The Indian growth story will remain the same, unless India's leaders and businessmen take remedial measures to overcome the situation.

Corruption is recognised as a fact of life in cities and towns of India. India's poor ranking on corruption indices provided by reputed organisations like Transparency International is a matter of great concern. Allocated funds for social welfare are misused and Social welfare activities remain a distant dream for people living in rural and urban areas. Money that is actually meant for development, anti-poverty programs, energy security and the growth of our economy is being accumulated in bank accounts of corrupt officials and leaders in the name of welfare work.

It is really a sad scenario that scams come to light only after the financial damage is incurred to the country and the money of taxpayers has been spirited away by unscrupulous officers and politicians.

It is being observed that Indian farmers are committing suicide as they are overburdened with financial losses and are unable to repay the loans of unscrupulous moneylenders. No contestants for the political throne in India say a word in real sense to permanently solve the problems of farmers in India. Even latest kids on the block such as a young anti-graft party are mum on this issue.

Lives are being lost and Indian farmers are constantly struggling against poverty, exploitation and ruin for which the actions of thoughtless leaders and officials are responsible to a large extent. The sad part of the whole issue is that no corporate sector honcho or leading businessman shows any interest in offering a solution to the problem which has been prevalent in the society for long.

Agriculture is an important sector for our country where farmers produce the raw materials that are used by large companies to make huge profits by utilising raw materials for making useful costly products. What is the reason that our so-called leaders and smart entrepreneurs mum on this issue? Those who have the resources and funds should try to solve the farmers' problems by helping farmers if they are really eager to see India as a superpower by 2030.

When foreign investors visit our country, they see grand buildings alongside dirty slums. This does not instil confidence in the minds of investors that India in any way can become a superpower in near future. Those who think realistically in our country also keep the similar opinion. Fodder scams and spectrum allocation scandals are only a small part of the bigger problem. In fact, the issues are much deeper and complex than this.

In a situation when a heinous rape is committed in the capital city of New Delhi and even in such situation, the opposition or the ruling leaders do not take much needed decisive action to utilise funds to help women so that they could lead safe and secured lives, it compels one to step back and think who still will have the confidence to claim that India will become a superpower in near future somewhere by 2030, or even by 2050? When a terrorist act takes place in the financial capital of Mumbai and one minister of the government while holding a press conference says that 'in such a big city, one or two incidents happen' and after such callous statement also, his power and position remain intact, how can India think or hope to acquire a superpower status by 2030?

The situation is very serious and unless the leading rulers take note of gravity of the problem and take a strong stand, corporate India will face all kinds of difficulties to peddle the growth story of India to foreign media and experts. Any one editorial or article in foreign newspapers about growing poverty or funds mismanagement in India is sufficient enough to send a message to even magnates of Indian origin abroad that they should not think of investing in India. It's time we wake up and take collective responsibility for the burdens that our country is undergoing so that India's effort to become a superpower is met with minimum hurdles.

Unity among political parties is the need of the hour in nation building instead of bickering. Unless this is done, the best solutions can never be found. Businessmen will have to display a sense of social conscience instead of just focusing solely on commercial interests. If this is not done, India's dream to achieve superpower status by 2030 will simply remain an empty dream for which all will be responsible.

4. BRICS Summit, Goa (2016): A Time to Recognise India

The Eighth BRICS Summit was held in Goa, India under the theme 'Building Responsive, Inclusive and Collective Solutions' where the key topics that were discussed are as follows:

1. **Terrorism:** The most important topic of this BRICS summit that was of biggest significance revolved around terrorism. To be more specific, the cross-border terrorism, a catchphrase usually used for Pakistan-sponsored terrorism was at the centre stage. The intensified Indian sentiments after the attack of terrorists at the Uri army base and India's punitive action on Pakistan supported terrorist centres through surgical strikes, it was quite obvious and natural that the issue of terrorism would draw great importance and attention in India.

   Though the declaration of the summit called for action against all terrorist organisations designated by the UN, it put forth the name of only the Islamic State and the Al-Nusra which were primarily responsible for causing threat to Chinese and Russian interests in the regions of Afghanistan and Syria. But the summit declaration did not mention the names of Pakistan-based terrorist organisations like Lashkar-e-Taiba and Jaish-e-Mohammad. There was only indirect reference to cross-border terrorism that came in the form of leaders agreeing on the 'responsibility of all states to prevent terrorist actions from their territories'. On completion of the summit, many seemed to suggest that India needs to work more on strengthening its grouping, especially China, so that India could be in a position to compel China to mention Pakistan-based groups like the JEM, which has been declared as a terrorist organisation by the UN.

2. **NSG Bids:** The declaration at BRICS Summit agreed that nuclear energy is an important component of India's attempts in the fight against climate change, and that with a stable government in New Delhi, it will be in a better position to guide nuclear trade judiciously. These two arguments were put forth by India to get the support of countries to get entry into the NSG, an elite club of countries that is well recognised to control trade in nuclear technology and fissile materials. This is really a significant development but what is most important here is how India approaches and persuades China in order to get its support in this regard as NSG works through consensus.
3. **Growth of Trade and Economy:** BRICS countries contribute to a total trade of only 5 per cent of whole grouping's global trade. It took BRICS eight summits to come to a customs agreement with an aim to promote trade among member countries. However, talks are yet in progress to come to an agreement of free trade pact. Though BRICS countries have dissimilar political situation, shouldn't become a hurdle for speeding up the economic cooperation among the countries.
4. **Idea of Russia to Set Up an Energy Cooperation Agency:** Russia was compelled to think in terms of setting up an energy cooperation agency because of the fact that there was a constant fall in global oil prices and production of oil and gas by Iran, Iraq and African countries increased and at the same time, the production of US shale gas also increased. All these developments made Russia consider searching for stronger energy partnerships. With similar energy needs, India and China too will need more energy resources in order to boost their growth. Though this idea might be of Putin, it is worth following because it offers a win-win situation for both sellers and buyers.
5. **Environment:** The members of BRICS accepted environment to be an important issue. The bloc not just welcomed the Paris Agreement but also advised countries to abide by the agreement and provide monetary assistance, technology and capacity building aid to developing countries.

   The leaders at the summit also underlined the comprehensive, balanced and ambitious nature of the Paris Agreement and described it to proclaim the principles of the UN Framework Convention on Climate Change. It not only contained the principle of equity but also common but distinguished responsibilities along with respective capabilities.

6. **2030 Agenda:** The members at the summit gave support to adopt landmark 2030 Agenda to abide by Sustainable Development and its Sustainable Development Goals during the UN Summit on Sustainable Development that took place on 25 September 2015. They also provided support to the adoption of Addis Ababa Action Agenda at the Third International Conference on Financing for Development. The BRICS leaders hailed the people-centered and holistic approach to sustainable development that was enshrined in the 2030 Agenda that emphasised on equality, equity along with quality-life to all. The leaders at the summit extended support for the reaffirmation of the guiding principles of the implementation of the 2030 Agenda, along with the principle of Common but Differentiated Responsibilities (CBDR).
7. **Empowerment of Women:** The leaders not only hailed the deliberations of the BRICS Women Parliamentarians' Forum in Jaipur on 20–21 August, 2016 but also commended the acceptance of Jaipur Declaration, centered on sustainable development goals. The emphasis was to strengthen parliamentary strategic partnerships on all the three dimensions of sustainable development, promoting gender equality and empowerment of women.

CREDIT RATING AGENCY (BRICS): MOVING AWAY FROM ISSUER-PAYS MODEL TO INVESTOR-PAYS MODEL

In 2016 BRICS Goa summit, member countries decided to set up a credit rating agency which would be based on market associated principles. The five biggest rising economies Brazil, Russia, India, China and South African at BRICS gathering wants to challenge the current credit rating framework and change it to another credit rating agency in which case the forthcoming financial specialist will make the payment for the rating of an issuer of a debt instrument.

In the present estimating model of rating organisations, which is known as Issuer-pays Model, the organisation or foundation that issues securities pays the rating agency to be appraised while in new BRICS rating agency, the speculator desires to put resources into the organisation that will make the payment for the rating of the organisation an investor-pays display.

An argument was put forth that it would lead to further consolidation of the global governance architecture. This is a change which is much required to happen. This will help the experts explore the possibility of setting up an independent BRICS Credit Rating Agency that is entirely based on market-oriented principles, so that the worldwide economic governance is further strengthened.

FUTURE CHALLENGES OF BRICS

There are a number of difficulties that come in the way of BRICS. Since each of the developing economies have dissimilar development ways with varying needs, they therefore lack a single agenda.

Since all the five nations of the group hold significant weight in worldwide financial and political aspects, their proceeding with engagement would certainly serve well for the stable development prospects in the regions of these countries. This is why these countries should come out of their individual agenda, which is very essential to realise the benefits of feasible developmental works and the proposed BRICS credit rating agency which were once supported by year-old New Development Bank.

In that sense, it should be the all-out effort of the BRICS members to follow an all-around financial development for their regions so that their relevance is not ignored at global level. Despite such an order be actually restricted, looking purely to advance speculations and business joint effort, they would likewise be in a position to perpetually reflect the dynamism of these five intense economies.

5. Commercial Surrogacy: Boon or Bane

India has helped itself become a universal centre of commercial surrogacy. In India, its general business sector was calculated at $450 million by a well-known organisation, Indian Council of Medical Research (ICMR), however the most broadly utilised 'legendary quality' for this business sector that is unregulated is $2.3 billion. So, it was regarded as the 'pot of gold' by none other than the Law Commission of India in 2009. Perhaps low expenses and advantageous directions, (for instance, getting the name of appointing guardians on the birth declaration and supervising the surrogates steadily for nine months in a lodging) pulled in planning guardians from across the globe.

India is known for its world-class well-being and medical facilities, where quality services are provided at much lower costs as compared to the most first world nations. With a goal for Medical tourism, India has now been acknowledged globally as a noteworthy country for medical tourism in India. A number of renowned and expensive healing facilities in the country give excursions to touring and help show India as part of the 'Bharat Darshan.'

Be that as it may, the multiplication of the business has led to uncovering a couple of darker spots also. One among such issues that has strengthened the foundation of tourism in India is popularly known as 'commercial surrogacy.' Surrogacy is a term which means a woman is prepared to carry a child to term for its intended parents through various fertility techniques along with IVF implantation. She gets compensation for carrying and developing the child in her body, and therefore, the term commercial surrogacy.

Commercial surrogacy was given permission in India without precedent for 2002 and since then has got converted into a vast industry in the field of medicine. Though there is no access for reasonable monetary numbers, a World Bank study that was conducted in 2012 showed the surrogacy business to be worth about $400 million every year, with 3,000 fertility clinic all across India.

Despite surrogacy in India being a multi-billion industry, surrogate moms do not get even a tenth of what they get in countries like the US. The flourishing of IVF centres, nonattendance of an administrative structure, and the poor ladies willingness to lease their wombs has created India to be an attractive choice for non-natives planning to have a surrogate kid. There are a number of questions that have been put forth over the alleged exploitation of surrogate mothers, and their need to safeguard the rights of child and the commissioning parents.

THE VIEW OF SC ON THE SUBJECT OF SURROGACY

In 2008 Baby Manji Yamada versus Union of India case, Supreme Court gave a verdict in which it said that commercial surrogacy is passable in India. A charge was made against baby Manji by Japanese guardians (through an obscure egg giver and the spouse's sperm) and was destined to be a surrogate mother in the state of Gujarat. The guardians due to some reasons separated before the child could conceive. The genetic father wanted to own the child's guardianship, but Indian law banished single men from doing this, while law of Japan didn't perceive surrogacy. In such a situation, a visa was at last allowed to be possessed by the child, though the case underlined the need to have an administrative structure in place for surrogacy in India. This led to the dawn of the ATR Bill (Assisted Reproductive Techniques) (Regulation) Bill, 2014. Now legitimate confusion still remains surrounding commercial surrogacy.

Though the guardianship of the child was at the end given to her grandma, it raised many questions for years regarding a practice. But, at the end of these questions gave rise to passing of India's draft Surrogacy (Regulation) Bill that got approved by the Cabinet in the month of August in the year 2016.

What are the Significant Points of the Newly Drafted Bill?

The newly drafted bill provides the provision of surrogacy as one of the options to parents:

1. who have been in relationship of marriage for five years and could not naturally produce children,
2. who have limited access to other reproductive technologies,
3. who are willing to produce biological children and find a desirous participant from among their relatives in doing so.

Under the present provisions of the bill, a number of fertility centres in India would get huge blow, as their activities will get prohibited under the new bill. Commercial surrogacy will lead to a situation wherein it will bring about 10 years' of detainment.

The bill likewise makes an attempt to show the lawful position of such a chills and guarantees, to the point that a child who is conceived of surrogacy will now have all the legitimate assurance of every right as a citizen. It would thus give abroad Indians, non-natives, unmarried couples, gay people, and live-in couples all the legitimate right to go into a surrogacy plan. The surrogate mother has to be a lady who herself has borne a youngster and she should neither be a non-Resident Indian (NRI) nor an outsider. A couple can't commission a surrogate child who has organic or received kids.

With no surprise, this Surrogacy bill has caused a great deal of verbal confrontation both in the country and abroad. People with inverse perspective or feeling think that, by permitting surrogacy for selective classes of residents on the basis of their way of life, sexual introduction, and life decisions, the bill is going to disregard natives' Fundamental Rights as laid down under the provisions of Article 14 of the Indian Constitution.

In any case, the bill make an effort to overcome the dilemma that could have arisen in the absence of this bill. Besides, gay rights are another burning issue that have to be addressed in India. Though the Supreme Court of India is perched on an audit appeal on Section 377 of the Indian Penal Code that relates to the status of gay rights, nothing much has been achieved as regards to reasonable legitimate position on the issue. Henceforth now, providing lawful rights to a surrogate tyke to gay guardians would simply put the privileges of the kid in danger. The Surrogacy (Regulation) bill can ensure the rights for gay populations once these bigger legitimate questions (for instance, the status of gay marriage) have been addressed. Thus now, if surrogacy is confined to connections which have a reasonable remaining according to law, it will help secure the privileges of the youngster and guarantees consonance with Article 14 of the Indian Constitution as against not abiding by it.

The second real issue related to prohibiting commercial surrogacy and limiting outsiders from profiting out of surrogacy in India. Right from the starting of commercial surrogacy, many occurrences have started disagreeable legitimate questions that move around commercial surrogacy including outsiders. In the year 2012, for example, an Australian couple who got twins through surrogacy subjectively dismisses one while choosing the other one. Such issues highlight the complexities that surround commercial surrogacy.

Meanwhile, we should try contemplating the misuse of ladies for the purpose of commercial surrogacy. In the year 2014, Al Jazeera put forth a story which showed how Indian ladies were misused for the purpose of commercial surrogacy. While these ladies really worked diligently for carrying a kid for about nine months, richness facilities continuously took more than 50 per cent of the amount that was given to them. Throughout the years, different news reports have showed similar comparable stories. A few examples are present today where surrogate moms have overcome adversity of being paid what they merited; most of them have landed up in despondency and misery.

Thinking on these lines, it may not be shocking that most nations of the world have put a ban on commercial surrogacy. Thailand, which was not long ago was once counted as commercial surrogacy manufacturing plant of the world, put a ban on the practices after an event in which Australian couple who had twins through commercial surrogacy made a choice to leave the kid who was suffering from Down's disorder while tolerating the sound tyke. Today, there is a flat out ban on commercial surrogacy in different countries of the world, with a full prohibition on all kinds of surrogacy in a couple. In wake of this, it is worth noting that the Indian government also has tried moving towards a boycott in consonance with worldwide standards (not at all like the Hague Convention on Adoption, in any case, there happens to be no reasonable convention on surrogacy all across the globe).

Then, putting a ban on commercial surrogacy can possibly open up entryways for selection also. In countries like India, where one comes to hear stories of kids being deserted by their folks out of destitution or social shame, particularly young ladies, putting a ban on commercial surrogacy could cause guardians to look towards reception as a method to satisfy their dreams of parenthood.

The draft Surrogate (Regulation) Bill makes all efforts to fully resolve different aspects associated with surrogacy in India. Though there are arrangements that will evolve in course of time, the heart of the bill beyond a doubt is putting a ban on commercial surrogacy. This is without doubt a stage in the right direction. Getting profits from a lady's womb by using her vulnerability is simply a wrong thing to do. A society is considered developed only when that society makes all efforts to secure the privilege of every person. Undoubtedly, a poor lady is among those whose voices are usually not heard in India, and the draft Surrogacy Bill 2016 looks to secure such people.

6. Crisis of European Refugee

In recent time, Europe has been witnessing one of the most severe refugee crises since the World War-II. In early part of 2015, about 3 lakh people knocked the door of asylum. This is apart from the 6.25 lakh applications that were received in the year 2014.

According to an estimate of the Office of the United Nations High Commissioner for Refugees (UNHCR), the influx of migrant continues to grow as Syria, Iraq and Afghanistan are still facing a number of problems like terrorism, sectarian violence along with unrest among the civil population.

INFORMATION ABOUT THESE REFUGEES

Though for Europe, the African originated refugee problem has more or less become chronic, influx in recent times has a number of new sources.

Most of the refugees are from Syria, a country that is completely war-torn. Since the very beginning of civil war in the year 2011, about 2 million people were compelled to leave the country to neighbouring countries like Turkey, Jordan and Lebanon. These people were given shelter along with other basic facilities in the camps sponsored by the UN.

However, very recently, as the refugee camps have got overcrowded and there seems to have no end to the ongoing conflict in Syria, refugees started moving to safe heavens in Europe for their safety, security and well-being.

Apart from Syria, Iran, Iraq, Turkey, Libya, Afghanistan, Eritrea, Egypt, Sudan, Ethiopia, and Somalia are among other major source countries.

REASONS FOR THEIR MIGRATION TO EUROPE

There are many reasons for the influx of migrants to Europe. These reasons however differ from one country to another and thus, can be classified under two parts: Push factors and Pull Factors.

PUSH FACTORS

- Terrorist activities as a regular affair in countries like Syria, Iraq and Afghanistan
- Sectarian violence of Shia-Sunni in countries like Syria and Iraq
- Gross violations of human rights that get manifested as compulsory national service in Eritrea forcing about 5000 people migrate from the country
- Absence of a rule of law because of power vacuum in Somalia compelling the citizens to cross the Mediterranean

PULL FACTORS

- Proximity due to geographical location: For most asylum seekers, only the Mediterranean Sea is safe way between their trouble-ridden present and wishful future. Therefore, the crisis is considered a synonym to the phrase Mediterranean Migrant Crisis.
- Trust in the European Administration: The firm belief of the refugees that they won't be denied the legitimate basic right to life in the rule bound and humane government of Europe, they are reluctant to seek asylum in the well-off Arab countries like Saudi Arabia, Oman, etc. despite their cultural affinity to these countries.
- Opportunities for employment: The European labour market is mature enough to provide the migrants immediate employment opportunities so that they could restart their lives.

ISSUED CONCERNED

The issues that are intertwined with the ongoing migration crisis in the Europe are as follows:

Dublin Procedure: According to the Dublin procedure, the first EU country where a migrant or refugee enters is held accountable for processing asylum claim. This in turn puts a huge pressure on countries like Greece and Italy where most of the people seeking asylum arrived first.

Since most asylum seekers wish to go to Germany, Sweden or France, questions here arise as to why register and house asylum seekers in a country where they themselves are not willing to stay in any case.

Opening Up of Fault Lines within the EU: The crisis led to the opening up of structural fault lines within Europe. Most of the smaller countries having low financial resources, like Hungary, do not want to share the burden.

Even, some of them are of the view that the big countries like France and Germany should come forward and take upon them the burden because such a situation has arisen due to their participation in the NATO-led war in the source countries.

Further, a growing disagreement among the larger nations is seen on the formula of relocating refugees within the European Union.

Moral Dilemma of Europe: Since most of the European economies are still under the shadow of the global financial crisis of 2008, it would be a matter to be seen as how far they could accommodate the migrants' interests without austerity measures.

Besides, if the rights to legitimate asylum seekers is denied, it is nothing but the violation of the article 18 (Right to Asylum), Article II-78 and Article III-266 of the European Constitution which is the foundation of EU.

Schengen Agreement: In the last one month, countries such as Germany and Hungary came forward to suspend the implementation of the agreement so as to keep a control over the migrant influx whose only purpose is to ease people movement across international borders without any compulsory checks.

Integrating the Migrants: One of the most relevant problems related to migrant rehabilitation is to what extent their integration will be successful provided the presence of anti-Islam sentiment in the European society because of many reasons.

MEASURES THAT HAVE BEEN TAKEN TILL DATE

At a summit level meeting on 23 September 2015, the European Union nations came to an agreement to offer an extra 1.1 billion euros to the UN agencies known to indulge in rehabilitating the migrants.

EU increased funding to maritime surveillance so as to avoid drowning incidents in the Mediterranean. According to an estimate, in 2014 itself, 3500 people were found dead or missing in the sea while moving through the route to nearby European islands.

The European Commission put forth a proposition of internal relocation of 120000 migrants based on a mandatory distribution key by making use of objective and quantifiable criteria, 40 per cent of the size of the population and the GDP, 10 per cent of the average number of past asylum applications and the unemployment rate.

Further, the formula is applied to nationalities of applicants who have an EU-wide average recognition rate of 75 per cent or more.

Additionally, Europe, the USA and Australia were having the desire to accommodate 10000 and 12000 refugees respectively in the next one year.

LEARNING FOR INDIA

Refugee problem has never been a new problem to India as it faced a sudden outburst of migrants from Bangladesh in the year 1971, from Afghanistan because of USSR's intervention in 1979 and from Sri Lanka due to the civil war between the armed forces and the LTTE.

Still, learning from the ongoing crisis, India should strenthen its diplomatic engagement so as to bring out a special convention on climate refugees.

For India, the engagement is quite important as half of Bangladesh is situated in the Low Elevation Coastal Zone (LECZ), within 10 meters above sea level which usually submerges as sea levels are set to rise because of the changes in climate.

Further, Maldives, another neighbour, is also under the threat of extinction because of similar reasons.

CONCLUSION

The ongoing crisis is a grim remainder of the fact that most communities in the world are still far from the essentials because of chronic problems such as hunger, poverty, terrorism, mal administration, along with sectarian violence, etc.

Though we have made a big progress in nurturing peace, security and socio-economic development, millions of people are still struggling for basic needs of life.

It is right time when the world leaders come together and find solution to the problem of migration on a permanent basis in order to ensure timely achievement of recently adopted Sustainable Development Goals.

7. Net Neutrality

The Principle of Net Neutrality or Internet Neutrality means Internet Service Providers (ISPs) have equal treatment of all data over the Internet. The term was created in 2003 by Columbia University media law professor Tim Wu as an extension of the established notion of a common carrier.

On the basis of this principle, the Governments and ISPs should equally treat every data transmitted over the Internet, without offering priority delivery or differential charges on the basis of the type of user (Business or Domestic), content (voice or video or data), platform, application, type of attached equipment or mode of communication.

PRESENT DEBATE SURROUNDING NET NEUTRALITY IN INDIA

Besides the intended policy shift by the TRAI, there are many developments in the telecom market that led to a rise in nationwide debate over the compliance of the principle.

In December 2014, India's major telecom giant Bharati Airtel decided to charge subscribers additional amount for using social networking applications like Skype and Viber which brought severe criticism, making the company rethink and put a stay on the implementation. The company put forth its argument that by providing communication services, these applications are eating away the revenues of the company.

In February 2015, Reliance Communications made an offer of few selected websites and applications free of cost for its customers in partnership with the internet.org of social networking giant Facebook.

On 6 April 2015, Airtel Zero programme was launched, according to which the Airtel subscribers can have an access to some specific websites and applications, which have got registered with the company, free of cost.

The above incidents show the intent of the ISPs in the direction of building new partnerships with content providers which is contrary to the principle of Net Neutrality.

Arguments Put Forth in Favour of Net Neutrality Principle

The most important benefit from the principle is that it has provided a level playing field by providing access of the Internet to the content providers if those are Internet monopolies such as Google and Facebook or new set-ups in the neighbourhood.

Any concession by the ISPs in abiding by the principle is nothing but an wrong business practice, as recently viewed by the Chairman of the Competition Commission of India (CCI), as it leads to preferential treatment of select websites and applications.

The argument such as this that social networking sites are eating into the revenues of telecoms seems completely absurd as the revenue foregone as approximated by the telecoms is fictional and not based on factual evidence.

The principle's violation will cause an adverse effect on the start-ups as the Internet giants with excess funds can make a payment of higher fees to ISPs with a purpose to push their data on the Internet on a preference basis.

To sum up, the exponents of the principal view that principle is very significant in protecting the openness of Internet.

Arguments that are Put Forth against the Net Neutrality Principle

ISPs do have some arguments that it costs them billions of dollars to buy spectrum from the government, construct Optic Fiber Cable (OFC) networks along with other required infrastructure. Hence, as an authorised supplier of the Internet services, just like the logistics service provider in the physical world, they should be given power to impose differential chargers on content providers and consumers based on their demands so as to access the Internet on a priority basis.

The ISPs also have another argument that, the above measure is in the interest of public as it acts as an incentive for them to expand and bolster their networks, which in turn gives an assurance of much desired last mile network access in the country.

The telecoms are also of the view that neutrality of social networking sites is not maintainable and an immediate need of the hour is to create a revenue sharing relationship because these applications are making huge revenue by making use of the infrastructure provided by them.

Some cyber experts are of the opinion that the present practices keep the consumers away from making the choice of availing priority delivery of the desired content. So, they end up paying additional money for faster bandwidth which delivers the irrelevant and desirable content at the same speed.

Argument is also put forth that the principle is not favourable to the rise of start-ups because of the inability of the market to operationalise innovative revenue models based on faster delivery of content.

In sum, those who oppose the principle argue that in an attempt to maintain equitable access to the Internet, the regulators have so far chosen the method that makes the internet equitably slow and expensive for everyone which is visible from high data charges and low bandwidth in the country.

Is There any Mid-Ground for its Solution?

Instead of relooking the very basic principle of Net Neutrality that has arisen due to proliferation of few monopolies such as Facebook and WhatsApp, the TRAI can make an effort to address the problem of revenue foregone directly by putting regulating mechanisms on the interconnection rates between external networks and Indian networks (since most of the monopolies operate from external networks) or by referring the matter to the CCI.

GLOBAL DIMENSION

In February 2015, the Federal Communications Commission of USA made a classification of Internet Services as public utility services which refers to the ISPs not authorised to make violations of the Net Neutrality principle.

Europe is making all efforts to correct a 2013 proposal for Net neutrality, in which privileged access was permitted to specialised services.

In 2014, Chile put a ban on zero-rated schemes, similar to Airtel Zero Programme, under which social media access is given free of cost to telecom subscribers.

CONCLUSION

Since our country is having the problem of digital divide between rural and urban areas in the form of lower penetration of internet in rural areas as compared to that of urban areas, it is essential that regulator come forward to keep the openness of the Internet intact and fulfil its responsibility so as to achieve the goals of Digital India programme.

8. The Masks of New Imperialism

It has been seen that globalisation and economic liberalisation have brought new hopes and prospects in the whole world. The World Trade Organisation is one of the most important organisations committed to this cause. Big claims, assurances and promises were given to the weaker unions when the WTO got started. Among the basic principles of WTO are trade involving no discrimination, free trade, transparency, economic equality among the countries. All these hopes were put down once the organisation started functioning. Its principles seemed better only on paper but not on real ground. The failure of Doha Agenda which witnessed only some promises/ prospects for the developing and under developed countries failed to fructify. All these instances indicate that WTO has given birth to a clash with neo-imperialism.

Perhaps Hang Kong and Macau are among the last few territories of the old imperialistic regimes i.e.: the Europeans. By the end of World War II, the conquerors began retreat, resulting in many nations becoming free and emergence of a new-world order governed by trade. When one of the last countries was achieving freedom from imperialistic forces, a new form of neo-imperialism force was blooming as 'Old bottle, new wine'. The name given to the new colonial force is globalisation. Globalisation since its beginning has taken different forms, the most recent being the World Trade Organisation (WTO) which is described as decentral commander of globalisation. Trade and economy are its two important weapons. The old imperialistic forces prevailed, expanded and conquered other nations utilising their links. Likewise, the new force also followed the old theory in the name of trade and economies, these countries have established themselves as the rulers of the new world. The old forces believed in the cheat conflicts to defeat and capture, but the new forces believed in other means such as trade sanctions, blockage of Buds and other assistance in the name of democracy and development. Thus, weaker nations are forced to comply with their demands like exporting oils, minerals, raw natural products and so on.

Through unequal conditions of economic exchange, Neo imperialism means supremacy of some countries over others. In other words, existence of neo-imperialism is observed when one nation is dependent on other nation because weaker nation is not in a position to survive economically in the modern world without the help of the powerful countries. Unlike other forms of imperialism, Neo imperialism is not established based on the direct imposition of political power by one society upon another, instead, neo-imperialism makes use of the money power in the modern world as a method for developed countries to keep poorer countries front stepping outside fill, roles that the developed countries have designed for themselves.

Due to a few developed nations, WTO is more or less becoming a tool to keep a watch on the trade among the member countries and control the economies of the world. The developed countries before the inception of the WTO had made an effort to convince the developing countries with the argument that in the present era, enhanced economic cooperation and mutual exchanges are very necessary for the success of the world economy. It became very obvious by the functioning of the WTO ministerial conferences that the organisation was brought to satisfy the narrow-minded and biased interests of the developed world instead of removing the road blocks in the economic development of the world. In the name of liberalisation, even the productions in countries like India get guided by the Multinational Companies (MNCs) that are under the regulations of developed countries. Even the media, the fourth pillar of the India democracy is more and more getting controlled by these MNCs. When the developing countries made efforts to raise the issues of cheap labour and low profits, the developed world came to give fatal punch by raising environmental issues to be detriment of the developing countries during Seattle Summit. After that considering overall functioning of the WTO, it becomes clear that the organisation has become one of line most powerful weapon of the developed countries and the MNCs to keep a control on the economics including the politics of the developing countries like India.

For import of technology, loans and economic cooperation, the developing and the underdeveloped countries have been tied with developed countries. Even the national security of some of the countries is controlled by the developed world but the latter in the guise of the same have controlled the economics of the former throughout multinational companies and investment. Thus, the developing world got trapped in the web of loans and interests as Indians experienced during the British period. Today, there is a lack of cooperation among the developing countries. Though there is an emergence of regional groupings, there are either disagreements among the members or they are incapable of taking an independent path. For some reasons, they are forced to toe the lines of the developed world. Be it ASEAN or SCO or SAARC or NAM or IBSA or BRIC, all in some way or the other have got influenced by the USA. Their inactivity or underperformance, if not impotence, has made them dependent on the developed world.

Hong Kong summit of the WTO in 2005 showed some hopes for the developing countries at the cost of sonic compromises on the Singapore issues. The developed countries at least in principle expressed approval to cut down and, remove the trade distorting subsidies in agriculture and trade assistance. However, during the operationalisation of Doha Development Agenda, the developed world could not do enough to lose their control by facilitating the developing countries.

The last decade showed increased attempt by the developed countries to overlook the interests of the developing countries. The interests of the two groups havocked at cross purpose. Developing countries, by the consolidation of the NAM and G-20, have given a good challenge to the monopoly of the USA, Britain, France, Australia etc. at the WTO. The no negotiating approach of the US led to the failure of Cancun round and the Singapore round. Developing countries have at least started using their courage to fight so as to protect their own interest. Now, they do not seem to be in a mood to bow down under ruthless exploitation nor are they ready to succumb to the unjustified and irrational US pressure. G20 countries have clearly conveyed that till the implementation of Doha promises, they would not move ahead to any event. Thus, in other words, WTO has become a forum of clash of interests between the developed and the developing world.

For their progress and growth, the developed world desires to utilise WTO as an effective instrument. This however doesn't seem to be possible. Such an unjust process can no longer continue for long. No one can deny that it is possible to be isolated from WTO but the success of the organisation will be at stake if all the nations do not be compassionate enough towards each other's concerns. Among the priorities of the developing countries, elimination of hunger, poverty, unemployment, economic and social disparity and increase of capital are important. The priority of the developed countries is to ensure their economic progress by monopolising the world trade. Rich nations like the US often use the forum of WTO to expand neo-imperialism while the weaker nations are still making an attempt to get out of the vicious circle of exploitation.

Thus, the hope of the developing countries since the inception of the WTO has clearly turned into a gloomy reality. It is the complete selfishness of the developed world that has led to the clash between the two which has been on the increase of and on. Perhaps such a clash was foreseen by the former UN Secretary General when he warned that if the WTO failed to accommodate the interests of the developing nations, they would question the whole effort of creating WTO and will thus lead to end the whole process. It is however hard to even imagine that the rich nations would be willing to work against their own interests to follow the basic principles of WTO. So, the developing and under developing nations needs to come together and muster up courage to overcome the hegemony of the developed world.

The conclusion could be evident through the words of the great economist Bhagawati, 'It is useful to remember that interdependence is a non-native attractive and soothing word, but when actions are unequal it also leads to dependence mid hence to possibilities of perverse policies; interventions and aggressively imposed coordination policies with outcomes that liana the social good acid the welfare of (lies dependent nations while advancing the interest of the powerful nations.'

Besides, old terrorism has been showing the new mask with which imperialism demonises the governments that it desires to conquer. Recall that George W. Bush, after his people were bombed by terrorism clearly linked to Saudi Arabia, the country having largest oil reserves in the Middle East, already regulated by the United States, resolved to attack Iraq without finding any link to it, in order to regulate the third-largest reserves also: those in second place belong to Iran, which the U.S. also has in its sights.

During the meeting at the Capitol on November 17, 2010, the radicals of the Republican Party made all effort to connect Venezuela, Bolivia, and Ecuador–which also happen to be oil-exporting countries–with the Islamic terrorism supposed to be promoted by Iran. They started mentioning that these governments are hostile to the U.S., and declared them anti-American and they are moving closer to Iran, becoming 'friends of our enemies,' and thus, they are already a threat involving weapons of mass destruction.

The settlers who established their colonies in America did so not only for religious freedom, but also for govern themselves in their own way so as to develop and protect their interests. Afterwards, they made a declaration for the independence from England with a purpose to avoid paying taxes without representation, and that's how the United States came into being. Leaving the rhetoric, no one can see the concept of freedom for the people. It was completely missing from the real motives for independence, and thus a country continued to be a slave country and in which millions of Indians were exterminated to make possible its expansion.

It cannot be denied that the country's laws were aimed to ensure the protection of the economic interests to which everything else was subordinated. That is the reason why conservatives always have supported the status quo, which, nonetheless, because of its brutality, could not be openly supported, and thus, compelling them to act as though they were clinging to the past only to maintain their 'traditional family values.' In fact, every change and evolution in thinking were always a threat to their original advantages with which they founded the country.

That is the possible explanation for why the humanisation of US society had to be fought for, and that it costs a stream of blood. The emancipation of the slaves, for example, got inspired by change, which was strongly opposed by the defenders of the status quo with a Civil War that left 618,000 dead and 412,000 wounded. But, with the victory of the north, the struggle did not get completed, because the new union continued to be an oligarchic society, as unjust as it was averse to the principle of humanity. A huge and long struggle was done to end racial segregation, and achieve human rights, public education, breakup of the monopolies, abolition of child labour, a minimum wage, rights of women, and so on. The conservatives were all opposed to these basic rights for human beings although they are now reckoned by the world as the most admirable part of our country: the human part that has united us as a people and impacted the rest of world.

The nation is in fact powerful, and the conservatives boast of defending their supremacy, but in doing so they delete mentioning the enormous human cost. The history of North American power is, therefore, one of expansion with the extermination of the Indians, of agricultural prosperity with slavery, of industrial progress with the exploitation of labour, of wars waged with an aim to expand our power abroad while people with progressive thinking fought for human rights at home, and, most recently, of wasting trillions in wars against 'terrorism' abroad when the country's economy is getting shattered.

It's a more like irrational reality that can be understood only by taking note of the fact that the US is the result of two ideological currents with opposing objectives. Global supremacy is without a doubt the Republican objective, and its foreign policy is, logically, the irritant in the relations with the rest of world. North American imperialism along with its corresponding anti-imperialism are consequently no more than the globalisation of the internal conflicts of North American reality. The Republicans call themselves patriots because they are able to defend the original postulates of the republic, as wrong as those may have been. They quote quite often from the Bible to justify their 'traditionalism,' while defending the interests of the rich who identify so much with money; and they are so few in relation to the people that they represent in reality the individualism and greed that generates poverty for the many. They put blame on the Democrats of being anti-American, socialists, communists, and, therefore, traitors to the 'capitalist' homeland founded by their ancestors. Abroad, they also accuse progressives of being anti-American in order to show them as 'a danger to national security, and terrorists by association.' Terrorism can have nothing to do with anti-imperialism as the former is a crime against humanity that caused deaths around the world long before it was used by Islamist extremists against the US. They, too, surely have their own reasons to fight against empires, but unlike the anti-imperialists, they do not do it with the use of vote power in a democracy.

Under no circumstances, terrorism is justifiable, and, therefore, should be removed from the face of the earth just like imperialism. But, till that happens, humanity cannot allow itself to get confused by the religious radicals of both extremes. Anti-imperialism is as legitimate as it is democratic, and represents, further, the internationalisation of the noblest progressive North American ideals: the right to life, liberty, dignity, health, social justice, and, of course, family. That is our connection with others and, therefore, with the flow of life. The Republicans happen to be so disconnected from that life that they found the shortcut of attributing it to God, with whom they presume to have a direct connection.

The difference between the anti-imperialists and the imperialists, accordingly, gets reduced to the difference between progressives and conservatives: the old dilemma of 'to be or not to be'... part of humanity.

9. Boom of BPO in India

Business Process Outsourcing (BPO) is important for Business Strategy of major organisations across the globe. BPO has been positively related to the quest for more efficient organisational designs: reduced cost, growth in productivity and innovative capabilities. So, BPO is important source for strategic advantage. There are a number of recent market research surveys that have indicated the CEOs around the world in all the companies feel that BPO is key for survival in today's extremely competitive atmosphere of business. There are multiple benefits of BPO. It allows the organisation to focus on their core activities by releasing resources which have constrained in non-core activities. It helps organisation reduce costs by cutting down the HR Costs – salary bills, perks, employee benefits, administration overheads. The client only has to make payment for useful quality work duly accomplished by BPO. It goes a long way in reducing recruitment and training expenses. This also improves the quality of service and productivity by ensuring greater accountability and transparency in production standards. This enables an organisation achieve huge volume of paperwork and routine administration work done very quickly at significantly lower cost. BPO also offers 24 × 7 service throughout the year which is crucial to operations related to customer service.

Almost a century ago, George Santayana noticed that, 'Those who cannot remember the past, are condemned to repeat it.' Today, the same sentiment is applicable to Indian BPO aspirants. When I hear about companies—Indian and foreign—creating a near frenzy in setting up BPO operations in India and dominating the world back office processing marketplace, I only hope that they have spent time studying the history of the Indian IT Services industry.

Let's look at this history. Today, Indian IT services providers are ensuring huge growth in their revenue. The success of IT services providers has been attributed to skilled IT services at a much reduced cost as compared to American or European companies. This business model has its origin in the history of Indian companies offering low cost data entry services. The formula for 'winning' business from indigenous, well-established companies was based on the creation of a market by providing programming services at a much cheaper rate. Y2K helped feed this frenzy and many Indian IT services companies got into the business. It also helped India produce well-qualified software engineers from its schools and that there was an availability of a ready labour pool to persue low cost programming. The mantra thus became: 'Come to India, where IT is done cheaper.'

BPO or Business Process Outsourcing in itself is a complete industry wherein businesses in a certain country outsource some of their operations (most often back office) to other places in the world to reduce costs through the use of cheap labour in these countries. This helps them enhance their profits and focus on their core business activities. The Business Process Outsourcing industry in India offers primarily to Western business activities of multinational corporations. BPO provides annual revenues of about $11 billion, around 1% of GDP.

In the early 1980s, outsourcing of businesses to India got started when many European airlines began using the national capital of Delhi as a base for back office operations. Later, American Express consolidated its JAPAC (Japan and Asia Pacific) back office operations into New Delhi. The head of this centre was Raman Roy. In the 1990s, Jack Welch of GE was persuaded to consider Gurgaon as a base for back office operations. By 2002, all important Indian software organisations were having BPO, among these, Infosys, HCL, Satyam, TCS and Patni were important. The international 3rd party BPO players such as Convergys and SITEL also entered and strengthened the BPO movement in India. Service arms of organisations such as Accenture, IBM, Hewlett Packard and Dell also established shop in India. The BPO industry bloomed in India because of its service delivery at a reduced cost. But due to increases in infrastructure costs, real estate costs, and salaries, BPO cost was significantly increased. So, Indian BPOs saw a shift of their operations from Tier-1 cities like Chennai, Bangalore, Hyderabad, Delhi and Mumbai to Tier-2 and Tier-3 cities like Mysore, Trivandrum, Kochi, Chandigarh, Mohali, and so on.

The transformation of rural India brought about the emergence of rural BPOs. The estimated global BPO Industry is worth 120-150 billion dollars. India has 5-6% share of the total industry, and 63% share of the offshore component. BPOs have spawned many industries which depend on them like Catering, BPO training and recruitment, transport vendors, (for home pick up and drops for night shifts), Security agencies, Facilities management companies, etc.

Indian IT companies achieved quality certifications (CMM, ISO etc.) so as to build a service value besides lower labour rates. However, my experience says that not much has changed. Lower cost is still the major factor put forth by Indian companies. It makes one wonder: what is the value proposition? Cheaper rates; where is the service advantage? Cheaper rates. Where is the differentiation with the Western market place? Cheaper rates. The new mantra still is: 'Come to India, where CMM level 5 IT service is done cheaper.'

Yet based on their history of moving from low priced data entry services to low price programming services, Indian companies do not seem to have learned the lessons of the past. What do you see on looking at the offerings from these companies? Most of them are touting 'low level' transaction processing services at a lower price. For instance, they offer a staffed call centre (popularly called as Customer Relations Management (CRM) services), or an accounts payable/receivable operation popularly called as Cash Management services. A bankcard application data entry and processing centre is called a 'Credit Management services center' and keypunching services are disguised in new name, medical transcription services. In the name of BPO, these companies are building a business niche where rates will prepare the battleground, cheaper services will be the value proposition and competition will be among each other. To me, the mantra is: 'Come to India where transaction processing services are done cheaper.'

Some controversies have caused an eruption around the industry. BPO employees are scornfully considered as cyber coolies. Also, some cases of rape and murder of a few female employees by cab drivers underlined the safety issues surrounding BPO industry. In spite of this, undoubtedly BPO industry has lifted the standard of life for many young Indians and resulted in increasing the ranks of the Indian middle class and building an atmosphere of economic boom. However, recently emerging trends of global economic downturn has affected the industry negatively as new contracts from countries like the US and other client nations might dry up due to the demands of jobs within the borders of these countries.

10. Significance of NAM in Today's World

Probably it is not a hyperbole that today's world is completely presenting a new scenario altogether–communist regimes in Eastern Europe has ended, 15 new republics have got created instead of the erstwhile Soviet Union, a united Germany is in full shape along with a new Europe with a new socio-economic and political identity.

The argument some people give is that the Non-Aligned Movement (NAM) teas the product of cold war and biopolarism and it is said that after the end of the cold war and the Erstwhile Soviet Union, NAM is believed to have lost its relevance.

It is correct to say that NAM emerged as a child of the cold war but during the three decades of its formation, it has established its identity on its own and thus, it can no longer be defined just in terms of cold war politics. NAM is a movement that has achieved dynamism of its own and has got different third world issues as its agenda and not just super power rivalry and confrontation.

Some others are of the view that NAM's task has, more or less, been achieved. For example, independence of colonies and dismantling of apartheid. The phase of cold war is also over now. Foreign bases have lost their relevance and due to disintegration of alliances, there is no need for non-alignment any more.

These people will have to understand that the primary concern of NAM, both as a national policy of many newly independent states and as a global movement, has been the liquidation of economic imperialism in order to strengthen economic growth and development. In addition to this, a number of issues NAM have to address in the coming years. Those issues can be like the democratisation of international relations, particularly in context of the UN Security Council, security for small and weak nations, disarmament, collective efforts for economic growth, overcoming the burden of debt of the developing countries, working on deteriorating terms of trade, the North-South dialogue, human rights, environmental issues, drug trafficking, international terrorism, ethnic and religious conflicts, new international economic order, new international information and technological order and so on.

Secondly, those skeptics who are of the view that the need for Non-Align Movement is losing its importance should bear in mind that despite many drastic changes in the 350 years old sovereign-state-system, the system has constantly and continuously maintained two important features: Great power hegemony and the opposition of the overwhelming majority of other states to that hegemony. So, the Non-alignment has a brief answer that works against the hegemonies or whoever is dominating the world.

There are some other who are of the view that NAM should no longer be continued because of its being less dynamic and is characterised by slow response to today's rapidly changing world. The example of NAM's poor response to the recent Gulf crisis is often cited. However, organisations cannot lose relevance just because of a few defects. The decisions should not be in haste about the relevance and significance of old organisations. Therefore, instead of having second thoughts about the relevance of NAM just because of its poor response to the Gulf crisis, we should take steps to strengthen NAM just like other organisations such as the UN.

Former President R. Venkataraman while delivering the Indira Gandhi Memorial Lecture to the Association of Indian Diplomats made an apt remark that 'Non-alignment is not an Ism. It cannot become outdated any more than common sense can become outdated. The cold war has ended. That does not make the UNO charter irrelevant. Non-aligned countries represent the will and voices of three-fourth of mankind. No nation, no group of nations can disregard the NAM. There must be something to it fix China to seek membership and Germany to get observer status of NAM.... From the Fifties through to the Eighties NAM spearheaded the struggle against colonialism and racialism. It must today raise its voice against the injustices and inequities of the emerging 21st century.'

The Non-Aligned Movement is considered the largest peace movement in the world. But when dealing with NAM, it is important to distinguish between Non-alignment as an International movement and Non-alignment as a Foreign Policy choice. In context of an International movement, it may have its limitation or it may not be performing the role assigned to it but NAM as a Foreign Policy choice--an assertion of independence in foreign affairs-has always remained, still remains and will always remain valid and relevant. However, both are equally significant and need not have water-tight compartmentalisation between the two as the success of one depends on the support of the other.

RELEVANCE

'Our approach to peace may then be called 'neutrality' if such a nebulous word can be used to define a policy.'

-Vijayalakshmi Pandit, President, UN General Assembly (1953)

Because of this statement that possibly laid bare the basic flaw in her argument and defence of policies such as the Non-Aligned Movement in her book 'India's

Foreign Policy'. Besides, the mistake of her brother Jawaharlal Nehru with regards to foreign policy was the dichotomous approach he took on it which he laid down as 'a choice between peace and the hydrogen bomb'. Nehru could still be forgiven because of the fact that perhaps India, which was taking the first step in the direction of recovery after 200 years of British rule, could not probably afford entering a wrong alliance in a post-World War situation. However, world has changed a lot since 1945 and, therefore, our approach should also change accordingly. If the debate is taken ideologically, there can be two grounds based on which it can be said that the previous Non-Aligned Movement has lost its significance or relevance in today's world. The belief on which the foundation of the Non-Aligned Movement was laid was that all the founding nations like India, Indonesia, Yugoslavia and Egypt aimed to establish peace and this also helped these countries to develop after years of enslavement. However, despite more than six decades of independence, though not fully developed, we have undoubtedly made progress in different fields. Today, though we happen to be reckoned for the second fastest growing economy, largest conventional armed forces, very decent track record of democracy, higher rate of literacy, higher standards of living (as against 1947), if we have not made enough development to come out of our cocoon then when and how will we ever achieve our unique identity on the global stage?

Nature does not suffer a vacuum, especially power never shows this character. It is absolutely correct that even with the decline of power of the United States and the Western World, the world is seen to become more and more multi-polar. However, it may also be a passing phase. There cannot be so many equals in the world. In words of Orwell, 'there will always be some more equal than the others'. Today or tomorrow, some nation or the other will definitely attempt to be at the top spot and while doing so will certainly undercut others in the process. India being in that race, common sense suggests that it will be finally our alliances that will ensure our safety and security from overambitious competitors. Therefore, alignment should not be considered an anathema to us.

THE GROWING POWER OF CHINA

The Middle Kingdom is not unwilling to acknowledge itself as probably the next global leader in a post-American world. Its economic might has got translated into diplomatic and military clout very steadily for some time. Perhaps, there is one country that can overtake China's aspirations to lead the world. India is growing by leaps and bounds for this top position. China completely understands this threat posed by India. So, it has been making systematic efforts to hinder the Indian growth story. A three pronged strategy has been designed by China with an aim to ensure that India does not reach a stage where she becomes too powerful to be contained.

a. Denial: Denying India to any influential position like the UN Security Council which will provide veto power to the country.
b. Provocation: Instigating India with frequent false claims over the territory of Arunachal Pradesh and issues like stapled visa, etc.

c. Intimidation: Threatening with building up of huge infrastructure near the borders.

In fact, some Indian strategists believe that China may plan to attack India by the end of 2017. Their claims to some extent get a backing from Wiki leaks disclosure that mentions a report provided by the Pentagon to the US Congress. According to the report, China has been making all attempts to deploy nuclear capable CCS5-MRBM missiles near the border regions with India. (The Indian Express, 25 August 2011). Now, though one can accept that it is not desirable to pander to the paranoia of war mongers, preparing for the worst will always be a wise thing to do. And the attack by China will mean a realisation by India for alliances as she may not be in a position to combat a Chinese blitzkrieg on her own. Russia may still have a tremendous power though may not be in her previous glory days of the USSR. The most important thing is that Russia has been an all-weather friend to India and she can be safely trusted for an alliance as a possible shield against China. After all, the Soviets alone helped India combat the pressure from Pakistan, the US and China at the time of Bangladesh War. This move may not please the US but may finally agree to have a similar understanding as they would understand a greater priority for containing China first in the region.

THE DECLINE OF PAKISTAN

It is unlikely that a nation state born out of anti-India sentiments will ever give away such sentiments despite our confidence building measures that we choose. At some point, we will have to realise that the day when Pakistan makes a choice to resolve all its problems with India will also be the day when it will give up its existing legitimacy as a nation (ideologically). Today, a downward spiral of Pakistan can be observed vividly as its national fabric is being torn to shreds because of the problems like fundamentalism and hate used against India. No doubt, it continues to follow the path of self-destruction, and in doing so, it will definitely make some more attempts to hold itself together and whip up the old enemy India. Pakistan may also consider attacking India and in the process can damage us considerably despite its inferior military capabilities. In other words, though we may end up getting victory in the war, it is not possible that we emerge unscathed. Therefore, the need of the hour is to align with nations such as the United States that has the ability to reign in Pakistan.

THE SURGE OF REGIONALISM

A country willing to command global influence must first start maintaining regional influence. Though fairly good relations have been maintained by India in its neighbourhood (exceptions: Pakistan and China), the peak of those good relations will only be realised through an alliance aimed to protect each other's interests. It is high time that India not just look to have 'cordial relations' but also build credible and long-lasting alliances with neighbouring countries like Sri Lanka, Nepal, Bangladesh, Afghanistan, Mongolia, Burma, Bhutan, Thailand, and so on.

THE FOREIGN POLICY WITH CHANGING ROLE

In the Nehruvian days, India might have allowed its foreign policy to highlight its moral position across the world, but in today's context, the situation has changed completely and India's foreign policy is focusing more on securing her energy interests. The growth story of India is also dependent on her abilities to look for cheap and reliable energy suppliers and thus the previous policy of global moral grandstanding and non-alignment can be abandoned to forge a pragmatic and well-crafted alliance that looks to promote national interests at all costs. Therefore, though it may still be debatable as whom to align with, need to have an alliance can no longer be delayed. In sum, the death knell of non-alignment has been sounded. Now, it is on India if it is listening.

RELEVANCE OF NON-ALIGNED MOVEMENT IN TODAY'S WORLD

Non-alignment, as the word indicates, can be referred to as a decision in which one does not associate completely with any of the groups. People following non-alignment remain neutral and do not back any of the blocks in case of a conflict, be it a conflict over land ownership or oil, as they believe in the ideals of sovereignty.

But the question still exists: Is NAM a relevant organisation in today's world?

Nihal Rodrigo, a former secretary-general of the South Asian Association for Regional Cooperation (SAARC) is of the view that NAM still has an important role to play, however the organisation may not be important as considered before. The very aim of formulating NAM was to combat the bi-polar ideology existing during the civil war. The group has its own importance at a political level.

Ever since its institution in April 1955, the rotation of the chairmanship among the third world countries and some developing countries including India has been done every 3 years.

Within the body itself, a lot of division and conflict on various economic and political issues can be observed as the members usually do not completely agree on any issue. The body does not put any kind of pressure upon its members for any rules and regulations of the body.

Today, NAM is losing its significance because of its inability in putting its influence on the member countries. At the global level since the movement does not create any major economic power, they are not really holding that much importance.

Their power, if any, actually comes only out of being consumers of product and services. To get the actual status of a world leading organisation, the movement must correct the efficiencies in each member country's social and economic issues. They should also focus on doing research and have sound evidence that they could be utilised while dealing with other international bodies and countries.

The movement must also realise and make efforts to be a unified force or else no one will take them seriously.

Is the existence of NAM relevant in this Unipolar world? Nilava Nandi (20 November, 2008) questions if the non-alignment movement is relevant only in a bi-polar world.

It is believed that it is not relevant now when the world is unipolar. But it is actually correct to say that the policy of non-alignment has its own relevance even today.

The new developments in different realms of politics and emerging contemporary approaches in political science have created confusion about the so-called unipolar world among the students of international relations. This situation has a lot of significance with regards to international relations, especially in context of the foreign policy of a nation. Among them, one relates to the repeated relevance of the non-alignment policy to the multitude of states of the non-aligned movement.

As the emergence of policy was observed in a bipolar world in the late 1940s, when the Cold War was in place, many believe it to relate only to a bipolar world. But when the Cold War began to retreat in the 1970s with the first wave of easing strained relations between countries, some writers began to question the relevance of non-alignment policy. In the 1980s, the mistake was noticed. But from 1988 onwards, some writers inadvertently committed a mistake with the emergence of a new détente between superpowers. People started making a view that in the changed context, non-alignment no longer continues to show its relevance.

The fact is that the non-alignment policy was not fully correlated with a bipolar world and the Cold War between the two blocks of superpowers. It is simply that non-alignment flourished in the post-World War phase, after struggle against the hegemony of superpowers by small or weak countries for about 350 years since the emergence of sovereign states in the mid-17th century in Europe. So, whatever be the situation of the world – bipolar, multi-polar or unipolar, non-alignment will be used as a foreign policy of the small/ weak states. In other words, the policy is going to last till the time sovereign nation states exist.

It seems meaningless for a person to question today the continuing relevance of the policy which over the years has become fundamental to the operations and functioning of sovereign nation-states. The jaded question of the day is non-alignment with whom. However, the answer is simple as before, non-alignment with the hegemony of superpowers. Though practising non-alignment may not be easy in a unipolar world, its relevance as a policy cannot be said to cease.

Till the time the functioning of sovereign nation-states is interrupted by power politics, i.e. till the time system starts operating as per the theory of sovereignty (independent and equal) of states in real sense, the policy of non-alignment will hold its validity and relevance in international relations despite periodical or marginal changes in the system.

It is the great tragedy of NAM that one member of the NAM (Iraq) has brought about a blatant violation of the UN Charter and NAM norms against a fellow member of both (Kuwait). Today the extant multilateralism is considered to be pretty weak but the community of states are not going to desert them. Earlier, they have survived bi-polarism and now they will survive uni-polarism too. Because of the huge progress made in the developing international law and international organisations, it can never be considered that they would allow the resurgence of the hegemony of one or more superpowers over the rest of the states.

NON-ALIGNMENT MOVEMENT AND ITS RELEVANCE IN THE 21ST CENTURY

In the present-day global situation, non-alignment or to be precise, its role and utility in general has caused a lot of controversy today as against before. Thus, the movement is going through a critical phase in its life. Today, it is at the crossroad and finds it tough to understand the path it has to rake. It is making all efforts to find its own recognition, reorient its viewpoint in a bid to ensure the role it has to perform in the changed international relations situation. This has led to a heated debate with regards to the validity and contemporary relevance of NAM and non-alignment as foreign policy behaviour in the newly created 'unipolar world'. As in the case of UN, the purpose of establishing NAM is more to be seen on a long-term basis.

The Jakarta Summit conference 1992 made a declaration in favour of NAM that has contributed to the ending of bipolar world and elimination of the cold war. These new developments in fact completely vindicate the validity and relevance of Non-Alignment. They accepted that NAM's role is ensuring 'its full participation in the building of the new world order'. This is the reason that the NAM membership has more than quadrupled from about 25 states in 1961 to 118 today. Though Non-Alignment had emerged as a new foreign policy behaviour during the period of the cold war and the bipolar world, it has little to do with either of the context today. It is further important to note that the policy was approved and accepted by the Non-Alignment minister conference that took place in Accra in 1991. It was again at the Non-Alignment summit conference that took place in Jakarta in Sept. 1992 and more recently at Durban, 1998, Kulalampur 2003, Havana, 2006, Sharm-el-Sheikh Egypt 2009, the relevance of the Non-Alignment movement has been validated.

Today, the world in a way is still divided into two blocks, one block having the nuclear weapons and the other without them. It is in this context, the relevance of NAM can still be validated as from the very beginning and even in more recently meets at Havana in 2006 and Sharm-el-Sheikh, Egypt in 2009 NAM always urged for the complete destruction of all nuclear weapons within a time bound framework but was opposed to treaties on Weapon of Mass Destructions which is not universal. However, NAM is of the opinion that the countries should have the right to use nuclear power for peaceful purposes. In these contexts, NAM is still known to put forth the views of developing countries on different international issues with high moral standing.

NAM along with the Group of 77 (G77–most of the members are from NAM) has succeeded in keeping Third World issues at most of the UN forums and agencies because of their high numerical strength. In the UN Educational, Scientific and Cultural Organisation (UNESCO), NAM and the G77 have been giving a lot of emphasis on the New World Information and Communication Order (NWICO) in order to improve the perceived imbalances in information and communication flows between the North and the South.

In the UN General Assembly, NAM also made an important contribution in transferring the permanent seat in the UNSC previously filled by the Republic of China (Taiwan) to mainland China.

In words of former PM of India Narasimha Rao, he said in June 1992 in a speech in Tokyo that 'the pursuit of a Non-Alignment policy is even more relevant to ever before NAM basically consists of the espousal of the right of nations to independence and development, regardless of the bloc phenomena. Whether there is one bloc or more at a given movement the urge of a non aligned country would continue to maintain its independence, to take decisions according to its light not tagging itself in advance to other'. Later in April 1997 New Delhi at the Foreign Minister summit, IK Gujral said, 'NAM affords its members forum where they can discuss their common problems, evolve solutions and work out positions in trying to tackle the international problems of peace, security, development, environmental safety, human rights etc'.

In words of the Foreign Minister of Colombia, Dr. Maria Emma Mejiva Velez, who perhaps once best echoed the thoughts of many people with regard to the significance of NAM in today's world when she said through a story that today Non-Alignment is much more than 'not being aligned to the great power bloc'. The statement meant that nations instead of just being non-aligned with military alliances should look for ways to bring in peace in the Middle East region. She also brought the attention in this submit that NAM in today's world has to address a number of issues that concern future rather than the past because the need of the hour is the development of the countries with environmental protection being at the core.

The recent 14th NAM submit in Havana further highlighted the relevance of NAM when it condemned all forms of terrorism irrespective of purposes and urged countries not to extend political, diplomatic, moral or material support or favour in any form to terrorism under the UN charter.

Probably the most significant role for NAM today lies in designing a concrete economic agenda with an aim to establish a just and fair international economic order. The globalisation and liberalisation trends worldwide have led to a number of complex economic problems. The rich-poor divide has got increased. The WTO rules and procedures have failed to provide adequate economic gains to the Third World. WTO summits have failed to bring about a consensus on a number of global issues. In this context, the role of NAM becomes important so as to keep the interests of developing countries without any partisan considerations.

The spectrum of NAM should further be expanded as there have been rising concern worldwide over issues like greenhouse gas emissions, health concerns such as AIDS, drug trafficking, increasing poverty, food crisis and unemployment particularly in the NAM members and LDC countries, the increasing digital divide between the rich and poor including fight against all forms of extremism, xenophobia, ethnic nationalism and regional wars.

In conclusion, despite the end of the cold war, there are many global issues of less developed countries for which justice is still awaited and, therefore, for such issues NAM can still play an important role. In reality, today cold war has taken a new dimension as the world is witnessing the ongoing confrontation between US and Russia over issues like eastward expansion of NATO, Kosovo's freedom and the Georgian crisis. As the world still has the fear of war or conflicts of some form, the world requires effective forums for the resolution of world problems for which NAM can be highly instrumental. In fact unless the world gets free from war and world peace is not guaranteed, the development of the Third World counties in real sense is not going to happen. Further since the past concept of colonialism has taken the place of neo-colonialism because of which there is economic exploitation by the MNC in the name of LPG (liberalisation, privatisation, and globalisation), the NAM has to contribute positively in making the globalisation inclusive and achieve a faire, just international economic order. In other words, Non-Alignment does not seem to lose any of its relevance rather it has been instrumental in protecting and preserving the interest of the Third World countries just as it did in the past, so it is also expected to serve their interest in the coming future too with all authority. Thus, it can be concluded that even today the philosophy of NAM has the relevance for the Third World as it was ever before.

11. Role of BRICS in Today's World

The idea BRIC (Brazil, Russia, India and China) was first envisaged in 2001 by Goldman Sachs as part of an economic modelling exercise in order to anticipate the trends of global economy over the next half century. The acronym BRIC was first mentioned in 2001 by Goldman Sachs in the Global Economics Paper No. 66, 'The World Needs Better Economic BRICs'. On 21st September 2010, BRIC Foreign Ministers at their meeting in New York conceded that South Africa may be invited to join one of the most prestigious world body BRIC. In accordance with this understanding, China, as the host of 3rd BRICS Summit, sent an invitation to South African President to attend the Summit in Sanya on 14 April 2011 along with other BRIC Leaders. The BRICS countries – originally Brazil, Russia, India, and China, and now South Africa – have proved to be a source of global economic progress and essential to upcoming generations. The centre of global economic activity is showing a noticeable change from industrialised nations in the west to developing economies in Asia, Africa, and Latin America. By the end of 2010, South Africa made an entry into the BRIC. Indonesia may also be given entry into the BRICS to give representation to the large developing countries that are quite central to global production and consumption.

In economics, BRICS is used to make a reference to the combination of Brazil, Russia, India, and China and South Africa making over 48% of the whole population of the world. These nations will have a lot to contribute to the future global economy. In the year 2000, the four countries in BRIC with Indonesia contributed to just 18 per cent of global GDP, whereas industrialised countries contributing to about 65 per cent. In the year 2010, BRIC countries contributed to more than a quarter of the world's GDP, at 27 per cent while the rich countries' share got reduced to

56 per cent. During 2000 to 2010, BRIC's GDP rose by an incredible 92.7 per cent, as against the global GDP growth of just 32 per cent, with industrialised economies showing a very moderate GDP growth of 15.5 per cent. The increasing significance of BRICS economies can be evident by the growth of imports. Their import and service demands, at about $2 trillion, contribute to 13.5 per cent of global imports, a rise from just 6 per cent 10 years ago. This underlines a 277 per cent growth in imports. Growth of imports globally during this period was just 92 per cent, while imports in industrialised economies increased only 72.3 per cent.

The source of imports have been diversified by BRICS countries and are trading more with other great emerging economies and developing countries. They contribute significantly to the global economy, and their role in the future of global economics seems more visible.

From 2000 to 2010, in the area of new businesses, the market capitalisation of BRIC companies took an upswing from $1.2 trillion to $6.4 trillion, a significant increase of 641 per cent. Their companies contribute about 18 per cent of global market capitalisation, a hike from a very modest 3.8 per cent in the year 2000. If the same trend continues, by 2025, BRICS companies will contribute to more than half of global market capitalisation. Demographic shifts are important events that are taking place and BRICS states, particularly India and China with much of the world's youth population, could have been driving the growth of consumer spending and innovation.

Their large domestic markets are bound to create economies of scale that form BRICS' geographies central to production and demand of the world. And they will be emerging as centres of innovation and development of new product. In the last two decades, India-China relations have seen a remarkable change: they are becoming broader and are with more substance. The most important component of that is the economy. The relations have seen a drastic change from China being an insignificant player to largest trade partner of India, with a trading of about $62 billion of goods in the year 2010. There are a number of Indian manufacturing and IT companies that are showing their great prospects in high-tech engineering, software development, banking and foreign exchange trading.

BRICS countries will have to work jointly with an aim to formulate strategies for the future. This could involve alliance on a wide variety of issues such as energy, food security, access to natural resources, climate change, governance along with international trade policies. The essential to maintain is the wide-ranging cooperation among BRIC countries so as to have a stake in each other's economy and strengthening this trade and business relations among them is an important component of that.

On 29 March 2012, the Fourth BRICS summit was organised in New Delhi. The agenda of the summit was BRICS partnership with an aim for Global Stability, Security and Prosperity. India, Brazil, Russia, China and South Africa took part at the summit and by the end of the summit, Delhi Declaration was released. Two agreements wer signed by the Development banks of BRICS: i) Master agreement to offer credit facility in local currency. ii) BRICS Multilateral letter of credit confirmation facility agreement. The five banks that took part in it are Banco Nacional de Desenvolvimento Economico e Social-BNDES, Brazil; State Corporation Bank for Development and Foreign Economic Affairs-Vnesheconom bank of Russia; Export-Import bank of India; China Development Bank Corporation, and Development Bank of Southern Africa. These two agreements are likely to further cooperation among development banks of the BRICS and are significantly going to enhance trade with the BRICS.

KEY POINTS OF DELHI DECLARATION

BRICS nations came to an agreement to work towards the reform of IMF and World Bank.

Brazil, India, China and South Africa congratulated the Russian Federation on its accession to the WTO.

BRICS countries expressed their commitment to play their role in the global fight against climate change and will put in all efforts in dealing with climate change issues at global level.

In the New Delhi summit, leaders of the BRICS group [Thursday, 29 March 2012] tried putting pressure on Western powers to cede more voting rights at the IMF this year and severely criticised the developed world's reflationary monetary policies that hampered global economic stability. Promised changes to voting rights at the IMF have not yet been affirmed by the United States, leading to dissatisfaction over the G7 and the U.N. Security Council reform, for which India and Brazil have been trying hard for years for permanent seats. The BRICS leaders also put the blame on rich countries for destabilising the world economy even after five years of global financial crisis by the creation of enormous global liquidity. It also noted the right of Iran to make use of nuclear energy for peaceful purposes. The member countries believed that the crises over Iran's nuclear programme should be resolved using diplomatic channels and the situation should not be allowed to intensify or worsen.

China expects the summit to exhibit the BRICS spirit of unity and win-win partnership, strengthen coordination and cooperation on global economy, finance, development along with other important issues of common interest, pushing forward practical cooperation in various fields, sending a collective message for the economic stability and recovery in the world, providing momentum for improving economic governance at global level and contribute to common development in the whole world. It can also be hoped that the summit will go a long way in strengthening institutional building of BRICS cooperation, mapping out future plans, and laying a solid footing for the growth of BRICS cooperation in the long run. Presently, a large number of emerging markets and developing countries have undergone speedy economic growth and become a vital force in the promotion of world peace and common development. With a firm commitment to peaceful development, cooperative development and harmonious development, these countries play an important role in common development of the world, which is essential for more balanced world economy, better international relations, more productive global governance and long-lasting world peace.

Since the beginning of the international financial crisis in 2008, these countries have led from front for ensuring global recovery by means of their own development. Their steady enhanced representation and their greater control over global economic governance have led the international order towards greater fairness and rationality. What has happened testifies once again that in the absence of emerging markets and developing countries, there will not be complete prosperity in the world; and that in the absence of stability in these countries, world peace and stability cannot exist. The development of these countries leads to have a constructive effect on the international landscape. The global community need to look at these countries keeping in mind a long-term and strategic perspective and actively provide all assistance for their development.

BRICS countries are playing an important role in defending and promoting the interests of developing countries. In their cooperation, BRICS countries have shown commitment for promoting South-South cooperation and North-South dialogue, aimed to execute the U.N. Millennium Development Goals, worked for the early achievement of the goals set out in the mandate for the Doha development round negotiations, worked harder to ensure a greater say for developing countries in global economic governance and strived hard against all forms of protectionism. Partnership among BRICS countries is made essential by the existing economic globalisation and democratisation in global relations. It is necessary keeping in mind the trend of the times identified by peace, development and cooperation, and fully conducive to establishing a harmonious world of long-lasting peace and common prosperity.

For BRICS to make practical cooperation in the near future, China desires to see efforts made in the two areas of high significance: First, laying a solid foundation. We should make all efforts to strengthen the existing cooperation programmes keeping in mind the practicality and efficiency and design a number of flagship projects. Second, being innovative. We should properly look for new spheres of cooperation keeping in mind the needs of economic and social development in BRICS countries, utilise the cooperation potential and infuse new vitality into the system of BRICS cooperation.

12. Investment in Private Sector in India: Future Road Ahead

A private investment in public equity takes into account the selling of publicly traded common shares or some kind of preferred stock or convertible security to private investors. It refers to allocating shares in a public firm in a stock exchange not through a public offering.

STATISTICS AND EMERGING TRENDS

In 2015, India has reported a 10-year low in investments in public-private sector which added to contraction that brought down the global investment.

As per the report of the World Bank, though global private infrastructure investment in 2015 showed similar pattern as compared with the previous year, it was 10 per cent lower as against the previous five-year average as a result of dwindling commitments in countries like China, Brazil, and India.

NEW ECONOMIC REFORMS

In the past few years, the government has adopted a few steps which are favourable to ensure the growth of private investment. Some of the highlights of these reforms are:

- Raising investment in public infrastructure.
- Introducing structural reforms in important sectors like power.
- The long-awaited Insolvency and Bankruptcy Code.
- Recent reforms in Foreign Direct Investment (FDI) that increased the limits on FDI in important sectors.
- Legislative and policy measures like introducing Goods and Service Tax (GST), Make in India along with reforms in areas like labour.

HURDLES TO PRIVATE INVESTMENT

Public investment in India have been facing a number of constraints because of increase in public debt and the government's strategy causing fiscal consolidation.

The balance sheets of India's financial and corporate sector have been highly stressed in recent times due to the credit-led corporate leverage. This is showing its effect on the short-term growth of credit.

Demand side corporate vulnerabilities have also led to lowering the level of private investment.

The corporate bond market in India is still in the stage of its infancy and is comparatively small.

Weak profitability along with excessive indebtedness, curbs the potential of the Indian corporate sector.

The problem of indebtedness exists persistently because of weak institutions associated with bankruptcy.

The Public Private Partnership (PPP) Model requires restructuring with institutional reforms making it more feasible.

Bank credit growth particularly to industry has been showing a significant decline in recent times reflecting weakening of capital, profitability and asset quality of a number of public-sector banks. These public sector banks have financed a good share of infrastructure.

A scenario of risk inversion in the Indian banking and investment sectors.

As a result of the global financial crisis in 2008, the external environment has stayed weak and dim ever since.

NEXUS BETWEEN BANKS AND CORPORATE SECTOR PLAYERS

The growth of investment in our country is hampered mainly because of the inter relatedness between the performance of banks and the players of corporate sector.

This is a big problem that needs an early solution. India has brought in a number of measures with an aim to deal with the bank-corporate nexus:

- Raising the banks' loan loss provisions.
- Reforming corporate governance of public-sector banks, recapitalising them, and restructuring stressed assets in the long run in a sustained way by means of asset-restructuring schemes.
- Better recognising the scope of the problem by following the Asset Quality Review (AQR).
- Introducing the new bankruptcy code.
- Executing out-of-court debt-restructuring mechanisms.

WAY AHEAD

- Ensuring rapid execution of steps for keeping a watch on further increasing non-performing assets and helping faster recovery of investment.
- The government, through the Budget every year, should follow an accelerated approach in the direction of recapitalisation and also recommend incentives for performance and resolution of debt.
- The government should take all steps so as to achieve completely transparent and provisioned public sector bank balance sheets by the completion of this financial year.
- Steps should be taken by the government also in order to accelerate plans so as to restructure weak public banks and divest non-core assets. The financial requirements because of these steps can be shaped into the medium-term fiscal consolidation plan very smoothly. This will help in both, expanding debt markets and improving financing inclusion.

CONCLUSION

All these existing hurdles are indicative of the persistent and detrimental impact on growth due to the delays in tackling high levels of impaired assets, stunted profitability, and bleak capital positions of banks that have diminished the availability of bank credit. Therefore, it should be ensured that the problems are nipped in the bud in order to avoid any lowering of credit ratings, economic growth predictions and making the revival of private sector investment possible.

13. 'For the Ills of Democracy, Social Movements may be the Cure, not Revolutions'

Democracy is a popular political setup in which people make a choice of their representatives and these representatives ensure legitimate control over the people of their constituencies. Democracy is described as an institution that finds its origin in French Revolution which was guided by the rule of law, division of power and a protest to monarchy rule. Democracy has been helpful in increasing political participation, distributive justice, enhanced values of equality, brotherhood and inclusion. After the completion of two world wars, a number of countries achieved freedom and followed democracy as it goes a long way in preventing concentration of power and offers required political stability, social inclusiveness and economic development. After two centuries of imperialism, India made a clear choice of democracy with an aim to promote social, economic and political freedom and justice along with universal adult franchise etc.

However, for decades since the rise of democratic ideology, a number of questions have been put forth that concern the impeccability and infallibility of democracy. It is under stress due to elevated intervention by state in questions relating to individuals' private affairs, increased corruption in public life, heightened rift between political executive and common people, illegitimate land acquisitions under the garb of development, amplified evils of society, lack of proper attention towards the minority and marginalised sections, suppressing freedom of speech and expression, clandestine approach of the government, police apathy towards the common people etc. It has been maintained that internal colonialism replaces external colonialism.

The increasing intolerance and hatred towards the ills of democracy get the shape of revolution and social movements. Both are meant to mobilise the citizens with former possibly being armed rebellion or military coup or use of force while latter is usually a peaceful protest and positive criticism of the government by means of petitions, organisation of pressure groups in a non-violent manner etc.

The rise of intolerance among the common masses must not lead to revolution which is usually not considered good for democracy and is described as mobocracy. Some of the instances of revolutions such as naxalism can never expect to establish a new social order. It can only cause chaos, spread extremism, encourage factionalism and lead to an instability in the political system of the country. The recent coups in African nations are testimonies to the fact that most of revolutionary movements do not pay any heed to public concern and existing system of government without offering any feasible alternative. The revolutions are characterised by bloodshed and use of armaments. The likes of Arab Spring and the fight between Syrian and Rebellions in most recent times tell the real story. Revolution has caused gross barbarity, killings, abductions, sexual assaults etc. and despite all that the purpose remains unclear. Now the global community also has made a mention of an internal process.

Besides, social movements have contributed a lot to the history of transition. As an organisation, the Congress party started its work by bringing social revolution in India. The momentum of such revolution was generated by various exponents of socio religious movements who can be listed prominently as Ishawar Chand Vidya Sagar, Raja Ram Mohan Roy, Jyotiba Phule, etc. The peaceful social mobilisation was also supported by Mahatma Gandhi on a mass scale. This ultimately brought about the independence of India, however, the role of a strong support from revolutionaries and social movements cannot be ignored completely in creating a national base for raising the voice against the imperialism. Similar instances of protests can be seen by different traders, merchants during American war of independence which ultimately forced Britain to withdraw heavy taxes on export of American goods. Mass social movements offer direct participation of people in democracy which offers some kind of direct powers to people and helps bring in positive change in the existing system. They would result in giving rights to collective groups of people instead of just an individual. Organising groups of people around single issues would result in direct influence on power.

The recent example of such movement is the protest against corruption by civil society organisation. Some of the global examples include Occupy Wall Street movement, movement for legalising LGBT. In Indian context, social movements led by various organisations namely PUCL for transparency in the appointments of government, fixing accountability of the political executives have created the right ground for keeping a watch on the ills of democracy. Social movements have also been led by people for the emancipation of women, giving them legal rights, raising their voices on political platform. Social movements have been helpful in putting pressure on the government to enact specific laws to ensure higher efficiency and transparency. There has been a rise in the social movements because of people becoming more educated and assertive who are aspiring for better societies for the common good. Social movements help remove the gap between individual interest and collective prosperity while revolutions have caused second and third wave of movement in Middle East countries like Yemen etc.

Therefore, it can be concluded that social movements are the hallmark to bring about social change, and revolution ensures the growth of an anomic society with an unstable political setup with elevated vulnerability. On the other hand, social movements through the mouth of NGOs and other organisations have brought about change in the course of existing world order. They have spread to almost every part of the society for addressing people concerns and bring in change in the normal discourse.

14. Dependence, Not Inequality, is the Real Misfortune

A quote by Albert Einstein 'Before God, we are all equally wise, and equally foolish' perfectly defines that God has created all of us equal. It is only humans that have created inequality on the basis of class, gender, caste, etc. Inequality sneaked in human society in various forms at community and national levels traversing across various dimensions such as social, economic and political aspects.

In simple words, inequality is uneven distribution of resources. For example, economic inequality is the result of uneven distribution of wealth; gender inequality is caused by uneven treatment of individuals based on gender. The same sense applies to racial inequality, political inequality and other such forms. But does having inequality alone pose problems in the society?

As Thomas Jefferson says 'Dependence leads to subservience'.

In ancient societies, men and women were treated equal, activities were evenly distributed and women were given dignity and respected. Uniformity was the main binding factor for unity in society. Perspectives also changed as humans evolved from primitive to modern society. As the activities were evenly managed in the primitive societies, there was no scope for dependence to creep in. In modern society, because men are given more powers and freedom, they have high economic benefits, political gains and societal respects. On the other hand, women are considered biologically inferior and are societally forced to take low-end jobs, giving them low stratum status in the society. The main problem surfaces because of the dependency of women on men and others in the society. Being treated not at par with men makes a condition unfortunate for women as they have to be dependent on others for livelihood. A woman remains dependent on others since birth to death: She is dependent on father in her childhood days for education, nutrition and health; when she reaches puberty age, brother is there for safety and security reasons; after marriage, she is dependent on husband; and finally in her old age, she is dependent on sons.

Britain set its foot in India with an aim to exploit the wealthy bird of gold. There existed much difference between India and the Britain with regard to military advantage and technological advancements. However, the real problem arose when India became dependent on the Britain for institutional changes, trade, agricultural development, etc. This led the Britain to have a complete control over India. It took 190 years to get freedom from the Britain. In the modern and liberalised era, everyone is dependent on other for one need or the other: people depend on the government for welfare schemes and governance; nations depend on one other based on the 'Theory of comparative advantage' and least developed and developing nations are forced to depend on the west for financial aids, capacity building and knowledge transfer.

It is unfortunate that India is unable to eliminate dependency from various levels to only result in poor socio-indicators. The recent Global Hunger Index prepared by IFPRI basically reveals the struggle that poor people are going through to fight malnourishment and poverty. Although the initiatives such as Integrated Child Development Scheme, Mid-Day Meals and Sabla are commendable steps by government, it is also important to trace the targets efficiently, create jobs and improve their standard of living.

Inequality can also be seen in the form of distribution of minerals, metals, water, etc.

As we will be the most populous country in next few years, the demand for resources to feed our population will also increase. To fulfil that increasing demand, it is required to establish a network of trade with other nations to make the population content. Our dependence on other countries in Middle East for oil makes us vulnerable to the price volatility due to conflicts in these nations. As India has abundant sunlight and inexhaustible resources of thorium, energy security can be achieved by using these natural resources. India's quest to explore nuclear energy got a boost after incorporation of India into international nuclear corporation and NSG. Low prices of solar PV cells, constant attempts by government in form of solar parks, ultra-mega parks are all commendable initiatives taken by government to use solar energy more efficiently in future.

Inequality also exists in non-humans. However, being dependent is not always bad as we live in an ecosystem where each species is dependent on other for survival. Food chain makes the important factor in the survival of all the species on the planet. Humans, who are part of the ecosystem, depend on plants, animals and decomposers for survival. Keystone Species plays a crucial role in the way an ecosystem works. If it doesn't exist, ecosystem would be dramatically different or cease to exist altogether.

In some instances, although it is not possible to eliminate dependency, it could be minimised gradually. For example, Third world nations are reliant on international institutions and the west mainly for their economic development. Some of the initiatives to bring backward people and nations into the mainstream include US Development assistance, WHO role in the treatment of HIV/AIDS, Australia's aid program and India's capacity building and aid programs to develop Sub-Saharan African countries.

India also cannot sustain and progresses alone as it is reliant on France for solar technology, Germany for wind technology, Russia for military armaments and Gulf countries for oil. Although it is important to establish trade relations and exchanges in the era of globalisation, it is also the need of the hour to devise strategies to help deficit areas. For example, ISRO has done a commendable job in launching multiple satellites for other countries and developing reusable satellites and own navigation system IRNSS.

It is time that Indian government should address the issue of inequality in terms of wealth, gender, caste, etc. Education, skill development per market and domestic demand, nutrition, sanitation and hygiene are necessary to make India a developed country. Special attention should be paid to the vulnerable sections such as SCs, STs, Divyangs and elderly. Initiatives such as Dalit capitalism, Reservation quota, Sugamya Abhiyan and pension schemes for old age have been undertaken to improve their standard of living. However, it is also important to monitor the progress of these schemes by devising a monitoring system. In addition, behavioural changes should also be brought in the society to eradicate issues such as social stigmas on Dalits and violence on women.

'There is no dependence that can be sure but a dependence upon one's self'. Overall, the culture of dependency should be reduced if not eliminated to ensure more freedom at all levels, which will be the perfect route to sustainable living.

15. Need of Referendum and Initiative in Our Democracy

INTRODUCTION

After Independence, India has embraced democracy, a move touted as one of the large-scale experiment worldwide. Although many nations after being unchained from the shackles of colonial rule fell prey to either dictatorship or military rule, India came out a winner to remain a democracy, irrespective of the large size and diversity. Even as we feel proud to be world's largest democracy, it is the need of the hour that we start finding out the solutions to the problems and challenges that are being faced by Indian democracy. To reflect on the extent we have achieved since Independence in terms of core issues related to democracy, and recurring issues of scams, criminal records of elected representatives and disorder in Parliament, a more relevant issue need to be addressed: how democratic, actually, is Indian democracy?

India is a representative democracy, where elections are held every five years so that people can select their representatives to discuss their problems in Parliament. Even though the idea of 'Of the People, by the People, for the People' is advertised in democracy, in India, it is disheartening to see that people's participation has merely been limited to voting once in five years. The irony of today's time is that although the government is elected by people, they are given less priority over big shots and corporate houses to cater to their interests against being funded while elections, resulting in people's interests being side lined. So, what institutional mechanism do the people have to make their voice heard, if their representatives do not represent their interests?

REFERENDUM AND INITIATIVE

India has seen a rise in demand to increase people's participation in policy formation. Although India still lags behind to find any amicable solution, many democracies worldwide have searched for solutions, Referendum (R) and the Initiative (I), to this structural defect. These instruments are used in a situation when some issues of policy and law-making are 'referred' to a direct vote by the electorate, instead of being solely adjudged by their representatives. They present citizens with a chance to have their say through an institutional channel in any issue, if it is felt that they are not being adequately represented by their representatives.

Switzerland was pioneer to announce these instruments, as far back as 1848. Although 36 other countries, mainly in Europe and Latin America, use these instruments at a national level, and various other countries like Germany, Brazil and the United States, at the state and regional levels. However, India is one among only five democracies never to have gathered courage to use them.

The Referendum (R): Referendum is an instrument that vests citizens with the power, by a direct vote, to take a call whether a legislation passed by Parliament should be rejected. If citizens are not sure of credibility of any legislation passed by the Parliament, they can, by acquiring signatures of a small per centage of the electorate, force a direct vote, by the entire electorate, on the law or policy in question. If a majority vote stands out against the legislation, then Parliament has no other option than to scrap the same. In Switzerland, to initiate a referendum, only support of 1 per cent of electorate is needed.

For instance in 2000, the 'Electricity Market Law' was constituted by the Swiss Parliament to liberalise and deregulate the electricity market. As apprehensions about law being anti-public service grew, the required number of signatures were collected and the law was put to vote. Finally, the law was scrapped as majority of the people opposed it.

The Initiative (I): Although the Referendum only lets citizens to accept or reject legislation passed by the Parliament, an 'Initiative' gives them the power to initiate a new legislation or constitutional amendment that they seem is required for them. Then, a bill prepared a group of citizens and supported by at least 2 per cent of the electorate (again established by signatures) is put to a nationwide direct vote. Finally, the draft is eligible to become is law if the same is supported by majority.

A classic example of people's victory by initiative can be cited by the vote held in Uruguay in 2002. In 2002, after making commitment to International Monetary Fund (IMF) to privatise the supply of drinking water and sanitation services of the entire nation, the Uruguay government had to take the law back in 2004 after facing successful opposition from people, who with the help of Initiative voted against the proposal of government.

BENEFITS

I&R mainly aims to bring legislative behaviour in line with the public opinion. The mere existence of I&R, even if not used, keeps the government on toes to not make any law or policy that may face opposition from the I&R channel to 'trump' them. For instance, in Uruguay in 2002, privatisation of the state-owned mobile phone operator was opposed by citizens. The government was forced to repeal the law even before the referendum could be held as the citizens have already collected required signatures to initiate the process of referendum.

Second, significant governance reforms are the result of I&R. The legislature hesitates to bring transparency in process of framing policy as it will typically curtail their own power. Due to conflict of interest, the lawmakers normally overlook or even damage such reforms. For instance, in India, there has been a long wait of 42 years to get the Lokpal Bill passed as it could investigate and prosecute corrupt lawmakers. In contrast, California has voted on 67 Initiatives on governance between 1912 and 2006, where policies related to campaign finance and prevention of elected representatives holding other offices have been made possible via Initiatives.

Third, the I&R process has played a positive role in forming more politically informed and participative citizenry by having the educative and transformative effect on people. Scholars are of the view that people are well informed and have more opportunities for direct political participation in Switzerland and American states where I&R is active.

CHALLENGES

There exist a few challenges in announcing I&R as it comes with many responsibilities to handle it properly.

First is the logistical challenge in conducting direct voting at the national or even state level. This challenge can be handled by the use of the information and communication technologies (ICT) in innovative ways. In addition, the content of the ballot is required to be formatted in a way that is easily understood by a wide variety of voters with varying linguistic backgrounds and levels of literacy. Here again, various solutions exist.

Another challenge is related to the competence of voter in making clear and effective judgment on matters of law and policy. An answer to this concern is that if our elected representatives (who are not experts on many of the issues they take decisions on) are able to make decisions on laws and policies with the help of experts, so can the people. The fact that referendums play a role in making informed and ideologically consistent choices can be established by the finding that even when voters fail to understand the complexity of issues, they are able to take simple cues, for example, who is supporting or opposing the proposition. It also motivates citizens to know about the issues to be voted by listening to the experts and engaging in debate. It is necessary to devise a framework that provides a diverse expert opinions for people to frame their mind.

Another challenge is to foil monetary special interests from affecting the I&R process, such as by funding high-spending deceptive campaigns. This important issue was traced some American states like California, Oregon and Colorado. For instance in 2006, an amount of $34 million was collected by two oil companies to rout an initiative for the funding of renewable energy research and production by oil companies.

CONCLUSION

It is noted that it turns out to be difficult and costly to influence large number of citizens for monetary special interests than to convince a smaller set of lawmakers through lobbying. With the view to limit or eliminate campaign financing in the I&R process, it is required to put a system in place to avoid it.

Irrespective of the challenges expected to be faced while announcing such democratic reform, it is the high time that people start to track government to implement such measures to do justice to the meaning of democracy. As the constitution of democracy falling short on this count, the I&R process has the potential to ensure that citizens' voices counterbalance a legislature unresponsive to peoples' interests. This is the time when everyone has to stand to help reinstate the core value of democracy, that is, 'Of the People, by the People, for the People'.

16. India's Stand in the Suez Canal Crisis

The Suez Canal Crisis was of utmost significance to approach that India had towards the region in general and the rise of Arab nationalism. India was unaware of the root causes that led to the crisis in the first place, and India has many lessons to learn from the way it was handled.

The crisis started when Egyptian territory was invaded by Israel, Britain and France on 29 October 1956. Although the crisis lasted only for 10 days, it was considered a moment of deep anxiety for India and indeed for relations between newly independent or rapidly decolonising states and their former colonisers.

Nehru expressed his views regarding the crisis to John Foster Dulles, 'the whole future of the relations between Europe and Asia' hung in the balance. The Indian government expected to be affected both economically and politically, as any 'restriction of traffic through the canal or blockade or imposition of higher tolls would have (had) harmful results and might (have) even prejudice (d) the progress of the Second Five Year Plan.'

In 1956, the economic progress of Egypt was depended mainly on guiding the flooding of the Nile, which was to be attained by completing the building of the Aswan Dam across the river. The Soviets and the Americans, who had initially proposed to grant economic support for building the dam, withdrew support due to economic incapacity of Egypt.

The President of Egypt, Gamal Abdul Nasser, was angry at the fact that even though former colonisers and the post-war super powers were earning good profit from traffic through the canal's waterways, none was coming ahead to fund the dam. In forceful retaliation, he announced nationalising the Suez Canal and that Egypt would build its own dam. Nehru, being unaware of Nasser's planned response, decided to distance India from being perceived as being complicit in this decision.

India after Independence had developed a special relationship with Egypt. As Nasser came to power in 1954, western powers started mocking him as an 'Asiatic Mussolini,' 'imitator of Hitler' and a 'would-be dictator.' Interestingly, Nasser's Arab nationalism was also seen a threat to their interests in Africa, and, indeed, in West Asia by both London and Paris. India, on the other hand, sensed a chance to build wider and friendlier relations within the region under 'the wise leadership of President Nasser'.

INDIA'S SUCCESSFUL DIPLOMACY

Understanding the Nehru's idea of 'spirit of brotherliness', Nasser counted heavily on Nehru for guidance on issues of international security. The Arab–Israeli conflict was the most prominent subject of talks between the two, especially that the 'Gaza strip was totally indefensible', with Nasser concerned that 'ever since Ben Gurion's come back, Israel had become more and more aggressive.' In addition, India also maintained its distance from the Western position on Israel and had instead made efforts to inspire secular nationalism in West Asia.

Considering Nasser as a potential partner in the process of developing regional security, Nehru had advised Nasser not to join any defence pacts and instead adopt a non-aligned posture. In its early years of collaboration, Tito's Yugoslavia, Nasser's Egypt and Nehru's India became a motif of the unity of the non-aligned across Europe, Africa and Asia.

Thus, when Nasser took the step of nationalising the canal, the burden fell on India to expect the worsening of the crisis. Nehru was, of course, of the view to 'prevent hostilities and to have a peaceful settlement which would ensure the use of the Canal as before' as he repetitively stressed.

Yet, the British and the French were decidedly adamant in their attitudes. Equally concerned with these developments, Eisenhower proposed that the British host a conference of interested and affected parties; this came to be known as the London Conference that, unfortunately, failed.

Not paying heed to the dialogues or the hearing to be conducted at the UN Security Council, Israel attacked Egyptian soil on October 29. Condemning the conflict, Britain and France initially issued ultimatums to both Israel and Egypt, but later supported Israel in the attack on Egyptian airfields only two days later.

Shocked and provoked by this 'dastardly action', Nehru took immediate measures to stop the conflict. Nehru was aware of the fact that Egyptian military was losing its feet and that 'Nasser proposed to lay down his life fighting.' Thus in a hush-hush move, India's Permanent Representative to the UN, Arthur Lall, was directed to actively court collaboration with the Egyptian delegate Omar Loutfi. The Uniting for Peace resolution, backed by USA, passed on 2 November 1956, dragged fighting forces behind armistice lines, and proposed the way for what came to be known as the Eisenhower–Nehru formula.

In an effort to end the war, the US kept on moving with its heft at the UN in handling western powers, while India brought on board Asian and African nations, resulting in moving a 19-member Asian-African resolution two days later, urging full compliance with previous UN resolutions calling for a ceasefire.

The first UN peacekeeping force, the UN Emergency Force I (UNEF I), was formed by the resolution moved by Canada, Columbia and Norway. As drawing troops from any of the five permanent members was not allowed, the structure of the UNEF I took on an urgent character and even the British invited India 'to come in heavily and assist in bringing about a speedy settlement.'

The Indian troops (a first instance for India to send armed troops for peacekeeping) left for the Suez on 15 November 1956 and was then positioned in the Sinai Peninsula. Indian peacekeepers built repute for themselves, acting as Nehru had besought them to, 'with credit to India and her gallant army.'

India's continual demands for the decolonisation of Asia and Africa at the UN and India's support of the Egyptian position did not hinder her from discussing with both sides, helping substantially in closing the crisis. It also cast India's relations with West Asia in a certain mould, altered only recently with India's perceived closeness with and adoration of Israel.

India's experience in Suez has been essential in gaining global repute by being non-committal, and at the same time being engaged at the level of the UN, a policy known at that time as non-alignment.

Following exacting and exhaustive debates, main elements of the policy that are of relevance to Indian diplomacy towards that region could be rescued and restituted. In fashioning that foreign policy, growth can only be attained by focussing on the antecedents of India's relations with that particular region, and certainly not with hubris toward its history.

17. Regional Comprehensive Economic Partnership (RCEP)

The Regional Comprehensive Economic Partnership (RCEP) is a trade deal that was being negotiated between 16 countries. They include the 10 Association of Southeast Asian Nations (ASEAN) members (Brunei, Cambodia, Indonesia, Laos, Malaysia, Myanmar, the Philippines, Singapore, Thailand, and Vietnam) and the six countries with which the bloc has free trade agreements (FTAs) — India, Australia, China, South Korea, Japan, and New Zealand. The purpose of the deal is to create an "integrated market" spanning all 16 countries. This means that it would be easier for the products and services of each of these countries to be available across the entire region.

The RCEP is billed to be the "largest" regional trading agreement. The countries involved account for almost half of the world's population, contribute over a quarter of world exports, and make up around 30% of the global Gross Domestic Product (the value of all goods and services produced in a year). Negotiations to chart out the details of this deal have been on since 2013, and all participating countries had earlier aimed to finalise it by November 2019.

INDIA'S CONCERNS

India on November 5, 2019 refused to sign the agreement. Key issues that have prevented India from coming on board include "inadequate" protection against surges in imports. This is a major concern for India, as its industry has voiced fears that cheaper products from China would "flood" the market. India had been seeking an auto-trigger mechanism that would allow it to raise tariffs on products in instances where imports cross a certain threshold. India has also not received any credible assurances on its demand for more market access, and its concerns over non-tariff barriers. RCEP participants like China are known to have used non-tariff barriers in the past to prevent India from growing its exports to the country.

India had also reportedly expressed apprehensions on lowering and eliminating tariffs on several products from the country. Its concerns on a "possible circumvention" of rules of origin — the criteria used to determine the national source of a product — were also not addressed. Current provisions in the deal reportedly do not prevent countries from routing, through other countries, products on which India would maintain higher tariffs. This is anticipated to allow countries like China to dump in more products.

India had sought to safeguard the interests of its domestic industry through measures like seeking a 2014 base year for tariff reductions instead of 2013, when negotiations on RCEP began, as it has raised import duties on several products between 2014 and 2019. Using a base year before 2014 would mean a drastic drop in the import duties on these products.

India's trade deficit with the ASEAN bloc – Brunei, Cambodia, Indonesia, Laos, Malaysia, Myanmar, the Philippines, Singapore, Thailand, Vietnam and the five others in the RCEP pact – China, Japan, South Korea, Australia, and New Zealand is already massive, and only increasing every year. Trade deficit with the above countries which stood at $54 billion in 2013–14 had increased to $105 billion in 2018–19.

India's trade deficit with China alone is $53 billion. Electrical machinery, equipment, appliances, plastic articles, iron and steel, aluminum, ceramic products, man-made fibres and furniture are a few of the many goods that China dumps into India every year. Thus, manufacturers of the above products fear increased dumping from China post the RCEP deal. The NITI Aayog report of 2017 makes an interesting point on how China's entry into a market can change the scenario completely. Since the enactment of the ACFTA (ASEAN-China Free Trade Agreement) in 2010, ASEAN-6 countries' (Indonesia, Malaysia, Thailand, Vietnam, Philippines, Singapore) the value of the goods traded with China has gone from a surplus of $53 billion to a deficit of $54 billion in 2016.

India's dairy farmers feared that dairy products could be dumped from milk-surplus countries such as New Zealand and Australia, if India joined the deal. As projected by the NITI Aayog, India's milk production is likely to touch 330 million tonnes (MT) by 2033, from the current about 180 MT. But the projected demand is likely to be about 292 MT. This shows that India would continue to have sufficient surplus to meet its own requirement, hence there was no case for allowing import of milk products even after a decade.

INDIA'S PAST EXPERIENCE WITH FREE TRADE AGREEMENTS (FTAs)

Post 2000, India started aggressively signing bilateral trade agreements, including the first bilateral FTA with Sri Lanka (ISFTA). This came into effect in March 2000. After that, India had signed bilateral trade agreements with Malaysia, Singapore and South Korea. It had also become a partner in many Regional Trade Agreements (RTAs) like the ASEAN CECA.

However, India has always been at the receiving end of the FTAs. According to the data, the imports from FTA partners have been more than India's exports to them after the signing of FTAs. In fact, in a report published by the NITI Aayog two years ago, India's exports to FTA countries have not outperformed the overall export growth or exports to rest of the world.

Among the domestic manufacturing industries, the metal industry has been hit the most by FTAs. A 10 per cent reduction in FTA tariffs for metals has increased imports by 1.4 per cent, says the report. In the agricultural commodities basket, it is dairy products, pepper, and cardamom, which will face the heat of higher dumping if India had signed the RCEP. At present, cheap imports of cardamom and black pepper from Sri Lanka and ASEAN countries have been hurting farmers in Kerala. The same has been the case with rubber farmers as rubber at cheaper rates from Vietnam and Indonesia are getting dumped into India. Coconut farmers too are distressed with coconut oil cakes coming-in from the Philippines and Indonesia.

WAY OUT

India before signing RCEP and FTAs must strengthen its domestic sector. At present India's economy is going through a slowdown. It is imperative that India makes its domestic industry more competitive by increasing competition between domestic players, strengthening the Micro, Small and Medium Enterprises (MSME) sector so that they can get integrated into the global value chain.

The contribution of the manufacturing sector to India's GDP has remained stagnant at around 17% since the 1990s, and the sector needs a big push in order to drive potential GDP growth. The focus on the manufacturing sector is critical for sustainable economic growth. Manufacturing not only creates strong positive backward and forward linkages in the economy, but, according to estimates, every job created in manufacturing has a multiplier effect of creating jobs in other sectors. Industrial revolutions don't happen overnight. They require careful planning, policy interventions, regular upgrades, and innovations and investments at every stage of development.

The central and state governments must come together to strengthen India's manufacturing sector by creating a single window approval for all regulations to set up a manufacturing unit. India's plans for the manufacturing sector need support in the form of a new industrial policy that creates incentives for key sectors. Strategies to enhance domestic competitiveness and to protect the industry from a surge in imports due to trade diversion are sorely needed. If the domestic industry has to thrive, protection, product market reforms and enabling conditions have to be created. When India's manufacturing sector is competent, India stands to benefit from RCEP and various FTAs. India must most importantly protect its agriculture, plantation and dairy sector from FTAs. These sectors must not be within the ambit of FTAs.

18. Anti-Defection Law

The anti-defection law is contained in the 10th Schedule of the Constitution. It was enacted by Parliament in 1985. It came into effect on 1st March 1985. The seeds of the anti-defection law were sown after the general elections in 1967. For a long time, the Indian political scene was affected by political defections by members of the legislature. This situation brought about greater instability in the political system. The infamous "Aaya Ram, Gaya Ram" slogan was coined against the background of continuous defections by the legislators. Legislators used to change parties frequently, bringing about chaos in the legislatures as governments fell. In this backdrop, P. Venkatasubbaiah, a Congress MP in Lok Sabha proposed the setting up of a high-level committee to make recommendations to tackle the "problem of legislators changing their allegiance from one party to another".

The Lok Sabha agreed to the setting up of a committee to examine the problem of political defections. The then Home Minister, Y B Chavan, headed the committee. The panel defined defection — and an exception for genuine defectors. According to the Chavan Committee, defection was the voluntary giving up of allegiance of a political party on whose symbol a legislator was elected, except when such action was the result of the decision of the party.

In its report, the Chavan Committee noted "that the lure of office played a dominant part in decisions of legislators to defect". It pointed out that out of 210 defecting legislators in seven states, 116 were given ministerial berths in governments which they helped form by their defections. To combat this, the Committee recommended a bar on defecting legislators from holding ministerial positions for a year or until the time they got themselves re-elected. It also suggested a smaller Council of Ministers both at the levels of the Centre and the States. The Committee was in favour of political parties working together to help evolve a code of conduct to effectively tackle disruptions.

THE TENTH SCHEDULE

The Bill to amend the Constitution was introduced by Rajiv Gandhi's Law Minister Ashoke Kumar Sen. The statement of objects and reasons of the bill said: "The evil of political defections has been a matter of national concern. If it is not combated, it is likely to undermine the very foundations of our democracy and the principles which sustain it."

The amendment, by which the Tenth Schedule was inserted in the Constitution, did three broad things. Firstly, it made legislators liable to be penalised for their conduct both inside (voting against the whip of the party) and outside (making speeches, etc.) the legislature. The penalty being the loss of their seats in Parliament or the state legislatures. Secondly, it protected legislators from disqualification in cases where there was a split (with 1/3rd of members splitting) or merger (with 2/3rds of members merging) of a legislature party with another political party. Thirdly, it made the Presiding Officer of the concerned legislature the sole arbiter of defection proceedings.

CHALLENGES

No sooner was the law put in place than political parties started to stress-test its boundaries. The issue of what constitutes a spilt in a political party rocked both the V P Singh and the Chandra Shekhar governments. The role of the Presiding Officers also became increasingly politicised. The intervention of the higher judiciary was sought to decide questions such as what kinds of conduct outside the legislature would fall in the category of defection, and what was the extent of the Speaker's power in deciding defections. The Supreme Court, while upholding the supremacy of the Speaker in defection proceedings, also held that the Speaker's decisions were subject to judicial review.

91ST CONSTITUTIONAL AMENDMENT ACT, 2003

A Constitutional amendment bill was introduced in the Lok Sabha to address deficiencies in the Tenth Schedule. A committee headed by Pranab Mukherjee examined the bill. The Committee observed: "The provision of split has been grossly misused to engineer multiple divisions in the party, as a result of which the evil of defection has not been checked in the right earnest. Further it is also observed that the lure of office of profit plays dominant part in the political horse-trading resulting in spate of defections and counter defections."

The one-third split provision which offered protection to defectors was deleted. Now only a merger of two-third members of a political party in the legislature with members of another political party in the legislature can take place. The amendment also limited the size of the Council of Ministers to fifteen per cent of the members of the Lok Sabha and the Vidhan Sabha, and preventing defecting legislators from joining the Council of Ministers until their re-election.

ABUSE OF THE LAW

Recent events in Karnataka and Goa have demonstrated, these amendments have had only limited impact. The removal of the split provision prompted political parties to engineer wholesale defections (to merge) instead of smaller 'retail' ones. Legislators started resigning from the membership of the House in order to escape disqualification from ministerial berths. The ceiling on the size of the Council of Ministers meant an increase in the number of positions of parliamentary secretaries in states.

The Speakers started taking an active interest in political matters, helping build and break governments. The anti-defection law does not specify a timeframe for Speakers to decide on defection proceedings. When the politics demanded, Speakers were either quick to pass judgment on defection proceedings or delayed acting on them for years on end. In Telangana, some members of the Congress legislature party became members of the Telangana Rashtriya Samiti (TRS) without being disqualified on grounds of defection as the speaker delayed the defection proceedings.

ROLE OF THE SPEAKER

A Constitutional challenge to the Tenth Schedule was settled by the apex court in Kihoto Hollohan (1992) case involving the speaker of the Manipur Legislative Assembly. The principal question before the Supreme Court in the case was whether the powerful role given to the Speaker violated the doctrine of Basic Structure i.e. certain basic features of the Constitution cannot be altered by amendments by Parliament, laid down in the landmark judgment in Kesavananda Bharati vs State of Kerala (1973). The petitioners argued whether it was fair that the Speaker should have such broad powers, given that there is always a reasonable likelihood of bias. The Supreme Court stated that Schedule's provisions were intended to strengthen the fabric of Indian Parliamentary democracy by curbing unprincipled and unethical political defections.

An independent adjudicatory machinery for resolving disputes relating to the competence of Members of the House is envisaged as an attribute of the democratic system which is a basic feature of our Constitution. The tenure of the Speaker, who is the authority in the Tenth Schedule to decide this dispute, is dependent on the continuous support of the majority in the House and, therefore, he does not satisfy the requirement of such an independent adjudicatory authority; and his choice as the sole arbiter in the matter violates an essential attribute of the basic feature. The Speaker's decision disqualifying a Member of a House under paragraph 6(1) of the Tenth Schedule is not immune from judicial scrutiny. It is subject to judicial review by High Courts and the Supreme Court.

REFORMS

The Anti-defection Law in India needs urgent reforms. Firstly, any member of the legislature who defects from one political party to another political party must not only be disqualified but also be barred from contesting election for the Lok Sabha or legislative assembly till its term expires. This can prevent defections and curb buying of MLAs in the event of hung assembly.

Secondly, a time frame of fifteen to thirty days must be provided for the Speaker to adjudicate on defection proceedings. The Speaker cannot be allowed to postpone indefinitely adjudication on defectors.

Thirdly, independent members must be allowed to join a political party within a time frame of six months. This will give political stability in the Lok Sabha or the state legislature, which will help in curbing defections from one party to another.

Fourthly, there should be a fixed time for conducting the floor test. A floor test is the determination on the floor of the House whether the Prime Minister or the Chief Minister commands the support of the majority of the MPs or the MLAs. This can be done necessarily by means of a recording the vote of each MP or MLA in the House. This determination of majority is done in a sitting of the legislature, for which the legislature has to be convened. There should be live telecast of the floor test and voting must be done by open ballot which will curb defection of MPs or MLAs to make it more transparent.

19. Article 370

Article 370 of the Indian Constitution gave special status to Jammu and Kashmir conferring it with the power to have a separate constitution, a state flag and autonomy over the internal administration of the state. The article was drafted in Part XXI of the Constitution: Temporary, Transitional and Special Provisions. The Constituent Assembly of Jammu and Kashmir, after its establishment, was empowered to recommend the articles of the Indian Constitution that should be applied to the state or to abrogate the Article 370 altogether. After consultation with the state's constituent assembly, the 1954 Presidential Order was issued, specifying the articles of the Indian Constitution that applied to the state. Since the Constituent Assembly dissolved itself without recommending the abrogation of Article 370, the article was deemed to have become a permanent feature of the Indian Constitution.

This Article, along with Article 35A, defined that the Jammu and Kashmir state's residents live under a separate set of laws, including those related to citizenship, ownership of property, and fundamental rights, as compared to residents of other Indian states. As a result of this provision, Indian citizens from other states could not purchase land or property in Jammu & Kashmir.

On 5 August 2019, the Government of India issued a constitutional order superseding the 1954 order, and making all the provisions of the Indian Constitution applicable to Jammu and Kashmir based on the resolution passed in both houses of India's Parliament with two-third majority. As a result all clauses of Article 370 except

Clause 1 were made inoperative. In addition, the Jammu and Kashmir Reorganization Act was passed by the parliament, enacting the division the state of Jammu and Kashmir into two union territories to be called Union Territory of Jammu and Kashmir and Union Territory of Ladakh. The reorganization took place on 31 October 2019.

IS ARTICLE 370 DELETED?

The Constitution (Application to Jammu and Kashmir) Order, 2019, issued by President Ram Nath Kovind in exercise of the powers conferred by Clause (1) of Article 370 of the Constitution, has not abrogated Article 370. While this provision remains in the statute book, it has been used to withdraw the special status of Jammu and Kashmir.

The Presidential Order has extended all provisions of the Indian Constitution to Jammu and Kashmir. It has also ordered that references to the Sadar-i-Riyasat of Jammu and Kashmir shall be construed as references to the Governor of the state, and references to the Government of the said State shall be construed as including references to the Governor of Jammu and Kashmir acting on the advice of his Council of Ministers.

This is the first time that Article 370 has been used to amend Article 367 (which deals with Interpretation) in respect of Jammu and Kashmir, and this amendment has then been used to amend Article 370 itself. Article 367 is meant to act as a guide, it helps the interpretation of certain laws. It is to this article that the Presidential Order adds a new clause to help interpret provisions applicable to the state of Jammu and Kashmir. This clause alters the interpretation of Article 370, switching out the words "constituent assembly" with "legislative assembly" in the proviso to Clause 3 of Article 370.

Clause 3 of Article 370 made it clear that if the President wishes to change anything within Article 370, he needs the recommendation of Jammu and Kashmir's Constituent assembly. But the J&K Constituent assembly was dissolved in 1957, so it could not possibly give a recommendation. The Constitution (Application to Jammu and Kashmir) Order, 2019 changes that language to make it the legislative assembly, rather than the constituent assembly.

Still, the clause mandates that the President get the approval of the legislative assembly. But Jammu and Kashmir did not have a governor in August 2019, since it's legislative assembly was dissolved in 2018 and replaced with first Governor's rule and later, President's rule. So how did the government get around that?

When a state is under President's rule, the power to make laws for the state is vested in the Indian Parliament. Jammu and Kashmir is currently under President's rule. So effectively, the government's move allows Parliament to act on behalf of the Jammu and Kashmir assembly to change the character of the state.

IS THE DIVISION UNCONSTITUTIONAL?

The petition filed in the Supreme Court on August 22, 2019 by six citizens challenging the constitutional validity of the president's amendments to Article 370 and the J&K

Reorganization Bill has claimed that these orders were unconstitutional, violative of the basic structure of the Constitution and violative of fundamental rights. The petition has listed several reasons why the petitioners believe the reading down of Article 370 and the reorganization of the state were bad in law.

It states that Article 370(3) prescribes the conditions under which Article 370 would cease to operate. It says that Article 370 can cease to operate only on the recommendation of the Constituent Assembly of the state and thereafter a public declaration by the president. However, the petition charged, there has been no such recommendation by the Constituent Assembly before such a declaration was made by the President of India.

Referring to the Presidential Order 2019 relating to Jammu and Kashmir, through which an amendment has been made to Article 367 of the Constitution of India by which the reference to the expression "Constituent Assembly of the State" has been read as "Legislative Assembly of the State", the petition stated that this amendment is a colorable exercise of power. It has claimed that the amendment seeks to achieve indirectly what cannot be achieved directly. It seeks to force an interpretation of Article 370(3) which would not be possible on a plain reading of the terms of the Article 370(3) of the Constitution of India. At present, there is no Constituent Assembly which is in existence and hence a fundamental condition for the effectuation/invocation of Article 370(3) is absent.

The petition also points out that the Legislative Assembly of Jammu and Kashmir does not have the power to alter the State's relationship with India on account of Article 147 of the Constitution of Jammu & Kashmir (amendment of Constitution of J&K). It has also stated that this act would undermine the very basis on which the (erstwhile) state of Jammu & Kashmir was integrated into India. Both the Instrument of Accession as also Article 370 envisage a special autonomous status of the State of Jammu & Kashmir which could only be changed upon a recommendation of the Constituent Assembly.

The present action, the petition noted, which has been effectuated without ascertaining the will of the people either through its elected Government or legislature or public means such as referenda, violates the basic principle of democracy, federalism, and fundamental rights. At present the matter is pending before the Supreme Court of India.

Salient Features of the Jammu and Kashmir Reorganization Act, 2019

- This Act divides Jammu and Kashmir into two UTs i.e. the Union Territory of Ladakh and the Union Territory of Jammu and Kashmir.
- Jammu and Kashmir will have a legislature whereas Ladakh will be a UT without legislature.
- The Union Territory of Ladakh will have Kargil and Leh districts, and the Union Territory of Jammu & Kashmir will comprise the remaining territories of the existing state of Jammu and Kashmir.

- The Reorganization Bill, 2019 envisages total number of Legislative Assembly seats 107 in Jammu and Kashmir. Out of these 107 seats 24 seats will remain vacant because these seats are in the Pakistan occupied Kashmir (PoK) which is illegally occupied by the Pakistan. After delimitation the maximum strength of the legislative assembly of the UT of Jammu and Kashmir will be enhanced to 114.
- Some seats will be reserved for scheduled castes and scheduled tribes in proportion to their population in the union territory of Jammu and Kashmir. In addition to this, the Lieutenant Governor may nominate two women members if they are not adequately represented.
- Powers related to police and public order shall remain with the union government.
- The Union Territory of Jammu and Kashmir will have a Council of Ministers to aide and advise the Lieutenant Governor. The size of council of Minister will not be more than 10% of the total number of members in the Assembly.
- The High Court of Jammu and Kashmir will be the common High Court for the Union Territories of Jammu & Kashmir and Ladakh. In addition to this there would be an Advocate General to provide legal advice to the government of the Union Territory of J&K.
- The Legislative Council of the state of Jammu and Kashmir will be abolished. Upon dissolution, all Bills pending in the Council will lapse.

20. Economic Slowdown in India

A slowdown means that the pace of the GDP growth has decreased. Countries like India and China are currently faced with an economic slowdown. It means the production and earnings of these economies are not growing at the same pace as, say, last year. A situation in which GDP growth slows but does not decline. For example, if GDP goes from 5% growth to 3% growth, an economy is experiencing a slowdown. Most analysts do not consider a slowdown to be a recession, but unemployment may rise and productivity may decline.

An economic recession signifies a drop in the Gross Domestic Product (GDP). The GDP is the total value of all the goods and services produced or created in a country in a year. When this value falls, the country's economy is said to be in recession. It means that the country is producing and earning less than what it did, say, six months ago. An economic recession is marked by low consumer spending because people lose confidence in the growth of the economy. This decrease in the demand for goods and services, in turn, leads to a decrease in production as companies reduce the output to match the demand. The GDP must decline for two consecutive quarters for it to be called recession.

India's real or inflation-adjusted Gross Domestic Product (GDP) grew at 5 per cent in the June 2019 quarter of financial year 2019–20 (Q1FY20), the slowest growth in six years (25 quarters). There is a debate whether India's slowdown is a cyclical or a structural one.

A cyclical slowdown is a period of lean economic activity that occurs at regular intervals. Such slowdowns last over the short-to-medium term, and are based on the changes in the business cycle. Generally, interim fiscal and monetary measures, temporary recapitalization of credit markets, and need-based regulatory changes are required to revive the economy.

A structural slowdown, on the other hand, is a more deep-rooted phenomenon that occurs due to a one-off shift from an existing paradigm. The changes, which last over a long-term, are driven by disruptive technologies, changing demographics, and/or change in consumer behaviour. India's slowdown is both cyclical and structural. There are various reasons for the slowdown.

DEMONETIZATION AND GOOD AND SERVICES TAX (GST)

On 8 November 2016, the Government of India announced the demonetization of all ₹ 500 and 1,000 banknotes. It also announced the issuance of new ₹ 500 and 2,000 banknotes in exchange for the demonetized banknotes. The Prime minister of India Narendra Modi claimed that the action would curtail the shadow economy and reduce the use of illicit and counterfeit cash to fund illegal activity and terrorism. The announcement of demonetization was followed by prolonged cash shortages in the weeks that followed, which created significant disruption throughout the economy.

Demonetization over a period of time resulted in cash crunch in the economy. India has a substantial informal economy that runs on cash. A large portion of this involves legitimate activities that are below the tax threshold and, therefore, should not be thought of as part of the black economy. Agriculture, for example, constitutes around 15 per cent of GDP, runs mainly on cash, and is mostly tax-exempt. The farm economy was hit by the sudden withdrawal of cash from the system during demonetization.

The Centre for Monitoring Indian Economy reported that 1.5 million jobs were lost in the unorganised sector during January–April 2017, just after demonetization. This led to reverse migration to villages. This further led to a substantial increase in demand for MGNREGA work.

Even as the aftershocks of demonetization were being felt, the government introduced GST from 1 July 2017 in such haste that it delivered another huge blow to the economy. GST is a structural reform that was introduced after much deliberations and debate over a period of time. However, it was badly implemented. For example, sourcing from MSMEs took a hit as bigger companies preferred to purchase from suppliers who could provide GST receipts. In other cases, imports were preferred over sourcing from small Indian companies who barely qualified under the GST net. Entire supply chains were disrupted.

There are also reports of increased harassment of taxpayers by overzealous tax authorities. The complex, multiple-slab GST framework, the constant changing of rules, along with the procedural problems, has also hurt small and medium businesses. Together with demonetization, GST has caused substantial job losses, particularly to our most vulnerable workers.

AUTO SECTOR

Automobile sector is facing its worst crisis in twenty years. But what signals a deeper problem is the Society of Indian Automobile Manufacturers (SIAM) report that three hundred dealerships have shut down in recent times. Sales of cars, tractors, two-wheelers have declined considerably. SIAM said about ten lakh jobs have been hit in the auto component manufacturing industry. A lot ancillary industries which provide spare parts are shutting down due to decreasing demand for automobiles.

REAL ESTATE

The health of real estate is a massive indicator of the state of Indian economy. It has links with about many ancillary industries i.e. bricks, cement, steel, furniture, electrical, paints etc. and affects them all if there is a boom or gloom in the sector. Reports are that the volume of unsold houses over the past one year has increased in the top cities of the countries. According to real estate research company Liases Foras, the unsold inventory currently stands at 42 months. This means it will take three-and-a-half years for the existing unsold flats/houses to clear up.

FMCG

The Fast-Moving Consumer Goods (FMCG) companies have reported decline in volume growth in the April–June quarter. This has been blamed on a sluggish rural demand, which, in turn, indicates less availability of money in villages. Reports say that the demand for FMCG in rural India was growing at 1.5 times of the urban demand. The rural demand has come down to the level of urban growth or below. FMCG major Hindustan Lever reported volume growth of 5.5 per cent in April–June quarter compared to 12 per cent last year. Dabur posted a growth of 6 per cent against 21 per cent last year. Britannia Industries recorded a volume growth of 6 per cent against 12 per cent in the same period last year. Asian Paints saw its volume growth decrease from 12 per cent in April–June quarter last year to 9 per cent this year.

BANK'S LENDING TO MSME

The Micro, Small and Medium Enterprises (MSMEs) are the backbone of economic development in any country and more so in India, with its large population needing products and services for their livelihood. At macro-level, lending by banks to industries shows a significant jump from 0.9 per cent in April–June quarter in 2018 to 6.6 per cent for the same period in 2019. The credit to big industries grew by 7.6 per cent during April–June compared to 0.8 per cent last year. Lending to MSME by banks has actually slipped from 0.7 per cent in 2018 to 0.6 per cent this quarter.

MEASURES NEEDED

At the top of its priorities, the government must radically simplify and rationalise the GST regime, even if it means a loss of revenue in the short term. Once, a measure of stability is brought into revenues, it is easy to undertake reforms in the structure and operational details. Reducing the number of tax rates is important and it should begin by getting rid of the 28% category altogether and transferring them to the 18% slab. In the next stage, the 12% and 18% categories can also be merged at 15%.

Secondly, the government must find innovative ways to start rural consumption and revive agriculture. Money must be put back in the hands of the people through targeted transfers. There is, however, a strong case to be made for an improved MGNREGA to serve as the vehicle for delivering a rural stimulus. By design, the MGNREGA is a demand-driven scheme (work is provided to anyone who seeks a job). More important, the programme is designed to incentivize participation of agricultural labour, not just farmers. MGNREGA, thus, has the potential of boosting incomes across all sectors of the rural economy.

Thirdly, the government must tackle the lack of credit for capital creation. It is not only the public sector banks, but also the NBFCs that are not lending.

Fourthly, key job-intensive sectors like textiles, auto, electronics and affordable housing must be revived and assured priority lending, especially for MSMEs.

Fifth, we need to find ways to address export markets that have opened up as a result of the trade wars between the United States and China.

Lastly, there needs to be a credible roadmap for massive public infrastructure development, including through private investment.

21. Election Funding

A staggering ₹ 55,000–60,000 crore was spent in the Lok Sabha elections, 2019, according to a study by the Centre for Media Studies (CMS), a not-for-profit multi-disciplinary development research think-tank. The figure is almost twice the amount estimated by the CMS for the last general polls in 2014 at ₹ 30,000. As of now, corporate donations, which come in various forms, mainly through individual corporate/businesses contributions and electoral trusts, cover more than the two-third of total funds collected by the political parties. This will further increase in the years to come, with the recent changes in the laws and the introduction of new tools such as electoral bonds.

HISTORY

The history of funding of political parties in India goes back to the freedom movement. The Birlas were one of the leading donors of the Indian National Congress. After Independence, the business class as a whole secured some leverage over the shaping of the Congress government's economic policy. It contributed the majority of donations towards poll spending in the post-independence era. In the 1960s, the Congress and the Swatantra Party were the main beneficiaries of donations from big conglomerates such as the Tatas and the Birlas, who together accounted for 34 per cent of the total company contributions between 1962 and 1968.

In 1969, the Indira Gandhi government imposed a complete ban on corporate funding (via deletion of the Section 293A of the Companies Act) to break the nexus between politics and businesses. However, this proved counterproductive. To beat the ban, political parties started raising funds by publishing souvenirs, in which advertisements were placed by the business houses. Businesses also resorted to tax evasions, black-market operations and other illegal mechanisms due to political compulsions and the threat of selective raids and nationalisation. This period also saw the rise of "briefcase politics" through which vast amounts of black money was transferred into the Congress Party account. In the era of license permit raj, this arrangement also suited the businesses. However, a forward-looking Rajiv Gandhi government, intending to end the culture of license permit raj, took a crucial decision of lifting the ban in 1985.

Post-liberalisation, real estate and manufacturing have been the two big sources for political funding. This is possibly because land is a core element in both sectors. Due to the regulatory restrictions on land, politicians wield enormous discretionary power over business activity in these areas. Politicians help builders negotiate the complex network of regulatory permissions dealing with land in exchange for cash infusions around election time. An analysis of the liabilities declared by MPs elected in the 2014 Lok Sabha election reveals how many of them raised huge loans from many big and small real estate companies.

RECENT CHANGES

The Central Government has introduced three major changes since in the mechanics of political funding in India-political parties can now receive foreign funds; any company can donate any amount of money to any political party; and any individual, group of people or company can donate money anonymously to any party through electoral bonds. The removal of a cap on corporate donations and introduction of electoral bonds have further strengthened corporate influence in political decision making. Among the known sources of donations to parties, between 2012 and 2016, corporate contributions formed a staggering 89 per cent of the total funds.

The 2017 Finance Act lifted the cap on corporate contributions from 7.5 per cent of the net profit of a company's past three financial years and removed the obligation to report such contributions in the company's profit and loss account. Besides, such donations do not require the approval of a company's board of directors. This provision is a convenient loophole for unscrupulous elements to route black money through bogus companies.

Introduced in 2013, electoral trusts was the government's way of creating a layer of opacity in the process of corporate donations to parties. These trusts could receive contributions from various companies and disburse them to various parties, with the public not knowing which company was really donating funds to which party or any quid pro quo transactions. In 2017–18, 86 per cent of the contributions to the 22 registered electoral trusts went to the ruling party. Between 2013 and 2016, donations from trusts accounted for one-third of all funding that parties disclosed.

ELECTORAL BONDS

In May 2017 the EC wrote to the Union Ministry of Law and Justice expressing apprehensions that electoral bonds might lead to increased use of black money for political funding through shell companies. The commission wanted the rollback of electoral bonds. The Commission called the introduction of electoral bonds a retrograde step in its submission to a parliamentary panel. The Electoral Bonds were originally meant for the Lok Sabha elections but it was later on extended to the state assembly elections.

On January 30, the RBI responded with objections to an amendment to the Reserve Bank of India Act (required to introduce the bonds). RBI called the electoral bonds a type of bearer bond that would not lead to transparency. Instead the purchasers of the bonds would remain secret.

The central government had on January 29, 2018, notified the electoral bond scheme. It is like a promissory note that can be bought by any Indian citizen or company incorporated in India from select branches of State Bank of India. The citizen can then donate the same to any eligible political party of his/her choice. Money received from electoral bonds will be deposited in a bank account verified by the Election Commission. All the transactions for electoral bonds can be done only through that account. These cannot be bought with cash, and the buyer must submit know your customer (KYC) details to the bank. Parties can encash these bonds in their designated SBI accounts.

The donor does not need to disclose which party he has donated to and the party does not need to reveal from whom it got the bonds. This code of secrecy ensures that only the ruling party has access to the information about which individual or company has donated to which party. This will result in people donating only to the ruling party. Electoral bonds militate against a fundamental premise: that the citizens have a right to know who is funding whom, and, thereby, possibly influencing policy outcomes.

First, the lack of anonymity creates a bias in favour of the ruling party. If a big corporate company does not donate to the ruling party, it could be punished later if the party is returned to power. The bulk of the donations, therefore, goes to the ruling party, thereby enhancing its chances of returning to power. Although perfectly legal, electoral bonds are heavily biased. Second, bonds cannot prevent the practice of cash donations. These transactions remain off the record books and leave no audit trail. Citizens will never know the amounts, their distribution across parties, and the names of donors. Third, bonds cannot prevent foreign agencies from financing Indian elections and looking for favours from the new government. This can easily be done through the creation of shell companies and making donations appear legitimate. The overwhelming number of electoral bonds sold was of very high denominations. The donors, in all probability, were corporates and businesses that wished to remain on the right side of the government.

PUBLIC FUNDING OF ELECTIONS

Direct state funding of political parties is practised in 86 per cent of the European countries, 71 per cent in Africa, 63 per cent in the Americas and 58 per cent in Asia.

Its supporters say that public finance can help protect the political process from direct, quid pro quo kickbacks or corruption and create a level playing field for parties, candidates with less resources and new entrants. There is, however, no guarantee that public finance will reduce election expenditure. In countries like Italy, Israel and Finland, which have experimented with public finding, there has been no significant drop in expenses. In the US, election expenditure continues to soar. Only a handful of countries like Germany and Japan have been able to reduce their poll expenditure by any significant extent. Besides, despite public finance, the reliance on private donations has not decreased in countries such as the US and Israel.

The success stories of Canada, Sweden and, to some extent, Japan, tell that an effective public funding model has two elements: reducing the dependency on corporate or private money by strict restrictions on expenditure limits, strong regulations and disclosures, and infusing white money through state funding or incentivising other funding options, such as tax-free donation.

WAY FORWARD

The Election Commission has sent a long list of suggestions for electoral reforms to the Union Government. Among these reforms was the proposal to reintroduce the provision in the Companies Act, 2013, which allowed a company to donate a maximum of 7.5 per cent of its average three-year net profit as political donations through electoral bonds. The government had done away with this restriction after the electoral bond scheme was introduced in 2017, leading to concerns that shell companies could be set up for the sole purpose of political donations. The commission is of the view that the earlier provisions ensured that only profit making companies with a proven track record provide donations to political parties and accordingly, it is recommended that this provision may be reintroduced. This is not the first time the EC has written to a central government on the issue. Like in the past, the government has taken little action on the suggestions related to electoral funding, except in limiting cash donations to ₹ 2,000. India's political finance reform has been stymied by two major factors: a lack of political will for reform, and an economy in which the state exerts a heavy hand, thus incentivising illicit funding.

The roots of the proliferation of unaccounted money in elections can be traced to the structure of political funding, which allows parties to manipulate their accounts any way they want. According to Association of Democratic Reforms (ADR), the six national parties declared an income of ₹ 1,559 crore in 2016–17, of which ₹ 711 crore, or 46 per cent, came in donations from unknown sources, such as sale of coupon, relief fund, miscellaneous income, voluntary contributions, and contribution from meetings. Full transparency should be paired with better enforcement, independent audits of the accounts of political parties and a zero tolerance policy towards those who lie or manipulate their official campaign expenditure statements. Political parties must come within the ambit of the Right to Information Act (RTI) as it will make the working of the political parties more transparent in terms of election funding.

22. Impact of the New Economic Measures on Fiscal Ties between the Union and the States in India

Fiscal federalism deals with division of revenue between the Centre and the States. The Government of India Act 1919 and 1935 formalized the tenet of fiscal federalism and revenue sharing between the Centre and the States, aimed at enhancing political, economic and administrative efficiency, and granting increased autonomy to the provinces of India.

Typically, federations face vertical and horizontal imbalances. A vertical imbalance arises because the tax systems are designed in a manner that yields much greater tax revenues to the Central government when compared to the State governments. The horizontal imbalances arise because of differing levels of attainment by the states due to differential growth rates and their developmental status in terms of the state of social or infrastructure capital.

After India achieved its Independence, the Indian Constitution prescribed for federal structure of government and defined fiscal relations between centre and states. It ensured distribution of powers through central, state and concurrent list which also divided the taxing and expenditure power between centre and states. The Central government has been given powers in respect of custom duties, excise duties, income tax, taxes on capital values, estate duty in respect of property other than agricultural land, terminal taxes on goods or railway passengers carried by railway, sea or air, taxes other than stamp duties on transactions in stock exchanges and future markets.

The State governments have been given exclusive tax powers in respect of land revenue, taxes on agricultural income, duties in respect of succession to agricultural land, estate duty in respect of agricultural land, taxes on land and buildings, excise duties on goods containing alcoholic liquors for human consumption. The Constitutional Amendment Act, 1956 empowered states to impose sales tax under Central Sales Act 1956.

The Constitution also provided for distribution of net proceeds of taxes between centre and states and allocation between states based on recommendation of Finance Commission. Taxation power and devolution of its revenue between centre & states are governed by list of constitutional articles such as Article 268–271. This tax arrangement between centre and the states has been dynamic and has been amended from time to time as per requirements e.g 88th Constitutional Amendment Act 2003, introduced Service Tax to be collected and appropriated by centre and states (Article 268-A).

The Central government also established the Planning Commission which was a non-statutory body for socio-economic planning of states and devolution of revenues to states in form of discretionary aid. The devolution and transfer to states mainly comprised of states share in taxes, grants in aid and loans to states. However, after the economic reforms of 1991, the government became a facilitator rather than a provider of services. This era also witnessed rise of income inequalities among states which caused regional imbalances and state and central government schemes failed to ensure necessary services. Recently, the Central government initiated various economic measures for empowering the states financially.

NITI AAYOG

A nation like India not only requires fiscal federalism to meet to need of the governments but also cooperative federalism to address some complex common problems. However the planning process remained centralized with inception of planning commission which proceeded with top down approach and one size fit all formula. Moreover the state did not have any direct say in policy planning by the Planning Commission. As a result the plans failed to address diverse regional issues in the country.

The NITI Aayog replaced the Planning Commission on 1 January, 2015 to inculcate the spirit of cooperative federalism in India through active involvements of all state governments and structured support initiatives and mechanisms with the states on a continuous basis, recognizing that strong states make a strong nation. One of its functions is to design strategic and long term policy and programme frameworks and initiatives, and monitor their progress and their efficacy. But the NITI Aayog is primarily a think tank with no power to have a say in budgets of state governments. The Planning Commission acted as an advisor to state governments on budgetary matters of state governments so that they could make economic transformation in their states.

NITI Aayog should be mandated to create an independent evaluation office which will monitor and evaluate the efficacy of the utilization of grants given to state governments. This office must also advise state governments on economic matters through various reports. It should not be involved in budget making of state governments.

FOURTEENTH FINANCE COMMISSION (FFC)

The FFC has increased the amount that the centre has to transfer to the states from the divisible pool of taxes by 10 per centage points, from 32 per cent to 42 per cent. Compared with the previous two Finance Commissions (FCs) that increased the share going to the states by 1 and 1.5 per centage points, respectively. Due to greater devolution, state governments would have greater resources at its disposal to undertake social and economic transformation in their states. The FFC also recommended grants to rural and urban local bodies, a performance grant and grants for disaster relief. The recommendations of the FFC have the potential to redefine Indian federalism in a long overdue and desirable manner.

CENTRALLY SPONSORED SCHEMES (CSS)

The centrally sponsored schemes cover several areas of state subjects which are crucial for realizing national development goals. These schemes are implemented by state government based on in guidelines of Union Government. However a number of CSS often overlapped with each other and its rigidity and centralized tendency prevented it in addressing regional needs.

The Union Government has reduced CSS from 66 to 28 umbrella schemes. Reduction of schemes with increased devolution helps the state government to address the several areas effectively without being dependent on centre. The flexibility inculcated in these schemes allow state government to design them as per their requirements in order to improve their efficiency.

GOODS AND SERVICE TAX (GST)

GST came into effect from 1 July, 2017 through the One Hundred and First Constitutional Amendment Act, 2016. The Goods and Services tax is a uniform indirect tax levied on all goods and services produced in the country and all goods and services imported from abroad. GST will be a single uniform indirect tax which will treat India as one market. It will replace all Central and state indirect taxes like CENVAT, excise, customs, VAT, state excise, etc. The GST has resulted in a single price of a product across the country, lower working capital for companies and a more simplified tax system.

The Amendment also created the GST Council by inserting Article 279-A in the Constitution. The Council comprises the union finance minister as chairman and state finance ministers as members. The Council shall make recommendations on matters relating to the GST. In the Council, the votes of the Central government will weightage of one-third of the total votes cast. Rest two-third weightage is given to the states. The Council with the cooperation of the centre and the states has resulted in cooperative federalism in the matter of indirect taxes.

PUBLIC FINANCIAL MANAGEMENT SYSTEM (PFMS)

Public Financial Management System (PFMS) is a financial management platform for all plan schemes, a database of all recipient agencies, integration with core banking solution of banks handling plan funds, integration with state treasuries and efficient and effective tracking of fund flow to the lowest level of implementation for plan scheme of the Government.

Due to the monitoring of funds through PFMS, one can know the actual status of utilization of funds by the multiple implementing agencies of the central and the state governments. The ultimate purpose of implementing any Scheme is to ensure that the benefits must reach to the last mile.

Funds under the centrally sponsored schemes flow almost entirely to the state government treasuries and a substantial part of the funds under the central sector schemes are also spent in the states through various central government agencies. The improvements brought-out in the management of public funds through PFMS, will have a cascading beneficial impact on the management of state government public finances as well as efficient delivery of public services by the states. PFMS, therefore, reflects the true spirit of Cooperative Federalism with the Centre and the

State Governments combining their efforts to improve public finance management for ultimate public good.

These new economic measures are well intended to transform fiscal relations between the centre and the states. But these measures are not perfect. GST needs improvement in terms of procedure, longer period of compensation to states in case of deficit of rev nue, than the mandated period of five years.

23. National Register of Citizens (NRC)

The register is meant to be a list of Indian citizens living in Assam. For decades, the presence of migrants, often called outsiders, has been a contentious issue here. Assam saw waves of migration, first as a colonial province and then as a border state in independent India. The First National Register of Citizens was compiled in 1951, after the Census was completed that year. The Partition of the subcontinent and communal riots had just triggered vast population exchanges at the border. Since 2015, the state has been in the process of updating the 1951 register. One of the stated aims of the exercise is to identify so-called "illegal immigrants" in the state, many of whom are believed to have poured into Assam after the Bangladesh War of 1971.

HISTORY

In 1979, about eight years after the war, the state saw an anti-foreigners' agitation. Assamese ethnic nationalists claimed illegal immigrants had entered electoral rolls and were taking away the right of communities defined as indigenous to determine their political future. In 1985, the anti-foreigners' agitation led by the All Assam Students' Union came to an end with the signing of the Assam Accord. Under this accord, those who entered the state between 1966 and 1971 would be deleted from the electoral rolls and lose their voting rights for 10 years, after which their names would be restored to the rolls. Those who entered on or after March 25, 1971, the eve of the Bangladesh War, would be declared foreigners and deported.

The National Register of Citizens now takes its definition of illegal immigrants from the Assam Accord – anyone who cannot prove that they or their ancestors entered the country before the midnight of March 24, 1971, would be declared a foreigner and face deportation. This means a person could be born in India in 1971 to parents who crossed the border in that year, and still be termed an illegal immigrant at the age of 48.

NEED FOR NRC

The mechanism for detecting so-called foreigners had previously been delineated by the Illegal Migrants (Determination by Tribunals) Act of 1983. This was struck down by the Supreme Court in 2005, on a petition which argued that the provisions of the law were so stringent, they made the "detection and deportation of illegal migrants almost impossible". That same year, the decision to start updating the National Register of Citizens was taken at a tripartite meeting attended by the Centre, the

Assam Government as well as the All Assam Students' Union and chaired by then Prime Minister Manmohan Singh. In 2013, the Supreme Court asked the Centre to finalise the modalities to update the new National Register of Citizens. The project was launched in earnest from 2015, monitored directly by the Supreme Court.

PROCESS OF NRC

The mammoth counting process went through several phases. First, there was data collection. Most individuals applying for inclusion into the NRC had to prove not only that their ancestors had lived in Assam pre-1971 but also their relationship with the ancestor. Then came the verification process. Documents were sent to the original issuing authorities while NRC officials conducted field verification. Once the data was submitted, the applicant's blood relations were plotted on a family tree.

NRC FINAL STATUS

A total of 3,30,27,661 persons had applied for inclusion of their names in the updated list of NRC Assam. More than 19 lakh people in Assam were excluded from the final list of the NRC that was released by the government on August 31, 2019 while over 3.11 crore persons were included.

As per the guidelines issued by the Central government, the excluded persons can approach one of the 400 foreigners' tribunals and appeal against their exclusions within 120 days of the publication of the final list. The tribunals are set up the government to hear the appeals of those who have been excluded from the Assam NRC List. The foreigners' tribunal will also issue certificates to the excluded people and explain them why they have been left out of the final list of NRC.

Under the provisions of Foreigners Act, 1946 and Foreigners Tribunal Order, 1964, only the tribunals are empowered to declare a person as a foreigner. Hence, non-inclusion of a person's name in the final list of the NRC does not by itself amount to him/her being declared a foreigner.

NRC AND CITIZENSHIP

Citizenship signifies the relationship between individual and state. It begins and ends with state and law, and is thus about the state, not people. Citizenship is an idea of exclusion as it excludes non-citizens. There are two well-known principles for grant of citizenship. While jus soli confers citizenship on the basis of place of birth, jus sanguinis gives recognition to blood ties. From the time of the Motilal Nehru Committee (1928), the Indian leadership was in favour of the enlightened concept of jus soli. The racial idea of jus sanguis was rejected by the Constituent Assembly as it was against the Indian ethos.

Citizenship is in the Union List under the Constitution and thus under the exclusive jurisdiction of Parliament. The Constitution does not define the term 'citizen' but gives, in Articles 5 to 11, details of various categories of persons who are entitled to citizenship. Unlike other provisions of the Constitution, which came into being on

January 26, 1950, these articles were enforced on November 26, 1949 itself, when the Constitution was adopted. However, Article 11 itself confers wide powers on Parliament by laying down that "nothing in the foregoing provisions shall derogate from the power of Parliament to make any provision with respect to the acquisition and termination of citizenship and all matters relating to citizenship". Thus Parliament can go against the citizenship provisions of the Constitution.

The Citizenship Act, 1955 was passed and has been amended four times—in 1986, 2003, 2005, and 2015. The Act empowers the government to determine the citizenship of persons in whose case it is in doubt. However, over the decades, Parliament has narrowed down the wider and universal principles of citizenship based on the fact of birth. Moreover, the Foreigners Act places a heavy burden on the individual to prove that he is not a foreigner.

CITIZENSHIP AMENDMENT BILL, 2019

As the Citizenship Act does not differentiate between foreigners on religious lines, the government plans to bring an amendment to the law to make Hindu, Sikh, Buddhist, Jain, Parsi, and Christian illegal migrants from Muslim-majority Afghanistan, Bangladesh and Pakistan eligible for citizenship of India without detention.

Under the present citizenship law, one of the requirements for citizenship by naturalisation is that the applicant must have resided in India during the last 12 months, as well as for 11 of the previous 14 years. The Amendment relaxes the second requirement from 11 years to 6 years as a specific condition for applicants belonging to these six religions, and the aforementioned three countries.

The Amendment in the Foreigners (Tribunals) Order, 1964, issued by the Central Government on May 30, 2019, empowered district magistrates of all States and Union Territories to set up tribunals to identify foreigners living in India illegally. The process of detaining illegal immigrants will have to be overseen by the local police. The state governments will also be required to build detention centres for illegal immigrants.

PAN INDIA NRC

The government has decided to prepare a National Population Register (NPR) by September 2020 to lay the foundation for rolling out a citizens' register across the country. The NPR will be a list of usual residents of the country. The NPR is a register of usual residents of the country. It is being prepared at the local (village/sub-town), sub-district, district, state and national level under provisions of the Citizenship Act 1955 and the Citizenship (Registration of Citizens and Issue of National Identity Cards) Rules, 2003. Once the NPR is completed and published, it is expected to be the basis for preparing the National Register of Indian Citizens (NRIC), a pan-India version of Assam's National Register of Citizens (NRC). For the purpose of NPR, a usual resident is defined as a person who has resided in a local area for past six months or more or a person who intends to reside in that area for the next six months or more. The main purpose of the NPR is to have an elaborate record or database of every resident in the country. This database comprises both demographic as well as biometric particulars.

24. Triple Talaq

The Supreme Court on August 22, 2017 held triple talaq as unconstitutional. Three of the five judges on the Constitution Bench — Justices Rohinton F Nariman, Uday U Lalit and Kurian Joseph — called the practice as un-islamic and arbitrary and disagreed with the view that triple talaq was an integral part of religious practice. But the minority ruling of Chief Justice JS Khehar and Justice Abdul S Nazeer underlined the primacy of Muslim Personal Law and said the practice enjoyed constitutional protection and was beyond the scope of judicial scrutiny. The Triple Talaq Bill thrice passed by the Lok Sabha over a period of 19 months received the approval of the Rajya Sabha on July 29, 2019. The Muslim Women (Protection of Rights of Marriage) Act, 2019, makes the practice of triple talaq a penal offence. The practice of instant triple talaq by Muslim men will be punishable by a jail term of three years.

INSTANT TRIPLE TALAQ

Instant triple talaq or talaq-e-bidat is a practice that was challenged in the court. It is different from the practice of "talaq-ul-sunnat", which is considered to be the ideal form of dissolution of marriage contract among Muslims.

Talaq-ul-sunnat consists of talaq-e-ahsan and talaq-e-hasan. Talaq-e-Ahsan is the 'most proper' form of talaq in which the husband expresses divorce in single sentence. And then has to wait till the iddat period is over. Iddat period for a woman who has been divorced by her husband is usually three monthly periods and during this time, she cannot marry another man. If before the completion of iddat, the husband resumes co-habitation with his wife or says that, the divorce is revoked. In case the woman is pregnant, the iddat period lasts until she gives birth. The waiting period for a woman after menopause is three months.

Talaq-e-Hasan is the 'proper' form of talaq. In this form, three successive pronouncements of talaq are made by the husband in three successive tuhrs (when the woman is not menstruating). In case of a non-menstruating woman, its pronouncement may be made after the interval of a month or thirty days between the successive pronouncements. This form of talaq can be revoked any time before the third pronouncement.

In the practice of talaq-e-biddat, when a man pronounces talaq thrice in a sitting, or through phone, or writes in a talaqnama or a text message, the divorce is considered immediate and irrevocable, even if the man later wishes to re-conciliate. The only way for the couple to go back to living together is through a nikah halala, which requires the woman to get remarried, consummate the second marriage, get divorced, observe the three-month iddat period and return to her husband. The practice of talaq-e-biddat has been viewed as abhorrent in theology but upheld as valid by law. Declaring the practice of talaq-e-biddat as "unconstitutional" may not balance out the gender parity among Muslims, because men still reserve the right to talaq without resorting to legal course of action.

THE SUPREME COURT JUDGEMENT

The issues in the case were so complicated that there are as many as three judgments. Chief Justice of India J S Khehar authored one opinion, with which Justice S Abdul Nazeer agreed. The second opinion was authored by Justice Kurian Joseph. The third judgment was written by Justice Rohinton F Nariman on behalf of himself and of Justice Uday U Lalit. Justice Kurian agreed with Justice Khehar on some points, and with Justice Nariman on others. Let us understand the judgments and reasons for the different opinions. All the opinions have clearly stated that they are dealing just with instant triple divorce, and not with other forms of divorces under Muslim Personal Law.

Justice Nariman: He held that instant irrevocable triple talaq not preceded by the efforts at reconciliation is unconstitutional, as it is contrary to the right to equality, which includes the right against arbitrariness. The basis of his decision is the recognition of triple divorce by the Shariat Act, 1937. The Act laid down that in matters of talaq, gift, will, inheritance etc., "the rule of decision where parties are Muslims shall be Muslim Personal Law". He quoted the 1932 decision of the Privy Council in which triple divorce was held as valid under Sharia to conclude that since instant triple divorce is "manifestly arbitrary", the Shariat Act, to the extent it recognised triple divorce, is ultra vires the Constitution.

He has struck down Section 2 of the Shariat Act, which recognises and enforces triple divorce. All parent laws, subordinate legislation and executive orders are subject to fundamental rights, and must be struck down if they are not compatible. Justice Nariman dissented with the judgment of the CJI on the issue of the judiciary not being the right forum to dispose of such matters. The Supreme Court cannot refuse to decide when approached by a litigant under Article 32 against the violation of his/her fundamental rights, and put the ball in Parliament's court, he said.

Justice Khehar: His judgment is the most detailed — 272 pages — and a major milestone in the history of freedom of religion in India. For the first time in Indian judicial history, freedom of religion subject to restrictions given in Articles 25 and 26 has been held to be "absolute". After quoting Constituent Assembly debates on Articles 25 and 44, the CJI held that personal law is part of the freedom of religion, which courts are duty-bound to protect. He also said courts are not supposed to find fault with provisions of personal law, which are based on beliefs, not logic. Personal law, he said, is beyond judicial scrutiny.

The CJI explicitly said that accepting the petitioner's prayer to hold triple talaq unconstitutional would amount to negating freedom of religion. He equated triple divorce to fundamental rights. Disagreeing with Justice Nariman, he observed that since the recognition of Muslim Personal Law by the Shariat Act of 1937 does not give it statutory status, and because Muslim Personal Law is not 'law' as held by the Supreme Court, the Shariat Act, or triple talaq under it, cannot be held unconstitutional.

Justice Joseph: The third and most important judgment was delivered by Justice Joseph who fully endorsed the CJI's opinion on freedom of religion, thereby ensuring its majority. He agreed with Justice Nariman on triple divorce not being an essential part of Muslim Personal Law. But he disagreed with Justice Nariman on the interpretation of the Shariat Act — concurring, rather, with Justice Khehar's opinion that the Shariat Act is not a legislation regulating triple divorce.

TRIPLE TALAQ IN OTHER COUNTRIES

The Supreme Court, in its judgment cited laws from 19 countries including Pakistan and Egypt which have abolished the practice. The panel referred the book 'Muslim Law in India and Abroad' by Tahir Mahmood and Saif Mahmood. The Arab States that have abolished the triple talaq includes Algeria, Egypt, Iraq, Jordan, Kuwait, Lebanon, Libya, Morocco, Sudan, Syria, Tunisia, United Arab Emirates and Yemen along with Southeast Asian countries like Indonesia, Malaysia and Philippines. Pakistan, Bangladesh and Sri Lanka also have enacted laws against the Muslim divorce practice.

In Algeria, divorce cannot be established except by a judgment of the court preceded by an attempt at reconciliation for a period not exceeding three months.

In Egypt, a Talaq pronounced under the effect of intoxication or compulsion shall not be effective. A conditional Talaq which is not meant to take effect immediately shall have no effect if it is used as an inducement to do some act or to abstain from it. A Talaq accompanied by a number, expressly or impliedly, shall not be effective except as a single revocable divorce. Symbolic expressions of talaq, i.e., words which may or may not bear the implication of a divorce, shall not effect a divorce unless the husband actually intended it."

GENDER JUSTICE

The majority of Muslims would welcome a formal end to the practice of triple talaq, but would be unhappy that the courts have interfered in what they have been led to believe is a matter of their faith. The five-member Constitution bench did not reach a unanimous decision on the matter. The three judges who supported quashing triple talaq did not follow the same logic to reach that decision. Two held this provision of the Muslim personal law to be arbitrary and, therefore, violative of the Constitution. One held the provision to be bad in law because the overwhelming purport of quranic injunctions on divorce is for fair treatment of the woman.

The two judges who gave the minority view that it requires legislation rather than a court decision to remove triple talaq also strongly disapproved of the practice. Triple talaq is the third and most undesirable form of divorce, even in the eyes of those who deem the practice to be legal. But the first two i.e. talaq-e-ahsan and talaq-e-hasan also fail the test of gender equity: they give men the unilateral right to divorce their wives, even if over an extended period of time that offers scope for reconciliation, rather than instantaneously.

The judges have thrown the door open for challenging the two remaining methods of divorce in the Muslim Personal Law on grounds of violating the right to equality. The chief justice, one of the authors of the minority view, stated that the first two methods of divorce, talaq-e-ahsan and talaq-e-hasan, too privilege the male and, thus, violate the right to equality, while calling upon the legislature to find a remedy by changing the law.

Champions of gender justice can challenge talaq-e-ahsan and talaq-e-hasan, on grounds of discrimination against women. Denying women democratic rights in the name of protecting religious custom weakens democracy and erodes minority rights.

ESSAYS ON BIHAR RELATED ISSUES

1. Poverty in Bihar

Poverty in Bihar, one of the most populous states in India, is a significant problem. The state is among the poorest in the country, with a high percentage of people living below the poverty line. The poverty rate in Bihar is estimated to be around 33.7%, which is higher than the national average of 21.9%.

Recently, Bihar has been ranked as the poorest state in the country in the Multidimensional Poverty Index, 2021 released by NITI Aayog. According to the report, 51.91% of the population of Bihar is poor. Whereas Kerala is the least poor state in the country, Bihar's 51.88% population (highest in the country) is malnourished.

According to the data of the National Family Health Survey-4 (2015-16) of the report, 39.86% of the population of Bihar was away from access to electricity, while according to the provisional data of the National Family Health Survey-5 (2019-20), only 3.7% of the population is out of reach of electricity, which shows the remarkable progress of Bihar in the field of electricity. Bihar has got a score of 0.265 in this multidimensional Index, out of which the MPI score of rural areas is 0.286 and the MPI score of the urban areas is 0.117, which indicates that the rural areas of Bihar have more poverty.

There are several reasons for the high poverty rate in Bihar. One of the major factors is the low level of economic development in the state. The lack of industrialization and a strong service sector means that there are limited employment opportunities for the large population. Additionally, the state has poor infrastructure, which makes it difficult for businesses to thrive. The poor state of infrastructure also means that access to basic services like healthcare and education is limited.

Another factor that contributes to poverty in Bihar is the low level of social development. The state has a high illiteracy rate, with many people unable to read or write. This lack of education is a significant barrier to social mobility and economic advancement. Additionally, Bihar has a high infant mortality rate, and access to healthcare is limited, particularly in rural areas. Literacy rate in Bihar is 61.80% as per the latest population census. Of that, male literacy stands at 71.20% while female literacy is at 51.50%.

The agricultural sector is the largest employer in Bihar, and many people rely on it for their livelihoods. However, agricultural productivity in the state is low, and farmers often face challenges like droughts and floods. This results in low yields and low incomes, which perpetuate poverty.

To address the issue of poverty in Bihar, the government needs to focus on improving economic and social development. This could involve measures like investing in infrastructure, promoting industrialization, and improving access to education and healthcare. Additionally, the government could provide targeted support to farmers, such as subsidies for fertilizers and improved irrigation systems.

Overall, poverty in Bihar is a complex issue that requires a multifaceted approach to address. While progress has been made in recent years, much more needs to be done to improve the lives of the people living in this state.

One of the biggest challenges in tackling poverty in Bihar is the lack of political will to address the issue. Corruption and inefficiency in the government are major obstacles to development in the state. Many resources that are allocated for poverty reduction are lost due to corruption and mismanagement. Therefore, it is important to increase transparency and accountability in government to ensure that resources are used effectively.

Another issue is the social inequality that exists in Bihar. The state has a large population of marginalized communities, such as Dalits, Adivasis, and Muslims, who are often excluded from mainstream development programs. These communities face discrimination and are often denied access to basic services like healthcare and education. Therefore, any efforts to reduce poverty in Bihar must address these inequalities and ensure that all sections of society have equal access to opportunities.

The COVID-19 pandemic has exacerbated poverty in Bihar, as it has in many other parts of the world. The pandemic has had a devastating impact on the state's economy, with many people losing their jobs or livelihoods. The government needs to focus on providing support to vulnerable communities and ensuring that they have access to essential services during the pandemic.

In conclusion, poverty in Bihar is a complex issue that requires a long-term, sustainable approach to address. While there is no single solution to the problem, improving economic and social development, increasing transparency and accountability in government, addressing social inequality, and providing support to vulnerable communities are all important steps towards reducing poverty in the state. With concerted effort and political will, it is possible to improve the lives of the millions of people living in poverty in Bihar.

2. Low Industrialisation in Bihar

Bihar, one of the most populous states in India, has historically had low levels of industrialization. Despite being home to a large population, the state has not been able to generate significant economic growth through industrialization. This lack of industrialization has contributed to the state's overall underdevelopment and high poverty levels.

Compared to the national average of 20.1%, Bihar's industrial sector accounts for just 3.2% of the state's net domestic product in terms of income. Food processing, IT & electronics and textiles & leather are the state's three highest-priority industries. Some of the rapidly expanding sectors in the state that are bringing in investment prospects in Bihar are food processing, dairy, sugar, manufacturing and healthcare.

Most of the industries are based on agriculture. The Dutch founded the first sugar-producing enterprise in 1840. The Bihar State Milk Cooperative Federation (CONFED) was founded in 1983. Silk industry growth has enormous potential in the Bhagalpur region. Bihar is also home to the tea industry. The Kishanganj district in Bihar is where the majority of the tea industry is located. The Purnia district's Maranga is being transformed into Jute Park. Along with other industries, the leather industry is also located in Bihar. Muzaffarpur and Mokama are the main centres for the leather industry. The majority of the raw materials travel to Kolkata, Kanpur, and Chennai as a result of the limited number of operating industries.

- **Barauni Refinery:**
  - It is owned by Indian Oil Corporation.
  - It is located in Begusarai.
  - It gets its oil from the Assamese oilfield of Numaligarh.
- **Bihar Industrial Area Development Authority (BIADA):**
  - It was established under the BIAD Act of 1974 to support Bihar's industrialization.
  - With locations in Patna, Darbhanga, Muzaffarpur and Bhagalpur, it has 4 regional offices.
- **Bharat Wagon and Engineering Company Limited:**
  - The PSU is situated in Mokama. It manufactures rail wagons.

There are several reasons why industrialization in Bihar has been slow. One of the main reasons is the lack of infrastructure. The state has poor road and rail connectivity, which makes it difficult for businesses to transport goods and access markets. Additionally, the state has a limited power supply, which makes it difficult for industries to operate efficiently. The lack of infrastructure also makes it difficult to attract foreign investment, which is crucial for industrial development.

Another factor is the lack of skilled labour. Bihar has a high population, but the education system is weak, and many people lack the skills necessary to work in modern industries. This means that businesses have to invest in training, which adds to their costs. Additionally, the lack of skilled labour makes it difficult for industries to adopt modern technology and processes.

The political and regulatory environment in Bihar is also not conducive to industrialization. Corruption and red tape are major issues, and it can take a long time for businesses to obtain permits and approvals. The state also has a poor law and order situation, which makes it difficult for businesses to operate safely.

To address the issue of low industrialization in Bihar, the state government needs to take several steps. One of the most important is to invest in infrastructure. The state needs to improve road and rail connectivity, as well as increase the power supply. This will make it easier for businesses to operate and attract investment.

The government should also focus on improving the education system and skilling the workforce. This will provide a pool of skilled labour for businesses to draw on and make it easier for industries to adopt modern technology and processes.

The regulatory environment needs to be streamlined and made more transparent. The government should also take steps to address corruption and improve the law and order situation in the state. This will make it easier for businesses to operate and create a favourable environment for investment.

Another important factor that has contributed to low industrialization in Bihar is the lack of access to finance. The state has a limited banking system, and many businesses, especially small and medium-sized enterprises, struggle to access credit. This makes it difficult for them to invest in equipment, expand operations, and improve productivity. The government needs to work with financial institutions to develop products and services that cater to the needs of small businesses and entrepreneurs.

In addition to addressing the factors that have hindered industrialization, the state government can also promote specific industries that have the potential to thrive in Bihar. The state is rich in natural resources, including agriculture and mineral deposits. The government can work to promote agro-based industries, such as food processing and packaging, which can add value to the state's agricultural output. Additionally, the state has significant reserves of coal, iron ore, and other minerals that can support the development of industries such as steel, cement, and chemicals.

The state government can also leverage its strategic location to promote trade and commerce. Bihar is situated at the crossroads of several major transportation routes, including the Grand Trunk Road and National Highway 19. The state can take advantage of its proximity to major markets in India and neighbouring countries like Nepal and Bangladesh to promote trade and commerce. The government can establish industrial parks and special economic zones that offer tax incentives and other benefits to attract investment.

In conclusion, low industrialization in Bihar has been a significant barrier to the state's economic development. To address this issue, the government needs to focus on improving infrastructure, skilling the workforce, creating a favourable regulatory environment, and promoting specific industries. With the right policies and investments, it is possible to promote industrialization in Bihar and generate economic growth that will benefit the state's population.

3. Agricultural Status of Bihar

Agriculture is the backbone of Bihar's economy, with the majority of the state's population dependent on the sector for their livelihood. Bihar has been divided into four primary agro-climatic zones based on soil characteristics, rainfall, temperature, and topography. Foodgrains like rice, paddy, wheat, jute, maize and oil seeds are the primary crops. The state grows a variety of vegetables, including cauliflower, cabbage, tomatoes, radishes, carrots and beets. Some of the non-cereal crops farmed include sugarcane, potatoes and barley. Gopalganj and Madhepura have the highest net sown area. Modern agricultural techniques and contract farming methods are being accepted by farmers, which is a positive development for the agriculture sector. In Bihar, there are three distinct crop seasons: Kharif, Rabi and Zaid. Despite this, the agricultural sector in Bihar faces several challenges, including low productivity, poor infrastructure, and limited access to finance.

Bihar is known as the "rice bowl of India" and is one of the largest producers of rice in the country. The state also produces significant quantities of wheat, maize, and other crops. However, agricultural productivity in Bihar is low compared to other states in India. The state's soil is highly fertile, but farmers face several challenges, including poor irrigation facilities, a lack of quality seeds, and limited access to modern farming techniques and technologies.

One of the key challenges facing farmers in Bihar is access to credit. Many farmers lack access to formal banking services, which makes it difficult for them to obtain loans for inputs such as seeds, fertilizers, and equipment. This limits their ability to invest in their farms and improve productivity. The state government has taken several steps to address this issue, including setting up a state-level agriculture credit plan and partnering with financial institutions to provide loans to farmers.

Another challenge is the lack of infrastructure in rural areas. Poor roads and transportation systems make it difficult for farmers to transport their produce to markets. This results in higher costs and lower profits for farmers. The government has been working to improve infrastructure in the state, including building new roads and bridges and setting up market yards and godowns for storage.

The state government has also launched several schemes to promote agriculture and improve the livelihoods of farmers. The Bihar Agriculture Roadmap, launched in 2007, is a comprehensive plan to transform agriculture in the state. The plan focuses on improving productivity through the use of modern technology and best practices, increasing access to credit, and improving infrastructure. The government has also launched the Mukhyamantri Kisan Aaye Badhotri Yojana, which aims to double farmers' incomes by 2022.

Despite the challenges, agriculture in Bihar has the potential to grow and contribute to the state's overall development. The state has a large population engaged in farming, and there is significant potential for the adoption of modern technology and best practices. The government needs to continue investing in infrastructure, promoting access to credit, and supporting farmers in adopting modern farming techniques.

There are several initiative taken for ansuring improvement in agriculture and allied sector:

The following canals are used to irrigate several regions of Bihar:

- **Kosi Canal:**
  - Two canals taken out from Hanuman Nagar reservoir.
  - Eastern Kosi Canal – irrigates Purnia, Madhepura and Saharsa.
  - Western Kosi Canal – irrigates Darbhanga district.
- **Sone Canal:**
  - Eastern Sone Canal taken out from Barun – irrigates Patna, Jahanabad, Aurangabad and Gaya.
  - Western Sone Canal has been taken out from Tishri – irrigating Ara, Buxar and Rohtas.
- **Kamla Canal:**
  - It is taken out from the Kamla River in Darbhanga.
  - It irrigates mainly the Madhubani district.
- **Triveni Canal:**
  - It is taken out from Gandak river at Triveni.
  - It irrigates the West Champaran district.
- **Gandak Canal:**
  - Two Canals taken out from the dam at Valmiki Nagar.
  - Saran Canal – irrigates Saran, Gopalganj and Siwan.
  - Tirhut Canal – irrigates Muzaffarpur, Vaishali and East Champaran.

Bihar is richly endowed with rainfall, healthy soil, and readily available groundwater, but the state failed to exploit its great agricultural potential, which contributed to rural poverty, poor nutrition, and labour migration within the state. Agriculture in Bihar is prone to natural calamities, especially floods in north Bihar and drought in south Bihar. Utilising suitable crop technology and providing crop insurance to all farmers can reduce the risk of natural disasters.

In conclusion, agriculture is the backbone of Bihar's economy, and the state has significant potential to improve productivity and contribute to the state's overall development. The state government needs to focus on improving infrastructure, promoting access to credit, and supporting farmers in adopting modern farming techniques. With the right policies and investments, Bihar's agricultural sector can grow and generate economic growth and prosperity for the state's population.

Another challenge facing the agricultural sector in Bihar is the impact of climate change. Bihar is prone to floods, droughts, and other extreme weather events, which can have a devastating impact on crops and farmers' livelihoods. The state government has taken steps to address this issue by investing in flood control infrastructure, promoting the use of climate-resistant crop varieties, and encouraging the adoption of sustainable agricultural practices.

Bihar also has a significant potential for agro-based industries. The state produces a large quantity of agricultural products, including fruits, vegetables, and dairy products, which can be processed and value-added to generate higher incomes for farmers. The government needs to promote the establishment of food processing and packaging industries in the state to create employment opportunities and generate additional revenue.

Another challenge facing the agricultural sector in Bihar is the lack of mechanization. Farming in the state is still largely manual, with farmers relying on traditional methods and techniques. The government needs to promote the adoption of modern farming technologies, such as farm machinery and equipment, to increase productivity and efficiency. This would require providing farmers with access to credit and training to enable them to invest in and use modern equipment.

In conclusion, agriculture remains an important sector in Bihar's economy, and the state has the potential to significantly increase productivity and improve farmers' livelihoods. The state government needs to focus on improving infrastructure, providing access to credit, promoting modern farming techniques, and value-adding to agricultural products. With the right policies and investments, Bihar's agricultural sector can become a major contributor to the state's economic development.

4. Flood in Bihar

Bihar is one of the most flood-prone states in India with 76% of population in the North Bihar living under the recurring threat of flood devastation. Bihar makes up 16.5% of India's flood affected area and 22.1% of India's flood affected population. About 73.06% of Bihar's geographical area, i.e. 68,800 square kilometres (26,600 sq mi) out of 94,160 square kilometres (36,360 sq mi), is flood affected. On an annual basis, they destroy thousands of human lives apart from livestock and assets worth millions. Every year, the state faces severe floods that cause extensive damage to infrastructure, crops, and homes. Floods in Bihar are caused by several factors, including heavy monsoon rains, overflowing rivers, and inadequate drainage systems.

The impact of floods in Bihar is devastating, with thousands of people losing their homes and livelihoods. Floods also cause significant damage to infrastructure, including roads, bridges, and buildings. The state government has taken several measures to mitigate the impact of floods, but more needs to be done to address the root causes of the problem. Out of 38 districts, 28 districts get flooded (of which 15 districts are worst affected) causing huge loss of property, lives, farmlands and infrastructure. During the 2008 Kosi floods, over 350,000 acres of paddy, 18,000 acres of maize and 240,000 acres of other crops were adversely affected, impacting close to 500,000 farmers.

One of the main causes of floods in Bihar is the lack of adequate drainage systems. The state has a network of rivers and canals, but many of them are poorly maintained and silted. This reduces their capacity to carry water during heavy rains, leading to flooding in low-lying areas. The government needs to invest in improving drainage systems and dredging rivers and canals to ensure they can carry water effectively.

Another factor contributing to floods in Bihar is deforestation. The state has seen a decline in forest cover over the years, which has resulted in soil erosion and reduced the ability of the land to absorb water. This increases the risk of floods and landslides. The government needs to take steps to promote afforestation and reforestation to improve soil health and reduce the risk of floods.

Climate change is also exacerbating the problem of floods in Bihar. The state is experiencing more frequent and severe rainfall events, which are causing flash floods and landslides. The government needs to take steps to adapt to the changing climate by investing in flood warning systems, building more resilient infrastructure, and promoting sustainable land use practices.

The impact of floods in Bihar is not just limited to infrastructure damage and loss of livelihoods. Floods can also lead to the spread of water-borne diseases and increase the risk of epidemics. The lack of clean drinking water and sanitation facilities during floods creates a breeding ground for diseases such as cholera, typhoid, and malaria. The government needs to prioritize the provision of clean water and sanitation facilities during floods to prevent the spread of diseases.

Floods also disproportionately affect the most vulnerable sections of society, including women, children, and the elderly. Women and children are often the most affected as they are responsible for household chores such as collecting water, cooking, and cleaning. During floods, they are forced to travel long distances to collect water and food, which can put them at risk of abuse and exploitation. The government needs to take steps to protect the rights of vulnerable groups during floods and provide them with access to basic services such as healthcare and education.

The impact of floods in Bihar can also be felt beyond the state's borders. The floods often cause damage to infrastructure such as roads and bridges, disrupting trade and transport links with neighboring states. This can have a cascading effect on the economy and lead to a reduction in economic activity. The government needs to prioritize investments in infrastructure and promote regional cooperation to mitigate the impact of floods on the wider economy.

In conclusion, floods are a major problem in Bihar that requires urgent attention from the government. The government needs to take a comprehensive approach to address the root causes of floods and invest in improving infrastructure, promoting afforestation, and adapting to the impacts of climate change. By doing so, the government can reduce the impact of floods on people's lives and ensure that the state can continue to grow and prosper in a sustainable way.

5. Water Management in Bihar

Water management is a critical issue in Bihar, a state that is predominantly agricultural and heavily dependent on water resources. The state has several rivers and an extensive network of canals, but water scarcity is a major issue in many parts of the state, particularly during the dry season. Effective water management is therefore essential to ensure sustainable development and the well-being of the people of Bihar.

Water resources, an effective instrument of poverty alleviation which plays a key role in the economic development of the state, is not getting due attention of the planners and policymakers in Bihar. There is an uneven distribution of surface water and groundwater resources in the state, leading to an acute shortage of potable water in several regions. The state water policy is yet to be made effective for ensuring optimum utilisation of water resources, point out experts.

One of the key challenges in water management in Bihar is the inadequate infrastructure for water storage and distribution. Many parts of the state do not have adequate storage facilities such as dams and reservoirs, leading to wastage of water during the monsoon season and water scarcity during the dry season. The government needs to invest in building more storage facilities to ensure that water is available throughout the year.

Another challenge in water management in Bihar is the inefficient use of water in agriculture. The state is heavily dependent on agriculture, and inefficient irrigation practices lead to water wastage and reduced productivity. The government needs to promote the use of modern irrigation techniques such as drip irrigation and sprinkler irrigation to improve water use efficiency.

Water pollution is also a major issue in Bihar, with many rivers and water bodies contaminated by industrial effluents and sewage. This poses a threat to public health and can lead to the spread of water-borne diseases. The government needs to enforce stricter regulations to control pollution and promote the use of eco-friendly technologies.

Groundwater depletion is another issue in water management in Bihar. Many parts of the state rely on groundwater for irrigation and drinking water, but over-extraction of groundwater has led to a decline in the water table. The government needs to promote sustainable groundwater management practices such as rainwater harvesting, recharging of groundwater, and regulation of groundwater use.

The government of Bihar has taken several initiatives to improve water management in the state. The state government has launched several programs such as the Mukhyamantri Jal Jeevan Hariyali Yojana and the Jal Jivan Hariyali Mission to promote water conservation and management. The Mukhyamantri Jal Jeevan Hariyali Yojana aims to provide financial assistance to farmers for the construction of rainwater harvesting structures, while the Jal Jivan Hariyali Mission focuses on rejuvenating water bodies and promoting water conservation.

The government has also taken steps to promote the use of renewable energy in water management. Solar-powered pumps and sprinklers have been introduced to reduce the dependence on grid electricity for irrigation. This has not only reduced the carbon footprint of agriculture but has also made it more affordable and accessible to farmers.

In addition, the state government has set up the Bihar State Water and Sanitation Mission to ensure effective implementation of water and sanitation programs. The mission aims to provide safe drinking water and sanitation facilities to all households in the state by 2030.

Assured irrigation from the groundwater source in Bihar state can help in a long way in food security. With a decadal growth rate in population of approximately 21%, the per capita availability of renewable fresh groundwater stands at approximately 251 m^3 per year in the state of Bihar. The stage of groundwater development in most of the blocks in the state remains below 50%. It can safely be increased up to 90%, provided a regular monitoring of the renewable groundwater resource as well as the trend of water level is done. Artificial groundwater recharge should be adopted in the areas underlain by hard rocks and marginal alluvial areas in the SGP augment the groundwater resource availability.

The role of community participation in water management cannot be overstated. The government has recognized this and has promoted the formation of water user groups to manage water resources at the local level. These groups are responsible for the management and maintenance of water supply systems and for promoting water conservation practices at the community level.

In conclusion, water management is a critical issue in Bihar that requires the collective efforts of the government, civil society, and the community. The government needs to continue its efforts to improve infrastructure, promote modern irrigation techniques, control pollution, and promote sustainable groundwater management practices. With the right policies and programs, Bihar can ensure that its water resources are used sustainably and that its people can continue to thrive in a healthy and prosperous environment.

6. Economy of Bihar during the Covid–19 Pandemic

The entire world saw an unprecedented crisis during the entire year of 2020–21 and at least in the first half of 2021–22 due to Covid–19 pandemic. This pandemic had a negative impact on the health as well as economic activities of people in almost all the countries. The pandemic has also laid grave impact on India due to loss of life and economic recession. Almost all the sectors of economy has been affected because both domestic demand as well as exports had come down. During this period a lot of ups and downs in economic activities were witnessed and the process to overcome this situation could be started only in the later half of 2021–22.

In fact, this observation in the economy is also good for the economy of Bihar. If we leave the duration of pandemic aside, then the economy of Bihar has been performing good for the remaining period and this positive trend had started around a decade ago. This strong process of growth along with different welfare schemes launched by the government of Bihar has built a new environment of hope and self-confidence in the state. Due to its commendable development oriented growth, Bihar has been able to gradually reduce the difference present in the per capita income of the whole country. As far as the welfare programs are concerned, there are many such programs that are implemented but the main focus has been on '*Saat Nishchay*–I and II'. The sectors that were included in *Saat Nishchay*–I were Welfare of Youth, women employment, supply of electricity to all households, clean drinking water, road communication, toilet facilities and higher technical education. It should be noted that implementation of *Saat Nishchay*–I ended in year 2020. It was replaced by *Saat Nishchay*–II that included welfare of youth, women empowerment, irrigation facilities to all agricultural land, clean villages, clean cities, accessible transport communication and health care facility for all.

Management of Covid–19 pandemic was probably the most challenging agenda for the state government during the recent years. In this context it is worth mentioning that the state government was able to face this challenge in the most efficient manner with its quadrilateral activity – regular checking, investigation, finding out the contact point, keeping it in check, management of covid care centres, treatment of the infected in notified covid hospitals, appointment of extra medical staffs for covid hospitals, helpline services through call centres and vaccinations.

Impact on the Economy of Bihar

There was a greater impact during the second wave of Covid–19 because localised lockdowns were implemented in various states. According to data released by Central Statistical Organisation (CSO) there was a reduction of 7.25 percent in the National

Economic Production measured in terms of Gross Domestic Product (GDP) in year 2020–21. As compared to this negative trend, the Gross State Domestic Product (GSDP) of Bihar during the same period of 2020–21 recorded a growth of 2.5 percent. This commendable performance by the economy of Bihar was seen during the year 2019–20 as well when the state recorded a growth rate of 7.41 percent as compared to national growth rate of 4.4 percent. By comparing the mean of the growth-related indices of the state and the country we come to know that both have recorded almost same growth rate.

Comparison of Per Capita Net State Domestic Product of states

The data of Per Capita Net State Domestic Product of states at the constant prices of 2011–12 are regularly released by the Central Statistical Organization (CSO). The Per Capita Net State Domestic Product of Bihar increased by 1.3 percent from ₹ 30,621 in 2019–20 to ₹ 31,017 in year 2020–21. It should be noted that Bihar and Tamil Nadu recorded an increase in Per Capita Net State Domestic Product in year 2020–21. All the other states witnessed a reduction. In year 2020–21 the Per Capita Net State Domestic Product of Bihar was ₹ 31,017 while the national average was ₹ 86,659.

Sector Wise Growth Rates

In order to decide on the performance of any economy it is important to analyse not only its comprehensive growth but sectoral growth rates as well. In Bihar the average growth rates of the three main sectors were as follows: primary sector – 2.3 percent, for secondary sector 6.4 percent and for tertiary sector it was 6.7 percent. Whereas for India the rates for primary sector was 3.2 percent, for secondary sector 4.0 percent and for tertiary sector it was 6.2 percent. These sectoral growth rates mark the prominent features of comprehensive growth process of economy of Bihar.

Huge Regional Disparity

In addition to huge economic adversity, huge regional (among the districts) disparity is also a mark of economy of Bihar. Per Capita Gross Domestic Product across the districts is a prime indicator of this disparity. In year 2019–20 highest Per Capita Gross District Domestic Product of ₹ 1.31 lakh was recorded in Patna and the lowest of 0.19 lakh in Sheohar. Per Capita small savings across various districts is another indicator of internal disparity in economic growth, the two districts with maximum prosperity and maximum poverty can be identified in this context as well. The most prosperous districts are Patna and Saran and the two most poor districts are Araria and West Champaran.

After considering the rankings of various indicators as a whole, the districts of Bihar that are relatively more developed are Patna, Begusarai, Muzaffarpur and Shekhpura. Whereas on the other hand Araria, Sheohar, Banka, Kishanganj and West Champaran are the most backward districts.

Agriculture and Allied Sectors

In order to achieve the stable growth target of year 2030 the growth of agriculture and its allied sectors is very important for Bihar. During the past five years (2016–17 to 2020–21), the primary sector which includes crops, livestock, forestry and timber production, fishing and hydroponics have increased with a rate of 2.1 percent. Total crop area in year 2019–20 was 72.97 hectares and the total crop density was 144 percent. Food grain production in year 2018–19 was 16.31 lakh tonne which increased at a rate of 4.9 percent and became 17.95 lakh tonne in year 2020–21. The total expenditure on irrigation in year 2019–20 was ₹ 2,114.87 crore. Irrigation water to every field (har khet tak sinchai ka pani) is an ambitious initiative of the state government under *Saat Nishchay*–II. It aims to provide assured irrigation to every agriculture land in the state.

During the past five years (2016–17 to 2020–21) the Gross State Value Added (GSVA) of the state in agriculture and its allied sectors was highest with 9.3 percent whereas for livestock it was 6.6 percent. It is quite clear that the reduction in share of crop sector in gross state value added was compensated by the increase in livestock and pisciculture during the recent years. Keep in mind that after the partition of state in year 2000 the mineral reserves of state had gone to Jharkhand, development of agriculture and its allied sectors is very important for the development of the state. Its vital front-end and back-end links contribute immensely in the rise of growth rate of the entire economy, create employment opportunities and reduce poverty. The contribution of crop sector in gross state domestic product for agriculture sector was the highest at 48.7 percent in year 2020–21. The livestock sector has also gained importance and it contributed for 34 percent in the agriculture sector in gross domestic state product.

Land Resources

Bihar is a state located in the eastern part of India with no seashores that shares its boundary with West Bengal in the east, Uttar Pradesh in the west, Nepal in the north and Jharkhand in south. On the basis of rainfall, temperature, soil and region the state is divided into three climate zones – north western alluvial plains, north eastern alluvial plains and alluvial plains of southern Bihar. The state has to face drought and flood frequently which impacts the agriculture. In addition to this almost 90 percent of cultivable land is either small or marginal in nature which causes a concern in terms of profitability and adoption of modern techniques in agriculture. As a result there is immense pressure of population on agriculture in the state.

Land Use Pattern

There has been no recognizable change in the land use pattern of the state during the past few years (2017–20). The share of total geographical area of Bihar in the total geographical area of the state is 94 lakh hectares. The contribution of total forest area in the total area of the state is constant at 6.6 percent. While, the total barren and uncultivable land is 4.6 percent, gardens is 2.7 percent and cultivable barren land is 0.5 percent and permanent grazing field is 0.2 percent which had been stable for three years (2017–20). Net sowing area was 50.77 lakh hectares and total crop area was 72.97 lakh hectare in year 2019–20 which makes crop density 1.44. the total uncultivable land in year 2017–18 was 41.18 lakh hectare which increased marginally to 42.82 lakh hectare in year 2019–20 which is 45.8 lakh percent of the total area. Land is a sparse resource and growing population is exerting more pressure on it through agriculture and other subsidiary activities which is manifested in the land productivity pattern of the state.

Crop Production and Productivity Pattern

The total food grain production of Bihar in year 2018–19 was 16.31 lakh ton which increased at an annual rate of 4.91 percent and became 17.95 lakh ton in year 2020–21. Whereas, increasing at an annual rate of 5.27 percent the grain production jumped from 15.86 lakh ton in 2018–19 to 17.57 lakh ton in 2020–21. In addition to this the productivity of grains also increased from 2,636 kg per hectare in year 2018–19 to 2961 kg per hectare in year 2020–21. The credit for this can be mainly attributed to technical reforms, assured irrigation, supply of certified seeds and provision of extension services. Among the major crops, production of rice, maize and wheat witnessed a remarkable growth. During the past three years (2018–19 to 2020–21) the productivity growth rate for rice was 9.6 percent, for maize 5.0 percent and for wheat it was 1.3 percent. The credit for increase in production of rice and maize can be given to increasing productivity and not to the increase in cultivation area. The production of rice and maize in year 2020–21 was 2,447 kg per hectare and 5,229 kg per hectare respectively.

This rising trend in productivity carried on to the production of coarse grains as well which recorded a growth rate of 4.3 percent during the past three years and the production reached to 3.55 lakh ton in year 2020–21. Sorghum and millets are the chief coarse grain crops of Bihar whose growth rate during the past three years was 31.1 percent and 16.4 percent respectively. But the decreasing trend in production of all the pulses is an area of concern. Fortunately, kharif pulse crops like udad, moong and ghagra recorded an increase in production. The productivity of kharif pulse crops increased from 793 kg per hectare in 2018–29 to 896 kg per hectare in 2020–21 which shows a growth rate of 6.3 percent.

Industrial Sector

For industrial development in Bihar the state government is trying to build favourable environment for the establishment of new infrastructure units in the state through various strategical measures. Bihar Industrial investment encouragement policy 2016 has served as the foundation of the industrial development of the state.

During the recent years Bihar State Milk Co-Operative Federation Ltd. (COMFED) has expanded throughout barring the duration of the pandemic. By including ethyl alcohol and production of electricity as a sub product of sugar, the sugar industry has also expanded its production base. In order to encourage the production of ethanol and to provide promotional amount the state government has formulated the Ethanol Production Promotional Policy, 2021. In recent years both agricultural sector as well as agriculture based sectors have witnessed a positive trend in their industrial expanse. During the crisis of Covid–19 pandemic, the state government had also formulated the Oxygen Production Promotion Policy 2021 in order to cater to the growing demand of oxygen for medical purposes. The state government has also adopted Mukhyamantri scheduled castes/Scheduled Tribes/extremely/backward Classes Entrepreneurship Development Scheme to promote entrepreneurship among the disadvantaged social groups in the state. In the case of minerals, the collection of the state government has increased significantly. The arrival of tourists in the state has come down drastically during the pandemic. However, the state government has utilized this period to develop additional amenities and facilities in many tourist places of the state.

In recent years, the state government has been making tireless efforts for industrialization in Bihar. In this direction, the policy makers have adopted several policies to help industries flourish. The state government has set up several dedicated institutions to remove bottlenecks and promote industries. It is expected that through this process, the state's position will change from a supplier of raw materials to other parts of the country for industrialization, to the supplier of finished goods inside and outside the country.

The annual growth rate of the secondary sector of Bihar's economy has been witnessing ups and downs over the years. Final estimates of the growth rate for the year 2018–19 are available. The major sectors driving the growth were mining and quarrying, electricity, gas, water supply and other utility services (EGWS) and construction. What is more important is that, the annual growth rates of sectors such as mining, quarrying, manufacturing, electricity, gas, water supply and other utility services and construction have also fluctuated over the years. In order to eliminate uncertainty and make these industries significant contributors to the overall economic development of the State, the State Government has taken several policy measures relating to certain industries. It can be seen from the data that between the year 2015–16 to the year 2019–20, the contribution of the industrial sector in the gross state value addition has decreased in both Bihar and India. Although the decline in Bihar is very small (20.3 percent to 20.1 percent), but in the case of India, this decline has been quite significant (31.6 percent to 29.6 percent).

Conclusion

From the above exegesis, it becomes quite clear that if we leave aside the duration of corona pandemic then the economy of Bihar is showcasing a developing tendency.

Although, due to Covid–19 pandemic, not only the economy of India was affected but the economy of Bihar was also hit. Like other states, the pandemic held an impact on every sector of economy in Bihar as well. But even during the corona pandemic, many sectors of economy of Bihar also witnessed a positive trend. By looking at this positive trend it can be concluded that in coming years the economy of Bihar will be able to put aside the impact of corona and move forward on the path of growth and development.

7. Disaster Management in Bihar

One of the poorest states of India, Bihar is often face to face with natural calamities like floods, droughts, earthquakes and cyclones. Considering the state's vulnerability to disasters, Disaster management is a serious issue in Bihar which have badly affected human lives and economy. The Bihar State Disaster Management Authority (BSDMA) is the agency responsible for managing disasters and mitigating their impact on the people and economy of the state. The state has seen several major disasters in the past, including the Kosi floods of 2008 and the Bihar floods of 2020. Therefore, disaster management in Bihar has been a top priority for the state government and various measures are being taken to ensure preparedness, mitigation and response to natural disasters.

Major Calamities

Flood: There are many reasons for flood in Bihar – huge water flow in rivers flowing from Himalaya to north Bihar. Due to the deposition of silt in the rivers, the depth of the basin is reduced, the course of the rivers in Bihar is changed, even the small rivers of the plains of North Bihar get flooded due to heavy rains and present the scene of flood. Rainfall is mainly focused in three months of monsoon during which the water flow in rivers rises up to 50 percent. Out of the total land area of 94,160 sq km of Bihar 73 percent of the total area is flood prone. 28 districts of Bihar fall under the flood prone zone.

Earthquake: Bihar is situated on the boundary of tectonic plate which is included in the Himalayan tectonic plates along the Nepal border. Main regions of the state have been classified as Earthquake prone zone–IV and V by the Risk Atlas of India, which means high intensity and highly sensitive to earthquakes. 15.2 percent of total area of Bihar have been classified as zone v where as 63.7 percent area is classified as zone–IV.

Drought: Although the climate and agricultural land of Bihar is favourable for production of many crops but the agriculture in the state is dependent upon monsoon and rainfall distribution. The distribution of monsoon is vey different among various regions of the state. Due to abnormal presence of rainfall most of the parts including the part of north Bihar is affected by flood whereas the southern and south wester part experiences extreme drought condition quite often.

Other calamities: In addition to the above mentioned calamities, the state is also affected by cold and hot winds, cyclones (high speed winds) etc.

Quick and Permanent Measures for Disaster Management

To help the people to bring back their normal life disrupted due to natural calamity i.e. until the people are fully provided with the facility of living space and the damage caused by the disaster is not compensated, till then it will be the responsibility of the Bihar State Disaster Management Authority to provide all kinds of help to those people. In such situation, some temporary relief is provided by the government which is as follows:

Temporary Accommodations or Tents: At the time of disaster like flood, drought, temporary accommodation or tents are first arranged by the teams formed by the Bihar State Disaster Management Authority, so that arrangements can be made for the living of the people.

Health Camps: All the responsibility to provide people with health care services due to a disaster also lies with this committee. Medicines for the old people or medicines for the people affected by flood, medicines for pregnant women, medicines for children and all the medical kits that could be used during any unforeseen health related issues is available in the health camps where after a thorough check-up, people are given medicines if needed.

Food Arrangements: When people are fighting natural calamities then the job of supply of food material to them is also done by a dedicated team. Food items and food packets are distributed to the disaster affected people and quick arrangements are made for food and water as per the requirement.

At the time of disaster, pregnant women and children below 6 years are specially given nutritional feeding, that is, they are given food and nutrition as per their requirement so that they can get well soon.

Other items: Other items such as tarpaulin sheets, halogen tablets, bleaching powder and other equipment or items are arranged for the affected area to help the people who are distraught and distressed due to natural calamity.

In addition to all the above mentioned temporary measures, there are many functions of the Disaster Management Department which is expected to be completed before the disaster or for the management of the disaster.

Preparedness is the key to effective disaster management and the Government of Bihar has taken several steps in this direction. The state has a State Disaster Management Authority (SDMA) which oversees the activities in disaster management in the state. The SDMA is responsible for coordinating with various departments and agencies to develop and implement disaster management plans. The state has also set up an Emergency Operation Center (SEOC) to provide a centralized platform for disaster response and management.

Apart from SDMC and SEOC, the state government has also set up district level disaster management to ensure effective response at the local level. These authorities are responsible for developing and implementing disaster management plans for their respective districts. They work closely with the various community to identify disaster prone areas and populations and develop evacuation plans.

The Government of Bihar has established the Bihar Institute of Disaster Management (BIDM) to provide training to disaster management professionals to enhance the capacity of its management workforce. The institute runs various courses on disaster management including search and rescue, first-aid and emergency response. It also conducts simulation exercises to test the preparedness of disaster management personnel.

Mitigation is an inherently important aspect of disaster management. One of the mitigation measures taken by the government is the construction of embankments along the rivers to prevent floods. The government has also taken measures to raise the groundwater level, such as the construction of check dams and water harvesting structures. These measures help in mitigating the impact of drought and flood on the agriculture sector, which is an important source of livelihood for the people of Bihar.

Several measures are also being taken by the State Government to strengthen disaster resistant infrastructure. Under this, the use of earthquake resistant construction material has been made mandatory in all government buildings and subsidy has been provided to private builders who use such material. The government has also started a program of retrofitting existing buildings to make them more earthquake resistant.

Response is the last step of disaster management and the Government of Bihar has taken several measures to ensure effective response to natural calamities. It has established a quick reaction force which can be deployed in case of emergency. The state government has also set up relief camps for the people affected by the calamities to provide them food, water and medical aid. The government has also provided financial assistance to those who have suffered losses due to natural calamities.

Thus, disaster management in Bihar is an important issue that needs to be addressed to protect the lives and livelihood of the people of the state. In this direction, several measures are being taken by the state government to enhance preparedness, mitigation and response to natural disasters. BSDMA has made progress in managing disasters and mitigating their impact, however there is still a long way to go in terms of capacity building and infrastructure development. Therefore, to keep the people of Bihar safe from the effects of natural disasters, the state government should continue to invest in disaster management.

8. Women Empowerment in Bihar

Equal participation of women and their development in all development processes is women empowerment. The demand of women for their rights in the economic, social, cultural and political spheres of life comes under women empowerment. For the empowerment of women, many schemes are started from time to time by the Central Government and the State Governments. In this context, many ambitious schemes have also been launched by the Bihar government. During the Eighth Plan (1992-97) for the first time the empowerment of women was recognized and accepted as a distinct strategy. This was taken forward in the Ninth Plan (1997–2002) by introducing the concept of the Women's Component Plan. Through this, it became necessary for the identified ministries to provide information about the flow of funds for women's programs. Later in the Twelfth Plan (2012-17), key indicators were identified to work on gender equality in the planning process through economic, social and cultural empowerment. During the years 2013–14 to 2019–20, the total expenditure for improving the status of women increased 4.5 times and in the year 2020–21, the share of women in the total state budget was 16.0 percent. At the same time, in 2020–21, the development of women in the percentage of gross state domestic product has also been increased to 3.7 percent.

The direct interventions of the state government to deal with gender equality can be summed up in two main parts – the Mukhyamantri Kanya Utthan Yojana to promote the birth of girls for child protection and prevent female feticide, and start of Lakshmi Bai Social Security Pension Scheme, Kanya Vivah Yojana and Nari Shakti Yojana etc for social and economic security schemes. The objective of Mukhyamantri Kanya Utthan Yojana is to promote the birth of girl child and prevent female feticide and gender imbalance. This scheme was launched in 2018. Under this scheme, at the time of birth of a girl child, ₹ 2,000 is transferred to her mother's/father's/guardian's account and after completion of one year and registration of Aadhaar, ₹ 1,000 more is transferred to that bank account. On the other hand, the Mukhyamantri Kanya Vivah Yojana aims to help families with a monthly income of less than ₹ 60,000 at the time of the girl child. Under this programme, girls' education is promoted and child marriage is prohibited. Under this, 5,000 rupees are given to the girl in the bank account through direct benefit transfer. Similarly, through two other schemes, work is done to remove social and economic concerns through financial protection and moral support. In the year 2019–20, among the four flagship schemes the maximum expenditure of 74.3 per cent was spent on Lakshmi Bai Social Security Pension Scheme.

Apart from this, for the economic empowerment of women, 35 percent reservation was provided to them in government services. Also, 50 percent reservation was given to women in Panchayati Raj institutions and municipal bodies. Apart from this, the state government has also established women police stations and reserved 35 percent posts for women in the Bihar Reserve Service.

Social empowerment of women is also necessary. In this direction too, the government has implemented some schemes through which social upliftment of women will be possible. Prominent among these is Jeevika Yojana. Under this, many initiatives have been taken to solve the main problems related to human development including food, health, safety and domestic cleanliness. To address the problem of food security, the concept of Food Security Fund (SAF) has been introduced at the village organization level, while Health Risk Fund (HRF) is another assistance program at the village level to meet health-related credit needs. The Jeevika Yojana has implemented Health Risk Fund in 51,089 villages which helps in meeting the health needs of the poorest sections of the society.

Under the Protection of Women from Domestic Violence Act 2005 and Prohibition of Human Trafficking Act 1986, the scheme of short stay homes has been implemented in all the districts of Bihar for the rehabilitation of socially and economically oppressed women. Various types of training and entrepreneurship development have been arranged to increase the capacity of women oppressed by society or family. Till now 12 out of 38 approved short stay homes are operational and these are being run by Mahila Vikas Nigam.

Under the comprehensive scheme of social, economic and cultural empowerment of women, women and adolescent girls who are victims of domestic violence and human trafficking are also provided free socio-psychological support and legal aid by the Government of Bihar. Efforts like setting up of women helpline, protection homes, short stay homes, foster homes, promotion of inter-caste marriages and capacity building are also going on for women and children who are victims of domestic violence.

Establishment of Defence Home in the state is another component of social empowerment aimed at rehabilitation of women and adolescent girls under the Protection of Domestic Violence Act 2005. In these shelters, women are made self-reliant so that they become empowered and capable of earning a living.

Didi Ki Rasoi is a commendable initiative started by the Bihar government. In this, community managed canteens are being run by the self-help group members themselves in respected hospitals of different districts (Buxar, Sheikhpura, Purnia and Vaishali). Inspired by the success of these canteens, the state government has decided to hand over the canteens of all government hospitals to women under the Jeevika scheme.

To promote cultural empowerment, decorative products like paper lamp, file, folder, laptop bag, saree etc. are being promoted by Jeevika using Madhubani painting and stone art. In October 2018, a company named Shilpgram Mahila Producer Company Limited was also established. The products made by these women are being sold offline (fairs, Khadi malls, wellness malls, B2B, B2C) or online through portals like shop.brips.in, GeM, Amazon, flipkart etc.

Bihar government is trying for the upliftment of women in the field of education as well. Under this, the name of Meena Manch can be taken. It is a group of 20 girls, including 15 upper primary school girls and 5 school dropouts after completing fifth grade. This forum is responsible for enrolling girls and boys in age-appropriate classes in schools, ensuring regular attendance of students, and motivating students to complete elementary education. Along with this, they are also motivated by the platform to take decisions about their progress and for personality development etc.

Women are half of our society, but do women and men have equal status in reality. Like other states, there is still a lot of work to be done in the field of women empowerment in Bihar. In many districts in India, the life of most of the women remains confined to the four walls of the house, Bihar is also included in these districts. About 95 percent of the women here are unemployed. The number of working women in Bihar is very less as compared to other states. However, with changing times, traditions are changing and social and cultural values are also changing. Due to the influence of changing generations in Bihar, new attitudes and new values are also being established, but still there is no significant change in the status of women. The women and child development department of the state is making every possible effort for the upliftment of women and government and non-governmental organizations are also trying for the development of women at their own level. I believe that social media can prove to be a better medium to make people aware about women empowerment. This is because in many criminal cases, the victims got justice through social media.

Apart from this, social media has also encouraged women for self-reliance. Information about news and schemes broadcast in newspapers and on TV has also had a wide impact on women's thoughts. It is hoped that the efforts of the state government for women empowerment will be fruitful and the reforms in the condition of women in Bihar will speed up.

9. Status of Education in Bihar - Challenges and Solutions

In the last few decades, the literacy rate of Bihar has increased to 63.8 percent. But still, it is less than other states of the country. Actually, there is a fundamental difference between literacy and education, which has to be understood. In the era of Make in India, Atmanirbhar Bharat and Digital India, the field of education is constantly being ignored, which is the foundation of all these schemes. The condition of the education system in Bihar is also worrying. In the last few years, the government has been active in promoting higher education institutions and initiatives have been taken to open several engineering and medical colleges and hospitals. The government believes that by increasing the number of colleges, more and more students will get benefited. Development is visible in the field of education, but even after so much development, the basic problems of Bihar's education system have not been solved. In order to bring necessary changes in the current education system prevalent in Bihar, special attention needs to be paid towards elementary education, so that the foundation of children can be strengthened right from the beginning. Annual Status of Education Report (ASER

Report–2022) has recently released the annual educational status report for the year 2022. According to this report, there has been a significant decline in the reading and writing ability of students from class 1 to 8 in rural schools across the country, and this decline is very high in Bihar. According to this report, only 35.6 percent of the state's fifth grade students were able to solve division problems in Maths and about 22.5 percent of students were able to read English sentences. Primary schools are suffering from lack of basic facilities. Even if some facilities are also available that is just for show. Although some people claim that there has been a lot of improvement in the education system in Bihar as compared to earlier. But there is no doubt that most of the children studying in schools do not have the basic skills of reading, writing and calculation, that is, they are not learning the knowledge and skills required for all round development as prescribed in the Right to Education Act. However, while working seriously on all these points, the Bihar government is continuously making efforts to improve the level of mathematics and linguistic proficiency at the primary level and reading and writing at the secondary level in the state.

Flaws in Education System

The flaws in the education system in Bihar are as follows:

Lack of basic facilities: The lack of basic infrastructure in primary schools is keeping the condition of school education weak in the state. Ten percent of the schools do not have pucca buildings. Fifty percent don't even have boundary walls. Close to 10 per cent schools lack separate toilets for boys or girls. In such a situation, children do not go to school at all.

Shortage of teachers: On an average only one teacher is available for 63 students in the state. While the national average rate of availability of teachers is 40, that is, it is mandatory to have one teacher to teach every 40 students.

Question mark on the qualification of teachers: The teachers who have been appointed to give a better future to the children in the school, their own education and knowledge are seen standing in the dock. They don't have the level of information that they can educate students by giving them. Apart from this, even if some teachers are qualified, their absence has been observed. Lack of level knowledge has been seen in the teachers selected by the Bihar Teacher Eligibility Test. In such a situation, the question of flaw in the examination system also arises. Government's efforts to improve the qualification of teachers have not been successful.

Delay in academic support: Children do not even get academic support on time. Till 2017, there was a provision by the government to give free books to the children from class 1 to 8, but half the session used to pass in this too. Now they get money for books, although sometimes even that is not available to the children on time.

Lack of academic monitoring: According to the rule, educational activities in the block should be monitored up to the cluster level, but the whole system runs only for formalities. Officers at every level are busy with teachers' salaries and other works, due to which children's education takes a back seat.

This situation is not of today but has been prevalent for the last several decades. Various reports have also expressed their concern on this issue.

Measures to Improve the Level of Education

Infrastructure Development in Educational Institutions: A lot needs to be done to ensure a child-friendly learning environment where all children benefit from the presence of advanced facilities of water, sanitation and mid-day meals. Education should be such that it basically helps them to acquire the skills of reading, writing and calculation, irrespective of the strata of the society. They should not be discriminated against on any grounds and should participate in the process of reading joyfully without fear. Though significant progress has been made under the provision of school infrastructure through various interventions of Sarva Shiksha Abhiyan and Rashtriya Madhyamik Shiksha Abhiyan, there is still a lot to be done.

Active Child Participation: It should be ensured that every child goes to school and studies. Important changes will have to be promoted by the government by working in the field of education. For this, promoting gender equality, keeping children healthy and safe and ensuring that schools are accessible to all sections of the society and they can easily enroll children are of paramount importance.

Child-Centered Pedagogy: Use innovative strategies such as play and art pedagogy in early language and numeracy learning to improve learning outcomes in children.

Recruitment of teachers: It is very important for a teacher to be qualified for good education. Therefore, caution should be exercised while recruiting teachers. Along with this, the presence of the teacher should be mandatory in all the classes. According to the subject, posting of adequate teachers should be done before the commencement of the session.

Efforts for capacity development of teachers: Revision of activity-based teaching material for primary classes and support for capacity development of teachers on language development. Support for developing remedial programs to improve the teaching arena in upper primary grades, digitization of teaching material and establishment of online teacher feedback system are innovative initiatives that can help teachers by removing disparity in teaching level.

Special attention to language: The main reason for the decline in the quality of education is that both the students and teachers do not have proper command over the language. Language is the medium of communication and the subject can also be explained through language only. If there will be authority over the language only then the students will be able to make a hold on the particular subject.

Making education development-oriented and business-oriented: The present education has to be made development-oriented and business-oriented so that it can help in achieving the constitutional goals of social, economic and political equality. Children can become confident citizens by getting education.

Freedom of government school teachers from non-academic work: For quality improvement in education, teachers should be freed from non-academic work and appropriate resources should be made available so that teachers can make good use of them.

Skill based education: There are two factors to enhance the quality of education – one is to update the curriculum regularly and the other is to focus on skill based education. With the regular updating of the syllabus, the students will be aware of the changes taking place at the country and global level and skill-based education will create new skills in them and the education will be employment-oriented.

Keeping in mind the motto 'Education is the right of every child', many government schemes have also been implemented by the state for the progress of education, which are as follows –

Mukhyamantri Poshaak Yojana
Bihar Shataabdee Mukhyamantri Baalika Poshaak Yojana
Mukhyamantri Kishori Svaasthy Kaaryakram
Mukhyamantri Chhaatravrtti Yojana
Mukhyamantri Baalak / Baalika Saikal Yojana
Mukhyamantri Vidyaarthee Protsaahan Yojana
Mukhyamantri Baalika Protsaahan Yojana
Mukhyamantri Baalika (Intar) Protsaahan Yojanan
Bihar Student credit card Yojana

After observing the status of education in Bihar, it would be appropriate to conclude that in this knowledge-centred world of 21st century, if we lag behind in the field of education, then we will not be able to stay anywhere. In such a situation, there will be no meaning of justice and development. In today's time, every parent stresses on educating the children on their behalf. Therefore, the state government should also pay attention to this. The government should form an inquiry committee to check the qualifications of the teachers so that qualified teachers can be appointed in the schools. The first step in improving the education system is 'appointment of qualified teachers' and attendance of all children in school. It is not very difficult to adopt all these measures, so the government is making efforts in this direction. Keeping in mind the implementation of the new National Education Policy–2020, the state government is laying emphasis on the Mission genius program for the children. This is the reason that the government has increased the education budget for the financial year 2022–23 by ₹ 1,155.94 crore. This time the total education budget is ₹ 37,191.87 crore. While the education budget in the last financial year 2021–22 was ₹ 38,035.93 crore. But still many areas of the state are backward in the field of education, where the shortcomings have to be removed and raised on the level of education.

10. Transport and Communication in Bihar

Bihar, located in the northern part of India, is one of the most populous and important states of the country. The state has a rich cultural and historical heritage and is known for its ancient universities and Buddhist sites. The transport system in Bihar plays an important role in connecting different regions of the state and promoting economic development. In this essay we will discuss the steps taken by the state government to improve the infrastructure and various modes of transport in Bihar.

Roadways

The road network in Bihar is quite extensive, which includes national highways and rural roads. National Highways are maintained by the National Highways Authority of India and they connect Bihar to other states of the country. The major national highways passing through Bihar are NH–2, NH–19, NH–28, NH–31, NH–31C, NH–80 and NH–83. State highways are maintained by public works departments and connect major cities within the state. Village roads connect small villages to the nearest town or city.

Despite having a vast road network, the road condition in Bihar is not good and the state is facing many issues like traffic congestion, poor condition of roads and accidents. The state government has taken several initiatives to improve the road infrastructure in Bihar. The government has started construction of four-lane highways and widening of existing highways to reduce traffic congestion. Bihar State Road Development Corporation (BSRDC) has been set up for the construction and maintenance of state highways. BSRDC is also working on construction of new roads around major cities to reduce traffic congestion.

The state government has also launched a new scheme called Mukhyamantri Gram Sampark Yojana to improve road connectivity in rural areas. Under this scheme, the government is getting roads constructed to connect remote villages to the nearest town or city.

Railway

Bihar has an extensive railway network which is part of the Indian Railways. The railway network connects Bihar to different parts of the country and several major railway stations are located in the state. Major railway stations in Bihar include Patna Junction, Darbhanga Junction, Muzaffarpur Junction and Bhagalpur Junction. The East Central Railway and the North Eastern Railway serve Bihar and the state has a total of 4,481 km of rail lines.

The railway network in Bihar is an important means of transportation of people and goods in the state. Railway lines are used to transport goods from one part of the state to another and also to other states of the country. The railway network is also important to the state's economy. The state government is taking several steps to improve the railway network in Bihar. The government is working on electrification of railway lines, construction of new railway stations and upgradation of existing stations.

Airways

There are many airports in Bihar but only a few are operational. Major airports in Bihar include Lok Nayak Jai Prakash Airport and Gaya International Airport in Gaya. Airports connect Bihar to other parts of the country and the world.

The state government is working on improving the existing airports and building new ones in different parts of the state. The government has started the construction of a new airport at Darbhanga which is expected to be operational soon. Work is also underway on the construction of a new airport at Bihta, which is expected to be operational in the near future.

Waterways

Bihar has a meagre network of waterways which are mainly used for the transportation of goods. The Ganges and its tributaries flow through Bihar and these waterways are used to transport goods from one state to another. The Inland Waterways Authority of India is responsible for the development and maintenance of waterways in Bihar.

To promote inland water transport, the state government is working on the development of waterways in Bihar. To facilitate the movement of goods, new river ports and ghats are being constructed. The government has launched a project to develop the Ganga River Front in Patna which is expected to boost tourism and increase economic activity.

Challenges and Future Prospects

Despite significant progress in transportation infrastructure in Bihar, the state continues to face several challenges. Such as the road network is inadequate and the existing roads are in poor condition, the railway network requires significant investment to improve its capacity and efficiency, airports in Bihar are limited and the state needs to develop new airports and upgrade existing airports. Investment is needed to improve and underutilize waterways in Bihar and significant investment is needed to develop inland water transport.

Several initiatives have been taken by the state government to improve the transport infrastructure in Bihar. The government is working on building new highways, developing new airports and improving the railway network, and is promoting public-private partnerships to garner investment.

Ultimately, the transport system is important for promoting economic growth and development and several initiatives are being taken by the state government to improve the transport infrastructure, but more efforts are needed. The government needs to invest in developing new highways, improving the railway network and adding new airports to improve connectivity within the state and with other parts of the country.

❑❑

LIST OF PROBABLE ESSAY TOPICS

1. North-eastern India. Special attention needed
2. Nuclear power plants in India! Whether India should focus more on them, etc.
3. Attack on Africans in India
4. Farmer suicides
5. PM Modi's agricultural schemes
6. Demonetisation
7. Prohibition on liquor and its effects
8. 100 per cent FDI in e-commerce
9. Freedom of expression versus nationalism
10. Digitisation and Indian democracy
11. Pros and cons of 2017 Union Budget
12. Pollution in India! Environmental crisis
13. India's responsiveness to natural disasters like flooding, etc.
14. Make in India
15. Swachh Bharat Abhiyan
16. Beef politics
17. India against terrorism
18. Energy security in India
19. Syrian crisis
20. Jallikattu protests in Tamil Nadu
21. Intolerance debate in campus
22. Social media versus conventional media
23. India's educational system
24. Relevance of Gandhi today
25. Pros and cons of a cashless economy
26. Relevance of SAARC today
27. Relevance of BRICS
28. Water disputes between Indian states
29. Value education in India and corruption
30. Trial by media
31. Tiger conservation in India
32. Development and Green India
33. Poverty and crime
34. 'I do not know with what weapons World War III will be fought, but World War IV will be fought with sticks and stones.' (Albert Einstein)
35. Inclusion of women in the armed forces. More combat roles for women
36. Superstition in India
37. Is socialism relevant?
38. 'Good fences make good neighbours'. (Robert Frost)

39. Freedom of press in India
40. India's role in the changing global order
41. Poverty and gender equality
42. Beti Bachao
43. 'If you educate a man you educate an individual, but if you educate a woman you educate a family'. (Kwegyir-Aggrey)
44. Juvenile crime in India
45. Crime against women in India
46. Should there be priority for India's space missions amidst pressing issues like poverty, unemployment, etc.?
47. Corruption in the armed forces
48. Scrapping of the Planning Commission
49. 'No country for old men'.
50. 'The death of dogma is the birth of morality'. (Emmanuel Kant)
51. Population Growth and Explosion
52. Employment and Unemployment
53. Literacy and Illiteracy
54. Child Labour and Street Children
55. Drug Addiction and Trafficking
56. HIV and AIDS
57. Smoking and Alcoholism
58. Ragging
59. Generation Gap and Modernity
60. Marriage and Divorce
61. Nuclear and Joint Family
62. Old Age and Geriatric Care
63. Maintenance for Senior Citizen
64. Social Reforms
65. Human Rights Abuse and Violation
66. Status of Women
67. Crime/Violence Against Women
68. Professional Career Oriented Women
69. Discrimination /Hardships at Work Place
70. Dowry
71. Corruption and Integrity
72. Transparency and Accountability
73. Bribery
74. Casteism and Caste Politics
75. Religion and Society
76. Secularism Communalism and Communal Harmony
77. Social Problems
78. Superstitions
79. Cultural Heritage and Monuments
80. Unity in Diversity
81. National Integration
82. Festivals
83. Rural Development
84. Droughts and Hunger
85. Water Pollution
86. Global Warming and Climate Change
87. Globalisation
88. Role of Media
89. Impact of Television
90. Indian Cinema and Image of Women
91. Role of Advertising
92. Role of Youth
93. Role of Intellectual
94. NGOs
95. Begging
96. Terrorism
97. Adultery

98. Beauty Contests
99. Brain Drain
100. Capital Punishment/Death Penalty
101. City Problems and Metropolitan Mess
102. Impact of Computers
103. Impact of Mobile Phone/Smart Phones
104. Social Networking Sites
105. Electoral Reforms
106. Female Feticide
107. Environmental Conservation
108. Mercy Killing (Euthanasia)
109. Mars Expedition
110. Antarctic Expedition
111. Role of Forests
112. Strike
113. Human Cloning
114. Role of IT
115. Role of Internet
116. Nationalism
117. Panchayati Raj
118. Reservation Policy
119. Role of Ethics in Politics
120. Wildlife Conservation
121. Biodiversity Depletion and Species Extinction
122. Infrastructural Development
123. Disability Rights
124. Impact of Newspapers and Print Media
125. Nation Building
126. Role of Science and Technology
127. Science and Society
128. Rape, Molestation and Sexual Abuse
129. Examination System Reform
130. Prostitution
131. Student Politics
132. Lesbians, Gays, Bisexual and Transgenders
133. Role of School Uniforms
134. Internal Security
135. Civil Defence
136. Cyber Crime
137. School Curriculum
138. Education for All
139. Goals and Aims of Education
140. Sports and Society
141. Teacher Grading
142. Politics and Corruption
143. Vulgarity and Society
144. Coalition Government
145. Arrange Marriage and Love Marriage
146. Gender Justice
147. Aadhaar Card
148. Khap and Honour Killing
149. Multiculturalism
150. Tourism and Society
151. Public Administration
152. Good Governance
153. Impact of Computer Virus
154. Impact of Cinema on Society
155. Reservation for Women
156. Yellow Journalism
157. Politics and Crime
158. Participatory Democracy
159. Police Reform
160. Prison Reform
161. Uniform Civil Code
162. Polio Eradication
163. India as a Soft State
164. Judicial Activism and Advocacy
165. T-20 Cricket
166. POTA
167. Urbanisation
168. Sustainable Cities
169. Privatisation of Education
170. Women Empowerment
171. Energy Crisis
172. Power Pricing
173. North-East Students' Problem

174. Minority Politics
175. Distributive Justice
176. Religious Tolerance
177. Participatory Decentralised Development
178. Family Planning & Population Control
179. Torture and Custodial Death
180. Conversion
181. Freedom of Expression
182. Social Responsibility of Advertising
183. CSR: Corporate Social Responsibility
184. Adolescence and Teenage Violence
185. Foreign Universities
186. Foreign Media
187. Sustainable Development
188. Natural Disasters
189. Disaster Management
190. Non-Violence of Peace
191. English as Second Language
192. Materialism in Society
193. Animal Rights
194. Gandhism
195. Media Freedom
196. Child Welfare
197. Road Rage
198. Green Activism
199. Natural Resource Management
200. Value-Based Education
201. Space Travel
202. Food Security
203. Human Development Index
204. Communal Violence Bill
205. Child or Underage Marriage
206. Indian Slums
207. Widow Remarriage
208. Democracy and Development
209. Politics and Religion
210. Apolitical Defence Force
211. India's Defence Requirements
212. United Nations Challenges
213. Economic Liberalisation in India
214. Privatisation of Indian Economy
215. Law and Social Change
216. Law, Ethics and Morality
217. Impact of Television on Society
218. Politics of Information
219. Scientific Temper and Attitude
220. Science and Arts
221. Science and Literature
222. Science and Religion
223. Information Science
224. Colonisation
225. Media Freedom and Privacy of Individual
226. Cyber Stalking and Internet Abuse
227. Future of Nation-State
228. Liquor Prohibition
229. Freedom of Criticism
230. Smoking in Public Places
231. Reading Habit
232. Peace Use of Nuclear Energy
233. Advances in Biotechnology
234. Scientific Research and Innovation in India
235. Space Programme of India
236. Educating the Girl Child
237. Sex-Education
238. Upcoming Career Opportunities
239. Distance Education
240. Online Education
241. Role of Private Universities
242. Studying Abroad
243. Brain Drain
244. Rural Development in India
245. Character Building

246. Courageous Life
247. Wisdom and Knowledge
248. Leadership
249. Importance of Humour
250. Patriotism
251. Art of Living
252. Self-Reliance
253. Moral and Spiritual Deprivation
254. Happy Life
255. Planning in India
256. Service Sector in India
257. Special Economic Zone (SEZs)
258. India's Foreign Trade
259. MNCs (Multinational Corporations)
260. Land Reforms in India
261. Indian Agricultural Sector
262. Food grains Management
263. Indian Industrial Sector
264. India's Public Sector
265. India's Private Sector
266. India's Small Scale Industry
267. Banking Sector in India
268. Energy Sector in India
269. Tourism Sector in India
270. Poverty in India
271. Inflation and Price Rise
272. Presidential System of Government
273. Constitutional Review, Reform and Amendments
274. Centre-State Relations
275. India's Neighbourhood Relations
276. Bangladesh Immigrants in India
277. Indian Diaspora
278. Pravasi Bhartiya and NRIs
279. Women's Quota in Parliament
280. Immoral Trafficking
281. Malls/Brand Culture
282. World Peace
283. WTO (World Trade Organisation)
284. World Financial Crises and Global Depression
285. Hindu Identity
286. State Repression in India
287. Maoism and Naxal Movement in India
288. Nuclear Non-Proliferation
289. Collapse of Socialism
290. Racism in World
291. Drug Menace in Third World
292. New World Economic Order
293. Peace-keeping, Peace-Building
294. UNDP (United Nations Development Programme)
295. UNEP (United Nations Environment Programme)
296. NAM (Non-Aligned Movement)
297. Piracy at Sea
298. Global Armament and Arms Build-up
299. Global disarmament
300. UN Security Council
301. Indian Bureaucracy
302. Indian Judiciary
303. Regional Parties in India
304. Multi-Party System in India
305. India's Foreign Policy
306. Bank Scams in India
307. Stock Market in India
308. India's Economic Policy Agenda
309. India's Industrial Policy Reforms
310. Public Sector Privatisation in India
311. Dunkel Draft
312. Intellectual Property Rights
313. Natural Wealth of India
314. Coalgate in India
315. Communication Regulation in India
316. Farmers' Suicide in India
317. CSIR and Indian Industry
318. CSIR and Global Patents
319. Health-Hazards in India
320. Tourism and Environment
321. Environment Hazards in Himalayas
322. Ethnicity in India
323. Cultural Renaissance of India
324. Integrated Indian Culture

325. Green Tribunal
326. Positive Thinking
327. Kundankulam Reactors
328. Operations Vijay
329. Revival of Cold War
330. Severe Acute Respiratory Syndrome
331. National Counterterrorism Centre (NCTC)
332. Right to Reject/Recall
333. Indo-UN Nuclear Deal
334. Ozone Depletion
335. Nuclear and Hazardous Waste Disposal
336. Nuclear Energy Revival
337. Solar Energy
338. Small Island Development Programme
339. Coastal-Zone Management
340. Wind Energy
341. Marine Pollution
342. Budget Airlines
343. Global Aviation Industry
344. Nuclear Submarine Disasters
345. Tsunami
346. Cyclones and Typhoons
347. Deforestation and Desertification
348. Anti-Defection Law
349. National Register of Citizens (NRC)
350. Citizenship Amendment Act (CAA) 2019
351. National Population Register (NPR)
352. Economic Slowdown in India
353. Article 370
354. Internal Security and Prosperity of Country
355. Margin to mains term: trans gender community
356. Sustainable development : Gross future
357. Self reliance foster self: respect
358. Credibility in Indian electronic media
359. Social Justice : A human right

❑❑❑

LAST 32 YEARS ESSAY QUESTIONS

1. UPSC/PCS Essay Paper Section-wise Essay Paper–UPSC/PCS Civil Service Main 2022

SECTION-A: 125 MARKS

Write any one of the following essays in 1,000–1,200 words:

1. Forests are the best case studies for economic excellence.
2. Poets are the unacknowledged legislators of the world.
3. History is a series of victories won by the scientific man over the romantic man.
4. A ship in harbour is safe, but that is not what ship is for.

SECTION-B: 125 MARKS

Write any one of the following essays in 1,000–1,200 words:

1. The time to repair the roof is when the sun is shining.
2. You cannot step twice in the same river.
3. A smile is the chosen vehicle for all ambiguities.
4. Justice because you have a choice, it does not mean that any of them has to be right.

2. Essay-list: Topic-wise of Last 32 Years (1991–2022)

ECONOMY AND DEVELOPMENT

1. Economic growth without distributive justice is bound to breed violence. (1993)
2. Ecological considerations need not hamper development. (1993)
3. Multinational corporations—Saviours or saboteurs? (1994)
4. Urbanisation is a blessing in disguise. (1997)
5. Resource management in the Indian context. (1999)

6. Globalisation would finish small-scale industries in India. (2006)
7. Protection of ecology and environment is essential for sustained economic development. (2006)
8. Globalisation would finish small-scale industries in India. (2006)
9. BPO boom in India. (2007)
10. Special economic zone: boon or bane? (2008)
11. Are our traditional handicrafts doomed to a slow death? (2009)
12. The focus of health care is increasingly getting skewed towards the 'haves' of our society. (2009)
13. Should a moratorium be imposed on all fresh mining in tribal areas of the country? (2010)
14. Is the criticism that the 'Public-Private-Partnership' (PPP) model for development is more of a bane than a boon in the Indian context, justified? (2012)
15. GDP (Gross Domestic Product) along with GDH (Gross Domestic Happiness) would be the right indices for judging the well-being of a country. (2013)
16. Was it the policy paralysis or the paralysis of implementation which slowed the growth of our country? (2014)
17. Tourism: Can this be the next big thing for India? (2014)
18. Innovation is the key determinant of economic growth and social welfare.
19. Crisis faced in India – moral or economic? (2015)
20. Can capitalism bring inclusive growth? (2015)
21. If development is not engendered, it is endangered. (2016)
22. Near jobless growth in India: An anomaly or an outcome of economic reforms? (2016)
23. Farming has lost the ability to be a source of subsistence for majority of farmers in India. (2017)
24. Poverty anywhere is a threat to prosperity everywhere. (2018)
25. Forests are the best case studies for economic excellence. (2022)

EDUCATION

1. Restructuring of Indian education system. (1995)
2. Literacy is growing very fast, but there is no corresponding growth in education. (1996)
3. Value-based science and education. (1999)
4. Irrelevance of the classroom. (2001)
5. Modern technological education and human values. (2002)
6. Privatisation of higher education in India. (2002)
7. What is real education? (2005)
8. 'Education for all' campaign in India: myth or reality? (2006)
9. Independent thinking should be encouraged right from the childhood. (2007)
10. Is an egalitarian society possible by educating the masses? (2008)
11. Credit-based higher education system—status, opportunities and challenges. (2011)
12. Is the growing level of competition good for the youth? (2014)

13. Are the standardised tests good measure of academic ability or progress? (2014)
14. Education without values, as useful as it is, seems rather to make a man more clever devil. (2015)
15. Destiny of a nation is shaped in its classrooms. (2019)
16. Neglect of primary healthcare and education in India are reasons for its backwardness. (2019)
17. Culture is what we are, civilization is what we have. (2020)

INDIAN DEMOCRACY, SOCIETY, CULTURE AND MINDSET

1. The Indian society at the crossroads. (1994)
2. Modernisation and westernisation are not identical concepts. (1994)
3. New cults and godmen: a threat to traditional religion. (1996)
4. True religion cannot be misused. (1997)
5. The composite culture of India. (1998)
6. Youth culture today. (1999)
7. Mass media and cultural invasion. (1999)
8. Indian culture today: a myth or a reality? (2000)
9. Modernism and our traditional socio-ethical values. (2000)
10. Why should we be proud of being Indians? (2000)
11. Responsibility of media in a democracy. (2002)
12. Globalisations and its impact on Indian culture. (2004)
13. How has satellite television brought about cultural change in Indian mindsets? (2007)
14. National identity and patriotism. (2008)
15. 'Globalisation' versus 'nationalism'. (2009)
16. Geography may remain the same; history need not. (2010)
17. From traditional Indian philanthropy to the gates-buffet model—a natural progression or a paradigm shift? (2010)
18. Does Indian cinema shape our popular culture or merely reflect it? (2011)
19. In the context of Gandhiji's views on the matter, explore on an evolutionary scale, the terms 'Swadhinata', 'Swaraj' and 'Dharmarajya'. Critically comment on their contemporary relevance to Indian democracy. (2012)
20. Is the Colonial mentality hindering India's Success? (2013)
21. Is sting operation an invasion of privacy? (2014)
22. Fifty Golds in Olympics: Can this be a reality for India? (2014)
23. Dreams which should not let India sleep. (2015)
24. Cooperative federalism: Myth or reality? (2016)
25. Biased media is a threat to Indian democracy. (2019)
26. South Asian societies are woven not around the state, but around their plural cultures & plural identities. (2019)

27. Culture is what we are, civilization is what we have. (2020)
28. There can be no social justice without economic prosperity but economic prosperity without social justice is meaningless. (2020)
29. Patriarchy is the least noticed yet the most significant structure of social inequality. (2020)

INTERNATIONAL ISSUES

1. The global order: political and economic. (1993)
2. Restructuring of UNO reflect present realities. (1996)
3. India's contribution to world wisdom. (1998)
4. The world of the twenty-first century. (1998)
5. The implications of globalisation for India. (2000)
6. My vision of an ideal world order. (2001)
7. The masks of new imperialism. (2003)
8. As civilisation advances culture declines. (2003)
9. India's role in promoting ASEAN co-operation. (2004)
10. Terrorism and world peace. (2005)
11. Importance of Indo-US nuclear agreement. (2006)
12. Good fences make good neighbours. (2009)
13. Preparedness of our society for India's global leadership role. (2010)
14. Has the Non-Aligned Movement (NAM) lost its relevance in a multipolar world? (2017)
15. Technology as the silent factor in international relations. (2020)

QUOTE BASED PHILOSOPHY, ETHICS BASED ESSAY QUESTIONS

1. He would reigns within himself and folds his passions and desires and fears is more than a king. (1993)
2. Compassion is the basic of all morality. Elucidate? (1993)
3. Youth is a blunder, manhood a struggle, old age a regret. (1994)
4. Useless life is an early death. (1994)
5. Our deeds determine us, as much as we determine our deeds. (1995)
6. Disinterested intellectual curiosity is the life blood of civilisation. (1995)
7. Truth is lived, not taught. (1996)
8. The pursuit of excellence. (2001)
9. If youth knew, if age could. (2002)
10. The paths of glory lead but to the grave. (2002)
11. Search for truth can only be a spiritual problem. (2002)
12. There is nothing either good or bad but thinking makes it so. (2003)